103

The Routledge Dictionary of Philosophy

First published in 1976, the *Dictionary of Philosophy* has established itself as the best available text of its kind, explaining often unfamiliar, complicated and diverse terminology. Thoroughly revised and expanded, this fourth edition provides authoritative and rigorous definitions of a broad range of philosophical concepts.

Concentrating on the Western philosophical tradition, *The Routledge Dictionary of Philosophy* offers an illuminating and informed introduction to the central issues, ideas and perspectives in core fields such as metaphysics, epistemology and logic. It includes concise biographical entries for more than one hundred major philosophers, from Plato and Aristotle through to contemporary figures such as Dummett, McDowell, Parfit and Singer.

All major entries are followed by helpful suggestions for further reading, including web links, and contain extensive cross-referencing to aid access and comprehension. This edition also features a brand new guide to the most useful philosophy sites on the internet. *The Routledge Dictionary of Philosophy* is an invaluable and up-to-date resource for all students of philosophy.

Michael Proudfoot was Head of the Department of Philosophy at the University of Reading, UK, and is now an Honorary Fellow of the Department.

A. R. Lacey is formerly a Senior Lecturer in the Department of Philosophy at King's College, University of London, UK

The Routledge
Dictionary of Philosophy

Fourth Edition

Michael Proudfoot and A. R. Lacey

LONDON AND NEW YORK

10066041

First published 1976
Second edition 1986
Third edition 1996
Fourth edition 2010
by Routledge
2 Milton Park Square, Milton Park, Abingdon, OX14 4RN

Simultaneously published in the USA and Canada
by Routledge
270 Madison Ave, New York, NY 10016

Routledge is an imprint of the Taylor & Francis Group, an informa business

© 1976, 1986, 1996 A.R. Lacey; 2010 Michael Proudfoot and A. R. Lacey

Typeset in Sabon by
Taylor & Francis Books
Printed and bound in Great Britain by
CPI Antony Rowe, Chippenham, Wiltshire

British Library Cataloguing in Publication Data
A catalogue record for this book is available from the British Library

Library of Congress Cataloging in Publication Data
Library of Congress Cataloging-in-Publication Data
Proudfoot, Michael.
The Routledge dictionary of philosophy / Michael Proudfoot and
A.R. Lacey – 4th ed.
   p. cm.
   Rev. ed. of: Lacey, A. R. (Alan Robert) / A dictionary of philosophy.
1976.
   [etc.]
   1. Philosophy–Dictionaries. I. Lacey, A. R. (Alan Robert) II. Lacey,
A. R. (Alan Robert) Dictionary of philosophy. III. Title.
   B41.L32 2009
   103–dc22

ISBN10: 0-415-35644-X (hbk)
ISBN 10: 0-415-35645-8 (pbk)
ISBN 10: 0-203-42846-3 (ebk)

ISBN 13: 978-0-415-35644-2 (hbk)
ISBN 13: 978-0-415-35645-9 (pbk)
ISBN 13: 978-0-203-42846-7 (ebk)

Preface to the Fourth Edition

This is an extensively revised edition of the *Dictionary of Philosophy* by A. R. Lacey which originally appeared in 1976, with new editions revised by Lacey appearing in 1986 and 1996. In this Preface I incorporate material from Lacey's three previous Prefaces, explaining something of the aim and nature of this book.

The difference between an encyclopedia and a dictionary isn't simply one of length. It is true that the *Routledge Encyclopedia of Philosophy* extends to ten substantial volumes, but there are admirable single volume encyclopedias (including the concise version of the *Encyclopedia of Philosophy*). Encyclopedias characteristically consist of essays of varying lengths, dealing with a variety of topics, often surveying the history of the treatment of that topic and discussing the various different theories forwarded by philosophers. The aim of a dictionary, on the other hand, is to clarify the meanings of terms, and to indicate issues and problems associated with those terms. The entries in a dictionary are not intended to be mini-essays, nor do they attempt to evaluate philosophers or theories, as an encyclopedia article might very well legitimately do. They are generally brief, explanatory and fairly neutral in tone. A dictionary will have, compared to an encyclopedia of the same length, more, but correspondingly shorter entries.

This dictionary is intended for the general reader and university student. The earlier editions of the dictionary had a considerable emphasis on logic, metaphysics, philosophy of language and epistemology. I have increased the number of entries on other areas, for example, ethics, aesthetics and philosophy of religion, even though these additions had to be kept brief if the book were to remain a reasonable size. The emphasis has been on the commonest terms and notions that are likely to come up in philosophy courses in the English speaking world. I have not attempted to cover non-Western philosophy, important though that may be, except, in one or two instances, where there have been significant connections with the Western tradition (Avicenna, for example).

There are over 100 entries on individual philosophers. These are very brief guides to their major works and dates, with cross-references to other entries and, where appropriate, to useful introductory works about that philosopher.

Some of the longer entries start with a brief definition: this should be understood only as an attempt to give the general character of the term concerned, as it is used in philosophy. This is specifically a dictionary of philosophy, so it is not concerned with the meanings that some of these words have in general use, where that conflicts with the philosophical use.

Cross-references are denoted by small capitals, and are of two kinds, within entries and self-standing. The former are only given when they seem useful. The term referred to is often mentioned in an approximate or abbreviated, but obvious, form. For example, the entry called 'conversion' might be referred to within the context of an entry as 'converse'. The self-standing cross-references are not a guarantee that a term is treated fully, but they may be thought of as forming a sort of index. Terms with more than one word normally appear only once. RUSSELL'S PARADOX appears under R but not under P, and the discussion of innate ideas can be traced through IDEA. Cross-references which occur at the end of entries, preceded by 'See also' may refer to the preceding entry as a whole, not just the last paragraph.

The bibliographies are by no means intended to be comprehensive, nor necessarily to include the latest twists and turns in continuing debates on issues. Rather, they are intended to give guidance to a reader who wishes to pursue further reading on a topic. The items in the bibliographies are included for various reasons. They may be the original source of the concept concerned, or a good introductory discussion of the issues, or a collection of relevant articles on the topic. From these sources, further bibliographical help can be found. The information in parentheses after the work gives some indication of why they are included. Asterisked items might be particularly helpful as an introduction. In this edition, I have included, for the first time, references in the bibliographies to sources on the internet. For further information about philosophy on the internet, please see the 'Guide to Philosophy Online'.

In the earlier editions, A.R. Lacey quite rightly acknowledged by name the many colleagues and friends who had helped him with advice and suggestions. I, too, am in debt to many sources and people. I have found the *Routledge Encyclopedia of Philosophy*, and the Concise version in particular, and the online *Stanford Encyclopedia of Philosophy* very useful. I was enormously helped by the four anonymous readers whom the publishers asked to look at the previous edition for their suggestions about deletions, additions and changes, the vast majority of which I have incorporated into this edition, and sometimes verbatim. I also wish to thank the following for their help: Emma Borg, Jonathan Dancy, Max de Gaynesford, Simon Glendinning, Hanjo Glock, Brad Hooker, Søren Landkildehus, Rick Momeyer, David Oderberg, John Preston, Severin Schroeder, Philip Stratton-Lake, Mark Tebbit, Nigel Warburton and Daniel Whiting. In some cases, their help extended to drafting a whole entry for me, but in all cases I must take the entire responsibility for the final entries and therefore for any errors that there may be in them. But my greatest thanks must be to A.R. Lacey, whose entries in the original editions of this Dictionary, most of which are retained in this edition, are examples of knowledge, clarity and concision, and which have provided a standard to be aimed for, if not always reached.

Michael Proudfoot

Prefatory note to the previous editions

All three of the previous editions owed so much to other people as almost to constitute a joint work in themselves. Dr J.L. Watling, Dr D.M. Tulloch and Mr D.A. Lloyd Thomas sent me detailed comments on the entire manuscript, and Dr Watling discussed innumerable points with me over innumerable lunches. For the third edition Prof. T. Crane and Prof. J. Cargile sent me detailed comments, both general and particular, on the complete draft, Prof. Crane also doing so on my initial revisions and adding a hundred or more bibliographic suggestions, virtually all of which I adopted.

For very substantial help on individual items I am grateful to Dr K. Hossack, Prof. M. Machover, Dr C. Hughes, Mr J. Hopkins, Prof. R.M. Sainsbury and Prof. G. Segal. Others who provided invaluable help on individual entries or questions include Dr S. Botros, Dr D.M. Edgington, Prof. D.A. Gillies, Dr S. Guttenplan, Prof. D.W. Hamlyn, Miss R.L Meager, Prof. D. Papineau, Prof. A.B. Savile, Prof. P. Simons, Dr L. Siorvanes, Dr R. Spencer-Smith, Dr A. Thomas, Mr J.D. Valentine, Mr P. Wesley (who translated the second edition into Dutch) and Prof. P.G. Winch.

The following among my non-philosophical colleagues took great trouble in getting me to communicate comprehensively: Mrs J.H. Bloch, Prof. D.F. Cheesman, Dr G. Darlow, Dr D.R. Dicks, Dr M.R. Hoare, Dr E. Jacobs, Mr. T. Taylor, Miss E.C. Vollans, Dr G.H. Wright and Mrs. Helen Marshall.

Naturally none of all these people is responsible for the remaining faults, especially as I did not always follow their advice, or not fully. I was also helped at various points by Mrs M. Blackburn of the University of London Library – to say nothing of the indispensable resources of that library itself. Prof. T. Honderich helped me greatly at various stages throughout, and I am grateful to various typists and secretaries who came to my aid in time of need, as I am to Bedford

College Philosophy Department for allowing me two sabbatical terms (and Kings College Philosophy Department for allowing me one) at relevant times.

Among written sources my main debts apart from the items mentioned in the bibliographies are to P. Edwards (ed.) *The Encyclopedia of Philosophy* (8 vols., Macmillan 1967), J.O. Urmson (ed.) *The Concise Encyclopedia of Western Philosophy and Philosophers* (Hawthorn 1960) and D. Runes (ed.) *Dictionary of Philosophy* (Littlefield Adams 1942) for mainly its logical entries. The intermittent 'recent work in ... ' surveys in the *American Philosophical Quarterly* should also be mentioned. I am grateful as well to Gale Research International for letting me re-use some of the material I contributed to their *Dictionary of Theories* (1993), and to the sources mentioned in the acknowledgments to that volume.

Just to repeat one paragraph from my original preface: The wide-ranging reader must be prepared to find almost any term used in ways I have not mentioned. In particular, it can only mislead to offer brief and precise definitions of philosophical '-isms'. I have thus tried instead to bring out something of the general spirit of such terms, which often refer to features or aspects rather than to people or systems. Precision is similarly inapposite in recommending the use of a term like 'the causal theory of meaning' rather than 'causal theories of meaning'. Context or even whim will often decide whether one talks of different theories, or of variants of a single theory. Words like 'principle', 'law', 'rule', 'thesis', 'axiom', again, are used almost indifferently in phrases like 'the principle of ... '.

Finally, for the present edition my main indebtedness is of course to Michael Proudfoot, both for undertaking the somewhat thankless task of revising someone else's work and for making such an excellent job of it. I have learnt quite a lot myself from the nearly 150 new entries he has contributed and have been agreeably surprised at the amount of my own work he has felt able to leave standing despite pressures on space.

A. R. Lacey

A

Abandonment. In existentialist philosophy, especially in SARTRE's atheistic version, the idea that we are born into a world that God has created is rejected: instead we are abandoned in a world which has no pre-existing meaning. See EXISTENTIALISM.

Abduction. Originating in Aristotle, the logic of abduction was not fully developed until the time of PEIRCE, who presented it as a form of reasoning from mysterious or anomalous facts back to the hypothesis, which, if true, would explain those facts. In contrast to the more familiar forms of deductive and inductive reasoning, abduction is more spontaneous in its operation and more tentative in its conclusions, as it seeks the most economical, coherent, plausible and causally adequate hypothesis. See also INFERENCE TO THE BEST EXPLANATION.

Umberto Eco, *The Sign of Three*, Indiana University Press, 1983.
N. R. Hanson, *Patterns of Discovery*, Cambridge University Press, 1958.

About. See REFERRING.

Absolute. Term used in post-Kantian Idealism, for example, in Fichte, Schelling and Hegel, and later in Bradley. It means the totality of things as a unity, or the only proper subject of predicates, or the unconditioned ground of all being (somewhat like noumena or things-in-themselves). See BRADLEY, IDEALISM, NOUMENON.

Absolute idealism. Refers to HEGEL's monistic idealism, claiming the total and all-encompassing identity of thought and reality.

Abstract. An abstract entity may be one constructed by the mind through the process of ABSTRACTION. But the term is also sometimes

1

used for entities regarded as being outside space and time, as, e.g. numbers are for a Platonist philosopher of MATHEMATICS. When applied to properties, ideas, etc., 'abstract' usually has the former sense, though the criteria for when a property counts as abstract in that sense are various, such as being a universal rather than a TROPE, or being mind-dependent in a certain way. But certain spatiotemporal things are also sometimes called abstract particulars, such as actions and events and tropes (where tropes are distinct from other tropes they belong within a concrete object.)

K. Campbell, *Abstract Particulars*, Blackwell, 1990. (Constructs a metaphysics taking tropes as basic.)

N. Cartwright and R. Le Poidevin, 'Fables and models', *Proceedings of the Aristotelian Society*, supplementary vol., 1991. (A symposium containing some discussion of the abstract/concrete contrast.)

B. Hale, *Abstract Objects*, Blackwell, 1987. (Uses 'abstract' in second sense and defends Platonist view of abstract objects.)

R. Teichmann, *Abstract Entities*, St. Martin's Press and Macmillan, 1992 (Nominalist approach.)

Abstract ideas. How can one word, 'dog', for example, at the same time refer to all the various different sorts of dog? Both Locke and Berkeley thought the meanings of words were IDEAS, and that ideas were mental images. Locke argued that by a process of ABSTRACTION we form an idea that allows us to concentrate on just some aspects of a thing (its essential dogginess), from which we can generalize to all other things (dogs) that have just those aspects. Berkeley rejected this claim: how could there be such a mental image, of a dog both large and small, white and brown, with and without a tail, such that it could stand for any dog? See UNIVERSALS.

J. Bennett, *Locke, Berkeley, Hume: Central Themes*, Clarendon Press, 1971. (See particularly Section II.)

Abstraction. Process by which, allegedly, we form concepts on the basis of experience or of other concepts. On being confronted with red things, each of which has many other properties, we abstract the redness and so form a concept of red. Having done the same with blue, yellow, etc., we then abstract from these concepts themselves the concept of colour, and so on. Empiricists like Locke use abstraction to help specify how we build up our concepts on the basis of experience. It is unclear, however, that Locke properly distinguishes such things as forming a concept on the basis of repeated presentations of a quality, abstracting genera from species, abstracting determinables from DETERMINATES. Abstractionism is the view that the mind does operate in this way.

D. Bell, 'Objects and concepts', *Proceedings of the Aristotelian Society*, supplementary volume, 1994, § 1. (Defends abstractionism.)

P. T. Geach, *Mental Acts*, 1957, pp. 18–44. (Criticizes abstractionism.)

J. Locke, *An Essay concerning Human Understanding*, 1690, e.g. 2.11.9–10, 2.12.1, 2.32.6–8, 3.3.9.

J. R. Weinberg, *Abstraction, Relation, Induction*, 1965. (Historical.)

Absurdity. In EXISTENTIALISM, especially in CAMUS, the idea that without any pre-existing God-created meaning in our secular world, the human desire for clarity and explanation creates an absurd and ultimately fruitless struggle.

Academy, The. The public gymnasium in Athens at which PLATO taught, which, after his death, continued the Platonic tradition for more than 300 years. The term is used in general to refer to Plato's pupils and followers, known as 'academics', from which is derived the modern sense of an intellectual institution and its members.

Acceptance, acceptability. See BELIEF, CONFIRMATION, LOTTERY PARADOX.

Access. It has often been held that we alone have access to our own thoughts and sensations (private or privileged access). See also PRIVATE LANGUAGE, and (for a different use of 'access') POSSIBLE WORLDS.

W. Alston, 'Varieties of privileged access', *American Philosophical Quarterly*, 1971, reprinted in R. M. Chisholm and R. J. Swartz (eds), *Empirical Knowledge*, Prentice-Hall, 1973.

J. Heil, 'Privileged access', *Mind*, 1988, with discussions by N. Georgalis and A. Brueckner in *Mind*, 1990. (B. Brewer in *Mind*, 1992 is also relevant.)

N. Malcolm, 'The privacy of experience', in A. Stroll (ed.), *Epistemology*, Harper and Row, 1967. (Discusses an ambiguity, and then the issue itself.)

Accident. In philosophy, the term has two uses. In SCHOLASTIC PHILOSOPHY, it refers to what has no independent existence but is merely a property of, or inheres in, a substance. In Aristotelian logic, it refers to a CONTINGENT property of a SUBSTANCE – one that is not essential to that substance. See ESSENCE and FORM.

Achilles paradox. See ZENO'S PARADOXES.

Acquaintance, knowledge by. RUSSELL distinguishes knowledge by acquaintance, where one says, 'I know x', from knowledge by DESCRIPTION, where one says, 'I know that p'. Though this distinction is admittedly not clear ('I know the capital of France' might mean either 'I know Paris' in the sense that I have been there or 'I know that the capital of France is Paris' without ever having been there). Nevertheless, a distinction between what is in some sense directly known, through sense experience, and what is inferred is basic to foundationalist theories of knowledge. See EPISTEMOLOGY.

R. Fumerton, 'Knowledge by Acquaintance vs. Description', *The Stanford Encyclopedia of Philosophy* (Spring 2004 Edition), Edward N. Zalta (ed.). Available at: http://plato.stanford.edu/archives/spr2004/entries/knowledge-acquaindescrip/ (accessed 1 March 2009).

Acrasia (Akrasia). See INCONTINENCE.

Action. The doing of something or what is done. Problems about actions concern first of all what they are and how they relate to things like trying, choosing, willing, intending (cf. also BASIC ACTION); and how are persons related to their actions and how do they know about them? We talk of the action of rain and of reflex actions, but action of the central kind is what is done by rational beings. Only they can perform actions. Acting usually involves moving in some way, or at least trying to move, so how are actions related to movements? How is my raising my arm related to my arm's rising? What one intends is relevant here, and this involves the ways in which what happens can be viewed (cf. INTENSIONALITY). Consider (as relating to one occasion): making certain neurones in the brain fire, tightening one's arm-muscles, flexing one's finger, moving a piece of iron, pulling a trigger, firing a gun, heating a gun-barrel, shooting a man, shooting an ex-farmer, shooting the President, assassinating the President, earning a bribe, grieving a nation, starting a war.

Are all these descriptions of one action, or of an action and its consequences, or what? Two substantive questions are connected with this. First, since an action cannot cause itself, how is action related to causation? Indeed, is an action the sort of thing that can be caused at all? Second, what bearing has this on responsibility?

Further problems, which also bear on responsibility, concern omissions, inaction, negligence and also unintentional actions, as when one frightens a bystander, or involuntary ones, as when one unwillingly reveals one's feelings by gasping, but perhaps something can only be an action when it is something an agent could set out to fulfil, even if indirectly (firing neurones by flexing one's finger).

A historically important contrast, deriving from Aristotle, lies between action, as what someone or something does, and 'passion', in the sense of what is done to it.

The relations between acts and actions are complex and disputed. 'Act' seems more of a technical term, especially in phrases like 'mental act' and SPEECH ACT, and less connected to responsibility, etc. Sometimes it was the sense of 'actuality', contrasting with potentiality rather than with state or condition. See also EVENT.

M. Brand and D. Walton (eds), *Action Theory*, Reidel, 1980. (Specially written essays on various relevant issues.)

W. Cerf, 'Review of J. L. Austin, "How to do things with words"', *Mind*, 1966, pp. 269–76, reprinted in K. T. Fann (ed.), *Symposium on J.L. Austin*, Routledge, 1969, pp. 359–68.

A. B. Cody, 'Can a single action have many different descriptions?', *Inquiry*, 1967. (Cf. R.E. Dowling's discussion and Cody's reply, ibid.)

D. Davidson, *Essays on Actions and Events*, Clarendon, 1980. (Reprinted articles discussing inter alia action and causation, reasons, persons and intentions.)

L. H. Davis, *Theory of Action*, Prentice-Hall, 1979. (General discussion of relevant issues.)

*A. Donagan, *Choice: The Essential Element in Human Action*, Routledge, 1987. (Good introduction.)

J. H. Hornsby, *Actions*, Routledge, 1980. (Discusses many of the questions above, though harder than Langford.)

A. Kenny, *Action, Emotion and Will*, Routledge, 1963. (Chapter 7 distinguishes actions from relations.)

*G. Langford, *Human Action*, Macmillan, 1971. (Elementary discussion. Extensive bibliography.)

J. L. Mackie, 'The grounds of responsibility', in P.M.S. Hacker and J. Raz (eds), *Law, Morality, and Society*, Clarendon, 1977, p. 176. (Different views of act/action distinction.)

A. I. Melden, *Free Action*, Routledge, 1961. (Raising one's arm, etc.)

D. Owens, *Causes and Coincidences*, Cambridge UP, 1992, Chapter 8. (Action and causation.)

W. D. Ross, *The Right and the Good*, Clarendon, 1930, pp. 6–7.

I. Thalberg, *Perception, Emotion and Action*, Blackwell, 1977. (Attempts common approach to various problems in these areas.)

G. H. von Wright, *Explanation and Understanding*, Routledge, 1971, p. 69.

Action (philosophy of). See MIND.

Actualism. View that only what is actual exists, as against possibilism, which allows mere possibilities to exist. Actualism is a view about POSSIBLE WORLDS.

In ethics, 'actualism' has been used for the view that whether we ought to do X depends on what would happen if we did it, while possibilism tells us to do whatever action is best. Suppose X would be best but only if we also did Y, which we shall not in fact do (whether or not we ought to): then possibilism says Do X, while actualism says Don't do X.

F. Jackson and R. Pargetter, 'Oughts, options and actualism', *Philosophical Review*, 1986 (reprinted in P. Pettit (ed.), *Consequentialism*, Dartmouth Publishing Co., 1993). (Ethical sense.)

M. J. Loux (ed.), *The Possible and the Actual*, Oxford UP, 1979. (See its index.)

A. McMichael, 'A problem for actualism about possible worlds', *Philosophical Review*, 1983. (See first two sections for relations between actualism and possibilism, with references.)

E. Prior, *Dispositions*, Aberdeen UP, 1985. (Chapter 2 discusses different versions of actualism.)

Actuality and potentiality. In Aristotle actuality is what has FORM and can causally interact with other things, whereas potentiality is what has the possibility of having form, the power to effect change.

M. S. Cohen, 'Aristotle's Metaphysics', *The Stanford Encyclopedia of Philosophy* (Winter 2003 Edition), Edward N. Zalta (ed.). Available at: http://plato.stanford.edu/archives/win2003/entries/aristotle-metaphysics/ (accessed 1 March 2009). (See Section 12, 'Actuality and Potentiality'.)

Ad hoc. A solution 'for this' (Latin) situation or problem only and not generally: an improvised or makeshift solution. In philosophy, the term is often used when a theory is adjusted in some minor way to take account of objections that threaten to falsify it.

Ad hominem. A form of fallacious argument which irrelevantly criticizes the person (literally 'against the person') rather than the person's argument.

Ad infinitum. Latin for 'to infinity', having no end.

Adorno, Theodor. 1903–1969. German philosopher, musicologist and critical theorist, born in Frankfurt, where he worked until 1933. From 1934 to 1937 he studied in Oxford, then in 1938 moved to the USA, where he became an American citizen, and worked in New York and California until 1949 when he returned once more to Frankfurt. He was a prominent member of the so-called Frankfurt School (the Institute for Social Research, which started in Frankfurt, but in the war years moved to New York), along with Benjamin, Marcuse, Habermas and others, including Horkheimer, with whom he collaborated on the book *Dialectic of Enlightenment* (1947). This critique of civilization and reason argues that they tend to self-destruction. Adorno is critical of mass-produced popular culture and believes art, and modernism in particular, has an important role in challenging concepts. Adorno's thought has influenced aesthetics and, in particular, the philosophy of music.

T. W. Adorno, *Aesthetic Theory*, 1970, trans. R. Hullot-Kentor, Minnesota UP, 1997.

M. Horkheimer and T. W. Adorno, *Dialectic of Enlightenment: Philosophical Fragments*, 1947, ed. G. S. Noerr, trans. E. Jephcott, Stanford UP, 2002.

Aesthetics. Often called philosophy of art, although it also is concerned with our experience of the environment – both the natural world and non-artistic artefacts. Roughly, that branch of philosophy concerned with the creation, value and experience of art and the analysis and solution of problems relating to these. Major problems centre on what makes something a work of art. Must it exhibit certain formal e.g. geometrical, properties (formalism), or express certain emotions, attitudes, etc. (expressionism), or do other things? What in fact is the role of pleasure and emotion, and are special types of them involved? Is there a special kind of value involved? Does the work of art embody special properties, like beauty, sublimity, prettiness, and if so, how are these related to its other properties? How relevant are the object's function, the context of production and the artist's intentions? Does it matter how a work was produced, whether difficulties

audience (the reader, listener, spectator, etc.). Wimsatt and Beardsley identified this fallacy, following their attack on the INTENTIONAL FALLACY, as part of their insistence on objective criticism, and in response in particular to the subjective and impressionistic literary criticism of the early part of the twentieth century.

> W. K. Wimsatt and M. C. Beardsley, 'The affective fallacy', *Sewanee Review*, 1949, reprinted in W. K. Wimsatt, *The Verbal Icon*, Methuen, 1970.

Affirming the antecedent. Arguing that if the antecedent of a conditional statement is true, so is the consequent. 'If Judith goes out then she goes to see Lesley. Judith has gone out. Therefore she has gone to see Lesley.' This is a valid argument, often called MODUS PONENS, whereas AFFIRMING THE CONSEQUENT and DENIAL OF ANTECEDENT are fallacies.

Affirming the consequent. The fallacy of arguing that if the consequent of a conditional statement is true, the antecedent must be. It may be, but it needn't be. Thus, it is fallacious to argue from, 'If Jill wins the lottery, she will go on holiday to Spain', that if Jill has gone to Spain on holiday she must have won the lottery: there may be some other explanation. She may have inherited some money, or used her savings, for example. Sometimes, however, such an argument, though not logically valid, may be acceptable if regarded as an example of INDUCTION or ABDUCTION. Thus, one explanation of Jill's holidaying in Spain is that she has won the lottery, and this may, in the circumstances, be the best explanation. See AFFIRMING THE ANTECEDENT and DENIAL OF ANTECEDENT.

Agglomeration. If I can go out and I can stay in, the conjunction 'I can go out and I can stay in' must be true, but 'I can go out and stay in' does not follow. 'Can' is therefore not agglomerative. An important ethical issue concerns whether 'ought' is agglomerative.

> D. Owens, *Causes and Coincidences*, Cambridge UP, 1992, pp. 11–15. (Uses the notion to show why coincidences cannot be explained.)
> B. A. O. Williams and R. F. Atkinson, 'Consistency in ethics', *Proceedings of the Aristotelian Society*, supplementary vol., 1965.

Agnosticism. The view that reason is unable to prove either that God exists or that God does not exist. Hume and Kant provided the philosophical foundations of agnosticism. In common speech, an agnostic is someone who neither believes nor disbelieves in God (whereas an atheist disbelieves in God).

A. Plantinga, 'Is belief in God properly basic?', *Nous* 15 (1) 1981. (Yes.)

J. J. C. Smart, 'Atheism and Agnosticism', *The Stanford Encyclopedia of Philosophy* (Summer 2007 Edition), Edward N. Zalta (ed.). Available at: http://plato.stanford.edu/archives/sum2007/entries/atheism-agnosticism/ (accessed 1 March 2009). (On the differences between atheism and agnosticism.)

Algorithm. Procedure for answering a given problem or type of problem by the properly disciplined applying of certain already established steps which are guaranteed to yield the answer. The procedures for long division and for extracting a square root are algorithms in arithmetic. See also DECIDABLE, HEURISTIC, RECURSIVE.

Alienans. See ATTRIBUTIVE.

Alienation. A term, originating in Hegel and Marx, to refer to the separation of things which naturally belong together which occurs in capitalism, especially of people from their human nature leading to loss of AUTONOMY. It isn't necessary for alienation to exist for people to feel alienated. Workers can be alienated from their products in a factory production line or from political processes when they feel powerless. Alienation can also result from reflection on one's own beliefs and values, which can undermine those beliefs and values without replacing them with any others, so that they remain one's own, but fatally weakened.

B. Ollman, *Alienation*, Cambridge: Cambridge UP, 2nd edn, 1976. (Considerable portions of this book can be read on line. Available at: www.nyu.edu/projects/ollman/books/a.php (accessed 1 March 2009)).

J. Wolff, *Why Read Marx Today?* Oxford UP, 2002. (Also good introduction.)

A. Wood, *Karl Marx*, Routledge, 1981. (Part I provides a good introduction.)

Aliorelative. See REFLEXIVE.

Alternation. See CONJUNCTION.

Altruism and egoism. Altruism (a term introduced by COMTE) is the virtue of considering others' interests before one's own and for their own sake. While altruism says one's duties are only to others, egoism says that each person's duties are only to themselves (to be distinguished from the extreme form, presumably never explicitly held except perhaps by a few dictators, that everyone's duties are only to me, the dictator or whatever). These should be distinguished from universalism (e.g. utilitarianism, etc.). See UNIVERSALITY. Ethical egoism, as above, should be distinguished from psychological egoism, which claims that people always act out of self-interest. HOBBES's political philosophy is based on psychological egoism. He claims that apparent examples of altruism are actually disguised cases of self-interest. Philosophers have continued to debate whether true altruism is possible: examples of saintly or heroic actions involving self-sacrifice are produced as ultimate examples of altruism.

T. Nagel, *The Possibility of Altruism*, Clarendon Press, 1981. (Defends altruism as rational.)

J. O. Urmson, 'Saints and heroes', in A. I. Melden (ed.), *Essays in Moral Philosophy*, University of Washington Press, 1958. (Examples of saintly and heroic action. Urmson is concerned with the possibility of SUPEREROGATION.)

Ambiguity. The property, had by some terms, of having two or more meanings. Ambiguity is not the same as VAGUENESS. 'Bald' is vague (how many hairs can a bald man have?) but not ambiguous. An ambiguous term can be quite precise in each of its senses. Also, it can be argued that ambiguity applies to terms, vagueness to concepts. 'How ambiguous is 'ambiguous'?' is a favourite philosophical question. Ambiguity may apply to words, phrases and sentences, considered in the abstract, or to utterances considered as uttered on a given occasion.

'Bank', connected with rivers and money, may be treated as two words with the same sound but different meanings or as one word with different meanings. Philologists would call 'bank' two words if its uses have different etymologies, but philosophers often arbitrarily treat it as one word or two. Such words, especially when treated as one word with different meanings, are often called equivocal, or homonyms.

Phrases or sentences can be ambiguous while none of the words in them is so. In 'little girls' camp' either the girls or the camp may be little. This is sometimes called amphiboly.

The ambiguity of 'Jack hits James and Jill hit him' depends not on the meaning of 'him' but on who is being referred to by 'him' on the particular occasion of utterance; 'him' here has ambiguity of

12

reference. Where the ambiguity depends on the structure of the sentence or expression, as here and with amphiboly, we have syntactical ambiguity. Where it depends on the meanings of individual words or expressions, we have semantic ambiguity. 'Pretty little girls' is a mixed example, where the semantic ambiguity of 'pretty' affects its syntactic role according as 'pretty' qualifies 'girls' or modifies 'little'. Pragmatic ambiguity is ambiguity in what is done in saying something, as 'You're a fine fellow!' may be sincere or sarcastic. 'Ambiguity' itself is sometimes used in wider, sometimes in narrower, senses.

Some words seem to have senses which differ, but are related. A healthy body is a flourishing one, while a healthy climate produces or preserves health and a healthy complexion is a sign of it. 'Healthy' is therefore often said to have focal meaning (Owen). It senses 'focus' on one dominant sense. Words like 'big', which are syncategorematic (see CATEGORIES), have something like focal meaning, in that it makes a difference what standards we use in applying them. A big mouse is not a big animal, so that to call something 'big' without further ado, can be ambiguous; see ATTRIBUTIVE.

When the ambiguities of an expression can be predicted according to a rule, the expression has systematic ambiguity. On the theory of TYPES, words like 'class' are systematically or typically ambiguous because their meaning varies according to the type to which they belong.

Other kinds of ambiguity, or related notions, include analogical and metaphorical uses of expressions, e.g. God is sometimes called 'wise' in a sense different from, though analogous to, that in which men are wise. Since many terms are ambiguous in this way when applied to God and men, this can be regarded as a case of systematic ambiguity; it is also related to focal meaning.

Some pervasive ambiguities are given special names, such as process/product ambiguity of words like 'vision' which can mean the power of seeing or something seen, or 'statement' which can mean act of stating or what is stated. Many philosophically important terms have this ambiguity. See also OPEN TEXTURE.

D. W. Hamlyn, 'Focal meaning', *Proceedings of the Aristotelian Society*, 1977–8. (Discussions of focal meaning and its significance in Aristotle (small amount of Greek in Owen). Cf. particularly § 2 of latter, and also (for a related concept) R. Robinson, 'The concept of knowledge', *Mind*, 1971, p. 20.)
W. Leszl, *Logic and Metaphysics in Aristotle*, Editrice Antenore, Padua, 1970, Part II, Chapter 1. (Kinds of ambiguity in Aristotle.)

G. E. L. Owen, 'Logic and metaphysics in some earlier works of Aristotle', in
I. During and G. E. L. Owen (eds), *Aristotle and Plato in the Mid-Fourth
Century*, Almquist and Wiksell, Göteborg, 1960, and 'Aristotle on the
snares of ontology', in R. Bambrough (ed.), *New Essays on Plato and
Aristotle*, Routledge, 1965.

W. V. O. Quine, *Word and Object*, Wiley, 1960, § 27–9. (Various kinds of
ambiguity, § 216 discusses vagueness.)

Amphiboly. See AMBIGUITY.

Analysis. See PHILOSOPHY.

Analogical arguments. Or arguments from analogy conclude that two
things or states of affairs similar in some respects are therefore similar
in other respects. For example, 'Jill lives in Florida and is rich, Sam
lives in Florida, therefore Sam is rich'.

Such arguments may fail for a variety of reasons, the most common
being that the similarities in the premise are not relevant to the inferred
similarities in the conclusion. These arguments may also involve
EQUIVOCATION. The best-known examples of arguments from
analogy are William Paley's argument from design for the existence of
God and MILL's argument for the existence of other minds. Paley
argued that if we were to come across a watch lying on the ground,
the complexity of its mechanism would persuade us that it must have
been manufactured – that it had a maker. In a similar way, he argues,
the complexity of the universe should persuade us that it has a maker.
One problem with this argument is that it is precisely the complexity
of the design of the watch in contrast to natural objects that per-
suades us it has a maker; yet the argument then invites us to conclude
that those natural objects, too, had a maker. The analogy between the
watch and the universe is just too weak to allow the conclusion to be
drawn. Mill argues that because I know that when I am pain (or have
other sensations), I react and behave in certain ways, I may therefore
conclude that when I see others react and behave in similar ways that
they are in pain (or have those sensations). This argument was
attacked by WITTGENSTEIN in *Philosophical Investigations*: he
argues that we learn to use the concepts of pain and sensation
through their application to people in general, and that therefore the
use of such concepts, whether in application to others or to ourselves,
actually presupposes that others feel pain and have sensations.

Analysis. See PHILOSOPHY.

Analysis (paradox of). The paradox that arises when we attempt to analyse, say, the concept brother into the concept male sibling. If they are the same concept differently named, no analysis has occurred; if they are different concepts, how can one analyse the other? Hence, the analysis must apparently be either trivial or wrong. This raises the question, among others, of what CONCEPTS are.

C. H. Langford, 'Moore's notion of analysis', in P. A. Schilpp (ed.), *The Philosophy of G. E. Moore*, Northwestern UP, 1942. (Analysis in Moore. See p. 323 for the paradox, and pp. 660ff. for Moore's reply.)

Analytic. The analytic/synthetic distinction is first explicitly made by Kant. A proposition is analytic, on Kant's view, if the predicate is covertly contained in the subject, as in 'Widows were once married'. A proposition where the predicate is attached to the subject but not contained in it is synthetic, as in 'Widows are sad'. The contradictory of a synthetic proposition is always synthetic whereas the contradictory of an analytic proposition is usually called 'analytically false'. Kant's distinction was partly anticipated by Leibniz, who distinguished 'truths of reasons' from 'truths of fact', and had the idea of containment; and by Hume, who distinguished 'relations between ideas' from 'matters of fact'.

Kant's distinction can easily be extended to conditional propositions, which are analytic if the consequent is contained in the antecedent, e.g. 'If she is a widow, she was married', and otherwise synthetic. Some other kinds of propositions raise difficulties, for instance, existential propositions like 'There exist black swans', where containment does not seem to apply, and the notion of containment is anyway hard to analyse. In general, in 'Sad widows are sad' the containment is straightforwardly verbal. But in what sense precisely is the predicate 'contained' in the subject in 'Widows were married', or the consequent in the antecedent in 'If all men are mortal and Socrates is a man, then Socrates is mortal'?

Kant himself proposed an alternative definition now often adopted: a proposition is analytic if its negation is, or is reducible to, a contradiction or inconsistency; otherwise, the proposition is synthetic. A proposition which is true because it exemplifies a certain logical FORM, as 'Bachelors are bachelors' exemplifies the form 'x's are x's', can be called explicitly analytic. A proposition which is true because of certain definitions, as 'Bachelors are male' is true because of the definition of 'bachelor', is implicitly analytic or true by definition. Explicitly analytic propositions, and sometimes implicitly analytic ones too, can be called logically true or logically necessary.

R. Robinson, 'Analysis in Greek geometry', *Mind*, 1936, reprinted in his *Essays in Greek Philosophy*, Clarendon, 1969. (Greek origins of analytic and synthetic methods.)

F. Waismann, 'Analytic-synthetic' (in six parts). *Analysis*, 10, 11, 13, (1949–53); reprinted in his *How I See Philosophy*, Macmillan, 1968.

Analytical hypothesis. See TRANSLATION.

Anaxagoras of Clazomenae. 500–428 BC. Greek PRE-SOCRATIC philosopher. Believed in the fundamental unity of the world, 'all things were together', and that each part latently contains all other parts – 'everything in everything'. Influenced Socrates, Plato and Aristotle, was teacher of the great statesman Pericles and the poet and playwright Euripides.

Ancestral relation. If a relation connects every two adjacent terms in a series there must be a relation which connects any two terms in the series. This relation is the ancestral of the original one. 'Ancestor of' is the ancestral of 'parent of', but a better example (since people have two parents) is that 'greater than' among whole numbers is the ancestral of 'greater by one than'. See also DEFINITION.

And. See CONJUNCTION.

Angst, angoisse. See EXISTENTIALISM.

Anscombe, G.E.M. 1919–2001. British philosopher, born in Ireland, worked in Oxford and Cambridge. Student of, then translator and commentator on the works of WITTGENSTEIN, one of his three literary executors. Wrote influentially in many areas of philosophy, including philosophy of mind (intention, first person), philosophy of action (brute facts), philosophy of language, ethics (she coined the term 'CONSEQUENTIALISM', which she opposed, though she meant by it any sort of non-absolutist view, and changed the course of ethics towards virtue ethics), also epistemology, metaphysics, history of philosophy and philosophy of religion. Was married to the philosopher Peter Geach. *Intention*, 1957. *An Introduction to Wittgenstein's Tractatus*, 1959. *Three Philosophers*, 1961, with P. T. Geach (on Aristotle, Aquinas and Frege). *Causality and Determination*, 1971. *Times, Beginnings and Causes*, 1975. *The Collected Philosophical Papers of G. E. M. Anscombe*, 3 vols., 1981: *1. From Parmenides to Wittgenstein*, *2. Metaphysics and the Philosophy of Mind*, *3. Ethics,*

Religion and Politics; Human Life, Action and Ethics: Essays, 2005.
See APPLIED ETHICS, CAUSATION, CONSEQUENTIALISM,
FACTS, NATURALISM.

Anselm, St. 1033–1109. Born in Aosta, he studied in France and
became archbishop of Canterbury in 1093. He originated the
'ONTOLOGICAL ARGUMENT' for God's existence in his *Proslo-
gion* (his *Monologian* contains related proofs of God's existence). He
also wrote on truth (*De Veritate*) and on logic and problems such as
that of universals (*De Grammatico*).

> D. P. Henry, *The Logic of St Anselm*, Clarendon, 1967. (Henry has also
> translated the *De Grammatico*, 1964.)

Anthropomorphism. The tendency to attribute human qualities to
non-human things.

Anthropic principle. The idea that the universe is so organized as to
permit life as we know it to exist, because were the universe not
organized in precisely this fashion, human beings would not exist and
so could not observe the universe.

> J. D. Barrow and F. J. Tipler, *The Anthropic Cosmological Principle*,
> Oxford UP, 1986. (Three versions, weak, strong and final proposed.)
> N. Bostrom, available at: www.anthropic-principle.com/ (accessed 1 March
> 2009). (Excellent website.)
> M. Gardner, in 'WAP, SAP, PAP, and FAP', *The New York Review of
> Books*, May 8, 1986, and S. Hawking, *A Brief History of Time*, Bantam
> Books, 1988, (p. 174) strongly criticizes Barrow and Tipler.

Antilogism. An inconsistent set of three propositions. The two premises of a valid SYLLOGISM with the CONTRADICTORY of its
conclusion, or more generally three propositions, any two of which
entail the contradictory of the third. Also called inconsistent triad.
The principle of antilogism says that if two propositions together
entail a third, then either of them and the contradictory of the third
together entail the contradictory of the other, e.g. if 'All men are
mortal' and 'Socrates is a man' together entail 'Socrates is mortal',
then 'All men are mortal' and 'Socrates is not mortal' together entail
'Socrates is not a man'.

Antirealism. See REALISM.

Apodictic. See MODALITIES, IMPERATIVES.

Apologetics. The systematic defence of a position and the rebuttal of counter-arguments, especially in connection with religion. From Socrates' speech in his own defence at his trial in Plato's *Apology*. Christian apologists have included Anselm, Thomas Aquinas, Pascal, Butler, Paley, Kierkegaard, Cardinal Newman and C. S. Lewis.

Aporetic. Raising and discussing problems without solving them.

A posteriori. See A PRIORI.

Apperception. In Leibniz, reflective consciousness rather than mere passive perception. In Kant, consciousness of oneself as a unity, on the empirical or transcendental level. Other writers use the term in fairly similar senses. Perhaps the unifying thread in its main senses is awareness of the self as that which judges. It plays little part in contemporary philosophy.

Applied ethics. Also called practical ethics. Practical ethics is the critical inquiry into the norms embedded in particular social practices: that branch of ethics which is concerned with the application of ethical principles to the consideration of real-life practical moral problems, such as abortion, euthanasia, animal rights, ecology, race and gender issues, the morality of war and so on. Although philosophers in the past had discussed such issues (for example, Hume on Suicide, Kant on a whole range of problems in his *Lectures on Ethics*, Mill on the death penalty) by the late 1960s there was widespread criticism of the academic discipline of ethics as dry and arid by Anscombe and others. Since then applied ethics has become an increasingly important subject, and areas such as business ethics, environmental ethics, medical ethics have rapidly developed. See ETHICS.

*P. Singer, *Practical Ethics*, Cambridge UP, 2nd edn, 1999. (Highly influential utilitarian treatment of some of the central topics.)

H. LaFollette (ed.), *Ethics in Practice*, 2nd edn, Blackwell, 2002. (Useful collection of articles, grouped by topic.)

R. G. Frey and C. H. Wellman (eds), *A Companion to Applied Ethics*, Blackwell, 2004. (50 essays by contemporary writers on wide range of topics.)

A priori. A priori knowledge is that which has its justification independently of experience, though it may presuppose experience from which we can obtain the concepts it involves; many philosophers (though not all: see Lehman) regard mathematical knowledge as a priori, though children can't acquire it until they have experience of the world. Knowledge which can only be justified by at least some appeal to experience (basically the five senses, and perhaps introspection) is called a posteriori or empirical. A proposition, judgement, etc. is a priori or empirical according to whether knowledge of it is one or the other. Originally, in Aristotelian philosophy, a proposition was a priori if it was based on, or inferred from, something prior to it in the sense of being its cause or ground. A proposition was a posteriori if it was inferred from its effects. When it was later assumed that the main way of knowing a proposition through its effects was to know it through sense-experience, 'empirical' largely replaced 'a posteriori', and 'a priori' took on the meaning given above.

The philosophical and epistemological question of how our claims to knowledge can be justified is different from the psychological question how we in fact came to our knowledge. Some of it we may be born with, but this will only be innate knowledge if it could be justified, whether a priori, as above, or empirically, through experience, though innate empirical beliefs, whether true or not, are likely to be called instinctive, especially if they manifest themselves only in action rather than in conscious awareness. However, these philosophical and psychological questions have often been conflated, sometimes through confusion, but sometimes through the thought that the psychological question should properly replace the philosophical one, as in naturalized EPISTEMOLOGY (cf. NATURALISM). Also the way we acquire a belief, especially if we acquire it by reasoning or intuitive insight, may well coincide with the way we could justify it – but not always: we know that a belief we 'acquire' by its being innate may well be false (for more on this see INNATE). Kant, in particular, usually talks of our a priori, rather than innate knowledge, meaning knowledge which we cannot get by experience because only if we already have it can we make any sense of experience. Innate ideas or concepts are also often called a priori, and a proposition can be regarded as absolutely a priori if all the concepts in it are a priori, e.g. 'No proposition is both true and false', and as relatively a priori if they are not, e.g. 'Nothing can be simultaneously red and green all over'. 'Relatively a priori' could also apply to the everyday sense in which an empirical proposition is knowable independently of a given context, as when a detective says, 'I haven't yet found any clues, but I know a priori that money is a motive for murder'.

It has usually been assumed that for any given sense of 'a priori' and the corresponding sense of 'empirical' every proposition is either a priori or empirical. But sometimes a proposition is not justified by experience, nor known a priori, but simply postulated. Those postulated as regulative principles to guide scientific procedure can be called non-empirical, though they are often classed as a priori, or sometimes, 'weak' a priori. 'Non-empirical' can also cover the a priori in general. The term 'pragmatic a priori' (C. I. Lewis) has been applied to propositions we decide by fiat to make immune to falsification by experience, e.g. 'Through a point not on a given straight line infinitely many straight lines parallel to the given one can be drawn', as a postulate of a non-Euclidean geometry.

The epistemological a priori/empirical distinction has often been thought to coincide with the metaphysical necessary/contingent distinction (see MODALITIES) and the logical ANALYTIC/synthetic distinction (concerning the structure of propositions). Kant, however, split the third distinction from the other two, calling some a priori and necessary propositions synthetic, while more recently Kripke has split the first two distinctions, arguing that some propositions are both a priori and contingent ('The standard metre rod is one metre long'), while others are both empirical and necessary ('Water is H_2O').

See also INNATE, RATIONALISM, INTUITION.

Aristotle, *Posterior Analytics* I. 1, 2.

D. Bostock, 'Necessary truth and a priori truth', *Mind*, 1988. (Complex but often illuminating defence of claim that a priori/ empirical and necessary/ contingent distinctions come apart, though for different reasons than Kripke gives.)

D. W. Hamlyn, *Theory of Knowledge*, Macmillan, 1970, Chapter 9. (General discussion of a priori knowledge.)

I. Kant, *Critique of Pure Reason*, 1781, 2nd edn 1787, B1–6.

J. J. Katz, 'What mathematical knowledge could be', *Mind*, 1995. (Defends a priori knowledge in maths, etc. as not requiring causal or quasi-perceptual contact with abstract objects.)

P. Kitcher, 'A. priori knowledge', *Philosophical Review*, 1980. (Offers analysis of a psychologistic or materialistic kind. For criticism, and defence of a moderate version of a more traditional type, see D. M. Summerfield, 'Modest a priori knowledge', *Philosophy and Phenomenological Research*, 1991.)

S. Kripke, *Naming and Necessity*, Blackwell, 1980 (originally published 1972).

H. Lehman, *Introduction to the Philosophy of Mathematics*, Blackwell, 1979. (Part ii defends an empiricist view of mathematics. Cf. also I. Lakatos, 'A renaissance of empiricism in the recent philosophy of mathematics', *British Journal for the Philosophy of Science*, 1976, tracing reactions to various unsettling developments like GÖDEL'S THEOREMS.)

C. I. Lewis, 'The pragmatic conception of the a priori', *Journal of Philosophy*, 1923, reprinted in H. Feigl and W. Sellars (eds), *Readings in Philosophical Analysis*, Appleton-Century-Crofts, 1949.

*P. Moser (ed.), *A Priori Knowledge*, Oxford UP, 1987. (Reprinted selections.)

A. Quinton, *The Nature of Things*, Routledge, 1973, pp. 132–4 ('A priori' and 'instinctive'.)

M. Thompson, 'On a priori truth', *Journal of Philosophy*, 1981. (Argues that it concerns our thinking itself, not any subject matter it has.)

Aquinas, St Thomas. c. 1224–74. He came from Aquino, near Naples, and worked at the University of Paris and elsewhere. His work largely consisted in continuing the efforts of his teacher Albert the Great to reconcile Greek philosophy with Christianity, and he was similarly influenced by the Arabs. He went beyond Albert in the extent to which he created a full-blooded philosophy, based on that of ARISTOTLE but developed it to fit in with Christian dogma; this involved original treatments of notions like BEING and analogy. He wrote prolifically, but his philosophical work is largely contained in monographs on particular questions, e.g. *On Being and Essence* (c.1253), *Disputed Questions on the Power of God* (c.1265); in more general works like *Disputed Questions on Truth* (1256–9); and in commentaries on Aristotle's main philosophical writings. It is summed up in the *Summa contra Gentiles* (c.1259–64) and the *Summa Theologica* (c.1265–73). He is also known for his 'five ways' of proving God's existence (see RELIGION). His philosophy, with that of his followers, is called Thomism. See also AUGUSTINE, COSMOLOGICAL, MARITAIN, METAPHYSICS, OCKHAM, ONTOLOGICAL ARGUMENT, PHILOSOPHY, SCOTUS, SUBSTANCE.

R. Goodwin (ed. and tr.), *Selected Writings of St Thomas Aquinas*, Macmillan, 1965. (Metaphysics, etc. Includes *On Being and Essence* and three other short works.)

A. C. Pegis (ed.), *Basic Writings of Saint Thomas Aquinas* (2 vols), Random House, 1945. (Theology. Vol. 1: *God and the Order of Creation*, vol. 2: *Man and the Conduct of Life*.)

Aretaic. In recent moral philosophy, and especially within VIRTUE ETHICS, there has been an interest in and focus upon human character and personality which has been called the Aretaic turn. This has

marked a contrast to the concentration on duty and rules of deontological ethics, and upon actions and their consequences in utilitarian
ethics. The word is derived from the Greek 'aretē', meaning excellence
or virtue.

Argument. See FUNCTION.

Aristotle. 384–22 BC. Pupil of PLATO, after whose death he travelled
round the Aegean (and was tutor to Alexander the Great), and then
founded Lyceum in Athens (355 BC; also called Peripatos; hence 'Peri-
patetics'). His interests were encyclopaedic, and he contributed to
most of the main branches of philosophy and natural science, as well
as initiating the systematic study of logic. His major works of current
interest include the *Organon* (set of treatises mainly on logic), *Metaphysics*, *Physics*, *De Anima (On the Soul)*, *Nicomachean Ethics*, *Poli-
tics*, *Poetics* (fragmentary). See also ALBERT, AMBIGUITY, A
PRIORI, AQUINAS, AUGUSTINE, BACON, BRENTANO, BEING,
CATEGORIES, CAUSATION, COSMOLOGICAL, DIALECTIC,
DIFFERENTIA, ELENCHUS, ENTELECHY, ETHICS, EXPLANA-
TION, FORM, FREEWILL, GOOD, INCONTINENCE, LOGIC,
MEANING, METAPHYSICS, MIND, MODALITIES, NEOPLATO-
NISTS, OCKHAM, PLEASURE (bibliography), PLENITUDE,
POLITICAL, PROPERTY, REASON, SCOTUS, SENSES, SOCRATES,
SPACE, SUBSTANCE, SYLLOGISM, THIRD MAN ARGUMENT,
TRANSCENDENTAL ARGUMENTS, TRUTH, UNIVERSALS,
ZENO'S PARADOXES.

J. L. Ackrill, (ed.), *Aristotle the Philosopher*, Oxford UP, 1981.
J. Barnes (ed.), *Oxford Translation of Aristotle*, 2nd edn, Princeton UP, 1984.
J. Barnes (ed.), *The Cambridge Companion to Aristotle*, Cambridge UP, 1995.
G. J. Hughes, *Routledge Philosophy Guidebook to Aristotle on Ethics*,
    Routledge, 2001.
A. Kenny, *Aristotle's Theory of the Will*, Yale UP, 1979.
M. Nussbaum and A. Rorty, *Essays on Aristotle's* De Anima, Clarendon, 1996.
J. O. Urmson, *Aristotle's Ethics*, Blackwell, 1988.

There are excellent entries on Aristotle in *The Stanford Encyclopedia
of Philosophy* (all accessed 1 March 2009) as follows:

S. M. Cohen, 'Aristotle's Metaphysics', *The Stanford Encyclopedia of Philo-
    sophy (Winter 2003 Edition)*, Edward N. Zalta (ed.). Available at: http://
    plato.stanford.edu/archives/win2003/entries/aristotle-metaphysics/.

R. Kraut, 'Aristotle's Ethics', *The Stanford Encyclopedia of Philosophy (Spring 2009 Edition)*, Edward N. Zalta (ed.). Available at: http://plato.stanford.edu/archives/spr2008/entries/aristotle-ethics/.

H. Mendell, 'Aristotle and Mathematics', *The Stanford Encyclopedia of Philosophy (Summer 2004 Edition)*, Edward N. Zalta (ed.). Available at: http://plato.stanford.edu/archives/sum2004/entries/aristotle-mathematics/.

F. Miller, 'Aristotle's Political Theory', *The Stanford Encyclopedia of Philosophy (Fall 2002 Edition)*, Edward N. Zalta (ed.). Available at: http://plato.stanford.edu/archives/fall2002/entries/aristotle-politics/.

C. Rapp, 'Aristotle's Rhetoric', *The Stanford Encyclopedia of Philosophy (Summer 2002 Edition)*, Edward N. Zalta (ed.). Available at: http://plato.stanford.edu/archives/sum2002/entries/aristotle-rhetoric/.

C. Shields, 'Aristotle's Psychology', *The Stanford Encyclopedia of Philosophy (Winter 2005 Edition)*, Edward N. Zalta (ed.). Available at: http://plato.stanford.edu/archives/win2005/entries/aristotle-psychology/.

R. Smith, 'Aristotle's Logic', *The Stanford Encyclopedia of Philosophy (Winter 2006 Edition)*, Edward N. Zalta (ed.). Available at: http://plato.stanford.edu/archives/win2006/entries/aristotle-logic/.

Aristotelianism. 'Modern' philosophy (starting with Descartes) and Renaissance interest in science is often portrayed as a reaction to the prevailing stifling Aristotelianism of the learned world, in which appeal to Aristotle was said settle the matter in any argument, whether philosophical or scientific: Aristotelianism is taken as a synonym for extreme conservatism and appeal to authority.

Aristotle's philosophy profoundly influenced many different schools of philosophers at many different times. Aristotle, 'The Wise Man', was extensively studied and commented on by Islamic philosophers such as AVERROES and AVICENNA. It was as a result of their works that the study of Aristotle flourished in Europe in the scholastic period of the twelfth and thirteenth centuries, and the assimilation of his work to make it compatible with Christian doctrine, by, for example, THOMAS AQUINAS. Later, in the Renaissance period, a variety of different interpretations and assimilations of Aristotle's work led to a wide variety of different forms of Aristotelianism. While there was a deference to the word of Aristotle, nevertheless that often concealed, in Islamic, Scholastic and in Renaissance Aristotelianism, original philosophical thought introduced covertly as interpretation of 'The Great Teacher'.

C. B. Schmitt, *Aristotle and the Renaissance*, Harvard UP, 1983. (Clear distinctions between various different forms of Aristotelianism.)

Armstrong, David M. 1926–. Born in Melbourne, he has worked mainly at Sydney, and is a leading representative of Australian materialism, which he combines with a moderate realism. After some early work on epistemology, he has written mainly on the philosophy of mind and metaphysics. His publications include *Perception and the Physical World*, 1961; *Bodily Sensations*, 1962; *A Materialist Theory of Mind*, 1968 (2nd edn, 1993); *Universals and Scientific Realism, vol. 1: Nominalism and Realism* (critical), *vol. 2: A Theory of Universals* (positive), 1978; *What is a Law of Nature?* 1983; *Universals: An Opinionated Introduction*, 1989 (partly revised 1978, vol. 2); *A Combinational Theory of Possibility*, 1989; *A World of States of Affairs*,1997; *The Mind-Body Problem: An Opinionated Introduction*, 1999; *Truth and Truthmakers*, 2004.

Arrow paradox. See ZENO'S PARADOXES.

Arrow's paradox. See VOTING PARADOX.

Art (philosophy of). See AESTHETICS.

Assertion sign. The symbol '⊢' invented by Frege, who drew its two parts from a complex system of symbols. It means either that what follows it is being asserted and not merely mentioned for consideration, or, more usually, that what follows can be asserted as a truth of logic, or as a theorem in a system (see AXIOM SYSTEM), 'p, q ⊢ r' normally means that proposition r is assertable if propositions p and q are given as true.

Assertoric. See MODALITIES.

Atheism. Atheism is disbelief in the existence of God, or, more strongly, affirming God's non-existence. Within Western philosophy this has taken the form of criticizing the traditional arguments for the existence of God and providing further reasons for supposing that God does not exist – for example, that the concept of God is a logically inconsistent one, or that the existence of evil in the world is incompatible with the existence of the traditionally conceived omniscient, omnipotent and benevolent Christian God (see THEODICY). See AGNOSTICISM (and Smart's article listed there).

D. Dennett, *Breaking the Spell: Religion as a Natural Phenomenon*, Penguin, 2006.

R. Le Poidevin, *Arguing for Atheism*, Routledge, 1996. (Clear, introductory work that aims at provoking discussion.)

M. Martin, *Atheism: A Philosophical Justification*, Temple UP, 1989, and 1992. (Is what the title says.)

J. Thrower, *A Short History of Western Atheism*, Pemberton, 1971.

Atomic sentence. A logically simple sentence containing no logical OPERATOR.

Atomism. The theory that matter consists of very small irreducible atoms, which can be traced back to Ancient Greece, where Leucippus fl. 450–420 BC and Democritus c.460–c.370 BC claimed that all objects consisted of a mixture of atoms and space, and that change simply consisted in the rearrangement of these fundamental atoms in space. Aristotle's rejection of the theory led to its neglect until with the development of modern science, it was revived in the writings of BACON, BRUNO, HOBBES, GALILEO, DESCARTES and others. LOGICAL ATOMISM is a quite separate theory, developed by RUSSELL and WITTGENSTEIN about the smallest and irreducible atoms of thought.

Attributive. An adjective stands in attributive position if it goes with its noun, ('A red house') and in predicative position if it occurs after a verb ('The house is red'). It is grammatically attributive if it can only occur attributively ('veritable') and grammatically predicative if it can only occur predicatively ('well', 'over', meaning 'finished'). It is logically attributive if a significant noun or equivalent must always be understood after it. Thus 'That mouse is large' is normally taken to mean 'That mouse is a large mouse' – while it is large for a mouse, it need not be large for an animal in general. 'Logically predicative' has no use.

Attributives are of different kinds. A large mouse is large for a mouse, but a mere child is not mere for a child. Adjectives like 'bogus' or 'alleged', which repudiate or cast doubt on the application of the following noun, occasionally called alienans, may or may not be called attributive. See also CATEGORIES, GOOD.

J. Brentlinger, 'Incomplete predicates and the two-world theory of the Phaedo,' *Phronesis*, 1972, p. 71 note 13. (Brief discussion, with references.)

P. T. Geach, 'Good and evil', *Analysis*, vol. 17, 1956–7. (Explains distinction and claims 'good' is always logically attributive.)

W. V. O. Quine, *Word and Object*, MIT Press, 1960. (See p. 103 for 'mere child' example.)

Augustine, St. 354–430. Born in North Africa, he was converted to Christianity in his early thirties, and became bishop of Hippo in 395 or 396. His philosophical interests turned progressively into theological ones, and he strongly influenced medieval thought, in ways somewhat contrasting with the current represented by ARISTOTLE and AQUINAS. His personal religious experience urged him to extricate himself from scepticism, and led him to study the types of knowledge (perception, reason, etc.). He tried to work out the nature of human beings in a Christian framework, and studied problems concerning the universe and its creation, the mind/body problem, freewill, and, now often regarded as his most lasting philosophical contribution, the nature of time (see SPACE). He also discussed ethical and (in the *City of God*) political topics. He started from a generally PLATONIC and NEOPLATONIC base. His important writings containing philosophical material include the *Confessions* (400), *On Free Choice of the Will* (freewill, and proof of God's existence), *City of God* (late in life and largely theological), *On the Literal Meaning of Genesis* (late; a commentary on Genesis).

> W. J. Oates (ed.), *Basic Writings of Saint Augustine* (2 vols), Random House, 1948. (Vol. 1 has *Confessions* and other works; vol. 2 includes *The City of God*.)

Austin, John L. 1911–60. British philosopher who worked in Oxford where he was one of the leaders of 'linguistic PHILOSOPHY' after the Second World War. He emphasized the philosophical significance of the nuances of ordinary language, and is mainly noted for his theory of SPEECH ACTS. 'Ifs and Cans', 1960. 'A Plea for Excuses', 1956 (two lectures relevant to FREEWILL, and reprinted in his *Collected Papers*, 1961.) *Sense and Sensibilia*, 1962 (attacks SENSEDATUM theory of AYER). *How to Do Things with Words*, 1962 (main source for speech act theory). See also CONDITIONALS, EPISTEMOLOGY, LANGUAGE (PHILOSOPHY OF), MEANING, SCEPTICISM, TRUTH. Not to be confused with John Austin (1790–1859), who was a legal philosopher noted mainly for his theory that the law is the command of the sovereign. *The Province of Jurisprudence Determined*, 1832.

Autological. See HETEROLOGICAL.

Autonomy. In politics, self-determination, self governing, not under anyone else's authority. Extended from its political sense (used

28

originally of the ancient Greek city-states) to be an important quality in persons in Kant's philosophy. Only through the exercise of reason, in the application of laws that we give to ourselves, does Kant say we achieve actions that are both truly moral and the actions of autonomous beings. Also used of ethics, the autonomy of ethics lying in its non-reducibility to non-ethical claims.

G. Dworkin, *The Theory and Practice of Autonomy*, Cambridge UP, 1988 (on political autonomy).

Averroes (Ibn Rushd, Abu'l Walid Muhammad). 1126–98. One of the most important Islamic philosophers, born in Spain. Worked in Spain and Morocco as a judge. Commentator on Aristotle. He argues for the compatibility of religion (and Islam in particular) and philosophy. His emphasis both on philosophy as an important form of truth, and on the importance of philosophers having a role in the state, is very reminiscent of Plato's *Republic*.

O. Leaman, *Averroes and His Philosophy*, Clarendon, 1988.

Avicenna (Ibn Sina, Abu 'Ali Al-Husayn). 980–1037. Born in Bukhara (now in Uzbekistan), physician and scholar, worked mainly in what is now Iran. One of the most important medieval Arab philosophers. He gives a comprehensive systematic account of God and Being, giving an important role to Reason. Strongly influenced both other Islamic philosophers and Christian philosophers, including Thomas Aquinas.

L. Goodman, *Avicenna*, Routledge, 1992. (Useful introduction.)

Avowals. Certain first-person utterances, like 'I am in pain', which when sincere seem to be infallible. Another person saying 'He is in pain' about oneself could be mistaken. Problems arise about whether avowals can, or need, be justified, and whether they are assertions.

D. Gasking, 'Avowals', M. E. Lean, 'Mr Gasking on avowals', in R. J. Butler (ed.), *Analytical Philosophy*, 1st series, 1962. (Relation of avowals to justification and fallibility.)

F. E. Sparshott, 'Avowals and their uses', *Proceedings of the Aristotelian Society*, 1961–2. (Avowals and their relations to similar utterances.)

Axiology. From the Greek, axia, meaning value. The philosophical study of values in general – not just moral, but aesthetic, and other

forms of value as well. Associated historically with the work of
BRENTANO, MOORE and ROSS. Revival of interest in recent
years. Often now termed 'value theory'. See ETHICS.

Nicholas Rescher, *Value Matters: Studies in Axiology*, Ontos Verlag, 2005.

Axiom system. Any system wherein certain expressions are derived in
accordance with a given set of rules from a decidable initial set of
expressions taken as given (and called axioms). The axioms themselves of such a system form an axiom set. 'Axiom system' is often
used for 'axiom set'. The formation rules specify what elements or
symbols the system is going to use and what combinations of them
are to count as expressions that can serve as axioms or be tested to
see whether they can be derived from the axioms. These expressions
are called well-formed formulae or wff, for short, and those of them
that can be derived from the axioms are called theorems. The formation rules are analogous to rules of grammar, and the wff are
analogous to meaningful sentences. The axioms themselves will count
as theorems if, as in most systems, they are trivially derivable from
themselves. For reasons of economy and elegance the axioms should
be independent, i.e. not derivable within the given system from each
other. The axioms may be infinite in number, provided rules for
selecting them are given. Such a rule will define an axiom scheme
by saying 'All wff of such and such a kind are to count as axioms'.
The transformation rules say what wff can be derived from others,
and so govern what the theorems of the system will be, given the
axioms.

In an abstract axiom system the expressions are simply symbols, or
marks on paper. But if the system is applied to a certain subject
matter we have a MODEL or interpretation of the system, and the
subject matter is said to be axiomatized. To axiomatize a subject is
thus to systematize it, and show how most of it can be derived if
certain selected axioms and transformation rules are taken for granted. These are so selected that the system shall be CONSISTENT and,
where possible, COMPLETE. The axioms are therefore either true
propositions, which need not be simple or obvious, or propositions
which can be postulated as true without leading to contradiction, as
in non-Euclidean geometries (see SPACE). The transformation rules
are related to VALIDITY as the axioms are to truth. See also
MODELS, BOOLEAN ALGEBRA.

C. Glymour, *Thinking Things Through*, MIT Press, 1992.

Ayer, Alfred J. 1910–89. British philosopher, born in London, who worked mostly in Oxford and London. He introduced logical POSITIVISM to Britain in 1936, and subsequently defended an empiricist outlook, writing mainly on perception and meaning, as well as on various historical issues. *Language, Truth and Logic*, 1936, 2nd edn (with important new 'Introduction') 1946. *The Foundations of Empirical Knowledge*, 1940 (the book criticized by AUSTIN). *Philosophical Essays*, 1954. *The Problem of Knowledge*, 1956. *Probability and Evidence*, 1972. *The Central Questions of Philosophy*, 1973. See also BASIC STATEMENTS, NEGATION, PHENOMENALISM, PRAGMATISM, PROBABILITY, SENSE DATA, SENTENCES.

B

Bacon, Francis. 1561–1626. Philosopher, essayist and politician, he was born and lived in London, was created Lord Verulam and Viscount St Albans, and appointed Lord Chancellor. His main philosophical work lay in the philosophy of science, where he tried to replace what he saw as the a priorism of the Aristotelian tradition by a new and thoroughgoing empiricism. His political writings rely heavily on the scientific optimism which he thought this method justified. *Essays*, 1597, expanded later. *The Proficience and Advancement of Learning*, 1605 (later revised as *De Dignitate et Augmentis Scientiarum* 1623). *Novum Organum*, 1620, P. Urbach and J. Gibson (eds and trans.), Open Court, 1994). This and the *De Dignitate et Augmentis* form part of the projected *Instauratio Magna*. *New Atlantis*, 1627 (a scientific Utopia.) Not to be confused with Roger Bacon (died 1292), who was a student of sciences and languages, and who wrote commentaries on various works of Aristotle and tried to institute a 'universal science'. See also MILL.

Bad faith. In Sartre, a kind of self-deception, where this involves behaving as a mere thing rather than realizing, in acts of authentic choice, the true type of being for a human being (what Sartre calls 'existence', or being 'pour soir' and not merely 'en soi'). This distinction is metaphysical, but has moral effects, for in 'bad faith' we evade responsibility and 'anxiety' by 'not noticing' possibilities of choice, or by behaving in a role others expect of us. A famous example is Sartre's 'waiter'. See also EXISTENTIALISM, INCONTINENCE.

H. Bergson, *Laughter*, Macmillan, 1911, French original, 1900. (Bergson's theory of the comic has some affinity to Sartre's view of bad faith, though Bergson and Sartre wrote quite independently.)

H. Fingarette, *Self-Deception*, 1969. (Self-deception in general. Cf. D. W. Hamlyn and H. O. Mounce, 'Self-deception', *Proceedings of the Aristotelian Society*, supplementary vol. 1971.)

J.-P. Sartre, *Being and Nothingness*, 1943, trans. 1956, Part 1, Chapter 2. (See also his *Essays on Existence* (ed. W. Baskin), Citadel Press, 1965 (selections from his writings. For waiter example see pp. 167ff.).)

Bald man (paradox of). See HEAP.

Barber paradox. Suppose a barber shaves all the men in a town, except those who shave themselves. Does he shave himself? If he does, he is one of those excepted group whom the barber (himself) does not shave. If he doesn't shave himself, then he is one of the group who is shaved by the barber (himself). So he both does and does not shave himself. So the original supposition ('Suppose there is a barber ... ') is false. Less important than RUSSELL'S PARADOX, etc., because there is no reason to assert the existence of such a barber.

M. Clark, *Paradoxes from A–Z*, London: Routledge, 2002.

Basic action. Action not involving further action as its cause, or which we do not perform by performing another action; e.g. moving our hands but not steering our car, which we do by moving our hands.

A. Baier, 'The search for basic actions', *American Philosophical Quarterly*, 1971. (Develops and criticizes the notion, giving references.)

S. Candlish, 'Inner and outer basic actions', *Proceedings of the Aristotelian Society*, 1983–4 (Further development and references.)

L. H. Davis, *Theory of Action*, Prentice-Hall, 1979. (Mainly on action in general, but see its index.)

Basic beliefs. Beliefs that do not rely on other beliefs for justification (for example, beliefs based on sense-experience, self-evident beliefs, incorrigible beliefs). See FOUNDATIONALISM.

A. Plantinga, *Faith and Rationality*, Notre Dame, 1983, pp. 39–44.

Basic statements. Also sometimes called protocol statements (sentences) or (by Carnap) primitive protocol statements. Statements which, according to logical POSITIVISTS in particular, are needed as the basis for the rest of our empirical knowledge. But the various conceptions of them have little else in common. Their subject matter varies, with different writers, from immediate personal experience to the common world. Their role may be to give a foundation for the individual's own knowledge (Ayer), or for INTERSUBJECTIVELY testable knowledge (O. Neurath). In a variant of the latter role they provide tools for testing universal hypotheses, and are therefore themselves mainly singular existential statements, saying that something exists or occurs at a certain place and date (Popper; e.g. the statement 'There is a black swan in Sydney now' could be used to test the hypothesis 'All swans are white').

A. J. Ayer, *Language, Truth and Logic*, Gollancz, 1936. (See 2nd edn 1946, p. 10.)

R. Carnap, *The Unity of Science*, Kegan Paul, Trench, Trubner, 1934, particularly pp. 43–4.

O. Neurath, 'Protocol sentences', in A. J. Ayer (ed.), *Logical Positivism*, Free Press, 1959 (trans. from German original in Erkenntnis, vol. 3, 1932–3).

K. R. Popper, *The Logic of Scientific Discovery, Hutchinson*, 1959 (German original, 1934), particularly § 28–9.

Bayes's theorem. Theorem of PROBABILITY calculus, variously formulated and developed by and after T. Bayes (1702–61). Briefly, where p and q are propositions, the probability of p, given q, is that of q, given p, multiplied by the prior probability of p and divided by the prior probability of q. The prior probability of a proposition is the probability it has by itself, not its probability 'given' another proposition. 'Bayesian' inductive procedures take the theorem to imply that the increase in probability that a hypothesis gains when its consequences are verified is proportional to the improbability of those consequences. The theorem's validity is undisputed, but its applications and usefulness are controversial (cf. CONFIRMATION). One form of the law of large NUMBERS, unrelated to the above, is also sometimes called 'Bayes's theorem'. 'Bayesian' is also often used by adherents of the subjectivist theory of PROBABILITY for the process which they think ought to govern changes in degrees of belief. A Bayesian approach to probability allows hypotheses, etc., to have probabilities, while a frequentist approach, using the frequency theory of PROBABILITY, confines probabilities to repeatable events.

H. E. Kyburg, *Probability and Inductive Logic*, Macmillan, 1970. (See its index.)

Beauty. Truth, goodness and beauty are NORMATIVE concepts which, in Ancient Greek philosophy, were thought to have a single origin, and, although truth and goodness have remained central concepts in philosophy and metaphysics, beauty has received somewhat less attention. Plato claimed that beauty was one of the transcendent FORMS. As with goodness, there are disputes between realists and antirealists, with the former claiming that beauty is a non-relational property. In the eighteenth century, it was thought of as a sensory property. It was often claimed that beauty was what was common to all works of art, the defining property of art. But not all works of art are beautiful: they may, for example, be terrifying, awe-inspiring or disturbing without being beautiful. In the eighteenth century, a contrast was drawn between the beautiful and the SUBLIME, both to be found in nature as well as in art. In the mid-twentieth century, Austin claimed that aesthetics had become too preoccupied with beauty and should pay attention instead to such concepts as the dainty and the dumpy. Although aesthetics has, indeed, subsequently studied a whole range of other concepts, discussion of beauty has more recently made something of a comeback. See AESTHETICS, REALISM.

F. Hutcheson, *An Inquiry concerning Beauty, Order, Harmony, Design*, 1725. (P. Kivy has edited an edition with useful introduction and notes, Martinus Nijhoff, 1993.)

M. Mothersill, *Beauty Restored*, Adams Bannister Cox, 1991. (Influential modern treatment.)

F. Sibley, *Approach To Aesthetics: Collected Papers On Philosophical Aesthetics*, (ed.) J. Benson, B. Redfern and J. Roxbee Cox, Clarendon, 2001. (Discussion of concepts other than beauty, including ugliness.)

N. Zangwill, *The Metaphysics of Beauty*, Cornell UP, 2001. (Excellent introduction to aesthetics.)

Beauvoir, Simone De. See DE BEAUVOIR, SIMONE.

Bedeutung. See MEANING.

Begging the question. Or *petitio principii*: assuming something in order to prove it. An argument whose premises already contain the conclusion. Often used of a question that assumes the truth at issue – 'Have you stopped beating your wife?' Increasingly in common usage the phrase is (controversially) used to mean simply 'raises the question'.

Behaviour. What an object, particularly a living creature, does. There are problems and ambiguities: is intention, or at least controllability, needed for behaviour? Are heartbeats behaviour? Must behaviour affect the outer world and be publicly observable? Is silent thinking behaviour? Must behaviour described in one way (e.g. waving one's arms) also be behaviour when described in another (accidentally breaking a vase)? Can the utterances of a parrot be called verbal behaviour? Should an uncontrollable reflex action, like a knee jerk, be called behaviour of the knee but not of the person? See also ACTION.

D. Davidson, 'Psychology as philosophy', in S. C. Brown (ed.), *Philosophy of Psychology*, Macmillan and Barnes and Noble, 1974, with comments and replies, reprinted with replies but without comments in Davidson's *Essays on Action and Events*, Oxford UP, 1980. (One view of behaviour, causation and rationality.)

D. W. Hamlyn, 'Behaviour', *Philosophy*, 1953. (Revised on one point in his 'Causality and human behaviour', *Proceedings of the Aristotelian Society*, supplementary vol. 1964.)

G. H. von Wright, *Explanation and Understanding*, Routledge, 1971, p. 193, n. 8 (Knee-jerk.)

Behaviourism. Doctrine or policy of reducing mental concepts to publicly observable BEHAVIOUR. In psychology it involves an experimental, and often physicalist and operationalist approach (see POSITIVISM), which rejects introspection, and is concerned with prediction and control rather than understanding. Logical or analytic behaviourism defines mentalistic terms using only behavioural or physiological terms. Metaphysical or philosophical behaviourism refuses to see more than physical behaviour where claims for mentality are made. Methodological behaviourism insists on behavioural tests but is neutral on the philosophical implications. Radical behaviourism is similar, but more rigorous; it rejects hypothetical constructs and intervening variables (see LOGICAL CONSTRUCTIONS). See also COGNITIVE, PSYCHOLOGISM.

N. Block (ed.), *Readings in the Philosophy of Psychology*, vol. 1, Harvard UP and Methuen, 1980. (Includes section on behaviourism.)

G. Ryle, *The Concept of Mind*, Hutchinson, 1949. (Classic work, usually taken to support analytical behaviourism.)

Being. Being seems at first to be a property of everything, or at least of everything there is, for how can anything have a property unless it is there to have it? Do unicorns have, say, the property of being vegetarian? Or is it only that they would have it if there were any unicorns? But if we accept this latter view, being cannot be a property after all, for anything which was to have it would have to have it already in order to do so, which is absurd; to say that something exists is not to say something about it. This point, that being is not a property, or, as it is commonly expressed, that 'exists' is not a (logical as against grammatical) predicate, was insisted on by Kant who used it to attack the ONTOLOGICAL ARGUMENT, though others have disagreed (see Strawson). It raises the question: what counts as being a property or (logical) predicate?

A position to some extent like Kant's is that of Aristotle, who insisted that being could not be an all-embracing genus (as animal is the genus of horse, cow, etc.), and that to call something existent is not to add to its description. (He said the same about unity and, for a different reason, about goodness.) Out of this arose the medieval doctrine of transcendentals. Aquinas listed 'being', 'one', 'true', 'thing', 'something', 'good' as transcending the CATEGORIES and applying to everything. Some other writers, e.g. Duns Scotus, use 'transcendentals' rather more widely, and Aristotle said of 'good' not, with Aquinas, that everything real was somehow good, but that 'good' was predicable in all the categories – a substance, quality, relation, etc. could be good. These transcendentals are usually included among the syncategorematic terms (see CATEGORIES (end)). They were intended to delineate the characteristics of being qua being, another notion originating in Aristotle, who made it the subject matter of metaphysics. In English, 'being' can be a participle ('Being fat, I ate less') or a gerund ('Being fat is unhealthy'), but Greek distinguishes, and Aristotle uses the participle, sometimes in the plural ('beings qua beings'). Interpretations of it differ. It may refer to everything that is, considered just as being, or to something which somehow accounts for the being of everything else. This may be substance in general or the highest kind of substance like God, or the movers of the cosmic spheres. On this latter view, God and the movers account for the being of other substances, and substance accounts for that of qualities, relations, etc.

Despite the difficulties in supposing that there are things which do not exist, philosophers have often been reluctant to put into one basket all the things that in some sense have being. Aristotle shows this reluctance in his doctrine of CATEGORIES (see *Metaphysics*, Book 4, Chapter 2), but more recently, different kinds of being have been distinguished in another way. Existence is sometimes distinguished from subsistence and other notions. Meinong, for instance, evidently thinking that a thing must in some sense be there for us to talk about it at all, thought that material objects in space and time exist, along with other things in space and time like shadows and gravitational fields, while things like UNIVERSALS, numbers and the difference between red and green, subsist. Fictional or imaginary objects, which can be concrete (unicorns) or abstract (the prime number between eight and ten), are sometimes said to subsist, but for Meinong they neither exist nor subsist; he says simply that they 'are objects' and have Sosein which means, literally, being so, or essence. But 'exist' and 'subsist', like 'existent' and 'subsistent', are often used interchangeably, especially when it is said that certain things, such as universals, do have being in some sense, and are not, as nominalism holds, analysable in terms of mere words.

Existence and subsistence, etc. can here be regarded as different grades or kinds of being. One strand of idealism treats being rather as having different degrees. Reality as a whole, the 'absolute', exists fully, while its parts derive their reality from their relations to it and to each other, and exist, but less fully, in proportion to their comprehensiveness.

Carnap divided questions of existence into those internal and external to a given system, e.g. that of arithmetic. 'Is there a prime number between six and nine?' is an internal question and belongs to arithmetic. 'Do numbers exist?' is an external question and belongs to philosophy, along with similar questions about universals, propositions, etc.

These various problems about fictional and timeless objects connect metaphysics with philosophical logic, and two further questions arise here. First, how do we tell to what ontology (i.e. list of things that are) a philosopher has committed himself? What counts as holding that, e.g. universals do or do not exist? Quine introduced this question to replace the traditional question, 'What is there?' He answered with the slogan, 'to be is to be the value of a variable'; i.e. we are committed to the reality of a thing or kind of things if and only if we cannot state our views in formal (i.e. logical) language without using affirmative statements where VARIABLES ranging over the thing or things in question are bound by the existential quantifier (see QUANTIFICATION). The second question is what the laws of logic themselves commit us to. In particular, can we prove by logic alone that there must be at least one object? By the predicate CALCULUS (let F stand for some predicate and a for any arbitrary individual) the seemingly undeniable logical truth 'Everything is F or not F' implies 'a is F or not F'. This in turn implies 'At least one thing is F or not F', and therefore that there is at least one thing. Various attempts to avoid this have been made. Both these questions are bound up with the interpretation of 'is' in the existential quantifier. Does it signify existence in a substantial sense, and if not, then what does it signify?

Many philosophers, especially the medievals and the existentialists, have contrasted a thing's essence, or what it is, with its existence (though in the case of God, these have been thought by Aquinas to coincide – but the sense of 'existence' ('esse') here is controversial). Some forms of existentialism contrast being or essence with existence. Being belongs to animals and inanimate things, and existence only to humans, who can create themselves and are not products of the environment.

A linguistic question concerns the different senses often ascribed to the verb 'to be'. The main senses are: existential ('These things shall be', 'There is ... '), predicative or copulative ('This is red'), classifying ('This is a shoe'; often subsumed under predicative), identifying ('This is Socrates', 'Tully is Cicero'). In ancient Greek it seems to have had also a veridical sense (' ... is true'). Other senses, some rather technical, have been suggested, including constitutive ('This house is bricks and mortar') and presentational ('The meaning of 'bald' is: hairless'). Sometimes 'is' signifies the present tense as in 'He is hot', but sometimes it is timeless as in 'Twice two is four' or 'Chaucer is earlier than Shakespeare'. What makes these senses different is that different things can be inferred from statements made by sentences containing them. 'Tully is Cicero' implies 'Cicero is Tully', but 'This book is red' does not imply 'Red is this book', where 'red' is the subject. But these differences are complex and controversial in detail, and so is the question what, if anything, links the senses together. (Aristotle thought that at least some senses were linked by 'focal meaning'; see above, and AMBIGUITY.) Some think the attempt to distinguish definite senses is mistaken (Kahn).

See PHENOMENOLGY and DASEIN for phenomenologists' discussion of being.

See also SUBSTANCE, REFERRING, ESSENCE, CATEGORIES.

Aristotle, *Metaphysics*, 998b22–7 (being not a genus; cf. Topics, 144a32–b4); 1003b26 ('one' and 'existent' not descriptive; cf. 1045a36–b8); Book 4, Chapters 1–3, Book 6, Chapter 1 (being qua being). *Nicomachean Ethics*, 1096a19–29 ('good').

J. Barnes, *The Ontological Argument*, Macmillan, 1972, Chapter 3. (Also has bibliography, to which add S. Read, '"Exists" is a predicate', *Mind*, 1980 (watch for misprints), discussed by L. Chipman, 'Existence, reference and definite singular terms', *Mind*, 1982.)

R. Carnap, *Meaning and Necessity*, 2nd edn, Chicago UP, 1956, supplement, A, § 2, reprinted in C. Landesman (ed.), *The Problem of Universals*, Basic Books, 1971. (External and internal questions.)

L. J. Cohen, *The Diversity of Meaning*, Methuen, 1962, § 33. (Does logic prove the universe cannot be empty?)

P. T. Geach, 'Form and existence', *Proceedings of the Aristotelian Society*, 1954–5, reprinted in A. Kenny (ed.), *Aquinas*, Doubleday, 1969, Macmillan, 1970. (Essence and existence in Aquinas.)

C. H. Kahn, 'The Greek verb "to be" and the concept of being', in *Foundations of Language*, 1966. (Attacks rigidity of distinction into senses.) See also his *The Verb 'Be' in Ancient Greek*, part 6 of J. W. M. Verhaar (ed.), *The Verb 'Be' and its Synonyms*, Reidel, 1973.

I. Kant, *Critique of Pure Reason*, 1781, 2nd edn 1787, B626–9. (Classic attack on existence as predicate.)

L. Linsky, *Referring*, Routledge, 1967. (Discusses theories of Meinong and later writers, playing down the metaphysical extravagance often attributed to Meinong.)

E. J. Lowe, *Kinds of Being: A Study of Individuation, Identity and the Logic of Sortal Terms*, Blackwell, 1988. (Distinguishes uses of 'is', and claims mutual dependence of individuals and kinds.)

A. Meinong, 'The theory of objects', trans. in R. Chisholm (ed.), *Realism and the Background of Phenomenology*, Free Press, Glencoe, 1960.

Plato. Relevant passages include *Republic*, 476e ff., *Timaeus*, 27d.

W. V. O. Quine, 'On what there is', in *Review of Metaphysics*, 1948, reprinted in his book *From a Logical Point of View*, Harper and Row, 1953; in L. Linsky (ed.), *Semantics and the Philosophy of Language*, Oxford UP, 1952; in Landesman (above); and (with comments and contributions from others on the same theme) in *Proceedings of the Aristotelian Society*, supplementary vol. 1951. ('To be is to be the value of a variable'. Cf. also his defence of this in 'Ontology and ideology revisited', *Journal of Philosophy*, 1983.)

W. Sellars, 'Grammar and existence: A preface to ontology', *Mind*, 1960, reprinted in Landesman (above). (Rather more technical criticism of Quine.)

P. F. Strawson, 'Is existence never a predicate?', *Critica*, 1967, reprinted in his *Freedom and Resentment*, Methuen, 1974.

J. J. Valberg, 'Improper singular terms', *Proceedings of the Aristotelian Society*, 1970–1, p. 132. (Presentational being.)

G. J. Warnock, 'Metaphysics in logic', in A. Flew (ed.), *Essays in Conceptual Analysis*, Macmillan, 1956. (Criticizes Quine's use of logic to solve ontological problems.)

D. Wiggins, *Sameness and Substance*, Blackwell, 1980. (Constitutive 'is'; see index.)

Belief. Assent to or acceptance of the truth of propositions, statements or facts (but see CONFIRMATION (end)). The proposition forms the content of the belief, and to believe is usually regarded as in some sense involving, and perhaps as standing in a certain relation to, the relevant proposition, so that belief is a propositional attitude (cf. SENTENCES). Belief is rather like JUDGEMENT except for being a state rather than a mental act. It is often regarded as a DISPOSITION, and as such need not be constantly manifesting itself: we have many beliefs we are not currently thinking of, and sometimes may not even be aware of having. But presumably it must manifest itself sometimes, or at least be able to do so (though the REALISM/ antirealism debate raises difficulties here), and this raises problems in some cases: can we believe TAUTOLOGIES, and even contradictions? Where p is a proposition, can we believe p and believe not-p (to be distinguished from not believing p). And does this entail believing p and not-p? Also, can we believe what we know is false (or regard as improbable), and can we be mistaken about whether we believe something? When are beliefs justified? These questions link belief with knowledge and rationality (see EPISTEMOLOGY).

A belief may be *de dicto* or *de re* (see MODALITIES) according as it matters, or does not, how what it is about is described. Suppose I believe a certain spy should be hanged, without realizing that the spy is my sister. Then I believe *de re*, but not *de dicto*, that my sister should be hanged – I believe it of her. See INTENSIONALITY AND INTENTIONALITY. But the distinction is controversial.

Further problems concern how belief relates to other notions, such as desires, actions, inner experiences and language. In fact, difficulties in isolating activities in the brain that could correspond to belief have even led some people to say there is no such thing as belief. Like meaning and thinking, belief also raises the sort of problems discussed under INTERNALISM. Also, how far is belief, assuming it does exist, voluntary, and can we have a duty to believe something (the ethics of belief)? Often, however, 'believe' is a parenthetical verb, in the sense that 'I believe it's raining' or 'It's raining (I believe)', is meant to be about the weather, not about the speaker. See also Moore's PARADOX about belief.

Finally, we can 'believe in' the existence, occurrence, truth, validity or value of something, or in something we think ought to be or occur. We often use 'believe in' for what is good rather than bad; we 'believe in' Smith's generosity but not his malevolence.

R. M. Chisholm, 'Firth on the ethics of belief', *Philosophy and Phenomenological Research*, 1991. (Relations between ethical and epistemological requirements.)

D. Dennett, 'Beyond belief', in A. Woodfield (ed.), *Thought and Object*, Clarendon, 1982, reprinted with afterthoughts and other relevant items in his *The Intentional Stance*, MIT Press, 1987. (General problems about belief (see particularly pp. 54ff. (pp. 168ff. in reprint) on *de re/de dicto* distinction.)

*A. P. Griffiths (ed.), *Knowledge and Belief*, Oxford UP, 1967. (Articles and bibliography, with introduction. See article by Braithwaite for a dispositional account.)

J. Heil, 'Believing what one ought', *Journal of Philosophy*, 1983. (Can it ever be reasonable or right to believe against the evidence? See also his 'Doxastic incontinence', *Mind*, 1984, and A. Michalos, 'The morality of cognitive decision-making', in M. Broad and D. Walton (eds), *Action Theory*, Reidel, 1980. For classic discussion see W. K. Clifford, 'The ethics of belief' in his *Lectures and Essays*, vol. 2, Macmillan, 1879, and see P. Helm, *Belief Policies*, Cambridge UP, 1994, for discussion of this and related issues. Clifford's essay, and William James's response, *The Will to Believe*, together with A. J. Burger's contemporary response to James, *An Examination of 'The Will to Believe'*, available at: http://ajburger. homestead.com/ethics.html (accessed 1 March 2009).)

K. Lehrer, 'Acceptance and belief reconsidered', in P. Engel (ed.), *Believing and Accepting*, Kluwer, 2000. (Makes distinction between ordinary, unconsidered, beliefs, and those that are more considered, and central to one's 'epistemic mission'.)

W. G. Lycan, 'Tacit belief', in R. J. Bogdan (ed.), *Belief: Form, Content and Function*, Clarendon, 1986.

R. B. Marcus, 'A proposed solution to a puzzle about belief', *Midwest Studies in Philosophy*, vol. vi, 1981. (Presents and discusses a puzzle raised by Kripke and also discusses belief and assent. See also her 'Rationality and believing the impossible', *Journal of Philosophy*, 1983. For Kripke's puzzle see his article in N. Salmon and S. Soames (eds), *Propositions and Attitudes*, Oxford UP, 1988, reprinted from A. Margalit (ed.), *Meaning and Use*, Reidel, 1979, where a comment by Putnam is added.)

D. H. Mellor (ed.), *Prospects for Pragmatism*, Cambridge UP, 1980. (Essays in honour of F. P. Ramsey (1903–30), many of which are relevant to belief. Mellor's own contribution, on 'Consciousness and degrees of belief', develops a theory of conscious belief, linking it to the subjectivist theory of probability, and is reprinted in his *Matters of Metaphysics*, Cambridge UP, 1991.)

J. Perry, 'The problem of the essential indexical', *Nous*, 1979, reprinted in N. Salmon and S. Soames (eds), *Propositional Attitudes*, Oxford UP, 1988, (Difficulties raised by the fact that some beliefs seem to involve indexicals or TOKEN-REFLEXIVES essentially.)

H. H. Price, 'Belief "in" and belief "that"', *Religious Studies*, 1965, reprinted in B. Mitchell (ed.), *The Philosophy of Religion*, Oxford UP, 1971.

S. P. Stich, *From Folk Psychology to COGNITIVE Science: The Case Against Belief*, MIT Press, 1983. (Discusses how cognitive science has tried to rehabilitate FOLK PSYCHOLOGY from the ravages of BEHAVIOUR-ISM, but expresses 'reluctant scepticism' (p. 5) over whether this will be ultimately possible. Cf. critical discussion by T. Crane in 'The language of thought: No syntax without semantics', *Mind and Language*, 1990 and also J. A. Fodor, *Psychosemantics*, MIT Press, 1987.)

Bentham, Jeremy. 1748–1832. Moral, political and legal philosopher, who was born in London and worked mainly there. He is generally regarded as the first major UTILITARIAN thinker, though he also had some interest in the theory of meaning, where he held a nominalist position, treating abstract entities as 'fictions'; this position underlay his treatment of moral and legal notions. He also devoted much of his writing to working out the practical applications of his theoretical views, in such fields as prison reform and the writing of constitutions. *A Fragment on Government*, 1776 (attacks the then fashionable legal theorist W. Blackstone). *An Introduction to the Principles of Morals and Legislation*, 1789.

R. Harrison, *Bentham*, Routledge, 1983. (Good introduction to Bentham's philosophy.)

Bergson, Henri L. 1859–1941. Worked mostly in his native Paris. He is perhaps most famous for his doctrine of 'creative evolution', which tried to supplement Darwinism by postulating an *élan vital* which causes variations as species develop. He combined this with a double view of time, as time in physics and time as experienced (*durée*), of which only the latter was continuous and flowing. He also made a famous study of laughter and the comic. *Time and Free Will*, 1889. *Matter and Memory*, 1896. *Laughter*, 1900. *Creative Evolution*, 1907. *The Two Sources of Morality and Religion*, 1932. See also INTUITION, MARITAIN, METAPHYSICS.

Berkeley, George. 1685–1753. Born in Kilkenny, Ireland, he mainly stayed in Ireland, though with visits abroad, including one to America, and he became bishop of Cloyne. He is considered one of the 'British EMPIRICISTS', and his philosophy starts from LOCKE's 'new way of ideas', but rejects abstract ideas and the possibility of real existence outside perception. This slogan 'esse est percipi' ('to be is to be perceived') sums up much of his philosophy, which is commonly known as 'subjective IDEALISM', though he himself called it 'immaterialism'; cf. PHENOMENALISM. However, among percipients Berkeley included God. *An Essay towards a New Theory of Vision*, 1709. *A Treatise concerning the Principles of Human Knowledge*, 1710. *Three Dialogues between Hylas and Philonous in Opposition to Sceptics and Atheists*, 1713. *De Motu* (on motion), 1721. *Alciphron, or the Minute Philosopher*, 1732 (largely theological, but with philosophical passages). See also SENSATION, SENSE DATA, SUBJECTIVISM.

A. A. Luce and T. E. Jessop (eds), *The Works of George Berkeley*, 9 vols, Nelson, 1948–57.

J. Bennett, *Locke, Berkeley, Hume: Central Themes*, Clarendon Press, 1971.

W. E. Creery (ed.), *George Berkeley: Critical Assessments*, (3 vols), Routledge, 1991.

J.P. Dancy, *Berkeley: An Introduction*, Blackwell, 1987.

Lisa Downing, 'George Berkeley', *The Stanford Encyclopedia of Philosophy* (Winter 2004 Edition), Edward N. Zalta (ed.). Available at: http://plato.stanford.edu/archives/win2004/entries/berkeley/ (accessed 1 March 2009).

R. J. Fogelin, *Berkeley and the Principles of Human Knowledge*, Routledge, 2001.

J. O. Urmson, *Berkeley*, Oxford UP, 1982.

Berlin, Isaiah. 1909–97. Born in Riga, lived in England from 1921 onwards, and worked in Oxford for most of his life. A political philosopher, whose best-known and most influential work, 'Two Concepts of Liberty' (1958), distinguished positive and negative liberty. Positive liberty emphasizes autonomy and self-determination, as in Kant's moral philosophy, while negative liberty is characterized by the absence of constraints or restrictions on action. He argued that although both were important and proper ideals, the pursuit of positive liberty could be dangerous and lead to state control and totalitarianism. Berlin also contributed to the philosophy of history: his essay 'Historical Inevitability' (1953) which asks whether history has been decisively influenced by exceptional individuals or, rather, by impersonal forces irrespective of human actions and intentions. *Four Essays on Liberty*, Oxford UP, 1969 (contains both essays mentioned above). *Liberty* (revised and expanded edition of *Four Essays On Liberty*), Oxford UP, 2002. *Concepts and Categories: Philosophical Essays*, Hogarth Press, 1978.

Bernoulli's theorem. See NUMBERS (LAW OF LARGE).

Berry's paradox. The phrase 'the least integer not nameable in fewer than nineteen syllables' seem to name a number. But the number concerned must be not nameable in fewer than nineteen syllables since the phrase does name it, yet nameable in fewer since the phrase itself has only eighteen. The paradox is of the kind sometimes called semantic (see PARADOX, and also RUSSELL'S PARADOX, TYPES).

M. Clark, *Paradoxes from A–Z*, Routledge, 2002.

E. Teensma, *The Paradoxes*, Van Gorcum, 1969, pp. 34–5. (Exposition with brief discussion.)

Bertrand's box paradox. Three boxes hold respectively two gold coins, two silver, one of each. A coin drawn randomly is gold. What is the probability that the other coin in the same box is gold? The box chosen must be double gold or mixed, so the probability is a half. Yet the coin must be the first or second in the gold box, or the gold in the mixed box; two of these three alternatives makes the other coin gold, so the probability is two-thirds. The paradox affects the classical theory of PROBABILITY, by suggesting that it is indefinite what the alternatives are.

M. Clark, *Paradoxes from A–Z*, London: Routledge, 2002.

Best (principle of the). See SUFFICIENT REASON.

Best explanation, inference to. See INFERENCE TO THE BEST EXPLANATION, ABDUCTION.

Better. Not always the comparative of 'good'. Something can be 'better but not yet good', and it may be easier to decide whether one thing is better than another than whether either is good.

S. Haliden, *On the Logic of 'Better'*, 1957. (Full formal treatment.)

A. Sloman, 'How to derive "better" from "is"', *American Philosophical Quarterly*, 1969. (Makes 'better' more fundamental than 'good', and defines it in logical terms.)

G. H. von Wright, *The Varieties of Goodness*, Routledge, Humanities Press, 1963, p. 26. ('Better' as non-TRANSITIVE.)

Between. Two main senses: (i) that in which a term lies between two other terms in some ordering; (ii) that in which a relation holds between two terms, as in 'difference between' and 'resemblance between'. In 'The Rhine passes between France and Germany' we have (i), but some cases seem less clear: 'The Rhine stretches between Switzerland and Holland'; 'The Rhine is the link between Switzerland and Holland'; 'the link between these events is such-and-such'. The analysis of 'distance between' is relevant to questions about empty space.

A. N. Prior, 'On a difference between "betweens"', *Mind*, 1961.

Biconditional. The connective (see CONJUNCTION) 'if and only if' (often abbreviated to 'iff') or a sentence comprising two clauses connected by it. Where p and q are propositions, 'p iff q' stands for 'If p then q and if q then p'.

Bivalence (principle, law of). See EXCLUDED MIDDLE.

Body, philosophy of. The fact that we are embodied creatures profoundly affects our experience – of ourselves, of others, of the world. But it is a fact which Western philosophy in the past largely neglected. However, in the twentieth century – partly through the influence of phenomenology and philosophers like HEIDEGGER and MERLEAU-PONTY, and partly through FEMINIST philosophy – philosophical interest in the body has increased.

M. Johnson, *The Body in the Mind: The Bodily Basis of Meaning, Imagination, and Reason*, University of Chicago Press, 1987.
M. Merleau-Ponty, *Phenomenology of Perception*, 1945, trans. C. Smith, Routledge, 1962. (Influential classic.)
M. Proudfoot (ed.), *The Philosophy of Body*, Blackwell, 2003. (Collection of specially commissioned articles).

Boethius, Anicius Manlius Severinus. c.480–525. Roman Christian philosopher, who helped to preserve the Greek classics and translated some of Aristotle's logical works in to Latin. Wrote on universals, the problem of evil, music and theology. His most famous work is *The Consolation of Philosophy*, 524, written while in prison awaiting execution for treason, and advocating a stoical acceptance of hardship and suffering.

Boethius, *The Consolation of Philosophy*, trans. V. E. Watts, Penguin, 1969.
H. Chadwick, *Boethius: The Consolation of Music, Logic, Theology and Philosophy*, Clarendon, 1986. (Authoritative discussion of his life, background and work.)

Boolean algebra. Algebra or, strictly, set of algebras, invented by G. Boole (1815–64) for the CALCULUS of classes; later developed further and given other applications, e.g. to electrical circuits, computing, etc. It resembles ordinary numerical algebra limited to one and zero (so that $x^2 = x$), but differs from it because classes are now confined to the universal and null CLASSES.

C. Glymour, *Thinking Things Through*, MIT Press, 1992, Chapter 4.

G. E. Hughes and M. J. Cresswell, *An Introduction to Modal Logic*, Methuen, 1968, Chapter 17 (beginning).

P. H. Nidditch, *The Development of Mathematical Logic*, Routledge, 1962, Chapter 6.

Bound. See VARIABLE.

Bracketing. See PHENOMENOLOGY.

Bradley, Francis H. 1846–1924. Born in Clapham (London), he worked in Oxford, and is usually considered the main British objective IDEALIST. He developed a MONISTIC system whereby the Absolute is the only subject of predicates, and the only fully true proposition would be one completely describing it. No other propositions can be more than partly true. He argued that relations were always internal to their terms (an argument MOORE criticized) though he also thought that they were illusory. He criticized the psychologism of empiricists like MILL in their use of terms like 'IDEA'. His logic is now particularly known for his views on negation, his ethics for his criticism of hedonism and the anti-utilitarian stance of his essay on 'My Station and its Duties'. He also wrote on the philosophy of history in *The Presupposition of Critical History*, 1876. *Ethical Studies*, 1876 (contains 'My Station … '). *Logic*, 1883 (2nd edn, revised especially on negation, 1922). *Appearance and Reality*, 1893. *Essays on Truth and Reality*, 1914. See also HEGEL, NATURALISM, OUGHT, UNIVERSALS.

A. Manser and G. Stock, (eds), *The Philosophy of F.H. Bradley*, Clarendon, 1984. (16 essays, discussing his work from a contemporary perspective.)

Brain process theory. See IDENTITY THEORY OF MIND.

Brains in vats. I seem to experience a world in which I live and move around. But might I be merely a brain in a vat of sustaining liquid, its neurons stimulated by electrical impulses (perhaps from a powerful computer) in such way as to make me think that I am a fully embodied person moving around in the world? This thought, exploited in many films, for example, *The Matrix*, has been central to disputes about knowledge and scepticism, and has its origins in DESCARTES' evil demon argument. It raises the question whether we have good grounds for any of our beliefs.

A. Brueckner, 'Brains in a Vat', *The Stanford Encyclopedia of Philosophy* (Winter 2004 Edition), E.N. Zalta (ed.). Available at: http://plato.stanford. edu/archives/win2004/entries/brain-vat/ (accessed 1 March 2009).

H. Putnam, 'Brains in a Vat', in K. DeRose and T. A. Warfield (eds), *Skepticism: A Contemporary Reader*, Oxford UP, 1992.

A. Zuboff, 'The Story of a Brain', in D. R. Hofstadter and D.C. Dennett (eds), *The Mind's I*, Basic Books, 1981. (Can also be found, with Hofstadter and Dennett's comments, available at: http://themindi.blogspot. com/2007/02/147.html (accessed 1 March 2009).)

Brentano, Franz C. 1839–1917. Born near Boppard (Germany) he worked mainly in Würzburg and Vienna and retired to Florence. He was a Catholic priest for a short period. He is particularly remembered for his claim that mental phenomena can be identified as those that are 'intentional' in nature (see INTENSIONALITY). He also studied certain interrelations between ideas, judgements, and emotions of love and hatred, and elaborated a theory of truth, which based it on 'evidence' in the sense of evidentness. His analysis of mental phenomena was especially influential on PHENOMEN-OLOGISTS like HUSSERL, and on MEINONG, and on English-speaking writers such as CHISHOLM, and less directly on the recent concern with intentionality (see MIND). He was himself much concerned with the study of ARISTOTLE. *Psychology from an Empirical Standpoint*, 1874. *The Origin of Our Knowledge of Right and Wrong*, 1889. *The Foundation and Construction of Ethics*, 1952 (more elaborate than previous item). *The True and the Evident*, 1930.

Broad, Charlie D. 1887–1971. Born in Harlesden (London) he worked mainly in Cambridge. Broad's contribution lay chiefly in his systematic exposition and thorough examination of a large number of philosophical theories in widely different spheres, and in his refusal to be browbeaten by current fashions into rejecting unpopular views. Like RUSSELL, he appreciated the importance of modern science, and he also, like SIDGWICK, took psychical research seriously. His views were often unfashionable as compared with those of his more POSITIVIST contemporaries on topics such as causation and induction, perception and the synthetic a priori, but they were elaborated to take account of current scientific and philosophical thought. Other topics to which he contributed in this way include time, substance, determinism, the body/mind problem and certain ethical issues. *Perception, Physics, and Reality*, 1914. *Scientific Thought*, 1923. *The Mind and Its Place in Nature*, 1925. *Five Types of Ethical Theory*, 1930. *Examination of McTaggart's Philosophy*, 2 vols., 1933, 1938. See also PROBABILITY, SELF-REGARDING, SPACE.

P.A. Schlipp (ed.), *The Philosophy of C.D. Broad*, Tudor, 1979. (Large volume, containing 21 critical essays with Broad's 'Reply to My Critics' and his 'Autobiography'.)

Bruno, Giordano. 1548–1600. Born in Nola, Italy. Became a Dominican friar, but in 1576 left the order, and, fearing the Inquisition, travelled widely in Europe, and lived for some time in Oxford and London, where some of his works were published. He was a supporter of Copernicus, an anti-Aristotelian who held Pantheist views. He also wrote on the art of memory and on magic. Burnt at the stake in Rome for heresy.

Buber, Martin. 1878–1965. Born in Vienna, lived mainly in Germany and Israel. Wrote on a variety of subjects, including theology and philosophy of religion. His best-known work is *Ich und Du* (*I and Thou*) which argues that self-consciousness, my awareness of myself and my identity, arises from my experience of and relationship with others. He contrasts two different ways of relating to others: 'I-It', or relating to others as objects, and 'I-Thou', a reciprocal relationships with another, and simultaneously with God, whom he describes as 'the eternal Thou'. *Ich und Du*, 1923, trans. W. Kaufmann, *I and Thou*, Charles Scribner's Sons, 1970.

Buridan's ass. A paradox, in fact found in Aristotle, but named after the fourteenth-century French philosopher, Jean Buridan. The rational donkey, faced with a choice between two absolutely equally desirable piles of hay, cannot decide between them, for it has no reason to prefer one to the other, and so starves to death. But it would be rational to make an arbitrary choice rather than starve to death. See SUFFICIENT REASON.

Burke, Edmund. 1729–97. Born in Dublin, British/Irish politician, a Whig MP from 1765 to 1794, and philosopher. He wrote influentially on Aesthetics and Political Philosophy. In his *Philosophical Enquiry into the Origin of our Ideas of the Sublime and Beautiful*, 1757, he distinguishes two contrasting responses to art and nature. Our enjoyment of beauty is associated with pleasure, while our experience of the sublime is a form of terror, associated with the fear of death: nevertheless 'a sort of delightful horror' which may take the forms of astonishment, awe, reverence and respect. Supported the American revolution but opposed the French Revolution. In *Reflections on the Revolution in France*, 1790, he expressed a particularly British form of Conservatism, involving a distrust of government based on abstract principles, the importance of continuity, custom and tradition, and support of the institutions of monarchy and the established Church.

Butler, Joseph. 1692–1752. Natural theologian and moralist who was born at Wantage and became bishop of Bristol and then of Durham. His contribution to moral philosophy consists in his examination of moral psychology, including the roles of self-love and benevolence, and his treatment of conscience as a principle having overriding authority. In natural theology he claims to see an analogy between the course of events in nature and what religion teaches, and so to derive confirmation of the latter, and he emphasizes the 'progressive' rather than 'static' nature of the afterlife. He also discusses personal identity with reference to LOCKE. *Fifteen Sermons*, 1726 (his moral philosophy). *The Analogy of Religion, Natural and Revealed, to the Constitution and Course of Nature*, 1736 (including appendix on personal identity).

C

Calculus. A general name, applied to a subject, for the body of principles governing reasoning in the subject. One can talk of an AXIOM SYSTEM for the propositional calculus, etc. Sometimes such systems are themselves called calculi.

The propositional calculus (also called the sentential calculus, calculus of unanalysed propositions, calculus of truth values or calculus of truth functions) concerns truth FUNCTIONS of propositions, but with the restriction that the propositions are regarded as either the same as each other or completely different. Partial similarities like that between 'All cats are black' and 'Some cats are black' are ignored. Its theorems are the relevant TAUTOLOGIES. When the restriction is lifted and the structure of propositions is taken into account, we have the functional or predicate calculus, or the calculus of relations. When the predicates are limited to MONADIC predicates, we have the monadic predicate calculus. The predicate calculus is called extended or second-order when predicates are quantified over (see QUANTIFICATION). When only INDIVIDUALS are quantified over, it is called restricted or first-order. There is also an extended propositional calculus, where propositions are quantified over.

The calculus of classes concerns classes and their members. It is structurally the same as the monadic predicate calculus. ('x is red' is interchangeable with 'x belongs to the class of red things', though RUSSELL'S PARADOX raises a difficulty for the view that every predicate defines a class.) It is the elementary nucleus of set theory, which treats problems arising out of the calculus of classes and goes beyond it by treating, for example, classes whose members are ordered, and problems specific to infinite classes. The relations between set theory and logic are important in connection with logicism (see philosophy of MATHEMATICS).

51

The calculus of individuals concerns the part/whole relationship, and is linked to MEREOLOGY.

For the calculus of chances see PROBABILITY.

The hedonic calculus, or calculus of pleasures, is the set of principles which would govern any system claiming that pleasures can be measured, added and, in general, systematically compared. But whether such a calculus could be constructed is controversial. BENTHAM attempted to formulate such a calculus, which he calls 'the felicific calculus', which compares the total amount of pleasure produced by an action in terms of various elements: the Intensity, Duration, Certainty or Uncertainty, Propinquity or Remoteness (how soon it will occur), Fecundity (how likely other pleasurable sensations will follow), Purity (how likely unpleasurable sensations will follow) and Extent (how many people are affected) of the pleasure.

N. Goodman, *The Structure of Appearance*, Harvard UP, 1951, Chapter 2. (Calculus of individuals.)

D. Hilbert and W. Ackermann, *Principles of Mathematical Logic*, 1928; 2nd edn 1938, trans. Chelsea, NY, 1950. (A standard account of the main logical calculi. Elementary introductions to symbolic logic, covering similar ground, are legion.)

D. C. Makinson, *Topics in Modern Logic*, Methuen, 1973, Chapter 5. (Set theory and logic. Cf. also Introduction to P. Benacerraf and H. Putnam (eds), *Philosophy of Mathematics*, Cambridge UP, 1964).

Cambridge change. Something undergoes a Cambridge change whenever any predicate starts or stops being true of it, including predicates like 'is an uncle', which do not seem to involve any real or intrinsic change in the subject itself. Similarly, if I stay the same while you grow bigger than me, we both undergo Cambridge changes, though only you would be said to undergo a real change. Normally, however, the term 'Cambridge change' is reserved for changes which are not real but are properly speaking 'mere' Cambridge changes, so that I but not you would be said to undergo a Cambridge change in the above example, i.e. 'Cambridge change' normally means 'mere Cambridge change'. So called from alleged popularity of 'mere' Cambridge change among some early twentieth-century Cambridge philosophers.

S. Shoemaker, *Identity, Cause, and Mind*, Cambridge UP, 1984, pp. 207–9. (Develops the notion further.)

Cambridge Platonists. Seventeenth century movement associated with Cambridge University, including Ralph Cudworth, Henry More, Benjamin Whichcote, Peter Sterry, John Smith and Nathaniel Culverwell (sometimes 'Culverwel'). Among the first to write philosophy in English. Although they were inspired by Plato, they had a strong interest in contemporary science and philosophy (More corresponded with Descartes) and aimed to reconcile science and religion. They were critical of Hobbes, Calvinistic determinism, conventionalism (and believed in natural kinds) and empiricism. They believed in the power of reason, and its ability to prove the existence of a benevolent God and of immortality. They were influential not only on British thinkers, including Newton and Shaftesbury, but also throughout Europe.

> C. A. Patrides (ed.), *The Cambridge Platonists*, Cambridge UP, 1968. (Selection of their writings.)

Camus, Albert. 1913–60. French philosopher and writer born in Algeria, worked in Algeria and France. Awarded the Nobel Prize for Literature in 1957. His writings, in the form of essays and novels, for example, *L'Étranger* (*The Stranger* or *The Outsider*), 1942, espouse a view of the absurd human endeavour to understand human existence in a world devoid of meaning. This fruitless struggle is encapsulated by Sisyphus, in the *Myth of Sisyphus*, 1942, who was condemned to roll a heavy stone up a hill, only for the stone, once it reached the top to roll down to the bottom again, and for Sisyphus's task to continue, endlessly. His views are very close to those of EXISTENTIALISM, though Camus rejected the label. See ABANDONMENT, ABSURDITY.

Cancelling-out fallacy. The assumption that where two partially identical expressions mean the same, one can cancel out the identical parts and the remaining parts will mean the same as each other, e.g. if 'Socrates killed Socrates' means the same as 'Socrates was killed by Socrates', then 'killed Socrates' means the same as 'was killed by Socrates'.

> P. T. Geach, *Reference and Generality*, Cornell UP, 1962. (See index.)

Cantor, Georg. 1845–1918. German philosopher of mathematics, who developed the fundamentals of set theory, and who showed by means of a diagonal procedure (see RICHARD'S PARADOX) that there exists more than one infinite number. Cantor's paradox starts with the presupposition that any class has more subclasses than members. Now suppose there were a class of all classes. Its subclasses, being classes, would be members of it. So there can be no class of all classes (and also no greatest cardinal NUMBER, not even among infinite numbers).

M. Clark, *Paradoxes from A–Z*, Routledge, 2002.

Carnap, Rudolf. 1891–1970. German logical POSITIVIST, born in Ronsdorf, and a member of the Vienna Circle. He migrated to America where he worked mainly in Chicago and Los Angeles. He tried to show that METAPHYSICS arose through our confusing talk about the world with talk about language (cf. FORMAL MODE). He sought to apply his positivism to scientific method by his physicalism (see POSITIVISM), and later in an elaborate examination of CON-FIRMATION and probability. *The Logical Structure of the World*, 1928. 'Die physicalische Sprache als Universalsprache der Wissenschaft', *Erkenntnis*, 1932 (trans. separately as *The Unity of Science*, 1934; physicalism). 'Testability and meaning', *Philosophy of Science*, 1936–7. *Meaning and Necessity*, 1947, enlarged 1956. *Logical Foundations of Probability*, 1950. *The Continuum of Inductive Methods*, 1952. See also BASIC STATEMENTS, BEING, EXPLA-NATION, FUNCTION, ISOMORPHIC, MEANING, MEANING POSTULATES, PROBABILITY, REDUCTION SENTENCES, SENTENCES, TRUTH, TYPES.

Cartesian. Connected with Descartes, or his ideas.

Cartesian circle. Refers to the allegedly CIRCULAR REASONING by Descartes to prove that whatever he clearly and distinctly perceives is true. It is true, he says, because God exists and is no deceiver. But this relies on his earlier proof of God's existence, of which we can be sure, he says, only because we clearly and distinctly perceive it.

Andrea Christofidou, 'Descartes' dualism: Correcting some misconceptions', *Journal of the History of Philosophy*, 2001.
Harry Frankfurt, *Demons, Dreamers, and Madmen: The Defense of Reason in Descartes' Meditations*, Bobbs-Merrill, 1970; reprinted by Princeton UP, 2007. (Defends Descartes against the charge of circularity.)
Bernard Williams, *Descartes: The Project of Pure Enquiry*, Penguin, 1978.

Casuistry. See ETHICS.

Categorical imperative. See IMPERATIVE.

Categories. Ultimate or fundamental divisions or kinds. For much of its history the search for categories has wavered between seeking distinctions among things in the world and distinctions among our ways of thinking or talking about the world. Much of the difficulty in each case has lain in knowing what distinctions to count as sufficiently fundamental. It is mainly by being ultimate or fundamental that categories differ from mere classes.

This wavering appears in Aristotle, who first explicitly introduced categories. His 'official' list contains ten categories, but the most important are SUBSTANCE, quantity, relative and quality, and his main interest seems to lie in distinguishing substance from the others. The list is clearly derived from different kinds of question that can be asked about a person, like 'How big is he?', 'What is he doing?'

Sometimes Aristotle seems to take a 'metaphysical' view, treating categories as the highest genera into which things in general can be divided, so that the world contains substances, qualities, etc., and anything one picks out such as a horse or red, can be classed under one of these headings. He sometimes lets categories overlap, so that the same item appears in more than one (end of Chapter 8 in his *Categories*). At other times he seems to take a 'logical' view and to be classifying the things one can say about something, and in particular about a substance, such as what it is, what qualities it has, how it is related to other things. Here he might be described as classifying predicates, but he often seems to regard predicates themselves as things in the world and not as linguistic expressions, so that the 'metaphysical' and 'logical' approaches are not clearly separate. Aristotle's classification is not very exhaustive. The terms 'one', 'good', 'being', he said, did not belong to any one category. These were later called transcendentals (see BEING). There are many others, some of which he discussed, which have no obvious place, including 'surface', 'sound', 'chance', 'proposition', 'necessity'; and complex terms like 'multiple of three', 'knowledge of French'. Aristotle also argues that there cannot be a single all-embracing genus like being or unit.

Many writers have followed Aristotle in elaborating sets of categories, usually more systematic than his. The Stoics had a set of four and they apparently wanted to classify at least some of the world's contents by examining the questions one can ask about a thing.

Among modern writers the most important contribution is that of Kant, who had a system of four groups of three. He intended these as a classification, whose correctness and exhaustiveness he claimed to prove, of the ways in which any mind recognizably like the human mind necessarily had to perceive and think about the appearances it was presented with. The categories were not a classification of things in themselves (NOUMENA), for Kant thought we could never know these and so never apply categories to them. The categories could only be applied to material given by experience, but they could not themselves be derived from experience, since all use of experience presupposes them. Kant's general idea is that we can only make sense of the world by imposing some structure originating from the mind upon it, e.g. to choose two of his categories, by seeing it as a set of substances in causal relationships. Many who accept this general idea reject the particular list he gave, and deny that there is some one list that is valid for all people and times. There is still much dispute about such related questions as whether there are certain features every language must share (cf. philosophy of LANGUAGE, INNATE).

In the last century two converging streams of thought aroused interest in categories. First there are the logical PARADOXES, which led Russell to construct his theory of TYPES. This theory divides the world up by insisting that things of different 'types' cannot be put together into a single class. It leads to corresponding divisions in language, e.g. two sentences of which one refers to the other are on different 'levels', and cannot be joined into a single sentence by 'and'. In fact 'type' and 'category' are sometimes used synonymously. Secondly, thinkers like Husserl and Ryle, among others, have tried to construct a doctrine of categories to systematize the ways in which a sentence can go wrong, and in particular the distinction between the false and the meaningless. Roughly speaking, the ideal of this approach would be to divide things into non-overlapping groups so that what could be said truly or falsely, but not nonsensically, of the members of one group differed radically from what could be said of the members of another, rather as most of the things that can be said of a cat differ from what can be said of a wish or of a day of the week. Sentences which say about a subject in one category something that can only be sensibly said about a subject in another category, are called CATEGORY MISTAKES or type confusions, e.g. 'Saturday is in bed'. Such a doctrine cannot tell us when a sentence makes sense if we must already know this before constructing the doctrine. But the doctrine could systematize the situation and throw useful light on individual cases through comparisons.

Many difficulties arise concerning categories. It sometimes seems to be thought that, if they exist at all, they must belong to the world and not language, because they must be found out and not created by us. But even if we create a language, we can still discover things about it. We may choose what our sentences shall mean, but once we have chosen we are committed to the implications of our choice, and we do not choose these implications. The main difficulties seem to be of two kinds. First, to think of subjects and predicates that will not go together is perhaps too easy, for we may reach so many categories that the doctrine becomes rather trivial, and 'category' becomes a pompous name for 'class' as often happens in ordinary speech. Are spoons and forks in different categories because 'This fork has lost one of its prongs' becomes nonsensical when 'fork' is replaced by 'spoon'? A distinction between absolute and relative categories has been found necessary in facing this problem (Strawson).

The second kind of difficulty, connected with the first, centres round the notion of meaninglessness. There are many ways in which something might be meaningless, nonsensical or absurd, as the following examples illustrate: 'Horse whether the', 'My wish has whiskers', 'I have found', 'I have any apples', 'He sleeps like milk'. Some of these may be given senses in special cases, but which of them serve to distinguish categories? One can ask how clearly in fact is the meaningless distinct from the false? 'Absurd' can cover both. And is every kind of predicate relevant? Are two things in the same category merely because the predicate 'being thought about by me now' can apply to both of them? One controversy arising out of all this is whether categories can be ultimately founded on grammatical distinctions (called syntactical in logic), or whether considerations of meaning independent of mere grammar must be used (in which case categories will have a semantic basis; cf. SEMIOTIC).

'Categorial' means 'having to do with categories'. 'Categorical', though often misused for 'categorial', has something like its ordinary meaning of 'definite' or 'downright', but refers to a certain form of proposition, one which says something is the case without reference to conditions or alternatives. 'That's a cat' is categorical, 'If that's a cat, it's an animal' is hypothetical. 'That's either a cat or a dog', is disjunctive. 'Mongrel categorical' is Ryle's name for a statement overtly categorical but covertly including a hypothetical statement; e.g. 'He drove carefully' says, for Ryle, not only that he did something but that he would have done certain things if certain events had occurred. See also categorical IMPERATIVE.

Aristotle, *Categories*, trans. with commentary by J. L. Ackrill in Clarendon Aristotle series, 1963, reprinted (without the commentary) in the 2nd edition of the *Oxford Translation of Aristotle*, J. Barnes (ed.), Princeton UP, 1984. (See also his *Topics*, Book I, Chapter 9, and for argument that being is not a genus see *Metaphysics*, 998b22–7.)

K. Campbell, *Abstract Particulars*, Blackwell, 1990. (Uses tropes as basis of a one-category metaphysical system, in contrast to Aristotle's.)

A. D. Carstairs, 'Ryle, Hillman and Harrison on categories', *Mind*, 1971. (Discusses some of their recent work.)

R. Grossmann, *The Categorial Structure of the World*, Indiana UP, 1983. (Discusses categorial status of individuals, properties, relations, classes, numbers and facts. Full table of contents.)

I. Kant, *Critique of Pure Reason*, 1781, 2nd edn 1787, trans. by N. Kemp Smith in 1929. (See its index.)

S. Körner, *Categorial Frameworks*, Blackwell, 1970. (Discusses basic frameworks of our thinking, allowing that these may legitimately change.)

*J. Passmore, *Philosophical Reasoning*, 1961, Chapter 7. (Somewhat sceptical approach.)

J. M. Rist, 'Categories and their uses', in A. A. Long (ed.), *Problems in Stoicism*, Athlone, 1971. (Stoic categories.)

*G. Ryle, 'Categories', *Proceedings of the Aristotelian Society*, 1938–9, reprinted in A. Flew (ed.), *Logic and Language*, 2nd series, Blackwell, 1953. (Attempts to construct theory of categories on semantic basis, resulting in so many category differences that the notion seems in danger of becoming trivial. See also his *The Concept of Mind*, Hutchinson, 1949, particularly p. 16 (p. 17 in Peregrine edn) for category mistakes, and particularly p. 141 (p. 135 in Peregrine edn) for mongrel categoricals.)

F. Sommers, 'Types and ontology', *Philosophical Review*, 1963. (One of several articles by Sommers elaborating a semantic theory of categories more rigorous than Ryle's.)

T. L. S. Sprigge, *Facts, Words and Beliefs*, Routledge, 1970, pp. 70–2. (Syncategorematic properties. Cf. N. Griffin, *Relative Identity*, Oxford UP, 1977, pp. 10–11 on 'polymorphous predicates'.)

P. F. Strawson, 'Categories', in O. P. Wood and G. Pitcher (eds), *Ryle*, Doubleday, 1970. (General discussion of possibility and usefulness of categories, starting from Ryle. See p. 199 (Paperback edn, 1971) for absolute and relative categories.)

Category mistake. Ryle claims that to think of the mind as something existing separately from the body is to make a Category Mistake. It is to fail to realize that mind and body belong to different CATE-GORIES or logical types: it is like thinking of team spirit as an extra player a football team must have, in addition to the other 'ingredients' such as forwards, backs, goal-keeper.

G. Ryle, *The Concept of Mind*, Hutchinson, 1949.

Catharsis. It seems a paradoxical feature of our experience of art that we enjoy tragedy. Aristotle's explanation (in his *Poetics*) is that the often overwhelming emotions we feel watching a tragedy serve a cleansing or purgative effect on us that rids us of undesirable feelings. This is the process of catharsis, Greek for 'purification' or 'cleansing'. An alternative reading is that catharsis is not so much getting rid of emotions, but rather a cleansing or clarification of them.

> N. Pappas, 'Aristotle' in B. Gaut and D. M. Lopes (eds), *The Routledge Companion to Aesthetics*, Routledge, 2001. (For the alternative reading.)

Causal theory of knowledge. Causal theories of knowledge, responding to GETTIER's challenge to the traditional TRIPARTITE ANALYSIS OF KNOWLEDGE, claim that a person can only be said to know a proposition p if there is some causal connection between the fact that makes p true and that person's belief in p.

> A. Goldman, *Epistemology and Cognition*, Harvard UP, 1986. (Prominent defence of the causal theory. See also Goldman's earlier 'A causal theory of knowing', *Journal of Philosophy*, 1967, which is reprinted with discussions in G. S. Pappas and M. Swain (eds), *Essays on Knowledge and Justification*, Cornell UP, 1978.)
> R. Shope, *The Analysis of Knowing*, Princeton UP, 1983.

Causal theory of memory. See MEMORY.

Causal theory of perception. See PERCEPTION.

Causation. Roughly, the relation between two things when the first is thought of as somehow producing or responsible for the second.

But to elaborate this intuitive idea is difficult, since it seems impossible to find or even conceive of any active production going on in nature. Why then do we think in terms of such production? Where do we get the 'idea of causation' from, and when in fact is it correct to apply it? Modern discussions of causation stem primarily from Hume's claim that our idea of causation cannot be gained in any simple way from either reason or observation: it cannot come from reason because reason can only tell us of logical relations, and if the cause and effect were logically related, i.e. if the occurrence of the cause entailed (see IMPLICATION) that of the effect, they would not be 'distinct existences' as Hume thought they should be; one proposition ('This has shape') can entail a distinct one ('This has size'), but there it does not make sense to suppose the first true and the second false, whereas it should make sense to suppose a cause exists without its effect. All this is not to deny that causal statements can be ANA-LYTIC, like 'Whatever causes cancer causes cancer'. If something correctly described as the cause of cancer exists, then cancer must exist – otherwise the first thing could not be called its cause. Hume thought observation can only tell us that some things regularly follow on other things. It cannot reveal that special 'force' or 'necessity' that we feel a causal situation must contain.

Causation may involve regularities (though this is disputed; see Alexander), but is that all it involves? Regularities may be causally significant or they may be accidental, and in trying to distinguish these we meet problems about natural laws and counterfactual CONDITIONALS. Furthermore what regularities are relevant? Per-haps, in the case of singular causal statements, i.e. those about given occasions, to say that *a* caused *b* is to say that *a* was followed by *b*, and that *a*-like things are regularly followed by *b*-like things; but how like *a* and *b* must the things in question be? If I say that striking that match caused it to light, am I saying that all matches light when struck, or only that all dry matches do, or what? One view (David-son) is that in saying '*a* caused *b*' we imply that there exists some true non-accidental generalization of the form, 'Things like *a* in certain respects are followed by things like *b* in certain respects', but we need not know what generalization.

Since the world is an interlocking whole, so that exact repetition of all circumstances is presumably impossible, and the course of events leading to a given event is enormously complex, a looser view of causes has often been taken. On one view an event's cause is some condition, or set of conditions, which is either necessary or sufficient, or both, for the event (see NECESSARY AND SUFFICIENT CON-DITIONS). This condition is singled out because it is rare or striking in some respect, or is amenable to human control. If matches were usually wet, and so did not light when struck, we might call its dry-ness the cause when some particular match did light when struck. As things are, we call the striking the cause because it is controllable and matches are usually dry.

We could tighten this up by calling an event's cause the set of those things which are separately necessary and together sufficient for its occurrence, perhaps with a proviso that general background condi-tions (the stars in their courses, etc.) can be excluded as irrelevant. But two difficulties arise. First, this would not distinguish causal from logical relations (see NECESSARY AND SUFFICIENT CONDITIONS).

Secondly, if *a* is a necessary condition of *b*, *b* is a sufficient condition of *a*, and vice versa. So if *a* is a necessary and sufficient condition of *b*, so is *b* of *a*. But then if *a* causes *b* we must say that *b* causes *a*, which seems absurd. (Variants of this 'tightening up' procedure are possible, but with similar disadvantages.)

There are problems about how causation is related to time. We often feel that a cause should precede its effect, but since time is continuous this seems to imply that there must be a gap between cause and effect. But when 'cause' is being used strictly, and not just to pick out what is striking or unusual, such a gap, whether temporal or spatial ('action at a distance'), seems mysterious. As Hume observed, once the total cause exists, how can it not have its effect there and then? Yet if cause and effect are simultaneous everything should happen at once. It seems no better to say, alternatively, that the gap is filled by a chain of infinitely many causes. Some kinds of causes, however, do seem simultaneous with their effects, e.g. forces or objects: 'Gravity caused him to fall', 'The dog caused the accident'. It has even been suggested that an effect could precede its cause (Dummett).

One way of explaining why causation seems to be a one-way relation, so that things cannot cause each other (though they can sustain each other, like the stones in an arch) is to derive the idea of causation from our experience of our own activity. To cause something is then to bring it about, and we call causes those things that could serve us, at least in principle, as recipes for producing their effects. On a primitive version of this view, nature itself does the bringing about, but we need not assume this. Even things clearly outside our control, like stellar processes, can be viewed as if they were in our control and we need not attribute activities to nature. Why we refuse to allow effects to precede their causes may then be because we cannot make sense of bringing about the past, because we have no experience of it in our own activities. We could always explain the case where the later event seems to cause the earlier (Dummett) by saying the earlier causes the later but by a process that has escaped us; but cf. von Wright (under DUMMETT).

Heisenberg's uncertainty principle (1927) says that we cannot in principle discover both the momentum and the position of a fundamental particle, because the process of discovery will always affect what is being discovered. (Whether the particle has both a momentum and a position is disputed.) Also, the behaviour of individual particles is often unpredictable in quantum mechanics. We can, however, attribute probabilities to the behaviour of such particles, and then use

PROBABILITY theory to predict with virtual certainty the behaviour of swarms of particles, i.e. of ordinary objects. This, coupled with the fact that physicists usually talk in terms of equations rather than one-way relations, raises three questions: Has physics abandoned or even undermined causation? Does it make sense to suppose that individual sub-atomic movements are caused, even though we cannot in principle discover their causes? Can there be ultimate causal tendencies, i.e. cases where a cause is followed by its effect, say, 90 per cent of the time and where this cannot be explained by pointing to an underlying 100 per cent generalization? (If 90 per cent of matches light when struck, this might be because 100 per cent of dry matches light when struck.) Clearly the answers will depend on how we view causation. The 'recipe' view might say causation is irrelevant for physics, not undermined by it, and that virtual certainty is all that causation requires. Alternatively we may say that a cause is simply something which makes its effect more probable.

A further important question about causation, which may affect the answers to some of the above questions, is how far it is really a metaphysical notion connected with necessitation and how far an epistemological notion connected with explanation, and how causation is related to coincidences (Sorabji and Owens). How are causation and causal explanation related? (See e.g. Owens, p. 23.)

What sort of things can be causes? Objects, events, forces, facts, states, processes, even absences ('The absence of oxygen caused his death'), can be described as causes. Which, if any, of these has the prior claim to the title of cause is disputable. No doubt the 'striking-ness' mentioned above can explain much here. But sometimes what appear to be near synonyms have been explicitly distinguished, notably 'effects', 'results' and 'consequences'.

An important question in recent philosophy of mind concerns whether actions can be caused, and if so, whether this affects our notion of responsibility (see FREEWILL). Obviously the word 'because', which we use in giving reasons for our actions, need not be causal. It can, e.g. signify logical relations, as in '141 cannot be a prime number because the sum of its digits is divisible by 3'. But even 'cause' may imply causality less than 'causal' does. We might accept 'My wife's profligacy caused me to sell my house', while rejecting 'The relation between my wife's behaviour and my action was a causal one.' Aristotle's four causes, here illustrated by reference to a man, are the material cause (flesh, etc.), formal cause (FORM of man), efficient cause (father), final cause (end or purpose, e.g. to live in a certain way). The notions are, however, less clear cut than this suggests, and the Greek word is wider than 'cause'. It means something like 'responsible factor'. An exemplary cause is a pattern or exemplar playing the role of Plato's 'FORMS'. God was sometimes called the exemplary cause when these Forms were regarded as IDEAS in His mind.

P. Alexander and P. B. Downing, 'Are causal laws purely general?', *Proceedings of the Aristotelian Society*, supplementary vol., 1970.

G. E. M. Anscombe, 'Causality and determination', in Sosa and Tooley, 1993, and also, with other items on causation, in her *Collected Philosophical Papers*, vol. 2, Blackwell, 1991. (Insists that causality need not involve regularity.)

Aristotle, *Physics*, book 2. (Four causes.)

B. Blanshard, *The Nature of Thought*, Allen and Unwin, 1939, Chapter 32, § 10–21. S. Shoemaker, *Identity, Cause, and Mind*, Cambridge UP, 1984, Chapter 10, particularly pp. 222ff. (Both these connect causation with logical necessity. E. Nagel, *Sovereign Reason*, Free Press, 1954, pp. 387–95, criticizes Blanshard.)

M. Brand (ed.), *The Nature of Causation*, 1976. (Readings.)

F. Copleston, *A History of Philosophy*, vol. 2, 1950. (Exemplary causes. See its index.)

D. Davidson, 'Causal relations', *Journal of Philosophy*, 1967, reprinted in his *Essays on Actions and Events*, Clarendon, 1980, and in Sosa and Tooley, below. (Singular causal statements.)

M. Dummett, 'Bringing about the past', S. Gorovitz, 'Leaving the past alone', *Philosophical Review*, 1964. (Cf. G. H. von Wright, *Explanation and Understanding*, Routledge, 1971, Chapter 2, § 10, and S. Waterlow, 'Backwards causation and continuing', *Mind*, 1974, which also contains a bibliography, to which add P. B. Downing, 'Subjunctive conditionals, time order and causation', *Proceedings of the Aristotelian Society*, 1958–9.)

E. Fales, *Causation and Universals*, Routledge, 1990, particularly Part I. (Defends realist view of causation as relation between universals.)

D. Gasking, 'Causation and recipes', *Mind*, 1955, reprinted in A. Sesonske and N. Fleming (eds), *Human Understanding*, Wadsworth, 1965, and in Brand (above). (Cf. von Wright (above), Chapter 2, § 8, 9.)

H. L. A. Hart and A. M. Honoré, *Causation in the Law*, Clarendon, 1959. (Standpoint of philosophy of mind.)

J. Heil and A. Mele (eds), *Mental Causation*, Oxford UP, 1994. (Specially written essays.)

D. Hume, *Treatise*, 1739, I 3, § 2, 3, 7. (Classic statement of problem. Cf. his *Enquiry concerning Human Understanding*, 1748, § 4, 7.)

*J. L. Mackie, *The Cement of the Universe*, Oxford UP, 1974. (Basically empiricist treatment but taking full account of directionality, necessity, etc. For extended summary see preface to paperback edition (1980).)

D. H. Mellor, 'The singularly affecting facts of causation', in P. Pettit *et al.* (eds), *Metaphysics and Morality*, Blackwell, 1987, reprinted in Mellor's *Matters of Metaphysics*, Cambridge UP, 1991. (Causation primarily links facts, not events. Cf. also his *The Facts of Causation*, Routledge, 1995.)

D. Owens, *Causes and Coincidences*, Cambridge UP, 1992. (General discussion, defining causation in terms of coincidences and linking it to explanation.)

D. Papineau, 'Probabilities and causes', *Journal of Philosophy*, 1985. (Discusses various views connecting these notions.)

B. Russell, *Analysis of Mind*, Allen and Unwin, 1921, Chapter 5, particularly beginning. (Can a cause precede its effect? Cf. his *Our Knowledge of the External World*, Allen and Unwin, 1914, Chapter 8.)

R. Sorabji, *Necessity, Cause and Blame*, Duckworth, 1980, Chapters 1 and 2. (Causation, necessitation, explanation, coincidences.)

*E. Sosa and M. Tooley (eds), *Causation*, Oxford UP, 1993. (Readings.)

Z. Vendler, 'Causal relations', *Journal of Philosophy*, 1967. (Criticizes Davidson and treats causes as facts. Also discusses effects, results and consequences, on which see also Hart and Honoré (above), pp. 25–6, and symposium in R. J. Butler (ed.), *Analytical Philosophy*, 1st series, Blackwell, 1962; Vendler's contribution to this is revised in his *Linguistics in Philosophy*, Cornell UP, 1967. On results and consequences see also S. Candlish, 'Inner and outer basic actions', *Proceedings of the Aristotelian Society*, 1983–4, particularly pp. 86–7.)

G. J. Warnock in A. Flew (ed.), *Logic and Language*, 2nd series, Blackwell, 1953. (Discusses 'Every event has a cause'.)

Causes: material, formal, efficient and final. Aristotle's four causes. See CAUSATION (end).

Cave, the allegory of the. Plato, through the character of Socrates, in *Republic* (Book 7 514a–520a), likens our condition to that of a prisoner in a cave who is chained, facing a wall. Behind the prisoner is a fire, and shadows are cast on to the wall by people he cannot see directly, carrying objects, including models of animals. The prisoner knows only the shadows, and takes them to be real things. The prisoner may come to realize they are only shadows, and may eventually break out of the cave, and will at first be blinded, but will come to see objects illuminated by the sun. The prisoner will want to return to the cave to enlighten those still there, but they will not listen to him, and he, used to daylight, will no longer be able to make out the shadows. To the prisoners he will seem blind. Plato uses the myth of the cave, along with metaphor of the sun, and the idea of the divided line, which precede the myth of the cave, to help explain his Theory of Forms. See PLATO and FORMS.

Central state materialism. See IDENTITY THEORY OF MIND.

Certainty. To be certain of something is not the same as knowing it, for a necessary condition of knowing that p is that p is true (see TRIPARTITE analysis of knowledge) whereas someone may be certain of something that is false, even though they strongly believe it.

> N. Malcolm, 'Knowledge and belief', *Mind*, 1952, and reprinted in his *Knowledge and Certainty*, Cornell UP, 1963.
> L. Wittgenstein, *On Certainty*, Blackwell, 1996.

C-function. See CONFIRMATION.

Charity (principle of). Principle that when interpreting an unknown language one should make the most favourable assumptions possible about the speaker's intelligence, knowledge, sense of relevance, etc., so as to make as much as possible of what is said come out true. Important in connection with radical interpretation (see TRANSLATION). However, it has come to be replaced, more realistically, by the principle of humanity, according to which, in interpreting, one must assume that the speaker's beliefs and desires are related to each other and the speaker's behaviour in the way that one's own are. This amounts to a requirement that, in interpreting what a speaker says, one views his or her words as the expression of the beliefs and desires that one would have oneself in his or her situation. The principles of charity and humanity are thought by some to be not simply necessary for successful interpretation but constitutive of it. The principles can be usefully employed in the interpretation of the texts of philosophers from the past.

> R. Grandy, 'Reference, meaning and belief', *Journal of Philosophy*, 1973, pp. 439–52. (Introduces the principle of humanity.)
> I. Hacking, *Why Does Language Matter to Philosophy?* Cambridge UP, 1975, pp. 146–50. (Discusses with historical references. Cf. also S. Evnine, *Donald Davidson*, Polity/Blackwell, 1991, Chapter 6.)

Chinese room argument. If a suitably programmed computer successfully answers questions put to it and thereby *appears* to understand them, why can't we say that it *does* understand them?

Searle's Chinese Room Argument is directed against what he calls 'Strong AI' (artificial intelligence), to show that merely simulating understanding isn't the same as actually understanding. Strong AI claims that to instantiate a computer program is enough to constitute intentionality, i.e. 'that feature of certain mental states by which they are directed at or about objects and states of affairs in the world' (cf. INTENSIONALITY AND INTENTIONALITY). Searle argues that something could always instantiate a program, and thereby simulate understanding, without duplicating it, and without itself actually understanding. To illustrate this he imagines that, knowing no Chinese, he is locked in a room and presented with Chinese characters together with rules for correlating the characters and producing some in response to others. These rules might be such that the characters he produced could serve as meaningful answers to questions represented by the characters presented to him. Yet however far this process was elaborated, Searle claims, he would not be understanding Chinese. What the argument in fact shows has been much disputed. See TURING TEST.

*T. Crane, *The Mechanical Mind: An Introduction to Minds, Machines and Mental Representation*, Penguin, 1995, Chapter 3. (Contains elementary introduction.)

J. M. Preston and M. Bishop (eds), *Views into the Chinese Room: New Essays on Searle and Artificial Intelligence*, Oxford UP, 2002. (19 essays by scientists and philosophers, including Searle, Block, Copeland and Penrose, with useful bibliography.)

J. R. Searle, 'Minds, brains and programs', *The Behavioral and Brain Sciences*, vol. 3, 1980, pp. 413–57. (Includes discussions and Searle's reply. For quotation see p. 424 n. 3.)

Chomsky, Noam. 1928–. American linguistics pioneer and political radical. Educated at University of Pennsylvania and works at MIT. His theories of generative grammar and universal grammar have profoundly influenced philosophy of language and philosophy of mind. For further details and more bibliographies, see GRAMMAR, STRUCTURE, TACIT AND IMPLICIT KNOWLEDGE.

R. Larson and G. Segal, *Knowledge of Meaning: An Introduction to Semantic Theory*, MIT Press, 1995. (Gentle introduction to Chomsky's approach.)

J. Lyons, *Chomsky*, Fontana, 1970, expanded 1977. (Elementary. For more elaborate treatment see J. Lyons, *Introduction to Theoretical Linguistics*, 1968.)

Church's theorem. See DECIDABLE.

Circular reasoning. See BEGGING THE QUESTION.

Class. Loosely, a group of objects or things. In many non-technical contexts (including most of this entry) 'class' and 'set' are synonymous. But there are technical reasons, associated with J. von Neumann, K. Gödel and P. Bernays, who hoped to avoid RUSSELL'S PARADOX, for saying some classes are not members of any other classes (as the class of cats is a member of the class of animal-classes). 'Set' is then limited to those classes which are members of other classes, the rest being called proper classes. The terms 'set theory' and 'CALCULUS of classes' are conventional, irrespective of this variation in usage.

Roughly, but only roughly, a class is closed if it has finitely many members and these are theoretically enumerable. It is open if it has infinitely many members, or if its membership is indeterminate (e.g. the class of horses, if it is indeterminate how many there will be).

It is important to distinguish class-inclusion from class-membership. A class is included in any class containing at least the same members. The class of cats is included in, but is not a member of, the class of animals for it is not an animal. It is a member of, but is not included in, the class of animal-classes for cats are not animal classes. Class-inclusion is TRANSITIVE, but class-membership is non-transitive. Smith may be a member of a union, and the union a member of the TUC, without Smith being a member of the TUC. For extensional and intensional definitions of classes see UNIVERSALS.

A unit class (or singleton) is a class with exactly one member. The universal class is the class containing everything, or everything in a given sphere.

The null, or empty, class is the one class with no members '[a, b]' means the class whose members are a and b. '<a, b>' means the ordered class whose members are a and b, in that order.

Class paradox. See RUSSELL'S PARADOX.

Closure. A notion easiest to explain by example. Let p, etc., be propositions, and suppose that whenever p is true, so is 'p or q' (as indeed is the case in classical logic). Then truth is said to be 'closed under' disjunction (the or-relation: see CONJUNCTION). The idea is presumably that when p is true the truth of 'p or q' is no longer an open question but is settled or closed. Closure is not limited to truth, however. The principle of epistemic closure says that someone who knows that p, and knows that p entails q, also knows that q; in this case knowledge is closed under known entailment. It is not closed under plain entailment, since we cannot know the infinitely many things entailed by what we know, but even allowing it to be closed under known entailment can lead to scepticism, by suggesting that quite modest claims to knowledge can commit us to false claims, and so must themselves be rejected.

> R. Nozick, 'Knowledge and scepticism', in J. Dancy (ed.), *Perceptual Knowledge*, Oxford UP, 1988. (Extracted from his *Philosophical Explanations*, Harvard UP, Oxford UP, 1981. Argues that knowledge is not closed under known entailment. For discussion, see J. Dancy, *An Introduction to Contemporary Epistemology*, Blackwell, 1985. See its index.)

Clusters. See UNIVERSALS.

Cogito. Latin for 'I think'. 'Cogito ergo sum' (I think therefore I am) is Descartes' argument for the certainty of my existence. See DESCARTES.

Cognitive. Those mental processes involved in understanding, believing as distinct from volitional processes such as wanting or intending. Also used of utterances that are either true or false, as distinct from those that are not, such as orders and exclamations, which are called non-cognitive. Are moral judgements cognitive or non-cognitive? See NATURALISM.

Cognitive psychology, cognitive science. The psychology of the cognitive processes involved in intelligence and in thinking. When extended to cover the study of artificial intelligence and areas bordering on cybernetics and other sciences it becomes cognitive science. One form it takes is that of computational psychology, which grew up as an attempt to mediate between purely behavioural and purely introspective approaches to the mind by postulating and studying events in the brain which 'represent' inferences, etc., in the way in which computer programs can represent things. Sometimes also 'cognitive science' itself is regarded as an alternative term for computational psychology.

Two comprehensive collections of essays:
W. Bechtel, and G. Graham (eds), *A Companion to Cognitive Science*, Blackwell, 1998.

W. Bechtel, P. Mandik, J. Mundale and R. S. Stufflebeam (eds), *Philosophy and the Neurosciences: A Reader*, Blackwell, 2001.

M. A. Boden and D. H. Mellor, 'What is computational psychology?' *Proceedings of the Aristotelian Society*, supplementary vol., 1984, (Critical discussions.)

*A. Clark, *Mindware: An Introduction to the Philosophy of Cognitive Science*, Oxford UP, 2001. (Excellent readable introduction.)

C. E. M. Dunlop and J. H. Fetzer, *Glossary of Cognitive Science*, Paragon House, 1993. (Brief explanations of cognitive science terms and relevant philosophical ones.)

A. I. Goldman (ed.), *Readings in Philosophy and Cognitive Science*, MIT Press, 1993. (Wide-ranging anthology. Cf. also his *Philosophical Applications of Cognitive Science*, Westview Press, 1993.)

J. Heil, 'Does cognitive psychology rest on a mistake?', *Mind*, 1981. (Yes. Treats 'cognitive psychology' as a synonym for 'computational psychology'. See also his *Perception and Cognition*, California UP, 1983, particularly Chapter 7.)

Cognitivism. Knowledge, belief, thinking and intellectual processes are called cognitive, and cognitivism can be any theory which appeals to such processes. In ethics especially, there has been, since the days of logical POSITIVISM (with premonitions in the eighteenth century), a debate between cognitivism, which treats ethics as concerned with truths, which by one means or another are accessible to human knowledge; and non-cognitivism, which treats ethics rather as concerned with emotions, prescriptions or similar attitudes. However, in the last third of the twentieth century the sharpness of the distinction became blurred, in keeping with complex treatments of notions like truth and objectivity. Some recent cognitivists regard the issue not as whether or not value-judgements are true or false, but whether or not they can be rationally justified. See also NATURALISM, SUBJECTIVISM.

J. Dancy, *Moral Reasons*, Blackwell, 1993. (Includes defence of cognitivism in the context of discussing moral motivation.)

F. Jackson, G. Oppy and M. Smith, 'Minimalism and truth aptness', *Mind*, 1994. (Attacks the attempt to defend cognitivism in ethics and elsewhere by watering down the notion of truth.)

Coherence theory of truth. See TRUTH AND FALSITY.

Coherentism. Coherentism and Foundationalism are the two main rival theories of the justification of belief – epistemological theories to be distinguished from theories about truth (for the coherence theory of truth see TRUTH AND FALSITY). Coherentism claims that for a belief to be justified it must belong to a system of beliefs that cohere with one another. This coherence involves various elements. The beliefs must be consistent with each other, with no contradictions. The beliefs should support one another, with one belief making others more probable. And the system should be comprehensive: the more it explains and covers the more coherent it is. See FOUNDATIONALISM.

L. BonJour, *The Structure of Empirical Knowledge*, Harvard UP, 1985.

K. Lehrer, *Theory of Knowledge*, Westview, 1990, completely revised 2nd edn 2000.

E. Olsson, *Against Coherence: Truth, Probability, and Justification*, Oxford UP, 2005. (Critiques of BonJour, Lehrer and many others.)

Collingwood, Robin G. 1889–1943. Philosopher and archaeologist who was born at Coniston and worked mostly in Oxford. Most of his philosophical work concerns aesthetics, philosophy of mind, philosophy of history and metaphysics. His theory of art, influenced by CROCE, bases art on expression and imagination, which leads him to a treatment of language. In philosophy of history he treats the historian's task as that of reconstructing the thoughts that lay behind or were embodied in historical actions. His later metaphysics is rather similar in nature, in that he sees its task as limited to the reconstruction of the 'absolute presuppositions' of an epoch in the history of thought (see IMPLICATION). *The Principles of Art*, 1938. *Autobiography*, 1939. *An Essay on Metaphysics*, 1940. *The New Leviathan*, 1942 ('an attempt to bring the Leviathan [of HOBBES] up to date' (preface)). *The Idea of History*, 1946.

Common Sense, School of. See REID, THOMAS.

Compatibilist. See FREEWILL AND DETERMINISM.

Complete. An AXIOM SYSTEM, in the sense of a set of axioms and rules of inference, is complete in a weak sense if all the truths of the kind it caters for can be derived within the system. It is complete in a strong sense if the addition of any other proposition of the relevant kind as an independent axiom makes the system inconsistent. There are further refinements. In particular, formalizations of the propositional CALCULUS can be complete in both senses; formalizations of the first-order predicate CALCULUS can only be weakly complete.

Also a set of axioms in a formal language is called complete if for every sentence S in the language either S or not-S follows from the axioms. In this sense no explicitly definable set of axioms rich enough for elementary arithmetic is complete (see GÖDEL'S THEOREMS); in fact no such set is complete in any sense mentioned above.

A. H. Basson and D. J. O'Connor, *Introduction to Symbolic Logic*, 3rd edn, University Tutorial Press, 1959. (See its index.)

E. J. Lemmon, *Beginning Logic*, Nelson, 1965. (See its index.)

A. N. Prior, *Formal Logic*, Clarendon, 1955. (See its index.)

Composition and division. 'Someone sitting could walk' might be interpreted in the composite sense (*sensus compositus*) to mean 'Someone could walk while sitting', or in the divided sense (*sensus divisus*) to mean 'Someone sitting could walk instead'. In a fairly intuitive sense the former puts walking and sitting together, while the latter keeps them apart. To wrongfully infer the expression interpreted in the composite sense from the same expression interpreted in the divided sense is to commit the fallacy of composition. The converse fallacy of division occurs if, e.g. we are given 'Everyone is male or female' in the composite sense, that each person is male or female, and take it in the divided sense, that everyone is male or everyone is female.

Other forms of the fallacy occur when we infer that what holds of a whole must hold of its parts, or what holds of a class must hold of its members (division), or vice versa in each case (composition); e.g. that if a solid made of atoms is coloured each part must be coloured; or that if X is an aggressive country X-ians must be aggressive individuals (division); or that if each vote fails to elect the candidate all the votes fail to do so; or that if each citizen is not numerous the citizens are not numerous (composition).

In modal contexts 'composite' and 'divided' have been thought to correspond respectively to '*de dicto*' and '*de re*' (see MODALITIES).

'All cats may be black' can mean 'Possibly all cats are black' or 'Any given cat may be black'. In the former (*de dicto*, composite) cats and black go together, with the modal term ('possibly') outside. In the latter (*de re*, divided) the modal term comes essentially between cat and black.

I. M. Copi, *Introduction to Logic*, Macon, NY, 6th edn, 1982 (1st edn. was 1953), Chapter 3 § 3.

A. N. Prior, *Formal Logic*, Clarendon, 1955, (See 'composition' in index.)

Comprehension. See INTENSIONALITY AND INTENTIONALITY.

Computational psychology. See COGNITIVE PSYCHOLOGY.

Comte, I. Auguste M. F. X. 1798–1857. Born in Montpellier, he lived mainly in Paris, holding various minor academic posts. From 1817 he was secretary for some years to the social reformer C. H. de Saint-Simon (1760–1825) and was influenced by him. His main work consisted of the development of POSITIVISM. *Cours de philosphie positive*, 6 vols, 1830–42. *Discours sur l'esprit positif*, 1844 (popular exposition). *Système de politique positive, ou traité de sociologie, instituant la religion de l'humanité*, 4 vols, 1851–4. (Comte also applied the title *Système de politique positive* to the second edition (1824) of a small work published in 1822.)

> A. Comte, *Introduction to Positive Philosophy*, Bobbs-Merrill, 1970, Haskett, 1988. (Transl. of first two chapters of *Cours de philosophie positive*.)

Concept. 'Concept' has taken over some uses of the ambiguous term 'IDEA', perhaps partly because 'idea' suggests images, etc.; but 'concept' is ambiguous between a logical sense, associated with Frege, and a (more usual) psychological sense, where it is the content of a thought (Newman), or the mode of presentation of a property (Peacocke). Concepts, however, are connected with UNIVERSALS, and on one view concepts are 'of' universals, so that to have a concept of, say, dog, is to be related to a non-material object like a Platonic FORM. But the 'concept of dog' is perhaps best taken as a single linguistic unit, like 'dog-concept', so that one is not tempted to seek some entity that 'dog' stands for.

A closely related view, conceptual realism, makes the concept itself a substantial entity, to which one is somehow related when one 'has' the concept. This leads to the 'paradox of ANALYSIS'.

Whereas conceptual realism says, in effect, that concepts are universals, conceptualism says that universals are concepts, but leaves open what concepts in the psychological sense are. They seem to be mind-dependent but common to many minds.

It may be that to have a concept is to have a means for classifying together things of a certain kind, and in some way thinking or reasoning about them, though some would insist that to have a concept of something one must also know what that thing is. This perhaps suggests that concepts are abilities, so that to have a concept of dog is to be able to think about dogs. How much the ability must cover is disputed. Has an animal, or a machine, a concept of dog if it reacts differentially to dogs? Can a person blind from birth have a concept of red? Does having a concept involve being able to use a word? Perhaps 'having a concept' is ambiguous in these respects. We must distinguish between the public concept of dog, or the concept dog, and an individual's concept of dog (though perhaps 'conception' might be used here: see below). An individual may include foxes, or think that dogs must by definition have tails; but if he diverges too far his concept will no longer be one of dog.

For Frege 'concept' is a logical term, contrasted with OBJECT. 'A concept is the referent of a predicate', while only an object can be the referent of a subject. Concepts can indeed be talked about, but only rather obliquely, in the way that 'There is at least one square root of four' talks about the concept square root of four. In 'Arkle is a horse' 'Arkle' introduces an object while 'is a horse' introduces a concept. Concepts are thus somehow incomplete: 'Arkle' can stand by itself, as a name, in a way that 'is a horse' cannot. Frege expressed this by calling objects saturated and concepts unsaturated (but cf. Dummett, pp. 31–3). Frege in fact defined a concept as 'a FUNCTION whose value [see VARIABLE] is always a TRUTH-VALUE'. Since what is referred to by a subject-term is automatically an object, Frege concluded paradoxically that 'the concept horse is not a concept' since we are referring to it. For Peacocke concepts are modes of presentation of properties.

Concepts are normally general (the concept dog covers dogs in general), but there can be individual concepts (e.g. the concept of the Atlantic; cf. also HAECCEITY).

Conception normally has only its everyday senses, perhaps tightened up a little, in philosophy (but see Woodfield). For conceptual scheme see RELATIVISM. See also POLAR CONCEPTS.

P. T. Geach, *Mental Acts*, Routledge, 1957. (Discusses nature and acquisition of concepts. Sometimes difficult.)

P. T. Geach and M. Black (eds), *Translations from the Philosophical Writings of Gottlob Frege*, Blackwell, 1952. (Contains his 'Concept and Object'. See also p. 30 for 'concept' and 'function', pp. 47–8 for concept as reference of predicate; for discussion of 'horse' paradox see J. Valberg, 'Improper singular terms', *Proceedings of the Aristotelian Society*, 1970–1, and D. Wiggins, 'The sense and reference of predicates', *Philosophical Quarterly*, 1984, reprinted in C. Wright (ed.), *Frege: Tradition and Influence*, Blackwell, 1984. Also see M. Dummett, *Frege: Philosophy of Language*, Duckworth, 1973.)

A. Newman, 'The material basis of predication and other concepts', *Australasian Journal of Philosophy*, 1988. (See particularly pp. 334, 341, for psychological/logical ambiguity.)

C. Peacocke, *Sense and Content*, Oxford UP, 1983. (See p. 89.)

K. R. Popper, *The Logic of Scientific Discovery*, Hutchinson, 1959 (German original, 1934), § 14. (Individual concepts. See also Leibniz, e.g. *Discourse on Metaphysics*, § 8.)

A. Woodfield, 'Conceptions', *Mind*, 1991. (See particularly pp. 548–50 for concepts and conceptions, and also D. Wiggins, *Sameness and Substance*, Blackwell, 1980, p. 79, n.1, and R. Shiner in *Journal of the History of Philosophy*, 1979, pp. 71–2.)

Conceptualism. See UNIVERSALS, CONCEPT, IDENTITY.

Conditionals. 'Conditional' and 'hypothetical' are normally used synonymously before terms like 'proposition' or 'statement'. Standardly a proposition of the conditional form. 'If p then q', is taken to entail its CONTRAPOSITIVE, 'If not-q then not-p'. There are cases, however, whatever their ultimate analysis, which seem not to be of this kind, e.g. 'If you want it, there's some bread here' does not entail 'If there's no bread here, you don't want it'. Austin uses this concerning freewill. Also an antecedent may be followed by a question or command as in 'If it rains, stay in'.

As there is a problem about relating entailment to strict IMPLICATION and its 'paradoxes', so there is one about relating the standard 'if' of ordinary thought to material implication and its 'paradoxes'. One cannot truly say 'If p then q' when p is true and q is false, i.e. when p does not materially imply q. But can one say it in all other cases? or must p and q be somehow relevant to each other? Or must some other condition be fulfilled? Some say that relevance has nothing to do with the *meaning* of 'If p then q', but that general conventions forbid us to utter it when p and q are mutually irrelevant. 'If that's so, I'm a Dutchman' may be an exception to these conventions, relying for its effect on contrast to the normal case (Strawson; see IMPLICATION (last paragraph)). Also, should we distinguish between asserting a conditional and conditionally asserting its consequent? Perhaps in saying 'If p then q' we are simply asserting q conditionally, in which case when p is false, 'If p then q' is neither true nor false but simply inapposite.

A particular source of difficulty lies in subjunctive and counterfactual conditionals or counterfactuals (also called contrafactual (Quine), contrary-to-fact, unfulfilled). Strictly subjunctive conditionals and counterfactuals are not the same. Counterfactuals may be conditionals with a false antecedent. Or they may be conditionals interpreted as entailing or presupposing that their antecedents are false. Or other analyses may be offered. (In the first case they will not have a special analysis, for the analysis of something should not depend on whether it or part of it is true or false; but the fact that a conditional can have a false antecedent will then affect the analysis of conditionals in general.) Subjunctive conditionals are those normally expressed in the subjunctive in English or related languages, and may include some open conditionals, which leave open whether or not the antecedent is taken as true ('Were it to rain tomorrow we should get wet'). However, the relevant problems are largely common to counterfactuals and subjunctive conditionals, and so are often expressed in terms of either. '□→' and '>' are sometimes used as symbols for counterfactual implication.

An important analysis of counterfactuals is offered by Lewis in terms of POSSIBLE WORLDS. Roughly, the idea is that a counterfactual is true if in the nearest possible world in which the antecedent is true the consequent is also true. More strictly (since there may not be a 'nearest' possible world) a counterfactual is true if any possible worlds in which the antecedent is true and the consequent false are further from the actual world than some possible world in which the antecedent is true and the consequent also true. How worlds are to be compared in terms of 'nearness' (i.e. similarity) raises problems, especially when we try to balance changes in initial conditions against breaching laws of nature. Counterfactuals and subjunctive conditionals seem even more remote from material implication than ordinary conditionals. They also provide problems for the verification theory (POSITIVISM) and the correspondence theory of TRUTH, and have a puzzling element of indefiniteness. After 'If Bizet and Verdi had been compatriots' should we put 'Bizet would have been Italian' or 'Verdi would have been French'?

Counterfactuals are also important in connection with LAWS of nature, PHENOMENALISM, and dispositional statements like 'This glass is brittle', which seems to imply that had it been struck it would have broken. Some writers distinguish natural laws from accidental generalizations ('All the coins in my pocket are silver', 'All ruminants are, as it happens, cloven-hoofed') by saying laws entail counterfactuals (or 'sustain' them, a looser term used in case counterfactuals are not, properly speaking, statements, and because on some views laws of nature do not make, and so cannot entail, assertions about the world). Counterfactuals have also, however, been divided into 'purely hypothetical' ones of the Bizet–Verdi type and 'nomological' ones, which we accept only if they accord with laws or similar acceptable statements. We accept 'If it were snowing it would be cold (since snow is always cold)' rather than 'If it were snowing snow would be hot (since today is in fact hot)' (Rescher). But obviously one cannot, without circularity, explain natural laws in terms of counterfactuals and explain counterfactuals in terms of natural laws. Other views about conditionals say that they state relations between propositions. They state that the antecedent proposition implies, in some sense, the consequent. Alternatively, conditionals may be condensed arguments (Mackie), or rules or sets of instructions for making inferences. See also CAUSATION.

P. Alexander and M. Hesse, 'Subjunctive conditionals', *Proceedings of the Aristotelian Society*, supplementary vol., 1962. (Connection between them and natural laws.)

J. L. Austin, 'Ifs and cans', in his *Philosophical Papers*, 1961, reprinted in B. Berofsky (ed.), *Free Will and Determinism*, Harper and Row, 1966. (Relevance of senses of 'if' to freewill problem.)

J. Bennett, 'Counterfactuals and temporal direction', *Philosophical Review*, 1984. (Full discussion of some different kinds of counterfactuals.)

R. B. Braithwaite, *Scientific Explanation*, Harper, 1953, p. 295. (Distinguishes 'conditional' from 'hypothetical'; cf. also P. Edwards (ed.), *Encyclopedia of Philosophy*, 1967, 4, p. 128.)

D. Edgington, 'On conditionals', *Mind*, 1995. (Long survey and discussion of various modern views, particularly on indicative conditionals. See also J. Bennett, 'Classifying conditionals' in same volume.)

N. Goodman, *Fact, Fiction and Forecast*, Athlone Press, 1954, revised in later editions. (Difficulties in using material implication to analyse counterfactuals.)

S. Hampshire, 'Subjunctive conditionals', *Analysis*, vol. 9, 1948, reprinted in M. Macdonald (ed.), *Philosophy and Analysis*, Blackwell, 1954. (Problems raised by subjunctive conditionals.)

F. Jackson, *Conditionals*, Blackwell, 1987. (Full treatment.)

*F. Jackson, G. Oppy and M. Smith, 'Minimalism and truth aptness', *Mind*, 1994. (Claims that one cannot defend the status of if/then statements as true or false by watering down the notion of truth.)

D. Lewis, *Counterfactuals*, Blackwell, 1973. (Offers extended analysis. See especially Chapters 1, 3, 4. For discussion of some issues see W. A. Davis, 'Indicative and subjunctive conditionals', *Philosophical Review*, 1979. Cf. also E. J. Lowe, 'Indicative and counterfactual conditionals', *Analysis*, vol. 39, 1979.)

J. L. Mackie, 'Counterfactuals and causal laws', in R. J. Butler, (ed.), *Analytical Philosophy*, 1st series, Blackwell, 1962. (Counterfactuals as argument forms. Develops Rescher.)

N. Rescher, 'Belief-contravening suppositions', *Philosophical Review*, 1961. (Differences among counterfactuals.)

G. Ryle, '"If", "so" and "because"', in M. Black (ed.), *Philosophical Analysis*, Cornell UP, 1950, Prentice-Hall, 1953. (Conditionals as instructions for inferences.)

*E. Sosa (ed.), *Causation and Conditionals*, Oxford UP, 1975. (Readings. The items on conditionals reprinted with some extra items in F. Jackson (ed.), *Conditionals*, Oxford UP, 1991.)

*P. F Strawson, *Introduction to Logical Theory*, Methuen, 1952, Chapter 2 § 7, Chapter 3 § 9. (Distinguishes 'if' and material implication. For 'Dutchman' see p. 89.)

D. Wilson, *Presuppositions and Non-Truth-Conditional Semantics*, Academic Press, 1975, pp. 120–3. (Nature of counterfactuals.)

Confirmation. A weak form of verification. To verify something is to show that it is true, or else to test it in a way that will reveal its truth if it is true. Often, however, we can only show that something is more likely to be true than it was, or was thought to be. This is one sense of confirmation. In logic, 'confirmation' usually lacks its everyday senses of verifying or making definite ('I confirmed the booking', 'The facts confirmed my hypothesis'). The opposite of confirmation is usually called disconfirmation, occasionally infirmation.

Confirmation is closely related to PROBABILITY, though both terms are used in various senses. Speaking only generally, confirmation is the process by which probability is conferred on a hypothesis, and probability is what is conferred by confirmation. The problems in this area therefore, especially in earlier writings, concern the two notions in this way: Problems about confirmation concern the methods that can make a hypothesis more probable, while problems about probability concern what it is that we are saying about something when we say that it is probable. The two sets of problems overlap, however, and the difference is not clear cut. Probabilify means 'make probable to some degree' (not necessarily more probable than not), and so is synonymous with one sense (see below) of 'confirm'.

So far we have taken 'confirmation' to cover any process by which a scientific hypothesis is made more probable. In this sense its problems approximate to those of INDUCTION. One way to support a hypothesis is to eliminate its rivals, and through much of its history induction has been viewed as an eliminative process. But a hypothesis can only be established in this way if all its rivals are eliminated, which in practice is seldom possible. It is difficult even in theory, unless it can be shown that its rivals are finite in number. Eliminating merely some of them will help only if there is some way of assigning probabilities to those that remain. Only if there is such a way can we talk of confirming by partial elimination. In fact confirmation has sometimes been contrasted with elimination and confined to some real or alleged process of giving positive support to a hypothesis – a process not dependent on eliminating any of its rivals. To find such a process is one aim of confirmation theory. Another aim is to account for how it is we can talk, as we do, of evidence being favourable even to a hypothesis we know to be false. These aims, especially the second, have led recently to technical notions of confirmation as a logical relation holding between a set of evidence propositions and a conclusion. ('Support' is often then used for the original notion, though it has other uses too.) One such relation (according to Carnap and Hempel) holds whether or not the conclusion is true, and even if we know it is false.

Confirmation is here a relation between some evidence and a conclusion, and holds irrespective of any other evidence. (Whether a conclusion is 'probable' in the ordinary sense depends on how far it is confirmed by all the available evidence.) Confirmation in this sense resembles entailment (see IMPLICATION), but is weaker, and the conclusion is not (as with entailment) contained in the premises. (There are further differences, e.g. where p, q and r are propositions, if p entails q then, normally, p-and-r entails q; this does not hold for confirmation.) For other writers (e.g. Popper, Swinburne) the confirmation given to a conclusion by some evidence is not the probability the conclusion acquires, but the ratio between that probability and the probability the conclusion had previously, usually on the basis of all the available evidence. Here confirmation is an increase in probability.

An enquiry into confirmation can ask three main questions (Hempel). First, what is confirmation? Second, when is one conclusion more highly confirmed by some evidence than another? Third, can numerical values be given to degrees of confirmation?

In treating the second problem Catnap, like most of those who elaborate a logic of induction, relies on the calculus of chances (PROBABILITY) and BAYES'S THEOREM. He considers a finite model, which can later be extended to an infinite one. He imagines a world containing a definite number of objects and a definite number of properties, and considers the various states that world might be in according to how the properties were distributed among the objects; e.g. if the objects were Tom and Bill and the properties tall and short, four state-descriptions could be given of the world, namely 'both tall', 'both short', 'Tom tall, Bill short', 'Tom short, Bill tall'. The confirmation given to a conclusion by evidence is then expressed in terms of a ratio between the number of state-descriptions compatible with the evidence and conclusion together and the normally larger number compatible with the evidence considered by itself. An important complication, however, is that not all state descriptions need be treated equally, and part of the task is to devise a 'measure' which will give a certain weighting to any given state-description. A favoured way is to give equal weight to different structures in the world. In the above example, 'both tall' and 'one tall, one short' represent two structures and have equal weight. They are structure-descriptions ('both tall' is also a state description). 'Tom tall, Bill short' and 'Tom short, Bill tall' share the structure-description 'one tall, one short', and so each has half the weight of 'both tall'. The resulting formula by which confirmations are worked out is called a confirmation-function or c function (in particular, c^*, which is based on structure-descriptions, as opposed to $c\dagger$, which is based on state-descriptions).

What ultimately justifies a given c-function is presumably that it gives results that tally with our intuitions of what should confirm what. But there is a difficulty about applying c-functions. If a proposition is entailed by something we know, we can assert it, but if it is only confirmed it may be absurd to assert it. That Smith is twenty no doubt confirms that he will live another forty years, but we would not assert that he will if we also knew that he had acute heart disease. Carnap therefore insisted on the requirement of total evidence, that we should not apply a confirmation argument unless the premises represent our total knowledge. This naturally raises practical difficulties over what can be excluded as irrelevant.

It is disputable how far Carnap has cut confirmation adrift from elimination, especially when we turn to the first of Hempel's three problems of confirmation and ask what confirmation is, and when one proposition confirms another.

Two paradoxes of confirmation are associated with Hempel and Goodman. Hempel's paradox begins from Nicod's criterion of confirmation. This says that 'All ravens are black' is confirmed by a black raven (strictly, by a sentence asserting the existence of one) and refuted by a non-black one, other objects being irrelevant. But it is plausible to say that whatever confirms a hypothesis in one formulation should confirm it in any logically equivalent formulation (the equivalence condition). A sentence like 'Here is a red shoe' confirms 'All non-black things are non-ravens' since a red shoe is a non-black non-raven. It should therefore also confirm the equivalent sentence 'All ravens are black', which seems absurd. Various questions arise from this, e.g. is there any difference between satisfying a hypothesis (i.e. being compatible with it) and confirming it? How is confirming a hypothesis related to increasing our knowledge about it, and to testing it?

Goodman's paradox concerns similar problems from a different point of view. Let 'grue' mean 'green if and only if first examined before time t, and otherwise blue'. Assuming t is still future, the fact that all emeralds so far examined have been green (and therefore also grue) seems to confirm 'All emeralds are grue' as much as it confirms 'All emeralds are green'. Yet surely it would be absurd to infer the former. (There are variants of the paradox, and also of the definition of 'grue'.) Many who have discussed this have tried to distinguish normal predicates like 'green' from odd ones like 'grue'. They could then rule that only the normal ones could be 'projected', i.e. used in inferences as above. However, it is not obvious that the problem concerns only 'odd' predicates, and it seems to resemble the curve-fitting problem: when two independently measurable features, such as the temperature and pressure of a gas, are plotted against each other on a graph the resulting set of points must be finite because we can only perform finitely many measurements. They may suggest a simple curve connecting them, but they are compatible with infinitely many curves. What, then, justifies us in choosing the suggested one?

These and similar problems have led to some scepticism about whether there is a logical relation of confirmation at all. (Goodman's paradox in particular also raises problems for INDUCTION.) Popper replaces confirmation by corroboration, which he defines in terms of falsifiability and the passing of tests. He insists that he is not claiming that the hypothesis corroborated is thereby more likely to be true. Others concentrate on acceptability, which differs from confirmation because to give rules for when it is rational to accept a hypothesis need not involve any reference to a logical relation and can take account of such things as what the accepter knows already, and what risks acceptance involves him in. (In fact Popper's rules for corroboration are acceptance rules.) Also, it may be rational to accept a hypothesis with a low probability, if its rivals have even lower probabilities; if there were just three competing hypotheses, with probabilities respectively of 40 per cent, 30 per cent and 30 per cent, it would be rational to accept the first, even though its probability was less than a half. See also PROBABILITY, INDUCTION, LIKELIHOOD.

P. Achinstein, 'On evidence: A reply to Bar-Hillel and Margalit', *Mind*, 1981. (Defends an earlier article on relations between evidence, probability and explanation.)

S. Blackburn, *Reason and Prediction*, Cambridge UP, 1973. (See Chapter 4 for discussion of 'grue' paradox.)

R. Carnap, *Logical Foundations of Probability*, Routledge, 1950, Chicago UP, 1962. (Full treatment of confirmation and two kinds of probability, with chapter summaries.)

L. J. Cohen, *The Implications of Induction*, Methuen, 1970. (Develops theory of confirmation not based on calculus of chances, though he prefers to call it 'support'. Also discusses acceptability.)

C. Glymour, *Theory and Evidence*, Princeton UP, 1980. (Develops a theory of confirmation, with extensive use of actual case studies, and criticisms of various different theories.)

N. Goodman, *Fact, Fiction and Forecast*, Athlone Press, 1954, revised in later editions. (Introduction and discussion of 'grue' paradox.)

C. G. Hempel, 'Studies in the logic of confirmation', *Mind*, 1945, reprinted with additions in his *Aspects of Scientific Explanation, Free Press, 1965*. (Starts with discussion of his paradox, and then elaborates his own theory of confirmation. See index of *Aspects* for discussion of requirement of total evidence.)

J. Hullett and R. Schwartz, 'Grue: Some remarks', *Journal of Philosophy*, 1967. (Survey of ways of treating Goodman's paradox. Several other relevant articles in same and preceding volume. Cf. also D. Stalker (ed.), *Grue! The New Riddle of Induction*, Open Court, 1984. (Fifteen essays, about half specially written, with introduction and 176-page bibliography summarizing, often in great detail, 316 items.)

W. Kneale, *Probability and Induction*, Oxford UP, 1949. (Introduction to these subjects, though getting more technical towards end. § 23 discusses confirmation and elimination.)

K. Popper, *The Logic of Scientific Discovery*, Hutchinson, 1959 (German original 1934). (Chapter 10 introduces corroboration.)

I. Scheffler, *The Anatomy of Inquiry*, Knopf, 1963, Routledge, 1964. (Contains discussion of Hempel and Goodman paradoxes.)

R. Swinburne, *An Introduction to Confirmation Theory*, Methuen, 1973. (See first chapter for confirmation and probability.)

Conjunction and disjunction. A compound sentence is a conjunction if its component sentences are joined by 'and'. It is a disjunction if they are joined by 'or'. The component sentences are, respectively, conjuncts, which are conjoined, and disjuncts, which are disjoined. 'Conjunction' and 'disjunction' can also mean the logical operations of forming such expressions. 'And' and 'or' here have only their joining force, without signifying, e.g. temporal order (as in 'He came and went'). 'Or' is usually inclusive ('either and perhaps both'), but can be exclusive ('either but not both'). Sometimes alternation replaces 'disjunction', with alternant and alternate for 'disjunct' and 'disjoin'. Occasionally 'disjunction' and 'alternation' are distinguished, 'disjunction' being kept for the exclusive sense. Conjunctions in the ordinary sense ('and', 'or', etc.) are in logic called connectives, and are among constants (see VARIABLE) and OPERATORS. See also AGGLOMERATION.

P. F. Strawson, *An Introduction to Logical Theory*, Methuen, 1952, pp. 77–92. (Connectives in logic and ordinary language. Cf. R. E. Gahringer, 'Intensional conjunction', *Mind*, 1970. (Brief note on senses of 'and').)

Connected. A relation is connected or connective if it holds, one way or the other, between any two among those objects which can, without absurdity, have the relation to something. It is connected in a domain (i.e. sphere, class) if it is connected when only the objects in that domain are considered, e.g. earlier than is connected in the domain of years (of any two years one is earlier than the other), but not in that of events (two different events can be simultaneous).

Connectionism. Any group of theories of the mind which model it on information processing systems known as 'neural networks', using the idea of 'parallel processing', whereby several different sets of interactions between nodes in a computer network occur simultaneously, or in parallel. In this way, separate elements to carry separate pieces of information are not needed, in contrast to theories like the trace theory of MEMORY or the LANGUAGE OF THOUGHT hypothesis. How far this represents a fundamentally new approach is disputed.

B. Beakley and P. Ludlow (eds), *The Philosophy of Mind: Classical Problems/Contemporary Issues*, MIT Press, 1992. (Part iv includes relevant items.)

W. Bechtel and A. Abrahamsen, '*Connectionism and the Mind: Parallel processing, dynamics, and evolution in networks*, Blackwell, 1991; 2nd edn 2002. (General introduction.)

*P. N. Johnson-Laird, *The Computer and the Mind: An Introduction to Cognitive Science*, Fontana, 1988, Chapter 10. (Elementary introduction). Cf. also T. Crane, *The Mechanical Mind: A Philosophical Introduction to Minds, Machines and Representation*, Penguin, 1995, pp. 154–62.

Connective. See CONJUNCTION, CONNECTED.

Connotation. See MEANING.

Conscience. Being aware of the morality of one's actions: often thought of as a sort of 'internal voice' or judge, and by some as the 'voice of God' within us. Sometimes seen as a manifestation of our moral values, and sometimes as the source of those values. BUTLER thought of conscience as a principle having overriding authority. There are several questions. Is conscience a cognitive or non-cognitive state? Can conscience motivate by itself? KANT seems to believe that conscience is a cognitive state (the thought that I ought to do some act) which can motivate me to act, whereas HUME, for example, thinks that because conscience is motivational it cannot be a cognitive state.

J. Butler, *Fifteen Sermons*, 1726, in his *Collected Works*, Vol 2, W. E. Gladstone (ed.), Clarendon, 1896.

J. D. Wallace, *Virtues and Vices*, Cornell UP, 1978.

Consciousness. Consciousness has presented a problem for philosophy: how can it arise? Does it, indeed, even exist? The word 'conscious' seems to have more than one sense, a fact which may have led to confusion on some of the topics mentioned below. In particular, two senses need distinguishing. In a strong sense, to be conscious involves reflective awareness and perhaps a conception of oneself as opposed to other things. In this sense, consciousness involves some intellectual or rational capacity and may be limited to the human level. But in a weaker sense anything that can have sensory experiences, especially that of feeling pain, can be called conscious. Problems will then also arise about the relations between these senses, and perhaps others: where, for instance, do being conscious *of* something and being conscious *that* something fit in, and what sort of things can one be conscious of? It seemed that phenomenal, i.e. subjective, experience was non-physical, thus inexplicable, leaving an 'explanatory gap'.

In the early and mid-twentieth century the influence of verificationism led to a decaying of introspective psychology and encouraging of behaviourism and materialism, at least in their methodological versions; consciousness therefore, while seldom denied outright, received little attention, in either of its senses. Consciousness came to be thought of as eliminable.

Recently, however, it has returned to favour. How far can any description be given of what seems ineffable, e.g. the colour red as it appears to our sight? Cf. QUALIA and the problems mentioned there. Can consciousness, without necessarily being denied, be dispensed with in describing our mental life in physical or FUNCTIONALIST terms? Can consciousness be studied and defined in its own right, or can it only be regarded as a feature of various mental phenomena, such as feelings, thoughts or emotions? Are animals conscious, and could artefacts ever be so? What would count as their being so? Freud taught us that desires, etc., can be unconscious, so what account should we give of these?

Maybe the problem of consciousness is insoluble because it is simply beyond our cognitive capacities (Nagel, McGinn). See MIND.

P. Carruthers, 'Brute experience', *Journal of Philosophy*, 1989. (Claims non-human animals are not conscious.)

D. Chalmers, 'Consciousness and its place in Nature'. Available at: http://consc.net/papers/nature.html (accessed 1 March 2009). (Overview of the metaphysics of consciousness by leading exponent.)

M. Davies and G. W. Humphries (eds), *Consciousness*, Blackwell, 1993. (Essays, both new and reprinted, covering psychological and philosophical issues, and with a long introduction.)

D. C. Dennett, *Consciousness Explained*, Little, Brown, 1991. (Offers to explain how consciousness arises.)

F. Dretske, 'Conscious experience', *Mind*, 1992. (Consciousness of and consciousness that, etc.)

O. Flanagan, *Consciousness Reconsidered*, MIT Press, 1992. (Claims that consciousness, though real, is 'neither miraculous nor terminally mysterious' (p. xi), and can be explained in terms of the science of the brain.)

R. Kirk, *Raw Feeling*, Clarendon, 1994. (Claims to bridge the gap between physical phenomena in the brain and conscious phenomena like sensations by showing that there are essential links between them.)

W. G. Lycan, *Consciousness*, MIT Press, 1987. (Defends a version of functionalism.)

C. McGinn, *The Character of Mind*, Oxford UP, 1982. (Excellent introduction to problems.)

T. Nagel, 'What is it like to be a bat?', *Philosophical Review*, 1974, often reprinted. (Influential in rehabilitation of interest in consciousness.)

K. V. Wilkes, 'Is consciousness important?', *British Journal for the Philosophy of Science*, 1984. (No.)

Consequences. See CAUSATION.

Consequential characteristics. See SUPERVENIENCE.

Consequentialism. Doctrine holding that whether an act is wrong depends solely on how the act's consequences compare with the consequences of alternative acts (act consequentialism), or on how the consequences of rules or practices or motives that allow the act compare with the consequences of rules or practices or motives that prohibit the act (rule consequentialism). UTILITARIANISM is one form of consequentialism. On the difficulty of distinguishing acts from their consequences cf. ACTION. Consequentialism is much the same as teleology in ETHICS. Teleology in ethics is the view that moral action has a goal; the goal could include some or all of the following: welfare, equality, freedom and other intrinsic values such as honesty, kindness, justice. Consequentialism was thought not to accord intrinsic value or disvalue to kinds of act or to character traits. But now the term 'consequentialism' is used interchangeably with 'moral teleology'. See also bibliography for UTILITARIANISM.

R. Brandt 'Some merits of one form of rule-utilitarianism', *University of Colorado Studies in Philosophy*, 1997. (Widely reprinted, for example in S. Darwall (ed.), *Consequentialism*, Blackwell, 2002).

P. Foot, 'Utilitarianism and the virtues', *Mind*, 1985. (Attacks consequentialism. Discussed by S. Scheffler, ibid.)

B. Hooker, *Ideal Code, Real World: A Rule-consequentialist Theory of Morality*, Oxford UP, 2000. (Influential defence of rule-consequentialism.)

D. McNaughton and P. Rawling, 'On defending deontology', *Ratio*, 1998.

*T. Mulgan, *Understanding Utilitarianism*, Acumen, 2007.

D. Parfit, *Reasons and Persons*, Oxford UP, 1986. (Part 1 discusses consequentialism.)

P. Pettit, 'The consequentialist perspective' in M. Baron, P. Pettit and M. Slote, *Three Methods of Ethics*, Blackwell, 1997.

S. Scheffler, *The Rejection of Consequentialism*, Clarendon, 1982. (Tentatively defends compromise between consequentialism and deontology.)

*S. Scheffler (ed.), *Consequentialism and its Critics*, Oxford UP, 1988. (Anthology.)

H. Sidgwick, *The Methods of Ethics*, Macmillan, 1874, final version, 1907, Part 3.

Consistent. One or more propositions form a consistent set if no contradiction can be deduced from the set. An AXIOM SYSTEM is consistent if no contradiction can be derived within it, i.e. by the rules it specifies. For some purposes, e.g. for systems without negation, other definitions are given, such as that a system is consistent if not every well-formed formula (see AXIOM SYSTEM) of the relevant kind can be derived in it. But the equivalence of different definitions cannot be taken for granted. Usually it is held that a logically false proposition or a contradiction is inconsistent with every proposition since every set it belongs to will imply a contradiction. But some have rejected this and insisted that whether two propositions are consistent with each other cannot be determined on the basis of either alone (Nelson); they would say, e.g., that 'Twice two is five' is consistent with 'Twice three is seven', but not with 'Twice two is seven'. See also VALID (for 'sound').

W. A. Hodges, *Logic*, Penguin, 1977. (See its index.)

E. J. Lemmon, *Beginning Logic*, Nelson, 1965. (See its index.)

E. J. Nelson, 'Intensional relations', *Mind*, 1930. (Consistency as involving both of two propositions.)

Constant. See VARIABLE.

Constatives. See SPEECH ACTS.

Constructivism. See INTUITIONISM.

Content. A term whose use has altered between its appearance in the nineteenth century and its present-day uses. Propositional attitudes (attitudes which involve propositions, like belief, desire, fear, doubt, thought, imagination, surmise) have something which they are or consist in and something (real or unreal) which they are of or directed towards. Meinong called the former the idea and the latter the object; he then distinguished within the idea the act itself and the content, being among the first to insist on this distinction between content and object. Later writers, however, use 'content' rather differently, and more in the sense in which Meinong used 'object'. The content of a belief is the proposition or state of affairs towards which it is directed, while the object is the thing (real or unreal) which the belief is about; both of these seem nearer to what Meinong meant by 'object', and the content is no longer part of the propositional attitude (or 'idea') itself. If I believe that Napoleon won at Waterloo, you believe that Wellington won at Waterloo, and Smith believes that Don Quixote won at Waterloo, then the contents of our respective beliefs are the propositions that Napoleon won at Waterloo, that Wellington did so, and that Don Quixote did so, while the objects of the beliefs are respectively Napoleon, Wellington and Don Quixote.

Perception too has a content, though this may differ from the content of judgements based on it. I might see a statue as a man, or the sun as larger at sunset than at noon, without being deceived in either case. My perception has a content representing the world as containing a man before me, or as containing an enlarged sun, while my judgements have contents conflicting with these. A further question is whether perceptual content always involves the perceiver's having the relevant concepts. Could a child's perception represent something (rightly or wrongly) as being, say, octagonal, if the child lacked the concept of an octagon?

An important distinction in the philosophy of mind has recently been made between broad (or wide) and narrow content in analysing a mental state. This corresponds to the distinction explained in the first paragraph of INTERNALISM AND EXTERNALISM. The broad content of a mental state is that content which it would have on an externalist analysis, while the narrow content is that which it would have on an internalist analysis. There is then a question about whether some or all of those mental states that have a content in the sense we are discussing can have both types of content. The terms 'broad' (or 'wide') and 'narrow' are applied similarly to various related notions. See also INDIVIDUALISM.

P. A. Boghossian, 'The status of content', *Philosophical Review*, 1990. (Argues against irrealism (see REALISM) concerning content.)

*T. Crane, *The Mechanical Mind: A Philosophical Introduction to Minds, Machines and Mental Representation*, Penguin, 1995, chapter 1. (Elementary introduction.)

F. Jackson and P. Pettit, 'Functionalism and broad content', *Mind*, 1988. (Claims that functionalism as a theory of mind can cope with the broad/narrow distinction. Cf. also discussion by M. Rowlands in *Mind*, 1989.)

A. Meinong, *On Emotional Presentation*, Northwestern UP, 1972 (German original, 1917). (See chapter 7.)

J. A. Passmore, *A Hundred Years of Philosophy*, Duckworth, 1957, 2nd edn, 1966. (See pp. 179–83; pp. 178–81 in Penguin edn, 1968.)

C. Peacocke, *Sense and Content*, Oxford UP, 1983, chapters 1 and 2. (Distinguishes sensational properties and representational content in the case of perception, followed by applications of the distinction. Cf. also his

'Analogue content' in *Proceedings of the Aristotelian Society*, supplementary vol., 1986, for a (difficult) discussion of non-conceptual content in the case of perception, going beyond his former position: see p. 16, and for further references p. 14, n. 11. See also T. Crane (ed.), *The Contents of Experience*, Cambridge UP, 1992, chapters 5 and 6, and J. McDowell, *Mind and World*, Harvard UP, 1993, Lecture III, claiming content that is to be available for rational thought must itself involve concepts (difficult).)

S. Sajama and M. Kamppinen, *A Historical Introduction to Phenomenology*, Croom Helm, 1987. (Historical discussion of earlier treatments of content.)

A. Woodfield (ed.), *Thought and Content: Essays on Intentionality*, Clarendon, 1982. (General essays on the nature, types, structure and roles of content.)

Contextualism. In general, any view emphasizing the importance of appeal to a context in answering a given question. In aesthetics, the doctrine that a work of art can only be appreciated in terms of its context. In philosophy of science, the doctrine that theoretical terms like 'electron' have meaning (contextual meaning) only by appearing as terms in deductive systems containing theorems which are empirically testable. In ethics, the doctrine that all values are instrumental (see GOOD), or else that moral problems both arise and can be solved only when we already accept some moral principles. These principles can be questioned only in the light of further principles. Within epistemology, a species of contextualism has many contemporary adherents, for example, Cohen, Lewis.

S. Cohen, 'Knowledge and context', *The Journal of Philosophy*, 1986.

D. K. Lewis, 'Elusive knowledge', *Australasian Journal of Philosophy*, 1996, 74, pp. 549–67. (Reprinted in E. Sosa and J. Kim (eds), *Epistemology*, Blackwell, 2000, which also contains Cohen's 1998 article, 'Contextualist Solutions to the Epistemological Problems: Scepticism, Gettier, and the Lottery'.)

Contingent. Normally, neither necessary nor impossible. See MODALITIES.

Contradiction. A proposition false on logical grounds, or (though less commonly in philosophy) the propounding of something inconsistent, either in itself or with something already propounded. The law or principle of contradiction (also called that of noncontradiction) says that nothing can simultaneously have and lack the same property, or that a proposition and its negation cannot both be true. Two propositions are contradictories if one is the negation of the other, or if they cannot both be true nor both false ('X is black', 'X is not black'). They are contraries if they cannot both be true but can both be false ('X is black', 'X is white'), and sub-contraries if they cannot both be false but can both be true ('X is not black', 'X is not white'). These terms can also be applied to predicates. 'Black' and 'white' are contrary predicates because 'X is black' and 'X is white' are contrary propositions. But contraries need not be opposites, i.e. at opposite ends of a scale which does not stretch further in either direction. 'Black' and 'grey' are contraries but not opposites, and so are red and yellow if regarded as on a scale stretching towards purple at one end or green at the other or both. Of two contradictory terms one and only one must apply to anything in their range of significance, but neither need apply to things outside that range. 'Black' and 'not black' are contradictory predicates even if neither is true (or false) of, say, numbers. But if we say both are false of numbers they become contraries. In a loose sense a proposition contradicts its contraries, since it entails (see IMPLICATION) their contradictories. 'X is black' contradicts 'X is white', if it entails 'X is not white'.

Contraposition. In a categorical proposition of traditional formal logic, replacement of a proposition by another (its contrapositive) which follows logically from it and is obtained by negating the subject and predicate and interchanging them. The contrapositive of 'All cats are animals' is 'All non-animals are non-cats'. Contraposition can be validly carried out on only some of the traditional types of proposition. Contraposition of a conditional or hypothetical proposition negates its antecedent and its consequent and interchanges them. 'If grass is green, snow is white' has as contrapositive 'If snow is not white, grass is not green'. This latter process is occasionally called transposition. See QUANTIFIER WORDS.

Contraries. See CONTRADICTION.

Contravalid. See VALID.

Conventionalism. In logic and mathematics, any doctrine according to which A PRIORI truths or necessary truths are thought to be true by linguistic convention. Applied to science, conventionalist views emphasize that the laws and hypotheses we accept or postulate depend on convention (though we may have good reason for adopting one convention rather than another): we can explain the data of astronomy by Ptolemaic epicycles, it is claimed, though at the price of extreme complexity. For a conventionalist, a law found to be successful for predicting, etc., becomes analytic, i.e. nothing is any longer allowed to count as falsifying it. On some views, it is only at this stage that it becomes a law. The real issue is perhaps how far convention enters in.

Conventionalism is close to INSTRUMENTALISM and PRAGMATISM.

See also MODALITIES, and cf. the views of Quine as discussed under ANALYTIC and TRANSLATION.

K. Britton, J. O. Urmson and W. C. Kneale, 'Are necessary truths true by convention?', *Proceedings of the Aristotelian Society*, supplementary vol., 1947.

H. Poincaré, *Science and Hypothesis*, 1902, trans. 1905. (Supports a conventionalist view of science.)

K. R. Popper, *The Logic of Scientific Discovery*, Hutchinson, 1959 (German original, 1934). (Critical of some aspects (only?) of conventionalism in science.)

W. V. O. Quine, 'Truth by convention' in his *The Ways of Paradox and Other Essays*, Random House, 1966 (originally published 1936 and variously reprinted). (Quine's early view, developed in his later writings.)

A. Sidelle, *Necessity, Essence, and Individuation: A Defense of Conventionalism*, Cornell UP, 1989.

Convention T. See MEANING.

Conversion. In traditional formal logic, replacement of a proposition by a logically equivalent one (its converse) having as subject the original predicate (simple conversion). 'No dogs are cats' is the converse of 'No cats are dogs'. In conversion *per accidens* the converse is implied by, but does not imply, the original. 'Some pets are dogs' is the converse *per accidens* of 'All dogs are pets'. Conversion of either type can be validly carried out only on some of the traditional types of proposition. See QUANTIFIER WORDS.

Correspondence Theory of Truth. See TRUTH AND FALSITY.

Corroboration. See CONFIRMATION.

Cosmological argument. An argument for God's existence, originating with Aristotle but taking various forms. Some versions of it are called the first cause argument. This is that everything requires a cause and God must exist to be the first cause – usually not first in time (Aristotle thought the universe was eternal) but as a sustaining cause. Aristotle gives the example of a stick moving a stone but itself simultaneously moved by a man. Another version of the cosmological argument, which is due to Aquinas, is that the universe exists only CONTINGENTLY (see MODALITIES), and therefore must depend on something which exists necessarily, namely God. Kant claimed that this version shared the main defect of the ONTOLOGICAL ARGUMENT. The argument is called cosmological because it argues from the nature of the cosmos or universe, which the ontological argument, and that from religious experience, do not. However, the argument from DESIGN, which also argues from the nature of the universe, is usually treated as distinct from the cosmological argument.

W. L. Craig and D. Smith, *Theism, Atheism, and Big Bang Cosmology.* Clarendon, 1993. (Debate between theist and atheist in alternate chapters. Sometimes technical. For historical account, distinguishing three importantly different versions, see W. L. Craig, *The Cosmological Argument from Plato to Leibniz*, Macmillan, 1980.)

A. Flew, *An Introduction to Western Philosophy*, Thames and Hudson, 1971, revised edn, 1989, chapter 6.

A. Kenny, *The Five Ways*, Routledge, 1969. (Aquinas's arguments for God's existence. First three are relevant.)

J. L. Mackie, *The Miracle of Theism*, Clarendon, 1982, chapter 5. (This and Flew are critical of the argument.)

Cosmology. In metaphysics, cosmology deals with theories about the universe as a whole, 'everything that is', including theories about space and time. In modern science, cosmology is the study of age and structure of the universe.

Counterfactuals. See CONDITIONALS.

Counterpart. See POSSIBLE WORLDS.

Count noun. Roughly, count nouns have plurals and can take numerical adjectives (e.g. 'cat'), while mass nouns (mass words, mass terms) do neither of these things (e.g. 'snow', in its main sense). Many words are both, in different senses (e.g. 'wood'). Count nouns, if defined in this grammatical way, need not provide a principle of counting (see SORTAL); 'thing' is grammatically a count noun, but one cannot unambiguously count the things in a room: what constitutes one thing? Mass nouns may or may not include some abstract nouns. See also SORTAL.

N. Griffin, *Relative Identity*, Oxford UP, 1977, chapter 2. (Count terms and mass terms. See also review by H. W. Noonan, *Mind*, 1979, p. 300.)

F. J. Pelletier (ed.), *Mass Terms: Some Philosophical Problems*, Reidel, 1979. (Includes bibliography.)

R. Smith, 'Mass terms, generic expressions, and Plato's theory of Forms', *Journal for the History of Philosophy*, 1978. (Mainly on Plato, but includes discussion of relevant issues.)

Covering law model. See EXPLANATION.

Craig's theorem. Theorem in mathematical logic, expounded by the American philosopher William Craig in 1953. The theorem states that any recursively enumerable set of (well-formed) formulae of a first-order language is (primitively) recursively axiomatizable. (See RECURSION.) The theorem has been taken to have a consequence for the description of scientific theories, namely, that a formal description, an axiomatization, of a scientific theory can be given which contains only observational terms and no theoretical terms, which thus seems to lead to the reductionist suggestion that theoretical terms are dispensable. Cf. RAMSEY SENTENCE.

Creation. The belief that the universe was created out of nothing (*ex nihilo*) as a free act by a single god is common to Christianity, Judaism and Islam. As well as creating it in the first place, it is further believed that god sustains the continued existence of the universe. There is disagreement whether cosmological theories such as the Big Bang Theory supports these beliefs.

Creationism. The acceptance of the 'literal truth' of the account of the creation of the world in the Bible, and, in particular, the belief that the universe is much younger than science generally takes it to be, which thus goes with a rejection of much geological and evolutionary science.

Criterion. Something providing a conclusive way of knowing whether something exists, or whether a word is used correctly. Criteria must be logically, and not merely inductively, evidence for what they are criteria of. Philosophical interest in criteria stems mainly from

Wittgenstein, though what precisely he meant by the term is disputed. If some disease is defined as the presence of a certain bacillus, then finding that someone has the bacillus gives us a criterion for saying he has that disease, while finding simply that he has an inflammation gives us only a symptom. A symptom is something that we know from experience always accompanies the thing in question, but it does not have to do so by definition. Symptoms are therefore one kind of evidence of the thing's presence. Another kind is what only sometimes accompanies the thing. Wittgenstein emphasizes that criteria and symptoms fluctuate as circumstances differ or alter.

Glock gives the three crucial characteristics of a criterion for Wittgenstein as (a) criteria determine the meaning of the words they govern; (b) criteria are ways of telling how one knows something; and (c) the criteria of some words are defeasible. The combination of (a) and (c) led to new developments in the philosophy of mind and epistemology because they offer a more flexible middle way between the black-and-white alternative of necessary and sufficient conditions and merely inductive evidence: something can be defeasible evidence and yet be constitutive of a concept. Arguably that contributes considerably to the solution of the problem of other minds.

A criterion, though linked by definition with what it is a criterion of, need not be present in every case. Horses are by definition quadrupeds, so that being a quadruped is part of a criterion for being a horse, but occasional freaks may have five legs. More importantly, we only have a concept of pain, Wittgenstein thinks, because there are publicly accessible criteria for telling when someone is in pain – but pain or its absence can be simulated. This suggests that criteria are important for applying a concept in general rather than in particular cases (Hamlyn). Cf. also Wittgenstein's 'family resemblance' view of UNIVERSALS. A concept may have more than one criterion.

A feature is often loosely called a criterion of something if it is one of a set of features which jointly constitute a criterion of it in the strict sense. If being maned, neighing and a quadruped is a criterion of being a horse, being maned is loosely a criterion of it, though not all maned things are horses. See GOOD for meaning and criteria, which some writers (e.g. Hare) relate differently in the case of value terms like 'good' than in the case of other terms.

Sometimes epistemological and metaphysical senses of 'criterion' are distinguished (MacDonald), though these may be aspects of the same thing.

For Criterion T see MEANING.

R. Albritton, 'On Wittgenstein's use of the term "criterion"', *Journal of Philosophy*, 1959, reprinted with afterthoughts in Pitcher (below). (Thinks Wittgenstein had two views on criteria. Many detailed references to text.)

J. W. Cook, 'Human beings', in P. Winch (ed.), *Studies in the Philosophy of Wittgenstein*, Routledge, 1969. (Both these discuss criteria and their use in philosophy of mind.)

*H. J. Glock, *A Wittgenstein Dictionary*, Blackwell, 1995. (Very clear entry on 'criteria'.)

D. W. Hamlyn, *The Theory of Knowledge*, Macmillan, 1970, pp. 68–75. (Concepts and criteria.)

R. M. Hare, *The Language of Morals*, Oxford UP, 1952, chapter 6. (Meaning and criteria, with reference to 'good'.)

S. MacDonald, 'Aristotle on the homonymy of the good', *Archiv fur Geschichte der Philosophie*, 1989. (See p. 159 n. 26.)

J. McDowell, 'Criteria, defeasibility, and knowledge' in J. Dancy (ed.), *Perceptual Knowledge*, Oxford UP, 1988. (Offers interpretation of 'criterion' in context of how we know of someone else's feelings or thoughts, and more generally of a world independent of ourselves.)

L. Wittgenstein, *The Blue and Brown Books*, Blackwell, 1958, written much earlier, pp. 24–5. (Nearest Wittgenstein comes to defining 'criteria'. Cf. section on criteria in N. Malcolm's review of Wittgenstein in *Philosophical Review*, 1954, revised and reprinted in Malcolm's *Knowledge and Certainty*, 1963, and in G. Pitcher (ed.), *Wittgenstein*, Macmillan, 1966, and cf. for further references N. Griffin, *Relative Identity*, Oxford UP, 1977, p. 49 n. 3).

C. Wright, *Realism, Meaning, and Truth*, 2nd edn, Blackwell, 1993. (Chapters 12 and 13 (7 and 8 in 1st edn, 1987) discuss role and usefulness of criteria in theory of meaning, tending to sceptical conclusion.)

Critical realism. In the philosophy of perception, critical realism is the theory that some of our sense data (for example, those of primary qualities) can and do accurately represent external objects, properties and events, while other of our sense data (for example, those of secondary qualities and perceptual illusions) do not accurately represent any external objects, properties and events. In short, critical realism refers to any position that maintains that there exists an objectively knowable, mind-independent reality, whilst acknowledging the roles of perception and cognition.

Critical realism refers to several schools of thought. These include the American critical realists (Roy Wood Sellars, George Santayana and Arthur Lovejoy) and a broader movement including Bertrand Russell and C.D. Broad. In Canada, the Jesuit Bernard Lonergan developed a comprehensive critical realist philosophy. More recently it refers primarily to the work of Roy Bhaskar and his followers. It is also a label used by some in the debate about how science and religion relate.

Croce, Benedetto. 1866–1952. Born in Abruzzo, he worked mainly in Naples. Though he wrote also on economics, ethics, politics and history, he is now best known for his work in aesthetics and literary criticism, in which he influenced COLLINGWOOD. His system was idealist in flavour, influenced by HEGEL and VICO, and centred on art as the expression of 'intuition', which is a certain kind of knowledge. Croce claims that aesthetics ends up as the general study of language. *Aesthetic*, 1902. *The Essence of Aesthetic*, 1912 (shorter but denser work).

Curve-fitting problem. See CONFIRMATION.

Cybernetics. From a Greek word for 'steer', cognate with 'govern'. The science of self-steering or self-adjusting machines, raising questions for philosophy like 'Can machines think?'

> M. A. Arbib, *The Metaphorical Mind: An Introduction to Cybernetics as Artificial Intelligence and Brain Theory*, Wiley, 1972, 2nd edn, 1988.
> N. Wiener, *Cybernetics, or Control and Communication in the Animal and the Machine*, MIT Press, 1948, corrected and expanded, 1961. (Introduction by a pioneer in it. See also J. F. Young, *Cybernetics*, Iliffe Books/ Elsevier, 1969, who accuses Wiener of unnecessary mathematics.)

Cynics. A group of thinkers (none of whose works survives) in Ancient Greece, from around the fourth century BC, the best known being Antisthenes and Diogenes of Sinope. Known through anecdotes about their lives, which emphasize their rejection of convention ('cynics' means literally 'doggy' ones), and a belief in acting naturally, in accordance with nature, and often a form of asceticism, they had a considerable influence on the STOICS.

Cyrenaics. The Cyrenaics, a Greek hedonistic school of philosophy associated with Aristippus of Cyrene, a follower of Socrates in the fourth century BC, believed that pleasure was the supreme good and, in particular, that immediate and bodily pleasures were to be preferred to deferred and mental pleasures. They thus differed from the Epicureans (and, much later, Mill). They held generally sceptical beliefs about the possibility of knowledge of anything beyond our immediate sensations. See EPICUREANS, HEDONISM, PLEASURE, UTILITARIANISM.

D

Dasein. Term used by HEIDEGGER meaning 'being there'. Humans exist in a world of objects and other people with which they interrelate and about which they care. This existence, or Dasein, is marked both by a realization of our purposiveness and potentiality and a tendency to ignore or lose this potentiality through absorption in present activities, leading to a state Heidegger calls unauthenticity. See EXISTENTIALISM.

Davidson, Donald. 1917–2003. Born in Springfield, Massachusetts, he worked mainly in Stanford, Chicago and Berkeley. He is notable equally for his contributions to the philosophies of language and of mind. In particular, he has used an idea of TARSKI's to analyse meaning in terms of TRUTH CONDITIONS, given an important role to EVENTS, and made causation respectable in explanations of action with his 'anomalous MONISM'. *Essays on Actions and Events*, 1980. *Inquiries into Truth and Interpretation*, 1984. *Problems of Rationality*, 2004. *Truth, Language, and History: Philosophical Essays*, 2005; (all four of these reprint important earlier articles). *Truth and Predication*, 2005.

De Beauvoir, Simone. 1908–86. French EXISTENTIALIST writer and philosopher and pioneer of feminism, friend of and influence upon SARTRE. Her book *The Ethics of Ambiguity*, 1947, is a good introduction to French existentialism. *The Second Sex*, 1949, in which she analyses the position of women in society, as the subordinate Other, has been enormously influential. Her assertion, 'One is not born a woman, but becomes one', famously encapsulates one of the central themes, the social construction of gender.

Debra Bergoffen, 'Simone de Beauvoir', *The Stanford Encyclopedia of Philosophy* (Fall 2004 Edition), Edward N. Zalta (ed.). Available at: http://

plato.stanford.edu/archives/fall2004/entries/beauvoir/ (accessed 1 March 2009). (Excellent introduction, summary and bibliographies.)

Decidable. A theory is decidable if there is an ALGORITHM for deciding, for any well-formed formula (see AXIOM SYSTEM), whether that formula is a theorem of that theory. Theories, in the sense in which arithmetic is a theory, are decidable if formalizations exist for them which are COMPLETE. In systems without CONTINGENT propositions, such as formalizations of arithmetic, a well-formed formula is decidable if and only if it or its negation is a theorem. Where contingent propositions enter, as in formalizations of the propositional CALCULUS, a well-formed formula is decidable if and only if one can prove whether it is logically true, logically false or neither. A decision procedure (one kind of ALGORITHM) lets one decide this mechanically by simply following a rule in finitely many steps. Decision procedures exist for the propositional and monadic predicate CALCULI, but not, in general, for more complex systems. Proof that such a procedure exists, or does not exist, for a given sphere is called a positive or negative solution, respectively, to the decision problem. The negative solution for the predicate calculus (beyond the monadic) is Church's theorem (1936).

See also RECURSIVE.

Decision problem. See DECIDABLE.

Decision procedure. See DECIDABLE.

Decision theory. The mathematical theory of how it is rational to act when confronted with alternatives which have various utilities and various probabilities. Where one is playing against rational opponents, not against nature or 'blind chance' (e.g. in taking account of the weather), we have game theory or theory of games. But game theory is sometimes treated as a part of decision theory. See also PRISONER'S DILEMMA, ZERO SUM GAME.

M. Bacharach and S. Hurley (eds), *Foundations of Decision Theory: Issues and Advances*, Blackwell, 1991. (Set of essays treating the issues from various angles.)

*M. D. Davis, *Game Theory*, Basic Books, 1970. (Elementary.)

Deconstruction. A philosophical approach, particularly associated with DERRIDA and Paul De Man, which involves a close reading of a text, looking for explicit or implicit contradictions and tensions, with the aim of revealing different possible interpretations and meanings. Words, concepts, have histories (see GENEALOGICAL ARGUMENTS). Their meaning is not fixed, for all time and so the meaning of the text is not fixed either. All texts have a variety of meanings: there is not just one meaning, fixed by the intentions of the original author. See bibliography for DERRIDA.

De dicto. See MODALITIES, SENTENCES, INTENSIONALITY.

Deduction. An argument is deductive if it draws a conclusion from certain premises on the grounds that to deny the conclusion while keeping the premises would lead to a contradiction. Given 'All men are mortal and Socrates is a man' we can deduce 'Socrates is mortal', because it would be contradictory to deny it. But 'deduction' is used more loosely by early philosophers and outside philosophy. See also NATURAL DEDUCTION.

Defeasible. Unlike those concepts which can be explained by necessary and sufficient conditions, a defeasible concept is one for which sufficient conditions cannot be stated, but can only be explained by means of an open list of exceptions or conditions which might 'defeat' it. HART, who introduced the term gives 'contract' as an example. A valid contract exists, so long as fraudulent misrepresentation, duress, lunacy, are absent (as well as an indefinitely long list of other possible defeating conditions). Another example might be 'free act': a human action can be assumed to have been free, so long as it was not coerced, or reflex, or … So, rather than there being something in common to, present in, all free actions, what explains why an action is free is the absence of defeating conditions. Concepts, and claims about where they apply, are called defeasible when they are always open to objection, and the objections are irredeemably heterogeneous; e.g. it is sometimes held that no definite criteria can be given for when concepts like freewill and responsibility apply. Compare the notions of imperfect and prima facie duties (see OUGHT).

H. L. A. Hart, 'The ascription of responsibility and rights', *Proceedings of the Aristotelian Society*, 1948–9, reprinted in A. Flew (ed.), *Logic and Language*, 1st series, Blackwell, 1951. (Hart has since withdrawn this paper, for reasons not affecting this reference.)

Definist fallacy. See NATURALISM.

Definition. A definition gives a *definiens* or defining expression for a definiendum or what is to be defined. 'Definition' itself can stand for the sentence doing the defining, for the process of doing it, or for the *definiens*. Various rules for definitions have traditionally been given, but these are now widely regarded as unduly restrictive, or as mere practical guides.

In a real or essentialist definition the definiendum is an essence or concept. A real definition is therefore an analysis of a concept (but, see Mill). In a nominal definition the definiendum is a term or word. 'Real' here means applying to the thing or concept, as against the word. 'Nominal' means 'applying to the word, as against the thing or concept'. The phrase 'real definition' is little used now. However, even a nominalist (i.e. here, one who accepts only nominal definitions) may reserve a word for a certain concept and then use a definition of the word to analyse the concept.

A definition may aim to clarify the meaning of an already existing term (lexical or dictionary definitions, e.g. '"Puppy" in English means "young dog"'); or it may introduce an abbreviation or stipulate how a term is going to be used (stipulative definitions, e.g. 'By "puppy" I shall mean any dog shorter than twelve inches'). Stipulative definitions are prescriptive in that they prescribe how a word is to be used, as are lexical definitions in so far as they do not merely report usage but prescribe standards of 'good' usage. Normally it is not the case that just any explanation of a term counts as a definition. A definition must have a certain adequacy, completeness and universality. A definition should normally state NECESSARY AND SUFFICIENT CONDITIONS for applying the definiendum. 'A puppy is a dog' is true, but not a definition for not all dogs are puppies.

Contextual definitions or definitions in use define a term indirectly by giving an equivalent for a whole context in which it occurs. One might define 'average' by explaining how it is used in sentences like 'The average man has two and a half children'. Two rather technical notions may be briefly mentioned. In a recursive definition the term defined occurs in the *definiens*, but in a way that avoids circularity. The term 'ancestor of' might be recursively defined as 'parent of, or ancestor of a parent of'. Cf. RECURSIVE. An inductive definition or definition by induction defines what it is for a term x in a series to have a certain property; it does this by defining what it is for the first term in the series to have the property, and then defining what it is for any term to have it, given that its predecessor has it. Taking the above example we define x as being an ancestor of y by saying that a parent of y is an ancestor of y, and any parent of an ancestor of y is an ancestor of y. Recursive and inductive definitions thus come to the same thing.

In an ostensive definition (not properly a definition at all) an instance of what the term applies to is physically pointed to ('Red is that colour there', or just 'Red!', said while pointing to a tomato). For impredicative definitions see theory of TYPES. In persuasive definitions an emotionally charged term is given a revised factual significance, to which the emotional charge then attaches. If one dislikes those who live on rent, one might redefine 'fascist' to include them. For extensional and intensional definitions, see UNIVERSALS.

What kinds of words can be defined will largely depend on the kind of definition, and on how rigorously we interpret 'definition'. A common problem is whether a given term can be defined without going outside a specified set of terms, e.g. can 'life' be defined in chemical terms?

Definitions are put to work within a conceptual role, or lexical, semantics, which discusses what the meanings are of expressions in natural languages, which is the main rival of theories which emphasize truth or reference (Davidson).

D. Davidson, *Inquiries into Truth and Interpretation*, 2nd edn, Oxford UP, 2001.

J. Fodor and E. Lepore, 'Why meaning (probably) isn't conceptual role', *Mind and Language*, 1991.

G. Harman, 'Conceptual role semantics', *Notre Dame Journal of Formal Logic*, 1982.

J. S. Mill, *A System of Logic*, Longmans, Green and Co., 1843, book 1 chapter 8. (See § 5 for real definitions.)

K. R. Popper, *The Open Society and its Enemies*, Routledge, 1945. (Vol. 2 includes famous attack on use of definitions outside technical contexts.)

R. Robinson, *Definition*, Clarendon, 1950. (Full-scale study, taking very liberal view of what counts as definition.)

C. L. Stevenson, *Ethics and Language*, Yale UP, 1945, chapter 9. (Persuasive definitions.)

A. Tarski (See bibliography to TRUTH AND FALSITY. Inter alia, distinguishes formal correctness and material adequacy of definitions.)

*D. Whiting, 'Conceptual role semantics', *The Internet Encyclopedia of Philosophy*. Available at: www.iep.utm.edu/c/conc-rol.htm (accessed 1 March 2009). (Excellent discussion of conceptual role, or lexical, semantics, with comprehensive bibliography.)

Deflationism. There are many differing deflationary theories of TRUTH. They have in common the claim that it is mistaken to think of truth as any kind of property or relation. To say that a statement is true is not to ascribe a property, truth, to it. FREGE, Ramsey and AYER held versions of it.

D. Stoljar and N. Damnjanovic, 'The deflationary theory of truth', *The Stanford Encyclopedia of Philosophy* (Summer 2007 Edition), Edward N. Zalta (ed.). Available at: http://plato.stanford.edu/archives/sum2007/entries/truth-deflationary/ (accessed 1 March 2009).

DeMorgan's laws. Named after the British logician Augustus De Morgan, 1806–71, a pioneer of making logic algebraic. He pointed out that in propositional logic (1) not (p and q) = not-p or not-q, and that (2) not (p or q) = not-p and not-q. So, for example, (1) if it is not true both that Henry is heavy and that he is tall, then either he is not heavy or he is not tall, and (2) if Laura is not either young or stupid, then she is both not young and not stupid. See CONJUNCTION AND DISJUNCTION.

Democracy (paradox of). See VOTING PARADOX.

Denial. See NEGATION.

Denial of antecedent. Fallacy of arguing that if the antecedent of a conditional statement is false, so is the consequent, e.g. 'If all cats are black, Tiddles is black; but not all cats are black; so Tiddles is not black'.

Dennett, Daniel. 1942–. American philosopher who has made significant contributions to philosophy of mind – particularly to debates about AI and consciousness (Can computers think?), cognitive science and free will – to the philosophy of evolution and to the philosophy of religion. Dennett argues for a close connection between empirical science and philosophical understanding and, in particular, claims that human qualities such as intelligence, consciousness, free will and interest in religion are natural phenomena which can be scientifically studied and which have to be understood against an evolutionary background. *Content and Consciousness*, 1969. *Brainstorms*, 1978. *The Mind's I: Fantasies and Reflections on Self and Soul*, co-edited with Douglas Hofstadter, 1981. *Elbow Room: The Varieties of Free Will Worth Wanting*, 1984. *The Intentional Stance*, 1987. *Consciousness Explained*, 1991. *Darwin's Dangerous Idea: Evolution and the Meanings of Life*, 1995. *Kinds of Minds: Towards an Understanding* *of Consciousness*, 1996. *Brainchildren: Essays on Designing Minds*, 1998. *Freedom Evolves*, 2003. *Breaking the Spell: Religion as a Natural Phenomenon*, 2006.

Denotation. See MEANING, INTENSIONALITY, DESCRIPTIONS.

Denoting phrases. See DESCRIPTIONS.

Deontic. See ETHICS, OPERATORS.

Deontological. See ETHICS.

De re. See MODALITIES, SENTENCES, INTENSIONALITY.

Derrida, Jacques. 1930–2004. French philosopher, born in Algeria, founder of DECONSTRUCTION. His many books discuss meaning, language, the difference between speech and writing, social structures, and, in his later work, political and ethical issues. He was initially strongly influenced by phenomenology and structuralism, but then saw himself as in opposition to them, characterizing his own philosophy as 'post-structuralist'. One of his central notions is that of 'the other', otherness: that to which is opposed to, or absent from, some more familiar subject, but the acknowledgement of which is necessary for the full understanding of the familiar subject. His work has been influential on literary theory, especially on the complexity of reading texts. Was unpopular among many analytic philosophers, partly because of his hostility towards analytic philosophy and philosophers. But there was a move towards a rapprochement towards the end of his life (see Glendinning). *Writing and Difference*, 1967. *Of Grammatology*, 1976. *Margins of Philosophy*, 1982. *Limited Inc*, 1988.

G. Bennington and J. Derrida, co-authors, *Jacques Derrida*, Chicago UP, 1993. (Exposition of Derrida's thought by Bennington, with running commentary by Derrida.)

S. B. Glendinning (ed.), *Arguing with Derrida*, Blackwell, 2001. (Comments, including Derrida himself, on the connection of his work with analytic philosophy.)

Two clear introductions: Christopher Norris, *Derrida*, Fontana, 1987, and B. Stocker, *Routledge Philosophy GuideBook to Derrida on Deconstruction*, 2006.

Descartes, René. 1596–1650. Born at La Haye in France and educated by the Jesuits, he travelled in his youth and then lived mostly in

Holland, but finally at the Swedish court. Usually known as the first of the 'continental RATIONALISTS', he contributed to mathematics, as well as philosophy, inventing 'Cartesian co-ordinates' and analytical geometry. In philosophy he aimed to establish a basis for certainty by pursuing SCEPTICISM as far as possible, using a 'method of doubt' until he reached something he could not doubt, his principle 'Cogito ergo sum' ('I think therefore I am'), on which he built up a systematic philosophy. He is particularly noted for his body/mind dualism. *Discourse on Method*, 1637. *Meditations on the First Philosophy*, 1641. *Principles of Philosophy*, 1644. See also ANALYTIC, CARTESIAN, FOUNDATIONALISM, HOBBES, INCORRIGIBLE, MALEBRANCHE, ONTOLOGICAL ARGUMENT, RYLE, SPACE, SPINOZA, SUBSTANCE, THINKING.

J. Cottingham, *Descartes*, Blackwell, 1986. (Best introduction to his work.)

J. Cottingham *et al.* (eds), *The Philosophical Writings of Descartes*, 3 vols, Cambridge UP, 1984, 1985, 1991.

Description, knowledge by. See ACQUAINTANCE, KNOWLEDGE BY and EPISTEMOLOGY.

Descriptions (theory of). Theory, devised by Russell to analyse sentences containing 'denoting phrases'. Russell originally recognized two ways of picking something out in discourse. One could name it. Or one could denote it, pick it out by using terms with a general meaning. 'Socrates' names Socrates. 'That man' does not name Socrates, or anyone, but might serve to pick Socrates out because of general rules for the use of 'that' and 'man'. Russell therefore recognized what he called denoting phrases. These were of two kinds. Definite descriptions begin with the definite article or its equivalent ('That man' equals 'The man over there'). Indefinite descriptions begin with the indefinite article. But because definite and indefinite descriptions can occur in meaningful sentences where there is nothing for them to denote, as in 'The present king of France is bald', he concluded that they cannot really function by denoting after all, and that the grammatical form of sentences containing them is misleading as to their logical form. In fact he abandoned denoting, though he temporarily kept the term 'denoting phrase'. The theory of descriptions says that the logical form of the above example is: 'There is exactly one present king of France, and there is no present king of France who is not bald.' Variant alternative formulations exist. Since what a sentence means should not depend on what happens to exist,

Russell applied this analysis to all denoting phrases, including 'the present queen of England' as well as 'the present king of France'. These phrases are then called incomplete symbols (see LOGICAL CONSTRUCTIONS).

Contrasted with denoting phrases are logically proper names, whose meaning is what they name. Ordinary proper names which do not name anything (and ultimately, for various reasons, all ordinary proper names) he regarded as disguised descriptions, and so as incomplete symbols, e.g. 'Apollo' stands for 'The Greek sun-god'. See MEANING.

K. Donnellan, 'Reference and definite descriptions', *Philosophical Review*, 1966. (Often reprinted. Distinguishes attributive and referential ways of interpreting definite descriptions.)

L. Linsky, *Referring*, Routledge, 1967. (Mediates between Russell and Strawson.)

S. Neale, *Descriptions*, MIT Press, 1990. (Develops and defends Russell's theory, in particular treating pronouns at length.)

B. Russell, 'On denoting', *Mind*, 1905, reprinted in his *Logic and Knowledge*, Allen and Unwin, 1956, and elsewhere. (Original version of theory of descriptions.)

R. M. Sainsbury, *Russell*, Routledge, 1979. (Chapter 4 discusses the theory.)

P. F Strawson, 'On referring', *Mind*, 1950, often reprinted. (Attacks the theory. Cf. also Strawson's 'Identifying reference and truth-values', *Theoria*, 1964, reprinted (with 'On referring') in his *Logico-Linguistic Papers*, Methuen, 1971. Russell replies in 'Mr Strawson on referring', *Mind*, 1957, reprinted in his *My Philosophical Development*, Allen and Unwin, 1959.)

Descriptivism. See NATURALISM.

Design (argument from). Argument, with many versions, for God's existence, relying on apparent pattern, design or purpose in the universe. Also called the teleological argument, and, by Kant, the physico-theological argument. See ANTHROPIC PRINCIPLE. See also COSMOLOGICAL ARGUMENT.

A. Flew, *An Introduction to Western Philosophy*, Thames and Hudson, 1971, revised edn, 1989, chapter 6. (Flew has since modified his views: see, for example, his interview with Gary Habermas, somewhat misleadingly titled 'My pilgrimage from atheism to theism', *Philosophia Christi* (Winter, 2004), available at: www.biola.edu/antonyflew/index.cfm (accessed 24 February 2009).

J. L. Mackie, *The Miracle of Theism*, Clarendon, 1982, chapter 8.

Designate. A name designates its bearer, and so only designates at all if it has a real bearer, though it may be quite intelligible without one ('Pickwick'). Occasionally 'designates' means 'connotes' (see MEANING). A rigid designator is a term which, if it designates an object at all, would designate it in any situation provided only that the object still exists and that language remains the same. 'Square of three' is a rigid designator of nine. 'Victor of Waterloo' is a non-rigid designator of Wellington, since he could have lost the battle. The proviso about existence distinguishes the weak (and usual) from the strong sense of 'rigid designator'.

S. Kripke, 'Identity and necessity', in M. K. Munitz (ed.), *Identity and Individualism*, New York UP, 1971, and in T. Honderich and M. F. Burnyeat (eds), *Philosophy as It Is*, Penguin, 1979. (See pp. 144–9 of original version for rigid designator.)

Designated values. See TRUTH-VALUE.

Determinates and determinables. 'Red' is a determinate of the determinable 'colour', while 'oak' is a species of the genus 'tree'. To be an oak is to be arboreal and deciduous, etc., but to be red is not to be coloured and something else; red is simple in a way oak is not.

W. E. Johnson, *Logic*, (1924) Dover, 1964, vol. 1, chapter 11. (Origin of the distinction.)

A. Prior, 'Determination, determinates and determinants'. *Mind*, 1949 (in 2 parts.)

J. R. Searle. 'On determinables and resemblance'. *Proceedings of the Aristotelian Society*, supplementary vol. 1959.

Determinism. See FREEWILL.

Dewey, John. 1859–1952. Educationalist and philosopher who was born in Vermont and worked in various American universities, the last being Columbia. His philosophical views are usually classed as PRAGMATIST and INSTRUMENTALIST. In particular, he is noted for his use of warranted assertibility in connection with the notion of truth. Also wrote on aesthetics. Much of his work was concerned with applying his pragmatist views to the study of educational theory and reform. *How We Think*, 1910. *Democracy and Education*, 1916. *Reconstruction in Philosophy*, 1920. *Human Nature and Conduct*, 1922. *The Quest for Certainty*, 1929. *Logic: The Theory of Inquiry*, 1938.

Diagonal procedure. See CANTOR, RICHARD'S PARADOX.

Dialectic. Literally, 'a method of conversation or debate' (etymologically akin to 'dialogue'). 'Dialectic' originally referred to debating tournaments, but Socrates and, at first, Plato thought that the cultivation of philosophy, and discovery of philosophical truths, could best be achieved by the interplay of opinions in co-operative enquiry by question and answer. Plato therefore used 'dialectic' for philosophical method in general, and came to apply it to whatever method of enquiry he favoured at the time, or to the highest stage thereof. Aristotle kept the sense of conversational interplay; but though he confined dialectic to serious enquiry rather than eristic or argumentativeness, he thought it an inferior, though sometimes indispensable, method of enquiry because it had to start from premises which were agreed to by the interlocutors rather than those which could be demonstrated to be true.

The use of 'dialectic' for debates where one reduced an opponent to contradiction helped to make 'dialectic' largely synonymous with 'logic' for the Stoics and the Middle Ages. The Aristotelian feature whereby dialectic relies on inadequate premises is seen again in Kant. In many later writers, notably Hegel and Marx, the sense of 'interplay' is transferred from the development of thought to that of the world itself. The world develops dialectically by the interplay of opposites. 'Hegelian dialectic' refers to a process (such as a series of historical events) in three stages: a thesis, which leads to a reaction, the antithesis, which contradicts the thesis, and then finally the synthesis which provides a resolution to the conflict. See also MATERIALISM.

R. Norman and S. Sayers, *Hegel, Marx and Dialectic: A Debate*, Harvester/ Humanities, 1980. (Has partly annotated bibliography. Conflicting interpretations by two British philosophers who agree a dialectical philosophy cannot be the mere dogmatism Marxism is often said to be.)

G. E. L. Owen (ed.), *Aristotle on Dialectic*, Clarendon, 1968. (Essays on dialectic up to Aristotle. Varying in difficulty. Most accessible are items by Ryle (controversial), Moreau and Moraux (both in French).)

H. H. Williams, *Hegel, Heraclitus, Marx's Dialectic*, Harvester Wheatsheaf, 1989. (Shows how Hegel and Marx have different approaches to notion originated by Heraclitus.)

Dialetheism. The view that some statements are both true and false. One motive for dialetheists is to deal with the logical PARADOXES, and to avoid triviality they accept a PARACONSISTENT logic (which others too may accept from different concerns, e.g. in connection with certain mathematical or scientific theories).

G. Priest, 'Contradiction, belief and rationality', *Proceedings of the Aristotelian Society*, 1985–6.

R. M. Sainsbury, *Paradoxes*, Cambridge UP, 1988 (revised 1995), chapter 6. (Balanced discussion.)

Dichotomy paradox. See ZENO'S PARADOXES.

Differentia. (Singular, plural is 'differentiae'.) What distinguishes a species from other species of the same genus. For Aristotle there was a problem about which CATEGORY the differentia of a substance-species (human, horse, etc.) belonged to.

Direct realism. The view that we directly, immediately, perceive physical objects and their properties. Indirect realism is the view that we perceive physical objects indirectly, by means of SENSE DATA, which we directly perceive: our perception of objects is mediated. The terms in which these views are expressed, as well as the views themselves, are controversial: for example, even those philosophers who find the concept of sense data useful might wish to say that they are essentially experiences, so had, rather than perceived. The argument from illusion is often invoked against direct realism. See PERCEPTION.

Disciplinary matrix. See PARADIGM.

Disjunction. See CONJUNCTION.

Disposition. Sometimes a disposition to behave in a certain way may be ascribed to something simply because it does so behave often, or, because it does so always when certain conditions are fulfilled, no matter why. But usually it is assumed that something underlies the disposition and causes its manifestations when the relevant conditions are fulfilled; then something may have a disposition without ever manifesting it, as a lump of sugar may be disposed to dissolve in water even if in fact it is never immersed. In principle, dispositions of either type can be acquired or lost; something may acquire a disposition of the first kind if it simply starts behaving in a certain way upon occasion, not having previously done so. 'Brittle', 'labile', 'greedy', 'intelligent' are typical terms for which a dispositional analysis may be offered. The usual contrast term to 'dispositional' is occurrent, used for what is actually in the process of happening. Sometimes 'dispositional' is contrasted with 'categorical'.

C. B. Martin, 'Dispositions and conditionals', *Philosophical Quarterly*, 1994. (Argues against conditional analysis of dispositions.)

D. H. Mellor, 'In defense of dispositions', *Philosophical Review*, 1974, reprinted in his *Matters of Metaphysics*, Cambridge UP, 1991. (He asserts that dispositions are real; they must be connected to other properties, but need not have a non-dispositional base.)

E. W. Prior, R. Pargetter and F. Jackson, 'Three theses about dispositions', *American Philosophy Quarterly*, 1982. (Claims that dispositions must have causal bases, but are different from them, and are themselves causally inert. For further development see Prior's *Dispositions*, Aberdeen UP, 1985.)

Distribution. In traditional SYLLOGISTIC logic the subject of a universal proposition (see QUANTIFIER WORDS for 'universal' and 'particular') and the predicate of a negative proposition are said to be distributed. This has been taken to mean that a universal proposition and a negative proposition say something about every member of the classes which their subject and predicate, respectively, denote. The laws or rules of distribution then say that in a valid SYLLOGISM the middle term must be distributed at least once, and any term distributed in the conclusion must be distributed in its premise.

The rationale, and indeed the need and effectiveness, of the doctrine have been much disputed. Perhaps the best interpretation is this (due to Fogelin and Sinnott-Armstrong): Let S stand for the subject, and P for the predicate, in the proposition concerned. Then universal affirmative propositions say that any S is identical to some P (e.g. 'All cats are black' says that any cat is identical to some black thing); universal negative propositions say that any S is distinct from any P; particular affirmative propositions say that some S is identical to some P; and particular negative propositions say that some S is distinct from any P.

This notion is unconnected with the distributive laws or rules of modern logical and mathematical algebras, which govern the interchange of 'and' and 'or' (or analogous notions).

*R. Fogelin, *Understanding Arguments: An Introduction to Informal Logic*, Harcourt, Brace, Jovanovich, 1978; 4th, revised, edn (with W. Sinnott-Armstrong), 1991. (Chapter 8 gives elementary introduction.)

P. T. Geach, *Reference and Generality*, Cornell UP, 1962, chapter 1. (Attacks distribution. Cf. also his *Logic Matters*, Blackwell, 1972, chapter 2 § 1, chapter 3 §2.)

D. Makinson, 'Distribution in traditional logic', *Nous*, 1969. (Defends and generalizes distribution. Moderately technical.)

W. C. Wilcox, 'Another look at distribution', *Mind*, 1971. (Another criticism. Moderately technical.)

Division. See COMPOSITION.

Double aspect theory. Theory that mind and matter as a whole (Spinoza), or that individual minds and their corresponding bodies, are two aspects of a single substance. See also IDENTITY THEORY OF MIND.

K. Campbell, *Body and Mind*, Macmillan, 1970. (See pp. 113–16 for brief account of the theory. For Spinoza see, e.g. his *Ethics*, part 2, p. 21 n.)

Double effect. See ETHICS.

Doxastic. Concerning or involving belief or judgement. Sub-doxastic has been used for implicit knowledge in the second sense (see TACIT, and the Smith and Davies references there, p. 131 n. 31), i.e. for a mental state which has CONTENT but in some sense does not amount to belief, though it contributes to the formation in the mind in question of states which do. Doxastic voluntarism is the view that one can choose, at least to some extent, what to believe. See also INCONTINENCE.

Dualism. Any view which claims to see in the universe as a whole or in some area of concern just two fundamental entities or kinds of entity or properties, e.g. the views that a person's mind and body are irreducibly different entities, or that physical and mental properties are of irreducibly different kinds, or that all propositions can be sharply and exhaustively distinguished into the ANALYTIC and the synthetic. Antidualists may claim the alleged distinction does not exist, or is not sharp, or is not exhaustive. See also MONISM.

Duhem, Pierre, M. M. 1861–1916. Born in Paris, he worked in various French universities. He did important scientific work, notably in thermodynamics, and also engaged in the history of science. In philosophy his chief contribution was to philosophy of science. His position was akin to positivism and to conventionalism, but while he insisted on the separation of science from metaphysics, he gave metaphysics the role of providing explanations and, it might be relevant to add, he remained a Catholic. Science itself, he thought, should elaborate theories, whose purpose was not to explain but simply to systematize phenomena in ways which science found convenient. *The Aim and Structure of Physical Theory*, 1906.

Dummett, Michael A. E. 1925–. Born in London, he has worked in Oxford, and is the leading exponent of antirealism (see REALISM), which he develops on the basis of mathematical INTUTIONISM. He is a leading interpreter of the philosophy of FREGE (and has also devoted much time to promoting racial harmony in the UK). His publications include *Frege: Philosophy of Language*, 1973; *Elements of Intuitionism*, 1977; *Truth and Other Enigmas*, 1978 (collected essays, probably the best introduction to his work); *The Interpretation of Frege's Philosophy*, 1981; *Frege and Other Philosophers*, 1991; *The Logical Basis of Metaphysics*, 1991; *Frege: Philosophy of Mathematics*, 1991; *Origins of Analytical Philosophy*, 1993 (German version, 1988); *The Seas of Language*, 1993 (mainly collected essays, supplementing *Truth and Other Enigmas*); *Truth and the Past*, 2005; *Thought and Reality*, 2006.

Duration. See SPACE.

Duty. See OUGHT.

Dworkin, Ronald. 1931–. American philosopher of law and politics, who has worked in the UK and America. He is a critic of HART and legal positivism, and attacks the idea that law is a system of rules: rather law is interpretive. He rejects Hart's rule of recognition as the sole determinant of legal validity. He holds there is a 'right answer' in most legal cases, including so-called 'hard cases'. We arrive at that answer by asking what interpretation of the law best explains and justifies past practice in the legal system. This interpretation gives the right answer. The right answer is found by looking for the one that fits best with precedent (past practice), but is also seen in its best possible light, in terms of moral and political values, such as justice, fairness, equality. This is illustrated by his imaginary 'chain novel', in which successive writers add chapters with the aim of fidelity to the foregoing, whilst striving to improve it in aesthetic terms. This mirrors the task of the judge, who interprets past law constructively to find the best legal and moral decision for the present case. While Hart argues for a clear demarcation between law and morality Dworkin sees the two as being essentially connected. He criticized BERLIN on liberty, holding that liberty and equality are interconnected and not in opposition. He is a liberal who has community and equality as ideals. *Taking Rights Seriously*, 1977 (new edn, with 'Response to critics', Harvard UP, 2007). *A Matter of Principle*, 1985. *Law's Empire*, 1986. *Life's Dominion*, 1993. *Freedom's Law*, 1996. *Sovereign Virtue: The Theory and Practice of Equality*, 2000. *Justice in Robes*, 2006.

S. Guest, *Ronald Dworkin*, Edinburgh UP, 1992. (Life and works, good bibliography.)

Dyadic. See MONAD.

E

Education, philosophy of. The study of general theoretical problems of an A PRIORI kind, about the possibility, nature, aims and methods of education.

The ancient paradox of learning (you can't learn what you don't know, because you won't know what to seek, and won't recognize it when found) is now dead as a paradox, but not before stimulating our thought on topics such as INNATE ideas, A PRIORI knowledge and referring; and one can still ask what is involved in learning.

How does education differ from indoctrination, training and programming and must indoctrination, etc., be totally, or only partially, excluded? What is presupposed in the learner, e.g. what degree of rationality? Is a teacher needed, or can one educate oneself, deliberately or accidentally? Can one be educated to be rational, in any sense, and what is involved in acquiring one's first language (cf. PRIVATE LANGUAGE)?

These questions about the nature of education affect questions about its aims and methods. Is the primary aim to instil knowledge, or to instil the ability to acquire knowledge, or neither? How far is education concerned with FACTS, and of what kinds? What is involved in education in morality and (aesthetic or other) taste? Does education aiming at knowledge differ from education aiming at action?

Questions of method largely belong to the theory and practice of education rather than to its philosophy, but answers to the above questions are relevant both here and to traditional questions on the roles of nature, training, practice, play, example.

S. C. Brown (ed.), *Philosophers Discuss Education*, Macmillan, 1975. (Five symposia from British conference).

W. Jaeger, *Paideia*, Blackwell, 1934 and after, trans. 1939–45. (Extended treatment of education and related topics in and before the age of Plato.)

J. Kleinig, *Philosophical Issues in Education*, St Martin's Press and Croom Helm, 1982. (Philosophical discussion of wide range of issues with full bibliographies.)

A. O'Hear, *Education, Society and Human Nature*, Routledge, 1981. (General introduction.)

R. S. Peters (ed.), *The Philosophy of Education*, Oxford UP, 1973. (Readings, with annotated bibliography.)

Plato, *Meno*, (Can 'virtue' (or excellence) be taught? (For paradox of learning see § 80–1). Cf. also *Protagoras*, *Republic*, books 2, 3, *Laws*, books, 1, 2, 7.)

B. Spiecker and R. Straughan (eds), *Philosophical Issues in Moral Education and Development*, Open UP, 1988. (Six papers from an international conference.)

R. Straughan and J. Wilson (eds), *Philosophers on Education*, Macmillan, 1987. (Views of some philosophers on education.)

R. Straughan and J. Wilson, *Philosophising about Education*, Holt, Rinehart and Winston, 1983. (Tries to induce critical thinking in the area.)

Effects. See CAUSATION.

Egocentric particulars. See TOKEN-REFLEXIVES.

Egocentric predicament. Predicament that EMPIRICISTS tend to find themselves in because of their view that our knowledge must start from what is directly accessible to us, namely our own sensations, images, ideas, etc. This makes it hard to see how we can ever know anything else, and so leads to solipsism (see SCEPTICISM). The term was invented by R. B. Perry (1876–1957).

Egoism (psychological and ethical). See ALTRUISM.

Eleatics. Parmenides and his disciple Zeno (not Zeno the STOIC) started a philosophy of extreme monism in Elea in south Italy in the early fifth century BC. As usually interpreted, Parmenides held that reality must consist of a single, undifferentiated and unchanging object, and Zeno defended him by revealing paradoxes in rival views. With Melissus of Samos (mid fifth century), who developed Parmenides, they influenced PLATO, among others. See also PARADOX, SPACE, SUBSTANCE, ZENO'S PARADOXES.

Elenchus. Usually, especially in Socratic context, an attempted refutation by questioning. In Aristotle it means refutation, sometimes limited to refutations in SYLLOGISTIC form. *Ignoratio elenchi*: ignoring the issue.

T. C. Brickhouse and N. D. Smith, *Plato's Socrates*, Oxford UP, 1996. (Chapter 1, critical of Vlastos.)

G. Vlastos, 'The Socratic Elenchus', 1983, in Vlastos, *Socratic Studies*, (ed.) M. Burnyeat, Cambridge UP, 1994.

Emergence. Roughly, a property or phenomenon is emergent if it appears in a system without appearing in the component parts of the system. But the relations between emergence and REDUCTIONISM are somewhat complex.

T. Nagel, 'Panpsychism', in his *Mortal Questions*, Cambridge UP, 1979. (Discusses emergence in the context of how conscious experiences can exist in organisms that seem to be purely physical. For two senses of 'panpsychism' itself see first and last paragraphs.) See also bibliography to REDUCTIONISM.

Emotivism. See NATURALISM.

Emotion. Although some philosophers recognized the importance of emotions (Aristotle, Hume), emotions have often been neglected or dismissed as irrelevant or inconveniently intrusive. They have been treated as if they were merely sensations, like itches and tickles, that come and go unbidden, independently of the will, and therefore not legitimate subjects of moral judgement, of praise or blame. But emotions, unlike sensations, are characteristically directed towards an object (an intensional object, see INTENSIONALITY): we are over-joyed at our team's success, or sad about a friend's illness, or frightened by the face in the dark. The success, the illness, the face are the objects of the emotions concerned. The emotions, therefore, are intrinsically connected, in a way sensations are usually not, with our beliefs: we would not be overjoyed unless we believed our team had won, and believed that to be a good thing. Our beliefs may be justi-fied, or unjustified, rational or irrational, morally suspect, the result of prejudice, and so on. Some emotions – shame, guilt, remorse – seem to have an intrinsically moral character: we may reveal something important about our own moral nature by the presence or absence of these emotions in us. So the emotions play a vital role in our moral life. They play an equally central part in our aesthetic experience, too, and so constitute an important area of study for aesthetics. Do works of art express emotions? Do they arouse or evoke emotions? How can we feel emotion for fictional characters and situations? See FEELINGS, JAMES–LANGE THEORY.

C. Calhoun and R. Solomon (eds), *What is an Emotion?* Oxford UP, 1984. (Collection of most important sources and articles from Aristotle to twentieth century.)

W. James, 'What is an emotion?', *Mind*, 1884. (Much reprinted, including in Calhoun and Solomon. Seminal work.)

*A. Kenny, *Action, Emotion and Will*, Routledge, 1963. (For the notion of the object of an emotion.)

D. Matravers, *Art and Emotion*, Oxford UP, 1997. (Arousal theory.)

J. Robinson, *Deeper than Reason: Emotion and its Role in Literature, Music, and Art*, Oxford UP, 2007. (Combines sophisticated philosophical discussion with latest psychological research.)

Empirical. See A PRIORI.

Empiricism. Any of a variety of views to the effect that either our concepts or our knowledge are, wholly or partly, based on experience through the senses and introspection. The 'basing' may refer to psychological origin or, more usually, philosophical justification. For some of the complexities see A PRIORI. Extreme empiricists may confine our knowledge to statements about SENSE DATA, plus perhaps ANALYTIC statements. Less extreme empiricists say that such statements must form the basis on which all our other knowledge is erected (cf. FOUNDATIONALISM). Other empiricists, however, may simply deny that there are any a priori propositions, or any synthetic or non-analytic a priori ones. Or they may say that if there are any a priori propositions, there are still no innate concepts. A weak form of empiricism may say only that we can acquire some knowledge through the senses. An empiricist view of some given concept or proposition bases it somehow on experience.

Sometimes empiricism has taken the form of a doctrine of meaning, saying that a word or sentence has meaning only if rules involving sense experience can be given for applying or verifying it. Analytic sentences are excepted. Such rules may further constitute the meaning. This is often called logical empiricism. For this and consistent empiricism see POSITIVISM.

Radical empiricism is a name for the philosophy of W. James; cf. PRAGMATISM.

Constructive empiricism is B. Van Fraassen's view that a scientific theory should imply all the truths that can be found by observation in the relevant sphere, even though the theory itself may postulate unobservable entities, 'Constructive' refers to its constructing models rather than seeking a logic of discovery.

'British empiricists' is a traditional label for Locke, Berkeley and Hume, in particular, and for sundry lesser or later figures regarded as sharing their general outlook. See also RATIONALISM.

H. Moritz (ed.), *Challenges to Empiricism*, Methuen, 1980. (Selections from leading philosophers, with partly annotated bibliography.)

D. Odegard, 'Locke as an empiricist', *Philosophy*, 1965. (Discusses senses of 'empiricist', in connection with Locke's philosophy).

B. Van Fraassen, *The Scientific Image*, Clarendon, 1980. (Constructive empiricism. See its index.)

R. S. Woolhouse, *The Empiricists*, Oxford UP, 1988. (Discusses Bacon, Gassendi and Hobbes, as well as Locke, Berkeley and Hume, and without prejudging how far they all are empiricists.)

Empiriocriticism. See POSITIVISM.

Enantiomorphs. See INCONGRUENT COUNTERPARTS.

En soi. See BAD FAITH.

Entailment. See IMPLICATION.

Entelechy. In Aristotle, actuality as against potentiality. He defines soul as the first entelechy of an organic body, meaning, roughly, the set of things the organism can do when active. The second entelechy is the actual doing of these things, though Aristotle does not use the phrase. It is unclear how far entelechy is general or particular, i.e. whether each individual animal, etc. has its own entelechy, or only has that of its species. In Leibniz, 'entelechy' is another term for 'MONAD'. The term also occurs elsewhere.

Aristotle, *De Anima* (*On the Soul*), book 2, chapter 1.

G. W. Leibniz, *Monadology*, 1714, particularly § 18–19, 63, 70.

Enthymene. Argument in which one or more premises, or interim conclusions, are silently assumed.

Environmental ethics. Ethical theories which include consideration of the natural world. Some such theories hold that the whole natural world possesses value and should be respected morally. Other theories hold weaker versions: that, for example, sentient creatures are worthy of moral respect, or that it is important for the well-being of human beings to respect their environment.

A. Brennan and Yeuk-Sze Lo, 'Environmental Ethics', *The Stanford Encyclopedia of Philosophy* (Fall 2008 Edition), Edward N. Zalta (ed.). Available at: http://plato.stanford.edu/archives/fall2008/entries/ethics-environmental/ (accessed 1 March 2009).

H. Rolston, *Environmental Ethics: Duties to and Values in the Natural World*, Temple UP, 1988.

Epicureans. Epicurus of Samos (342–271 BC) founded a school (sometimes called the Garden, from its meeting-place in Athens) which rivalled the STOICS till Roman times, though producing few famous names. Like the Stoics, the Epicureans were materialists, but they added the concept of empty space and were atomists (following Leucippus and Democritus of the fifth century). They also rejected determinism by allowing an uncaused 'swerve' to their atoms, though its exact nature and its role in their system are obscure. Like the Stoics they were interested in epistemology, but they were less interested in logic. In ethics, as well as rejecting determinism they advocated HEDONISM, but of a very restrained kind: their hedonism was largely a matter of emphasizing the role of feeling, but their stress on the pains that followed excess led to their recommendations differing little in practice from those of Stoicism. A version of the system is eloquently expounded in Lucretius's (c.99–c.55 BC) poem *De Rerum Natura* (*On the Nature of Things*). See also PHILOSOPHY, SUBSTANCE.

A. A. Long, *Hellenistic Philosophy*, Duckworth, 1974.

A. A. Long and D. N. Sedley, *The Hellenistic Philosophers*, Cambridge UP, 1987. (Vol. 1 contains translated texts and vol. 2 Greek texts with commentary.)

Epiphenomenalism. Doctrine that mental phenomena are entirely caused by physical phenomena in the brain or central nervous system, and themselves have no effects, mental or physical. An epiphenomenon is a by-product, itself, without (significant or relevant) effects, of some process.

Epistemic. Concerning or involving knowledge.

Epistemology. Also called theory of knowledge. Enquiry into the nature and grounds of knowledge. 'What can we know, and how do we know it?' are questions central to philosophy, and knowledge forms the main topic of epistemology, along with its relation to other cognitive notions like BELIEF, understanding, REASON, JUDGE-MENT, SENSATION, PERCEPTION, INTUITION, guessing, learning and forgetting. See philosophy of MIND (last paragraph) for philosophy of mind and epistemology.

Questions about knowledge can be divided into four main, though overlapping, groups, concerning its nature, its types, what is known and its origin. Knowledge clearly differs in its nature from purely psychological states like feeling sure, for in straightforward contexts the word 'know', like 'realize', 'REFUTE' and many other words, can only be used by a speaker who himself has certain beliefs on the matter in question. If I say 'Smith knows (or, Smith does not know) that fairies exist' I commit myself to their existence, which I do not if I say 'Smith believes (feels sure, is sure) ... ' Verbs like 'know' are sometimes called factive to express this feature. Knowing is usually thought to involve believing, though some say that it replaces belief, or that one can believe one thing while somehow knowing the opposite.

It is often thought that knowledge is justified true belief, but even if belief is involved there are objections to this view. No agreed account has yet been produced of what counts as justification, and sometimes no justification seems called for; do we have to justify claims to know our own intentions, or where our limbs are? Some say we have a special knowledge without observation of certain things, e.g. (in normal health) where our limbs are, which others can only know by observing us.

Justification may be internalist or externalist (see INTERNALISM AND EXTERNALISM). Internalist justification focuses on the knower's state of mind and demands that the knower be aware of (have at least a true belief in), and preferably be able to produce some adequate reason for the truth of, the relevant belief, though what counts as adequate can be disputed: obviously if one is in error one has not knowledge, but must error be not only absent but impossible (cf. INCORRIGIBLE)? If so, knowledge will be rare. Externalist justification stresses the difference between knower and known and demands some real connection between them. This may take the form of a suitable causal link whereby what is known causes the knower's belief, or is perhaps jointly with the belief caused by some third thing; this would allow for knowledge of the future, etc. The knower may be allowed to make inferences, but purely intellectual knowledge, e.g. of logic or mathematics, may be hard to cater for, since causation does not seem to apply there. Another difficulty is that causation was introduced to prevent the belief being merely accidentally true, but the causal chain itself may be of a deviant kind; e.g. suppose a volcano causes some lava to cover a field, which causes a farmer to remove it, which causes a conservationist fanatic to replace it, which causes a newcomer to perceive it and infer the volcano's existence: does the newcomer know the volcano existed?

Another externalist approach is reliabilism (sometimes used to include causal theories). This may be a criterion for knowledge, or simply for justification (whereby a belief is justified if it is produced by a method that normally produces true beliefs, even if it happens to be false this time; for knowledge of course it must be true). Reliabilism may, however, be partly internalist if it is insisted that the believer be aware of the method used and of its reliability. (Similarly a causal theory may become partly internalist if the knower must be aware of the relevant causal chain.) If a belief so produced is true it can be called knowledge, but an objection is that even a normally reliable method may sometimes produce a belief which is true but only by chance or for reasons unconnected with the method: would that still count as knowledge? Also has one knowledge if one is regularly right but can give no reasons, though the subject matter seems to demand them (e.g. successful soothsaying)?

Internalists and externalists agree that knowledge must in a certain sense be not accidental. Suppose that by chance I witness a traffic accident. The event was accidental (it could even be uncaused for all that concerns us here); and my knowing of it is accidental (I only saw it by chance); but it is not accidental that my belief that there was an accident is true.

Other accounts of knowledge introduce causation, or make 'know' a performative verb (see SPEECH ACTS) or say that to know is to be able to tell.

Does knowing involve knowing that one knows? How far do knowledge and the other cognitive notions involve consciousness and rationality: can humans have unconscious knowledge? Can animals and machines have knowledge at all?

The types of knowledge often occur in pairs. A PRIORI and empirical knowledge have long been contrasted (see also below on origins), and the ANALYTIC/synthetic distinction is relevant here. If a priori knowledge is analytic it risks having no content, since analytic propositions seem merely to repeat (part of) the subject in the predicate, explicitly or implicitly, or to do something analogous to that. Kant postulated synthetic a priori propositions, known by TRANSCENDENTAL ARGUMENTS, but their existence is controversial.

Knowing propositions or facts (propositional knowledge, e.g. knowing that Paris is the capital of France) is contrasted with knowing objects (i.e. knowing Paris). 'OBJECTS' must presumably be wide enough to include things like someone's character, and knowing objects may anyway involve knowing facts about them.

Russell distinguished knowledge by acquaintance from knowledge by description, a distinction only intelligible in the light of his theory of DESCRIPTIONS. If I am acquainted with an object it can be a constituent of a proposition I understand, and its logically proper name will be the subject of that proposition. If I know such a proposition to be true I have knowledge by acquaintance of the object. If on the other hand I know the proposition that the last French king was beheaded, whose subject is a description, I have knowledge by description of that king, whether or not I am also acquainted with him. By acquaintance, Russell apparently means a form of immediate knowledge which is not propositional but consists in confrontation. 'Immediate knowledge' might cover some propositional knowledge like knowledge without observation, some perceptual knowledge, telepathy and intuition, but there are difficulties over just what acquaintance, in Russell's sense, consists in.

Ryle contrasts knowing how and knowing that, and this distinction has been widely used in, for example, ethics and philosophy of mind, e.g. moral knowledge might consist in knowing how to behave.

Some types of knowledge are partly defined in terms of what is known, including memory, of the past, and precognition, of the future.

The objects we have knowledge of are legion and, apart from the general problems of SCEPTICISM, some of these objects raise special problems about how, rather than whether, we know them. One such sphere is knowledge about ourselves, especially about our existence, our feelings and their locations (when they have them; see SENSATIONS), our mental states and characteristics, and the position of our limbs (see above). A controversial notion relevant here is private or privileged ACCESS. Some philosophers, notably Wittgenstein, claim that we cannot have knowledge unless the idea of our being mistaken makes sense, e.g. we cannot know, nor not know, that we are in pain. Other such spheres include the past (including dreams), the future, general facts and scientific laws, logical and mathematical facts, philosophical, religious, moral and aesthetic facts. In many of these cases it is disputed whether, strictly, there are any such facts to be known.

RATIONALISTS and EMPIRICISTS have traditionally battled over the origin of knowledge. Can the mind to any degree actively originate its contents, or are those contents entirely built up from what it passively receives through the senses or introspection, as the tabula rasa or blank tablet theory suggests? The strong empiricist and sceptical trend in English-language philosophy early in the last century has now largely broken down as the issue has become less clear cut. Here too belong questions about conceptual schemes, or basic ways of looking at the world. How fundamental can differences between them be? E.g. must we view the world in terms of substances and attributes, etc., or could we substitute an alternative scheme? Cf. CATEGORIES.

Epistemology includes further questions somehow related to knowledge. Rigour and provability concern the acquisition of knowledge. TRUTH and PROBABILITY concern the assessment of it. MEANING and other notions relating to language concern the vehicle of it. METAPHYSICS, LOGIC, and philosophies of MATHEMATICS, SCIENCE and LANGUAGE are all relevant here.

Genetic epistemology, associated largely with J. Piaget (1896–1980) and his followers, studies empirically the acquisition of concepts and mental abilities by children, and belongs to psychology rather than philosophy. For moral epistemology see ETHICS.

Naturalized epistemology, a notion mainly associated nowadays with Quine though having its roots in Hume, is what results when instead of trying to justify in the traditional manner our claims to knowledge we offer a causal account, particularly in terms of evolution, of how we come, and inevitably come, to have the kinds of belief we have (cf. NATURALISM).

J. L. Austin, 'Other minds', in his *Philosophical Papers*, 1961. ('Know' as performative verb.)

L. BonJour, *The Structure of Empirical Knowledge*, Harvard UP, 1985.

E. Craig, *Knowledge and the State of Nature*, Clarendon, 1990. (Aims not to define knowledge but to account for it in terms of why we have the concept.)

*J. Dancy, *An Introduction to Contemporary Epistemology*, Blackwell, 1985.

J. Dancy (ed.), *Perceptual Knowledge*, Oxford UP, 1988. (Reprinted essays on knowledge as connected with perception.)

D. Davidson, 'On the very idea of a conceptual scheme' in his *Inquiries into Truth and Interpretation*, Clarendon, 1984. (Attacks idea that knowledge is relative to conceptual schemes.)

F. Dretske, *Knowledge and the Flow of Information*, CSLI, 1999.

E. L. Gettier, 'Is justified true belief knowledge?' *Analysis*, Vol. 23, pp. 121–23, 1963. Available at: www.ditext.com/gettier/gettier.html (accessed 1 March 2009).

A. I. Goldman, 'A causal theory of knowing', *Journal of Philosophy*, 1967. (Cf. also B. Skyrms, 'The explication of "X knows that p"', ibid. Goldman is reprinted with discussions in Pappas and Swain. For his later views see his *Epistemology and Cognition*, Harvard UP, 1986, which also discusses reliabilist criterion for knowledge (chapter 3) and for justification (chapter 5).)

D. W. Hamlyn, *Theory of Knowledge*, Macmillan, 1970. (More advanced introduction.)

K. Lehrer, Theory of Knowledge, Westview, 1990, completely revised 2nd edn 2000.

Midwest Studies in Philosophy, vol. 5, 1980. (Single topic journal issue entitled *Studies in Epistemology*.)

G. S. Pappas and M. Swain (eds), *Essays on Knowledge and Justification*, Cornell UP, 1978. (General readings.)

A. Plantinga, *Warrant: The Current Debate*. Oxford, 1993.

B. Russell, 'Knowledge by acquaintance and knowledge by description', in his *Mysticism and Logic*, Penguin, 1918. (Cf. INTUITION.)

G. Ryle, *The Concept of Mind*, Hutchinson, 1949, chapter 2. (Knowing how and that. For criticism see D. G. Brown, 'Knowing how and knowing that, what', in G. Pitcher and O. Wood (eds), *Ryle*, Macmillan, 1970, and for use in ethics see J. Gould, *The Development of Plato's Ethics*, 1955.)

G. Ryle, 'Epistemology', in J. O. Urmson (ed.), *The Concise Encyclopaedia of Western Philosophy and Philosophers*, 1960. (Brings out breakdown of rationalist/empiricist contrast.)

W. V. O. Quine, 'Epistemology naturalized', in his *Ontological Relativity and Other Essays*, Columbia UP, 1969. (Cf. also M. J. Woods, 'Scepticism and natural knowledge', *Proceedings of the Aristotelian Society*, 1979–80, D. Papineau, 'Is epistemology dead?', *Proceedings of the Aristotelian Society*, 1981–2.)

C. Sartwell, 'Knowledge is merely true belief', *American Philosophical Quarterly*, 1991, 'Why knowledge is merely true belief', *Journal of Philosophy*, 1992. (Defends this claim, first article answering objections and second giving positive account.)

G. N. A. Vesey, *The Embodied Mind*, Allen and Unwin, 1965, Chapter 7, § 5. (Discussion of knowledge without observation.)

D. Wilson, *Presuppositions and Non-Truth-Conditional Semantics*, Academic Press, 1971, Gregg Revivals, 1991. (See index for factives.)

Epoche. See PHENOMENOLOGY.

Equality. An unclear but important concept in ethics. While it is clear that people are not, in fact, equal with respect to almost any significant characteristic, the ideal of equality might be taken to mean that everyone should be treated equally. But that is also unclear, even if we add 'in the relevant respects'. Egalitarianism, or equality of outcome, for example, equalizing income or wealth, is to be distinguished from equality of opportunity. RAWLS argues that inequalities can only be justified if they benefit the worst off in society. See DWORKIN, JUSTICE, RAWLS.

I. Berlin, 'Equality', *Proceedings of the Aristotelian Society*, 1955–56.

G. A. Cohen, *If You're an Egalitarian, How Come You're so Rich?* Harvard UP, 2000.

R. Dworkin, *Sovereign Virtue: The Theory and Practice of Equality*, Harvard UP 2000.

H. Frankfurt, 'Equality as a moral ideal', *Ethics*, 1987, reprinted in Frankfurt, *The Importance of What We Care About*, Cambridge UP, 1988, and in L. Pojman and R. Westmoreland (eds), *Equality: Selected Readings*, Oxford UP, 1997.

S. Gosepath, 'Equality', *The Stanford Encyclopedia of Philosophy* (Fall 2007 Edition), Edward N. Zalta (ed.). Available at: http://plato.stanford.edu/archives/fall2007/entries/equality/ (accessed 1 March 2009).

T. Nagel, *Mortal Questions*, Cambridge UP, 1979.

T. Nagel, *Equality and Partiality*, Oxford UP, 1991.

J. Rawls, *A Theory of Justice*, Harvard UP, 1971, rev. edn 1999.

T. Scanlon, *What We Owe to Each Other*, Harvard UP, 1998.

*B. Williams, 'The idea of equality', in Williams, *Problems of the Self*, Cambridge UP, 1973, and in Pojman and Westmoreland (see above).

Equivalence. Reciprocal implication, in any sense of 'IMPLICATION'.

Equivalence class. See NUMBERS.

Equivalence relation. Any SYMMETRIC AND TRANSITIVE relation, e.g. equal in size to. Its terms are equivalent in the sense that there is some determinable property, like size, which they all have to the same degree or in the same determinate form, and whatever any of them has the relation to, so do the others. If a is equal in size to b, then if a is equal to c, b also is equal to c.

Equivocal. See AMBIGUITY.

Eristic. See DIALECTIC.

Erotetic. Concerning questions.

Error theory, in ethics. The theory that all ethical claims are false. A form of moral scepticism of which J. L. Mackie is the principal advocate.

Eschatology. The study of the end of the world, judgement day, heaven, hell.

Essence. A nominal essence is a group of terms used to define a concept. For example, if I define a horse as 'anything with a mane and four legs that neighs', then this phrase or group of terms forms the nominal essence of horse. A real essence may be a group of concepts or UNIVERSALS objectively given in nature independently of our definitions (e.g. Socrates' question 'What is courage, really and truly and irrespective of mere human opinions?' presupposes that courage has a real essence); 'essence' by itself usually means this, which derives from Aristotle and normally applies to species, though sometimes to individuals (see FORM, HAECCEITY). Alternatively (with Locke) a real essence is an underlying structure of an object, e.g. an atomic structure. See also FORM.

> J. Locke, *An Essay concerning Human Understanding*, 1690, book 3, chapters 3–6.

Essentialism. See MODALITIES.

Eternal recurrence. See METAPHYSICS.

Ethical intuitionism. Philosophers have often appealed to the 'pre-reflective' intuitions of common sense to act as a check on the acceptability of the conclusions they come to on theoretical grounds. Ethical intuitionism was an important moral theory through the eighteenth, nineteenth and early twentieth centuries. After falling out of favour for the most of the twentieth century, interest in ethical intuitionism has recently revived among a wide range of moral philosophers working in a variety of different areas and traditions. Ethical intuitionism is a form of moral REALISM, claiming that there are facts of morality, but that these facts cannot be reduced to any single principle nor to natural facts. To suppose they can is to commit the 'naturalistic fallacy' (Moore). Rightness and goodness are simply indefinable properties. The basis of our moral knowledge is our intuitive understanding of morality. See INTUITION, INTUITIONISM, NATURALISM, REFLECTIVE EQUILIBRIUM.

R. Audi, *The Good in the Right: A Theory of Intuition and Intrinsic Value*, Princeton UP, 2005. (Good example of recent revival.)

G. E. Moore, *Principia Ethica*, Cambridge UP, 1903. (Classic work, naturalistic fallacy).

W. D. Ross, *The Right and the Good*, Clarendon, 1930.

H. Sidgwick, *Methods of Ethics*, Macmillan, 1874, (7th edn and final version, 1907), particularly book 1, chapter 8. (Types of ethical intuitionism.)

P. Stratton-Lake (ed.), *Ethical Intuitionism: Re-evaluations*, Oxford UP, 2007. (12 contemporary essays.)

Ethics. Perhaps, on the dominant view, an enquiry into how people ought to act in general, not as means to a given end. The primary concepts are then ought, obligation, duty, right, wrong, though not in all their uses. For the other main view the primary topic is value and the primary concepts are the valuable, the desirable, the good in itself. All these notions are normally included under ethics, though the second group can also be excluded as belonging rather to axiology, the study of value in general (in aesthetics, economics, etc., as well as ethics). An ethics based primarily on value can be called an axiological ethics.

These two views *of* ethics correspond closely to two outlooks *in* it. For deontologists (notably Kant, W. D. Ross, H. A. Prichard) duty is prior to value, and at least some of our duties, such as promise-keeping, are independent of values. Deontological properly means connected with, or favouring, this outlook. Deontic means, simply, connected with duty and related notions, as in 'deontic LOGIC'. For teleologists, notably UTILITARIANS, our only duties have reference to ends and are to produce value, or perhaps to distribute it in certain ways; cf. CONSEQUENTIALISM. These views may not be sharply distinguishable, since deliberate action must always aim at some end; and even Kant emphasized moral worth. Also the slogan 'Do right, whatever the consequences' faces difficulties over distinguishing acts from their consequences (cf. ACTION).

However, though this distinction still holds, it has recently been supplemented with other approaches that are less easy to classify, notably rights-based ethics, where rights are prior to duties in the sense that duties are defined in terms of them; and a revival of Aristotelian VIRTUE-based ethics, where the promotion of the virtues and of actions based on them is taken as the proper aim.

The distinction between views of ethics and views in ethics is reflected in two groups into which ethical questions are often divided. These are usually contrasted as ethics/morals, metaethics/ethics, philosophical ethics/normative ethics or metaethics/normative ethics, the subject as a whole being called ethics, moral philosophy or sometimes morals.

In the first group are conceptual questions, which introduce other branches of philosophy, notably logic, philosophy of language and epistemology. During the last century questions about the meaning of ethical terms and the CRITERIA for applying them have been emphasized. How do the terms relate to each other, including the 'bad' terms, like 'bad', 'evil', 'wrong', etc., though in practice these 'bad' terms receive much less attention? How do moral uses of all these terms relate to non-moral uses and, in general, what distinguishes the MORAL as such? Other questions concern how we should analyse sentences containing these terms. Cf. NATURALISM, on the prescriptivist/descriptivist issue and the fact/value distinction. A connected question is whether there are any objective moral truths (as moral realism holds), and whether moral conclusions can be objective even if not strictly describable as 'true'. Questions about how such conclusions might be known and, in general, about how moral arguments can be justified, what part is played in them by reason, feeling and intuition, and about the nature and role of conscience, belong to moral epistemology. An important notion in this area is that of UNIVERSALIZABILITY, and the MORAL sphere can often be compared with others, e.g. the aesthetic or that of rational action in general. Cf. also GOOD, OUGHT.

Questions of the second main group mentioned above concern actual moral issues, like: What things are good, right, etc.? What are our duties? Are there any natural rights? Do animals have rights? When if ever is abortion, or genetic engineering and experimentation, permissible? When and how far can war be justified, especially when mass destruction is involved?

These two groups were sharply distinguished (and the first preferred) both by logical POSITIVISM because of its restrictions on what could be true or false, and by the succeeding linguistic PHILOSOPHY because in rejecting the restrictive dogmatism of the positivists it also thought the philosopher should avoid dogmatizing on substantial issues. However, this all implies that every position on questions of the first group is compatible with every position on those of the second. This compatibility results from the particular answers positivism and linguistic philosophy gave to questions of the first group.

These answers, and therefore the sharpness of the distinction, have been attacked because of doubts on the fact/value distinction and more willingness to allow reason a role in moral arguments, not just in factual or logical preliminaries. The second group has therefore received much more attention recently, and subjects such as business ethics, legal ethics, medical ethics, environmental ethics (the last two overlapping with bioethics or the ethics of life), are flourishing parts of what is often called APPLIED ETHICS.

Many questions seem not to belong to either group alone, such as analyses of particular virtues and vices, and questions about merit and responsibility and about moral ideals. Questions belonging to philosophy of mind rather than ethics, but clearly relevant here, concern FREEWILL, psychological HEDONISM and INCONTINENCE. Such borderline questions are often classified as moral psychology, along with analyses of notions like motive, intention, desire, voluntary, deliberation, pain, pleasure, happiness; ethics proper examines their moral relevance. Interest is a more specifically ethical notion, and the distinction between one's own and others' interests leads to questions about egoism and altruism.

One question involving both moral psychology and ethics concerns the Catholic double effect doctrine: we may not intentionally produce evils, but we may sometimes rightly do what we foresee will produce evils, provided we do not intend these, but regard them as unwanted side-effects, not as indispensable steps. Does this make sense? If so, is it psychologically possible? And is it morally acceptable?

Metaphysical and religious justifications for ethical positions are uncommon now, but one concept deserving mention is that of the FUNCTION of man, appealed to especially by Aristotle.

A distinction is sometimes made between agent ethics and spectator ethics because things like motives, and the difference between what is right and what the agent thinks is right, may play one role when one is deciding what to do, and another role when one is judging what someone else does or should do.

Casuistry is the application of moral principles to particular cases or types of case. Here it contrasts with situational ethics, or moral particularism, which insists on considering each moral situation as it arises, in isolation from others, and rejecting general principles. Casuistry has fallen into disrepute largely from the possibility of using ever more subtle features of a situation to reach a desired moral conclusion in the face of allegedly inadequate moral principles – 'inadequate' can be stretched to cover 'inconvenient'. Moral particularism, on the other hand, has become increasingly influential. Along with the rejection of general moral principles, moral particularists such as Dancy draw attention to the way examples are used in moral education, and to the role of sensitivity and judgement in making moral decisions.

Descriptive ethics examines what moral views are actually held by various people or societies, and whether any are universally held. Though such questions might seem scientific rather than philosophical, they often involve analysis and interpretation as well as mere fact-finding, and indeed illustrate the blurring of the philosophy–science distinction.

*B. Almond and D. Hill (eds), *Applied Philosophy: Morals and Metaphysics in Contemporary Debate*, Routledge, 1991. (Selections from *Journal of Applied Philosophy* on environment, personal relations, war, etc., justice and equality, and medical ethics. Cf. also B. Almond (ed.), *Introducing Applied Ethics*, Blackwell, 1995, and for a more theoretical and methodologically based collection, E. R. Winkler and J. R. Coombs (eds), *Applied Ethics: A Reader*, Blackwell, 1993, mainly new or revised essays with summaries linking them.)

Aristotle, *Nicomachean Ethics*. (Very influential, for methods rather than conclusions, on post-war British ethics; cf. R. Sorabji, 'Aristotle and Oxford philosophy', in *American Philosophical Quarterly*, 1969. See book 1 for functions, books 2–5 for virtues and responsibility, book 7 for incontinence.)

R. Audi, *The Good in the Right*, Princeton UP, 2004. (On intuitionism.)

M. Baron, P. Pettit, and M. Slote, *Three Methods of Ethics*, Blackwell, 1997. (Good contrast of Kantianism, consequentialism and virtue ethics.)

*J. Dancy, *Ethics without Principles*, Oxford UP, 2004. (Defends moral particularism.)

S. Darwall, A. Gibbard, P. Railton, 'Towards fin de siècle ethics: some trends', *Philosophical Review*, 1992. (Survey of developments from 1950 to 1990 with many references.)

*W. Frankena, *Ethics*, Prentice-Hall, 1963. (Short introduction, from modified Utilitarian standpoint.)

A. Gewirth, 'Metaethics and moral neutrality', R. C. Solomon, 'Sumner on metaethics', *Ethics*, 1968, G. H. von Wright, *The Varieties of Goodness*, Routledge, Humanities Press, 1963, particularly chapter 1, G. J. Warnock, *The Object of Morality*, Methuen, 1971. (All these illustrate the breakdown of the sharp metaethics normative ethics distinction.)

R. M. Hare, *Freedom and Reason*, Oxford UP, 1963. (Includes discussion of moral ideals. Cf. J. O. Urmson, 'Saints and heroes', in A. I. Melden (ed.), *Essays in Moral Philosophy*, 1958, reprinted in J. Feinberg (ed.), *Moral Concepts*, Oxford UP, 1969.)

B. Hooker and M. O. Little, *Moral Particularism*, Oxford University Press, 2000. (Detailed and clear critical discussion.)

R. Hursthouse, *On Virtue Ethics*, Oxford UP, 1999. (Leading contemporary version of virtue ethics.)

F. Kamm, *Intricate Ethics*, Oxford UP, 2006. (Intuitionism and rights.)

C. Korsgaard, *Creating the Kingdom of Ends*, Cambridge UP, 1996. (Influential essays from one of the leading contemporary Kantians.)

S. Kagan, *Normative Ethics*, Westview Press, 1998.

I. Kant, H. J. Paton (trans.) *The Moral Law: Kant's Groundwork of the Metaphysic of Morals*, Hutchinson, 1948. (Kant's most important ethical work.)

J. L. Mackie, *Ethics: Inventing Right and Wrong*, Penguin, 1977. (Antirealist approach, i.e. opposing moral realism. Cf. also S. Blackburn, *Spreading the Word*, Clarendon, 1984.)

J. S. Mill, *Utilitarianism*, 1861.

D. Parfit, *Climbing the Mountain*, Oxford UP, 2008. (Argues that the best versions of Kantian ethics and of contractualism dovetail with the best version of rule-consequentialism.)

J. Rawls, *A Theory of Justice*, Oxford UP, 1972. (Influential attempt to base morality on a hypothetical contract.)

W. D. Ross, *The Right and the Good*, Oxford UP, 1930 and 2002. (Leading example of pluralist deontology.)

T. Scanlon, *What We Owe To Each Other*, Harvard UP, 1998. (Influential discussion of reasons, value, contractualist ethics and responsibility.)

*P. Singer (ed.), *Applied Ethics*, Oxford UP, 1986. (Selected readings on various moral issues).

J. J. Thomson, *The Realm of Rights*, Harvard UP, 1992. (A careful account of various moral rights.)

*B. A. O. Williams, *Morality*, Penguin, 1972, (Elementary introduction. His *Ethics and the Limits of Philosophy*, Fontana, 1985, is fuller but rather harder.)

Eudaimonia, eudaimonism. see HAPPINESS.

Event. Generally regarded as either a change, usually of short duration, in the qualities or relations such as spatial relations of a thing, or as the possession of a property or relation by something at or for a time. Many of the problems about events concern how they are related to other things, e.g. OBJECTS, particulars (see UNIVERSALS), INDI-VIDUALS, UNIVERSALS, FACTS, states of affairs, propositions (see SENTENCES), changes, ACTIONS. Can events be classed under any of these? Indeed are events needed as a separate ontological category at all? Also are events of radically different kinds? Are some events recurrent (e.g. 'annual events' perhaps?) and some unique, some instantaneous and some enduring, some mental and some physical? An important ambiguity is that sometimes 'event' means 'kind of event'. How should we individuate events (i.e. tell when we have one and when another)? Are events always datable? A murder is presumably an event, but if I murder someone by slow poison, does the murder occur when I administer the poison or when the victim dies, perhaps years later (cf. ACTION)? And can events move or change?

J. Bennett, *Events and Their Names*, Oxford UP, 1988. (Full treatment. Cf. discussions of it, with reply, in *Philosophy and Phenomenological Research*, 1991, pp. 625–62.)

R. Chisholm, 'States of affairs again', D. Davidson, 'Eternal versus ephemeral events', *Nous*, 1970. (Events, propositions, particulars. Further references in Davidson).

D. Davidson, *Essays on Actions and Events*, Clarendon, 1980. (Reprinted essays. See also criticisms, with Davidson's replies, in B. Vermazen and M. B. Hintikka (eds), *Essays on Davidson: Actions and Events*, Clarendon, 1985 and S. Evnine, *Donald Davidson*, Blackwell, 1991, particularly pp. 25–33.)

T. Horgan, 'The case against events', *Philosophical Review*, 1978. (One example of this view. For criticism see I. Thalberg, 'A world without events?' in B. Vermazen and M. B. Hintikka (eds), *Essays on Davidson: Actions and Events*, Clarendon, 1985, itself criticized by R. H. Feldman and E. Wieringa, 'Thalberg on the irreducibility of events', *Analysis*, vol. 39, 1979.)

L. B. Lombard, *Events*, Routledge, 1986. (Full treatment.)

Z. Vendler, 'Causal relations', *Journal of Philosophy*, 1967, pp. 707–8. (Events and facts.)

Evidence (paradox of ideal). Suppose we assume that the a priori PROBABILITY of a certain penny falling heads on the next toss is ½ and that therefore it is rational to half-expect heads. Suppose we then find that in the past it has fallen heads and tails equally often. This evidence seems ideal justification for the rationality of this half-expecting. Yet the half-expecting was already the perfectly rational state of mind to adopt. Therefore the evidence seems superfluous. Offered by Popper as objection to (what he calls) subjective theory of PROBABILITY.

K. R. Popper, *The Logic of Scientific Discovery*, Hutchinson, 1959 (German original 1934), pp. 407–10.

R. H. Vincent, 'The paradox of ideal evidence', *Philosophical Review*, 1962. (Criticizes Popper.)

Evil, The problem of. See THEODICY.

Examination paradox. See PREDICTION.

Excluded middle (Law or principle of). Often abbreviated as LEM. Traditionally, 'A is B or A is not B' (any given thing either has or lacks any given property), or in the propositional calculus (where 'p' stands for a proposition) 'p or not p'. Under the influence of INTUI-TIONISM and antirealism (see REALISM) it has become standard to distinguish LEM from the principle or law of bivalence, that every proposition is true or false, a semantic rather than logical principle since it is about propositions and mentions truth. Intuitionism rejects LEM and bivalence, but replaces bivalence by a weaker principle, *tertium non datur* (there is no third truth-value), that no proposition is neither true nor false; for classical (i.e. non-intuitionist) logic this entails bivalence, but for intuitionism, which denies one half of the double NEGATION principle, it does not.

Many-valued logics (see TRUTH-VALUE) reject all three of these principles, a line taken (in effect) by Aristotle, followed by Lukasiewicz, in trying to avoid logical determinism (see FREEWILL, including its bibliography (Aristotle item)).

A traditional problem for LEM has lain in vague predicates like 'bald' (see HEAP). A vague predicate may be made precise ('pre-cisified') in various ways; 'bald' may be precisified as 'having fewer than 100 hairs', or as 'having fewer than 10 hairs', and so on. One approach, that of SUPERVALUATION, treats a vague proposition as true if it is true however the vague term is precisified. This view keeps LEM but rejects bivalence. This is because 'p or not p' may hold for every precisification ('Smith is bald or not bald' may be true whether we let 'bald' mean 'having fewer than 100 hairs', or 'having fewer than 101 hairs' or whatever), while p does not hold for every precisification, and neither does 'not p' (it need not be the case that 'Smith is bald' is true for all precisifications of 'bald', and the same applies to 'Smith is not bald': if Smith has exactly 100 hairs he will be bald, if 'bald' means 'having less than 101 hairs', but not bald if it means 'having less than 100 hairs' (though in either case, 'Smith is bald or not bald' will be true, and so LEM is saved)).

P. T. Geach and W. F. Bednarowski, 'The law of excluded middle', *Proceedings of the Aristotelian Society*, supplementary vol., 1956. (Pre-Dummett discussions of vague predicates.)

G. Rosen, 'The shoals of language' (a 'critical notice' of M. Dummett, *The Seas of Language*), *Mind*, 1995. (Useful on bivalence and realism.)

*R. M. Sainsbury (see bibliography to HEAP).

See also bibliography to INTUITIONISM, particularly pages xix, xxx and index of Dummett's *Truth and other Enigmas*, Duckworth, 1978.

Existential import. See QUANTIFIER WORDS.

Existentialism. A movement primarily associated with Kierkegaard, Jaspers, Heidegger, Sartre and Marcel, though many others are often included. Its exponents have widely differing outlooks, in religion and politics as well as in philosophy, but share certain general themes.

The most important of these themes is an interest in humanity as such and its relations to the world, and in the notion of BEING. Existentialists normally contrast the sort of being that applies to humans, what Heidegger calls DASEIN, with that which applies to things, and to humans only in so far as they are things. Existentialists tend to regard the being which applies to humans as something which they only attain sometimes, and ought to struggle for. Sartre contrasts the être-pour-soi which partly does, and partly should, belong to humans, with the être-en-soi which belongs to things but which humans fail to escape from when they live in BAD FAITH. There seems therefore to be a certain tension in existentialism about whether what is described is the inevitable human condition, or an ideal, perhaps never fully attainable. The two poles of this tension give existentialism its two philosophical footholds, in metaphysics and ethics.

A feature of human existence, for existentialists, is that humans are active and creative while things are not. Things are simply what they are, but humans might be other than they are. Humans must choose, and (at least on some versions) must choose the principles on which they choose. They are not, like things, already determined. 'Existence precedes essence' for humans: they make their essences as they go along, and do not live out a predetermined essence or blue-print (but see also Cooper, chapter 4). Humans are free, and the reality and nature of freedom is a major concern for existentialists. Furthermore, humans are conscious of the contrast between themselves and things, of their relations with other humans, of their eventual deaths, and of their power to choose and become what they are not. All this leads to a notion of not-being, or 'Nothing', which, to the despair of logicians, existentialists often appear to treat as a thing or condition in its own right. Sometimes this 'Nothing', and sometimes the contingency of things in general, provokes an emotion or condition of dread (despair, anguish, Angst, angoisse).

In elaborating what being is for humans, and how they are related to the world, recent existentialists have been strongly influenced by Husserl's PHENOMENOLOGY, though they reject some aspects of it.

J. Collins, *The Existentialists*, Regnery, 1952, Greenwood Press, 1977.

*D. E. Cooper, *The Existentialists: A Reconstruction*, Clarendon, 1990. (Sympathetic general introduction, stressing what is common to the different thinkers.)

A. C. Danto, *Sartre*, Fontana, 1975. (Introduction.)

M. Heidegger, *Sein und Zeit*, 1927, trans. as *Being and Time*, Blackwell, 1962. (His main work.)

N. Langiulli (ed.), *The Existentialist Tradition*, Doubleday Anchor, 1971. (Selections from many writers, with brief biographies and full bibliographies of them. Very difficult. Items by Abbagnano, Buber, Marcel, Sartre perhaps easiest.)

J. Macquarie, *Existentialism*, Hutchinson, 1972. (General introduction from theological point of view.)

A. R. Manser and A. T. Kolnai, 'Existentialism', *Proceedings of the Aristotelian Society*, supplementary vol., 1963. (Critical discussions of existentialist ethics.)

J.-P. Sartre, *L'Etre et le néant*, 1943, trans. as *Being and Nothingness*, Methuen, 1957. (His main work. Cf. also his. *Essays on Existentialism* (ed. W. Baskin), Citadel Press, 1965, translated selections on leading topics in his work, including famous examples of young man and the Resistance (pp. 42 ff.) and waiter (pp. 167 ff.).)

D. M. Tulloch, 'Sartrian existentialism', *Philosophical Quarterly*, 1952.

*M. Warnock, *Existentialism*, Oxford UP, 1970. (Elementary introduction, though limited in coverage.)

Explanation. The process of making something intelligible, or saying why certain things are as they are, or the account used to do these things. The account is sometimes called the explanans, and the thing to be explained is called the explanandum. An explanation may do things like reducing the unfamiliar to the familiar, thus enlightening people. Things it does in this way are called its pragmatic features and they are relevant to the question of whether an explanation should be relative to the receiver. A child, a lay adult and an expert seem to require different explanations of the same thing, since what is already familiar to them will differ. Yet a scientific explanation may be in terms hitherto unfamiliar even to the scientist, the lay person may study science to find 'the' explanation of something, and the familiar itself may need explaining, as Newton explained the falling of an apple by associating it with other, apparently quite unrelated, phenomena. Many writers have therefore regarded the pragmatic features as subjective and incidental, and have concentrated rather on various views of the logical form an explanation should take.

On one view, the covering law model, an explanation should state general laws and initial conditions which together logically entail the explanandum. 'All water heated at normal pressure to 100°C boils' and 'This water was so heated' together explain why this water boiled. The model can be adapted to explain laws themselves, and may have more complex applications, where covering laws are distinguished from supporting laws. However, not just any covering law will do. 'Whenever water is about to turn to steam it boils' and 'This water was about to turn to steam' do not explain the boiling. This suggests that an explanation must present what is 'more knowable absolutely' even though perhaps not 'more knowable to us' (Aristotle), and that pragmatic features are relevant, though they need not be subjective (cf. Dray, p. 74). An explanation therefore might present a cause, or something logically prior to the explanandum in the relevant system, as when the explanandum is a mathematical fact.

Often, however, scientific laws say that not all As are Bs, but that a certain proportion are. When the covering law model is extended to use laws of this type, explanations are called statistical or probabilistic. The previous kind, all As are Bs, are called nomological. Nomological explanations are DEDUCTIVE. The explanandum is deduced from the premises. Statistical explanations are usually (not always: see Hempel) INDUCTIVE. For reasons given under CONFIRMATION statistical explanations must be supplemented by Carnap's requirement of total evidence (or Hempel's weaker form, the requirement of maximal specificity).

It is disputed whether any but deductive explanations are properly called explanations at all, and also how many kinds of explanation there are. In particular, can the covering law model apply to subjects like history and psychology, and can teleological explanations, i.e. those in terms of purposes or final causes, be reduced to causal explanations? Also do questions beginning with Why? How? etc. call for the same type of explanation? Is there a basic difference between explaining why-necessarily and how-possibly (Dray)? Can the covering law model account for explaining what something is, or what people are doing?

Further, how is explaining something related to describing it, and also to predicting it? Darwinism explains the variety of species, but does not seem fitted for predicting new species. Thales allegedly predicted the eclipse of 585 BC by consulting records but he could almost certainly not explain it. Do explanation and predictability nevertheless ultimately go together?

So far we have left the explananda vague. When not themselves laws, are they events, states, processes, situations, actions, forbearances, or are they statements describing these? To explain a statement one needs to explain one or more features of the relevant event, while to explain the event itself in its infinite richness would seem a hopeless task. Explaining meanings raises special problems.

After asking what an explanation is, we can ask when one is adequate, and whether the same explanandum can be given more than one explanation.

Explication, when not simply a synonym for 'explanation', is the process whereby a hitherto imprecise notion is given a formal definition, and so made suitable for use in formal work. The definition does not claim to be synonymous with the original notion, since it is avowedly making it more precise. (This is a form of logical analysis: see PHILOSOPHY.)

Aristotle, *Posterior Analytics*, 71b33–2a6. ('More knowable absolutely' and 'to us'. See also early chapters for when scientific argument is explanatory.)

R. Carnap, *Logical Foundations of Probability*, Routledge, 1950, Chicago UP, 1962, chapter 1. (Explication. Cf. W. V. O. Quine, *Word and Object*, Wiley, 1960, § 53–4.)

W. H. Dray, *Laws and Explanation in History*, 1957. (Opposes covering law model for history.)

C. G. Hempel, *Aspects of Scientific Explanation*, Free Press, 1965. (Chapter 12 has full account of covering law model, and defends its adequacy in all fields. Chapter 9 (also in *Journal of Philosophy*, 1942) defends it regarding history. Cf. also his 'Explanation in science and in history', in R. G. Colodny (ed.), *Frontiers of Science and Philosophy*, 1962, reprinted in P. H. Nidditch (ed.), *The Philosophy of Science*, Oxford UP, 1968, and in W. H. Dray (ed.), *Philosophical Analysis and History*, Harper and Row, 1966, Greenwood Press, 1979.)

*J. Hospers, 'What is explanation?', *Journal of Philosophy*, 1946, reprinted in A. Flew (ed.), *Essays in Conceptual Analysis*, Macmillan, 1956, St Martin's Press, 1966, Greenwood Press, 1981. (Elementary defence of covering law model as adequate for explanations-why of events.)

P. Kitcher and W. C. Salmon (eds), *Scientific Explanation*, Minnesota UP, 1989. (Specially written papers, including long historical survey, with chronological bibliography. Cf. also Salmon's *Scientific Explanation and the Causal Structure of the World*, Princeton UP, 1984, defending appeal to causation rather than to deductive inference or necessitation.)

D.-H. Ruben, *Scientific Explanation*, Routledge, 1990. (Partly historical and partly constructive. Elaborates realist view, whereby explanation is not just relative to human knowledge or interests.)

D.-H. Ruben (ed.), *Explanation*, Oxford UP, 1993. (General anthology of reprinted items.)

C. Taylor, *The Explanation of Behaviour*, Routledge, 1964. (Distinguishes and defends need for, teleological and purposive explanations. T. L. S. Sprigge, 'Final causes', *Proceedings of the Aristotelian Society*, supplementary vol., 1971, assimilates teleological to causal explanations. Cf. also L. Wright, *Teleological Explanations: An Etiological Analysis of Goals and Functions*, California, 1976, which defends them.)

G. H. von Wright, *Explanation and Understanding*, Routledge, 1971. (Causal and teleological explanations regarding human actions, etc. Good bibliography.)

Explanation gap or explanatory gap. See CONSCIOUSNESS.

Explication. See EXPLANATION.

Extension. See INTENSIONALITY AND INTENTIONALITY.

Extensionality thesis. See LEIBNIZ'S LAW, INTENSIONALITY AND INTENTIONALITY.

Externalism. See INTERNALISM AND EXTERNALISM.

F

Fact. Usually, that which corresponds to a statement or makes it true (cf. the correspondence theory of TRUTH). As such, a fact has seemed somehow to exist in the world, independent of thought and language. Since statements have a structure, consisting of subject and predicate, etc., it has been thought that facts must also have a structure, so that the elements in the statement can correspond to elements in the fact; facts may simply be sets of objects in the world related in certain ways. If so, a cake will be a fact, which it is surely not, though its existence may be. Nor are facts quite the same as situations or states of affairs, for one can be 'in' these, and it is natural to talk of a situation, but less natural to talk of a fact, as enduring or being altered. This may suggest that while situations, etc., are indeed in the world, facts represent rather ways we choose to describe the world, though of course the world severely constrains how we can describe it; the ways will also be objective rather than evaluative (but see NATURALISM on the sharpness of this distinction).

The view that facts are things in the world corresponding to parts of thought and language has led to difficulties about whether there are any facts corresponding to statements involving words like 'not', 'or', 'all', 'some', 'if', since these statements seem to be less directly about the world than are simple statements (cf. LOGICAL ATOMISM).

If we abandon strict correspondence theories of truth, which need facts as entities in the world for statements to correspond to, we can tie facts more closely to thought and language. Are facts simple true propositions, or 'truths'? 'It's true that ... ' and 'It's a fact that ... ' mean much the same, and we can say 'What he says is a fact'. But expressions like 'His statement is borne out by (corresponds to) the facts' raise some difficulty. Facts but surely not true propositions can be causes ('The fact that the match was struck caused it to light'). (On propositions see SENTENCES.) Perhaps one should no more ask what facts are than what cases are when something 'is the case'. Some writers (e.g. Mellor) accept both these 'thin' facts and substantive facts.

Brute facts are either facts in general considered as given independently of how we see the world (emphasizing the objectivity mentioned above); or facts not holding in virtue of any other facts holding (cf. SUPERVENIENCE); or facts about the world not involving values, rules, or institutions, e.g. 'Grass is green', 'I like beer', but not 'Beer is good for you'. 'Smith scored a goal' is an example of an institutional fact, depending on rules or institutions.

'Factual' is used in various ways and in each case false statements as well as true ones can be called factual. Contrasted with 'fictional' it refers to the real world. Contrasted with 'evaluative' it refers to what is objectively and decidably there and not merely contributed by human attitudes as evaluation may seem to be. Contrasted with 'theoretical', it refers to what is decidable, directly even if not conclusively, by observation. Contrasted with 'logical' or 'necessary', it refers either to what concerns the world rather than thought or discourse, or to what is merely contingently true or false. However, since statements in logic can normally be proved to be true or false, one can also talk of facts of logic or mathematics (cf. MODALITIES). Whether one can talk of moral, etc., facts is disputed. See also SENTENCES, EVENTS.

G. E. M. Anscombe, 'On brute facts', *Analysis*, vol. 18, 1958.

D. Davidson, 'True to the facts', *Journal of Philosophy*, 1969, reprinted in his *Inquiries into Truth and Interpretation*, Clarendon, 1984. (Why facts cannot ground a correspondence theory of truth, and what should replace them.)

D. W. Hamlyn, 'The correspondence theory of truth', *Philosophical Quarterly*, 1962. (Defends a weak version.)

D. H. Mellor, *The Facts of Causation*, Routledge, 1995.

B. Rundle, *Facts*, Duckworth, 1993. (Discusses nature of facts, and their relations to theories and values. Short and non-technical, but best suited to those with some appreciation of the later philosophy of Wittgenstein.)

P. F. Strawson, 'Truth', *Proceedings of the Aristotelian Society*, supplementary vol, 1950, § 2, reprinted in G. Pitcher (ed.), *Truth*, Prentice-Hall, 1964, and in Strawson's *Logico-Linguistic Papers*, Methuen, 1971. (Rejects substantive facts.)

J. O. Urmson, *Philosophical Analysis*, Oxford UP, 1956, part 1, particularly § 5. (Facts and logical atomism.)

Factive. See EPISTEMOLOGY.

Fact/value distinction. See NATURALISM.

Fairness. What is a fair distribution of goods? Is that the same as a just distribution? It need not be an equal distribution: for some may deserve more of the goods, some may need more of the goods, and some may not want any of the goods. See EQUALITY, JUSTICE, RAWLS.

Faith. To have faith is to believe without reason or proof. How are faith and reason related? The view of AUGUSTINE and AQUINAS is that faith underlies or is prior to any sort of reasoning or knowledge, whereas LOCKE claims that faith can be achieved through reason. See FIDEISM.

A. Kenny, *What is Faith?* Oxford UP, 1992.
A. Plantinga and N. Wolterstorff (eds), *Faith and Rationality: Reason and Belief in God*, Notre Dame UP, 1983.
R. Swinburne, *Faith and Reason*, Oxford UP, 1984.

Fallacy. An argument of invalid, rather then VALID, form. An argument may have true premises and a true conclusion, but still be invalid. Thus 'Tiddles is a mammal, all cats are mammals, therefore Tiddles is a cat' is invalid, which can more clearly be seen by substituting 'Rover' for 'Tiddles'. This is an example of the fallacy of the undistributed middle. 'Fallacy' is often used more informally to mean any sort of error in thinking, not necessarily connected with the form of the argument. See DEDUCTION, SYLLOGISM.

Fallibilism. Doctrine that nothing or nothing about the world can be known for certain, or alternatively that knowledge does not require that the evidence be logically conclusive or the possibility of error totally absent.

False. See TRUTH AND FALSITY.

Fatalism. See FREEWILL.

Feeling. Any one of indefinitely many ways of experiencing situations, real or imaginary, in the world or in oneself. Feelings are akin to SENSATIONS, and many of the philosophical problems that arise are best treated under that head. Both can be bodily, in which case they partly coincide, but feelings can also cover emotions and attitudes, and also opinions, especially when one wishes to disclaim any but obscure reasons for these.

One problem concerns how feelings are to be identified and described. How far can they be distinguished from each other intrinsically and without reference to causes or accompanying inclinations or dispositions? What is their role in the emotions, and how far can emotions and things like consciousness and PLEASURE be elucidated in terms of these? How do we use feelings in acquiring knowledge of the world and of other people? How do we know that they exist, if we do, in ourselves or others? Can we be deceived about our own feelings? Pain in particular has been a prime example in the PRIVATE LANGUAGE dispute. See EMOTION.

S. R. Leighton, 'On feeling angry and elated', *Journal of Philosophy*, 1988. (Discusses feelings as they occur in emotions, with references.)

A. R. Mele, 'Akratic feelings', *Philosophy and Phenomenological Research*, vol. 50, 1989–90. (Can there be an analogue in feelings to INCONTINENT action?)

R. Moran, 'The expression of feeling in imagination', *Philosophical Review*, 1994. (The role of feeling in our aesthetic response to fiction.)

R. C. Roberts, 'What is an emotion? A sketch', *Philosophical Review*, 1988. (First main section discusses different kinds of feelings and relations between feelings and emotions.)

G. Ryle, 'Feelings', *Philosophical Quarterly*, 1951, reprinted in his *Collected Papers*, Hutchinson, 1971, vol. 2. (Various uses of 'feel' and relations between them. Cf. also his *The Concept of Mind*, Hutchinson, 1949.)

Felicific calculus. See CALCULUS.

Feyerabend, Paul K. 1924–94. Radical Austrian philosopher of science who worked mainly in America. Pupil and later critic of POPPER and falsificationism. Held an anarchistic view of science. There is no single thing which is 'scientific method': to think so is to restrict science. Rather, science advances when, as he put it, 'anything goes'. The scientific point of view is only one, and not necessarily a superior, way of looking at the world. *Against Method*, 1975, revised edn 1988.

J. M. Preston, 'Paul Feyerabend', *The Stanford Encyclopedia of Philosophy* (Spring 2007 Edition), Edward N. Zalta (ed.). Available at: http://plato.stanford.edu/archives/spr2007/entries/feyerabend/ (accessed 1 March 2009).

Fideism. The view that matters of faith, such as the existence of God and other religious doctrines cannot be proved by reason, which is irrelevant to, or even in opposition to, faith.

Figure. See SYLLOGISM.

Finitism. A mathematical method or system is finitist or finitary if it refuses to recognize any objects (numbers, etc.) which cannot be constructed (see INTUITIONISM) in a finite number of steps; but some variation exists about whether the construction must be possible in practice or only in principle. Finitism is thus, like intuitionism, a form of constructivism, but unlike intuitionism, appeals primarily to what can be done in a finite number of steps with a finite number of elements. It is therefore sometimes more rigorous than intuitionism, and is associated more with formalism (see INTUITIONISM). It is more of a method rather than, like intuitionism and formalism, a theory. Extreme forms of it, which allow only constructions which can be carried out in practice and in a feasible number of steps, or insist like Wittgenstein that a mathematical statement only gets sense from the way it is proved, are sometimes called strict finitism. One question which arises is whether there is a largest class. To say that there is goes beyond merely saying, with Aristotle, that the infinite is only potential and never actual (see METAPHYSICS).

P. Benacerraf and H. Putnam (eds), *Philosophy of Mathematics*, Blackwell, 1964, part 4. (Wittgenstein. Cf. particularly p. 505.)

S. Körner, *The Philosophy of Mathematics*, Hutchinson, 1960, particularly, pp. 77–9.

G. Kreisel in *The British Journal for the Philosophy of Science*, vol. 9, 1958–9, pp. 147–9. (For fuller treatment see C. Wright, 'Strict finitism', *Synthèse*, vol. 51, 1982, particularly p. 204 and the note at pp. 269–70 (which wrongly refers to Kreisel as 'volume 8').)

First cause argument. See COSMOLOGICAL.

Focal meaning. See AMBIGUITY.

Fodor, Jerry A. 1935–. American philosopher of mind and language. Argues that thinking is a kind of computation, but that the attempt to show this through artificial intelligence research is mistaken and has been a disaster. Holds that the mind is a computational engine, and that some mental processes are modular and specialized. There is, he says, a 'LANGUAGE OF THOUGHT': that is, thinking occurs in a mental language, which he calls Mentalese. *The Structure of Language*, with Jerrold Katz (eds), 1964. *The Language of Thought*, 1975. *The Modularity of Mind: An Essay on Faculty Psychology*, 1983. *Psychosemantics: The Problem of Meaning in the Philosophy of Mind*, 1987. *A Theory of Content and Other Essays*, 1990. *The Elm and the Expert: Mentalese and Its Semantics*, 1994. *Concepts: Where Cognitive Science Went Wrong* (The 1996 John Locke Lectures), 1998. *The Mind Doesn't Work That Way: The Scope and Limits of Computational Psychology*, 2000. *In Critical Condition: Polemical Essays on Cognitive Science and the Philosophy of Mind*, 2000. *The Compositionality Papers*, with E. Lepore, 2002. *Hume Variations*, 2003. See BELIEF, FOLK PSYCHOLOGY, FUNCTIONALISM, HOLISM, INDIVIDUALISM, METHODOLOGICAL SOLIPSISM, PSYCHO-SEMANTICS, SEMANTICS, TACIT KNOWLEDGE.

Folk psychology. The supposed commonsense 'theory' by means of which we explain actions in terms of ordinary beliefs and desires, etc. Folk psychology contrasts with more science-based theories, some of which even deny that there are such things as beliefs and desires. By analogy, 'folk' has come to be used more widely, e.g. 'folk physics'.

W. E. Lycan (ed.), *Mind and Cognition*, Blackwell, 1990. (Part vi has relevant articles, including Horgan and Woodward.).

S. P. Stich, *From Folk Psychology to Cognitive Science: The Case Against Belief*, MIT Press, 1983. (Expresses scepticism about folk psychology. For a defence of it see J. A. Fodor, *Psychosemantics*, MIT Press, 1987, and T. Horgan and J. Woodward, 'Folk psychology is here to stay', in *Philosophical Review*, 1985.)

Form. In metaphysics a form is a general nature or ESSENCE belonging to a species, or else a particular nature or essence belonging to an individual (see HAECCEITY). For Plato's transcendent Forms (often distinguished by a capital F) see IDEA, UNIVERSALS. For Aristotle, forms normally existed only in combination with matter (an exception may be God), though forms which did so could also exist in the mind qua known by the mind. A horse was a lump of flesh 'informed' by the form or essence of horse, i.e. made into something having the essential properties and powers of a horse. Basically therefore an Aristotelian form is that which makes an object what it is. It can also be called the formal cause of the object. In the Middle Ages this notion was called a substantial form. A substantial form classified an object as what it basically is, while an accidental form was any set of properties of an object, whether essential to it or not. It is not always clear whether there is a different substantial form for each individual object, or only for each type or species. The Aristotelian form is itself unclear in this respect.

In logic the form of a proposition is the kind or species to which it belongs; a proposition can be, e.g. universal or negative in form. The form is contrasted with the content or matter (cf. 'subject matter'), what the proposition is individually about. Form is also relative: 'All cats are black' and 'No dogs are brown' are of the same form in that both are universal, but of different forms in that only one is negative.

The distinction between form and content is often hard to make. A proposition's form seems to be an abstract pattern it exemplifies, in virtue of which formal inferences can be drawn from it. 'Every a is a b, so every non-b is a non-a' is a valid inference pattern, because an inference exemplifying it is valid irrespective of the meanings of whatever terms replace 'a' and 'b'. 'Smith is a bachelor, so he's unmarried' is valid, but only because of what 'bachelor' means. It is a non-formal inference. Formal inference also depends on what words like 'every' mean, and it is hard to say when a pattern is abstract enough to be called formal. Is 'x exceeds y and y exceeds z, so x exceeds z' an abstract pattern, i.e. can 'exceeds' count as a formal word?

Other questions include whether form really belongs to propositions. Does it belong to sentences instead? And how is logical form related to grammatical form? See also STRUCTURE.

G. E. M. Anscombe and P T. Geach, *Three Philosophers: Aristotle, Aquinas, Frege*, Blackwell, 1962. (See pp. 75–88 for substantial forms.)

Aristotle, *Metaphysics*, book 7 (also called Z), particularly chapters 4–6, 10–17. (His main discussion. Very difficult.)

J. Bennett, *Kant's Analytic*, Oxford UP, 1966, pp. 79–81. (This and Whiteley raise difficulties about form.)

A. Kenny, *Aquinas*, Oxford UP, 1980. (See its index for substantial forms.)

W. Leszl, *Logic and Metaphysics in Aristotle*, Editrice Antenore, 1972, part 6. (Includes discussion, largely intelligible by itself, of form and matter. Occasional Greek.)

D. Mitchell, *An Introduction to Logic*, Hutchinson, 1962, chapter 1. (Form and validity. Cf. also chapter 5 and pp. 151–3.)

Plato, *Phaedo, Republic*, books 5–7, *Parmenides*, § 126–37, *Timaeus* and, for Aristotle's criticism of Plato, see his *Metaphysics*, book 1 (also called A), chapters 6 and 9.)

R. M. Sainsbury, *Logical Form: An Introduction to Philosophical Logic*, Blackwell, 1991. (General treatment of philosophical logic, centring on notion of form.)

P. F. Strawson, *Introduction to Logical Theory*, Methuen, 1952, pp. 40–56. (Logical form, including its relations to patterns.)

*R. D. Sykes, 'Form in Aristotle: Universal or particular?', *Philosophy*, 1975. (Fairly elementary discussion.)

C. H. Whiteley, 'The idea of logical form', *Mind*, 1951.

Formalism. Any doctrine somehow emphasizing FORM against matter or content (e.g. in aesthetics; but not metaphysical doctrines emphasizing form in the way Platonists or Aristotelians do). In ethics, the doctrine that an action's value or rightness depends on what kind of act it is (e.g. one of promise-keeping), not on its consequences; cf. deontology (ETHICS). For formalism in mathematics see INTUITIONISM.

Formal mode. Sentences about words, such as '"Red" is a quality-word' or '"Red" is an adjective', are said to be in the formal mode. Sentences about objects, qualities, etc., are said to be in the material mode. Thus 'Red is a quality' is in the material mode. Philosophers, especially some logical POSITIVISTS, have sometimes thought that 'metaphysical' notions like substance, quality, etc., could and should be dispensed with by translating sentences involving them into sentences about language, i.e. out of the material mode and into the formal mode, as illustrated above. Such translation has been called semantic ascent.

R. Carnap, *The Unity of Science*, Kegan Paul, Trench, Trubner, 1934, pp. 37–42.

W. V. O. Quine, *Word and Object*, Wiley, 1960, § 56. (Semantic ascent.)

Formation rules. See AXIOM.

Foundationalism. The view that knowledge requires foundations, in the sense that unless we start from a set of beliefs that are properly basic, in that they either do not require justification themselves, or else are justified simply in virtue of the way in which we come to have such beliefs, and from which we can derive in various ways the rest of our knowledge, we can never know anything at all. A notable example of a foundationalist is Descartes. See also INCORRIGIBLE. Epistemological and psychological versions of foundationalism are possible, as they are of the rival coherentist view that our knowledge is mutually supporting, none being basic to all the rest.

R. Audi, 'Psychological foundationalism', *Monist*, 1978. (Different versions of foundationalism and coherentism.)

Four-term fallacy. Arguing in a SYLLOGISM whose premises are true, if at all, only if the middle term has a different sense in each, e.g. 'All cats miaow; that woman is a cat; therefore that woman miaows.'

Frankfurt School. See ADORNO.

Freewill and determinism. Our natural feeling that, special circumstances apart, we always could do otherwise than we do is often thought to conflict with the view that every event is caused and that human actions cannot be excepted. Resolutions of this conflict have naturally been viewed mainly in the light of how they affect moral responsibility.

Fatalism holds that the future is fixed irrespective of our attempts to affect it. Seldom held as a philosophical doctrine this view often appears in literature (e.g. the Oedipus legend). A view often leading to the same effects, though for quite different reasons (without appealing to the 'will of fate', etc.), is logical determinism. This argues that a given future event must either occur or not occur. Whichever happens, the prediction that it would happen will turn out to be correct, and therefore was correct all along, whether or not we knew it. Therefore, since one statement about the apparent future alternatives is already true, nothing we can do will alter matters. This puzzle affects the nature of TRUTH: can a statement (one about the future) be true at one time (when the future comes) and not at another (before the future comes), or is it senseless to talk of a statement as true 'at a time'? Or is logical determinism true but harmless, until we confusedly infer that the future is therefore already causally fixed, which suggests that deliberation is pointless? Strictly, 'logical determinism' is a misnomer, since the doctrine is not about things being determined but about certain statements being true.

Causal determinism says that everything that happens is caused; it allows that our choices and actions are effective as links in the causal chain, so that deliberation has a point, but insists that they are themselves caused. Determinists are sometimes divided into hard and soft. Hard determinists say that our actions are caused in a way that makes us not as free as we might have thought, so that responsibility, if it implies freewill, is an illusion. The causes may be physical and physiological (events in the brain), or else mental (e.g. conscious or unconscious desires, and childhood experiences which cause such desires). Soft determinists, by far the largest class in recent times, say that our actions are indeed caused, but we are not therefore any less free than we might be, because the causation is not a constraint or compulsion on us. So long as our natures and choices are effective as items in the causal chain, the fact that they are themselves caused is irrelevant and does not stop them being what they are. Indeterminists, however, insist that determinists, of whatever complexion, can give no sense to the sentence 'He could have done otherwise', where this means something more than simply 'He might have done otherwise (had his nature or circumstances been different)'. Soft determinists often hold that what justifies praise and blame is solely that they can influence action. This, say indeterminists, misses the point of these concepts, which are essentially 'backward-looking'. Hard determinists are incompatibilists, i.e. think freewill and universal causation are incompatible. Soft determinists are compatibilists. Indeterminists may be either, but are usually incompatibilists.

One difficulty with indeterminism is that mere absence of causation does not seem enough. If our actions are no more than random intrusions into the causal scheme of things how can we be any more responsible for them than if they were caused? Indeterminists are sometimes called libertarians. But more strictly, libertarians are those who postulate a special entity, the 'self', which uses the body to intervene from outside, as it were, in the causal chain of events, but is itself immune to causal influence. Sometimes this self is said to be immune only where moral considerations arise, with obvious difficulties about which considerations are MORAL.

Such a self must at least be open to pressure from things in the world (or why would it ever make a wrong or weak-minded choice?), and to define its actual relations to the world seems difficult. More usually now, indeterminists appeal not to a separate entity but to the very nature of those things (choosing, intending, deciding, acting, etc.) which characterize persons as such, whatever may be the relation between being a person and having (or being?) a body. It may not make sense for choices or actions to be caused. Reasons offered for this include the following: physical causes can only cause physical movements, like an upward movement of a leg, but not ACTIONS, like a kick, for actions always involve things like intentions and a context, which go beyond mere movement (Peters). On the other hand, alleged mental causes like desires, intentions, motives, etc., are not separate states or events: they are features of actions which provide ways of classifying them. (Ryle says one's greed is not something causing one to act but consists simply in one's acting in a greedy manner.) Another view (sometimes called the logical connection argument) is that a desire, etc., can only be specified as the desire to do a certain action, and so is not sufficiently independent of the action to be able to cause it, for a cause and its effect must be two separate things (Melden, though this oversimplifies Melden's view; cf. MODALITIES (para. beginning 'Non-contingent ... ')).

Recently these views have been attacked, and causation has returned to favour. But there are still difficulties about reason. If our beliefs are caused physiologically, or by non-rational mental events, why should we assume they are reliable? Yet are rational considerations, as such, suitable for being causes? On the other hand, we do not normally, if ever, choose our beliefs, but do not think our freedom diminished because we are 'compelled by the evidence' to believe something. Again reasoning, whether on theoretical or practical matters, and also choosing and deciding, seems to be possible only if we at least believe that their outcome is not yet determined. We cannot try, or even want (as against idly wishing), to do something we firmly think impossible.

A related problem concerns causation, prediction and explanation. To act freely is not to act unpredictably or inexplicably, as indeterminism in the sense of mere absence of causation seems to imply. However, even a caused event cannot be predicted without adequate information, and it seems that we could never know enough to predict our own actions strictly, since we cannot take into account the result of the prediction itself. (Cf. how opinion polls affect elections they predict.) Therefore, it seems that an action may be unpredictable even though caused, or predictable even though uncaused. This raises questions about what grounds are in fact available to us for predictions, and what sorts of explanation can be given of actions. All these problems clearly have bearings on the mind–body problem (philosophy of MIND). See also CAUSATION, REASON, EXPLANATION.

G. E. M. Anscombe (see bibliography to CAUSATION).

Aristotle, *De Interpretatione*, chapter 9, trans. with notes in J. L. Ackrill, *Aristotle's Categories*, Oxford UP, 1963. (Classic discussion of logical determinism. For modern development of Aristotle's view see also J. Lukasiewicz, 'On determinism' in S. McCall (ed.), *Polish Logic 1920–1939*, Clarendon, 1967, reprinted in Lukasiewicz's *Selected Works*, L. Borkowski (ed.), North-Holland, 1970. For Aristotle on freewill generally see his

Nicomachean Ethics, 3, 1–5, and on determinism and chance *Metaphysics*, book 6 (also called E), chapters 2–3 and *Physics*, book 2, chapters 4–6, with discussion by R. K. Sorabji in his *Necessity, Cause, and Blame*, Duckworth, 1980, chapters 1–2.

*B. Berofsky (ed.), *Free Will and Determinism*, Harper and Row, 1966. (Contains many classic discussions, including R. E. Hobart, 'Free will as involving determination and inconceivable without it', *Mind*, 1934; A. I. Melden, *Free Action*, Routledge, 1961 (selection. See text above); D. Davidson, 'Actions, reasons, and causes', *Journal of Philosophy*, 1963 (often reprinted. Rehabilitation of role of causation); A. C. MacIntyre, 'Determinism', *Mind*, 1957 (the role of rationality); J. L. Austin's 'Ifs and cans' (criticism of soft determinist analyses of 'could have … ' in terms of 'would have … , if … ', cf. also his 'A plea for excuses', *Proceedings of the Aristotelian Society*, 1956–7). For the rehabilitation cf. also D. W. Hamlyn, 'Causality and human behaviour', *Proceedings of the Aristotelian Society*, supplementary vol., 1964, reprinted in N. S. Care and C. Landesman (eds), *Readings in the Theory of Action*, Indiana UP, 1968, and G. Madell, 'Action and causal explanation', *Mind*, 1967.)

D. C. Dennett, *Elbow Room*, Oxford UP, 1984. (Defends version of compatibilism. Cf. also his 'I could not have done otherwise – so what?' *Journal of Philosophy*, 1984, with reply by van Inwagen.)

S. Evnine, *Donald Davidson*, Polity Press/Blackwell, 1991, pp. 47–9. (Brief discussion of logical connection argument, with references.)

H. G. Frankfurt, 'Freedom of the will and the concept of a person', *Journal of Philosophy*, 1971, reprinted in Watson below. (Appeals to the notion of second-order volitions.)

J. Heil and A. Mele (eds), *Mental Causation*, Oxford UP, 1994. (Specially written essays by many notable writers. Cf. also W. Child, *Causality, Interpretation and the Mind*, Clarendon, 1994, for a partly, though only partly, related issue involving compatibilism.)

P. van Inwagen, *An Essay on Free Will*, Oxford UP, 1983. (Defends incompatibilism. Cf. also his 'Ability and responsibility', *Philosophical Review*, 1978.)

R. Kane (ed.), *The Oxford Handbook of Free Will*, Oxford UP, 2002. (Includes articles by advocates of a modern 'successor' view to the hard determinist position, including Galen Strawson, see also below, who holds that true free will cannot exist.)

K. Lehrer, *Metamind*, Oxford UP, 1990 (Human freedom depends on our ability to have thoughts about thoughts.)

B. Libet, A. Freeman and K. Sutherland (eds), *The Volitional Brain: Towards a Neuroscience of Freewill*, Imprint Academic, 1999. (Essays on the impact of recent work in neuroscience, including Libet's seminal work.)

S. Morgenbesser and J. Walsh (eds), *Free Will*, 1962. (Includes medieval contributions.)

*D. F. Pears (ed.), *Freedom and the Will*, Macmillan, 1963. (Based on BBC series of popular talks. Two rather more advanced anthologies are T. Honderich (ed.), *Essays on Freedom of Action*, Routledge, 1973 and K. Lehrer (ed.), *Freedom and Determinism*, Random House, 1966).

R. S. Peters, *The Concept of Motivation*, Routledge, 1958.

K. R. Popper, 'Indeterminism in quantum physics and in classical physics', *British Journal for the Philosophy of Science*, 1950. (Prediction in people and machines.)

G. Ryle, *The Concept of Mind*, Routledge, 1949. (Classic discussion of, inter alia, emotions, motives, the will, terms like 'voluntary' and 'involuntary'.)

*G. Strawson, (1998, 2004). 'Free will', in E. Craig (ed.), *Routledge Encyclopedia of Philosophy*, Routledge. Available at: www.rep.routledge.com/article/V014 (accessed 1 March 2009).

*G. Watson (ed.), *Freewill*, Oxford UP, 1982. (Contains varied and important items.)

Frege, Gottlob. 1848–1925. German mathematical logician who was born in Wismar and worked in Jena. His work on the foundations of MATHEMATICS, which he hoped to derive from pure logic, was seriously interrupted when he was told of RUSSELL'S PARADOX by Russell. His greatest contributions to logic were his development of QUANTIFICATION and his elaboration of the distinction between sense and reference (see MEANING). Also influential were his distinction between CONCEPT and OBJECT, his use of the notion of FUNCTION, and his rejection of what was later called a 'speech act' analysis of NEGATION (which was later important for ethics: see NATURALISM). *Begriffsschrift*, 1879 (quantification). *The Foundations of Arithmetic*, 1884. *Die Grundgesetze der Arithmetik*, 2 vols, 1893, 1903. P. T. Geach and M. Black (eds), *Translations from the Philosophical Writings of Gottlob Frege*, Blackwell, 1952 (contains 'Function and concept', 1891; 'Concept and object', 1892; 'On sense and reference', 1892; and 'Negation', 1919, as well as chapter 1 of the *Begriffsschrift*). See also ASSERTION, FUNCTION, IDEA, IDENTITY, INTENSIONALITY AND INTENTIONALITY, NATURALISM, PSYCHOLOGISM, REFERRING, SENTENCES, UNIVERSALS.

M. Dummett, *Frege: Philosophy of Language*, Duckworth, 2nd edn, 1992. (Difficult but seminal.)

E. N. Zalta, 'Gottlob Frege', *The Stanford Encyclopedia of Philosophy* (Spring 2007 Edition), Edward N. Zalta (ed.). Available at: http://plato.stanford.edu/archives/spr2007/entries/frege/ (accessed 1 March 2009).

Frege argument. Also known as the 'slingshot'. Argument based on alleged doctrines of Frege and claiming that if we allow inter-substitution of coextensive terms, and also of logically equivalent sentences, in certain areas where this seems plausible, then certain philosophical claims can be reduced to absurdity. For instance, it is argued, if we claim that causation holds between facts then it can be shown that any fact will be the cause of any other.

S. Evnine, *Donald Davidson*, Polity Press/Blackwell, 1991. (Appendix gives clear exposition of main argument.)

S. Kneale, 'The philosophical significance of Gödel's slingshot', *Mind*, 1995. (Examines at length two main versions of the argument, and their effects on topics like the analysis of definite DESCRIPTIONS, the existence of facts and non-extensional logics.)

Function. (This entry is confined to logic and mathematics, except for its bibliography.) Some expressions have either numerical values or TRUTH VALUES which we can calculate once we give values to the VARIABLES in the expression. The rest of the expression is then called a function of the variables. Thus $3x + 7$ contains a variable, x, and a function $3() +7$. But 'function' is often applied to the whole expression, including the variables. The function is then called a function of x. Its value in either case depends on the value given to x. Again if p and q are propositions, p and q (but not p because q is a truth function of p and of q. We can know the truth value of p and q (but not that of p because q) once we know the truth values of p and of q.

A value assigned to a variable in a function is called an argument of the function, and contributes to the value of the function. $3x + 7$ has the value 19 for the argument 4.

Frege appealed to functions in analysing CONCEPTS and thereby predicates: ' ... is red' can be thought of as a function, because we can assign a truth value to x is red by assigning a value to x (i.e. replacing x by the name of something; x is red becomes true if we replace x by 'blood'), or alternatively by quantifying over x (see QUANTIFICATION).

'x is red' can be called a propositional, statemental (rare) or sentential function, according as blood is red is regarded as a proposition, statement or sentence. Sentential functions are often called open sentences. The term closed sentential function is occasionally used of ordinary sentences.

J. Bigelow and R. Pargetter, 'Functions', *Journal of Philosophy*, 1987. (Discusses and defends one of four biological senses of the term.)

R. Carnap, *Introduction to Semantics*, Harvard UP, 1942, § 37. (Ambiguities, here ignored, of 'function' and 'propositional function'.)

R. Cummins, 'Functional analysis', *Journal of Philosophy*, 1975. (Criticizes two basic assumptions of previous analyses, and then offers his own. 'To ascribe a function to something is to ascribe a capacity to it which is singled out by its role in an analysis of some capacity of a containing system' (p. 765).)

P. T. Geach and M. Black, *Translations from the Philosophical Writings of Gottlob Frege*, Blackwell, 1952. (Contains Frege's 'Function and concept' (cf. CONCEPT). Frege's symbolism is awkward and outdated. For sentences as referring to truth-values see his 'Sense and reference', ibid.)

P. Kitcher, 'Function and design', *Midwest Studies in Philosophy*, vol. 18, 1993. (Claims function implies design, but not intention or designer.)

R. Sorabji, 'Function', *Philosophical Quarterly*, 1964. (Non-logical senses.)

L. Wright, 'Functions', *Philosophical Review*, 1973. (Emphasizes their explanatory role, and offers an analysis which covers both conscious and natural functions, after discussing other views. For fuller development of appeal to natural selection which he makes see R. G. Millikan, *Language, Thought, and Other Biological Categories*, MIT Press, 1984, particularly chapter 1.)

Functionalism. Any view which analyses something in terms of how it functions, and especially in terms of its causes and effects. In particular, functionalism as an answer to the MIND/body problem defines mental states and properties in terms of what causes them, how they manifest themselves in behaviour, and how they interact with each other. Recently functionalism concerning the mind has developed from treating the mind as a kind of machine like a TURING MACHINE to treating it rather in terms of biological functions, on the grounds that this can better account for the mind's relation to the outer world (cf. INTENSIONALITY AND INTENTIONALITY). See also QUALIA.

N. Block (ed.), *Readings in the Philosophy of Psychology*, vol. 1, Harvard UP and Methuen, 1980. (Includes section on functionalism.)

T. Burge, 'Philosophy of language and mind: 1950–90', *Philosophical Review*, 1992. (See pp. 40–1 for a distinction between analytic and scientific functionalism.)

J. A. Fodor, 'The mind-body problem', *Scientific American*, January, 1981.

J. A. Foster, *The Immaterial Self*, Routledge, 1991, chapter 3. (Attacks functionalism.)

F. Jackson and P. Pettit, 'Functionalism and broad content', *Mind*, 1988. (Claims that the existence of broad (or wide) CONTENT is no objection to functionalism. Cf. also R. A. Wilson, 'Wide functionalism', *Mind*, 1994, which has further references as well.)

W. G. Lycan (ed.), *Mind and Cognition*, Blackwell, 1990. (See item by Sober, which defends functionalism by distinguishing two kinds, Turing machine functionalism and teleological functionalism, through ending with some reservations. See also part vii for discussions of functionalism and qualia.)

N. Malcolm, '"Functionalism" in philosophy of psychology', *Proceedings of the Aristotelian Society*, 1979-80. (Distinguishes and discusses four senses of the term.)

S. Shoemaker, *Identity, Cause, and Mind*, Cambridge UP, 1984, particularly chapters, 5, 8, 9, 12, 14, 15. (Defends functionalism. For definitions of it see pp. 111, 337.)

P. Smith and O. R. Jones, *The Philosophy of Mind: An Introduction*, Cambridge UP, 1986. (See particularly chapters xi–xii, xv, xvi for sympathetic discussion.)

G

Gambler's fallacy. Assumption that if, for example, a coin has come down heads many times in succession, it is more likely to come down tails next time to 'restore the balance'. If the coin and its throwing are unbiased the tosses will be independent of each other and the coin is equally likely to come down heads next time. No finite run of heads, however long, violates the 'laws of chance'. (A long run of heads might suggest the coin is biased, so that the laws of chance do not apply, or not in the same way, and further heads should be expected. The 'gambler' assumes that the laws of chance do apply, and that therefore tails are to be expected. His mistake lies in the 'therefore'.) Cf. von Mises's 'principle of the impossibility of a gambling system', and the frequency theory of PROBABILITY.

R. von Mises, *Probability, Statistics and Truth*, Hodge, 1939 (German original, 1928), chapter 1.

Game theory. See DECISION THEORY.

Genealogical Arguments. Term taken over by Michel Foucault, French philosopher and historian (in, for example, *The History of Sexuality*, 1976–84), from NIETZSCHE, *On the Genealogy of Morals*. Used for an investigation of the history of a social institution or idea, often in order to subvert it. Compare GENETIC FALLACY.

General. See SENTENCES.

Generality constraint. Condition introduced by Evans in analysing what it is for someone to entertain (without necessarily believing) the thought that a certain object has a certain property. The person must be able to entertain the thought, concerning the same object, that it has any of the properties he has a conception of and also to entertain the thought, involving the same property, that any of the objects he can think about has it. To entertain the thought that Tom is tall one must be able to entertain the thoughts that Tom is short, clever, etc., and that Bill, George, etc., are tall. Thoughts which would be meaningless, e.g. that the person Tom is a prime number, are excluded, but other attitudes as well as belief are relevant: the thinker must be able to doubt, suppose, wish, etc. that Tom is tall.

G. Evans, *The Varieties of Reference*, Oxford UP, 1982, particularly pp. 100–5, 148. (Cf. also the occurrences of this term in the book's index, most of which are concerned with the application of the constraint to thoughts about oneself.)

Generalization in ethics. See UNIVERSALIZABILITY.

Generative grammar. See CHOMSKY, GRAMMAR, PSYCHOLINGUISTICS.

Genetic fallacy. Assumption that because the origins of something can be traced, the thing in question is somehow illegitimate or only apparent; e.g. that conscience is illusory if it develops from childhood fears. Facts about origins should not be confused with justifications.

Genidentity. Sometimes things are said to have temporal parts or stages as well as spatial ones, the thing itself being regarded as a four-dimensional whole or 'space–time worm'. Two such parts of a single whole are then called genidentical (they are not of course identical since they are different parts). There are problems about when such stages do belong to the same whole, and whether things do have such temporal parts or stages is controversial. The term 'time-slice' is also used for 'temporal part'. I as I exist on Monday and I as I exist on Tuesday can be called time-slices of myself, but what is controversial is whether such time-slices are really parts of something, i.e. of a whole only part of which exists at any given time.

R. M. Chisholm, *Person and Object*, Allen and Unwin, 1976. (See particularly chapter 7 and Appendix A on identity through time and temporal parts.)

D. Lewis, *On the Plurality of Worlds*, Blackwell, 1986. (Doesn't use the term 'genidentity', but see its index under 'Persistence through time'.)

H. Reichenbach, *The Philosophy of Space and Time*, Dover Publications, 1957 (German original 1928), pp. 270–4.

Gettier cases. In 1963, Edmund Gettier published what became a highly influential article of just three pages, which challenged the traditional and, until then, generally accepted TRIPARTITE analysis of knowledge (which claims that a person, X, is said to know a proposition, p, if, and only if, (1) p is true; (2) X believes that p; and (3) X is justified in believing that p). Gettier shows that in some circumstances when all three conditions are be fulfilled, we would all the same not say that the person knew. These circumstances are where it is in some way a coincidence that all three conditions are fulfilled. Although Gettier's account has itself been criticized, it has led to many attempts to revise the tripartite analysis to meet his objections, for example, by insisting on causal connections between the traditional conditions. See CAUSAL THEORY, NOZICK, TRACKING THE TRUTH.

*J. Dancy, *Introduction to Contemporary Epistemology*, Blackwell, 1985. (Clear discussion, with good examples.)

F. Dretske, 'Conclusive reasons', *Australasian Journal of Philosophy*, 1971.

L. Floridi, 'On the logical unsolvability of the Gettier problem', *Synthese*, 2004. (Available at: www.philosophyofinformation.net/pdf/otluotgp.pdf.)

*E. L. Gettier, 'Is justified true belief knowledge?' *Analysis*, Vol. 23, pp. 121–23, 1963. Available at: www.ditext.com/gettier/gettier.html (accessed 1 March 2009).

A. Goldman, 'A causal theory of knowing', *The Journal of Philosophy*, 1967.

R. Kirkham, 'Does the Gettier problem rest on a mistake?' *Mind*, 1984.

K. Lehrer and T. Paxson, 'Knowledge: Undefeated justified true belief', *The Journal of Philosophy*, 1969.

R. Nozick, *Philosophical Explanations*, Harvard UP, 1981. (Attempt to meet Gettier's objections.)

Plato, *Theaetetus*, 201c–201d. (The origin of the tripartite account.)

Given. See PERCEPTION. Cf. also J. J. Ross, *The Appeal to the Given*, 1970.

God, arguments for God's existence. See COSMOLOGICAL ARGUMENT, DESIGN (ARGUMENT FROM), ONTOLOGICAL ARGUMENT.

Gödel, Gödel's theorems. Kurt Gödel, 1906–78, was an Austrian, then Czechoslovakian, then American, logician and philosopher of mathematics, whose work has been hugely influential. He was born in Brno in Moravia (then part of Austro-Hungary, later Czechoslovakia, now in the Czech Republic), and educated in Vienna. He moved to the USA in 1940 and spent the rest of his life working at Princeton. He was a strong advocate of Platonism in mathematics. He is best known for his fundamental theorems in logic. His completeness theorem, in his 1930 doctoral dissertation claims that the first-order predicate CALCULUS is weakly COMPLETE. Gödel produced his most famous theorem, on the incompleteness of formalized arithmetic, in 1931. In it, he shows that for any AXIOM SYSTEM adequate to axiomatize arithmetic, starting from DECIDABLE axioms, there will always exist at least one well-formed formula (see AXIOM SYSTEM) not decidable in the system, even though we can see on other grounds that it is true. He also showed that a system's CONSISTENCY cannot be proved within the system itself. These are respectively his first and second incompleteness theorems: either or both are called Gödel's theorem.

E. Nagel, J.R. Newman and D.R. Hofstadter, *Gödel's Proof*, Routledge, 1958, revised edn, 2002. (Remarkably clear exposition for layman.)

P. Smith, *An Introduction to Gödel's Theorems*. Cambridge UP, 2007.

R. Smullyan, *Gödel's Incompleteness Theorems*, Oxford UP, 1991.

Goldbach's conjecture. That every even number greater than two is the sum of two primes. Common example of proposition necessarily true or necessarily false, but unproved and unrefuted, so that both its truth and its falsity are epistemically possible (see MODALITIES) though only one is logically possible.

Good. Very roughly, the property or characterization of a thing giving rise to commendation. For PLATO the object of the Good is the highest form of knowledge, which can be achieved only after a long and arduous process of education in mathematics, metaphysics and so on. ARISTOTLE rejects Plato's metaphysical structure, including the FORMS, and rejects the notion that a knowledge of mathematics or science is necessary for virtue or goodness, which are for him autonomous. Reason, experience and practice enable us to understand what the right way to act in particular circumstances is.

Ever since Aristotle and his medieval followers failed to include 'good' in the scheme of CATEGORIES, except by making it apply in all of them (see BEING on transcendentals), 'good' has caused bewilderment by its many uses. Indefinitely many things seem desirable as good, and for indefinitely many reasons. So what is the goodness which they all share, for surely some sort of unity must underlie all these various uses?

A famous claim made in 1903 by G. E. Moore was that goodness, in its primary sense, is a simple, unique, intrinsic and indefinable property, rather like yellow, only 'non-natural' – a term he never properly explained but which involves at least that goodness is not detectable by the senses or by scientific means, nor even by reason, but only by a sort of intuition; attempts to define it committed the 'naturalistic fallacy' (see NATURALISM).

Other writers, however, distrusting the apparent 'mysteriousness' of this, have defied Moore's strictures and offered a 'naturalistic' definition of goodness as a relational property, such as that of causing pleasure, or satisfying certain desires or interests. Such definitions have the merit of explaining why goodness appeals to us, but another approach has been common among empiricists such as logical POSITIVISTS and linguistic PHILOSOPHERS, though having its roots in the eighteenth century. This stresses the role in our life of words like 'good', which are mainly used in connection with commendation, 'That's a good car' might mean 'I hereby commend that car'. Originally such analyses were open to objections about cases where no commending seems to be in the offing, such as, 'If it's a good car, it'll be expensive'. 'If I hereby commend that car ... ' even if this makes sense, is clearly inadequate (cf. Searle). However, more sophisticated analyses might be tried, along such lines as, 'If I commend that car, then I shall be committed to expecting it to be expensive.'

One source of problems is that goodness, so far as it is a characteristic at all, is usually a consequential characteristic; in terms of the examples discussed there, good is analogous to right rather than to red (see SUPERVENIENCE). Good is also sometimes said to be logically ATTRIBUTIVE. A good thief need not be a good person, and a knife good for cutting butter need not be good for cutting leather. But is good attributive in 'Pleasure, friendship and loyalty are all good'? All this suggests we should distinguish between the meaning of 'good' (or the nature of goodness) and the CRITERIA (loose sense) for applying it, i.e. the features which make a thing good. A good car and a good apple are not, or not obviously, good in different senses, but they are good for quite different reasons, and what may be good-making properties for one type of object may be bad-making ones for another (much as being red, round and luscious may make for beauty in a tomato, but not in a woman). Good-making properties may perhaps be logically or causally goodmaking. They are causally so if they cause their possessor to be good, as being an eater of certain foods may help to ensure that the eater is a good athlete. Logically, good-making properties, so far as they exist at all, may be expected mainly in artefacts or things with a function. Being sharp will cause a razor to be a good razor, but being able to remove beards in a short time while leaving the underlying skin intact may perhaps constitute being a good razor. Would it be contradictory to say a razor had this property but was not a good one, or perhaps was not a better one than an otherwise similar razor which did not have it? But here we return to the problems of SUPERVENIENCE.

As some of the above examples have implicitly shown, not all good things are intrinsically good. Things can be instrumentally good, i.e. good as a means to an end, be the end itself good or not; or they can be contributory goods, serving as parts, perhaps valueless in themselves, of a good whole, as an otherwise neutral patch of paint may contribute to the value of a picture. The highest good, *summum bonum*, may be either that thing or feature which taken by itself is better than anything else, or that total situation which contains more good than any other. (Kant used '*supremum bonum*' for the former and '*summum bonum*' for the latter.) Both of these are distinct from what is merely good on the whole, where other things may be better. A further kind of goodness is moral goodness, which is limited mainly to people, actions and intentions, and, perhaps, emotions, desires and institutions, and facts or situations involving these (cf. MORAL). People sometimes say things like, 'Pain is not really evil; only sin is evil'. Do they mean the substantive judgement that only moral good and evil are really good and evil at all, or the triviality that pain in itself is not a moral evil? (Cf. on the Stoics, especially, below.)

The substantive question, 'What things are good?' was rather soft-pedalled by the logical positivists and the linguistic philosophers, who, though for different reasons in each case, thought it their business to analyse, not to preach. But earlier and later philosophers have been less hesitant. Moore picked on certain aesthetic experiences and personal relationships (and heavily influenced the 'Bloomsbury set' of the first quarter of the twentieth century). Aristotle chose a life in accordance with (the highest) virtue as the main good, and the Stoics chose virtue as the only good, while Kant called the good will the only unconditional good. More recently an extremely influential view; especially among UTILITARIANS, has been that ultimately only states of mind can be good (Sidgwick); but this has been criticized on the grounds that the goodness of many states of mind presupposes that of other things desired for their own sakes (Wiggins). See also BETTER.

Aristotle, *Nicomachean Ethics*, book 1, (The good for man.)

P. T. Geach, 'Good and evil', *Analysis*, vol. 17, 1956, reprinted in P. Foot (ed.), *Theories of Ethics*, Oxford UP, 1967. (Claims that 'good' is attributive and descriptive (see NATURALISM). See short bibliography added in reprint for examinations of linguistic behaviour of 'good'.)

R. M. Hare, *The Language of Morals*, Oxford UP, 1952. (Speech act analysis. Meaning and criteria. Can just anything be good? On this last cf. P. Foot, 'Moral beliefs', *Proceedings of the Aristotelian Society*, 1958–9, reprinted in P. Foot (ed.), *Theories of Ethics*, Oxford UP, 1967.)

N. M. Lemos, 'Higher goods and the myth of Tithonus', *Journal of Philosophy*, 1993. (Defends view that some goods are incommensurably higher than others.)

G. E. Moore, *Principia Ethica*, Cambridge UP, 1903. (Good as a simple indefinable quality. Last chapter discusses what things are good.)

R. Nozick, *The Examined Life*, Simon and Schuster, 1989, chapter 10. (Criticizes Sidgwick's outlook, though without mentioning him.)

J. R. Searle, 'Meaning and speech acts', *Philosophical Review*, 1962, reprinted with discussions and additions in C. D. Rollins (ed.), *Knowledge and Experience*, Pittsburgh UP, 1962. (Attacks speech act analyses of 'good'.)

H. Sidgwick, *The Methods of Ethics*, Macmillan, final version, 1907 (1st edn 1874), book iv, chapter xiv.

D. Wiggins, *Truth, Invention and the Meaning of Life* (pamphlet), *Proceedings of the British Academy*, 1976, reprinted in his *Needs, Values, Truth*, Blackwell, 1987; see particularly § 1–6, 10–15. (Discusses, inter alia, whether the ultimate good can consist in states of feeling or the satisfaction of desires. Difficult.)

G. H. von Wright, *The Varieties of Goodness*, Routledge, 1963. (Full discussion of the different uses of 'good'.)

Goodman, Nelson. 1906–98. American philosopher whose work was in metaphysics, epistemology and aesthetics. Born in Massachusetts, educated at Harvard, and worked at University of Pennsylvania and at Harvard. His work was concerned with the nature of the symbols and other means we use to represent the world. He argued that there is no single, objective, way of seeing the world, for there are many different, and quite proper, ways of representing the world. We make our worlds, rather than find them. For Goodman's paradox, or riddle, of induction, see CONFIRMATION and INDUCTION. *The Structure of Appearance*, 1951. *Fact, Fiction, and Forecast*, 1955. *Languages of Art: An Approach to a Theory of Symbols*, 1968. *Ways of Worldmaking*, 1978. *Of Mind and Other Matters*, 1984. See CALCULUS, CONDITIONALS, MEANING, MEREOLOGY, REFERRING, REPRESENTATION, UNIVERSALS.

Grammar (depth, surface). See STRUCTURE (DEEP AND SURFACE).

Grammars (generative, etc.). A generative grammar is a set of elements and rules which will generate the grammatically acceptable sentences of a language in a way that reveals their grammatical structure. (Cf. the way the rules of chess generate possible situations on a chessboard.) N. CHOMSKY in his early work distinguishes three types of generative grammar, in order of increasing adequacy: finite state grammars, phrase-structure grammars, transformational grammars. To generate something, rules are given for replacing one set of symbols by another. Sometimes the rules of a phrase-structure grammar specify that the relevant symbols are replaceable only if they precede or follow certain other symbols. Such more powerful rules, and grammars containing at least one of them, are context-dependent (context-sensitive). The remaining replacement rules, and grammars limited to them, are context-free. Chomsky has more recently adopted a minimalist approach. See also STRUCTURE.

N. Chomsky, *The Minimalist Program*, MIT Press, 1995.

N. Chomsky, *Syntactic Structures*, Mouton, 1957.

N. Chomsky, *Knowledge of Language: Its Nature, Origins and Use*, Praeger, 1986.

G. Harman (ed.), *On Noam Chomsky: Critical Essays*, Doubleday Anchor, 1974. (See especially Searle's article, 'Chomsky's revolution in linguistics', for general introduction.)

Greatest happiness principle. See UTILITARIANISM.

Grelling's paradox. See HETEROLOGICAL.

Grue. See CONFIRMATION, GOODMAN.

H

Haecceity. Anglicized form of *haecceitas* (literally 'thisness'), introduced by SCOTUS for an individual essence, i.e. an essence peculiar to and distinguishing an individual, not an essence of a species. Haecceitism is the belief in haecceities, and anti-haecceitism their rejection, or else the rejection of primitive transworld identity (see POSSIBLE WORLDS).

R. M. Adams, 'Primitive thisness and primitive identity', *Journal of Philosophy*, 1979. (Discusses Leibniz's position, identity of indiscernibles, and defends primitive thisness and primitive transworld identities, though insisting they are different and independent notions.)

D. Kaplan, 'How to Russell a Frege-Church', *Journal of Philosophy*, 1975, pp. 722–3, reprinted in M. Loux (ed.), *The Possible and the Actual: Readings in the Metaphysics of Modality*, Cornell UP, 1979, pp. 216–17. (Haecceitism and anti-haecceitism.)

G. S. Rosenkrantz, *Haecceity: An Ontological Essay*, Kluwer, Dordrecht, 1993.

Happiness. John Stuart Mill claims an action is morally right if it leads to the greatest happiness for the greatest number. But he then (in *Utilitarianism*) goes on to discuss pleasures (higher and lower) as if they were the same thing as, or constitutive of, happiness. But pleasures seem to be states that are important at the moment of experiencing them, whereas happiness seems more often to be associated with longer periods ('the happiest years of my life', or 'call no-one happy til he's dead', as Solon said). Am I necessarily the best judge of whether I am happy? If happiness is simply a state of mind, perhaps I am. But if happiness is more to do with my whole situation, perhaps others (or myself in retrospect) can better decide. Subsequent UTILITARIAN philosophers have tended to write of well-being or human welfare as the things to be aimed for, and they are arguably more objectively determinable.

J. Annas, *The Morality of Happiness*, New York: OUP 1993. (Discusses ancient Greek conceptions of happiness, especially Aristotle.)

L. Sumner, *Welfare, Happiness, and Ethics*, Oxford: Clarendon Press, 1996.

Hare, Richard M. 1919–2002. British philosopher, born at Backwell near Bristol and worked in Oxford, then the USA, whose main contribution was to ETHICS, where his approach was inspired by 'linguistic philosophy'. He opposed NATURALISM, advocated a 'prescriptivist' analysis of moral judgements and treated moral judgements and philosophical analyses as distinct and independent of each other. He combined all this with an emphasis, derived from KANT, on UNIVERSALIZABILITY as what distinguishes moral from other evaluative judgements. *The Language of Morals*, 1952. *Freedom and Reason*, 1963 (develops his earlier book). *Moral Thinking: Its Levels, Methods and Point*, 1981. See also CRITERION, GOOD, IMPERATIVE, OUGHT, PHRASTIC.

Hart, H. L. A. (Herbert). 1907–92. British philosopher of law and political philosopher, educated and worked at Oxford, where he became Professor of Jurisprudence. His views involved him in a series of famous arguments with those who opposed them. He was a legal POSITIVIST whose position was attacked by DWORKIN. He believed in the separation of law and morality, which involved him in famous debates with Lon Fuller and Lord Devlin. Contributed important work on CAUSATION, and introduced the term 'DEFEASIBLE'. With Tony Honoré, *Causation in Law*, 1959, 2nd edn, 1985. *The Concept of Law*, 1961, 2nd posthumous edn 1994, *Law, Liberty and Morality*, 1963, *Punishment and Responsibility*, 1968 (essays on criminal law). See INTUITION, LAW, OUGHT.

Heap (paradox of). Also called 'sorites' (Greek for 'heaped') or (less often) 'bald man'. It seems that for any number n, if n grains form a heap so do n-1 grains; a heap cannot stop being a heap by losing just one grain. But if follows that any number of grains will form a heap, including one or even zero. The paradox affects all vague predicates, i.e. (it is usually claimed) most ordinary ones, and is important for the law of EXCLUDED MIDDLE; cf. also TRUTH, SUPERVALUATION. A special 'fuzzy logic' has been developed in connection with this. See also VAGUENESS.

M. Clark, *Paradoxes from A–Z*, London: Routledge, 2002.

J. A. Goguen, 'The logic of inexact concepts', *Synthese*, 1968–9. (Introduction to fuzzy logic, used to solve paradox.)

D. Raffman, 'Vagueness without paradox', *Philosophical Review*, 1994. (Appeals to psychological considerations to help solve paradox.)

*R. M. Sainsbury, *Paradoxes*, Cambridge UP, 1988 (revised, 1995) chapter 2. (Cf. also his 'Degrees of belief and degrees of truth', *Philosophical Papers*, 1986, which uses paradox to defend degrees of truth. Asterisk applies to first item.)

C. Travis, 'Vagueness, observation, and sorites', *Mind*, 1985. (Appeals to context of utterance rather than vagueness of predicates to solve paradox.)

Hedonism. Psychological hedonism has three main forms: that everyone desires only his own PLEASURE or HAPPINESS; that everyone necessarily aims only to maximize his own pleasure; that everyone always acts on his strongest desire. The term also sometimes applies to the theory that only pleasant thoughts can motivate actions. The three main senses can also (and the third properly speaking should) be called psychological egoism.

Ethical hedonism has two main forms: that only pleasure is ultimately good; that every action should aim to maximize pleasure (not necessarily the agent's).

For qualitative hedonism see PLEASURE.

The paradox of hedonism says that pleasure is often best attained by not seeking it. See also UTILITARIANISM.

Hegel, Georg W. F. 1770–1831. Born in Stuttgart, he worked at various German universities, especially Berlin, where he died. He is usually classified as an objective IDEALIST. His system is characterized by the use of a DIALECTIC of thesis, antithesis and synthesis (though some scholars warn against reading too much of this into Hegel), and could perhaps be described as an attempt to trace the development or emergence of 'spirit' or 'Geist', both systematically in a logical doctrine of categories and historically in the process of world history. He influenced such widely diverse thinkers as MARX, BRADLEY and CROCE, and stimulated vigorous hostility in KIERKEGAARD and SCHOPENHAUER. *Phenomenology of Spirit*, 1807. *Science of Logic*, 3 vols, 1812, 1813, 1816. *Encyclopaedia of the Philosophical Sciences*, 1817 (first part is often known as the 'Lesser Logic', second part concerns philosophy of nature, third part covers same ground as the Phenomenology). *Elements of the Philosophy of Right*, 1820 (or 1821). See also DIALECTIC, IDEA, METAPHYSICS.

F. C. Beiser (ed.), *The Cambridge Companion to Hegel*, Cambridge UP, 1993. (See pp. 488–90 for list of translations.)

Two good introductions: D. Knowles, *Routledge Philosophy GuideBook to Hegel and the Philosophy of Right*, 2002, and R. Stern, *Routledge Philosophy GuideBook to Hegel and the Phenomenology of Spirit*, 2001. (Clear introduction.)

Heidegger, Martin. 1889–1976. Born in Baden, he lived and taught in Germany, especially in Freiburg. He was a leading EXISTENTIALIST and his work centred round an investigation of 'being', both that which is proper to human beings, 'Dasein', and that which belongs to things in general. In his early days he was much influenced by HUSSERL. *Being and Time*, 1927. *Kant and the Problem of Metaphysics*, 1929. *Off the Beaten Track*, 1950. *Introduction to Metaphysics*, 1953. See also JASPERS, MARCEL.

Two clear introductions:

S. Mulhall, *Routledge Philosophy GuideBook to Heidegger and Being and Time*, 2005.

G. Pattison, *Routledge Philosophy GuideBook to the later Heidegger*, 2000.

Hempel, Carl. 1905–97. Born and educated in Germany, after 1939 worked mainly in the USA. Was a logical POSITIVIST (though he preferred 'logical empiricist'), associated closely with CARNAP and Neurath and the Vienna Circle. Wrote on truth, CONFIRMATION, INDUCTION and the nature of scientific explanation. *Philosophy of Natural Science*, 1966.

Hereditary property. If an object *a* stands in relation R to an object *b*, any property of *a* which must ipso facto belong to *b* is R hereditary. If R is the relation greater by two than, then the property of being even is R-hereditary among numbers, since if a given number is even then any number it is greater by (exactly) two than must also be even. Sometimes a property of numbers is called hereditary if it must belong to the successor of any number to which it belongs. Here R is being implicitly specified as 'has as its successor'.

Hermeneutic. Concerning interpretation. Hermeneutics, originating in Biblical studies, has developed, through F. Schleiermacher (1768–1834) and W. Dilthey (1833–1911) in particular, to an approach now associated especially with H.-G. Gadamer (1900–2002), which, in interpreting history and thought, denies both that there is a single objective true interpretation transcending all viewpoints and that we are for ever confined within our own viewpoint. Interpretation is rather something to be arrived at by a gradual interplay between the subject matter and the interpreter's initial position.

H.-G. Gadamer, *Philosophical Hermeneutics*, California UP, 1976. (Selected essays in translation. See editor's introduction, which links Gadamer with Wittgenstein and other Continental writers. Cf. R. Rorty, *Philosophy and the Mirror of Nature*, Blackwell, 1979, (see index), which also links hermeneutics with W. Sellars and Quine. For further connection with Anglo-Saxon philosophy see B. Harrison, *An Introduction to the Philosophy of Language*, Macmillan, 1979, pp. 166–7.

Heterological. Not applying to itself. 'German' (which is not a German word) and 'monosyllabic' (which is not a monosyllabic word) are heterological adjectives. Homological (or autological) means 'applying to itself'. 'English' (which is an English word) and 'polysyllabic' (which is a polysyllabic word) are homological adjectives.

The heterological paradox, attributed to K. Grelling (1886–1942, died in Auschwitz) and H. Weyl (1885–1955), asks whether 'heterological' is itself a heterological adjective. If it is, it does not apply to itself, and so is not heterological. If it is not, it does apply to itself, and so is heterological. A related, but different, paradox asks whether the attribute (not adjective) not-possessing-itself possesses itself. Both paradoxes are of the kind sometimes called semantic (see PARADOX, and also RUSSELL'S PARADOX, TYPES).

M. Clark, *Paradoxes from A–Z*, London: Routledge, 2002.
G. Ryle, 'Heterologicality', *Analysis*, vol. 11, 1951, reprinted in M. Macdonald (ed.), *Philosophy and Analysis*, Blackwell, 1954, and in Ryle's *Collected Papers*, Hutchinson, vol. 2, 1971.

Heuristic. Concerning discovery, as against proof. Heuristics is the study of methods and discovery. A heuristic is a procedure for achieving a result which does not consist simply in applying certain general rules which are guaranteed to lead to the result in question. Contrast ALGORITHM.

G. Polya, *How to Solve It*, Princeton UP, 1945, 1957, 1971, Doubleday, 1957.

Historical materialism. The analysis of history, pioneered by Karl MARX, in terms of social and economic forces, in particular, the ways in which humans interact and work to produce the means for survival.

G. A. Cohen, *Karl Marx's Theory of History: A Defence*, Princeton UP, 1978.

K. R. Popper, *Conjectures and Refutations: The Growth of Scientific Knowledge*, Routledge, 1963. (Marxist analysis of history as unfalsifiable. And see bibliography for HISTORICISM.)

D.-H. Ruben, *Marxism and Materialism: A Study in Marxist Theory of Knowledge*, Harvester, 1977, revised 1979. (Tries to mediate between Marxist and Anglo-Saxon philosophy. See Introduction for senses of 'materialism'.)

A. W. Wood, *Karl Marx* (*Arguments of the Philosophers* series), Routledge, 2004. (Discusses misinterpretations of Marx.)

Historicism. Originally, any of several views of emphasizing the importance of history, especially the view that things should always be seen in terms of their historical development. But for Popper, who uses historism for the above, historicism is the view that historical events are determined by inevitable laws, which history aims to predict, and that corporate wholes cannot be reduced to the individuals composing them.

D. E. Lee and R. N. Beck, 'The meaning of "historicism"', *American Historical Review*, 1953–4. (Cf. also G. D. Mitchell (ed.), *A Dictionary of Sociology*, RKP, 1968.)

K. R. Popper, *The Poverty of Historicism*, 1957, written earlier. (Cf. his *The Open Society*, RKP, 1945.)

Historism. See HISTORICISM.

History (philosophy of). History proper seems limited to the sphere of human action, natural events being included only so far as they affect or are affected by human action; things like the 'history of the universe' seem rather secondary. Problems in the philosophy of mind, about action, freewill, causation, rationality, are therefore especially relevant to the philosophy of history, and are connected to the question what is the aim of history: is this to describe the course of events or to explain it, and what sorts of EXPLANATION can be given? Are general laws to be sought, and if so, of what kinds? Is history a science?

Another set of problems concerns how history is possible and how historical claims can be justified. The reality of the past and the

justifiability of using memory are subjects for metaphysics and epistemology, but the philosopher of history asks how statements about
the past can be verified, both in general and taking account of the
various kinds of statement and kinds of evidence, and what is their
meaning. Are they really, as some logical positivists held, about the
extant evidence? On what principles are facts and topics to be selected, and how far can or should the historian be objective and neutral?
Should he 'stick to the facts'? What counts as doing this?

The purpose of history must be distinguished from purpose in history. Can purposes or patterns be discerned in history either as a
whole or in parts? Is history in any way cyclic? What can we learn
from it? Critical philosophy of history, as well as covering the questions mentioned previously, asks what kind of answers these latter
questions can have and what count as answers. The answers themselves are the province of speculative philosophy of history. Some
questions, e.g. the elucidating of concepts like progress, historical
event, historical period, may fall between these provinces.

Metahistory properly means philosophy of history, but is often
limited to the speculative branch. See also HISTORICISM,
EXPLANATION.

R. F. Atkinson, *Knowledge and Explanation in History: An Introduction to
the Philosophy of History*, Macmillan, 1978. (Covers relations between
philosophy and history, how we can know of the past, objectivity,
explanation, causation, values.)

A. Bullock, 'The historian's purpose', C. Dawson, 'The problem of
meta-history', *History Today*, 1951 (February, June). (Both on metahistory.)

W. H. Dray, *Philosophy of History*, Prentice-Hall, 1964. (This and Walsh are
two introductions to both critical and speculative sides.)

*S. Gardiner (ed.), *The Philosophy of History*, Oxford UP, 1974. (Anthology
on relevant issues.)

S. Hook (ed.), *Philosophy and History*, New York UP, 1963. (Discussions
between philosophers and historians.)

E. Loone, *Soviet Marxism and Analytical Philosophies of History*, Verso,
1992, trans. by B. Pearce from 1980 Russian original. (Discussion by
Estonian analytical philosopher with Marxist background. Foreword by
E. Gellner.)

W. H. Walsh, *An Introduction to Philosophy of History*, Hutchinson, 1951.

Hobbes, Thomas. 1588–1679. Born at Malmesbury he lived in England and France. He is now best known for his political philosophy,
defending an absolute sovereignty as the only way to ensure social

security and prevent life from being 'solitary, poor, nasty, brutish and short', as it would be in the 'state of nature'. This sovereignty he based on a social contract among men, but the sovereign had duties only to God. As usually interpreted, he based the duty of political obedience on self-interest. (Cf. also ROUSSEAU.) He also developed a nominalist view of UNIVERSALS, and a philosophy of nature which analysed everything, including human beings, in terms of matter and motion. He was also much influenced by his study of geometry. At one point he engaged in controversy with Descartes. *De Cive*, 1642, trans. 1651 as *Philosophicall Rudiments concerning Government and Society*, (political). *Leviathan*, 1651 (main political work, including also treatment of human beings). *De Corpore*, 1655, trans. 1656 as *Elements of Philosophy, The First Section, Concerning Body* (metaphysics and treatment of inanimate nature). See also COLLINGWOOD, MODALITIES.

G. Newey, *Routledge Philosophy GuideBook to Hobbes and Leviathan*, 1995. (Clear introduction.)

Holism. Any theory which approaches its subject matter as a whole rather than bit by bit. An example would be Quine's view that 'our statements about the external world face the tribunal of sense experience not individually but as a body', because we can always avoid accepting, or avoid rejecting, any given scientific view by making sufficient adjustments elsewhere in our system. Elsewhere holism may insist that the properties of a whole cannot be predicted or explained in terms of those of its parts, or (especially in political philosophy) that the whole is more important than the parts. Holistic explanation claims that certain things, especially in psychology, must be explained not in terms of individual beliefs or desires (say) but only of complete systems of them.

J. Fodor and E. Lepore, *Holism: A Shopper's Guide*, Blackwell, 1992. (Discussions of some notable modern views.)

C. Peacocke, *Holistic Explanation*, Oxford UP, 1979. (Discusses issues arising because explaining action requires appealing to both belief and desire, and explaining perception requires appealing to both one's location and what the world is like there. Difficult.)

W. V. O. Quine, 'Two dogmas of empiricism', *Philosophical Review*, 1951, revised and reprinted in his *From a logical Point of View*, Harvard UP, 1953. (For quotation see p. 38 of original, p. 41 of reprint. The second 'dogma' is the view that 'each meaningful statement is equivalent to some logical construct upon terms which refer to immediate experience' (opening paragraph).)

Homological. See HETEROLOGICAL.

Homophonic. See MEANING.

Humanity (principle of). See CHARITY.

Hume, David. 1711–76. Scottish, born in Edinburgh, and generally regarded as the greatest of 'British empiricists', Hume was a historian and a man of letters as well as a philosopher. His religious opinions stood in the way of his having an academic post but he was for a short time Chargé d'Affaires in Paris where he was much celebrated and he later came to hold the post of Under-Secretary of State in England from which he resigned in 1769. He examined meticulously our modes of thinking, both deductive and inductive, and claimed that they were far less powerful than we assumed. This led him to generally sceptical conclusions about such notions as REASON, CAUSATION and necessity (see MODALITIES), and about how far we are justified in postulating a world outside ourselves, or indeed a self for it to be outside (as against a mere set of experiences). (Cf. also NATURALISM.) He developed a philosophy based on 'impressions', and making substantial use of the then relatively new doctrine of the association of ideas; he drew out the implications of this philosophy also for psychology and ethics. KANT claimed that it was Hume who 'aroused him from his dogmatic slumbers'. *A Treatise of Human Nature*, 1739–40. *An Enquiry concerning Human Understanding*, 1748. *An Enquiry concerning the Principles of Morals*, 1751. (The two *Enquiries* are shorter and later versions of parts of the *Treatise*.) *Dialogues concerning Natural Religion*, 1779. L. Selby-Bigge (ed.), *Hume's Treatise of Human Nature*, Clarendon, 1888, and *Enquiries concerning Human Understanding and concerning the Principles of Morals*, Clarendon, 2 vol. edn, 1902. (These are the standard modern editions and contain full analytical indexes.) See also ANALYTIC, HUTCHESON, IDENTITY, MORAL SENSE (bibliography), NATURALISM, PERCEPTION, POSITIVISM, REID, ROUSSEAU, RUSSELL, SCEPTICISM.

N. Kemp Smith, *The Philosophy of David Hume*, Macmillan, 1941. (Classic study. New edn 2005 with good introduction by D. Garrett.)

W. E. Morris, 'David Hume', *The Stanford Encyclopedia of Philosophy* (Winter 2007 Edition), Edward N. Zalta (ed.). Available at: http://plato.

stanford.edu/archives/win2007/entries/hume/ (accessed 1 March 2009). (Useful introduction.)

Husserl, Edmund. 1859–1938. Born in Moravia, he spent his life teaching in German universities. He is usually regarded as the leading figure in PHENOMENOLOGY, which took two successive forms in his own work, descriptive and transcendental. His early work (1891) was still under the influence of PSYCHOLOGISM, which in his mature and phenomenological stages he vigorously rejected. His early phenomenology (1900–1) has some affinities with linguistic philosophy. He was influenced especially by BRENTANO and in turn influenced EXISTENTIALSIM. *Philosophy of Arithmetic*, 1891. *Logical Investigations*, 1900–1. *Ideas: General Introduction to Pure Phenomenology*, 1913. *Cartesian Meditations*, 1931. *The Crisis of European Sciences and Transcendental Phenomenology: An Introduction to Phenomenological Philosophy*, 1936 (in part; full edition 1954). See also CATEGORIES, HEIDEGGER, MERLEAU-PONTY, NATURALISM.

D. Woodruff Smith, *Husserl*, Routledge, 2007. (Clear introduction.)

Hutcheson, Francis. 1694–1746 (or 1747). Born in Ulster, he worked in Dublin and at Glasgow university. Though he also wrote on metaphysics and logic, he is important mainly as a theorist of the MORAL SENSE school who also anticipated some features of utilitarianism. He developed and systematized the work of SHAFTESBURY, and influenced HUME. F. Hutcheson, *An Inquiry concerning Beauty, Order, Harmony, Design*, 1725. (P. Kivy has edited an edition with useful introduction and notes, Martinus Nijhoff, 1993.) *An Essay on the Nature and Conduct of the Passions and Affections with Illustrations on the Moral Sense*, 1728. See also BEAUTY, PRICE, SMITH.

Hypothesis. See LAWS.

Hypothetical. See CONDITIONALS.

Hypothetical constructs. See LOGICAL CONSTRUCTIONS.

Hypothetical imperatives. See IMPERATIVE.

Hypothetico-deductive method. See INDUCTION.

I

Ibn Rushd, Abu'l Walid Muhammad. See AVERROES.

Ibn Sina, Abu 'Ali Al-Husayn. See AVICENNA.

Icons. See SIGN.

Idea. The Greek words idea and eidos, virtually synonymous, and etymologically linked with 'vision', may originally have meant 'visible
form' but by Plato's time could mean 'nature', 'essence' or 'kind'.
Plato's 'Ideas' were non-material objects outside the mind, though the
mind could know them. The translation 'Form' is therefore often
preferred as less misleading. (Cf. FORM, UNIVERSALS.) Plato considered but rejected the view that 'ideas' were something in our
minds. Some Stoics adopted it, but in later Greek and medieval
writings ideas tended to be in the mind of God.

For many modern philosophers 'idea' has been a technical term
important for their systems, used in many senses, often in the same
philosopher (notably Locke), but almost always for something in or
having reference to the mind.

Its meanings include: what is immediately present to the mind in an
experience (SENSE DATUM, feeling); what is before the mind when
it reflects, remembers, introspects, imagines (images, etc.); what the
mind preserves from its experiences, or finds within itself, or constructs in various ways out of simpler ideas (one's idea of red, colour,
gratitude, number); things like these latter but common to different
people ('the' idea of red); a quality in an object which causes experiences (Locke, but rarely even there); the meaning of a word; the
subjective associations of a word, contrasted with its meaning (Frege);
a representation of something that cannot be experienced (Kant,
based on Plato). For Hegel, 'idea' means something like the overall

pattern or purpose in the universe or is a term whose use centres on this. In aesthetics 'idea' is sometimes used in a Platonic sense, for what a work of art aims to embody or copy.

Because it is so ambiguous, particularly between uses for datable existents (sense datum, image, etc) and logical uses (meaning of a word, 'the' idea of … , etc.), 'idea' has largely been replaced for technical purposes by more specific terms like 'sense datum', 'image', 'CONCEPT'. See also IMAGERY, INNATE, SENSE DATA.

J. Bennett, *Locke, Berkeley, Hume: Central Themes*, Oxford UP, 1971. (Good discussion of multiple senses of 'idea'.)

F. H. Bradley, *Principles of Logic*, 1883, 2nd (revised) edition 1922. (Opening chapter, based on idealist standpoint, criticizes confusion due to ambiguity of 'idea').

I. Hacking, *Why Does Language Matter to Philosophy?* Cambridge UP, 1975. (Discusses seventeenth-century usage of 'idea'.)

Ideal. Entity or attribute of a kind suggested by 'IDEA'. 'Ideal' suggests freedom from the imperfections of the material world, together with unattainability (cf. Platonic 'Ideas'), but also the unreality of what depends simply on the mind. There is also the neutral sense, 'connected with ideas, or the mind'. The 'unreality' and 'neutral' strands are rather commoner in philosophy, especially before the twentieth century, than in popular usage.

Idealism. A doctrine, or set of doctrines, to the effect that reality is in some way mental. Idealism is concerned with 'IDEA' more closely than with 'IDEAL'. It is not primarily concerned with ethics or conduct, though certain ethical views have sometimes been associated with it. Idealism is contrasted primarily with REALISM, though also with MATERIALISM. Rarely, it means simply that the universe is spiritual in the sense of depending on God. Sometimes, however, views are called idealist which hold that reality is outside the mind, but can only be described from some point of view there are different ways of looking at reality, none of which is more correct that the others, rather as whether Oxford is to the right of Cambridge depends on where one is looking from. In this wide sense, such outlooks as PRAGMATISM and CONVENTIONALISM are idealist. Kant, similarly, held that reality existed independently, but that how it appeared to us was determined by the structure of the human mind. Public empirical knowledge was therefore possible, but only of appearances ('phenomena'). He called himself an empirical realist but a transcendental idealist, meaning by this that what we perceive is in general not illusory, but as real as perceptible things could be, but that nevertheless philosophy forces us to assume that they are appearances of things which in themselves are quite unknowable by us. Full-blooded idealism holds that reality is mental. 'To be is to be perceived', as Berkeley said. Matter does not exist except in the form of ideas in the mind, or as a manifestation of mental activity. The 'mind' in question may be one's own mind (solipsism: see SCEPTICISM), minds in general, or the mind of God (Berkeley).

Absolute idealism developed after Kant, notably with Hegel, and was popular in Britain from about 1865 to 1925. It takes many forms, but its central point is that there is only one ultimately real thing, the Absolute, which is spiritual in nature. Other things are partial aspects of this, or illusory appearances generated by it. Here idealism becomes a form of MONISM. The Absolute is so called because it alone does not depend on or presuppose anything and does not have its properties relative to something else.

A distinction is sometimes made between subjective and objective idealism. 'Subjective idealism' is used mainly of views that the only reality is ideas in the mind, especially the human mind. The term is often, however, applied to Berkeley, though he himself used immaterialism. 'Objective idealism', like absolute idealism, applies mainly to forms of idealism which place reality outside the human mind. It is used especially when the arguments in favour of idealism say that appearances are contradictory, and therefore are mere appearances of a reality lying behind them; subjective idealism, by contrast, says that appearances and minds are the only reality (cf. also PHENOMENALISM).

Plato's theory of IDEAS, or FORMS, is not usually called idealism now, since these Ideas, though not material, are not mental or mind-dependent. See also BEING.

A. C. Ewing, *Idealism: A Critical Survey*, 1934. (Sympathetic, though not himself an idealist.)

A. C. Ewing (ed.), *The Idealist Tradition*, Free Press, 1957. (Selections from leading idealists.)

J. Foster, *The Case for Idealism*, RKP, 1982. (Defence of a moderate version)

J. Hospers, *Introduction to Philosophical Analysis*, RKP, 1956, chapter 8. (Discusses subjective idealism in relation to other theories.)

R. Le Poidevin, 'Fables and models', *Proceedings of the Aristotelian Society*, supplementary vol., 1991. (See p. 73 for a distinction between idealism and phenomenalism.)

A. Quinton, *Absolute Idealism*, 1972. (Dawes Hicks lecture at British Academy, 1971).

Identically true, false. See IDENTITY.

Identity. Attribute of being a single thing or single kind. In ordinary speech two things may be called numerically identical (or one in number: 'Persia and Iran are identical'), or identical (or one) in type or species (exactly similar, as with 'identical twins'). Philosophers keep 'identical' for the first sense, using 'indiscernible' for the second (see LEIBNIZ'S LAW). But what is identity, in this first sense? Is it a relation between a thing and itself? If so, every true statement of identity should be trivial, or else senseless. Hume used time to solve the problem, saying that identity statements state that an object existing at one time is the same as itself existing at another, e.g. 'This chair is the same as the one here yesterday.' This could suggest that GENIDENTITY is in question, but anyway this covers only some cases. Suppose Smith is mayor of a certain town. Then 'Smith is Smith' is trivial but 'Smith is the mayor' is not, even though the words 'the mayor' refer to Smith. It was this that made Frege distinguish between sense and reference (see MEANING), saying that what gave content to an identity statement was the different ways in which the object was described.

A distinction exists between two approaches to identity statements. On a conceptualist approach one can only say '*a* is the same so-and-so as *b*' where 'so-and-so' is a SORTAL term. On a realist approach, 'so-and-so' can be replaced by a non-sortal term like 'thing' or 'object'. The identity is here given, as it were, in the world itself and does not depend on the concepts we apply. It is a further question, however, whether identity is relative, in the sense that *a* might be the same so-and-so, but not the same such-and-such, as *b*, e.g. was Nixon the same official (namely the American president), though not the same man, as Eisenhower?

This distinction between two approaches may be relevant to various problems which arise because things persist in time, for they may persist for different periods if described in different ways. Suppose a gold coin melts. Then it seems that the coin is destroyed but the piece of gold is not. If the coin is the piece of gold, then the same thing seems to be destroyed and not destroyed. If the coin is not the piece of gold, then we seem to have two things in the same place at the same time (though not throughout the same time). Perhaps the gold is not identical with, but 'constitutes', the coin (Wiggins; cf. BEING).

Furthermore, a coin which melts is presumably destroyed, but a baby which grows up is not destroyed, though it stops being a baby. But what stops being a baby and lives to be eighty? And how long does the baby last? Eighty years? (Terms like 'baby' are called phase terms or phase universals.)

Also can 'identity statements be contingent? 'Smith is the mayor' seems contingent. Yet 'Smith is Smith' seems necessary. See MODALITIES.

Sometimes *a* is called strictly identical with *b* if whatever can be said of one can be said of the other (INTENSIONALITY apart). Some would say that an adult is identical, but not strictly identical, with the baby he once was, on the grounds that the adult but not the baby could be called, for example, married: one can say, 'The baby you knew is now married.' But there are no married babies. 'Strict' or 'perfect identity' is also sometimes used for identity that cannot be reduced to GENIDENTITY.

Further problems concern the criteria of identity, both for objects and for events, properties, propositions, etc. Is the property red identical with that of reflecting or emitting light of certain wavelengths? Spatiotemporal continuity is an obvious criterion to use for objects, but a suit need not possess it (if trousers and coat are separated), and a sound or toothache can be intermittent. We must also ask, continuity of what? Not of matter, since a body, and still more a flame, are constantly changing their matter; and perhaps they change their shape and other properties too. Furthermore we must be able to individuate places and times themselves, i.e. tell when we have one and when another, if we are to use them to individuate objects. Particular attention has been given to the question of personal identity. What is a PERSON? How are persons, minds and bodies related? What role do things like memory and traits of character play?

Questions of identity are also important in aesthetics. How is Olivier related to Hamlet when it is true to say both that Olivier is now alone on the stage and that Hamlet is now alone on the stage?

On whether identity is intrinsic or extrinsic, and for the 'ship of Theseus' problem, see INTRINSIC AND EXTRINSIC.

To identify *a* with *b* is simply to claim, or assume, that *a* and *b* are identical. To identify *a* as *b* (or as a *b*) is to pick out *a* by either taking it to be identical with *b* or attributing *b*-type characteristics to it. I can identify Smith with a spy only if I already have some spy in mind, but I can identify him as a spy without this.

The law of identity, one of the traditional 'laws of thought', says that everything is what it is, or that if something is true, it is true. A proposition that is an instance of this law (e.g. 'A cat is a cat'), or one that can be transformed into such an instance by applying to it the rules of logic (e.g. 'If Tiddles is a cat, Tiddles does not fail to be a cat'), can be called identically true, and its negation identically false. For type/token distinction, see UNIVERSALS. See also LEIBNIZ'S LAW, IDENTITY THEORY OF MIND, GENIDENTITY.

D. Hume, *Treatise*, 1739, book 1, part 4, § 2 (pp. 200–1 in L. A. Selby-Bigge's edition, Clarendon, 1888 (1946 reprint)).

S. Kripke, *Naming and Necessity*, Blackwell, 1980, original version 1972. (Discusses, inter alia, both identity across POSSIBLE WORLDS and the nature of identity.)

J. Locke, *Essay concerning Human Understanding*, 1690, part 2, chapter 27. (Pioneering discussion of personal identity. See discussions by A. Flew, 'Locke and the problem of personal identity', *Philosophy*, 1951, and (more difficult) D. Wiggins, 'Locke, Butler, and the stream of consciousness: And men as a natural kind', *Philosophy*, 1976, both reprinted in Perry, and for elaboration and defence of Locke's view see C. Rovane, 'Self-reference: The radicalization of Locke', *Journal of Philosophy*, 1993.

M. K. Munitz (ed.), *Identity and Individuation*, New York UP, 1971. (Essays, including S. Kripke's 'Identity and necessity', which is also in S. P. Schwartz (ed.), *Naming, Necessity, and Natural Kinds*, Cornell UP, 1977, and (with editorial introduction) in T. Honderich and M. F. Burnyeat (eds), *Philosophy as It Is*, Penguin, 1979.)

H. Noonan (ed.), *Identity and Personal Identity*, Dartmouth Publishing Co., 1993. (Two wide-ranging volumes of essays. See also his own *Personal Identity*, Routledge, 1989, which discusses historical and modern views while developing his own.)

J. Perry (ed.), *Personal Identity*, California UP, 1975. (Important discussions, historical and modern, though less full than Noonan.)

A. O. Rorty (ed.), *The Identity of Persons*, Cornell UP, 1976. (Readings.)

M. Schechtman, 'Personhood and personal identity', *Journal of Philosophy*, 1990. (Traits of character, memory, etc., are inadequate as criteria for grounding personal identity.)

S. Shoemaker, *Self-Knowledge and Self-Identity*, Cornell UP, 1963. (Extended discussion of personal identity. See pp. 36–8 for 'strict' or 'perfect' identity as not reducible to genidentity (though not so called).)

D. Wiggins, *Sameness and Substance*, Blackwell, 1980. (Discussion of identity, substance, and personal identity. Conceptualist but claims identity never relative. Cf. his 'On being in the same place at the same time', *Philosophical Review*, 1968 (rather easier), and symposium with M. J. Woods, 'The individuation of things and places', *Proceedings of the Aristotelian Society*, supplementary vol., 1963. On identity and constitution see also H. W. Noonan, 'Constitution is identity', *Mind*, 1993.)

B. A. O. Williams, 'Personal identity and individuation', *Proceedings of the Aristotelian Society*, 1956–7. (Bases personal identity on bodily continuity.)

Identity of indiscernibles. See LEIBNIZ'S LAW.

Identity theory of mind. Theory that various conscious phenomena are identical with states or processes in the brain or central nervous system. Brain process theory, physicalism, central state materialism, or just materialism, are alternative names for the theory (the third for the version using the central nervous system). The conscious phenomena concerned may be limited to sensations and pains, or may include also thoughts, beliefs, desires, emotions. In the former case a BEHAVIOURIST explanation of emotions, etc., may be given.

The theory may take two main forms, called TYPE and TOKEN IDENTITY THEORY. The former identifies types of sensations, etc., with types of brain-states, etc., so that whenever a certain sensation (e.g. a certain kind of headache) occurs a brain-state of that type will be present and identical with it. The token theory claims merely that each occurrence of the headache will be identical with some brain-state. Early versions of the theory, in either form, insisted that the identity was contingent (see MODALITIES), like (it was claimed) that of a lightning flash with an electrical discharge. But since Kripke separated the necessary/contingent and a priori/ empirical distinctions (see A PRIORI) contingent identity has fallen into disfavour, and the claim is rather that the identity is empirical though still necessary. Criticisms of the theory include asking how it could be verified, and whether the IDENTITY could be strict. The theory stems largely from Australia in the mid-1950s, though akin to the DOUBLE ASPECT THEORY and to neutral MONISM.

D. M. Armstrong, *A Materialist Theory of the Mind*, Routledge, 1968, revised 1993.

G. Bealer, 'Mental properties', *Journal of Philosophy*, 1994. (Defends theory against four common objections, but then attacks it.)

C. V. Borst (ed.), *The Mind/Brain Identity Theory*, Macmillan, 1970. (Expository and critical essays, including several main original sources.)

T. Burge, 'Philosophy of language and mind: 1950–90', *Philosophical Review*, 1992. (Survey article with many references. See pp. 32–9.)

*K. Campbell, *Body and Mind*, Macmillan, 1970, chapters 5, 6. (Elementary discussion.)

C. S. Hill, *Sensations: A Defense of Type Materialism*, Cambridge UP, 1991.

J. O'Connor (ed.), *Modern Materialism: Readings on Mind-Body Identity*, Harcourt, Brace, and World, 1969. (Further essays, overlapping with Borst.)

J. Ross, 'Immaterial aspects of thought', *Journal of Philosophy*, 1992. (Claims thinking cannot be any physical process or any function of one.) See also bibliography for MIND (PHILOSOPHY OF).

Identity theory of predication. Theory that apparent subject/ predicate statements, like 'X is red,' are properly to be analysed as identity statements of the form 'X is identical with some red thing'.

Idiolect. A language considered as spoken or written by a given individual.

If. See CONDITIONALS.

Iff. If and only if.

Illocutions. See SPEECH ACTS.

Illusion (argument from). See PERCEPTION.

Imagery. Mental imagery fell into disrepute in the mid-twentieth century in both philosophy and psychology. Statements about one's images were not publicly assessable, and so fell foul of Wittgenstein's PRIVATE LANGUAGE argument, while psychology had no means of studying them or using them in scientific accounts of human beings. They also suffered from being apparently indeterminate in nature. Recently, however, scientists have found ways of studying them, and integrating their study with that of vision, and following this their study has become respectable again in philosophy too. (Cf. at least in part the similar revival of SENSE DATA.)

Interest has centred mainly on visual images, and two main theories are current about what these are, pictorialism and descriptionalism.

Pictorialists argue first that images do indeed exist and are used in solving various imaginative problems, and that they do so by representing the relevant material in a spatial manner. Pictorialists use experimental data, such as that when subjects are asked to say whether two diagrams are congruent, where this could be found by rotating one of them, the time needed to answer is proportional to the size of the angular rotation required; this, pictorialists claim, suggests that subjects do indeed mentally rotate one of them.

Descriptionalists emphasize such things as the indeterminacy of images, and claim that they represent things more as linguistic items do. A verbal description of a scene, for instance, will inevitably ignore many features of it altogether – which is different from representing them as blurred or hidden, as a picture might. An image of a red tomato represents something as a red tomato, but does not itself contain something red, as a picture normally would. Pylyshyn, a leading descriptionalist, insists that we must distinguish whether 'image' refers to 'what I experience when I imagine a scene, ... surely that exists in the same sense that any other sensation or conscious content does (e.g. pains, tickles, etc.)' or to 'a certain theoretical construct that is claimed to have certain properties (e.g. to be spatially extended) and to play a specified role in certain cognitive processes'. He gives a large role to 'tacit knowledge' (see TACIT AND IMPLICIT KNOWLEDGE), and also insists that in 'image of object X with property P', P belongs to the object, not the image; ignoring this, he thinks, is 'probably the most ubiquitous and damaging conceptual confusion in the whole imagery literature'.

However, pictorialists agree that there is no actual picture in the brain – it would involve an inner eye to see it, and how would that work? Imaging a red tomato does not involve a circular bit of the brain being red. Rather, as with the descriptionalists, we represent something as a red tomato, only the representing is spatial rather than linguistic. Also the indeterminacy objection does not hold, they claim: an ordinary stick-picture of a person may leave it indeterminate, and not merely blurred or hidden, whether it is male or female, clothed or unclothed, etc.

But now the issue itself is becoming blurred (see Block's 'Introduction' to *Imagery*), and others, such as Tye, present an alternative or compromise view.

B. Beakley and P. Ludlow (eds), *The Philosophy of Mind: Classical Problems/Contemporary Issues*, MIT Press, 1992. (Part iii has relevant items.)

N. Block (ed.), *Imagery*, MIT Press, 1981. (Includes important articles on both sides; see pp. 152, 153 for quotations from Pylyshyn. See also Block (ed.), *Readings in the Philosophy of Psychology*, vol. 2, Harvard UP and Methuen, 1981.)

S. Kosslyn, *Image and Brain: The Resolution of the Imagery Debate*, MIT Press, 1994. (Full discussion of images, defending their existence and importance with very extensive bibliography.)

W. G. Lycan (ed.), *Mind and Cognition*, Blackwell, 1990.

M. Tye, *The Imagery Debate*, MIT Press, 1991. (Discusses the two main views both philosophically and scientifically, offering his own alternative.)

Imitation game. See TURING TEST.

Immaterialism. See IDEALISM.

Imperative. Kant distinguishes two sorts of imperatives concerning actions. A Hypothetical Imperative is of the form 'If you want to achieve X, do Y' – for example, 'If you want to get fit, take exercise every day'. The imperative – 'take exercise every day' – is conditional on some end – getting fit. In contrast, a Categorical (or apodictic) Imperative has no such dependence on any antecedent condition: it is an unconditional moral imperative which enjoins us to moral actions without regard to our wishes or desires. Since he was concerned only with imperatives, of each kind, valid for all rational agents he recognized only one categorical imperative, which formed the basis of morality. He formulated it variously, but the general point was, roughly, that one should act only in ways that are UNIVERSALIZ-ABLE. The problems of the categorical imperative are largely those of universalizability. But is the hypothetical imperative really an imperative at all, and not just a statement that fully willing the end involves willing the means? Recently imperatives have been important in prescriptivist views of ethics (see NATURALISM), and there has also been discussion of what logical relations they can stand in.

R. M. Hare, *The Language of Morals*, Oxford UP, 1952, part 1. (Logic of imperatives. Also prescriptivism.)

J. H. McDowell, 'Are moral requirements hypothetical imperatives?', *Proceedings of the Aristotelian Society*, supplementary vol., 1978. (No.)

H. J. Paton, *The Moral Law*, Hutchinson, 1948. (Best translation of Kant's *Grundlegung*. Cf. also Paton's commentary, *The Categorical Imperative*, 1947.)

B. A. O. Williams and P. T. Geach, 'Imperative inference', *Analysis*, 1963 (supplement). (Can one infer one imperative from another?)

Implication and entailment. 'Implication' is the most general name for those relations between propositions or statements in virtue of which we can infer the truth of a proposition or statement from something else. A minimum condition for such a relation to hold (except contextual implication: see below) is that if one proposition, p, implies another, q, it is not the case that p is true and q is false.

180

Whenever this condition is fulfilled, and provided p and q are each either true or false, we say that p materially implies q. Hence a false proposition materially implies any proposition (for if p is false it is not the case that p is true and q false), and any proposition materially implies a true proposition; these facts are called the 'paradoxes' of material implication, though they are only paradoxical in the sense of sounding odd because 'implies' in ordinary speech suggests a stronger relation. Material implication is usually symbolized by '⊃', which is specific to it, or '→' which can also stand for other relations, including entailment.

Strict implication (C. I. Lewis) holds from p to q when it is logically impossible (see MODALITIES) for p to be true and q false. Hence it too has 'paradoxes', that an impossible (i.e. necessarily false) proposition strictly implies any proposition, and any proposition strictly implies a necessary proposition. Occasionally the impossibility and necessity involved may be not confined to the logical.

Entailment is a special relation introduced by Moore, who said it held from p to q when and only when q can be logically deduced from p. Entailment in this sense, as against the looser popular sense, can be called logical entailment (whether or not it is purely a logical relation: see below). Entailment is often thought to differ from strict implication, by requiring that the propositions that it links have some relevance to each other, or connection of meaning, so that the paradoxes of strict implication do not apply to it. On this view, entailment is not always purely a logical relation. Many writers have tried to formalize this relevance requirement and show that it avoids the paradoxes, but these attempts, sometimes called relevance logics, remain controversial.

Logical implication is implication that holds as a matter of logic, or is logically necessary. Though often equated with strict implication, logical implication is more general. It need not be limited to a relation whereby a contradiction implies any proposition and any proposition implies a necessary proposition. If entailment is a logical relation different from strict implication (so not purely a logical relation), 'logical implication' can cover both. 'Logical implication' is also used as a general contrast to 'contextual implication' (see below).

Presuppositions are carried by certain statements, questions, etc. 'Have you stopped beating your wife?' presupposes that you have one and have beaten her. Strawson and others distinguish presuppositions from entailments because when p entails q, if q is false p is false, but when p presupposes q, so does not-p, and if q is false p is neither true nor false (if you have no wife it is neither true nor false that you have stopped beating her). It is disputed, however, whether presupposition and entailment in fact exclude each other (Linsky). 'Absolute presuppositions' is Collingwood's term for statements which are not (as most statements are, he thought) answers to questions. They are neither true nor false, but underlie the thought of persons or epochs.

Contextual or pragmatic implication is related to, and not always easily distinguishable from, presupposition. 'Implicature' (Grice) is also used for much the same notion. Perhaps the main difference is that presupposition affects the truth of what is said, while contextual implication affects the rationality or correctness of saying it. Normally if one says something one contextually implies that one believes it. If I say 'It's raining' I contextually imply that I believe it is; but it could be raining even if I do not believe it is. 'A speaker in making a statement contextually implies whatever one is entitled to infer on the basis of the presumption that his act of stating is normal' (Hungerland). Gricean implicature has become important recently in connection with entailment, CONDITIONALS and other contexts involving the relations between formal logics and ordinary language. For both presupposition and contextual implication it is disputable what does the presupposing, etc. Is it what is said, the saying of it, or the sayer? Saying (which here includes asking, etc.) may even be replaced by something non-linguistic: 'By (deliberately) frowning he implied he was angry.' A non-deliberate frown could only 'imply' anger causally, rather as rainbows imply rain. Contextual implication lies between such a causal sense and logical implication. See also CONDITIONALS, INFERENCE.

A. R. Anderson and N. Belnap, 'Tautological entailments', *Philosophical Studies*, 1962 (Relevance logics. For fuller development see their *Entailment: The Logic of Relevance and Necessity*, vol. 1, 1975 (see index). See also G. Iseminger, 'Is relevance necessary for validity?', *Mind*, 1980.)

R. G. Collingwood, *An Essay on Metaphysics*, Oxford UP, 1940, particularly part 1. (Absolute presuppositions.)

H. P. Grice, 'Logic and conversation' in D. Davidson and G. Harman (eds), *The Logic of Grammar*, 1975, reprinted in revised form with other relevant material in Grice's *Studies in the Way of Words*, Harvard UP, 1989. See also his 'The causal theory of perception', § 3, *Proceedings of the Aristotelian Society*, supplementary vol., 1961, reprinted in G. J. Warnock (ed.), *The Philosophy of Perception*, Oxford UP, 1967, particularly § 3. (Some kinds of implication.)

I. Hungerland, 'Contextual implication', *Inquiry*, 1960. (Contextual implication and presupposition. For quotation see p. 255.)

C. I. Lewis and C. H. Langford, *Symbolic Logic*, Century, 1932, chapter 8. (Equates entailment with strict implication. Cf. also J. Bennett, 'Entailment', *Philosophical Review*, 1969, a general survey defending Lewis.)

B. Mates, *Stoic Logic*, California UP, 1961, chapter 4. (Philonian, Diodorean and Chrysippean implication, i.e. various Greek anticipations of modern discussions.)

G. E. Moore, *Philosophical Studies*, RKP, 1923, p. 291. (Entailment introduced.)

E. J. Nelson, 'Intensional relations', *Mind*, 1930. C. Lewy, J. L. Watling and P. T. Geach, 'Entailment', *Proceedings of the Aristotelian Society*, supplementary vol., 1958. T. J. Smiley, 'Entailment and deducibility', *Proceedings of the Aristotelian Society*, 1958–9. (All these try to separate entailment from strict implication. See also Anderson and Belnap (above).)

W. Sellars, 'Presupposing', P. F. Strawson, 'A reply to Mr Sellars', *Philosophical Review*, 1954. (These discuss Strawson's earlier views on presupposition, and its relation to entailment. Cf. also L. Linsky, *Referring*, 1967, chapter 6.)

G. H. von Wright, 'A note on entailment', *Philosophical Quarterly*, 1959. (Comments on Geach above.)

D. Wilson, *Presuppositions and Non-Truth-Conditional Semantics*, Academic Press, 1975. (Rejects logical and pragmatic presuppositions, preferring a non-logical but semantic 'suggestion'.)

Implicature. See IMPLICATION.

Incommensurability. If one person long jumps 7.82 metres and another jumps 24 feet 6 inches, we can work out who jumped the furthest because we can convert from metres to feet and inches, and vice versa – the two systems are commensurable. But, for example, temperature in Fahrenheit and volume in gallons are not – they are incommensurable. KUHN, FEYERABEND and others have argued that scientific revolutions radically change the meanings and contexts of the terms used in the new and old theories, so the theories are incommensurable and cannot be compared or evaluated. See KUHN, PARADIGM, PERSPECTIVISM.

D. Davidson, 'On the very idea of a conceptual scheme' in *Inquiries into Truth and Interpretation*, Oxford UP, 1984, 2nd edn. 2001. (Critical of the idea of incommensurability.)

T. S. Kuhn, *The Structure of Scientific Revolutions*, University of Chicago Press, 1962.

Incomplete symbol. See LOGICAL CONSTRUCTIONS.

Incompleteness. See COMPLETE, GÖDEL'S THEOREMS.

Incongruent or incongruous counterparts. Also called enantio-morphs. Pairs of things differing only as an object and its mirror-image do, or a pair of hands, or opposite spirals. The precise characterization of this difference (probably first attempted by Kant) is difficult, and may be important for studying the nature of space.

> J. Bennett, 'The difference between right and left', *American Philosophical Quarterly*, 1970.

Inconsistent triad. See ANTILOGISM.

Incontinence. Also called acrasia (akrasia), weakness of will. The 'Socratic paradox' that no one errs willingly (for a willing error is not an error) raises the problem whether one can act against one's better judgement, be the judgement moral or prudential, etc. Similarly, can one assent to something against the evidence, or deceive oneself (doxastic incontinence; cf. BAD FAITH)? (The Greek word here translated as 'err' can also mean, more ambiguously, 'goes wrong'.)

> *W. Charlton, *Weakness of Will*, Blackwell, 1988. (General introduction to topic, using ancient and modern discussions.)
> *D. Davidson, *Essays on Actions and Events*, Clarendon Press, 1980. (Includes important 1970 article, 'How is weakness of the will possible?')
> J. Gosling, *The Weakness of the Will*, Routledge, 1990. (1st half historical, 2nd half positive.)
> A. R. Mele, *Irrationality: An Essay on Akrasia, Self-deception, and Self-control*, Oxford UP, 1987. (Treats both action and belief. See Preface to paperback edition (1992) for references to his more recent work, and see bibliography to FEELINGS.)
> G. W. Mortimore (ed.), *Weakness of Will*, Macmillan, 1971. (Selections ancient and modern.)
> S. Stroud, and C. Tappolet (eds), *Weakness of Will and Practical Irrationality*, Clarendon Press, 2003. (Good collection of recent articles.)
> D. Wiggins, 'Weakness of will, commensurability, and the objects of deliberation and desire', *Proceedings of the Aristotelian Society*, 1978–9, reprinted with revisions in his *Needs, Values, Truth*, Blackwell, 1987, and in A. O. Rorty (ed.), *Essays on Aristotle's Ethics*, UCLA Press, 1981. (Fairly difficult.)

Incorrigible. A statement is incorrigible for someone if he cannot be in error in believing or disbelieving it. Whether such statements exist is disputed, but typical candidates are reports of immediate experience like, 'I now seem to see something red.' Incorrigible statements are not the same as necessarily true or false statements. The above example, if true, is only contingently true, and we can make mistakes about necessary statements (e.g. in mathematics). In a weaker (though etymologically more correct) sense a statement is incorrigible if we can be mistaken about it but there is no way of correcting us, e.g. perhaps statements reporting our dreams. (Such statements might be called incorrigible but not infallible.)

A statement is indubitable for someone if he cannot rationally doubt or reject it. I can reject the statement that I seem to see something red, but not, according to Descartes, the statement that I exist. 'Incorrigible' and 'indubitable' are often used more loosely, and even interchangeably. See also FOUNDATIONALISM.

J. L. Mackie, 'Are there any incorrigible empirical statements?', *Australasian Journal of Philosophy*, 1963. (No. Uses 'incorrigible' in weak sense, and 'indubitable' for strong sense.)

R. W. Miller, 'Absolute certainty', *Mind*, 1978. (Defends an analysis of it which, he claims, avoids danger of leading to scepticism.)

R. Warner, 'Incorrigibility', in H. Robinson (ed.), *Objections to Physicalism*, Clarendon, 1993. (Defends modified version of it.)

Independent. See AXIOM.

Indeterminacy. Used in a variety of contexts in philosophy. Quine claims that in translating from one language to another, multiple meanings are possible for any element in the language. For more on the indeterminacy of translation, see TRANSLATION. Legal indeterminacy is the idea that any ruling a judge may produce can be justified by legal arguments from existing law and precedent. If only one legal decision were possible, there should never be split decisions. Both the indeterminacy of translation and legal indeterminacy can be seen as examples of a more general idea, that any phenomenon can be explained by a multiplicity of theories.

For quantum indeterminacy, see Heisenberg's Uncertainty Principle in CAUSATION.

Indeterminism. See FREEWILL.

Indexicals. See TOKEN-REFLEXIVES.

Indicator terms. See TOKEN-REFLEXIVES.

Indifference (principle of). Also called principle of insufficient reason (different from Leibniz's principle of SUFFICIENT REASON). Principle that if we have no reason to expect one rather than another of n mutually exclusive and collectively exhaustive possibilities to be realized, we should assign a probability of 1/n to each of them. The principle's validity is disputed. See also PROBABILITY.

> W. C. Kneale, *Probability and Induction*, Oxford UP, 1949, § 31, 34. (Criticizes principle, but defends variant of it. Cf. S. Blackburn, *Reason and Prediction*, Cambridge UP, 1973, chapter 6 for another defence.)

Indirect realism. See DIRECT REALISM.

Indiscernibility of identicals. See LEIBNIZ'S LAW.

Individualism. In recent philosophy of mind and psychology, this has come to denote a view very similar to INTERNALISM in its main sense, holding that the content of an individual's thought or experience depends simply on that individual, and does not logically (though of course it may causally) depend on things in the individual's environment. Sometimes, however, a distinction is made between individualism as a doctrine about mental states and internalism as a doctrine about the contents of those states, and it is claimed that individualism does not entail internalism (Egan 1992). Methodological individualism covers various views to the effect that facts about societies are explainable in terms of facts about individuals, while methodological holism denies this.

> T. Burge, 'Individualism and the mental', *Midwest Studies in Philosophy*, vol. iv, Minnesota UP, 1979. (Cf. also his 'Individualism and psychology', *Philosophical Review*, 1986. Burge introduces individualism in this sense, arguing against it. M. Davies, 'Individualism and perceptual content' and G. Segal, 'Defence of a reasonable individualism', both in *Mind*, 1991, respectively defend and attack Burge's position.)
>
> F. Egan, 'Must psychology be individualistic?', *Philosophical Review*, 1991. (Attacks both Burge and Fodor, and claims the answer depends on the goal of the theorizing.)
>
> F. Egan, 'Individualism, computation, and perceptual content', *Mind*, 1992.
>
> J. A. Fodor, *Psychosemantics*, MIT Press, 1987, chapter 2. (Defends individualism in psychology. See also his 'A modal argument for narrow

content', *Journal of Philosophy*, 1991, for a distinction between individualism and internalism.)

D.-H. Ruben, *The Metaphysics of the Social World*, RKP, 1985. (See particularly pp. 150ff. for methodological individualism. See also K. R. Popper, *The Open Society and its Enemies*, Routledge, 1945, chapter 14.)

Individuals. There seem to be four main senses:

(i) whatever can be counted, one by one ('individuated'), or can be talked of or referred to (logical subjects: see MEANING). In this sense all particulars (see UNIVERSALS) are individuals, but not vice versa. Beauty is an individual. We can talk about it and distinguish it from other things, but it is a universal and not a particular (it seems not to exist 'all at once' like an object in space and time). Tennis is an individual, though not a particular, nor perhaps a universal ('tennis' does not seem to behave like words in '-ity', '-ness', '-hood', etc.). 'Individual' in this first main sense resembles 'OBJECT' when the 'existence' strand of that word is dominant.

(ii) In logic individuals are contrasted with predicates or functions (i.e. universals). They are what 'individual VARIABLES' range over, and so they are whatever the subject of a logical expression can refer to – but the expression must belong to the first-order (or 'restricted') predicate CALCULUS, and must not appear only in the 'extended' predicate calculus (where predicates can be referred to).

(iii) Same as 'particular'.

(iv) What cannot be further divided. On this view, absolutely specific properties will be individuals, e.g. if red can be divided into crimson and scarlet but scarlet cannot be further divided then scarlet will be an individual.

(ii) has affinities with both (i) and (iii), and the senses are not sharply distinguished. (iii) is the oldest sense.

R. Jackson, 'Locke's distinction between primary and secondary qualities', *Mind*, 1929, reprinted in C. B. Martin and D. M. Armstrong (eds), *Locke and Berkeley*, Macmillan, 1968. (Another individuals/particulars distinction.)

F. Sommers, 'Predicability', in M. Black (ed.), *Philosophy in America*, Allen and Unwin, 1965, particularly pp. 277 ff. (Defines individuals, in sense perhaps nearest to (iii), in terms of what can be predicated of them.)

P. F Strawson, *Individuals*, Methuen, 1959. (See particularly pp. 226–7, and his 'Categories' in O. P. Wood and G. Pitcher (eds), *Ryle*, Macmillan, 1970, pp. 196, 199. Cf. also Strawson's *Introduction to Logical Theory*, Methuen, 1952, p. 144.)

J. Valberg, 'Improper singular terms', *Proceedings of the Aristotelian Society*, 1970–1, particularly pp. 136–41. (Some difficulties in defining 'individual'.)

Indubitable. See INCORRIGIBLE.

Induction. In its widest sense, any rational process where from premises about some things of a certain kind a conclusion is drawn about some or all of the remaining things of that kind. An argument is inductive in a narrow or strict sense (to which the rest of this article is confined) if it claims to draw such a conclusion from such premises directly in a single step (as opposed, e.g. to Popper's method: see below). If this step consists in arguing that because some (or all observed) As are Bs therefore further (or all) As are Bs, we have simple or enumerative induction. Those who accept that induction is, given certain conditions, a rational process are often called inductivists.

The traditional form of simple induction, 'All observed As are Bs, so all As are Bs', can be regarded as a special case (where n = 100) of the general form (where n ranges from 0 to 100) 'n per cent of observed As are Bs so n per cent of all As are Bs'. Of course it will often be impossible for arithmetical reasons for the total population of As to have exactly the same ratio of Bs as the sample, but this does not affect the general idea. Some writers, notably J. S. Mill, think that inductive inference goes from particulars to particulars, i.e. to further instances, not to a generalization. Others think a conclusion about particulars can be reached only through a generalization, i.e. that one can only argue from 'All (or, for some value of n, n per cent of) observed ravens have been black' to 'The next raven will be black' by using the intermediate conclusion 'All (or n per cent of all) ravens are black'. Of course the smaller n is, the weaker the argument will be.

Anti-inductivists say that induction is not a rational process, and that inductive arguments in fact work in other ways. They may claim that inductive arguments are really DEDUCTIVE arguments, some of whose premises have been suppressed; if these premises were made explicit the deductive nature of the argument would become clear. Alternatively, they may claim that inductive arguments really work by the hypothetico-deductive method, whereby a hypothesis is set up and conclusions are deduced from it and tested against experience: if the conclusions turn out false the hypothesis is rejected. Inductivists can also use this method, but anti-inductivists, notably Popper, believe that the hypothesis cannot be directly supported: all we can do is try to falsify it.

Inductivists and anti-inductivists agree nowadays that no formal rules can be given for reaching (as opposed to confirming) the right hypothesis (cf. PSYCHOLOGISM), which does not imply that ways of reaching it cannot be assessed as rational. What distinguishes inductivists is that they think the hypothesis, however acquired, may be supported directly by evidence (not merely indirectly, by its surviving attempts to falsify it). Anti-inductivists tend to think that an INFERENCE, or a step in argument, is 'deductive or defective' (A. C. MacIntyre).

Hypotheses about objects that are not directly observable, such as electrons or magnetic fields, are sometimes called transcendent hypotheses. They cannot be reached or directly confirmed by simple induction. The process by which they are reached or confirmed has sometimes been called secondary induction (Kneale), especially when it is regarded as rationally assessable and not merely a matter of psychology. 'Secondary induction' can also refer to any induction whose premises themselves result from induction. We might conclude inductively that all ravens have feathers, and that all swans do, and then conclude by a further induction from ravens and swans that all birds do.

Much of inductive logic, i.e. the general study of induction, consists in asking whether induction has any place in scientific enquiry, and, if so, what rules can be elaborated to govern its use as a method of CONFIRMATION. The problem of induction has traditionally been the problem of justifying not so much particular rules as induction in general, and especially simple induction (sometimes by the backhanded method of reducing it to disguised deduction; cf. the first type of anti-inductivist above, and (ii) below). However, a major problem for inductivists has also been provided by Goodman's 'grue' paradox (see CONFIRMATION); this raises the question what counts as induction, i.e. what conclusion is the relevant inductive conclusion with respect to some given evidence. The main attempts to justify simple induction are as follows.

(i) Mathematical facts about the relations between samples and their parent populations are used.

(ii) Some grand overall premise is sought which can turn inductive arguments into deductive ones: that the future resembles the past, that nature is uniform, that every event has a cause, and that the variety in the universe is finite in amount, have been favourite candidates. The difficulties have concerned formulating these premises (how closely must the future resemble the past? What counts as a cause?) and then justifying them. (ii) is now unpopular.

(iii) Perhaps induction can be used to justify itself. This seems circular, but is the circularity only apparent?

(iv) The pragmatic or practicalist approach has it that induction cannot indeed be validated, in the sense of being shown to be likely to work, but it can be rationally justified as a practical policy because every alternative is less rational; the claim is here that induction is likely to work if any method is. 'Vindicated' is sometimes used here. We do not know what the actual universe is like. In some possible universes induction would work better than other methods, while in some (notably, chaotic ones) no method would work. But in no possible universe, it is claimed, would any method work better than induction. Infinitely many methods are possible, but we must distinguish alternatives which deliberately predict results conflicting with inductive predictions (negative induction or counter-induction) from those which are merely indifferent to induction (e.g. appeal to soothsayers). The former are easier to deal with. The 'long-term' problem of whether a certain method is rational if given an indefinitely long time to work in differs from the 'short-term', and more interesting, problem of whether it is rational when we are only interested in a finite time ahead.

(v) Induction may not need justification because it is a going concern. There are generally acknowledged criteria of inductive soundness. We may well study in detail what they are, but it is senseless to reject them because they are our touchstone for rejecting any inductive arguments, and so we should be appealing to them even in rejecting them (cf. PARADIGM CASE ARGUMENT).

(vi) (A strengthened form of (v).) Induction not only is a going concern but is inevitably so, since it is necessarily involved in one way or another in all rational thinking and behaviour; but we cannot abandon it, whether we want to or not. This is a form of TRANSCENDENTAL ARGUMENT.

Various processes called 'induction' must be distinguished from induction proper. Intuitive induction is a process where particular cases serve as psychological causes rather than rational justifications for generalizations whose justification is a priori. If we notice that something coloured is extended, this may make us realize rather than infer that all coloured things are extended. Proof by mathematical, recursive or course-of-values induction is the process whereby we prove that something holds for every term in a series (e.g. for every natural number) by proving that it holds for the first term, and that it holds for the successor of any term for which it holds. Cf. also DEFINITION by induction. 'Mathematical induction' is different from the use of simple induction as a preliminary move in mathematics. A mathematician might argue, 'All examined even numbers are the sum of two primes, so (perhaps) all even numbers are', and then try to prove this conclusion. Perfect induction or induction by complete enumeration (not by simple enumeration, which is simple induction) consists in asserting, e.g. 'All the chairs in this room are wooden' after checking them one by one. The 'inductive leap' consists simply in assuming that the chairs checked are all there are in the room. See also CONFIRMATION, PROBABILITY, CAUSATION.

S. F. Barker, 'Must every inference be either deductive or inductive?', in M. Black (ed.), *Philosophy in America*, Allen and Unwin, 1965.

M. Black, 'Self-supporting inductive arguments', *Journal of Philosophy*, 1958. P. Achinstein, 'The circularity of a self-supporting inductive argument', *Analysis*, vol. 22, 1962. (Both reprinted in P. H. Nidditch (ed.), *The Philosophy of Science*, Oxford UP, 1968. Cf. further debate between Black and Achinstein in *Analysis*, vol. 23, 1962–3, and see R. B. Braithwaite, *Scientific Explanation*, Harper 1953, chapter 8. All these are in Swinburne (below). Cf. also Mellor (below).)

S. Blackburn, *Reason and Prediction*, Cambridge UP, 1973. (Attempts justification by version of principle of indifference, and offers solution to 'grue' paradox.)

P. Edwards, 'Bertrand Russell's doubts about induction', *Mind*, 1949, reprinted in A. Flew (ed.), *Logic and Language*, vol. 1, Blackwell 1951 and in Swinburne below. (Claims induction needs no defence.)

N. Goodman, 'Seven strictures on similarity', in L. Foster and J. W. Swanson (eds), *Experience and Theory*, Duckworth, 1970. (Induction and resemblance.)

W. Kneale, *Probability and Induction*, Oxford UP, 1949. (Part 2 discusses various kinds of induction and pseudo-induction (intuitive, etc.).)

A. C. MacIntyre, 'Hume on "is" and "ought"', *Philosophical Review*, 1959. (See p. 453 for 'deductive or defective', a disjunction which MacIntyre rejects.)

D. H. Mellor, 'The warrant of induction' in his *Matters of Metaphysics*, Cambridge UP, 1991. (Inaugural lecture defending the existence of such a warrant.)

K. Popper, *The Logic of Scientific Discovery*, Hutchinson, 1959 (German original 1934). (Advocates hypothetico-deductive method, but based solely on falsification, without confirmation. Cf. Popper's 'personal report' in C. A. Mace (ed.), *British Philosophy in the Mid-Century*, 1957, reprinted in Popper's *Conjectures and Refutations*, RKP, 1963, chapter 1; and cf. his *Objective Knowledge*, Oxford UP, 1972, chapter 1.)

H. Reichenbach, *The Theory of Probability*, California UP, 1949 (German original 1935), final section. (Vindication of induction from point of view of frequency theory of PROBABILITY; cf. also his *Experience and Prediction*, Chicago UP, 1938, § 38–40, and also H. Feigl, 'De principiis non disputandum ... ?', in M. Black (ed.), *Philosophical Analysis*, Cornell UP, 1950, particularly pp. 129–39.)

B. Russell, *Problems of Philosophy*, Howe University Library, 1912, chapter 6. (Classic statement of problem of induction.)

R. Swinburne (ed.), *The Justification of Induction*, Oxford UP, 1974. (Includes several of above items, and also discussions of pragmatic approach by W. C. Salmon and J. W. Lenz.)

J. O. Wisdom, *Foundations of Inference in Natural Science*, Methuen, 1952. (Follows Popper in general. Chapter 24 offers vindication. Chapter 23 criticizes mathematical justification of simple induction.)

Infallibilism. The view that to be said to know that p, it must be that one cannot be wrong about p, or (a view rejected by most) that one knows that p only if one's belief that p is based on evidence that logically entails p. Contrasted with FALLIBILISM. See also EPISTEMOLOGY, GETTIER.

Inference. Assertion on the basis of something else. 'All cats are black, so this cat is black' represents an inference, though 'inference' can refer to the conclusion, 'This cat is black', as well as to the process. 'If all cats are black then this cat is black', where neither antecedent nor consequent is actually asserted, represents an IMPLICATION. Inferences need not necessarily be DEDUCTIVE (for J. S. Mill they cannot be, since deduction does not represent a substantial enough transition of thought).

In immediate inference, a conclusion is drawn from a single premise, especially by OBVERSION, CONVERSION, CONTRAPOSITION and INVERSION. In mediate inference, two or more independent premises are involved, as in a syllogism. This distinction, however, is not exact. See also INDUCTION.

M. Deutscher, 'A causal account of inferring', in R. Brown and C. D. Rollins (eds), *Contemporary Philosophy in Australia*, Allen and Unwin/Humanities, 1969.

J. S. Mill, *A System of Logic*, Longmans, Green, 1843, book 2, chapter 1. (Nature of inference.)

G. Ryle, '"If", "so", and "because"', in M. Black (ed.), *Philosophical Analysis*, Cornell UP, 1950. (Inference and implication.)

Inference to the best explanation. Sometimes called the method of hypothesis. Rooted in ABDUCTION, a method of reasoning central to the logic of scientific discovery which starts with facts and then seeks the best explanation of them. It has become increasingly popular in other areas, including artificial intelligence, the theory of knowledge and the various attempts to defeat epistemological SCEPTICISM. Different models of inference to the best explanation appeal to the most likely or the most aesthetically appealing hypothesis, with competing models of what is to count as the 'best' explanation.

G. Harman, 'The inference to the best explanation', *The Philosophical Review*, 74:1, 1965.

P. Lipton, *Inference to the Best Explanation*, London: Routledge 2001, (2nd edition).

Infinity. See METAPHYSICS.

Information, philosophy of. The study of philosophical issues arising in computer science and information technology, though it has its origins in the logical theory of information developed by PEIRCE.

L. Floridi, 'What is the philosophy of information?', *Metaphilosophy*, 2002.

Innate. Cf. A PRIORI throughout, and especially for the relations between it and 'innate'. 'Innate' means 'inborn' but what being innate amounts to is complex and disputed. Basically the innate is what is prior to experience, where the priority is the chronological or psychological one of acquisition rather than the epistemological one of justification. But an innate idea or concept may be any of the following: (i) an idea we can acquire without our being presented with an instance in experience, and without having to construct it from ideas so presented (as perhaps we construct unicorn from horse and horn); (ii) an idea we must so acquire, if we acquire it at all, since experience could not supply us with it, e.g. the ideas of validity or negation; (iii) an idea we can acquire without any experience at all, or never acquire but have always had; substance and cause may be examples; (iv) an idea we can apply without using experience; we do not use the senses to find whether an argument is valid – but perhaps this sort of idea might be better called a priori.

Similarly a belief or proposition may be innate in any of several senses: (i) a proposition we believe from birth; (ii) one we believe, or may come to believe as soon as we acquire the relevant ideas or concepts – for instance, once we acquire the ideas of red and green we may believe that nothing can be simultaneously red and green all over (cf. the relatively a priori under A PRIORI); (iii) one we assent to as soon as we are presented with it; (iv) one we cannot understand without believing it; and (v) one we cannot learn from experience but nevertheless do believe. Any of these may be called a priori to the extent that 'know' may properly be substituted for 'believe' or 'assent to'. But this cannot always be done. An innate belief may be false, and even when it is true we may require the support of observation before we can properly be said to know it. However, Leibniz thought that our innate beliefs must amount to knowledge, or God would be deceiving us, and sometimes an evolutionist justification is offered for claiming that at least most of our innate beliefs must be true, or we would not have survived the course of evolution, so that such beliefs do in general amount to knowledge, and are a priori to the extent that we do not need to appeal to current experience to justify them – though evolution could indeed produce a false belief (Quinton, pp. 133–4). In the mid-to-late twentieth century the appeal to innateness has taken a different turn with Chomsky's claim that we have an innate tendency to learn and use certain grammatical structures more easily than others, and could not otherwise learn our native language as quickly as we do. Nativism is the view that some ideas are innate.

B. Beakley and P. Ludlow (eds), *The Philosophy of Mind: Classical Problems/ Contemporary Issues*, MIT Press, 1992. (Part v has relevant items.)

N. Block (ed.), *Readings in the Philosophy of Psychology*, vol. 2, Harvard UP and Methuen, 1981. (Contains discussions, some with replies, mainly on Chomsky, etc.)

*N. Chomsky, *Reflections on Language*, Maurice Temple Smith and Fontana, 1976. (Fairly elementary exposition of his ideas.)

J. Locke, *Essay Concerning Human Understanding*, 1689, Book 1. (Attacks some versions of innate ideas. Criticized by G. W. Leibniz, *New Essays Concerning Human Understanding*, 1763, written earlier. See chapter 2 of Stich.)

*J. Lyons, *Chomsky*, Fontana, 1970, expanded 1977. (Elementary introduction to his ideas.)

R. Nozick, *The Nature of Rationality*, Princeton UP, 1993. See particularly chapter iv. (Offers partial evolutionist justification for treating innate beliefs as true.)

*A. Quinton, *The Nature of Things*, Routledge, 1973, pp. 132–4. (The innate, the a priori and the instinctive.)

S. P. Stich (ed.), *Innate Ideas*, California UP, 1975. (Discussions both of older material and of Chomsky.)

Inscription. A written token (see UNIVERSALS). Inscriptivism (inscriptionism) is any view making significant use of inscriptions, e.g. the inscriptional theory of intentionality explains intentionality (see INTENSIONALITY) in terms of relations between utterers and token sentences (considered as written, for convenience).

W. V. O. Quine, *Word and Object*, Wiley, 1960, pp. 214–15.

Institutional theory (of art). The theory, developed by George Dickie, partly from work by Arthur Danto, that what makes something a work of art is not anything to do with its content or intrinsic nature, but whether it has been deemed a candidate for appreciation by the social institution of the Artworld, the whole network of organizations and people including theatre, galleries, critics concerned with art. This definition of a work of art faced criticisms of circularity, and has been revised and refined by Dickie in successive works.

A. C. Danto, 'The Artworld', *The Journal of Philosophy*, 1964, also in J. Margolis, *Philosophy Looks at the Arts*, Temple UP, 3rd edn, 1987.
G. Dickie, *Art and the Aesthetic: An Institutional Analysis*, Cornell UP, 1974, and *Art Circle: A Theory of Art*, Spectrum Press, 1997.

Instrumentalism. Theory that scientific laws and theories are instruments for predicting observable phenomena, and are therefore to be judged by their usefulness and not classified as propositions which can be true or false. Somewhat similar to CONVENTIONALISM. 'Instrumentalism' is also used for a development of PRAGMATISM by Dewey, and for the view that values (generally, or in some sphere, e.g. aesthetics) are instrumental (e.g. in promoting satisfaction); see GOOD.

I. Hacking, *Representing and Intervening: Introducing Topics in the Philosophy of Natural Science*, Cambridge UP, 1983. (Discusses scientific objectivity ('representing') and experimental method ('intervening').)
K. R. Popper, *The Logic of Scientific Discovery*, Hutchinson, 1959 (German original, 1934), p. 423 (Critical, with references.)
S. E. Toulmin, *The Philosophy of Science*, Hutchinson, 1953. (Example of instrumentalist outlook.)

Insufficient reason (principle of). See INDIFFERENCE.

Intensionality and intentionality. Historically these terms have different origins, but whether there is really one notion or two underlying modern uses of them is disputed, and if two, how they are related. 'Non-extensional' is often used for 'intensional', perhaps to avoid this question. 'Extension' and its derivatives are always spelt with 's'. So far as they are different notions 'intensional' primarily concerns the sphere of logic and 'intentional' that of philosophy of mind. This entry treats them in order.

Intuitively, extensions can be thought of as the extents which certain kinds of terms range over and intensions as that in virtue of which they do so. Extensions correspond roughly to classes, and intensions to properties. A property like that of being a person determines at most one class. There is only one class of persons, though it may have sub-classes. But one and the same class may correspond to more than one property. The class of ruminants, for example, is the same as the class of cloven-hoofed animals. A class itself can be defined in extension or in intension; see UNIVERSALS.

So long as we are interested only in a group of objects and not in the properties in terms of which they are viewed, we can substitute for our first description of them any other description that picks out the same class (e.g. 'cloven-hoofed things' for 'ruminants'), and what we say will remain true, if it was true with the first description. If all ruminants are mammals, then all cloven-hoofed things are mammals. This is expressed by saying we can substitute the second description *salva veritate* (lit.: 'preserving truth'). Similarly if we study propositions only in respect of their TRUTH-VALUES (as logicians often do; cf. truth-FUNCTIONS), then for any proposition another with the same truth-value can be substituted *salva veritate*. Therefore, truth-values count among extensions. Propositions themselves, which cannot be substituted like this when our interests are less restricted, count among intensions, which are sometimes called intensional objects (but 'extensional objects' is not used).

Extensions are simpler than intensions, in that, to speak loosely and roughly, they concern things as they are in themselves rather than as picked out in terms of the various properties they have. Many logicians therefore prefer extensions, and would like to dispense with intensions, by translating statements containing intensional notions into statements free from them. The view that this can be done is called the extensionality thesis (cf. LEIBNIZ'S LAW) and is defended by LOGICAL ATOMISTS, logical POSITIVISTS, nominalists and, in general, those who prefer a sparse and austere universe. It is attacked by those who accept the richness and complexity of the universe at its face value and as indispensable. Its defenders, notably Quine, also argue that if it is not accepted then no coherent system of logic can be elaborated, i.e. they claim that there is no intensional logic. This view can itself be called a version of the extensionality thesis.

If, in a certain context, a referring phrase cannot, *salva veritate*, be replaced by another phrase referring to the same thing, the context is called opaque. Otherwise it is transparent. (Cf. MODALITIES on the *de dicto/de re* distinction). For example, if there are just nine planets we can say 'The number of the planets is the number of the planets' and 'The number of the planets is nine', but, it is claimed, while we can prefix 'necessarily', to the first statement we cannot prefix it to the second – there might have been some other number of planets. 'Necessarily' generates an opaque context. So far opacity is in effect the same as intensionality, though applied more narrowly. Contexts can be opaque. Properties, etc. can be called intensional, but not opaque. Perhaps opacity should be called an effect of intensionality.

Intentional situations may be thought of as those where a relation appears to exist but does not really, as 'want' in 'I want a unicorn' seems to relate me to a unicorn, though there are no unicorns for me to relate to (but there are difficulties: see next paragraph). This happens primarily in certain psychological contexts, and the basic problem concerning intentionality has been to define it so that it picks out and explains the peculiarities of just these psychological contexts. Sometimes, as we have seen with the 'number of planets' example, the truth of statements about an object depends on how the object is described. This is especially so with psychological notions like believing, thinking, wanting. Cicero and Tully are one man, but Smith may believe that Cicero is an orator without believing that Tully is one (though he believes of Tully that he is one, since his belief concerns that man (Cicero) who in fact is also Tully); cf. BELIEF on this use of the *de re/de dicto* distinction. Similarly he may believe that Hitler was hanged without believing that Hitler suffered the same fate as Goebbels, even if Goebbels was hanged, since he may not know this. Also the object may not exist. Smith may believe that Apollo is an orator, or that unicorns live in Africa. This gives an alternative criterion for opacity to the above substitutional one. Roughly, a context is opaque if it carries no implications about the existence of the thing it mentions. 'He saw Apollo' is transparent, but 'He worships Apollo' is opaque, since Apollo need not exist for him to do so. But on the former criterion 'He worships Apollo' is transparent, since, if Apollo is a beast, 'He worships a beast' must follow. But the substitutional criterion itself has its complexities. If Oedipus brought it about that Laius died he brought it about that his father died, so 'brought it about that' generates a transparent context; but it generates an opaque one in that one cannot substitute just any truth for 'Laius died', as one could after 'It is true that'. Since Brentano, who brought these issues to light and revived some medieval terminology, objects like Cicero, Apollo and unicorns, in these contexts, are called intentional objects, and are sometimes said to have intentional inexistence (existence in the mind, or as an object of the mind's activity). One can perhaps think of them as what the mind is intent upon, though this may be historically inaccurate (Kneale). Sometimes, as with Cicero but not Apollo, the intentional object corresponds to a real object. The relations between the two are then not clear. If they are identical, the intentional object of Smith's belief should also be Tully. If they are not identical, the intentional object seems to be merely in the mind, but this is unsatisfactory, since the belief, in both the Apollo and Cicero cases, claims to be about something outside the mind. The whole notion of intentional objects is thus difficult (cf. THINKING), and various theories exist about their nature and reality.

It is tempting to pick out the psychological contexts as those in which no assumptions are made about the existence or non-existence of the things mentioned, i.e. which are opaque by the second criterion above. Two sorts of difficulty arise here. First it is not clear how far the 'psychological' extends. 'John is shooting at unicorns' mentions a physical activity, though with a psychological aspect. Since, on one interpretation, it does not imply that there are any unicorns it is on that interpretation presumably intentional. On the other hand 'John knows (realizes, admits) there are unicorns' is presumably psychological and yet does imply there are unicorns. ('Know' is a 'factive' verb: see EPISTEMOLOGY). Moreover, perception and feeling pain are surely psychological but do not seem always to involve ways of looking at things, or assumptions about existence, i.e. they do not seem to be psychological in the way required.

The second difficulty is that whatever features are picked out to mark off the psychological contexts as intentional seem to apply also to many clearly non-psychological contexts, e.g. modal ones (see MODALITIES) 'Possibly unicorns are vegetarian' need not imply that there are unicorns or that there are not, and so seems to be intentional. It is this that raises doubts about the distinction between intentionality and intensionality (since modal contexts are agreed to be intensional).

However intentionality is to be defined, questions involving it have been central in recent philosophy of mind with its emphasis on analysing the CONTENT of mental states and its discussions of INTERNALISM AND EXTERNALISM.

Intentions in the ordinary sense form just one kind of intentional context, and have no special privilege in their connection with the intentionality here at issue. See also MEANING, THINKING, MIND.

*T. Crane, *The Mechanical Mind. A Philosophical Introduction to Minds, Machines and Mental Representations*, Penguin, 1995, chapter 1, particularly pp. 31ff. (Elementary introduction to intentionality and to its distinction from intensionality.)

P. T. Geach, 'Teleological explanation', in S. Körner (ed.), *Explanation*, 1975, particularly pp. 83–4. ('Brought it about that', etc.)

A. Kenny, *Action, Emotion and Will*, RKP, 1963. (Chapters 9 ff. discuss 'objects' of emotions, etc., referring to Chisholm, etc. Spells with 's'.)

Proceedings of the Aristotelian Society, supplementary vol., 1968. (Includes two relevant symposia: J. O. Urmson (easiest) and L. J. Cohen, 'Criteria of intensionality', equate intentionality with intensionality and discuss criteria stemming from R. Chisholm. W. C. Kneale and A. N. Prior, 'Intentionality and intensionality', distinguishing these notions and discuss various problems, including the relations of these notions to nominalism. Kneale includes historical material, for more of which see M. Spencer, 'Why the 's' in intension?', *Mind*, 1971.)

W. V. O. Quine, 'Reference and modality' in *From a Logical Point of View*, 2nd (revised) edn, Harvard UP/Harper and Row, 1961, reprinted with some (difficult) discussions following from it in L. Linsky (ed.), *Reference and Modality*, Oxford UP, 1971. (Opacity and its effects on modal logic and intensional logic in general.)

R. Scruton, 'Intensional and intentional objects', *Proceedings of the Aristotelian Society*, 1970–1. (Separates them and makes further distinctions within intentionality.)

J. R. Searle, *Intentionality: An Essay in the Philosophy of Mind*, Cambridge UP, 1983. (General discussion, distinguishing sharply between 's' and 't' versions; see its index.)

L. S. Stebbing, *A Modern Elementary Logic*, Methuen, 1943. (Chapter 6 discusses relevant terminology in traditional logic.)

Intentional fallacy. The fallacy, according to Wimsatt and Beardsley, of thinking that knowledge of the artist's intentions and, more generally, of the artist's biography, are relevant to understanding a work of art. The artist's intentions, expressed separately from the work of art, have no special status in determining its meaning: the work is public, not the artist's private possession. Wimsatt and Beardsley were pioneers of the 'New Criticism', which claims that a work of art stands on its own, can be objectively evaluated and understood, independently of its origins or its effects (see AFFECTIVE FAL-LACY). Authorial authority was also later challenged by Roland Barthes and by the post-modernists.

R. Barthes, 'The death of the author', *Aspen*, 1967, reprinted in his *Image-Music-Text*, Noonday, 1977.

F. Cioffi, 'Intention and interpretation in criticism' in Cyril Barrett (ed.), *Collected Papers on Aesthetics*, 1965, also in Margolis. (Many interesting examples, and a subtle discussion of the alleged fallacy).

A. Savile, 'The place of intention in the concept of art', *Proceedings of the Aristotelian Society*, 1969, reprinted in H. Osborne, *Aesthetics*, Oxford UP, 1972. (Intention important as it distinguishes art from what is not art.)

W. K. Wimsatt and M.C. Beardsley, 'The intentional fallacy', originally in the *Sewanee Review*, Summer 1946, reprinted in many places, for example, W. K. Wimsatt, *The Verbal Icon*, Methuen, 1970, chapter 1; or D. Lodge (ed.), *20th Century Literary Criticism*, Pearson, 1972; or J. Margolis, *Philosophy Looks at the Arts*, Temple UP, 3rd edn, 1987.

Intentionality. See INTENSIONALITY AND INTENTIONALITY.

Interactionism. The theory, most closely associated with DES-CARTES, that body and mind, though two different substances, can interact with each other. Physical events can cause mental events, and vice versa.

Internalism and externalism. A set of related dichotomies that apply in various spheres, notably philosophy of mind, epistemology and ethical theory. In general, internalism about something analyses it in terms confined to a certain relevant sphere, while externalism insists that the analysis must involve terms outside that sphere. In philosophy of mind, the debate concerns the contents of various mental states. Internalism treats them as confined within the person who has them and as independent of anything outside, so that to find whether a person has a given mental state we need only examine that person, while externalism insists that for at least some cases this may not be so, notably for thinking, believing, etc., where it may quote Putnam's slogan, '"Meanings" just ain't in the head!' Putnam imagines a world called Twin Earth. This is exactly like Earth (and is inhabited by counterparts or doppelgangers of ourselves) except that the liquid in its seas and lakes, etc., is not H_2O but has a different chemical composition, XYZ, but this can only be detected by scientists, since the liquid in ordinary situations behaves just like water. For Putnam, the liquid cannot then be water, but we could call it 'twater'. Twin Earthians, however, call it 'water', i.e. they use the same sound 'water' for it, since all the physical facts about them, including the sounds they utter, are the same as those true of us in the corresponding circumstances; 'water' is our word for their liquid, and they would only utter 'twater' if they envisaged some further Twin Twin Earth. Now suppose that Smith, on Earth, thinks, 'Water is wet'. His doppelganger on Twin Earth will also have a thought he will express as 'Water is wet', but he will be thinking not of water but of twater, the only liquid he has met.

Similarly, externalism claims, if I have never heard of, say, Vesuvius, and have had no kind of contact with it, then I cannot be thinking of Vesuvius, even if I have a mental picture that happens to resemble Vesuvius closely and I use the sound 'Vesuvius' to name it. In each case, for externalism, what one is thinking of depends essentially on something outside the thinker. Externalism grounds an apparent objection to the IDENTITY THEORY OF MIND, for if thoughts or sensations depend essentially on things outside the thinker, how can they be identical with states of the brain, which do not in the relevant sense depend on anything external?

For internal and external realism see REALISM.

For the epistemological sense of internalism and externalism see EPISTEMOLOGY.

In ethics, 'internalism' has been used of the view that reasons for acting, and especially moral requirements, must be capable of providing motivations for action if they are to be such; and of the view that they do provide such motivations. Externalism denies this need. Various versions of the distinction exist.

See also CONTENT, INTENSIONALITY AND INTENTIONALITY, INDIVIDUALISM, MIND.

T. Burge, 'Individualism and the mental', *Midwest Studies in Philosophy*, vol. iv, Minnesota UP, 1979. (Cf. also his 'Individualism and psychology', *Philosophical Review*, 1986. Burge is a pioneer in advocating externalism in philosophy of mind.)

S. Darwall, *Impartial Reason*, Cornell UP, 1983, particularly chapter 5. (Internalism and externalism in ethics. See also D. Brink, *Moral Realism and the Foundations of Ethics*, Cambridge UP, 1989, particularly chapter 3.)

R. Jay Wallace, 'How to argue about practical reason', *Mind*, 1990. (See p. 356 for ethical sense of 'internalism'.)

C. Macdonald, 'Weak externalism and mind-body identity', *Mind*, 1990. (Uses one version of strong/weak distinction to claim externalism is compatible with one version of identity theory of mind.)

C. McGinn, *Mental Content*, Blackwell, 1989. (Defends one kind of weak externalism and draws some implications. Cf. also review by D. Owens in *Mind*, 1990.)

H. Putnam, 'The meaning of "meaning"', in his *Mind, Language and Reality*, vol. II, Cambridge UP, 1975. (Putnam and Burge are pioneers of the main philosophy of mind debate in its modern form, though it has earlier roots. For slogan, see p. 227.)

Intersubjective. Something is intersubjective if there are ways of reaching agreement about it, even though it may not be independent of the human mind (and hence not objective), e.g. the hypothesis that a certain chemical tastes like pineapple might be intersubjectively testable. Intersubjectivity is usually contrasted with subjectivity rather than with objectivity, which it may include. See also SUBJECTIVISM.

Intervening variables. See LOGICAL CONSTRUCTIONS.

Intrinsic and extrinsic. In metaphysics, an 'extrinsic' view of identity holds that whether two apparently different things are in fact identical may depend on the existence or not of some further thing, while an 'intrinsic' view denies any such dependence. Hobbes's 'ship of Theseus' problem arises here: Theseus' ship was preserved, but gradually repaired plank by plank until all the planks had been replaced. The old planks were then gathered together and reconstituted into a ship. Which ship was the original? A related problem arises in philosophy of mind. For instance, suppose that after you die someone with all your memories and characteristics, etc., appears on Mars: will it be you? It may be tempting to say yes – but then what if two or more such people appear? As they are not identical with each other they cannot all be identical with you (assuming identity is TRANSITIVE), and then it may seem arbitrary to say that any of them is.

P. Mackie, 'Essence, origin and bare identity', *Mind*, 1987. (Defends what is in effect an 'intrinsic' view of identity, drawing some implications of doing so. Cf. discussion by B. Garrett in *Mind*, 1988, and Mackie's reply in *Mind*, 1989.)

H. Noonan, 'The closest continuer theory of identity', *Inquiry*, 1985. (Attacks this 'extrinsic' view of identity – for which see R. Nozick, *Philosophical Explanations*, Harvard UP, Oxford UP, 1981, chapter 1 – defending a rival 'intrinsic' one.)

Intuition. Generally a direct relation between the mind and some object, analogous to what common sense thinks is the relation between us and something we see unambiguously in a clear light.

Bergson contrasts intuition as a means of knowing reality as it is in itself with intellect as a means by which we manipulate reality for purposes of action.

What we are said to intuit may be objects not accessible to the senses (numbers, universals, God, etc.), or truths, and intuitions have been divided into 'intuitions of' in the former case and 'intuitions that' in the latter. The emphasis is on the directness of the relation, free from any influence of the environment or interpretation. Hence Kant used 'intuition' for our relation to sensible objects too, so far as this was considered as abstracted from anything contributed by the mind. Intuition thus considered has something in common with Russell's 'acquaintance' (cf. EPISTEMOLOGY), Locke claimed that we have intuitive knowledge of our own existence, Husserl that we have it of essences and Spinoza that we have it of elementary mathematics.

Intuition of truths may take the form of knowledge which we cannot account for, simply because we are unconscious of the reasons which led us to it. In the case of such 'hunches', investigation will often uncover the reasons. More philosophically important are cases where, allegedly, there are no reasons to be uncovered, and no means of checking the truth of apparent intuitions, except perhaps by their coherence with further intuitions.

Intuitions of this kind have been important especially in philosophy of mathematics (see INTUITIONISM) and ethics, and also in logic and metaphysics. Whether such intuitions can be accepted, and whether ultimately they are unavoidable, are disputed questions. Cf. RATIONALISM.

In ethics especially, and concerning topics like personal IDEN-TITY, philosophers often appeal also to the 'pre-reflective' intuitions of common sense to act as a check on the acceptability of the conclusions they come to on theoretical grounds. See ETHICAL INTUITIONISM.

H. L. Bergson, 'Introduction to metaphysics', 1903 (translated 1912 and in his *The Creative Mind*, Philosophical Library, 1946), *Creative Evolution*, 1907 (trans., Macmillan 1911).

D. Føllesdal and D. Bell, 'Objects and concepts', *Proceedings of the Aristotelian Society*, supplementary vol., 1994. (Includes discussion of Husserl on intuitions.)

H. L. A. Hart, G. E. Hughes and J. N. Findlay, 'Is there knowledge by acquaintance?', *Proceedings of the Aristotelian Society*, supplementary vol., 1949.

W. Hudson, *Ethical Intuitionism*, Macmillan, 1967. (Brief introduction.)

J. Locke, *Essay concerning Human Understanding*, 1690, book 4, chapter 9. (Intuition of the self.)

D. Pole, *Conditions of Rational Inquiry*, Athlone, 1961, chapter 1. (General discussion of intuition.)

B. Spinoza, *Ethics*, book 2, § 40 n. 2, *Treatise on the Improvement of the Understanding*, § 19, 22–4. ('*Scientia intuitiva*' introduced.)

Intuitionism. Any doctrine emphasizing the role of INTUITION. Mathematical intuitionism, associated especially with L. E. J. Brouwer (1881–1966) and A. Heyting (1898–1980), confines the subject matter of mathematics to what is given in intuition. In particular, it refuses to assume that infinite sets actually exist, though it allows rules which generate ever larger finite sets. It is a form of constructivism, which insists that we should postulate entities (numbers, etc.) only if we know how to construct them, i.e. how to specify them systematically in terms of things we already accept. But intuitionism insists further that in mathematics we should call something true or false only if we either know it intuitively or know how to prove or disprove it, using steps known by intuition. (Hence an acceptable proof of something's existence involves constructing it.) Intuitionism therefore introduces a special kind of negation for use in mathematics, which has the consequence that we can deny a (non-counter-intuitive) proposition only if we can disprove it. Since intuitionists think that some (non-intuitive) mathematical propositions cannot be proved or disproved, they insist that the law of EXCLUDED MIDDLE does not apply to this kind of negation. On negation outside mathematics they have no united view, though discussions of them usually refer to the above version.

Formalists too, limit mathematics to what is in a sense within our control. Some of them (e.g. H. B. Curry) make mathematics consist of formal systems whose elements are mere symbols or meaningless marks, to be operated on by fixed rules. Mathematics is not about abstract objects like numbers or classes that these marks might be thought to stand for. D. Hilbert (1862–1943), the most famous formalist, thought the logical paradoxes showed that non-finitary mathematics (see FINITISM) needed justifying. He therefore interpreted it as a formal system and used finitary means to prove the consistency of this system (cf. METAMATHEMATICS). See also ETHICAL INTUITIONISM.

P. Benacerraf and H. Putnam (eds), *Philosophy of Mathematics*, Blackwell, 1964, particularly pp. 66–77 (Brouwer), 134–51 (Hilbert).

M. A. E. Dummett, *Truth and Other Enigmas*, Duckworth, 1978. (Collected essays including many relevant and influential items. See particularly Preface, pp. xxiv–xxix, chapter 14. For revision of some of his views see his later *The Seas of Language*, Oxford, 1993, with its Preface.)

K. G. Hossack, 'A problem about the meaning of intuitionist negation', *Mind*, 1990. (Distinguishes strong and weak intuitionism and attacks former.)

W. and M. Kneale, *The Development of Logic*, Oxford UP, 1962. (See its index.)

G. T. Kneebone, *Mathematical Logic and the Foundations of Mathematics*, Van Nostrand, 1963. (Pp. 243–50 gives elementary account of intuitionism, showing link with Kant.)

S. Körner, *The Philosophy of Mathematics*, Hutchinson, 1960. (Includes full treatment of intuitionism and formalism.)

W. V. O. Quine, *Philosophy of Logic*, Prentice-Hall, 1970, pp. 87–8. (Intuitionism and constructivism.)

Intuitionism, ethical. See ETHICAL INTUITIONISM.

Inversion. In traditional formal logic, replacement of a proposition by another (its inverse), which follows logically from it (assuming, as the traditional logic did, that all the relevant classes have members) and has as subject the negation of the original subject, e.g. 'Some non-cats are non-black' is the inverse of 'All cats are black.' Inversion can be carried out on only some of the traditional types of proposition.

Inverted spectrum. Might your red be my green? Is it possible that two people use exactly the same colour vocabulary in exactly the same way, but nevertheless the colours they see are different? They both agree that tomatoes are red and grass is green, but the colour one sees when he looks at a tomato is the same colour the other sees when she looks at grass. We know that some people, the colour blind, see colours differently from those who are not colour blind, but we know this because the differences are detectable. Could there be undetectable differences in colour vision? Locke was the first to suggest this. If it were possible, it would seem to prove the existence of non-physical qualia: but the possibility has been criticized by many philosophers. See QUALIA.

A. Byrne, 'Inverted Qualia', *The Stanford Encyclopedia of Philosophy* (Fall 2008 Edition), Edward N. Zalta (ed.). Available at: http://plato.stanford.

edu/archives/fall2008/entries/qualia-inverted/ (accessed 1 March 2009). (Excellent introduction and discussion with good bibliography).

J. Locke, *Essay concerning Human Understanding*, II, xxxii, 15, 1689, Oxford UP, 1975.

S. Shoemaker, *Identity, Cause, and Mind*, particularly pp. 357–81, Cambridge UP, 1984. (The whole book is relevant.)

Isomorphic. Sharing the same structure. Two or more sentences are intensionally isomorphic (Carnap) if they are logically equivalent, and have the same number of component sentences, and any component sentence in one is logically equivalent to the correspondingly placed component sentence in each of the others. The definition can be extended to certain other expressions. Isomorphism is the property or state of being isomorphic.

R. Carnap, *Meaning and Necessity*, Chicago UP, 1947, pp. 56–9.

J

James–Lange theory. Sometimes called the peripheric theory. Theory that emotions are consequences, not causes, of bodily disturbances, that 'the bodily changes follow directly the perception of the exciting fact, and that our feeling of the same changes as they occur is the emotion'. 'A purely disembodied human emotion is a nonentity' (though not a contradiction).

W. James, *The Principles of Psychology*, 1901, vol. 2, chapter 25. (Quotations on pp. 449, 452.)

James, William. 1842–1910. Psychologist and philosopher, and brother of novelist Henry James, he was born in New York and spent his life partly travelling and partly working at Harvard. Philosophically he is best known as a leading PRAGMATIST, though also in connection with the JAMES–LANGE THEORY of the emotions and with neutral MONISM. *The Principles of Psychology*, 1890 (includes much philosophy too). *The Varieties of Religious Experience*, 1902. *Pragmatism*, 1907. *The Nature of Truth*, 1909 (supplement to *Pragmatism*). *Essays in Radical Empiricism*, 1912 (neutral monism). See also EMPIRCISM, SANTAYANA.

Jaspers, Karl. 1883–1969. Born in Oldenburg in Germany, he worked mainly at Heidelberg and Basel. He was a leading EXISTENTIALIST philosopher, whose work was much influenced by his early training in medicine and psychiatry, and has greater connections with contemporary social and political problems than does that of HEIDEGGER. He treats human existence in terms of various notions, including DASEIN, which he uses in a sense different from Heidegger's sense. *Philosophy*, 1932. *Reason and Existenz*, 1935 (5 lectures). *Philosophy of Existence*, 1938 (3 lectures). *The Question of German Guilt*, 1946 (on German war guilt). *Reason and Anti-Reason in Our Time*, 1950 (3 lectures). See also MARCEL.

Judgement. Act of judging, or, less commonly, proposition, or content of an act of judging. Acts of judging by different people or at different times, but with the same content, may, however, count as a single judgement (e.g. if you and I both judge that grass is green). Whether it is acts or contents that logic is primarily concerned with has been disputed. Idealists and pragmatists have tended to prefer acts, and formal logicians contents. Judgement is often equated with BELIEF, or with the formation of belief, though belief is a state or disposition rather than an act; 'judgement' itself, however, has a dispositional sense in phrases like 'in my judgement ... ', 'a person of judgement'.

Judgements are sometimes limited, in both 'act' and 'content' senses, to cases where an element of assessment or evaluation is concerned, e.g. moral judgements may be contrasted with statements of fact. See also SENTENCES, THINKING.

> P. T. Geach, *Mental Acts*, RKP, 1957. (One view of judgements. Fairly difficult.)

Justice. The discussion of justice can concern itself with desert (backward looking) 'corrective justice', or outcome (forward looking), distributive justice. Questions of desert are involved in criminal justice: questions of outcome in social justice – how should goods to be distributed in society? Claims for justice by previously disadvantaged groups and minorities are often based on the idea of equal treatment for equals. See EQUALITY, LAW.

Justification. See EPISTEMOLOGY.

K

Kant, Immanuel. 1724–1804. German philosopher who spent all his life in Königsberg (now Kaliningrad). He is often regarded as synthesizing the 'British EMPIRICIST' and 'Continental RATIONALIST' schools by standing back from the questions they asked ('What is the nature of the world?', 'How do we know about the world?') and saying we must first give a critique of our faculties; he asks what it is possible for any mind like the human mind to know. Hence his philosophy after 1781 is often called the 'critical' philosophy. Much of his philosophy centres round his defence of synthetic a priori propositions, see ANALYTIC. He also tried to derive morality from reason alone, and to elaborate a notion of the self compatible with our possession of freewill. *Critique of Pure Reason*, 1781 (2nd edn 1787). *Groundwork of the Metaphysic of Morals*, 1785 (see Paton, below). *Critique of Practical Reason*, 1788. *Critique of Judgment*, 1790. See also APPERCEPTION, A PRIORI, BEING, CATEGORIES, COSMOLOGICAL, DESIGN, EPISTEMOLOGY, ETHICS, FORM (bibliography), GOOD, HARE, HEIDEGGER, HUME, IDEA, IDEALISM, IMPERATIVE, INCONGRUENT, INTUITION, MANIFOLD, MODALITIES, NOUMENON, OUGHT, PHENOMENOLOGY, REASON, REID, SCHOPENHAUER, SPACE, STRAWSON, TRANSCENDENTAL ARGUMENTS, UNIVERSALIZABILITY.

N. Kemp Smith (trans.), *Immanuel Kant's Critique of Pure Reason*, Macmillan, 1929. (Standard translation.)

H. J. Paton (trans.) *The Moral Law: Kant's Groundwork of the Metaphysic of Morals*, Hutchinson, 1948. (Kant's most important ethical work.)

Kierkegaard, Søren A. 1813–55. Danish religious thinker and philosopher who, due to a large inheritance, lived and published independently. Based in Copenhagen he travelled a couple of times to Berlin where

Either/Or, 1843, was written. Berlin also figures prominently in *Repetition*, 1843. Along with *Philosophical Fragments*, 1844, *The Concept of Anxiety*, 1844, and *Concluding Unscientific Postscript*, 1846, the early works established him as an opponent of HEGEL's science of logic and its ambition to systematize existence. Thus, he is often considered a precursor to existentialism: however, in contrast to that movement, he stresses the ontological priority of God over human existence, as for example in *Works of Love*, 1847, *Sickness unto Death*, 1849, and *Practice in Christianity*, 1850. Whereas earlier he was concerned with the ethics of how to live, he was later pre-occupied with existential communication. In the year of his death, he launched a vitriolic attack on the Danish church in a series of pamphlets entitled *The Moment*.

G. Pattison, *The Philosophy of Kierkegaard*, Acumen, 2005.

Knowledge. See EPISTEMOLOGY.

Kripke, Saul A. 1940–. Born in Bay Shore, NY, he has worked mainly at Princeton. Coming to philosophy from mathematics he has worked mainly in logic and metaphysics, and more recently in the interpretation of Wittgenstein. He has developed a causal theory of the MEANING of names and 'natural kind words' (such as 'horse' and 'iron') and pioneered (with PUTNAM) a revival of essentialism, insisting also that the a priori/empirical and necessary/contingent distinctions do not, as usually then thought, coincide (see also PUTNAM). His publications include 'Naming and necessity' in D. Davidson and G. Harman (eds), *Semantics of Natural Language*, 1972 (republished as separate book, 1980); and *Wittgenstein on Rules and Private Language*, 1972.

Kuhn, Thomas S. 1922–96. American, originally a theoretical physicist. In his influential *The Structure of Scientific Revolutions*, 1962, Kuhn develops POPPER's thought that the history of science is a process of conjectures and refutations. For Popper, a scientific theory is a hypothesis or conjecture which seeks to explain the known facts in a particular area. When a counter-example is observed, the theory is refuted, and a new conjecture is produced which explains the new observation. Kuhn points out that this is not what happens: in fact, observations that might seem to refute existing theories are ignored, or dismissed as experimental errors. When such counter-examples accumulate in an area, a crisis point is reached, and there is a complete revolution in the shared assumptions which govern the way that area of science is understood, and a 'paradigm shift' takes place which incorporates the anomalous observations. See PARADIGM, SCIENCE.

T. S. Kuhn, *The Structure of Scientific Revolutions*, Chicago UP, 1962, 2nd edn with postscript, 1970. (For criticism see I. Lakatos and A. Musgrave (eds), *Criticism and the Growth of Knowledge*, Cambridge UP, 1970, and I. Hacking, 'Lakatos's philosophy of science', in I. Hacking (ed.) *Scientific Revolutions*, Oxford UP, 1981. See also P. Horwich (ed.), *World Changes: Thomas Kuhn and the Nature of Science*, MIT Press, 1993. (Conference papers reflecting Kuhn's influence and with 'Afterwords' by him).)

L

Language (philosophy of). Not the same as linguistic philosophy, nor as linguistics, which studies the general features of natural languages structurally (synchronic) or historically (diachronic, also called philology).

As a separate study, philosophy of language is a recent offshoot of logic, connected also to epistemology, metaphysics and philosophy of mind. It asks general questions about language as such, not (like linguistics) about particular languages. The latter, of course, provide examples.

The primary end of language is communication. Other ends, like getting people to do things, depend on this. Many things can be communicated – information, requests, commands, ideas, innuendoes, etc. (cf. SPEECH ACTS). Whether the primary function of language is to inform (or assert) may be disputed, but this function in fact receives most attention. Two concepts which are therefore of central importance are TRUTH and FACTS. The question of how communication is possible, or how language works, involves us in studying the notion of MEANING. CONCEPTS, propositions and statements (see SENTENCES) have been thought necessary to account for meaning, and they raise problems about what they are and what properties they have (e.g. the ANALYTIC/synthetic distinction).

A study of language in general will naturally ask whether there are any features every language must share. Such features might be ones without which a language could not exist. It might be claimed, for example, that every language must include ways of referring to particular objects, or ways of negating; or the features might be needed because human nature is what it is. (N. Chomsky claims that certain features of language are universal and throw light on how the mind works; cf. CATEGORIES.) It is also claimed (Davidson) that to be learnable a language must be compositional, i.e. the meanings of sentences must depend systematically on the meanings of words.

Further general questions about language include how far animals can have language, whether there can be a PRIVATE LANGUAGE and whether ideal languages are possible, of which natural languages are defective versions (as, for example, Russell and perhaps Plato thought). Artificial languages, whether used in science or computing or constructed for theoretical interest, can also be studied.

After the Second World War, naming and verificationist theories of MEANING were rejected, and there followed the piecemeal approach of linguistic philosophy, dominated by Wittgenstein and Austin. METAPHYSICS has also used philosophy of language on topics like SUBSTANCE. Recently there has been some return to large-scale theorizing stemming from CHOMSKY, whose contribution involves applying mathematical techniques to problems connected with the attempt to specify all the sentences constructable in a given language. There have also been substantial developments in the theory of meaning, pioneered by writers like Davidson and Putnam; see REALISM.

*W. Alston, *Philosophy of Language*, Prentice-Hall, 1964. (General introduction.)

J. L. Austin, *How to Do Things with Words*, Oxford UP, 1962. (Functions of language, by major exponent of speech act analyses.)

M. Bavidge and I. Ground, *Can We Understand Animal Minds?* Palgrave Macmillan, 1994.

J. F. Bennett, *Rationality*, RKP, 1964. (Can animals have language?)

S. Blackburn, *Spreading the Word*, Clarendon, 1984. (General introduction to philosophy of language, combined with positive philosophizing and developing his 'quasi-realism'.)

T. Burge, 'Philosophy of language and mind: 1950–90', *Philosophical Review*, 1992. (Survey article with many references. See particularly 1st half for philosophy of language.)

D. Davidson, *Inquiries into Truth and Interpretation*, Oxford UP, 1984. (Collected essays of major contributor to recent developments.)

*J. Lyons, *Chomsky*, Fontana, 1970, expanded 1977. (Elementary introduction. cf. also Chomsky's lecture series *Languages and the Problems of Knowledge*, MIT Press, 1988.)

H. Putnam, *Philosophical Papers, Volume 2: Mind, Language and Reality*, Cambridge UP, 1975.

P. F. Strawson, *Individuals*, Methuen, 1959. (Part 2 discusses role of referring.)

L. Wittgenstein, *Philosophical Investigations*, Blackwell, 1953. (Probably most important of his many books. Cf. his *Tractatus* (see bibliography to LOGICAL ATOMISM) for earlier stage in his thought.)

Language game. Wittgenstein discussed the way language works by inventing small-scale languages for special spheres, such as house-building, and asking how they might work and what they must be like. Comparing them to certain children's games he called them language games. He then compared them to the complexities of actual language, and used them to emphasize the role of words in certain human practices, like doing science and play-acting. He originally thought of them as primitive or autonomous, i.e. as not presupposing the rest of language. But 'language game' came to be applied also to certain parts or spheres of already existing languages, e.g. religious language, or language as used in connection with promising, can be called language games, though they could hardly exist except as parts of a language used more generally.

R. Rhees, *Discussions of Wittgenstein*, RKP, 1970, chapter 6. (Discussion of some difficulties by sympathizer.)

L. Wittgenstein, *Philosophical Investigations*, Blackwell, 1953, particularly part 1, § 7, 23.

Language of thought. Fodor's name for his view (also called the representational theory of mind) that mental states have a syntactic (see SEMIOTIC) structure corresponding to the semantical structure of the propositions which form their objects, i.e. that mental states represent their objects by having parts which represent parts of the objects in a systematic way. The language is also called 'Mentalese'.

*T. Crane, *The Mechanical Mind: A Philosophical Introduction to Minds, Mechanics and Mental Representation*, Penguin, 1995, chapter 4. (Elementary introduction; see pp. 154–62 for comparison of language of thought with CONNECTIONISM.)

J. A. Fodor, *The Language of Thought*, T. Y. Crowell, 1975, Harvester, 1976. (See also his *Psychosemantics*, MIT Press, 1987, particularly its Appendix, for briefer version and see bibliography to PSYCHOSEMANTICS and also W. G. Lycan (ed.), *Mind and Cognition*, Blackwell, 1990, part v.)

Law (philosophy of). The study of problems concerning prescriptive laws (as against laws of nature, often called descriptive, which are studied by philosophy of science. On 'natural law', see LAWS.)

There are widely different views about what a law is. Is it a command of the sovereign? Or a prediction of what judges will decide? Or a prediction that certain actions will be followed by sanctions? Or a statement of an intention to impose sanctions? Or something else? Are there formal conditions (as against conditions affecting its content) that a law must satisfy to count as a law at all, like being initiated in certain ways by a body with special authority, or not being inconsistent with itself or with other laws in the same system? Are there restrictions on content, e.g. is an alleged law not a law at all if it prescribes what is impossible, or violates divine, natural or moral law? And are these kinds of law, if they exist, all law in the same sense? Also is a law still a law if there is either no prescribed sanction or no power of enforcement?

Some of these questions raise issues of justification. To justify a law or to justify a legal system may be either to show that it really is one, or to show that it is good, fair, proper, impartial, etc. How closely these tasks are related is disputable. Other things that need justifying are judgements within a legal system, e.g. those of lawyers or of judges, and the duty of obedience. Closely related are questions about the justification of punishment, be it of punishment in general, of particular penalties for particular types of case, or of individual cases. The notions of intention and strict liability (i.e. liability irrespective of intention) are relevant here.

Certain problems concern the different branches of law (constitutional, civil, commercial, criminal) and how they relate to each other and to equity. Constitutional law in particular raises questions about how it can change. In other branches the role of judges in making law is relevant. Questions of sovereignty and sanctions lead to problems about the possibility and nature of international law.

R. Dworkin (ed.), *The Philosophy of Law*, Oxford UP, 1965. (Important articles by Dworkin, Hart, Devlin, Rawls and others.)

H. L. A. Hart, *The Concept of Law*, Oxford UP, 1961. (Full discussion of many problems.)

H. L. A. Hart, *The Morality of the Criminal Law*, Oxford UP, 1965. (Hart's side in famous debate with Lord Devlin, cf. P. Devlin, *The Enforcement of Morals*, 1959, reprinted with other relevant items in book of same title, 1965.)

T. Honderich, *Punishment: The Supposed Justifications*, Hutchinson, 1969.

R. S. Summers (ed.), *Essays in Legal Philosophy*, Blackwell, 1968, *More Essays in Legal Philosophy, Blackwell*, 1971. (First volume covers questions of analysis and justification. Second discusses historical figures. See Summers's introductions for survey of issues.)

M. Tebbit, *Philosophy of Law: An Introduction*, Routledge, 2000, 2nd revised edition, 2005.

Laws. The traditional distinction between 'prescriptive' laws (legal, moral, divine) and 'descriptive' laws (scientific) is convenient, but not necessarily accurate, 'Prescriptive' laws (see philosophy of LAW) may not be prescriptions, and 'descriptive' laws may not describe the world. The laws of logic and mathematics are simply accepted statements, usually important, in those subjects. The laws of thought are the logical laws of identity, contradiction and EXCLUDED MIDDLE. Whether they are more important than other logical laws is disputed. The rest of this entry mainly concerns scientific laws.

Generalizations may be closed (limited in space and time: 'All the coins now in my pocket are silver') or open ('All ravens, at all times and places, are black'). But on another interpretation open generalizations have the form, 'Anything whatever, if it is so-and-so, is such-and-such', where 'so-and-so' may or may not contain spatio-temporal restrictions like 'now in my pocket'. On this interpretation, both the first two examples would be closed, because they each have a limited subject matter (coins and ravens), and any generalization could be formulated as an open generalization of the second kind.

In so far as scientific laws are generalizations, they are usually regarded as open on the first interpretation (though this excludes those of Kepler (see below) and Galileo). They also are usually taken to imply counterfactuals (see CONDITIONALS): 'All ravens are black', if a law, implies 'If there were ravens on Mars (though there aren't) they would be black'. For both these reasons laws cannot be conclusively verified. Also, many laws seem to have no direct application: 'All bodies unacted on by forces move with constant velocity in a straight line' – but there are no such bodies. For these and other reasons, scientific laws are sometimes thought to be rules governing the scientist's expectations, and so prescriptive, or else idealized descriptions to which the world approximates, as triangles on a blackboard approximate to Euclidean triangles. On this last view, the point of Newton's first law of motion (quoted above) is that any deviation of an object from uniform rectilinear motion must be attributed to its being acted on by forces. Some writers refuse to call laws 'true' on the grounds that they are not straightforwardly descriptive.

Normally a hypothesis is a statement not yet accepted as true, or as a law, while a law is only called a law if it is accepted, whether or not we call it 'true'. But occasionally laws, though accepted, are still called hypotheses, e.g. 'Avogadro's hypothesis'. A lawlike statement is sometimes a statement resembling a law except that it is not accepted and is perhaps rejected, and sometimes a statement not general enough to be a law because it refers to individual objects (e.g. Kepler's 'laws' about how 'the' planets go round 'the' sun, which do not mention suns and planets in general). Occasionally it is a statement attributing dispositional characteristics, e.g. 'Glass is brittle.'

Theory has various meanings: (i) One or more hypotheses or law-like statements (either of first two senses), regarded as speculative. (ii) A law about unobservables like electrons or evolution, sometimes called a theory because evidence about unobservables is felt to be inevitably inconclusive. (iii) A unified system of laws or hypotheses, with explanatory force (not merely like a railway timetable). (iv) A field of study (e.g. in philosophy: theory of knowledge, logical theory). These senses sometimes shade into each other. A principle may be a high-grade law, on which a lot depends, or it may be something like a rule. To call all scientific laws principles suggests they hover between being rules and being idealized descriptions. Legal, moral, aesthetic, etc., principles may resemble scientific laws in being descriptions of ideal worlds, set up to govern actions as scientific laws are to govern expectations. However, they differ from them by not being idealized descriptions of the real world, to be rejected unless the real world approximates to them in the relevant ways. (Other uses of 'law' and 'principle' exist.)

Scientific laws are often called laws of nature or natural laws. Natural law (generic singular) is the moral law (i.e. set of laws) regarded as derivable from the general nature of the universe by reason alone, without appeal to revelation, feelings, interests, etc. See also EXPLANATION, MODALITIES, CONVENTIONALISM, INSTRUMENTALISM.

D. M. Armstrong, *What is a Law of Nature?* Cambridge UP, 1983. (A connection between universals.)

R. B. Braithwaite, *Scientific Explanation*, Harper, 1953. (Pp. 300–3 analyse scientific laws in terms of their explanatory function.)

J. W. Carroll, *Laws of Nature*, Cambridge UP, 1994. (Defends realist view of them, connecting with causation.)

A. P. D'Entreves, *Natural Law*, Hutchinson, 1951, 2nd edn republished with new introduction by C. J. Nederman, Transaction Publishers 1994. (Sympathetic discussion, more historical and less analytical than Finnis.)

J. Finnis, *Natural Law and Natural Rights*, Clarendon, 1980. (Full discussion from mainly philosophical rather than historical point of view. See also, for an anthology, J. Finnis (ed.), *Natural Law*, 2 vols, Dartmouth Publishing Company, 1991.)

W. Kneale, *Probability and Induction*, Oxford UP, 1949. (Part 2 discusses various kinds of scientific law, and claims that they express objective necessities.)

217

M. Singer, *Generalization in Ethics*, Eyre and Spottiswoode, 1963, chapter 5. (Moral rules and principles.)

S. E. Toulmin, *Philosophy of Science*, Hutchinson, 1953. (Advocates 'idealized description' view, though without so calling it, and discusses other views.)

Learning paradox. See EDUCATION.

Leibniz, Gottfried W. 1646–1716. German mathematician and philosopher who was born in Leipzig and, after holding various court posts, worked as a librarian and historian in Hanover. He and Newton, independently, invented the differential calculus. He is usually included among the 'Continental RATIONALISTS'. Also, in METAPHYSICS he claimed that all true propositions are really ANALYTIC, and that reality consists of independent MONADS, which mirror but do not influence each other, and contain within themselves a sort of blueprint of their entire life-histories, which they work through according to a 'pre-established harmony' arranged by God. Leibniz is also noted for LEIBNIZ'S LAW and, although he denied the reality of relations, he defended a relational view of SPACE and time (in letters to S. Clarke, who represented Newton). *Discourse on Metaphysics*, written 1685–6, published 1846. *Principles of Nature and of Grace, Founded in Reason*, written 1714, published 1718. *The Monadology*, written 1714, first published in German 1720. *New Essays on Human Understanding*, written 1704, published 1765 (critique of LOCKE's Essay). He also wrote important letters to A. Arnauld, See also APPERCEPTION, CONCEPT (bibliography), ENTELECHY, INNATE, INTENSIONAL1TY, OCCASIONALISM, PSYCHOPHYSICAL, SUBSTANCE, SUFFICIENT REASON.

G. W. Leibniz, *New Essays concerning Human Understanding* (trans. A. G. Langley), Macmillan, 1986. (Originally published, 1916. Includes also shorter relevant pieces by Leibniz and indexes. For more recent translation, with notes see G. W. Leibniz, *News Essays on Human Understanding* (trans. P. Remnant and J. Bennett), Cambridge UP, 1981.)

L. Loemker (ed.), *Gottfried Wilhelm Leibniz: Philosophical Papers and Letters*, Chicago UP, 1956. (Translated selections (c. 650 pp.), with long introduction. For a similar but shorter selection see R. Anew and D. Garber (eds), *G. W. Leibniz: Philosophical Essays*, Hackett, 1989. Both volumes include some of the shorter substantive works.)

A. Savile, *Routledge Philosophy GuideBook to Leibniz and the Monadology*, 2000. (Clear introduction.)

Leibniz's law. There are two principles which together form what is now called Leibniz's law, though Leibniz himself seems only to have held the first of them. The identity of indiscernibles is the principle that if a group of things have all their properties in common, or belong to exactly the same classes, they are identical in the sense of being really only one thing. The indiscernibility of identicals (Quine) is the principle that if a group of things are identical (i.e. are really one thing, though perhaps described in different ways), they have all their properties in common. Sometimes the term, 'Leibniz's law' is limited to the second principle.

The identity of indiscernibles can be held in various forms, which differ in strength according to what sort of properties are considered relevant. In a weak, and thereby more plausible, form spatiotemporal properties are included. The principle then says only that things sharing all their properties, including their positions in space and time, are identical. But a stronger form says that things will be identical if they have all their non-relational properties in common (i.e. properties which do not, like spatiotemporal ones, involve a relation to something else). This would mean there cannot be two or more things exactly similar. In the weaker form, but not in stronger ones, the identity of indiscernibles is the converse of the indiscernibility of identicals.

Leibniz himself often said that things are identical when they can be substituted for each other without making a true proposition false. This leads to apparent limitations of the law because of problems connected with intentionality (see INTENSIONALITY AND INTENTIONALITY and the Cicero example there). However, it is really words or descriptions, not things, that can be substituted for each other. The law, therefore (since, as viewed so far, it concerns things, not words), does not apply to the Cicero case, and so need not be limited. But the law might be regarded as giving rise to a principle of substitutivity, whose two halves will say that if whatever can be said of *a*, so described, can be said of *b*, so described, then *a* and *b* are identical (weak form of identity of indiscernibles), and vice versa (indiscernibility of identicals); co-referring terms can therefore be intersubstituted, thus preserving truth. It then seems necessary to allow exceptions to this principle. The view that these exceptions can, however, be ultimately dispensed with (or alternatively that only in so far as they can is formal logic possible) is called the extensionality thesis, principle, or (especially in formal contexts) axiom. See also IDENTITY, SPACE, INTENSIONALITY, SUFFICIENT REASON.

H. G. Alexander (ed.), *The Leibniz–Clarke Correspondence*, Manchester UP, 1956. (See Introduction, p. xxiii, for references to text.)

F. Feldman, 'Leibniz and "Leibniz' Law"', *Philosophical Review*, 1970. (What Leibniz himself held.)

L. Linsky, *Referring*, RKP, 1967. (Substitutivity distinguished from Leibniz's law on p. 79.)

M. J. Loux (ed.), *Universals and Particulars*, Anchor Books, 1970. (Includes items on identity of indiscernibles.)

P. F. Strawson, *Individuals*, Methuen, 1959. (Chapter 4 discusses a strong form of the identity of indiscernibles, partly in terms of Leibniz.)

D. Wiggins, *Sameness and Substance*, Blackwell, 1980. (Discusses significance for the nature of identity of various formulations of each of the principles, though keeping title 'Leibniz's law' for indiscernibility of identicals. See its index. Difficult.)

Lemma. The conclusion of one argument used as a premise for another: thus an intermediate conclusion on the way to a further conclusion.

Levinas, Emmanuel. 1906–95. Born in what is now Lithuania, studied and worked in France and became a French citizen in 1930. Studied under HUSSERL and HEIDEGGER, and promoted their work and PHENOMENOLOGY in France. He pioneered the phenomenological study of ethics, which he saw as the basis of philosophy. The fundamental nature of ethics lies in my individual relationship, face-to-face, with other people (the Other). *Totality and Infinity*, 1969. *Otherwise than Being*, 1981.

S. Critchley, 'Emmanuel Levinas: A disparate inventory', in *The Cambridge Companion to Levinas*, ed. S. Critchley and R. Bernasconi. Cambridge UP, 2002.

A. Peperzak, *To the Other*, Purdue UP, 1993. (Good introduction.)

Lewis, David K. 1941– 2001. Born in Oberlin, Ohio, he worked mainly at Princeton. He developed an influential analysis of counterfactuals (see CONDITIONALS) in terms of POSSIBLE WORLDS, and then went on to develop this latter notion, holding an extreme realist view of them whereby, though not actual, they are as real as the actual world but spatiotemporally disconnected from it. He also wrote on aspects of MEREOLOGY. His publications include *Convention*, 1969; *Counterfactuals*, 1973; *Philosophical Papers*, vol. 1, 1983 and vol. 2, 1986; *On the Plurality of Worlds*, 1986; *Parts of Classes*, 1991.

Liar paradox. 'This statement is false' seems to be false if true, and true if false. Traditionally attributed to Epimenides the Cretan in the (inadequate) form, 'All Cretans are liars', this paradox is often called a semantic PARADOX. It raises difficulties especially for the correspondence theory of TRUTH, for it is hard to find a fact for 'This statement is false' to correspond to, or fail to correspond to. This paradox was also mainly responsible for the semantic theory of TRUTH taking the form that Tarski gave it. See also RUSSELL'S PARADOX, TYPES.

J. Barwise and J. Etchemendy, *The Liar*, Oxford UP, 1987.

M. Clark, *Paradoxes from A–Z*, London: Routledge, 2002.

R. L. Martin (ed.), *The Paradox of the Liar*, Yale UP, 1970. (Brief history, followed by recent discussions. Extensive bibliography.)

R. L. Martin (ed.), *Recent Essays on Truth and the Liar Paradox*, Oxford UP, 1984. (Specially written essays, with discussions.)

G. Ryle (see bibliography to HETEROLOGICAL).

R. M. Sainsbury, *Paradoxes*, Cambridge UP, 1988 (revised 1995), chapter 5. (Compares the Liar with Russell's paradox.)

Liberty. May refer to freedom of the will: see FREEWILL AND DETERMINISM. MILL's *On Liberty* is the classic account of liberalism: society should be so organized that each person is at liberty to do whatever they want, without the interference of the state, so long as it does not curtail the liberty of others or cause them harm. BERLIN claimed there were two concepts involved in political freedom which should be distinguished. The negative conception of freedom is the absence of constraint (in important or relevant areas, for there cannot be total absence of any constraints). The positive concept is of autonomy, self-determination, self-government.

I. Berlin, *Liberty* (contains his classic 1958 article 'Two Concepts of Liberty'), Oxford UP, 2002.

J. S. Mill, *On Liberty*, 1859.

D. Miller (ed.), *Liberty*, Oxford UP, 1991. (Good collection of essays.)

J. Riley, *Routledge Philosophy GuideBook to Mill on Liberty*, 1995. (Clear introduction.)

Libertarianism. See FREEWILL.

Likelihood. If we know how a property is distributed in a population (e.g. how many of all the swans in the world are white) we can infer the probability of any given distribution of the property in any random sample. But the converse inference from sample to population involves a simple inversion, which (unlike the inversion involved in BAYES'S THEOREM) will not work for probabilities. R. A. Fisher (1890–1962) therefore introduced likelihood as a notion for which this simple inversion is valid. (But outside technical contexts 'likelihood' is usually synonymous with 'probability'.)

To see how Fisher's likelihood relates to probability, consider the probability that a ball is white when randomly chosen from a bag of three balls, each white or black. Let h_n be the hypothesis that the bag contains exactly n white balls and 3-n black balls. Let w/h_n and b/h_n signify the probabilities that the chosen ball is white or black, respectively, given h_n. $w/h_n + b/h_n = 1$, i.e. the probabilities on a given hypothesis add up to one. Now consider the four probabilities w/h_0, w/h_1, w/h_2, w/h_3. These, though exhaustive and non-overlapping, do not add up to one (but to two, in this case). They are therefore called likelihoods, but it is obscure what likelihoods are, unless we merely say they are probabilities grouped in a way that stops them obeying the laws of PROBABILITY theory They can indeed usually be mathematically manipulated to add up to one. But this does not lessen the difficulty.

A. W. F. Edwards, *Likelihood*, Cambridge UP, 1972; expanded edn, Baltimore, 1992. (Full technical treatment.)

I. Hacking, *Logic of Statistical Inference*, Cambridge UP, 1965. (See index.)

M. G. Kendall and A. Stuart, *The Advanced Theory of Statistics*, vol. 1, Griffin, 1958, chapter 8.

Locke, John. 1632–1704. Born in Somerset, he worked mostly in Oxford and London when not in exile because of his political activities against the Stuarts before 1688. His central work was in epistemology, where his 'new way of IDEAS' has led to his being regarded as the first main 'British EMPIRICIST'. He insisted that ideas could only come from experience, though connections between them could be known A PRIORI, and he elaborated the primary/secondary QUALITY distinction. He also wrote on political theory from a liberal point of view. *Letters concerning Toleration*, 1689 and after. *Two Treatises of Government*, 1690. *An Essay concerning Human Understanding*, 1690. See also BERKELEY, BUTLER, ESSENCE, IDENTITY (bibliography), INNATE (bibliography), MEANING, PERCEPTION, SHAFTESBURY, SORTAL, SPACE, SUBSTANCE.

E. J. Lowe, *Locke on Human Understanding*, Routledge, 1995. (Good introduction.)

Locutions. See SPEECH ACTS.

Logic. The central topic of logic is valid reasoning, its systematization and the study of notions relevant to it. This gives it two systematically related areas of concern, formal logic and philosophical logic (also called logical theory, though usage varies and philosophy of logic is sometimes confined to the study of logical systems and their applications).

The main task of formal logic is to axiomatize (see AXIOM SYSTEM) various subject matters, constructing in particular the propositional and predicate CALCULI. Theorems are then proved in and about the resulting systems to bring out their properties. The important properties include CONSISTENCY, COMPLETENESS and the possession of DECISION PROCEDURES. The study of such properties is often called metalogic.

Systems complex enough to axiomatize mathematics on the basis of DECIDABLE axioms turn out to have these properties only to a severely limited extent (see GÖDEL'S THEOREMS). Also, the logical PARADOXES make it harder to construct these systems. Much of modern formal logic consists in trying to avoid or minimize these limitations and difficulties. How relevant they are in the sphere of philosophical logic, or even outside it, is disputed. The main issues are the nature of truth, especially in view of the LIAR PARADOX, and the relations between formal systems and ordinary language. Some, especially adherents to linguistic PHILOSOPHY, have argued from these or other considerations that ordinary language has no exact logic (cf. OPEN TEXTURE). The study of ordinary language from this point of view is sometimes called informal logic, though this can also refer to the study of those inferences which depend on the content rather than form of the sentences concerned. We infer 'Smith is unmarried' from 'Smith is a bachelor' because of the meaning of 'bachelor' not because 'Smith is a bachelor' has a certain form. A formal inference from 'Smith is a bachelor' might yield 'Bachelors include Smith' (see FORM); this raises some of the problems concerning the ANALYTIC.

Formal logic also studies NATURAL DEDUCTION, and formal parts of modal and deontic logic (see below).

A topic related to formal logic is set theory (see CALCULUS). This and proof theory (see METAMATHEMATICS) are normally together called mathematical logic, and lead towards the philosophy of MATHEMATICS. Modern formal logic and mathematical logic are each, or together, often called symbolic logic, to mark the more intensive use of symbols, or logistic.

Deontic logic studies logical relations between propositions containing terms like 'obliged', 'commanded', 'permitted', 'forbidden', though the term tends to be confined to the construction of formal systems using deontic terms, and the problems these systems raise. A rather similar subject is the logic of preference, which asks, for example, what sets of preferences can consistently be held together (e.g. can one prefer *a* to *b*, and *b* to *c*, but *c* to *a*?) Cf. VOTING PARADOX.

Philosophical logic examines the concepts involved in formal logic and uses its results, but is not concerned with the mechanics of the various systems; however, the boundaries between these areas of logic are not sharp. It also studies the nature of logical systems as such, and whether there can be alternative logics (see below).

As a study devoted to valid reasoning, it naturally asks about reasoning in general and how many kinds of it there are. Is all reasoning, properly speaking, deductive, or is there also inductive reasoning (see INDUCTION, philosophy of SCIENCE), and perhaps other kinds, e.g. in morals, history, aesthetics? Are there several kinds of validity? Validity is closely connected to logical necessity, and thence to necessity in general and other modal concepts such as possibility and impossibility (see MODALITIES). Modal concepts are studied by modal logic, though in practice this term, like 'deontic logic', tends to be confined to the study of formal systems using modal terms. General analyses of necessity, etc. belong to philosophical logic, which also asks how these modal notions are related to the A PRIORI and the ANALYTIC.

Reasoning involves passing from premises to conclusions, and so involves a relation and the things which it relates. Both of these are subjects for philosophical logic. The relation in its most general form is IMPLICATION, which raises problems about its different kinds and its relation to INFERENCE. The things it relates are SENTENCES, propositions or statements, which again raise problems about what they are.

Attempts to relate logic to epistemology may be said to lie behind the development of INTUITIONIST logic, perhaps the main alternative to two-valued classical logic (recognizing only the two TRUTH-VALUES, truth and falsity). But other 'deviant logics' have also been developed for various purposes, such as the alleged needs of quantum mechanics.

Logic also studies meaning in general, of ordinary words as well as of formal words like 'all', 'and', etc., and of both words and sentences. This broadens into the study of language in general: how it does what it does and how it relates to the world (cf. above on relating ordinary language to formal systems). How are the various roles that words fulfil, such as meaning, referring, describing, predicating, to be distinguished and related? These problems now form a subject of their own, philosophy of LANGUAGE, but they still fall broadly under logic. Two further notions important in this area are DEFINITIONS and TRUTH (see above; truth also belongs to epistemology). Logic borders on metaphysics when we ask how far various logical views commit us to asserting that certain kinds of things, like propositions, exist, and how we should analyse existential QUANTIFICATION (cf. BEING).

Formal logic effectively began with Aristotle, who systematized immediate INFERENCE and the SYLLOGISM, which remained the basis of traditional logic until about a century and a half ago. Vigorous developments in both formal and philosophical logic were made by the Stoics, and in philosophical logic in the Middle Ages, but these were forgotten and have only recently been revived. The syllogism is now seen to form a small part of the predicate calculus.

A key feature in the history of modern logic since about the middle of the nineteenth century has been the development of a logic of relations. This comes from realizing, and taking seriously, that not all propositions consist of a subject and predicate linked by the copula, 'is' ('are'). Traditional logic had unduly restricted itself by assuming that they do, and could not formalize so simple an argument as 'Ten exceeds nine and nine exceeds eight, so ten exceeds eight', where the main verb stands for a relation. See also TOPIC-NEUTRAL, QUANTIFIER WORDS.

*I. Copi, *Introduction to Logic*, Macmillan 6th edn, 1982. (Covers formal, informal and inductive logic, and has many examples, some with answers. See also W. A. Hodges, *Logic*, Penguin, 1977. (Has exercises with answers).)

J. N. Crossley *et al.*, *What is Mathematical Logic?* Oxford UP, 1972. (Brief. Fairly elementary.)

*A. Grayling, *An Introduction to Philosophical Logic*, Harvester, 1982; 2nd edn, Duckworth, 1990. (Mainly elementary with two rather harder chapters at end.)

G. E. Hughes and M. J. Cresswell, *An Introduction to Modal Logic*, Methuen, 1968. (Comprehensive.)

J. N. Keynes, *Formal Logic*, 1884, 4th (revised) edn 1906. (Standard and full treatment of traditional logic.)

W. and M. Kneale, *The Development of Logic*, Oxford UP, 1962. (Very full treatment of historical development of the subject.)

*E. I. Lemmon, *Beginning Logic*, Nelson, 1965. (Adopts NATURAL DEDUCTION approach.)

B. Mates, *Stoic Logic*, California UP, 1953.

*W. V. O. Quine, *Philosophy of Logic*, Prentice-Hall, 1970. (General introduction from Quine's own point of view.)

*R. M. Sainsbury, *Logical Forms: An Introduction to Philosophical Logic*, Blackwell, 1991. (Claims to bridge gap between elementary formal logic and more advanced philosophical logic.)

P. F. Strawson, *Introduction to Logical Theory*, Methuen, 1952. (Represents 'linguistic philosophy' outlook, that there is no exact logic of ordinary language.)

G. H. von Wright, *The Logic of Preference*, Edinburgh UP, 1963. (Introduction.)

G. H. von Wright, *An Essay in Deontic Logic*, North-Holland, 1968. (Introduction, with bibliography.)

F. Waismann, 'Are there alternative logics?', *Proceedings of the Aristotelian Society*, 1945–6, reprinted in his *How I See Philosophy*, Macmillan, 1968. Cf. S. Haack, *Deviant Logic*, Cambridge UP, 1974, and *Philosophy of Logics*, Cambridge UP, 1978 (which includes glossary.)

Logical atomism. Theory associated mainly with Russell (middle period) and Wittgenstein (early period) which seeks to analyse thought and discourse in terms of indivisible components. Atomic propositions consist of a subject term and a predicate term ('John is clever'), or a set of terms linked by a relation term ('John hates Tom'), and they are true if they correspond directly to FACTS, which are all (for this theory, at least in its purest form) atomic. Molecular propositions are truth FUNCTIONS of atomic ones and correspond in complex ways to those same facts. This shows, it is claimed, that the logical connectives (see CONJUNCTION) do not name or correspond to elements of facts, or anything else. They simply connect propositions. However, it was not clear on this view how atomic propositions could be false, and various kinds of propositions supposed to be molecular in the above sense created difficulties when treated as such, e.g. general (see UNIVERSAL) and negative propositions; it was difficult to make them correspond, even in complex ways, to atomic facts.

As for the constituents of atomic facts, Wittgenstein left them unspecified, calling them simply 'objects'. Russell regarded 'John is clever', etc., as only apparently atomic, because only simple things we are acquainted with could be constituents of atomic propositions and named by logically proper names (see DESCRIPTIONS, MEANING), and such simples were confined to our own SENSE DATA (and UNIVERSALS), which made it hard for him to give any genuine examples of atomic propositions and therefore of atomic facts. See also INTENSIONALITY AND INTENTIONALITY (for the 'extensionality principle').

D. F. Pears, *Bertrand Russell and the British Tradition in Philosophy*, Fontana, 1967. (Fuller and harder than, and sometimes critical of, Urmson.)

B. Russell, 'The philosophy of logical atomism', *The Monist*, 1918, reprinted in his *Logic and Knowledge*, Allen and Unwin, 1956, and D. Pears (ed.), *Russell's Logical Atomism*, Fontana/Collins, 1972. (A popular account. The essay 'Logical atomism', in both these volumes is harder.)

R. M. Sainsbury, *Russell*, RKP, 1979, chapter II.

J. O. Urmson, *Philosophical Analysis*, Oxford UP, 1956. (Fairly elementary.)

L. Wittgenstein, *Tractatus Logico-Philosophicus*, 1921, trans. D. F. Pears and B. F. McGuinness, RKP, 1961. (Very difficult.)

Logical constructions. When we say 'The average person has 2.4 children' we are really saying something about Smith, Jones, etc. The sentence is analysable into a set of sentences in which the phrase 'the average person' does not appear. The average person is therefore a logical construction, and 'the average person' is an incomplete symbol. These notions were introduced by Russell.

Later writers, especially Wisdom, distinguished weak and strong senses of 'incomplete symbol'. A symbol was incomplete in a weak sense if (i) it purported to refer to something; (ii) the sentence containing it would be replaced, in a proper logical language, by sentences not containing it; but (iii) these new sentences would only be true, in simple affirmative cases, if the thing apparently referred to did indeed exist. If 'The present king of France is bald' is analysed by the theory of DESCRIPTIONS, 'the present king of France' is an incomplete symbol in a weak sense. A symbol was incomplete in a strong sense if, (i), like 'the average person', it disappeared when the sentence containing it was properly reformulated, but (ii) the reformulated version could be true, in simple affirmative cases, even though what the symbol apparently referred to did not exist (no person with 2.4 children exists). 'Logical construction' (or 'construct') was thereafter kept for what incomplete symbols in a strong sense purported to refer to, i.e. the average person, but not the present King of France, would be a logical construction. There is, however, a complication: Moore held that if 'the average person' is an incomplete symbol, then so is 'has 2.4 children'; but this latter does not seem, straightforwardly, to involve a logical construction.

Logical constructions, therefore, lost the role they had in the theory of descriptions, but they remained a powerful tool for reductive analysis (see PHENOMENALISM). Although Russell sometimes used the phrase logical fictions, logical constructions are not hypothetical, inferred, fictitious or imaginary entities. The average person is none of these. They are often contrasted with inferred entities (i.e. entities we infer to exist, but cannot observe). In scientific contexts those logical constructions which purport to be properties (as the average person purports to be an object), e.g. density, which can vary in degree, are sometimes called intervening variables, while inferred entities are called hypothetical constructs (but usage varies).

L. W. Beck, 'Constructions and inferred entities', *Philosophy of Science*, 1950, reprinted in H. Feigl and M. Brodbeck (eds), *Readings in the Philosophy of Science*, Appleton-Century-Crofts, 1953. (Compares treatment of things like electrons as logical constructions and as inferred entities.)

N. MacCorquodale and P. E. Meehl, 'Hypothetical constructs and intervening variables', *Psychological Review*, 1948, reprinted in H. Feigl and M. Brodbeck (above). (Discussed in succeeding volumes of *Psychological Review*.)

J. O. Urmson, *Philosophical Analysis*, Oxford UP, 1956, pp. 27–41. (Traces how strong sense incomplete symbols grew out of weak sense ones.)

J. Wisdom, 'Logical constructions', *Mind*, 1931–3. (Series of articles forming *locus classicus* for strong sense logical constructions. Cf. particularly 1931, pp. 188–95.)

Logical fictions. See LOGICAL CONSTRUCTIONS.

Logical geography. See SPACE.

Logically proper names. See MEANING, DESCRIPTIONS.

Logical subject. See MEANING.

Logical Positivism. See POSITIVISM.

Logicism. See MATHEMATICS.

Logics (many-valued). See TRUTH-VALUE.

Logistic. See LOGIC.

Logos. The Greek concept has two basic and interconnected strands: (i) the result of speaking, i.e. speech, discourse, theory (as against practice), sentence, story; (ii) the result of picking out or counting, i.e. account, formula, rationale, definition, proportion, reason (both as 'a reason' and as 'the power of reason'). For examples in English of how the two strands tend to merge cf. 'recount', 'all told'.

W. K. C. Guthrie, *A History of Greek Philosophy*, vol. 1, Cambridge UP, 1967, pp. 419ff.

Lottery paradox. In a fair lottery with 100 tickets the chance that any given ticket will lose is 99 per cent. It therefore seems reasonable, for any given ticket, to believe, or accept as a basis for action, the statement, 'This ticket will lose.' Yet the conjunction of such statements for all the tickets must be false, since some ticket will win, so we can hardly accept the conjunction. We seem to have to accept each statement separately, but not the conjunction of them. The paradox raises difficulties especially for the notion of the acceptance of inductive conclusions (cf. CONFIRMATION).

M. Clark, *Paradoxes from A–Z*, Routledge, 2002.
H. E. Kyburg, *Probability and Inductive Logic*, Macmillan, 1970, pp. 176–7, 179.

Luck, moral. See MORAL LUCK.

M

Mach, Ernest W. J. W. 1838–1916. Born in Moravia, he worked mainly in Prague and Vienna; in 1901 he became a member of the Austrian house of peers. He contributed significantly to physics as well as to philosophy of science, and his name is applied to various phenomena connected with shock waves. In philosophy of science Mach developed a form of POSITIVISM. *The Science of Mechanics*, 1883. *The Analysis of Sensations and the Relation of the Physical to the Psychical*, 1906. *Popular Scientific Lectures*, 1894 (or 1896). *Knowledge and Error: Sketches on the Psychology of Enquiry*, 1905.

Mach's principle. The principle that a body's inertial mass depends on the mass of every other body in the universe. This can be used to defend a relational view of SPACE because the 'fixed' stars, which form the main repository of mass in the universe, provide a frame for deciding when a body is rotating without appealing, as Newton did, to absolute space. Variants of the principle exist, and it is not explicit in Mach himself. One question is whether the stars cause the inertial mass to be what it is, or whether they merely provide a frame of reference (so that the dependence is merely metrical rather than causal).

I. Bradley, *Mach's Philosophy of Science*, Athlone, 1971, chapter 6.

Machiavelli, Niccolò. 1469–1527. Italian, specifically Florentine, politician and writer, often taken as an exemplar of devious, cynical political amoralism for gain. In his deliberately provocative treatise, *The Prince (Il Principe)*, written in 1513–14 and published post-humously in 1532, he does indeed argue that being morally good in conventional terms may not always be the most effective course of action for a prince and his people, given the unpredictable role of 'Fortuna' or chance. The most successful prince will privately balance moral action with immoral action according to circumstances, though remaining publicly above reproach. But this may be misleading. For the prince's aim should be good results (whatever the means) for the state, not personal gain. Also, his *Discourses on the Ten Books of Titus Livy* paints a different picture, praising civic virtue, love of God and country, and the rule of law, and places republics or government by the people as always superior to the rule of princes.

C. Nederman, 'Niccolò Machiavelli', *The Stanford Encyclopedia of Philosophy* (Fall 2005 Edition), Edward N. Zalta (ed.). Available at: http://plato.stanford.edu/archives/fall2005/entries/machiavelli/ (accessed 1 March 2009).

McDowell, John. 1942–. Born in South Africa, has worked in Oxford and Pittsburgh. Written on a wide range of subjects, but moral philosophy, the philosophy of mind and the philosophy of language in particular. Follows Wittgenstein in seeing the task of philosophy as primarily therapeutic, resolving confusions in our thinking, 'giving philosophy peace', rather than substantive theorizing. Although he sees his own theories as a form of NATURALISM, he is opposed to the reductive scientistic naturalism of many of his contemporaries. Although he is an EXTERNALIST about the mental, he claims that objective judgements can only be made from within the framework of our actual practices. In *Mind and World*, Harvard UP, 1994; with new introduction, 1996, he offers a broadly Kantian account of INTENTIONALITY. Both *Mind, Value, and Reality*, Harvard UP, 1998, and *Meaning, Knowledge, and Reality,* Harvard UP, 1998, are collections of many his papers up to their dates of publication, but he continues to write prolifically.

M. de Gaynesford, *John McDowell*, Blackwell, 2004.

T. Thornton, *John McDowell*, Acumen, 2004.

McTaggart, John E. 1866–1925. Cambridge metaphysician, born in London, who developed an idealist (and atheistic) system centring on the notions of substance and the part/whole relation (and also involving human reincarnation). He denied the reality of many things, such as material objects and space, but is now best known for his argument against the reality of time (see SPACE). *The Nature of Existence*, 1921 (vol. 1), 1927 (vol. 2).

C. D. Broad, *An Examination of McTaggart's Philosophy*, Cambridge UP, 1933 (vol. 1), 1938 (vol. 2). (Standard commentary.)

Magnitudes (extensive and intensive). A magnitude is extensive if (a) things can be ordered in accordance with it; and (b) there are units of it such that, for any number n, things with n such units can be constructed out of n things with one unit each. A magnitude is intensive if only the ordering is possible. Roughly, M is an intensive magnitude if 'more M than' makes sense but 'twice as M as' does not. It is extensive if both makes sense. Long is clearly extensive, and beautiful presumably intensive, but examples are often hard to classify.

H. L. Bergson, *Time and Free Will*, Allen and Unwin, 1910 (French original, 1889), chapter 1. (Criticizes notion of intensive magnitudes.)

B. Ellis, *Basic Concepts of Measurement*, Cambridge UP, 1966. (More extended and technical than Smart. See p. 85.)

J. J. C. Smart, 'Measurement', *Australasian Journal of Philosophy*, 1959. (Measurement in general. Confines 'magnitude' to extensive magnitudes.)

Major premise, term. See SYLLOGISM.

Malebranche, Nicholas. 1638–1715. Born in Paris, he became a member of the religious society called the Oratoire de France. Starting largely under the influence of DESCARTES he elaborated a system which is now known chiefly for his OCCASIONALISM and his doctrine that we 'see all things in God', i.e. that the objects of almost all our knowledge are ideas, which exist independently of us and in God; we know external objects only as represented by ideas. Malebranche also wrote on science and morality. *De la Recherche de la vérité*, 1674–5, trans. T. Lennon and P. J. Olscamp *The Search After Truth* and *Elucidations of the Search After Truth*, Ohio State UP, 1980. *Traité de la nature et de la grace*, 1680. *Traité de morale*, 1684. *Entretiens sur la métaphysique et sur la religion*, 1688.

Manifold. A variegated complex of elements considered as it is before being organized. For Kant especially, the sensory manifold is the as yet unstructured variety of material presented to the senses, which the mind then organizes through concepts, so that perception results.

Many-sorted logic. A logical system is many-sorted if different groups of individual VARIABLES in it are restricted to ranging over different kinds of things. Where all the individual variables have the same range the system is one-sorted.

Marcel, Gabriel. 1889–1973. French philosopher and dramatist born in Paris. He is usually classed as an EXISTENTIALIST, though of a theistic kind as opposed to SARTRE, HEIDEGGER or JASPERS (he joined the Catholic church in 1929), but the aptness of this classification has been disputed. *Journal métaphysique*, 1927. *Être et avoir*, 1935. *Presence et immortalité*, 1959. (These three volumes form a philosophical diary, trans. as *The Metaphysical Journal* by B. Wall, Henry Regnery Company, 1950.) *The Philosophy of Existence*, 1949 (republished as *Philosophy of Existentialism*, 1961; translated essays). *The Mystery of Being*, 2 vols, 1950–1.

Marginal utility, diminishing. For any good, the marginal utility of that good decreases as the quantity of the good increases. If I give you one orange, it may give you a certain amount of pleasure – x units, say. If I give you two oranges, you may obtain 2x units of pleasure – depending on how hungry you are. But if I give you three oranges, then it is unlikely you will obtain 3x units, and as the number of oranges goes up, the amount of pleasure each orange gives you diminishes – you are satiated with oranges, some of them will go bad before you can eat them, etc.
See PLEASURE, UTILITARIANISM.

Maritain, Jacques. 1882–1973. French Catholic philosopher born in Paris, who worked mainly there and in North America. After being influenced by BERGSON in his youth he became interested in Thomism (see AQUINAS), developing a system which particularly emphasized different kinds of knowledge (scientific, metaphysical, mystical). He also wrote prolifically on metaphysics, ethics, political philosophy and aesthetics, and helped to draft the *United Nations Universal Declaration of Human Rights*, 1948. *Degrees of Knowledge*, 1932 (his best known work: on the types of knowledge).

Marx, Karl H. 1818–83. Born in Trier, Germany, he worked in various cities of north-west Europe, and eventually in London. He was primarily a sociologist and economist, but his views have had considerable philosophical influence. He started from HEGEL's dialectic and, in collaboration with Engels, founded the doctrine of dialectical MATERIALISM, and developed a system of economic determinism which was supposed to govern human activities in every sphere. *Economic and Philosophical Manuscripts of 1844*, 1844. *The German Ideology*, written 1845–6 (with Engels). *The Poverty of Philosophy*, 1847 (criticism of P. J. Proudhon (1809–65)). *The Communist*

Manifesto, 1848 (with Engels). *Outlines of the Critique of Political Economy*, written 1857–8, published 1941, often referred to as the *Grundrisse*. *Das Kapital* (*Capital*), 3 vols, 1867, 1885, 1893. *Theories of Surplus Value*, written 1862–3.

Mass noun. See COUNT.

Materialism. Usually the view that everything, or everything in a certain sphere, is made of matter: only matter exists, and mind, spirit, etc. are either illusory (eliminative materialism) or (a commoner view) can be somehow reduced to matter (reductive materialism). A non-reductive and non-eliminative materialism may also be based on SUPERVENIENCE. The IDENTITY THEORY OF MIND is often called simply materialism, and along with 'physicalism' the term may apply to any theory saying that the mental is nothing over and above the physical. (Materialists may or may not also deny the independent reality of abstract things like universals.) In another sense, uncommon as a sense of the word in philosophy, materialism says mind, etc. are real enough but causally dependent on matter: a weak version would say that if there had been no matter there would be no mind; a stronger version would add that if matter were destroyed mind would vanish too. Also uncommon in philosophy is 'materialist' in the sense of 'emphasizing material values (food and drink, etc.)'. Dialectical materialism, however, which applies Hegel's DIALECTICAL process to a material rather than spiritual reality, does emphasize material values in that it makes economic considerations both the cause and the proper end of human, and especially social, action. See also REDUCTIONISM, HISTORICAL MATERIALISM and bibliography to IDENTITY THEORY OF MIND.

D. M. Armstrong, *A Materialist Theory of Mind*, Routledge, 1968, revised 1993. (Cf. also his *Universals and Scientific Realism*, Cambridge UP, 1978. Rejecting substantial universals but also extreme nominalism.)

T. Horgan, 'From supervenience to superdupervenience', *Mind*, 1993. (See particularly § 7 for kinds of materialism, with many references.)

A. Quinton, *The Nature of Things*, RKP, 1973. (Materialist standpoint.)

H. Robinson (ed.), *Objections to Physicalism*, Clarendon, 1993. (Specially written essays. See editor's 'Introduction', pp. 1–3, for uses of 'materialism' and 'physicalism'.)

D.-H. Ruben, *Marxism and Materialism: A Study in Marxist Theory of Knowledge*, Harvester, 1977, revised 1979. (Tries to mediate between Marxist and Anglo-Saxon philosophy. See Introduction for senses of 'materialism'.)

Material mode. See FORMAL MODE.

Mathematics (philosophy of). The study of concepts and systems appearing in mathematics, of the nature of mathematical knowledge, and of the justification of mathematical statements.

The basic objects of mathematics are NUMBERS, of which there are various kinds (cardinal, ordinal, natural, real, etc.; see Russell). Whether numbers are real entities, and how we decide this, are questions shared with metaphysics (cf. BEING). Platonists, or realists, think that numbers are ABSTRACT entities in the sense of being outside space and time, and that mathematical truths, including those about infinite numbers, exist independently of our researches. Constructivists emphasize the dependence of mathematics on the activity of mathematicians (see INTUITIONISM, FINITISM). Numbers have been defined in terms of CLASSES or sets which are themselves studied by set theory (cf. CALCULUS). In fact the definition of 'equinumerous class' helped G. CANTOR to elaborate the study of infinite numbers. One class is equinumerous ('equivalent' and 'equipollent' are other terms used here) to another if for each member of one there can be found exactly one corresponding member of the other. These definitions enable the calculus of classes, and set theory, to be used to axiomatize mathematics (cf. AXIOM SYSTEM, LOGIC). One difficulty about classes stems from RUSSELL'S PARADOX. Logicists, however (notably Frege and Russell), who claim to reduce mathematics entirely to logic, have used classes for this purpose. They claim that mathematical objects can be defined in logical terms, via classes, and also that mathematical proofs can be reduced to logical proofs. But there are difficulties in proving the existence of classes in general from axioms which can be reasonably regarded as purely logical.

Geometry was originally regarded as fundamentally different from arithmetic, and as dealing with space. Kant's views on space provoked questions about how different geometries relate to each other and to real SPACE. Arithmetic suggests the question of how different algebras relate to each other and to the world (cf. AXIOM SYSTEM). These questions are connected with the questions whether our knowledge of mathematical concepts and propositions is empirical as, in particular, J. S. Mill thought, or A PRIORI. Modern developments on all these questions have tended to unite arithmetic and geometry.

Other questions include: what is truth in mathematics, and how is it related to provability? Is every mathematical truth provable (cf. GÖDEL'S THEOREMS), and can we know mathematical truths by direct insight as well as by proof?

*S. F. Barker, *Philosophy of Mathematics*, Prentice-Hall, 1964. (Elementary.)

P. Benacerraf and H. Putnam (eds), *Philosophy of Mathematics*, Blackwell, 1964. (Important collection of readings, of varying difficulty.)

*G. Frege, *Foundations of Arithmetic*, Blackwell, 1884, trans. by J. L. Austin, 1950. (Fairly elementary discussion of numbers, etc., from Platonist and logicist viewpoint by a pioneer of modern logic. Includes more technical appendix on Russell's paradox.)

L. Goddard, '"True" and "provable"', *Mind*, 1958. (Cf. discussions in *Mind*, 1960, 1962.)

S. Körner, *Philosophy of Mathematics*, Hutchinson, 1960. (Rather more advanced.)

I. Lakatos, *Proofs and Refutations*, Cambridge UP, 1976, original version 1963–4. (Elaborate discussion, in dialogue form with historical notes, of genesis of some problems about proof.)

H. Lehman (See bibliography to A PRIORI.)

B. Russell, *Introduction to Mathematical Philosophy*, Allen and Unwin, 1919. (General.)

G. Ryle, C. Lewy and K. R. Popper, 'Why are the calculuses of logic and arithmetic applicable to reality?', *Proceedings of the Aristotelian Society*, supplementary vol., 1946.

*H. Wang, 'Process and existence in mathematics', in Y. Bar-Hillel *et al.* (eds), *Essays on the Foundations of Mathematics*, Magnes Press, 1962. (Brings out some of the issues in mainly simple language.)

Maximin principle. See ORIGINAL POSITION.

Meaning. Problems about meaning can be put into two main and inter-related groups: What is meaning, in the sense in which words and sentences have meaning? What different kinds of meaning are there, and how are they related to various other notions?

Discussions of what meanings are have mainly concerned words and sentences, which differ from each other: We construct sentences, and can understand ones we have not seen before. Sentences have meaning because of the words in them, while words only have meaning because they are fitted to play a role in sentences. Different words may have meaning in different ways, but whether all words have meaning is disputed. Do proper names (see below)? Does 'to' in 'I want to go'?

During the earlier part of the twentieth century notions like naming, referring to, or standing for have dominated such discussions. Naming (denotative, referential) theories of meaning say that a word's meaning is what it names or stands for, or else its relation to

that. Cf. the slogan *unum nomen unum nominatum*: 'For every name
there is exactly one thing named'. Proper names are taken as the primary case. Hence the nickname 'Fido' – Fido theory. The word 'Fido'
has as its meaning the dog Fido which it names. On this theory a
general word like 'dog' could stand for the UNIVERSAL, doghood
(Russell), or the class of dogs, or different dogs on different occasions
(also Russell). 'Red' could stand for the colour red, 'runs' and 'running' for the action of running, even perhaps 'if' for the notion of
doubt or conditionality.

Ideational theories make words stand for ideas or thoughts, etc.
(Aristotle, Locke). They provide a single kind of thing (ideas) for very
different kinds of words to stand for, though usually without
explaining the notion of standing for.

All these are relational or correspondence theories. They say that a
word's meaning is or involves a thing (physical, mental or abstract) to
which it is related. Largely through the influence of Wittgenstein they
have been much attacked, though they have also experienced a certain
revival recently.

This attack on relational theories implied that meanings are not
'things', and led to the slogan 'Don't ask for the meaning, ask for the
use'. Use theories explain meaning in terms of use. They provoke
questions about whether the connection between meaning and use is
the same for words and for sentences, whether meaning is as wide a
notion as use (see below on speech acts), and whether what matters
most is actual use or rules for use. This last distinction is one version
of that between de facto and de jure theories. De facto theories
explain meaning in terms of what happens or is the case, e.g. how
people actually do use words. De jure theories explain it in terms of
norms, rules, conventions, standards, or in general what ought to be
the case, e.g. they might claim that 'I didn't do nothing' cannot
properly mean 'I didn't do anything', despite Cockney usage.

Causal or stimulus/response theories explain the meaning of a word
or sentence in terms of its effect on the hearer or the cause of the
speaker's uttering it. They are examples of de facto theories, stemming from BEHAVIOURISM, and they claim the advantages of a
scientific approach. They become naming theories too, if they say that
the object named is the meaning while the object's effects are what
make it the meaning. A causal theory of names and 'natural kind
words' (like 'lion' and 'water') has recently been advanced by S.
Kripke and H. Putnam, in opposition to description theories like
Russell's (see below). The same authors have advanced a causal
theory of REFERENCE, whereby what if anything one refers to is

partly determined by the things to which one stands in certain causal relations.

A theory of sentence-meaning also stimulated by science is the verification theory, whereby a sentence's meaning is the method of verifying it; cf. logical POSITIVISM for this, and for the operationalist theory of word meaning. Picture theories are analogues for sentences of naming theories for words and like naming theories they are correspondence theories. They are especially associated with LOGICAL ATOMISM, and with the correspondence theory of TRUTH.

On picture theories sentences, whether true or false, have meaning because they picture possibilities; true sentences picture those possibilities which are facts. But can picture theories cater for the stating involved in stating facts?

A common modern theory says that to give the meaning of a standard indicative sentence is to give its TRUTH CONDITIONS. These, however, are not given for sentences individually but holistically, by constructing a 'theory of truth' for a whole language. This starts with axioms saying what the words mean and rules for combining them into sentences, in such a way that theorems can be derived, each of which says of some sentence that it is true if and only if so-and-so is the case, where 'so-and-so' represents what, intuitively, the sentence means. Such a theorem is called a T-sentence. An example would be, '"Snow is white" is true if and only if snow is white'. When, as here, what follows 'if and only if' is the same, without the inverted commas, as what precedes it, the T-sentence is called homophonic (literally, 'same-sounding'). A theory of truth whose axioms yield the intuitively right T-sentences is said to satisfy Convention (or Criterion) T. See also TRANSLATION (for 'radical interpretation'). Discussion of all this has largely concerned whether truth conditions alone can provide adequate resources for a proper theory of meaning. See REALISM. In a more limited sphere a truth conditions account of meaning has been offered as a way of avoiding positing the existence of certain properties, such as that of being present: '2009 is present' will get its meaning by being true if and only if uttered during 2009, so that no property of 'presentness' is needed.

With the general question of what meaning is belongs also the question of synonymy, i.e. when words or sentences have the same meaning.

Turning to the second of the original questions, about kinds of meaning, and related notions, we can for suitable words distinguish between intension and extension (cf. INTENSIONALITY AND INTENTIONALITY), and between various allied notions. Thus Mill distinguishes connotation from denotation. A word denotes the things it applies to, and connotes the attributes it implies that those things have. 'Person' connotes, perhaps, the attribute of being a rational animal, and denotes all persons. 'Connotation' can refer to the relation or to what is connoted, and 'denotation' similarly. The comprehension of 'person' is the whole set of properties shared by all persons, or else the set which (logically) must be shared by them.

Frege distinguishes Sinn and Bedeutung, standardly translated sense and reference respectively, though other translations exist, and 'meaning' has been used for each of them at different times. The phrases 'the evening star' and 'the morning star' have the same reference, Venus, but different senses. Frege uses this to explain why 'The evening star is the morning star' is not trivial, like 'Venus is Venus'.

The relations between these terms are complex. Roughly, a term denotes, independently of occasion, all those things we can refer to on a given occasion by using certain phrases containing the term. 'Cats' denotes cats in general, and we can use a phrase like 'that cat' to refer to, say, Tiddles on some occasion. Strictly it is we who refer to Tiddles by saying 'that cat', but the phrase 'that cat' can itself be said to refer to Tiddles on this occasion. ('Denote', especially, is often used loosely.)

A term has divided reference (Quine) if, like 'shoe' but unlike 'water' or 'red', it can be used, without additions like 'piece of', to refer to different objects.

The connotation/sense distinction is difficult, and controversial, but an example may illustrate one way of making the distinction. Is it contradictory to say, 'The queen of England is not queen at all but illegitimate'? Yes, if 'the queen of England' is interpreted as having connotation, since the statement then implies that the person referred to by the phrase has the property of reigning. But the sense of the phrase can be used to pick out the person, without committing the speaker to the truth of this implication, for a hearer, for example, who believes that Elizabeth II is legitimate. If the phrase is thus interpreted as still having sense, but not connotation, the statement is not contradictory. If Elizabeth II were not legitimate, the sentence could be used to say so without contradiction, and might be useful for ensuring that the supposed hearer knew who was being talked about. Sense and reference apply to subject expressions and sometimes to predicates and to sentences (Frege thought the reference of a predicate was a concept, and of a sentence was its TRUTH-VALUE). Connotation and denotation can apply to subject expressions and predicate expressions, but not to sentences. Sense is close to the non-technical notion of sense.

Proper names, which provide the model of meaning for naming theories, raise problems about whether they have connotation or sense or both. 'That woman there' picks someone out as being a woman and being in a certain place, but 'John' makes no obvious reference to any of its bearer's properties. In what sense are proper names words? Do they form part of a language? They are hardly meaningless, but they do not usually appear in dictionaries. Russell followed Mill in thinking they lack connotation. However, he thought this only of logically proper names, i.e. those names which were not abbreviated descriptions, as he thought ordinary proper names in fact were. He thought 'Socrates' was not really a name at all, but an abbreviation for, for example, 'the philosopher who drank hemlock', (cf. DESCRIPTIONS). This is the view criticized by Kripke and Putnam (above). A logical subject is either the subject of a sentence in a logically ideal language, i.e. a language where a sentence's real and apparent subjects coincide, or it is what such a subject refers to.

Under the influence of logical positivism, cognitive, descriptive or factual meaning has been distinguished from other kinds, notably emotive, evaluative and prescriptive (see NATURALISM). Arising out of these distinctions and generalizing from them is Austin's theory of SPEECH ACTS, which distinguishes between the meaning of what is said and what he calls the 'illocutionary force' of saying it. Attempts have been made to analyse the meanings of some words, including 'good', 'true', 'probable', in terms of speech acts they are used in making, and to ground meaning itself in illocutionary force (a kind of use theory). It is here that the different kinds of IMPLICATION (presupposition, implicature, etc.) and their roles become relevant.

It is also important to distinguish, especially concerning TOKEN-REFLEXIVES, between what meaning words and sentences have in general and what they mean, or what the speaker means by them, on a given occasion. This raises the question of how meaning is related to intention, for people can 'mean something' both in the sense of referring to something ('I mean you') and as intending to do something ('I meant to come yesterday'). They may also 'mean' something in the sense of suggesting something beyond what they mean in the direct sense ('In saying "Time's getting on" he meant it was late, and he also meant it was time for you to go'; cf. IMPLICATION again). An interesting question, discussed by Wittgenstein, concerns what it is to mean what one says.

In fact not only words, sentences and people can be subjects of the verb 'mean' but also actions, works of art, and natural events, states and processes. 'Mean' can have natural objects or events as its subject when there are symptoms ('Those spots mean measles') or causes ('clouds mean rain') or things having value or importance ('That locket means a lot to me'). 'His life has no meaning' seems to come between this last sense and the sense of pattern, order, idea in which works of art have meaning. Actions have meaning either in these ways or in the way sentences have it. Grice distinguishes the various kinds of meaning into two main groups, natural, the group applying natural events, etc., and non-natural, the group applying to people and symbols, words and sentences, etc.

A final question concerns meaninglessness; how many kinds of it are there, and how are they related to contradiction and falsity (cf. CATEGORIES)? See also REFERRING, AMBIGUOUS, DEFINITION, OPEN TEXTURE, REALISM, TRUTH CONDITIONS.

Aristotle, *De Interpretatione*, particularly chapters 1–4, trans. with commentary in J. L. Ackrill, *Aristotle's Categories and De Interpretatione*, Oxford UP, 1963. (Basis of Aristotle's theory of meaning, though only elementary.)

L. J. Cohen, *The Diversity of Meaning*, Methuen, 1962 (revised 1966). (Chapter 2 introduces de facto/de jure distinction.)

E. Daitz, 'The picture theory of meaning', *Mind*, 1953, reprinted in A. Flew (ed.), *Essays in Conceptual Analysis*, Macmillan, 1956.

D. Davidson, 'Truth and meaning', *Synthèse*, 1967, revised in 'Radical interpretation', *Dialectica*, 1973, both reprinted with other relevant material in his *Inquiries into Truth and Interpretation*, Clarendon, 1984. (Leading exponent of truth-conditions theory. See also for a contrasting view M. A. E. Dummett, 'What is a theory of meaning? II' in G. Evans and J. McDowell (eds), *Truth and Meaning*, Oxford UP, 1976, reprinted with other relevant material in his *The Seas of Language*, Clarendon 1993.)

G. Frege, 'Sinn und Bedeutung', 1892, trans. in P. Geach and M. Black, *Translations from the Philosophical Writings of Gottlob Frege*, Blackwell, 1952, and also in H. Feigl and W. Sellars (eds), *Readings in Philosophical Analysis*, Cornell UP, 1949.

N. Goodman, 'On likeness of meaning', *Analysis*, vol. 10, 1949, reprinted in M. Macdonald (ed.), *Philosophy and Analysis*, Blackwell, 1954, (Difficulties over synonymy.)

H. P. Grice, 'Meaning', *Philosophical Review*, 1957, reprinted in P. F. Strawson (ed.), *Philosophical Logic*, Oxford UP, 1967, and also, along with other relevant material, in Grice's *Studies in the Way of Words*, Harvard UP, 1989. (Criticizes causal theory and develops theory using intention (which might, however, itself be called a causal theory).)

J. N. Keynes, *Formal Logic*, 1884, 4th (revised) edn, 1906. (Full details of traditional terminology of intension and extension. For later terms cf. also R. Carnap, *Meaning and Necessity*, Chicago UP, 1947, chapter 3.)

S. Kripke, *Naming and Necessity*, 1980 Blackwell (original version, 1972). (Causal theory of names, natural kind words, and reference. Cf. also S. P. Schwartz (ed.), *Naming, Necessity and Natural Kinds*, Cornell UP, 1977, including inter alia articles by H. Putnam and G. Evans.)

E. Lepore, (ed.) *Truth and Interpretation*, Blackwell, 1986. (Important essays by Davidson, Dummett and others on truth-conditions theory.)

J. Locke, *An Essay concerning Human Understanding*, 1689, book 3. (An intentional theory.)

J. S. Mill, *A System of Logic*, 1843, Longmans, Green, book 1, chapter 2, particularly § 5. (Connotation/denotation distinction. Classic discussion of names. Cf. final footnote on senses of 'connotation'.)

A. W. Moore (ed.), *Meaning and Reference*, Oxford UP, 1993. (Includes several classic items.)

Plato, *Cratylus*. (Earliest surviving connected discussion of meaning.)

W. V. O. Quine, *Word and Object*, Wiley, 1960, § 19. (Divided reference.)

B. Russell, *An Inquiry into Meaning and Truth*, Allen and Unwin, 1940, particularly chapters 1–7, 13–15. (Complex theory of meaning of words and significance (as he calls it) of sentences. Cf. his *My Philosophical Development*, Allen and Unwin, 1959, chapters 13, 14.)

J. R. Searle (See bibliography to GOOD.)

D. Wiggins, 'The sense and reference of predicates', *Philosophical Quarterly*, 1984, reprinted in C. Wright (ed.), *Frege: Tradition and Influence*, Blackwell, 1984. (Relevant on sense and connotation, and on the interpretation (and correction) of Frege.)

L. Wittgenstein, *Philosophical Investigations*, Blackwell, 1953, particularly § 1–43. (Classic criticism of naming theories in favour of use theory.)

Meaning postulates. A device whereby implicitly ANALYTIC sentences, like 'Bachelors are male', are introduced into a formal language (one whose terms are rigorously defined) by postulates like 'Anything, if it is a bachelor, is (to count as) male'. More interestingly, 'Anything, if it is a raven, is (to count as) black' could be used as a meaning postulate to fix a sense of 'raven'. Anything we refuse to call black we will then refuse to call a raven.

R. Carnap, 'Meaning postulates', *Philosophical Studies*, 1952, reprinted in his *Meaning and Necessity*, 2nd edn, Chicago UP, 1956.

Meinong, Alexius. 1853–1920. Austrian, born in Lemberg (Lviv) in Ukraine, he worked mainly in Graz. He developed BRENTANO's view by insisting on a distinction between the content and the object ('Gegenstand') of a thought, and his philosophy largely concerns the various kinds of such objects. These include chairs and tables, which exist; 'objectives' like the being of chairs, which are always positive or negative; higher-order objects like the difference between red and green, which merely subsist; dragons and the golden mountain and the round square, which neither exist nor subsist but still have 'Sosein' ('being so'). Objects which were not objectives he called 'Objekta'. He also supplemented Brentano's distinction between ideas and judgements by introducing 'supposals' or 'assumptions' ('Annahmen'), and he elaborated a theory of value. *Über Annahmen*, 1902 (importantly revised in 1910, and translated and edited by J. Heanue, *On Assumptions*, California UP, 1983). 'Über Gegenstandstheorie', in A. Meinong (ed.), *Untersuchungen zur Gegenstandstheorie und Psychologie*, 1904 (translated as 'On the theory of objects' in R. Chisholm (ed.), *Realism and the Background of Phenomenology*, Free Press, 1960). *Über Möglichkeit und Wahrscheinlichkeit*, 1915. *Über emotionale Präsentation*, 1917 (translated as *On Emotional Presentation*, Northwestern UP, 1972). See also BEING, OBJECT, REFERRING.

Memory. In general a faculty of knowing, whose exercise can be called remembering, recollecting, recalling, being reminded, reminiscing; the relations between these form one of the problems involved, though 'remember' is the most general verb (it can also mean 'bear in mind'). 'Memory' can take the plural when it refers to experiences (or things experienced) which are remembered, or to rememberings of them.

We can remember people, places, objects, appearances, experiences, events, facts, as well as remembering to do things, how to do things, where to find things, etc. Memory involves some reference to the past, but what is remembered need not be the past; I can remember that five twelves are sixty, that tomorrow is Tuesday, as well as remembering to put the cat out. But I am not remembering something if the sole basis for what I am doing lies in the present. I can only remember to put the cat out if I have earlier had it in mind to put it out. Is remembering simply knowing because one has known? But there are difficulties with this (Martin and Deutscher, Munsat): not everything I know or knew (it is claimed) can be remembered; I can know, but can I remember, that if Hitler had won the war, British Jews would have perished? Perhaps only in the 'bear in mind' sense? Also if I tell someone a fact, forget it, and then learn it again from that person, I now know it only because I once knew it, but I am not remembering it; the causal theory of memory here faces an objection facing other causal theories too (e.g. of PERCEPTION), that of deviant causal chains: not just any old causal chain will do. It seems then that some 'trace' is needed, whether physical in the brain or mental, to be a causal link connecting my previous knowing with my present knowing. But the whole idea of 'traces' or causal theories of memory has been attacked on the grounds that no coherent account can be given of what properties such a trace must have, or of how it could operate without a further trace to set it going, i.e. of how the brain could 'pick out' the right trace without a 'little man' ('homunculus') inside it to do so. Stimulus/response theories might seem to solve this 'picking out' problem, but how do the stimulus and response get associated, since there can be indefinitely many responses to any stimulus? (See Bursen, in bibliography.)

Memory seems, at least in many cases, to give us knowledge of the past. Is this because we now have some mental item, e.g. an image, which represents the past (representative theory), or because we are now directly aware of the past, though distant in time, rather as we perceive things distant in space (realist theory)? Both theories raise problems. How can we know that such images do represent the past, and distinguish them from those which belong to imagination and don't? How could we be aware of a past no longer there to be known? How does this compare with seeing stars so distant they have already vanished? But must there anyway be some object we are aware of, be it past event or present image, any more than when we know a mathematical fact? Two further questions arise, a metaphysical one of whether the past must somehow be real if we are to know it or know about it, in whatever way, and an epistemological one: if, as the representative theory says, we are acquainted only with the present, how can we get a concept of pastness, and how can statements about the past have meaning if it is impossible in principle to verify them (cf. REALISM)? This leads on to the general question of scepticism about memory: how can we justify our reliance on memory, and how pervasive is that reliance? Can we know the world was not created five minutes ago with us and all our 'memories' ready made (Russell)?

Another question concerns how many different kinds of memory there are, and how they are related, for despite what was said above about memory not needing images and not always being of the past, sometimes we do suddenly remember something having a vivid image as we do so. How relevant is the image in these cases? Might we have a faculty similarly related to the future? How analogous are memory and precognition here? Do we discover facts about the past by inspecting the image, or must we, even in these cases, already know those facts in order to construct the image? What role is played by our intentions in constructing it? Is memory, even here, a source of knowledge, or only a kind of knowledge? It is these cases that make memory seem analogous to perception, and it is here that we talk of our 'memories' and say that we can only remember what we have witnessed: I remember that Caesar invaded Britain, but his doing so is not among my memories, and I cannot remember it. This suggests the question, in what sense can animals remember (see Munsat)? Also can we remember, or only seem to remember, what is false or did not happen?

Quasi-remembering, or q-remembering, is a notion developed recently in discussions of personal identity. A q-memory of an event must be preceded by an experience of that event, but that experience need not, as with ordinary memory, belong to the person doing the remembering. Ordinary memory, where the experience does belong to the remembered, is then regarded as a special case of q-memory.

Finally how is remembering related to forgetting, and what is forgetting? Some help can be got for this and previous questions by studying the grammar of words like 'remember' and 'forget'. We can say 'He remembers (remembered) putting the cat out, but can we say 'He forgets (forgot) ... ', as opposed to 'He has forgotten (had forgotten, no longer remembers) ... ' or 'He forgot that he had put the cat out' (cf. Munsat)?

H. A. Bursen, *Dismantling the Memory Machine*, Reidel, 1978. (Attacks causal theories, especially 'trace' theories.)

R. F. Holland, 'The empiricist theory of memory', *Mind*, 1954, reprinted in S. Hampshire (ed.), *Philosophy of Mind*, Harper and Row, 1966. (Discusses inter alia relations between memory and imagination, and role of images.)

*D. Locke, *Memory*, Macmillan, 1971. (Good introduction.)

C. B. Martin and M. Deutscher, 'Remembering', *Philosophical Review*, 1966. (Detailed discussion, advocating causal theory. Cf. also discussion in D. Owens, *Causes and Coincidences*, Cambridge UP, 1992, pp. 158–62.)

S. Munsat, *The Concept of Memory*, Random House, 1966. (Elementary introduction.)

D. Parfit, *Reasons and Persons*, Oxford UP, 1984. (See p. 220 for quasi-remembering, and cf. also S. Shoemaker, 'Persons and their pasts', *American Philosophical Quarterly*, 1970, reprinted in his *Identity, Cause, and Mind*, Cambridge UP, 1984, for that and related notions. For criticism of the notion of quasi-remembering see M. Schechtman, 'Personhood and personal identity', *Journal of Philosophy*, 1990, particularly § 3.)

B. Russell, *The Analysis of Mind*, Allen and Unwin, 1921. (See pp. 159–60 for world beginning five minutes ago.)

Mentalism. See PSYCHOLOGISM.

Mentioning. See REFERRING.

Mereology. Literally, 'theory of parts'. The relation between a whole and its parts, unlike that between a class and its members, is TRANSITIVE, and mereology names a theory of the Polish logician S. Lesniewski (1886–1939), which treated the structure of classes by using this transitive relation instead of the class–membership relation. He did this to avoid certain difficulties connected with the vicious circle principle and the theory of TYPES. (The term also has a technical use within the theory itself.)

Goodman also used the whole/part relation to deal with problems about stuffs, like water, or qualities, like red. He treated 'water' as a name for the whole quantity of water in the universe, so that the Pacific Ocean is a part of water. Similarly the colour red is treated as the totality of red things, a single large object split up over space.

Mereological essentialism is the theory that the parts of an object are essential to it, so that if any of its parts are lost or replaced it becomes a different object.

R. M. Chisholm, *Person and Object*, Allen and Unwin, 1976, Appendix B. (Mereological essentialism explained and defended.)

N. Goodman, *The Structure of Appearance*, Harvard UP, 1951 (3rd edn, Reidel, 1977).

C. Hughes, 'Is a thing just the sum of its parts?', *Proceedings of the Aristotelian Society*, 1985–6. (Defends mereological essentialism.)

P. Simons, *Parts*, Clarendon, 1987, chapter 1. (General treatment of the subject.)

J. T. J. Srzednicki, V. F. Rickey and J. Czelakowski (eds), *Lesniewski's Sytems: Ontology and Mereology*, Nijhoff, 1984. (Collected articles on and following Lesniewski.)

Merleau-Ponty, Maurice. 1908–61. Born in Rochefort in France, he worked mainly in Lyon and Paris. He is best known for his work on the PHENOMENOLOGICAL description of the phenomena of

consciousness, emphasizing particularly the role of the body. He dis-
agrees in some respects with Husserl, and has affinities with
existentialism. He also had ethical and political interests, and was a
friend and associate of SARTRE, though differing in his attitude to
Marxism. *The Structure of Behaviour*, 1942. *The Phenomenology of
Perception*, 1945. *Sense and Nonsense*, 1948 (collected essays).

T. Baldwin (ed.), *Reading Merleau-Ponty: On Phenomenology of Perception*,
Routledge, 2007. (British and American philosophers on Merleau-Ponty's
relevance to contemporary philosophy.)

T. Carman, *Merleau-Ponty*, Routledge, 2008. (Clear accessible introduction
to life, work and significance.)

Meta-. See PHILOSOPHY, METAPHYSICS.

Metaethics. Metaethics, unlike normative ethics (that is, ethical theory
and applied or practical ethics), does not try to evaluate actions or
people as good or bad, better or worse, but investigates the nature of
ethical properties, attitudes, judgements; the assumptions that lie
behind our moral practices. Within metaethics, views can be broadly
divided into realist or antirealist. Moral realism asserts the objectivity
of moral judgements, which are expressed in statements which are
true or false. Versions of moral realism include intuitionist, naturalist
and rationalist theories. In contrast, moral antirealism denies the
existence of objective moral values, or denies that moral judgements
are expressed in statements which are either true or false. Antirealist
views are either subjective, non-cognitivist or ERROR THEORY.
See COGNITIVISM, ETHICS, NATURALISM, INTUITIONISM,
REALISM.

G. Sayre-McCord, 'Metaethics', *The Stanford Encyclopedia of Philosophy*
(Fall 2008 Edition), Edward N. Zalta (ed.). Available at: http://plato.
stanford.edu/archives/fall2008/entries/metaethics/ (accessed 1 March 2009).

Metahistory. See HISTORY.

Metalanguage. A language rich enough for talking about some language
(which may or may not be itself, or part of itself) is a metalanguage
for the language talked about, which is an object language for it.
'Metalanguage' is thus a relative term, though a language rich enough
for talking about a metalanguage for a given object language is
sometimes called a metametalanguage relative to that object language;

for example, a language L2, could be a metalanguage for L1 while being an object language for L3, a situation likely to arise in systems where words like 'true' have 'typical' AMBIGUITY. 'Object language' means 'language which is the object of investigation'. A language lacking devices for talking about languages (i.e. lacking terms like 'word', 'true', 'say', or quotation marks) can only be an object language.

Metalogic. See LOGIC.

Metamathematics. Also called proof theory. Study of the concepts used in mathematics, especially of the properties of formal systems (see AXIOM). Often now confined to analyses springing from that of D. Hilbert (1862–1943), who insisted on FINITIST restrictions for metamathematics which he relaxed for mathematics itself; cf. INTUITIONISM (for formalism).

> D. Hilbert, 'On the infinite', in P. Benacerraf and H. Putman (eds), *Philosophy of Mathematics*, Blackwell, 1964.

Metaphysics. The original 'meta'-word, deriving from the title given to Aristotle's untitled treatise by his first-century BC editor Andronicus. It means that which comes after 'physics', the latter being the study of nature in general. Thus the questions of metaphysics arise out of, but go beyond, factual or scientific questions about the world.

A central part of metaphysics is ontology. This studies BEING and, in particular nowadays, what there is, e.g. material objects, minds, PERSONS, UNIVERSALS, NUMBERS, FACTS, etc. There is the question of whether these all 'are' in the same sense and to the same degree, and how notions like BEING, existence and subsistence are related together. One can also ask whether particular views on logic commit one to particular views on what exists (e.g. propositions, numbers). A particular theory about what exists, or a list of existents, can be called an ontology. Another question involving logic is whether or not existence is a predicate (or property). Ontology borders on philosophy of religion with questions like: Does anything exist necessarily (cf. ONTOLOGICAL and COSMOLOGICAL ARGUMENTS)? It is necessary that something, no matter what, should exist? Can any answer be given to the question, 'Why is there something rather than nothing?'? 'Ontology' is also a technical name for part of the system of S. Lesniewski (1886–1939).

Metaphysics is distinguished by its questions being general. As well as seeking an inventory of kinds of things that exist, it asks what can be said about anything that exists, just in so far as it exists. Can we classify all that exists, or in some sense is, or has being, into different fundamental kinds, in one or more ways (see CATEGORIES)? Is there any hierarchy among kinds of things? Do some depend on others for their existence or being? These questions involve the relations between very general notions like thing, entity, OBJECT, INDIVIDUAL, UNIVERSAL, particular, SUBSTANCE, and also EVENT, process, state. Here three metaphysical outlooks, overlapping though not exhaustive, may be distinguished. One outlook (e.g. Plato, the rationalists), takes one or more substances as the basis of the universe. A second takes act and potency (e.g. Aquinas); and a third (PROCESS PHILOSOPHY) takes events and processes (e.g. Heraclitus, the Stoics, Hegel, Bergson, Whitehead). These outlooks, especially the first and third, are connected with attitudes towards change. Adherents of the first outlook have often held either that change is not fully real, or that the most basic things in the universe do not change except in secondary or unimportant ways. The third outlook puts change at the heart of things. It does not deny all unity and constancy, which would result in unintelligible chaos, but makes these depend essentially upon change.

The distinction of act from potency, or actuality from potentiality, derives from Aristotle, as does that of FORM from matter and 'privation' (i.e. the absence of form where it could be present). Both these distinctions, it is claimed, are needed when we examine the nature and kinds of change, and they lead us to examine matter itself and its relations to space and substance. SPACE AND TIME in fact provide a whole range of problems about their reality, nature, absoluteness and uniqueness. Change is also closely related to IDENTITY and CAUSATION, both of which also raise special problems in philosophy of mind, concerning personal IDENTITY and FREEWILL.

These notions of change, identity and causation lead to further questions about the general pattern of change in the universe. Is it, in the long run, random or does it lead in a certain direction? Or is it cyclic or repetitive, a view commoner among the Greeks than today though revived on some views in modern cosmology? Is there even, as was believed by some Pythagoreans and Stoics, followed by Nietzsche, an eternal recurrence of the same cycle, an endless repetition of exactly the same world-history? Here we must distinguish between repetitions of the same participants, including ourselves, and repetitions of the same pattern with different participants, our 'doubles'. The same problems arise over 'mirror universes' (cf. SPACE, LEIBNIZ'S LAW, SUFFICIENT REASON).

Questions about space and time suggest further questions about infinity. Is the universe finite or infinite? Here, as in the last paragraph, philosophy and science may overlap. And which is 'higher' or more real, the finite or the infinite? There is a distinction here between Christianity, emphasizing the limitations of finite things, and the Greeks, especially the Pythagoreans and Aristotle, who regarded the infinite as essentially incomplete; Aristotle believed that there could not be an actual infinite, and that the infinite is only potential, so that to say that (e.g.) numbers are infinite may be to say merely that you can always take further numbers beyond those taken already.

All these enquiries about the overall nature of the universe lead to the question whether a necessary being, or God, must be postulated to explain the universe. What sort of EXPLANATIONS can be given? In particular, are teleological EXPLANATIONS needed or possible?

A further general question about the universe is whether in some relevant sense we should regard it as one (MONISM) or many (pluralism). Since monists must presumably admit that plurality is at least apparent, the real/apparent distinction becomes relevant, and with it questions about how far SCEPTICISM with regard to the reality of things can be consistently taken: how different can the world be from what it seems, and how far can we know things as they are? (Cf. EPISTEMOLOGY.) Another view which relies heavily on the real/apparent contrast, because it differs widely from common sense, is IDEALISM, which regards reality as basically mental or dependent on the mind. But idealism need not be sceptical.

An influential source of scepticism earlier in the twentieth century, however, has been interest in the influence of language. Some have thought, especially logical POSITIVISTS like Carnap, that the distinction between substance and attribute is simply a reflection of the grammatical distinction between noun and adjective (without asking how that itself arose), so that instead of talking of things and qualities we should talk of thing-words and quality-words. We will then see, it is claimed, that we need not regard (say) beauty as a metaphysical entity merely because we have the thing-word 'beauty' (cf. FORMAL MODE). How far does 'ontology recapitulate philology'? Philosophers like the logical positivists, who emphasized language, often reacted against speculative metaphysics (the construction of all-embracing systems that cannot be tested by observation). Many empiricists, notably Hume, do so too, though the mantle of empiricism has at least partly fallen on antirealism (see REALISM). Descriptive metaphysics claims to avoid the vices of speculative metaphysics, without abandoning metaphysics altogether. It confines itself to analysing various concepts, like SUBSTANCE, which it claims to show are basic and unavoidable.

Metaphysics also borders on ethics and aesthetics. It asks whether values are grounded in the nature of things, or contribute to the cosmic process, and what kind of reality is possessed by works of art and the things that make them up (e.g. the figures in a painting). Taken as the name of a subject 'metaphysics' is no longer a 'bad word', but the current mood, though far less restrictive than logical positivism, or linguistic philosophy, remains predominantly hostile to anti-common-sense speculations, including idealist or sceptical systems (though idealism has some following in the UK). At the same time it regards most forms of DUALISM as over-simplifying at best. The return of metaphysics is marked by a greater tolerance of large-scale systems, and also of such things as essentialism and substantive (not merely logical) necessity (see ESSENCE, MODALITIES). See also PROCESS PHILOSOPHY.

Aristotle, *Metaphysics*. (See particularly books 4 (or Γ) and 6 (or E), trans. with notes by C. Kirwan in Clarendon Aristotle series, 1971, 2nd edn, 1993, for Aristotle's conception of metaphysics. His *Physics* also contains much now regarded as metaphysics, including discussion of infinity in book 3.)

R. Carnap, *Meaning and Necessity*, 2nd edn, Chicago UP, 1956, supplement A, reprinted in C. Landesman (ed.), *The Problem of Universals*, Basic Books, 1971. (Holds that much metaphysics depends on language.)

*D. W. Hamlyn, *Metaphysics*, Cambridge UP, 1984. (General introduction from modern viewpoint, developing the speculative/descriptive contrast.)

P. van Inwagen, *Metaphysics*, Oxford UP, 1993. (Introduction by in-depth treatment of certain problems, though avowedly limited in scope.)

*J. Kim and E. Sosa, *A Companion to Metaphysics*, Blackwell, 1995. (Large alphabetically organized very useful guide, with more than 250 entries.)

S. Kripke, *Naming and Necessity*, Blackwell, 1980 (original version, 1972). (Influential in revival of essentialism. For an early example of this see also C. Kirwan, 'How strong are the objections to essence?', *Proceedings of the Aristotelian Society*, 1970–1.)

R. Le Poidevin, P. Simons, A. McGonigal and R. Cameron, *The Routledge Companion to Metaphysics*, Routledge, 2009. (Comprehensive guide in over 50 commissioned chapters.)

D. H. Mellor, *Matters of Metaphysics*, Cambridge UP, 1991. (Essays on various topics, amounting to a metaphysical position.)

Midwest Studies in Philosophy, vol. 4, 1979. (Single-topic journal issue entitled *Studies in Metaphysics*.)

W. V. O. Quine, *Word and Object*, Wiley, 1960. (See flyleaf for 'ontology recapitulates philology', attributed to J. G. Miller; cf. the biological slogan 'ontogeny recapitulates phylogeny'.)

A. Quinton, *The Nature of Things*, RKP, 1973. (Discussions both of and in metaphysics.)

P. F. Strawson, *Individuals*, Methuen, 1959. (Defends descriptive metaphysics. Fairly difficult.)

*W. H. Walsh, *Metaphysics*, Hutchinson, 1963. (General introduction from fairly traditional viewpoint.)

G. J. Warnock, 'Metaphysics in logic', in A. Flew (ed.), *Essays in Conceptual Analysis*, Macmillan, 1956. (Does logic commit one to metaphysical views?)

Methodological solipsism. In general, the view that one should adopt solipsism (see SCEPTICISM) as a device to help one investigate some sphere, without necessarily believing it. Usually, however, it appears as a term introduced into philosophy of mind by Putnam for 'the assumption that no psychological state, properly so called, presupposes the existence of any individual other than the subject to whom that state is ascribed', and used by Fodor as a consequence of his view that 'we should take it to be a condition upon specifications of mental operations that they apply to mental representations in virtue of their form'. Methodological solipsism holds that a belief, say, is what it is independently of whether it is true, or succeeds in referring to anything. The view is thus an INTERNALIST one, but does not imply that one should ignore 'the relations between an organism's behaviour and the effects of its behaviour in the course of developing theories of the organism's mental states'. One point critics have made is that methodological solipsism seems to allow varying degrees, according to just how much the specification of the mental state is supposed to be independent of. See also INDIVIDUALISM.

J. A. Fodor, 'Methodological solipsism considered as a research strategy in cognitive psychology', *The Behavioral and Brain Sciences*, vol. 3, 1980, pp. 63–109. (Includes discussions and Fodor's reply. For quotations see p. 103 and for critical point see p. 98. The article, without the discussions, also appears in Fodor's *Representations*, Harvester Press, 1981.)

H. Putnam, *Mind, Language and Reality* (vol. 2 of his *Philosophical Papers*), Cambridge UP, 1975. (See p. 220 for quotation.)

Methodology. See SCIENCE.

Metric. A set of rules, with suitable units, for measuring extensive MAGNITUDES. As an adjective 'metric' or 'metrical' means 'measurable' ('metric SPACE') or 'involving measurement' ('metric geometry').

Middle term. See SYLLOGISM.

Mill, John Stuart. 1806–73. The son of James Mill (1773–1836), who was a philosopher of somewhat similar tendencies, Mill was born in London where he worked in the India office. He is noted as an EMPIRICIST and early PHENOMENALIST, and in ethics as a (somewhat wayward) UTILITARIAN and defender of liberty. He also wrote on political philosophy. His logic is largely remembered for his distinction between connotation and denotation (see MEANING), his criticism of the SYLLOGISM, his elaboration of a philosophy of science along the lines of Bacon's and his empiricist treatment of basic MATHEMATICAL propositions. His approach was of the general type now called extensionalist. *A System of Logic, Ratiocinative and Inductive*, 1843. *On Liberty*, 1859. *On Representative Government*, 1861. *Utilitarianism*, 1861. *An Examination of Sir William Hamilton's Philosophy*, 1865 (contains his phenomenalist views). *The Subjection of Women*, 1869. See also BRADLEY, DEFINITION, INDUCTION, INFERENCE, MEANING, PLEASURE, RUSSELL, SELF-REGARDING, WHEWELL.

> J. Skorupski, *John Stuart Mill*, Routledge, 1989. (Good introduction to Mill's philosophy.)

Millet paradox. See ZENO'S PARADOXES.

Mind (philosophy of). Sometimes called philosophical psychology. Psychology deals with questions that can be settled by observation, experiment and measurement, while philosophy of mind settles its different questions by reflection. Before the twentieth century the subjects were hardly distinguished, and the sharp divisions that have prevailed through much of that century are now becoming blurred again as philosophy of mind becomes ever more reliant on the findings of subjects like cognitive science (see COGNITIVE PSYCHOLOGY, CONNECTIONISM). The philosophy of psychology is a rather narrower subject concentrating on philosophical problems that arise from studying the nature of psychology as a science, such as the problem of the scientific status of Freudianism.

Recent philosophy of mind has been perhaps primarily, though far from exclusively, concerned with two main problems: first that of what mind is and how it relates to body, known as the mind–body or body–mind problem; this is a very ancient problem with soul or spirit, especially in older literature, sometimes replacing and sometimes being added to mind. The second main problem is that of how the mind relates to the external world in its dealings with that world in terms of thought, belief, perception, etc. (see INTENSIONALITY AND INTEN-TIONALITY). This too is a problem with ancient roots but owes its modern revival partly to the influence of BRENTANO and others, and partly to the developments of cognitive science mentioned above.

For the second problem see, as well as INTENSIONALITY, INTERNALISM AND EXTERNALISM, INDIVIDUALISM, CON-TENT. Answers to the first problem range between idealist views that only the mind is real and materialist views that either the body alone is real (cf. BEHAVIOURISM) or mental phenomena are identical with certain physical ones (IDENTITY THEORY OF MIND). These views, along with the DOUBLE ASPECT THEORY, neutral MONISM, Strawson's view distinguishing bodies from PERSONS and Aristotle's view that mind is to body as FORM to matter, are all MONIST views, in that they deny that mind or mental phenomena and body or bodily phenomena are distinct things. DUALIST views assert this distinctness and include interactionism, EPIPHENOMENALISM, PSYCHO-PHYSICAL PARALLELISM and OCCASIONALISM. A weaker dualism, however, applies to properties rather than substances (and would include, e.g. Strawson's view). FUNCTIONALISM is compatible with both monism and dualism.

Idealist and most dualist views are currently in a minority, though not unrepresented, while the identity theory is still being vigorously discussed. The related topic of personal IDENTITY is important for questions like: Can a mind animate several bodies, successively, as in reincarnation, or at once? Can several minds animate the same body (one view of 'multiple personality' cases), or one mind many bodies ('corporate personalities')? Can a mind exist without a body at all, whether or not originally joined to one? Clearly much depends on what counts as a mind. This is one of the few areas where philosophy may affect our predictions of the future. Discussion has been stimu-lated by the logical possibility of brain transplants. Early work in psychical research has been relevant here and in connection with extrasensory perception, precognition, telepathy, etc. The question of whether causal relations can link mental phenomena with each other and with physical phenomena, and if so, how, arises here.

A topic linking philosophy of mind closely to ethics is philosophy of action. The FREEWILL question again makes us ask whether actions can be caused, e.g. by reasons or intentions, and calls for a general analysis of concepts like motive, intention, volition, wanting, trying. Are they the sort of things that could be causes? Are they mental states? Can they be identified or described independently of actions? Are there limitations on our irrationality (cf. INCONTINENCE)? Ethics as well as philosophy of mind can ask whether there are logical limits to what we can approve of or feel obliged to do. Are there things such that nothing would count as our approving of them?

CONSCIOUSNESS is a topic which has seen a big revival of interest recently. Its study also raises questions about pleasure and pain (cf. psychological HEDONISM), and about FEELINGS and EMOTIONS. In what sense, for example, are feelings 'in' the body or mind, and how are emotions to be analysed and distinguished from feelings and from each other? Many such questions, like many on perceiving and imagining, border on aesthetics.

This brings us to the more centrally cognitive notions like perception, sensation, judgement, together with more specific ones like attending, noticing, observing, and the more purely intellectual ones like thinking, understanding, believing, doubting, feeling sure, reasoning, inferring. Epistemology concentrates primarily on questions of justification, while philosophy of mind analyses these concepts rather from the point of view of what logical conditions someone must satisfy if he is to be said to be perceiving, thinking, etc. The second of the original main problems is relevant here. Knowledge is not in the above list, because knowing involves being correct or justified; its analysis therefore belongs to epistemology. Again, the question of whether believing is being disposed to act in certain ways belongs primarily to philosophy of mind, but the question of whether one can properly be said to believe something where one could not be wrong, such as believe one is in pain, belongs to epistemology. But the distinction is not rigid.

See QUALIA, INTENSIONALITY.

A. R. Anderson (ed.), *Minds and Machines*, Prentice-Hall, 1964. (Can machines think? and similar questions.)

D. M. Armstrong and N. Malcolm, *Consciousness and Causality: A Debate on the Nature of the Mind*, Blackwell, 1984. (Materialist and opponent debate issues concerning consciousness.)

P. Beakley and P. Ludlow (eds), *The Philosophy of Mind: Classical Problems/Contemporary Issues*, MIT Press, 1992. (Large anthology. Main headings: the mind–body problem, mental causation, mental imagery, associationism/connectionism, innate ideas.)

N. Block (ed.), *Readings in the Philosophy of Psychology*, 2 vols, Harvard UP/Methuen, 1980–1. (Mainly reprinted articles, in sections covering behaviourism, reductionism and physicalism, functionalism (vol. 1), mental representations, imagery, the subject matter of grammar, innate ideas (vol. 2).)

T. Burge, 'Philosophy of language and mind: 1950–90', *Philosophical Review*, 1992. (Survey article with many references, see particularly 2nd half, pp. 29ff., for philosophy of mind.)

*K. Campbell, *Body and Mind*, Macmillan, 1970. (Introductory.)

*T. Crane, *The Mechanical Mind: A Philosophical introduction to Minds, Machines and Mental Representation*, Penguin, 1995. (Elementary introduction.)

D. Davidson, *Essays on Actions and Events*, Clarendon, 1980. (Influential articles on various topics, including his 'anomalous MONISM' (chapter 11). See also B. Vermazen and M. B. Hintikka (eds), *Essays on Davidson: Actions and Events*, Clarendon, 1985, and E. Lepore and B. P. McLaughlin (eds), *Actions and Events: Perspectives on the Philosophy of Donald Davidson*, Blackwell, 1985.)

J. A. Foster, *The Immaterial Self*, Routledge, 1991. (Defends a dualist view.)

J. Glover (ed.), *The Philosophy of Mind*, Oxford UP, 1976. (Readings.)

J. Heil and A. Mele (eds), *Mental Causation*, Oxford UP, 1994. (Specially written essays.)

W. James, 'Does "consciousness" exist?', in his *Essays in Radical Empiricism*, 1912 (written 1904). (Neutral monist approach.)

A. Kenny, *Action, Emotion and Will*, RKP, 1963. (Discussion of these concepts.)

*C. McGinn, *The Character of Mind*, Oxford UP, 1982. (Introduction to some issues.)

D. Rosenthal (ed.), *The Nature of Mind*, Oxford UP, 1991. (62 articles and extracts covering wide range of topics. Main headings: problems about mind, self and other, mind and body, the nature of mind, psychological explanation.)

C. Rovane, 'Self-reference: The radicalization of Locke', *Journal of Philosophy*, 1993. (Defends view of personal identity that takes seriously multiple and corporate personalities.)

G. Ryle, *The Concept of Mind*, Hutchinson, 1949. (Classic attack on some dualist ('ghost in the machine') mind–body views, with discussions of feelings, emotions, etc.)

*P. Smith and O. R. Jones, *The Philosophy of Mind: An Introduction*, Cambridge UP, 1986.

J. Symons and P. Calvo (eds), *The Routledge Companion to Philosophy of Psychology*, Routledge, 2009. (Over 40 specially commissioned chapters on key topics.)

G. N. A. Vesey (ed.), *Body and Mind*, Allen and Unwin, 1964. (Selections from Descartes onwards.)

R. Warner and T. Szubka (eds), *The Mind–Body Problem: A Guide to the Current Debate*, Blackwell, 1994. (Mainly new essays, wide-ranging from physicalism to dualism.)

A. R. White, *The Philosophy of Mind*, Random House, 1967; Greenwood Press, 1978. (Combines general survey with detailed analyses.)

Minor premise, term. See SYLLOGISM.

Miracles. A miracle, in the precise sense discussed in philosophy, by, for example, AQUINAS and HUME, is an event caused by divine intervention 'beyond the order commonly observed in nature' (Aquinas), or 'in transgression of a law of nature' (Hume), and not merely a beneficial coincidence which does not involve such a contravention. Hume argues that there can be no justification for belief in a miracle, for

> A miracle is a violation of the laws of nature; and as a firm and unalterable experience has established these laws, the proof against a miracle, from the very nature of the fact, is as entire as any argument from experience can possibly be imagined.
>
> (*Enquiries*, p. 114)

That is to say, we should believe the whole accumulated evidence of multiple events which has established and confirmed the law of nature, rather than evidence for the single miraculous event which seems to contradict that law.

T. Aquinas, *Summa Contra Gentiles*, III, chapters 98–103.

D. Basinger and R. Basinger, *Philosophy and Miracle: The Contemporary Debate*, Edwin Mellen, 1986.

R.J. Fogelin *A Defense of Hume on Miracles*, Princeton UP, 2005.

D. Hume, (ed. L. A. Selby-Bigge), *Enquiries Concerning Human Understanding*, 1748. 3rd edn Oxford UP, 1975. (Chapter X, 'Of Miracles'.)

R. A. H. Larmer, (ed.) *Questions of Miracle*, McGill-Queen's UP, 1996. (Collection of articles.)

M. Levine, 'Miracles', *The Stanford Encyclopedia of Philosophy* (Fall 2005 Edition), Edward N. Zalta (ed.). Available at: http://plato.stanford.edu/

archives/fall2005/entries/miracles/ (accessed 1 March 2009). (Extensive discussion and critique of Hume, and long bibliography.)

Modalities. Ways in which something can exist or occur or be presented, or stand. Sense modalities are ways in which we perceive, namely seeing, hearing, etc. Alethic modalities are the necessity, contingency, possibility, or impossibility of something being true. 'Alethic' means 'concerned with truth'. Deontic modalities include being obligatory, being permitted and being forbidden. Among epistemic modalities are being known to be true, and being not known to be false. 'Epistemic modality' is potentially ambiguous as to whether it covers both being probable, certain, etc., and being believed, doubted, etc. Tenses are sometimes called modalities; cf. moods of a verb. 'Modality' is also used for the property of being or having a modality.

Unless otherwise specified, 'modal' and 'modality' normally refer to the alethic modalities, of which the most important are necessity, possibility and impossibility. Terms like 'necessary', 'possible', 'must', 'may' are called modal terms.

The relations between those modal terms are rather ambiguous. In particular, the possible may include everything not impossible, including the necessary; or it may be limited to what is neither necessary nor impossible; or it may be further limited to the merely possible as against the actual. The contingent is normally what is neither necessary nor impossible. 'Factual', like 'actual' in one sense, may denote what is neither necessary nor impossible nor merely possible; but it can also be opposed to 'logical', and so apply to a kind of necessity (see below). 'Actual', in this sense, is not used of statements, but 'factual' in both senses, 'possible' in all the above senses and 'contingent' can apply to false statements as well as to true ones (cf. FACTS). The logical relations between modal terms, e.g. whether being necessary entails being possible, clearly depend on the senses in which the terms are taken.

A statement or proposition is necessary if it must be true. A statement which claims that something is necessary, one containing (in its main clause) modal terms like 'necessary' or 'must', is called apodictic. One containing modal terms like 'possible' or 'may' is called problematic. One containing no modal terms is called assertoric. A necessary statement need not be apodictic. 'Twice two is four' is necessary in standard arithmetic, but not apodictic: it contains no word like 'necessary'. Nor need an apodictic statement be necessary. 'Necessarily all cats are black' is apodictic, but not necessary nor even true. In fact whether a statement is apodictic, problematic or assertoric is independent of whether it is necessary or possible, etc. A statement containing 'impossible' or its equivalents counts as apodictic. 'Apodictic' can also mean 'connected with demonstration', as often in 'apodictic necessity', and is sometimes synonymous with 'necessary'. (Kant uses 'apodictic', etc. slightly differently, to indicate how judgements are thought, not expressed; cf. also IMPERATIVE). 'N', 'L', '□' are among symbols for 'necessarily' or 'it is necessary that' ('L' is limited to logical necessity (see below); in POLISH NOTATION 'N' means 'not'). 'M', '◇' are among symbols for 'possibly' or 'it is possible that'. Statements containing modal terms are the subject matter of modal logic (see LOGIC), which is not always limited to the alethic modalities.

When a modal term is applied to a statement itself containing one, as in 'It is possible that that statement is necessary', we have nested or iterated modalities.

A difficult and controversial distinction, of medieval origin, is that between *de re* and *de dicto* modality. Roughly, cases where modal terms apply to the possession of an attribute by a subject are *de re* and cases where they apply to a statement or proposition are *de dicto*. '*De dicto*' means 'concerning the proposition'; '*de re*' means 'concerning the thing'. Consider the sentence, 'The number of the gospels necessarily exceeds three.' On a *de dicto* reading this means that the statement that the number of the gospels exceeds three is necessary, which is false: the gospels do amount to more than three, but not necessarily. On a *de re* reading it means that the number of the gospels, i.e. the number four, necessarily exceeds three, which is true, if we allow (*pace* Quine) that things like numbers have their arithmetical properties necessarily. On the other hand, consider the sentence, 'If I am sitting I am necessarily not standing.' On a *de dicto* reading this is true, since it is a necessary statement that if I am sitting I am not standing; I cannot be both. But on a *de re* reading it is false, since if I am sitting it is indeed a property of me that I am not standing, but not a necessary property; I could have been standing. But the notion of *de re* modality, and its relations to *de dicto* modality, are controversial. The difficulty concerns whether a thing's possession of its properties can be called necessary. On the *de dicto* interpretation only statements or propositions are said to be necessary. The view that *de re* modality is intelligible and that there are cases of it, even if ultimately they must be analysed in terms of *de dicto* modality, is the form usually taken in modern discussions by essentialism, when this means the doctrine that at least some objects have essences. Rejection of this is one form, or perhaps one aspect, of nominalism (cf.

DEFINITION). Essentialism has enjoyed a revival recently. The *de re/de dicto* distinction is also important, and controversial, concerning propositional attitudes (see SENTENCES for these and BELIEF for the distinction here).

Properly speaking, necessity and possibility are absolute. But in a secondary sense they may be relative to (conditional on) some expressed or tacit condition or premise. In particular the conclusion of an argument may have *necessitas consequentis*, which is absolute, if it is necessary independently of the argument, or *necessitas consequentiae*, which is relative, if it merely follows necessarily from the premises: 'No spaniels have visited the moon' follows necessarily from 'All spaniels are dogs' and 'No dogs have visited the moon', but is not itself necessary, even though it and the premises are true. It therefore has only *necessitas consequentiae*. A conclusion in itself impossible may be possible relative to (i.e. may be consistent with) certain premises: 'Humans live without air' is possible relative to 'Humans can do whatever fish can do'. If the impossibility is logical the situation is more complex: Is 'Twice two is five' consistent with 'Half five is two' (cf. IMPLICATION, CONSISTENT)? Similarly a conclusion possible in itself may be impossible relative to certain premises.

Epistemic possibility and necessity are relative to what we, or some given set of people, know, or to what we believe. Something possible given only what we know or believe may not be possible given everything that is the case, and something not possible given everything that is the case may be possible given only what we know or believe; similarly something necessary given everything that is the case may not be necessary given only what we know or believe, and something not necessary given everything that is the case may be necessary given only what we know or believe. In ancient times, it was epistemically possible that Mars was inhabited, and epistemically necessary that the earth was flat. Its flatness followed from other beliefs then current.

Necessity and possibility may also be logical, or physical (causal, scientific, natural, factual), or of various other kinds such as moral, legal, aesthetic. Logical necessity and possibility may be formal or non-formal (see ANALYTIC. 'Logically necessary' normally amounts to the same as 'logically true'.)

The nature of physical necessity and possibility has been long disputed, especially since Hume. Are they independent of logical necessity and possibility, or ultimately reducible to them, or merely illusory? Are the logical/physical and absolute/relative distinctions related? Perhaps a physically necessary statement is simply one that follows logically from (i.e. is necessary relative to) the laws of an accepted scientific system. But are not the laws themselves necessary in some sense, and if so, in what sense?

It is hard to define modal terms without begging the question. The logically or physically necessary is sometimes defined as what happens in all logically or physically POSSIBLE WORLDS, but what are these? Perhaps all conceivable worlds, or all worlds compatible with certain laws; but 'conceivable' and 'compatible' have modal endings ('-ble'), and are not the laws themselves necessary? Modal realism is the view that such possible worlds are in some sense real; see POSSIBLE WORLDS again.

Is a logically necessary statement one which nothing would count as contradicting, so that 'All cats are animals' is necessary if nothing would count as a cat that was not an animal? But how do we know that nothing would so count? Is it because 'cat' and 'animal' mean what they do, so that 'All cats are animals' says nothing about cats but exhibits a rule of language, and language depends on us? This is the CONVENTIONALIST or linguistic theory of logical necessity. But to apply a convention (in this case, the convention to use words in certain ways) involves following a rule, and if the rule is itself a convention we shall be led into an infinite regress. It seems that we cannot avoid logical necessity as a constraining force, and at most may hope to decide where it shall constrain us. We may alter our language but we shall always be committed to something. We can make 'Twice two is five' true by redefining 'five', but then we must accept 'Five is half eight' – unless we redefine 'eight', but we must stop somewhere.

Conceptually necessary is often loosely used as synonymous with 'logically necessary'. But if 'logically necessary' is confined to that whose denial is contradictory, 'conceptually necessary' can cover also that whose denial is unintelligible but not strictly contradictory. 'Nothing can be red and green all over' is perhaps an example (cf. ANALYTIC). But there is a problem about when something is contradictory.

Non-contingent is often used for 'logically necessary', but properly it denotes a looser relation: one might say that intention was non-contingently related to action. Any given intention need not be followed by the relevant action, and so the relation is not strictly a necessary one, but the concept of intention could hardly have arisen unless intentions were usually followed by the relevant actions.

Sometimes one can arrange different kinds of necessity in order of degree of stringency, and treat formally the resulting relations between them.

Further questions concern absolute possibility and actuality. Can there be possibilities which remain so throughout all time but are never actualized? Aristotle and Hobbes, among others, said no; cf. PLENTITUDE.

A logical possibility is anything not self-contradictory, but a real possibility may be either simply a physical possibility or something having at least some probability (or perhaps not too low a probability) that it will occur. See also ANALYTIC, CAUSATION.

Aristotle, *De Caelo (On the Heavens)*, book 1, chapter 12. T. Hobbes, *Elements of Philosophy: Concerning Body*, 1655, chapter 10, § 4. (Aristotle and Hobbes reject eternal unrealized possibilities.)

R. Cartwright, 'Some remarks on essentialism', *Journal of Philosophy*, 1968. (Defends intelligibility of *de re* modality, while doubting if it is analysable in terms of *de dicto* modality.)

I. Kant, *Critique of Pure Reason*, 1781, 2nd edn 1787, B.101. (His use of 'apodictic', etc.)

S. Kripke, *Naming and Necessity*, Blackwell, 1980 (original version, 1972). (Leading reviver of essentialism. Cf. S. P. Schwartz (ed.), *Naming, Necessity and Natural Kinds*, Cornell UP, 1977, for discussions, including items by fellow essentialist H. Putnam (who incidentally envisages a case where 'All cats are animals' is not even true: see p. 107). Cf. also C. Kirwan, 'How strong are the objections to essence?', *Proceedings of the Aristotelian Society*, 1970–1.)

N. Malcolm, 'Are necessary propositions really verbal?', *Mind*, 1940, pp. 189ff. (Defends linguistic view of logical necessity.)

Midwest Studies in Philosophy, vol. 6, 1986. (Issue devoted to essentialism.)

A. Plantinga, 'De re et de dicto', *Nous*, 1969. (Explains *de re* in terms of *de dicto* modality, criticizing W. C. Kneale in E. Nagel, P. Suppes and A. Tarski (eds), *Logic, Methodology and Philosophy of Science*, Stanford UP, 1962, who rejects the distinction. Cf. also Plantinga's *The Nature of Necessity*, Oxford UP, 1974, for defence of essentialism and *de re* modality.)

K. R. Popper, *The Open Society and Its Enemies*, RKP 1945. (Contains famous attack on one version of essentialism.)

W. V. O. Quine, 'Truth by convention', in H. Feigl and W. Sellars (eds), *Readings in Philosophical Analysis*, Appleton-Century Crofts, 1949. (Stresses limitations of conventionalist theory of logical necessity. His 'Reference and modality' in his *From a Logical Point of View*, Harper and Row, revised edn, 1961, represents one approach to the *de re/de dicto* distinction (though not so called), claiming that modal contexts are always opaque (see INTENSIONALITY AND INTENTIONALITY), and prefiguring but not accepting the revival of essentialism.)

Mode. See SUBSTANCE.

Models. A logical or mathematical model of an AXIOM SYSTEM, or of a sentence in an axiom system, is a set of entities, which may be numbers or classes and hence abstract, whose relations can be represented by that system or sentence. A structure of such entities is a model of a sentence S if S is true in the structure. The natural numbers, taken as related in the way they are by the relation successor of, are a model of Peano's axioms, since these are true of the natural numbers, so taken. ('So taken', because the axioms would not necessarily be true of the natural numbers if, e.g. these were taken in a different order.) Important problems concern what is true of all models of a given system. In some earlier literature a theory can be called a model of another theory, or can contain an interpretation of it, if the sets of objects they study are models of the same axiom system, when they are taken in the way in which they are studied (see previous parenthesis). A scientific model is normally a theory intended to explain a given realm of phenomena, or a sort of picture intended to explain a theory by replacing its terms with more perspicuous ones (Braithwaite).

Model theory concerns logical and mathematical models. It studies relations between formal languages and interpretations of them, i.e. problems connected with saying that a sentence of a formal language (e.g. the restricted predicate CALCULUS) is true in an interpretation. This interpretation may be an abstract structure or a world, e.g. the real world as it was in 1970. The starting-point for all forms of model theory is A. Tarski's semantic definition of TRUTH.

M. Brodbeck, 'Models, meaning and theories', in L. Gross (ed.), *Symposium on Sociological Theory*, Harper and Row, 1959. (Discusses many different uses of 'model'. On scientific models see also R. B. Braithwaite, *Scientific Explanation*, Harper, 1953, chapter 4.)

*J. N. Crossley *et al.*, *What is Mathematical Logic?* Oxford UP, 1972, chapter 3. (Brief fairly elementary account of model theory. For technical introduction, presupposing some mathematical logic, see J. E. Bell and A. B. Slomson, *Models and Ultraproducts: An Introduction*, North Holland, 1969, revised, 1971.)

A. Tarski, *Introduction to Logic*, Oxford UP, 1941, § 37. (Models in logic.)

Modus ponens. Literally, method which asserts. Argument that if a conditional statement and its antecedent are true, so is its consequent, e.g. 'If this, then that. This. Therefore that.' (Some refinements are omitted.)

Modus tollens. Literally, method which denies. Argument that if a conditional statement is true but its consequent is false, then its antecedent is false, e.g. 'If this, then that. But not that. Therefore not this.' (Some refinements are omitted.)

Monad. Literally, group of one. Either a numerical unit or an object which is essentially unitary and indivisible. For Leibniz, simple substances, which are what is ultimately real. Monadic means either 'concerning monads' or 'having only one term'. Predicates like '(is) red' are monadic (occasionally called monadic relations), since only one term needs adding to make a sentence. Relations proper are dyadic or two-term or two-place relations, or dyadic predicates, if two terms are needed (as with bigger than: 'a is bigger than b'). They are polyadic or many-term or many-place if more than two are needed (between needs three: 'b is between a and c').

G. W. Leibniz, *Principles of Nature and of Grace*, 1714; *Monadology*, 1714.

Monism. Any view which claims that where there appear to be many things or kinds of things there is really only one or only one kind. Weaker forms of monism may claim simply that the things in question are related together, or unified, in some significant way. What is said to be one in any of these ways may be the whole universe, or some lesser subject matter. The most famous extreme monist, holding (as most commonly interpreted) that there is only one object, is Parmenides, writing about 500 BC. Neutral monism is a particular doctrine claiming that physical and mental phenomena can both be analysed in terms of a common underlying reality, sometimes called neutral stuff. Among major philosophers it is associated with James and Russell. Anomalous monism says that every mental event is identical with some physical event (the token IDENTITY THEORY OF MIND) but that there are no laws for explaining or predicting mental events as such. See also SUPERVENIENCE, DUALISM.

D. Davidson, 'Mental events', in L. Foster and J. W. Swanson (eds), *Experience and Theory*, Duckworth, 1970, reprinted in Davidson's *Essays on Actions and Events*, Oxford UP, 1980. (Anomalous monism.)

W. James, *Essays in Radical Empiricism*, 1912, chapters 1 and 2, B. Russell, *The Analysis of Mind*, Allen and Unwin/Macmillan, 1921. (Two versions of neutral monism, which also appears, in effect though not in name, in H.-L. Bergson, *Matter and Memory*, Macmillan, 1910 (French original, 1896).)

Mood. See SYLLOGISM.

Moore, George E. 1873–1958. Born in Upper Norwood, he worked in Cambridge. He led the revolt against IDEALISM at the start of this century, and was one of the fathers of analytical PHILOSOPHY. He criticized the extravagances, as he saw them, of philosophers who flouted common sense with such doctrines as that time is unreal and that all RELATIONS are internal. He held influential, if somewhat idiosyncratic, views in ETHICS, and was particularly noted for his criticism of the 'naturalistic fallacy' (see NATURALISM). 'The refutation of idealism', *Mind*, 1903. *Principia Ethica*, 1903. *Some Main Problems in Philosophy*, 1953 (lectures given in 1910). 'External and internal relations', *Proceedings of the Aristotelian Society*, 1919–20. See also BEING, BRADLEY, ETHICAL INTUITIONISM, GOOD, IMPLICATION, PHENOMENALISM, SCEPTICISM, SENTENCES, TRUTH, UTILITARIANISM.

Moral. Concerning habits, customs, ways of life, especially when these are assessed as good or bad, right or wrong. Among things we call moral are theories, arguments, outlooks, rules, reasons, virtues, people, books, actions, intentions, and, perhaps, desires and feelings. There is an important ambiguity between 'moral' as against 'immoral' and 'moral' as against 'non-moral'. People are normally called moral only in the first sense; problems can be moral only in the second. An immoral principle is still a moral principle in the second sense, as against, say, a legal or aesthetic principle. 'Morality' is similarly ambiguous. 'Amoral' (which properly means 'non-moral', not 'immoral') is seldom used in philosophy.

Various ways of distinguishing the moral from the non-moral have been tried. A moral principle might be defined as one concerning things in our power and for which we can be held responsible. This would contrast moral principles with, for example, intellectual and aesthetic ones, which it might not be in our power to apply. Or a moral principle might concern the ultimate ends of human action, e.g. human welfare. Other views have it that a moral principle is one which people in fact prefer over competing principles, or else one which they should prefer. Others again make principles moral if a certain kind of sanction is applied when they are violated. UNIVERSALIZABILITY has also been used to define moral principles.

A view may offer a necessary condition of morality, or a sufficient condition, or both (see NECESSARY AND SUFFICIENT

CONDITIONS). A further distinction is that in defining morality one may be saying what counts as moral for a given person or society, or giving one's own view of what counts as moral.

G. Harman, *The Nature of Morality*, Oxford UP, 1977. (General introduction to various issues concerning morality, though less concerned with defining the moral as such.)

*G. Wallace and A. D. M. Walker (eds), *The Definition of Morality*, Methuen, 1970. (Selected essays.)

*B. Williams, *Morality*, Penguin, 1972, particularly penultimate chapter. (Brief elementary introduction.)

G. H. von Wright, *The Varieties of Goodness*, RKP, 1963, particularly chapter 1 (last paragraph), chapter 6, § 5ff. (Moral goodness and goodness generally. Acts and intentions. Assumes UTILITARIANISM).

Moral luck. The term, introduced by Bernard Williams, refers to the idea that a moral agent's character may be the proper object of moral evaluation, even though some aspects of that character might be beyond the agent's control. This seems counter-intuitive, for it might be thought that we can only be morally judged on those things for which we were responsible. Yet in practice we constantly morally evaluate people for things which are not under their control.

T. Nagel, *Mortal Questions*, Cambridge UP, 1979.

B. A. O. Williams, *Moral Luck*, Cambridge UP, 1981.

Significant extracts from both of these books can be found in the useful collection: D. Statman (ed.), *Moral Luck*, State University of New York Press, 1993.

Morals. See ETHICS.

Moral sense. An alleged sixth sense, whose existence was hotly disputed in the eighteenth century. Its proponents, who included SHAFTESBURY and HUTCHESON, held that our own and others' actions arouse agreeable or disagreeable 'sentiments', or feelings, in us according as the actions are, in conventional terms, virtuous or vicious, or when, for example, a successful murder is judged more harshly than an attempt which fails through pure chance. It is not always clear, however, what is the role of the sense, on this view, i.e. whether we perceive qualities by it, and if so, of what sort, or whether it simply arouses sentiments in us, or gives us a desire to act, when we perceive certain qualities in the ordinary way.

S. Darwall, A. Gibbard and P. Railton, 'Toward fin de siècle ethics: some trends', *Philosophical Review*, 1992. (A survey article. See pp. 152–65, on 'sensibility theories', for a modern outlook with some analogy to moral sense theories.)

D. D. Raphael, *The Moral Sense*, Oxford UP 1947. (Discussion, mainly historical.)

L. A. Selby-Bigge (ed.), *British Moralists*, 1897. (Vol. 1 contains selections from moral sense theorists, vol. 2 selections from their opponents. Cf. also Hume's ethical writings.)

Moving rows paradox. See ZENO'S PARADOXES.

Mutatis mutandis. Latin for 'with needed changes changed'. Used, when comparing cases or examples, to mean 'making due allowance for different circumstances', or 'making the necessary alterations in details'. 'For the election of the vice-chairman, the same rules shall apply as for the election of the chairman, *mutatis mutandis*' – by replacing, for example, the word 'chairman' by 'vice-chairman' in the appropriate rules.

N

Nagel, Thomas. 1937–. American philosopher, born in Belgrade, Serbia, but educated in and works in USA. Wide range of interests including political philosophy, ethics, epistemology and philosophy of mind. In his well-known article 'What is it like to be a bat?' and *The View from Nowhere*, he argues against reductionist accounts of consciousness, for although he is not a dualist, and he believes there are necessary connections between the physical and the mental, he does not believe these are logical connections. Central to his philosophy is the interplay between the subjective and the objective: every point of view is a view from somewhere, and the idea of an objective point of view, whether of judgement, or experience or reality in general, is the idea of a view from nowhere – an impossibility. He defends ALTRUISM and discusses MORAL LUCK. *The Possibility of Altruism*, Oxford UP, 1970 (reprinted, Princeton UP, 1978). *Mortal Questions*, Cambridge UP, 1979. (Includes 'What is it like to be a bat?' which was first published in *Philosophical Review*, 1974.) *The View from Nowhere*, Oxford UP, 1986. *What Does It All Mean? A Very Short Introduction to Philosophy*, Oxford UP, 1987. (One of the best short introductions to philosophy.) See also QUALIA.

Naturism. See INNATE.

Natural deduction. What relation holds between the premises and the conclusions of a valid argument? Natural deduction rules attempts to reflect and formalize the way logicians actually argue to their conclusions. Such rules systematizes those DEDUCTIONS that involve contingent propositions (see MODALITIES), not merely TAUTOLOGIES. They systematize the 'natural' arguments of everyday life. Associated especially with G. Gentzen (1909–45) and S. Jaśkowski (1906–1965).

E. Lemmon, *Beginning Logic*, Nelson, 1965. (Uses it to introduce formal logic.)

Naturalism. There are two main applications of the term 'naturalism' in modern philosophy, one in metaphysics, epistemology and philosophy of mind and the other in ethics. What they have in common is the belief that the universe is all one, in the sense that all objects in it and all aspects of it are equally accessible to study by scientific method.

The empiricist tradition of Locke, Hume, J. S. Mill and others made no sharp distinction between what would now be called philosophy of mind and psychology. Questions about the justification of mental states such as beliefs tended to be assimilated to questions about their psychological origins. Towards the end of the nineteenth century and beginning of the twentieth, this tendency was fiercely attacked, in particular by Bradley, Frege and (eventually but not at first) by Husserl, usually under the name of PSYCHOLOGISM. The empiricist revival that dominated the first half of the twentieth century accepted and indeed insisted on this distinction between epistemology and psychology, and the difficulty of finding epistemological justifications for various beliefs once psychological substitutes were discounted led to scepticism.

More recently, mainly under the influence of Quine, there has been a revival of naturalism but in a more self-conscious form, called naturalized EPISTEMOLOGY, in that epistemological questions are not just tacitly treated in a psychological manner but the change is avowed and deliberate. Among other writers this is also true of Hume, but Hume abandoned the search for justification, and tried to explain rather than justify our beliefs in such things as real causal connections and the existence of a world outside our own minds. (How far he either accepted those beliefs in fact or thought they could be disproved is disputed, but he claimed that scepticism, however irrefutable in theory, was impossible to accept in practice outside the philosophical study.) The recent revival is more inclined to claim that the psychological account itself constitutes a kind of justification. Cf. here reliabilism (see EPISTEMOLOGY).

The ethical version of naturalism claims that there is no unbridgeable gulf between ethics and other studies. It takes two main forms, that ethical terms can be analysed into non-ethical terms, and that ethical conclusions can be logically derived from non-ethical premises. Modern discussions start from two famous attacks on these two forms respectively, by Moore and Hume. Moore insisted that 'good' is indefinable, and that the questions what 'good' means and what things are good must be sharply distinguished, e.g. pleasure may be good, and even possibly the only good thing, but 'good' does not mean 'pleasant' or 'producing pleasure', etc. He called the neglect of this distinction the naturalistic fallacy, and said goodness is a non-natural quality. (He never successfully explained 'non-natural', which is now not used of qualities. For 'non-natural' see MEANING.) One of Moore's arguments was the open question argument: whatever definition of 'good' was offered, it would always be an open question whether what satisfies the definition is good. It is not clear, however, whether the naturalistic fallacy lies in defining 'good'; defining 'good' in non-ethical terms; defining any ethical notion in non-ethical terms; defining any notion in terms of notions in a different sphere; or indeed simply confusing one notion with another (cf. Prior). In this last form the fallacy is sometimes called the definist fallacy. It is difficult, however, to mark off different spheres or notions, and the errors, if any, are not strictly fallacies – no fallacious inference is involved.

Hume, as usually interpreted, attacked naturalism by denying that conclusions whose main verb is an 'ought', or an equivalent, can be logically derived from premises not containing such a notion; he maintains what is now called the is/ought distinction. Hume was primarily concerned with the moral OUGHT, but the question also arises of whether his view applies to other 'oughts' (e.g. 'doctor's orders').

The alleged distinction underlying both these attacks is often if loosely, called the fact/value distinction, though 'ought' is not strictly a value term (and the fact/value and is/ought distinctions are sometimes separated: Wiggins, who accepts the former but rejects the latter).

Moore made his distinction between different qualities, all of which objectively belonged to their possessors: whether a thing is good no more depends on the observer than whether it is, say, spherical. Various later writers, however, have tried to make the same distinction in other ways, asking how words have meaning, and what the speaker's own attitudes contribute. Thus a distinction grew up between straightforward descriptions which claim to state facts and impart knowledge, and utterances whose purpose is to express or evince emotions or attitudes, to issue prescriptions or recommendations, or to evaluate. Utterances of the former kind, and the words used in them, had descriptive, factual or cognitive meaning; those of the latter kind had emotive, evaluative, prescriptive or in general non-cognitive meaning, and were subject to a SPEECH ACT analysis. The terms in the former list in general coincide (but for ambiguities in 'factual' see FACTS). Those in the latter list do not all coincide – to express emotion is not the same as to prescribe action or attitudes – but they share the property of being contrasted with the former list. Many utterances, however, especially ethical ones, had both kinds of meaning. 'He is courageous' might mean 'He knowingly takes great risks' (factual), 'and I hereby express approval of his doing so' (emotive), or 'I hereby recommend you to follow suit' (prescriptive). 'He is rash' might have the same factual meaning but the opposite non-cognitive meaning, i.e. as above, but with 'disapproval' for 'approval' and 'forbid' for 'recommend'. Emotivists and prescriptivists analyse ethical utterances in this way, emphasizing emotive and prescriptive meaning, respectively, but descriptivists think that ethical utterances have meaning in the same way as factual ones do, i.e. they state facts, even if of an ethical kind. Descriptivism and naturalism are in practice closely similar, but Moore was a descriptivist but not a naturalist.

Understandably, the naturalist controversy is associated with another, concerning whether there are objective and agreed procedures for arriving at conclusions in matters of value or duty. Descriptivists and most naturalists claim that there are, even if they are hard to elaborate. They take the utterances in question to say something true or false about objective reality, and so to state facts. Their opponents may deny that there are such procedures. Hence the attempt common among POSITIVISTS and linguistic philosophers to confine ethics to certain questions only: see ETHICS. Alternatively, they allow that there are such procedures, but have special difficulty in elaborating them, since special kinds of reasoning seem needed to support conclusions claiming to do something other than state facts.

Recently the fact/value distinction has come under fire. There seems to be little unity on the value side, which has to cover expressions of emotion, commendations, prescriptions, etc., in each case sometimes moral and sometimes non-moral. Where a similar distinction seems viable it may still be relative (Anscombe). Emotivists and prescriptivists face objections connected with UNIVERSALIZABILITY. The theory that words like 'good' or 'ought' get their meaning by commending or prescribing, i.e. by their use in SPEECH ACTS, also faces difficulties (see GOOD).

The view that moral conclusions cannot be logically derived from non-moral premises may be called a weak non-naturalism or weak antinaturalism if it admits that there are limits to the possible contents of ethical statements, i.e. to what we can intelligibly be said to commend or prescribe as a duty. Would we, for example, understand anyone who seriously thought it his duty to blink every five seconds, regardless of circumstances? It is a strong non-naturalism if it denies that there are such limits (cf. the question whether just anything can be GOOD). The phrase 'autonomy of morals' or 'of ethics' can apply to both these versions of non-naturalism, and also to the view that practical moral questions can be separated from theoretical ethical analysis because any position on the former can be combined with any position on the latter. This last view too has been attacked because of universalizability, among other things.

Perhaps the most central question is whether there is any way of establishing ethical or other valuational conclusions. If there is, there may seem to be little objection to using terms like 'true' and 'fact' in connection with such conclusions, i.e. to adopting descriptivism; but this view has recently been disputed.

'Naturalism' is also used in other ways, notably in art, where it might be most obviously described as the attempt to represent nature (including human nature) as it is rather than in various stylized, symbolic, or romantic guises; cf. REALISM.

See also OUGHT, GOOD, MEANING, FACTS, ETHICS, SUPERVENIENCE.

G. E. M. Anscombe, 'On brute facts', *Analysis*, vol. 18, 1958. (Argues that distinction between 'brute' and 'institutional' facts is relative.)

R. F. Atkinson, 'The autonomy of morals', *Analysis*, vol. 18, 1958. (Defends fact/value distinction against some attacks of a logical nature.)

C. Beck, 'Utterances which incorporate a value statement', *American Philosophical Quarterly*, 1967. R. W. Newell, 'Ethics and description', *Philosophy*, 1968. (Two attacks on fact/value distinction.)

*P. Foot (ed.), *Theories of Ethics*, Oxford UP, 1967. (Includes several notable discussions of naturalism.)

D. P. Gauthier, 'Moore's naturalistic fallacy', *American Philosophical Quarterly*, 1967. (Discusses Moore and Prior and offers own view on naturalistic fallacy.)

A. Gewirth, 'Positive "ethics" and normative "science"', *Philosophical Review*, 1960. (Compares ethics and science as fields of enquiry.)

J. Griffin, 'Values: Reduction, supervenience, and explanation by ascent' in D. Charles and K. Lennon (eds), *Reduction, Explanations, and Realism*, Clarendon, 1992. (Throws doubt on the natural/non-natural distinction, and thereby on supervenience accounts of value: what exactly supervenes on what?)

*W. D. Hudson (ed.), *The Is/Ought Question*, Macmillan, 1969. (Discussions of Hume's attack on naturalism, plus some essays on evaluation.)

W. D. Hudson, *Modern Moral Philosophy*, Macmillan, 1970. (General introduction. Includes Hare's later views in discussing prescriptivism, etc. Cf. also p. 171 on terminology.)

F. Jackson, G. Oddy and M. Smith, 'Minimalism and truth aptness', *Mind*, 1994. (Argues against a too ready acceptance of terms like 'true' and 'fact' in connection with ethical statements.)

P. Kitcher, 'The naturalists return', *Philosophical Review*, 1992. (Extended survey of the revival of naturalism in metaphysics and epistemology.)

Midwest Studies in Philosophy, vol. 19, 1995. (Journal issue devoted to philosophical naturalism.)

G. E. Moore, *Principia Ethica*, Cambridge UP, 1903, chapter 1, particularly § B. (Locus classicus for naturalistic fallacy.)

L. Nochlin, *Realism*, Penguin, 1971. (Naturalism in art.)

D. Papineau, *Philosophical Naturalism*, Blackwell, 1993. (General discussion, relating naturalism to physicalism and applying it to problems in philosophy of mind and epistemology.)

A. N. Prior, *Logic and the Basis of Ethics*, Oxford UP, 1949. (Naturalistic fallacy in its historical setting.)

W. V. O. Quine, 'Epistemology naturalized' in his *Ontological Relativity and Other Essays*, Columbia, 1969. (Major influence in revival of naturalism.)

A. K. Sen, 'Hume's law and Hare's rule', *Philosophy*, 1966. (Uses universalizability to defend naturalism.)

S. J. Wagner and R. Warner (eds), *Naturalism: A Critical Appraisal*, Notre Dame UP, 1993. (Specially written essays mainly critical of naturalism from wide variety of viewpoints, with introduction and summaries.)

D. Wiggins, 'Truth, invention, and the meaning of life' (pamphlet), *Proceedings of the British Academy*, 1976, reprinted in his *Needs, Values, Truth*, Blackwell, 1987. (See particularly p. 96 (of reprint) for separation of fact/value and is/ought distinctions. Difficult.)

Naturalistic fallacy. See NATURALISM.

Necessary. See MODALITIES.

Necessary and sufficient conditions. A necessary condition for something is one without which the thing does not exist or occur. The presence of oxygen is a necessary condition for human life. A sufficient condition for something is one given which the thing does exist or occur. Prolonged absence of oxygen is a sufficient condition for human death. Necessary or sufficient conditions need not precede what they are conditions of. The existence of humans is a sufficient condition for the presence of oxygen. As this last example shows, a sufficient condition may be causally connected with what it is a condition of, without being a cause of it. But necessary or sufficient conditions do not have to be causal: fine weather is a necessary condition of my going out today – because I have so decided. They can also be logical (being an equilateral Euclidean triangle is both necessary and sufficient for being an equiangular Euclidean triangle), or just accidental: if all dodos were eaten, however accidentally, being eaten is a necessary (though not causally necessary) condition for being a dodo. But 'necessary' and 'sufficient' are often tacitly limited to the non-accidental. 'Sufficient conditions' (plural) may refer to conditions jointly sufficient for something, or to conditions each of which is itself sufficient.

Negation. A distinction is sometimes made between external and internal negation. In external negation a whole proposition is negated, in internal negation only part of one. 'It's not thought that he'll come' involves external negation if it means simply that people don't think he will come, but internal negation if it means they do think he won't. There is a similar distinction between negating a proposition and negating a predicate or term, e.g. between 'This isn't red' and 'This is non-red'. 'Denial' is sometimes kept for the negation of a predicate or term. It is also sometimes used for the rejection of a claim already made, as opposed to an assertion, which even if it includes a negative element still claims something about the world (Barwise and Etchemendy). 'Positive' and 'affirmative' are generally synonymous.

The double negation principle says that any proposition implies and is implied by the negation of its negation. INTUITIONIST logic rejects the second half of this.

Various problems arise: Can negative and affirmative propositions be separately identified? Or can one only say that two propositions are negations of each other, neither being 'the' negative one? Is negating something a special activity? Is affirming somehow prior to negating? Can language dispense with negation?

Privation is the view that evil is negative – the absence of good.

For 'Square of opposition' see QUANTIFIER WORDS.

See also INTUITIONISM, particularly Hossack in bibliography.

A. J. Ayer, 'Negation', *Journal of Philosophy* 1952, reprinted in his *Philosophical Essays*, Macmillan, 1954. (Definition, and dispensability, of negation.)

J. Barwise and J. Etchemendy, *The Liar*, Oxford UP, 1987. (See pp. 16–17 for treatment of 'denial'.)

G. Buchdahl, 'The problem of negation', *Philosophy and Phenomenological Research*, 1961–2. (Is affirmation prior to negation?)

G. Frege, 'Negation', in P. T. Geach and M. Black (eds), *Translations from the Philosophical Writings of Gottlob Frege*, Blackwell, 1952. (Is negating something a special activity?)

J. D. Mabbott, G. Ryle and H. H. Price, 'Negation', *Proceedings of the Aristotelian Society*, supplementary vol., 1929. (What does negation presuppose?)

B. H. Slater, 'Internal and external negations', *Mind*, 1979. (Uses the distinction to solve various problems.)

Neoplatonists. Various groups of philosophers influenced by Plotinus (AD 205–70) and claiming Platonic inspiration. Plotinus in his *Enneads* claimed to interpret and develop PLATO, basing himself especially on certain passages suggesting that reality is somehow derived from a single thing, called the One or the Good, which transcends existence (i.e. is on too high a plane to be said to 'exist') and is unknowable. Plotinus also developed an epistemology. The Neoplatonists also tried to unify Plato and ARISTOTLE. They are now often regarded as having misinterpreted Plato. Leading Neoplatonists after Plotinus include Porphyry (c.232–c.304), Iamblichus (c.270–c.330), Proclus (c.409–c.487), Philoponus (sixth century), Simplicius (sixth century), Boethius (c.480–525).

E. K. Emilsson, *Platonism on Sense-Perception*, Cambridge UP, 1988. (Plotinus' epistemology. First chapter also contains good introduction to Plotinus' general philosophy.)

R. T. Wallis, *Neoplatonism*, 1972.

Neustic. See PHRASTIC.

Newcomb's paradox. You are offered two boxes. The first contains a thousand pounds. The second contains either a million pounds or nothing. You can take either both boxes or the second alone. Many other people have made the choice. All or nearly all who chose both boxes found the second empty. All or nearly all who chose the second box found it full. Which should you choose? Induction suggests the second alone. Yet the boxes have already been arranged, so how can your now choosing both boxes affect the contents of the second? Surely then you should choose both?

M. Clark, *Paradoxes from A–Z*, London: Routledge, 2002.

J. L. Mackie, 'Newcomb's paradox and the direction of causation', *Canadian Journal of Philosophy*, 1977, reprinted in his *Logic and Knowledge*, 1985. (Non-technical discussion. See p. 200 for connection with PRISONER'S DILEMMA.)

R. Nozick, 'Newcomb's problem and two principles of choice', in N. Rescher (ed.), *Essays in Honor of Carl G. Hempel*, 1969. (Original place of publication of the paradox. Clear exposition followed by sometimes rather technical discussion of it and variants.)

R. M. Sainsbury, *Paradoxes*, Cambridge UP, 1988, revised, 1995. (See pp. 51–63 (53–65 in revised edn) for elementary introduction.)

Nietzsche, Friedrich. 1844–1900. Born in Prussia, he taught classes at Basel and then lived in Switzerland and Italy, and died after eleven years of insanity. He contrasted the Apolline and Dionysian elements in Greek tragedy, and in his view of ethics, where he contrasted 'master' and 'slave' morality and made pungent criticisms of utilitarianism and Christian ethics, and of notions, like equality, common in the Enlightenment. Linked with these latter views are his concepts of the 'will to power' and the 'superman' or 'ÜBERMENSCH'. How far his own ideal involves aggressive egoism is disputed. He also took a pragmatic, PERSPECTIVAL, attitude to truth and revived the PYTHAGOREAN and STOIC notion of eternal recurrence (see METAPHYSICS). He is sometimes associated with EXISTENTIALISM. See also ÜBERMENSCH. *The Birth of Tragedy*, 1872. *Beyond Good and Evil*, 1886. *Towards a Genealogy of Morals*, 1887. *Thus Spake Zarathustra*, 1883–5.

W. Kaufmann (ed. and trans.), *The Portable Nietzsche*, Viking Press, 1954, revised 1968, *Basic Writings of Nietzsche*, Modern Library, 1968. (Between them these contain the above works and five other works complete, with extracts from further ones.)

R. Schacht, *Nietzsche*, Routledge, 1983. (Detailed survey.)

M. Tanner, *Nietzsche: A Very Short Introduction*, Oxford UP, 2001. (Clear, readable, myth-dispelling.)

Nomic. See NOMOLOGICAL.

Nominalism. Normally any view which treats a given (apparently non-linguistic) subject matter in terms of words or language rather than in terms of substantial realities. In fact, however, there are two versions: (i) the view that there are no abstract entities, and that abstraction depends on things being described in certain ways; (ii) the view that there are no universals (also called PARTICULARISM). Only (i) falls under the opening definition above. (ii) is followed by Armstrong in particular (see bibliography to UNIVERSALS). See UNIVERSALS, BEING, DEFINITION, MODALITIES, REALISM, SUBSTANCE.

Nomological. Concerning or involving laws. Nomic means this, or sometimes 'lawlike' (see first sense of this under LAWS).

No-ownership theory. Theory that states of consciousness are not owned by anything, mental or physical.

> P. F. Strawson, *Individuals*, Methuen, 1959, chapter 3. (Critical, with references.)

Normative. A term or sentence, etc., is normative if its basic uses involve prescribing norms or standards, explicitly or implicitly, e.g. 'ought' is normative, and so is 'good' for anyone holding that, for example, 'Piety is good' either means or entails 'One ought to be pious'. Normativity is not only involved in ethics: epistemology, too, can be seen as normative, in so far as it is concerned with the justification of our beliefs, and with judging the rightness or wrongness of our cognitive states.

Noumenon. (Singular. Plural: 'noumena'. Adjective: 'noumenal'.) For Kant, a noumenon is a 'thing-in-itself', as opposed to its appearance or phenomenon. Noumena cannot be experienced and are unknowable: they can only be postulated, though without knowing what they are like, to account for the appearances (phenomena) we are confronted with. Kant also believed that the noumenal world is in some way accessible to us through our ability to act morally.

> I. Kant, *Critique of Pure Reason*, 1781, 2nd edn 1787. (See index to N. Kemp Smith's translation, MacMillan, 1929.)

Nozick, Robert. 1938–2002. American philosopher who contributed to a wide range of areas, including epistemology and political philosophy. He argued for an analysis of knowledge which overcame GETTIER's objections to defining knowledge as justified true belief by dispensing with the notion of justification as a criterion for knowledge, and introducing the idea of 'tracking the truth'. He holds that a belief amounts to knowledge if it 'tracks the truth', i.e. would not be held were it false, would be held were it true, and is in fact true. In political philosophy he argues for a libertarian position in response to RAWLS: he claims that a just state need not be based on the MAXIMIN principle, but could be one in which large inequalities exist, so long as this state was arrived at by a process of freely conducted negotiation between the state's members, and that there was a just starting position. *Philosophical Explanations*, 1981. (For 'tracking the truth' see chapter on 'Epistemology'; abridged version in J. Dancy (ed.), *Perceptual Knowledge*, Oxford UP 1988.) *Anarchy, State and Utopia*, 1974.

J. Wolff, *Robert Nozick: Property, Justice and the Minimal State*, Polity Press, 1991. (Good introduction to, and response to, Nozick's political philosophy.)

Numbers. The natural numbers (also called finite cardinal numbers or cardinals) are the non-negative integers: 0, 1, 2, ... They are nowadays often defined in terms of sets (see CLASSES). As Frege pointed out, two sets, whether finite or infinite, are equivalent if they can be paired off so that for each member of one there is exactly one corresponding member of the other. ('Equipollent' often replaces 'equivalent', which can then have a wider sense.) The equivalence class of a set is the class of all sets equivalent to it. If there are twelve apostles, twelve months of the year and twelve signs of the zodiac, these three sets are members of the same equivalence class and share the same cardinality. For technical reasons, their cardinal (12) is regarded as a particular set selected from this equivalence class by, for example, the following general method, due to J. von Neumann: 0 is the (unique) empty set; 1 is the set whose only member is 0; 2 is the set whose only members are 0 and 1, and so on; 12 is therefore the set whose only members are 0, 1, 2, ... 11, and in general each finite cardinal is the set of all smaller cardinals. This method can be extended to define infinite cardinals too.

Two equivalent sets, each ordered in a certain way, are similar or have equal order-types if they can be paired off so that each set preserves its own order; the apostles in any given order can be paired off with the months in any given order so that at each stage the next apostle goes with the next month. Finite equivalent ordered sets are always similar, but infinite ones (sometimes also called transfinite in mathematics) need not be; the set of positive integers in ascending order is not similar to the same set in the reverse or descending order (... , 2, 1, 0), because the latter has no first term to go with the first term (0) of the former. Ordered sets of which every non-empty subset has a first member are called well-ordered, and the order-type of a well-ordered set is an ordinal number or ordinal. The ordinal of one well-ordered set is greater than that of another if the second set as a whole is similar to an initial segment (only) of the first.

Philosophers are divided about whether numbers are real non-material entities, those who think they are, such as Plato or Frege, often being called Platonists. For other kinds of numbers (negative, rational, real, complex, transcendental, etc.) see dictionaries of mathematics.

See also MATHEMATICS (PHILOSOPHY OF).

A. A. Frankel, *Abstract Set Theory*, revised edn, North-Holland, 1961 (1st edn 1953). (See its index.)

A. W. Moore, *The Infinite*, Routledge, 1990. (General introduction, both historical and positive.)

Numbers (law of large). Various related theorems about possibilities for events, among them Bernoulli's theorem and Poisson's theorem. For a rough illustration of the general idea, suppose that a tossed coin is equally likely to fall heads or tails. Then, the law says, the longer the series of tosses, the greater the probability that the frequency of heads will be within some given distance of 50 per cent (e.g. between 49 per cent and 51 per cent; it cannot be exactly 50 per cent except after an even number of tosses). The law is not itself a prediction. If we assume, on whatever grounds, that the coin will behave in certain ways, e.g. that it will not show any bias, then the law spells out what it is that we are assuming. To see what lies behind this illustration, consider all possible results, in terms of heads and tails, that a series of tosses of a fair coin could yield. Then the longer the series the greater the proportion, among the possible results for that series, of results containing between 49 per cent and 51 per cent heads. See also BAYES'S THEOREM.

I. Hacking, *The Taming of Chance*, Cambridge UP, 1990. (See chapter 12 for some historical material on Bernoulli, Poisson and Chebyshev, who developed the law.)

J. R. Lucas, *The Concept of Probability*, Clarendon, 1970, chapter 5. (Offers proof of Bernoulli's theorem. See also W. C. Kneale, *Probability and Induction*, Oxford UP, 1949, § 29, who is clearer on what the theorem actually says.)

J. O. Wisdom, *Foundations of Inference in Natural Science*, Methuen, 1952, chapter 20. (Brief statement of some relevant theorems, with proof of one.)

Nussbaum, Martha. 1947–. Moral philosopher and 'liberal feminist', born in New York, educated at NYU and Harvard, and now at University of Chicago. Her work on Ancient Greek Philosophy and ethics discusses factors outside our control which have great moral significance and which might affect our ability to flourish, such as some of our emotions – compassion, grief, disgust, shame. *The Fragility of Goodness*, 1986. *The Quality of Life* (with A. Sen), 1993. *Cultivating Humanity*, 1997. *Sex and Social Justice*, 1998. *Hiding from Humanity: Disgust, Shame and the Law*, 2004.

O

Object. Literally, what 'lies before' something. What is experienced (the object), as opposed to what experiences it (the subject). Anything which has independent existence (qualities, etc., have dependent existence); or, and perhaps more commonly in philosophy, what a change is instigated to produce, or a mental attitude is 'directed at' (see INTENSIONALITY AND INTENTIONALITY on 'intentional objects'); cf. 'the object in my pocket', 'the object of my ambition'. These meanings are often intermingled. Kenny distinguishes what is perhaps a third sense: the object of an action is that which is changed by the action. (He spells 'intentional' with an 's'.) Meinong distinguished the object of an act like thinking from its content, but insisted that the object had something called 'BEING SO'. Frege treated objects as whatever can be named, and contrasted them with CONCEPTS. In this wide sense 'object' approximates to 'thing', though usually, when the 'independent existence' meaning is dominant, objects are limited to particulars (see UNIVERSALS). In the case of emotions, etc., the object may be hard to distinguish from the cause.

A. Kenny, *Action, Emotion and Will*, RKP, 1963. (See index.)

A. Meinong, 'The theory of objects' in R. Chisholm (ed.), *Realism and the Background of Phenomenology*, Free Press, 1960 (trans. from German original of 1904). (A famous and influential, though controversial, theory.)

J. A. Passmore, *A Hundred Years of Philosophy*, Duckworth, 1957, revised and expanded, 1966. (See index particularly pp. 176–87 (173–85 in Penguin edn) for Brentano and Meinong on objects.)

J. J. Valberg, 'The puzzle of experience' in T. Crane (ed.), *The Contents of Experience*, Cambridge UP, 1992, particularly § 4 (reprinted from Valberg's *The Puzzle of Experience*, Oxford UP, 1992.

Objectivism. See SUBJECTIVISM.

Object word. (i) Word standing for OBJECTS (in first sense) e.g. 'cat', but not 'red' or 'snow'; (ii) word in an object language (see METALANGUAGE).

Obligation. See OUGHT.

Obversion. In traditional formal logic, obversion negates the predicate of a categorical proposition and negates the proposition itself. The result (the obverse) is logically equivalent to the original. 'All cats are black' and 'No cats are non-black' are obverses of each other. See QUANTIFIER WORDS.

Occam. See OCKHAM.

Occasionalism. Doctrine that things or events are caused only by God, never by other things or events. God uses apparent causes as occasions (hence called occasional causes) for creating their apparent effects. Associated especially with Malebranche and others of his time, where however, the main emphasis is on the apparent causal relations between mind and body. Leibniz's similar view is not occasionalism, because his God programmed the course of events from the creation, and did not interfere on each occasion. See also PSYCHOPHYSICAL PARALLELISM.

> N. Malebranche, *Dialogues on Metaphysics and on Religion*, 1688, trans. 1923, 7th Dialogue.

Ockham, William of. c.1285–1349. English Franciscan theologian, born at Ockham (Surrey), who worked mainly in Oxford, Avignon and Munich. He worked against the same general background as AQUINAS and Duns SCOTUS, but he separated philosophy further from theology by severely limiting the extent to which God's existence can be proved. He is commonly regarded as a nominalist (see UNIVERSALS), and is famous for OCKHAM'S RAZOR. He contributed substantially to logic and the theory of meaning, among other topics. His writings include the *Summa Logicae*, *Quodlibeta Septem* (seven miscellanies), and commentaries on the *Sentences* of Peter Lombard and on various works of ARISTOTLE.

> P. Boehner (ed. and trans.), *William of Ockham: Philosophical Writings: A Selection*. Nelson, 1957, updated, Hackett, 1990. (Has Latin text with English translation.)

M. Loux (ed. and trans.), *Ockham's Theory of Terms: Part I of the Summa Logicae*, Notre Dame, 1974.

Ockham's razor. Principle attributed to William of Ockham, that 'entities are not to be multiplied beyond necessity' (not his own words), i.e. it is arbitrary to postulate the existence of things, or kinds of things, unless one has to. More generally, one should choose the simplest hypothesis that will fit the facts. A stronger form claims that only what cannot be dispensed with is real and that to postulate other things is not only arbitrary but mistaken.

Omnipotence (paradox of). See RELIGION.

Omniscience (paradox of). See RELIGION.

One-many problem. See UNIVERSALS.

One-sorted. See MANY-SORTED.

Ontological argument. An argument of God's existence, stemming from Anselm. Very roughly: God is by definition the most perfect being; it is more perfect to exist than not to exist; therefore God exists. In DESCARTES, existence is a perfection and cannot be separated from the concept of God any more than the fact that the angles of a triangle equal two right angles, so God must by definition exist, just as a triangle's angles by definition equal 180 degrees. More generally, any argument can be called an ontological argument which infers that something really exists because certain concepts are related in certain ways. Discussion of the topic has been closely linked with the question of whether existence is a predicate (or attribute).

J. Barnes, *The Ontological Argument*, 1972. (Detailed examination.)
J. Bennett, *Kant's Dialectic*, Cambridge UP, 1974, § 72–4. (Discusses existence as a predicate and necessary existence.)
J. L. Mackie, *The Miracle of Theism*, Clarendon, 1982, chapter 3. (Critical.)
A. Plantinga (ed.), *The Ontological Argument*, 1968. (Versions and discussions from Anselm to present day.)
A. Plantinga, *The Nature of Necessity*, Oxford UP, 1974, chapter 10. (Defends a version of the argument. See also, for criticism of him, M. Tooley, 'Plantinga's defence of the ontological argument', *Mind*, 1981, and Mackie.)

Ontology. See METAPHYSICS.

Opaque. See INTENSIONALITY.

Open question argument. See NATURALISM.

Open texture. Loosely, a term's indeterminacy of meaning. Waismann thought that with most empirical predicates (see A PRIORI) we cannot guarantee to be able to apply or refuse to apply them in all cases. However precise we made their meaning a borderline case could always turn up in the future. He called this feature open texture, and distinguished it from VAGUENESS, which is a feature of already existing uses of predicates, not of possible future uses (see AMBIGUITY). Vagueness can be minimized by giving more accurate rules, but open texture cannot because we cannot predict future borderline cases. He compared open texture to possibility of vagueness. Open texture and vagueness are important in connection with verifiability (see POSITIVISM) and the law of EXCLUDED MIDDLE. It is not clear that they are, as often thought, confined to empirical predicates.

F. Waismann, 'Verifiability', *Proceedings of the Aristotelian Society*, supplementary vol., 1945, reprinted in his *How I See Philosophy*, Macmillan, 1968, and in G. H. R. Parkinson (ed.), *The Theory of Meaning*, Oxford UP, 1968. (Open texture and verifiability.)

L. J. Cohen, *The Diversity of Meaning*, Methuen, 1962, chapter 9. (Significance of vagueness.)

I. Lakatos (see bibliography to MATHEMATICS). (Open texture of mathematical concepts.)

Operationalism. See POSITIVISM.

Operator. A logical operator is any expression whose function is to affect in a specific way the logical properties (e.g. the entailments) of an expression or expressions to which it is attached, e.g. 'and' operates on two propositions by joining them into a whole, which has entailments neither of them has separately. See also VARIABLE. For modal operators, involving necessity and possibility, see MODALITIES. Deontic operators are used in deontic logic, involving the principles connected with the concepts of obligation, permission and prohibition.

Opposition (square of). See QUANTIFIER WORDS.

Or. See CONJUNCTION.

Order. See TYPES (THEORY OF).

Original position. A device used by Rawls in constructing his theory of justice. Rawls imagines a set of people about to be incarnated into a society, which will be run on political and moral principles which they are now to choose. They are rather idealized figures, supremely rational and intelligent but situated, in this 'original position', behind a veil of ignorance. They have general scientific and economic knowledge, but no knowledge of the detailed arrangements in the society except that resources will not be over-plentiful, nor of their own position in it, nor of their own individual interests, abilities, tastes or opinions, or even of their conception of the good. They are motivated solely by their own interests, which need not be selfish, and indeed are to take account of the interests of their own immediate descendants, but they ignore the interests of their fellow choosers, with whom they cannot make bargains. The basic principle they will deploy, says Rawls, is the 'maximin' principle: they will choose that arrangement of society in which the least fortunate people in that arrangement are in the least unfortunate situation compared to other possible arrangements. Once the basic principles have been chosen, the veil of ignorance is gradually lifted to enable more detailed principles to be reached. Basically, justice is then defined in terms of the principles such choosers would unanimously choose. The result, however, is to be checked by comparison with our native intuitions, and the initial result and the intuitions are then to be allowed to modify each other in a process aimed at reaching a REFLECTIVE EQUILIBRIUM by modifying the conditions under which the original position is set up. Problems arise about how far such bloodless and abstract creatures as the choosers could come to any rational choice at all, and how far they can keep their present conceptions of the good when considering different conceptions that they may have later, and indeed how far they are allowed to differ from each other at all why not just have one chooser, who will naturally be unanimous?

> J. Rawls, *A Theory of Justice*, Oxford UP, 1972, particularly section 4 (for original position) and section 24 (for veil of ignorance).

Other minds problem. See SCEPTICISM.

Other-regarding. See SELF-REGARDING.

Ought, obligation, duty. Etymologically a corruption of 'owe it', 'ought' suggests a gap which requires to be filled. But the gap may not always exist: to say the kettle ought to be boiling when it clearly is boiling is normally pointless, but 'It ought to be boiling by now' does not imply that it is not; when told that it is boiling we can say 'and so it ought to be'. (But saying that it ought may often 'contextually imply' that it is not: see IMPLICATION.) Presumably what requires that the kettle should be boiling is the laws of science, plus statements that the gas is lighted, etc.

A term related to the closing of a gap is obviously well suited for use when guiding action. In 'You ought to take quinine' what requires it is presumably your state of health, the laws of medicine and your interest in recovering. It is harder to explain the moral 'ought'. There may be laws of morality corresponding to those of medicine, but what corresponds to the agent's interest in recovering, without which taking quinine would be pointless? This makes us ask how morality relates to self-interest. Does it presuppose it? In fact several questions concern 'ought' and motivation. Even if 'Smith ought to X' does not imply he already has a motive to X, must 'ought' carry a motive with it? i.e. can he coherently say, 'I acknowledge that I ought to X, but that gives me no motive to X'? Would this count as genuine acknowledgement? And can it be true that one ought to X, if one thinks one ought but remains completely unmoved? Also is it the case that we ought to act from certain motives?

Furthermore, what is requirement, which presumably is a metaphorical notion? If it is said that God does the requiring, so that the requiring is not metaphorical, why should we obey Him? And can we deduce moral conclusions (either general laws or statements about specific cases or kinds of case) from purely non-moral premises? (Cf. NATURALISM.)

We also use 'ought' to express what we ought to do, all things considered (see MORAL). How does this so-called 'final ought' relate to the moral 'ought', and in general is there really only one sense of 'ought'? Some think even the moral 'ought' ambiguous, according as it does or does not imply that we can do the relevant act, i.e. that the slogan 'Ought implies can' does or does not apply: if we do the more urgent of two competing moral acts, is there a sense in which we still ought to do the other, or ought to have done it, even though we could never have done both? Cf. AGGLOMERATION.

A further place for moral conflict can arise between what we ought to do and what we think we ought to do, when these differ. Is there a sense which what we think we ought to do can supersede in these cases what we ought to do, and become what we really ought to do, just because we think this? Or is this really incoherent? How far ought we to follow our conscience, as it is sometimes put? On the moral 'ought' see also IMPERATIVE, MORAL.

Obligations are normally things we incur because of specific circumstances (e.g. a promise or favours received). The basis of many obligations is a contract, which need be only implicit, if implicit contracts are possible. There may be many reasons why I ought to obey the law, but I only have an obligation to obey it if I have incurred that obligation, perhaps on some form of the social contract theory (see POLITICAL PHILOSOPHY). Obligations are primarily moral or legal. They are also to some moral agent (including corporations, God, etc.). If I buy a dog I no doubt ought to feed it, but any obligation I am under must be to the seller, or perhaps to society.

Being obliged is wider than being under an obligation. What matters now is the lack of alternatives, not the element of incurring. The alternatives excluded may be physically or prudentially rather than morally or legally impossible ('I was obliged, but not under an obligation, to hand over my purse'). Also one need not, though one may, be obliged to someone. But one cannot be obliged to do what is not morally at least excusable: a soldier is not obliged to flee the battle, however prudent that may be.

Obligatory belongs roughly with 'obligation'. It is not confined to the moral and legal (there can be obligatory moves in a game), but it presupposes rules and does not cover cases of being physically or prudentially obliged.

Duty is primarily connected with roles, whether or not these are voluntarily undertaken. One has duties as a secretary, father, son, etc. Duties tend to be of longer standing and less *ad hoc* than obligations: one meets one's obligations as one incurs them, but does one's duty or discharges one's duties in the normal course of things.

Duties and obligations are therefore special kinds of things we morally or legally ought to do, though it does not follow that we always ought to perform them, since they may be overridden, whether by other duties, etc., or even by something non-moral: see above on the 'final ought'.

Another question introduces rights. Must there be a correlative right wherever there is a duty or obligation, and vice versa? Do animals have rights, and do we have duties to them?

Since Kant, especially, 'duty' has often been used loosely for whatever we morally ought to do, and 'obligation' is often used with similar looseness. Kant, following others, distinguished perfect duties, which were absolute and could never be overridden, from imperfect duties, which could be overridden by other duties or even by inclinations (e.g. benevolence: we need not, perhaps could not, give to charity on every possible occasion, but must sometimes). This makes us ask whether the same act can be both dutiful and meritorious, and raises the question of supererogation, i.e. whether an act can be meritorious though not one that we ought to do. Prima facie duties (Ross) are general duties such as benevolence and promise-keeping, which may be overridden in a given situation. The term has been objected to because it implies that when overridden they cease to be duties at all; cf. DEFEASIBLE, and the discussion above of competing moral claims.

Finally, could there be religious, as against moral, duties?

F. H. Bradley, *Ethical Studies*, Oxford UP, 1876, essay 5 ('My station and its duties'). (Famous idealist account of basis of moral 'ought'.)

H. N. Castañeda, 'Imperatives, oughts and moral oughts', *Australasian Journal of Philosophy*, 1966. (Meaning of 'ought'. Moral and overriding ('final') 'ought'.)

W. K. Frankena, 'Obligation and motivation in recent moral philosophy', in A. I. Melden (ed.), *Essays in Moral Philosophy*, Washington UP, 1958.

D. P. Gauthier, *Practical Reasoning*, Oxford UP, 1963. (Includes discussion of obligation and duty.)

*R. M. Hare, *The Language of Morals*, Oxford UP, 1952, part 3. (Influential analysis of 'ought' and its relation to imperatives and to 'right' and 'good'.)

H. L. A. Hart, 'Legal and moral obligation', in A. I. Melden (ed.), *Essays in Moral Philosophy*, 1958.

P. Helm (ed.), *Divine Commands and Morality*, Oxford UP, 1981. (Why should we obey God? and related questions.)

D. A. Lloyd Thomas, 'Why should I be moral?', *Philosophy*, 1970.

J. K. Mish'alani, '"Duty", "obligation" and "ought"', *Analysis*, vol. 30, 1969.

E. Page, 'On being obliged', *Mind*, 1973. (Senses of 'obliged'.)

P. L. Quinn, *Divine Commands and Moral Commandments*, Clarendon, 1978.

W. D. Ross, *The Right and the Good*, Clarendon, 1930. (See chapter 2 for prima facie duties. Cf. also his later book, *Foundations of Ethics*, Clarendon, 1939 (sometimes called 'The righter and the better').)

B. A. O. Williams and R. F. Atkinson, 'Consistency in ethics', *Proceedings of the Aristotelian Society*, supplementary vol. 1965. (Conflict of duties.)

Ousia. Greek for 'being', 'essence'. See SUBSTANCE.

P

Panpsychism. The theory that mind is pervasive throughout the universe, that every thing (and not just humans and animals) has a soul or mind and is to some degree sentient. LEIBNIZ and SCHOPEN-HAUER held versions of the theory: more recently, Timothy Sprigge and Galen Strawson have defended it.

T. L. S. Sprigge, *The Vindication of Absolute Idealism*, Edinburgh UP, 1983.

G. Strawson, 'The self', in S. Gallagher and J. Shear (eds), *Models of the Self*, Imprint Academic, 1999.

G. Strawson, 'Realistic monism: Why physicalism entails panpsychism' in A. Freeman (ed.), *Consciousness and its Place in Nature: does Physicalism entail Panpsychism?* Imprint Academic, 2006. (Strawson's is the keynote paper, discussed by the other contributors, with Strawson's replies.)

Pantheism. The view that nature (and human beings) are part of God, modes of his being, not separate from or independent of him. Christianity has tended to reject the identification of God with nature. SPINOZA argued for pantheism.

Paradigm. A paradigm for a concept is an ideal instance of it which can be used for assessing other instances. Plato seems sometimes to have thought of his Forms (see IDEA, UNIVERSALS) as paradigms in this sense.

T. S. KUHN introduced 'paradigm' in a technical sense, or senses, into philosophy of science. Here a paradigm is basically a way of looking at things, a shared assumption which governs the outlook of an epoch and its approach to scientific problems; or an accepted theory, e.g. Ptolemaic or Copernican astronomy. These have remained the most important of the Kuhnian senses, though in his later work disciplinary matrix is used for approximately these senses, and paradigms become standard forms of solutions to problems (e.g. they become equations, formulae, etc.). These solutions are then used for solving further problems, and so govern the forms these further solutions take. Kuhn is largely concerned with how shifts of paradigms occur as science develops.

T. S. Kuhn, *The Structure of Scientific Revolutions*, Chicago UP, 1962, 2nd edn with postscript, 1970.

M. Masterman, 'The nature of a paradigm', in I. Lakatos and A. Musgrave (eds), *Criticism and the Growth of Knowledge*, Cambridge UP, 1970. (Extracts twenty-one senses of 'paradigm' from Kuhn and discusses, reducing to three groups. Cf. Kuhn's reply (ibid, § 6, and 'postscript' (above). For further discussions see bibliography to SCIENCE.)

Paraconsistency. The view that there are important logical theories that do not allow (as classical logic does) that a contradiction has every proposition among its logical consequences. A system containing contradictory propositions is inconsistent, but if it does not contain every proposition, it avoids being trivial. It is claimed that various scientific and mathematical theories are in fact of this nature, and so can be logically analysed by paraconsistent logics, and also defended as they stand, in that we need not assume that the inconsistencies in them are merely aberrations that must be removed before they can be properly studied. See also DIALETHEISM.

G. Priest, R. Routley and J. Norman (eds), *Paraconsistent Logic: Essays on the Inconsistent*, Philosophia Verlag, 1989.

Paradigm case argument. A type of argument claiming that certain things must exist or be real because certain expressions have a standard correct use in our language. It is claimed that there must be such a thing as freewill because there are standard situations, paradigm cases, where it is generally agreed to be correct to say, 'He did it of his own freewill.' Without such situations, it is argued, the word 'freewill' would have no meaning. An example seeming to support this is that only because red things exist or have existed can 'red' have the meaning it has. The argument is that certain things must exist because certain expressions have a meaning and therefore a correct use.

The argument has been attacked on various grounds. Even for 'red' to mean what it does, perhaps there need only seem to be red things. This assumes that there could seem to be red things though there were in fact none. If a certain expression is to have meaning, does this imply that something exists, or only that it could exist, or neither? And are there relevant differences between terms like 'red' and 'freewill'? Also how much can the argument show? Even if 'freewill' means what it does because situations exist where we are not subject to external constraint, hypnotism, etc., does this show that we have freewill in a philosophically interesting sense?

Appeal to the paradigm case argument is closely associated with linguistic PHILOSOPHY. See also TRANSCENDENTAL ARGUMENTS.

P. Edwards, 'Bertrand Russell's doubts about induction', *Mind*, 1949. (Applies the argument to legitimize induction, as does P. F. Strawson, *Introduction to Logical Theory*, Methuen, 1952, chapter 9.)

O. Hanfling, 'What is wrong with the paradigm case argument?', *Proceedings of the Aristotelian Society*, 1990–1. (Defends the argument.)

J. Passmore, *Philosophical Reasoning*, Duckworth, 1961, chapter 6. (Critical of this and related argument.)

R. J. Richman, 'On the argument of the paradigm case', *Australasian Journal of Philosophy*, 1961. (Attacks argument. Cf. discussions by C. J. F. Williams (ibid.) and Richman (ibid., 1962).)

J. W. N. Watkins, 'Farewell to the paradigm case argument', *Analysis*, vol. 18, 1957–8. (Cf. discussions in same volume.)

Paradox. Etymologically, 'against belief'. Full-blooded paradoxes which affect the basis of logic exist when some statement needed for logic can apparently be both proved and disproved. Among them, paradoxes depending on purely logical or mathematical terms are called logical paradoxes, or paradoxes of set theory (e.g. RUSSELL'S PARADOX) while paradoxes depending on notions like meaning, designation, etc., are called semantic paradoxes (e.g. LIAR PARADOX); these are sometimes distinguished from the logical ones. In pragmatic paradoxes there is a contradiction not in what is said but in what is done in saying it. 'It's raining, but I don't believe it is' is not contradictory for both parts could be true. But uttering the second part frustrates the normal intention of uttering the first. Strategic paradoxes offer problems for how it is rational to act, claiming that each of two inconsistent policies can be defended as preferable to the other (NEWCOMB'S PARADOX, PRISONER'S DILEMMA). Other paradoxes claim e.g. that apparently indispensable notions are inconsistent (e.g. ZENO'S PARADOXES), or that apparently possible situations are impossible (e.g. PREDICTION PARADOX). Loosely speaking a paradox may be little more than something odd or unexpected (e.g. material and strict IMPLICATION paradoxes). But how significant a given paradox is, is often disputed. See also theory of TYPES.

M. Clark, *Paradoxes from A–Z*, London: Routledge, 2002.
T. Baldwin, *G. E. Moore*, Routledge, 1990. (See pp. 226–32 for discussion of 'Moore's paradox', a pragmatic paradox.)
A. Pap, *Semantics and Necessary Truth*, Yale UP, 1958, chapter 9C. (Types of paradox, especially pragmatic.)
*R. M. Sainsbury, *Paradoxes*, Cambridge UP, 1988 (revised 1995). (General introduction.)

Parallelism. See PSYCHOPHYSICAL PARALLELISM.

Parenthetical verb. See BELIEF.

Parfit, Derek. 1942–. British philosopher who works in the USA at Harvard and at Oxford. His highly influential book *Reasons and Persons*, 1984, raises, in succession, problems about moral choice and rationality, about self-identity, possible futures for the world and their moral significance now. He brings out failings in consequentialism and self-interest theories of rationality, criticizes theories of personal identity, and shows how utilitarian arguments lead to repugnant conclusions when applied to future states of the world involving as yet unborn people. *Climbing the Mountain*, 2008, argues that the best versions of Kantian ethics and of contractualism dovetail with the best version of rule-consequentialism. See REDUCTIONISM.

Parmenides. See ELEATICS.

Particularism. The view that only particulars (see UNIVERSALS) exist, and more specifically that the properties and relations of particulars are themselves particulars, not universals (see TROPES).

Particularism resembles NOMINALISM, but a particularist might accept abstract particulars like numbers, seen as abstract objects. They would be particulars rather than universals because they do not have instances (there are instances or twoness, but not of the number two). Nominalists, however, would normally reject numbers seen as abstract objects.

For moral particularism, see ETHICS.

Particulars. See UNIVERSE, INDIVIDUALS.

Pascal, Blaise. 1623–62. French mathematician, scientist and philosopher, born in the Auvergne. He made many important contributions to mathematics, and planned a comprehensive apology for Christianity, which he did not live to complete, leaving the fragmentary and aphoristic, but highly influential, *Pensées*, published posthumously in 1670. These include Pascal's version of a pre-existing argument, known now as 'Pascal's wager'. The argument goes that if God and an afterlife exist we could face infinite suffering in Hell. Therefore it must be rational to act as though they do exist, however low the probability (above zero), since the resulting sacrifice of pleasure is only finite.

  I. Hacking, 'The logic of Pascal's wager', *American Philosophical Quarterly*, 1972.
  A. Krailsheimer, *Pascal*, Past Masters, 1980. (Introductory.)
  P. T. Landsberg, 'Gambling on God', *Mind*, 1971.

Paternalism. The view that it is justifiable to interfere with someone's liberty or autonomy against their will when it is in that person's interests to do so. Soft or weak paternalism justifies interference only when the person is in ignorance of crucial relevant facts, or is not acting in a fully voluntary way. Hard or strong paternalism, on the other hand, claims that someone else may know better what is truly in the interests of the individual concerned, even when they are acting a fully informed and voluntary way: people need to be protected against their foolish choices.

  J. L. Feinberg, *The Moral Limits of the Criminal Law*, vol 2, *Harm to Self*, Oxford UP, 1986. (Extensive discussion.)
  J. S. Mill, *On Liberty*, 1859. (Argues against paternalism.)

Peirce, Charles S. 1839–1914. Born in Cambridge, Massachusetts; he worked as an astronomer, government physicist and university teacher in America. He is especially famous as the first main PRAGMATIST, but he also developed an elaborate system of logic. This contributed to modern mathematical logic in many ways, notably by his development of a logic of relations, including the distinction between monadic, dyadic and polyadic relations (see MONAD). He also developed a metaphysics based on three categories which he called firstness, secondness and thirdness. Peirce published no books in his lifetime, but apart from his *Collected Papers*, 8 vols, 1931–58, some selections exist: *Chance, Love and Logic*, 1923; *The Philosophy of Peirce*, 1940. See also UNIVERSALS, SYNECHISM.

Perception. The faculty of apprehending the world specifically through the senses, or the general exercise of it, or particular cases of its exercise. Perception raises problems which form an important branch of epistemology.

The analysis of perceiving is complicated by the variety of its objects (cf. SEEING). How is perceiving the redness of Smith's face related to perceiving that his face is red, that he is angry, that he is subconsciously afraid? And can one perceive an object without perceiving facts about it?

Usually 'perceive' is a 'success' or 'achievement' word (cf. EPISTE-MOLOGY on 'factive'), i.e. we can only perceive what is there or is true. But this may not always hold, if we allow that Macbeth perceived a dagger, and it does not apply to 'perceive as' (cf. SEEING). We can misperceive, i.e. make mistakes about what we perceive.

Perception is thus a complex notion, and two main and connected problems concern its relations to sensory experience, and to intellectual notions like belief, judgement, inference.

Sense-perception obviously involves the senses, but exactly how? Very often we perceive things otherwise than as they are, sometimes knowingly and sometimes not. The penny seen from one side looks elliptical, the candle seen out of focus looks double, the whistle seems to change pitch as the train passes. All this has suggested, by the argument from illusion, that what we 'directly' or 'immediately' perceive or are aware of (often called SENSE DATA, etc.) sometimes or always differs from what is 'out there' in the world: we perceive objects by interpreting or inferring from these sense data. More radically, the fact that we sometimes seem to perceive when we are not strictly perceiving at all, as when we dream or hallucinate, suggests SCEPTICISM about how we can know that an external world exists at all. The former position may be reinforced because we know scientifically how the physical and physiological processes involved inevitably affect the information we get through our senses. (But if the presence of such processes means that we never perceive objects, even when the processes are not distorted, what is it that we never do? What would it be to 'really perceive' an object?)

If we do attempt to start from a basis limited to 'pure experience', it is difficult, as empiricists from Locke and Hume onwards have found, to get beyond it. The sense data, etc., supposed to serve as a bridge between us and the world end up as a drawbridge that keeps us from the world. This attempt has been attacked in two ways. Firstly, the arguments for it are suspect, and seem self-defeating. We can only contrast appearance with reality if we already have independent knowledge of reality, and the fact that we may be deceived on any occasion does not imply that we may, or even could, be deceived on every occasion. Secondly, it seems impossible to isolate and describe any 'pure experience' (the GIVEN). Not only does all describing involve language, and so memory, but experience is ineradicably affected by context and knowledge. The retinal image has two dimensions, but we see the world as having three, even with one eye closed. The penny looks round, as much as it looks elliptical (has 'looks' two senses here?), and continues to look so while being turned or moved (object constancy). We select part of what we see as foreground, seen against a background (the figure/ground theory emphasized by Gestalt psychologists), and there is the duck/rabbit phenomenon (see SEEING). As artists know, perceptual reduction, abstracting a basic 'pure experience' from our perceptions, is difficult or impossible.

Yet the facts remain that perception involves the senses, that perceptions are normally the basis for beliefs, and that illusions do occur. Any theory of perception should answer questions like these: Is there direct or immediate awareness or pure experience, and if so, has it special objects? If it has, how are these related to physical objects or parts of them, including their surfaces? Do words like 'looks', 'seems', 'appears', always imply doubt, or are they ambiguous between a sense that does and a sense that does not? Is perception something unitary, or has it two parts, a sensory part involving this 'direct' awareness and some process of interpretation or judgement based on this? If two parts, are they successive or simultaneous? Does a single account hold for different modes of perception such as seeing, hearing, etc.? Do we in fact perceive physical objects at all? Or do we only infer their existence? Or do we treat them as LOGICAL CONSTRUCTIONS (cf. PHENOMENALISM)? If we do perceive physical objects (and shadows, etc.), under what conditions do we do so? Must we know we are doing so? Must we notice or pick out the object? Are there really such things as unconscious and subliminal perception? What features of an object can we perceive? Its colour? Shape? Nature? Behaviour? Causal properties? Beauty? Suitability for this or that? Does the object play a causal role, and if so, what does it cause, our having an experience or our perceiving the object? And does this role enter the analysis of what we mean by saying we perceive the object, so that to say we perceive something is to say, among other things, that it causes us to do something? Or is it merely that our perceptions of it, or our accompanying experiences, are always in fact caused partly by it? And why does it matter by what route the causal chain operates (cf. MEMORY on deviant causal chains)?

Views giving causation a role in one of these ways are among CAUSAL THEORIES OF PERCEPTION. Representative (representational) theories say either that what we perceive is not the object but something else (sense data, etc.) representing it, or that we do perceive the object but only by being directly aware (etc.) of such representatives which may or may not be parts of the object. Causal and representative theories often go together.

Disjunctive theories claim that when someone believes he or she is perceiving an object then either he or she is, and it is therefore a veridical perception, or it is a hallucination, but that (unlike the causal theorist) there is no common perception in both cases, caused differently in each case.

Realist theories say that whatever it is that is perceived exists independently of being perceived. Naïve realism is properly the view, attributed to the 'plain man', that we not only perceive ordinary objects but normally perceive them as they are, by a direct relation without sense data, interpretations, etc., and with 'as they are' raising no problems. There is a paradox in attributing any philosophical view to the 'plain' non-philosophical man, and in practice 'naïve realism' often starts by meaning whatever the plain man would say without reflection (i.e. discounting illusions, etc.), and ends, as the argument develops, by meaning simply realism.

Perceptual usually applies to things as they appear to the perceiver. Thus, perceptual consciousness is the total conscious experience of the perceiver qua perceiver. Perceptual objects are whatever it is one perceives, be it sense data, physical objects, or whatever, considered as having just those characteristics they are perceived as having. These are perceptual characteristics (what these are may be unclear, as in the penny case above). Perceptible characteristics, however, are those accessible to perception (e.g. colour but not magnetism). The perceptual-field is the total of a person's perceptual objects at a given moment, not necessarily distinguished as separate objects. Perceived object refers usually to the physical or public object (or shadow, etc.) perceived, considered as having the characteristics it really has. Percept is similar to 'perceptual object'. It sometimes refers to sense data, but sometimes to the contents of perceptual consciousness for those not holding a sense datum theory (Firth). See also SENSES, SENSATION, SENSE DATA, SEEING, FEELING, PHENOMENALISM.

T. Crane (ed.), *The Contents of Experience*, Cambridge UP, 1992. (Essays, mainly specially written.)

J. Dancy (ed.), *Perceptual Knowledge*, Oxford UP, 1988. (Reprinted essays, more recent than Swartz. P. Snowden's 'Perception, vision, and causation' and J. McDowell's 'Criteria, defeasibility, and knowledge' defend versions of the disjunctive theory.)

R. Firth, 'Sense-data and the percept theory', *Mind*, 1949–50, reprinted with important addendum (p. 270) in Swartz. (Develops and discusses 'percept theory' as against sense datum theory, and discusses perceptual reduction).

E. H. Gombrich, *Art and Illusion*, Phaidon, 1960. (Argues against isolatability of experience in perception, from point of view of art and with plentiful illustrations.)

J. Heil, *Perception and Cognition*, California UP, 1983. (Perception involves acquiring belief in a certain way, but belief need not involve language and cannot be analysed in terms of internal representations (see also COGNITIVE PSYCHOLOGY).)

*R. J. Hirst, *The Problems of Perception*, Allen and Unwin/Humanities Press, 1959. (Introduction, advocating one view.)

E. Jackson, *Perception*, Cambridge UP, 1977. H. Robinson, *Perception*, Routledge, 1994. (Two defences of sense data theories).

M. Martin, 'Sight and touch', in Crane, 1992. (Brings out differences between these).

D. Owens, *Causes and Coincidences*, Cambridge UP, 1992. (See pp. 143–58 for defence of a causal theory.)

C. Peacocke, *Sense and Content*, Oxford UP, 1983, chapters 1 and 2. (Rehabilitates sensation as having a role in question about perception, distinguishing sensational and representational properties of experiences.)

*P. Smith and O. R. Jones, *The Philosophy of Mind: An Introduction*, Cambridge UP, 1986. (Chapter 7 attacks view that perception involves inner objects. Chapter 8 defends view that perception is acquisition of beliefs for which see Heil (above) and Armstrong in Dancy.)

P. Snowdon, 'How to interpret "direct perception"', in Crane, 1992. (Defends version of direct realism, taking sense data and argument from illusion seriously, though without accepting them.)

R. J. Swartz (ed.), *Perceiving, Sensing and Knowing*, 1965. (Reprinted essays with bibliography.)

I. J. Valberg, 'The puzzle of experience', in Crane, 1992. (See particularly pp. 18–32 for statement of argument from illusion. Cf. also his book *The Puzzle of Experience*, Oxford UP, 1992, from which this extract is reprinted.)

Perdurance. An ordinary object, like a table, is usually thought to be made up of spatial parts, and if it endures for say a week, it and each of its parts are said to be present on each day. But philosophers sometimes think of such objects as made up of temporal parts, say a Monday part, a Tuesday part, and so on. In that case, the object is never present as a whole and its Monday part is present only on Mondays, and so on. The object is then said to perdure. An object which either endures or perdures can be said to persist.

D. K. Lewis, *On the Plurality of Worlds*, Blackwell, 1986, p. 202.

Perfection (principle of). See SUFFICIENT REASON.

Performatives. See SPEECH ACTS.

Peripatetic. Literally 'performing while moving around'. Label attached to ARISTOTLE's followers; often used interchangeably with 'Aristotelian'. So called from *peripatoi* or covered walkway where Aristotle taught.

Peripheric. See JAMES–LANGE THEORY.

Perlocutions. See SPEECH ACTS.

Person. Certain modern writers use 'person' in a technical way to stand for a type of entity different from material objects and dis-embodied spirits. P. F. Strawson insists that persons are not reducible to these other things. He distinguishes M-predicates, applying to both material bodies and persons (e.g. weighing ten stone), from P-predicates, applying only to persons (e.g. thinking, going for a walk). Others have made a similar distinction. Some P-predicates, however, may apply to persons only because they have bodies (e.g. going for a walk). See also IDENTITY, philosophy of MIND.

T. Forrest, 'P-predicates', in A. Stroll (ed.), *Epistemology*, Harper and Row, 1967.
B. Smart, 'How can persons be ascribed M-predicates?', *Mind*, 1977.
P. F. Strawson, *Individuals*, Methuen, 1959, chapter 3.

Personalism. Any of a wide variety of views emphasizing the primacy, in the universe, of persons (non-technical sense), whether human or divine.

P. A. Bertocci, 'The perspective of a teleological personalistic idealist', in John E. Smith (ed.), *Contemporary American Philosophy*, 2nd series, Allen and Unwin, 1970.

R. T. Flewelling, 'Personalism', in D. D. Runes (ed.), *Twentieth-Century Philosophy*, 1943. (General survey.)

Perspectivism. The theory that there can be radically different and incommensurable conceptual schemes or perspectives, one of which we must, consciously or unconsciously, adopt, but none of which is more correct than its rivals; see RELATIVISM.

Perspectivism was named by J. Ortega y Gasset (1883–1955) and versions of it have been held by Nietzsche, E. Sapir (1884–1939), B. L. Whorf (1897–1941) and T. S. Kuhn (1922–1996).

Petitio principii. See BEGGING THE QUESTION.

Phase terms, phase universals. See IDENTITY.

Phenomena. See NOUMENON, PHENOMENOLOGY.

Phenomenalism. Literally, a theory based on appearances. Earlier phenomenalists analysed physical objects in terms of actual and possible sensations (Mill treated matter as a permanent possibility of sensation). More recently phenomenalism has taken a linguistic form. Its main claim has been that sentences about physical objects can be analysed without residue into sentences about SENSE DATA, which Moore and Russell distinguish from SENSATIONS. Its point, in both versions, is that we can only know appearances, but need not postulate unknowable objects lurking behind them, because belief or talk about such objects is really only a disguised form of belief or talk about the appearances themselves. The phenomenalist goal of providing detailed translations of statements about physical objects, vigorously pursued until just after the Second World War, is now widely regarded as unattainable, even in principle.

Like subjective IDEALISM, from which perhaps it developed, phenomenalism makes appearances central. Subjective idealism says physical objects are unreal. Phenomenalism says they are real, but are not what they seem – they are appearances, actual or possible. BERKELEY is hard to classify. Though usually called a subjective idealist, he held that physical objects were real but were ideas and not material objects. See also PERCEPTION, PHILOSOPHY.

Primarily phenomenalism is a doctrine about physical objects. More broadly, any view that uses LOGICAL CONSTRUCTIONS can be called phenomenalist.

A. J. Ayer, *Foundations of Empirical Knowledge*, Macmillan, 1940. (Defence of modern phenomenalism. Cf. his later view in 'Phenomenalism', *Proceedings of the Aristotelian Society*, 1946–7, reprinted in his *Philosophical Essays*, 1954.)

A. C. Grayling, *Berkeley: The Central Arguments*, Duckworth, 1986. (Generally sympathetic introduction to Berkeley).

*J. Hospers, *Introduction to Philosophical Analysis*, RKP, 1956, chapter 8. (Discusses phenomenalism in relation to other theories.)

R. Le Poidevin, 'Fables and models', *Proceedings of the Aristotelian Society*, supplementary vol., 1991. (See p. 73 for a way of distinguishing phenomenalism from idealism.)

J. S. Mill, *An Examination of Sir William Hamilton's Philosophy*, 1865, chapter 11, appendix to chapter 12. (Early version of phenomenalism.)

Phenomenology. Literally, the description or study of appearances. Any description of how things appear, especially if sustained and penetrating, can be called a phenomenology. The close attention given by linguistic PHILOSOPHY to the actual workings of language is sometimes called linguistic phenomenology. But more specifically 'phenomenology' refers to a movement starting with Brentano and associated especially with Husserl, and, later, Heidegger and Merleau-Ponty. This at first emphasized the description of human experience as directed onto objects, in the sense in which thoughts or wishes have objects, even if unreal ones ('intentional objects'; see INTENSIONALITY). In Husserl the emphasis shifted away from the mere description of experience towards a description of the objects of experience, which he called phenomena. Phenomena were things which appear. He saw them in fact as essences which the mind intuited, and the task of phenomenology was to describe them. This, however, was not an empirical task, but an a priori one. It resembled in fact what was later called conceptual analysis (see PHILOSOPHY), though it insisted that the essences were real things, not, for example, ways in which words were used. (We can still think of unreal things like unicorns; the essence of unicorn is real on this view.) Phenomenology also led on to the study of being, associated with EXISTENTIALISM. Husserl thought that studying essences as they were intuited involved laying aside various preconceptions derived from science; this laying aside was called reduction, epoche or bracketing the world.

D. Bell, *Husserl*, Routledge, 1990. (General discussion of his philosophy.)

H. L. Dreyfus, *Husserl, Intentionality and Cognitive Science*, MIT Press, 1982. (Relevance of phenomenology to contemporary philosophical issues.)

E. Husserl, *Cartesian Meditations*, 1931 (French), 1950 (German), Nijhoff, 1960 (English). Cf. also his *The Idea of Phenomenology*, 1907, Nijhoff, trans. 1964, and *The Paris Lectures*, 1929, trans. 1964.

D. Moran, *Introduction to Phenomenology*, Routledge, 2000. (Excellent introduction.)

G. Ryle, *Collected Papers*, vol. 1, Hutchinson, 1971. (Includes several relevant items. Chapter 10 brings out some connections with conceptual analysis, and chapter 12 some with existentialism.)

H. Spiegelberg, *The Phenomenological Movement*, Nijhoff, 1960. (Extended history, ending with philosophical summary.)

M. Warnock, *Existentialism*, Oxford UP, 1970. (Includes chapter on Husserl.)

Philosophy and analysis. An embarrassment for professional philosophers is that they cannot produce any succinct, or even agreed, definition of their profession. 'What is philosophy?' is itself a philosophical question.

Literally meaning 'love of wisdom', 'philosophy' came to stand for knowledge in general about man and the universe. The Stoics and Epicureans (c. 300 BC) divided knowledge into logic (including also what is now called epistemology), physics (including all that we now call science) and ethics (including also what we now call philosophy of mind and psychology). Natural philosophy, dealing with the world of nature, and moral philosophy, dealing with humanity, were the descendents of physics and ethics, respectively, in these senses, 'Natural philosophy' is now, when used at all, limited to physics while 'moral philosophy' is normally limited to ETHICS. Metaphysics, which the Stoics and Epicureans had largely assimilated into physics, became assimilated to natural theology, and became the centre of philosophy, after Aquinas had separated natural from revealed or dogmatic theology.

Only in the last century or two have the sciences become so specialized that philosophy appears as simply one discipline among others. There are two main ways of distinguishing it, by its subject matter or its methods. Many have held that its subject is in some way 'ultimate things', either about the universe as a whole or about matters affecting human fate and conduct in the most basic way. Now, however, philosophy is more commonly distinguished by certain methods, its subject being whatever is most suitably studied by them. In particular, philosophy avoids using the senses and relies on reflection. It is an a priori study. In developing from its older to its modern form it has shed the sciences one by one as they became amenable to systematic empirical study rather than armchair speculation – first physics and chemistry, and then the human sciences (economics, psychology, sociology). But philosophy also lacks any definite and systematic procedures for proving results. Mathematics has therefore always lain rather outside philosophy, and mathematical LOGIC, though needed more than ever as a tool by philosophy, is itself now becoming a separate subject, allied to mathematics.

All this circumscribes the subject matter of philosophy. Science tells us what particular things the world contains, but philosophy asks about the different ways in which we can classify whatever the world, or any world, contains; (cf. CATEGORIES, METAPHYSICS). Science gives us knowledge, but philosophy asks what we can know, and how (EPISTEMOLOGY).

One role, then, of philosophy is to look behind or after (meta-) the sciences and analyse the concepts (notions, ideas) and methods they use. A given science X, often has an associated 'philosophy of X' (or 'meta-X') which fulfils this role. METAPHYSICS, where 'physics' means the study of nature in general, is the most general of these studies, though questions of scientific method now fall under a separate study, philosophy of SCIENCE.

Analysis, in some sense, is always therefore an important part of philosophy. Under the influence of POSITIVISM and allied trends, much twentieth-century English-speaking philosophy (to which the rest of this entry is confined; for other kinds cf. EXISTENTIALISM, PHENOMENOLOGY, IDEALISM) has assumed that substantive results in subjects like ethics, politics and aesthetics could not be reached by rational argument. These subjects were matters of attitude and persuasion. Philosophy, it was often thought, should simply analyse concepts (conceptual analysis). It should become analytical philosophy, using philosophical analysis.

Analysis, however, is ambiguous. It can mean simply the explication of concepts like substance, cause, good, material object, asking, for example, what things count as material objects and what they all have in common. In this ordinary sense all philosophy involves analysis. There are, however, various kinds of analysis. One kind claims that what is being analysed is 'really' something else at a deeper level, which replaces it (cf. PHENOMENALISM and LOGICAL CONSTRUCTIONS); the original thing may or may not somehow survive the analysis rather than being eliminated (cf. REDUCTIONISM). Another kind, sometimes called logical analysis claims simply to show the correct logical form of ordinary sentences (cf. theory of DESCRIPTIONS), making no metaphysical claims about what really exists, etc. But even this is in fact reductive, since it condemns some ways of speaking and replaces them.

After the Second World War, a reaction against the restrictions of logical positivism and the failure of phenomenalism, suggested that any consistent outlook or set of concepts (e.g. in ethics or religion) was prima facie as good as any other, and that philosophy should analyse what is involved in everyday ways of speaking and thinking, without trying to judge between them. This emphasizes ways of speaking, but it is no longer reductive. It does not condemn some ways of speaking as fundamentally unjustified and seek to replace them. It is called linguistic or ordinary language philosophy, using linguistic analysis, and was often condemned as evading the real problems; though ordinary language philosophy need not, as its enemy Russell thought, be done in ordinary language, i.e. without technical terms. Philosophy of LANGUAGE is different from linguistic philosophy, being a subject, not an outlook.

The term analytical philosophy sometimes carries the implication that philosophy should confine itself to conceptual analysis and not claim to answer any substantive questions. In this sense it has come under attack in recent decades, especially since some philosophers, like Quine, would say that, since no clear account can be given of 'ANALYTIC', we cannot coherently seek the analytic truths about concepts that conceptual analysis demands. But there is a wider sense of 'analytical philosophy' in which it denotes the attempt to tackle philosophical problems piecemeal by analysing the problems themselves into manageable parts rather than trying to construct grand overall systems from which solutions to these problems emerge. In this second sense analytical philosophy is still the dominant outlook in English-language philosophy (despite a growing tolerance of large systems: see METAPHYSICS), and indeed is growing on the European continent in various countries on both sides of the old Iron Curtain.

Nevertheless analytical philosophical is now bolder in making substantive claims, and is much less isolationist. But it still, like linguistic philosophy, feels discomfort, if no more, at outraging common sense. It relies heavily, on the techniques of formal logic, but is more sensitive to its debt to the empirical sciences, e.g. physics and cognitive science (see COGNITIVE PSYCHOLOGY). This has blurred the edges between philosophy and science, though the philosopher must still have an eye for the difference between questions for reflection and questions for observation; observation may stimulate, but can never solve, philosophical problems. Partly for this reason and partly because of its own internal development, involving constant refinement and sophistication, philosophy has become much more technical than it used to be at the mid-century; philosophy of mind and philosophy of language have been particularly influenced in this respect and are both growth areas.

Since the late 1960s much of philosophy has been under the influence of a debate between REALISM and antirealism. The influence of Wittgenstein has been particularly strong on antirealist thinking. There has been a revival of interest in essentialism and innate ideas (the latter largely under the influence of Chomsky), while at the same time Berkeley's idealism has been taken more seriously than it used to be. The influence of language is still great, but not overriding.

See also AESTHETICS, EPISTEMOLOGY, ETHICS, LOGIC, METAPHYSICS, POLITICAL PHILOSOPHY, PROCESS PHILOSOPHY, SOCIAL PHILOSOPHY, Philosophies of BODY, EDUCATION, HISTORY, LANGUAGE, LAW, MATHEMATICS, MIND, RELIGION, SCIENCE.

A. J. Ayer, W. C. Kneale, G. A. Paul, D. F. Pears, P. F. Strawson, G. J. Warnock and R. A. Wollheim (eds), *The Revolution in Philosophy*, Macmillan, 1956. (Philosophy as it saw itself about 1950.)

*M. Hollis, *Invitation to Philosophy*, Blackwell, 1985. (Brief elementary introduction.)

T. Honderich and M. F Burnyeat (eds), *Philosophy as It Is*, Penguin, 1979. (Reprints of notable articles, with introduction to each by editors. Cf. also T. Honderich (ed.), *Philosophy through Its Past*, Pelican, 1984, modern articles on earlier thinkers.)

*T. Nagel, *What Does It All Mean?* Oxford UP, 1987. (Brief elementary introduction.)

*A. O'Hear, *What Philosophy Is*, Pelican, 1985. (Brief elementary introduction.)

J. A. Passmore, *100 Years of Philosophy*, Duckworth, 1957, revised and expanded, 1966. (Full, documented and readable. Tends to conflate important and unimportant.)

Philosophical Review, 1992. (The January issue is devoted to four survey articles, with many references, covering developments in various fields in philosophy from 1950 to 1990. See pp. 195–209 for discussion of relations between philosophy and its own history.)

R. Rorty (ed.), *The Linguistic Turn*, Chicago UP, 1967. (Essays on relations between language and philosophy in mid-twentieth century, with long introduction and full bibliography.)

R. Rorty, J. B. Schneewind and Q. Skinner (eds), *Philosophy in History*, Cambridge UP, 1984. (Specially written essays covering both theoretical questions and specific examples.)

*B. Russell, *The Problems of Philosophy*, Home University Library, 1912. (Dated in detail but still good introduction to philosophical thinking.)

B. Russell, *My Philosophical Development*, Allen and Unwin, 1959. (Final chapter attacks linguistic philosophy.)

*R. Scruton, *Modern Philosophy: An Introduction and Survey*, Sinclair-Stevenson, 1994.

*N. Warburton, *Philosophy: The Basics*, Routledge, 1992.

T. Williamson, *The Philosophy of Philosophy*, Blackwell, 2007. (Elaborate and sophisticated discussions of various aspects of the subject. Not for beginners.)

Phrastic and neustic. Sentences like 'The door is shut', 'Shut the door!', 'Is the door shut?' seem to have something in common as well as differences. R. M. Hare called what they had in common the phrastic (roughly, what is said, or the content) and what was peculiar to each of them the neustic (from the Greek for assenting or subscribing). The phrastic might be represented as 'The door being shut' and the respective neustics as 'Yes', 'Please', 'Query'. Thus the first sentence would be analysed as, 'The door being shut: yes.' Later Hare distinguished also the tropic, or sign of mood (from the Greek for 'mood'), from the neustic, which he kept for assent or subscription. See also SENTENCES, SPEECH ACTS.

R. M. Hare, *The Language of Morals*, Oxford UP, 1952. (See index. Original distinction. For tropics see his 'Meaning and speech acts', *Philosophical Review*, 1970, pp. 19ff, reprinted with appendix in R. M. Hare, *Practical Inferences*, Macmillan, 1971, pp. 89 ff.)

Physicalism. See POSITIVISM.

Physico-theological argument. See DESIGN.

Plato. 427–348/7 BC. Earliest European philosopher of whom substantial works survive. Pupil of SOCRATES, founder of Academy (probably c.385 BC), teacher of ARISTOTLE. Lived mostly in Athens, with occasional visits to Sicily where he tried unsuccessfully to put into practice the ideal state of his dialogue *Republic*. Contributed to all the main branches of philosophy, notably with his theory of 'FORMS' or 'IDEAS'. Wrote some thirty-four dialogues, which all survive. See also BEING (bibliography), DIALECTIC, EDUCATION (bibliography), EMPIRICISM, IDEALISM, LANGUAGE (PHILOSOPHY OF), MEANING, METAPHYSICS, NEOPLATONISTS, PLEASURE

(bibliography), POLITICAL (bibliography), PYTHAGORAS, SCEP-
TICISM, SOPHISTS, SUBSTANCE (bibliography), THIRD MAN
ARGUMENT, UNIVERSALS.

R. Kraut, 'Plato', *The Stanford Encyclopedia of Philosophy* (Fall 2008 Edition), Edward N. Zalta (ed.). Available at: http://plato.stanford.edu/
archives/fall2008/entries/plato/ (accessed 1 March 2009). (Excellent brief
introduction.)

Platonism. See UNIVERSALS, MATHEMATICS.

Pleasure. An agreeable quality of experiences or the experiences themselves. An ambiguity exists between 'pleasure' in general and
'pleasure' in the sense of a pleasant activity or experience, a source of
pleasure in the first sense. 'Pleasure' can also mean something like
'will' as in 'at the king's pleasure'.

Philosophers discuss primarily the first sense, and start by asking
what pleasure is. It has often, especially in connection with
HEDONISM, been regarded simply as 'agreeable feeling'. But competing accounts have been offered, especially recently. Pleasure has
been thought to be a process, or a kind of activity, or to be essentially
connected with attention or desire. Adverbial theories make pleasure
a modification of activity, so that 'experiencing pleasure' means
something like 'living pleasurably'. The relations between pleasure
and enjoyment, liking, pain, etc., are also topics for discussion. Special problems concern asceticism and masochism: Does anything
count as disliking or failing to like pleasure, or as liking or failing to
dislike pain?

Discussions of hedonism have raised the question of whether pleasure can be measured. Can pleasures, or amounts of pleasure, whether
of the same or different people, be compared and added together, or
arranged in order of magnitude, as some versions of UTILITAR-
IANISM demand? What would it be that was being measured? Are
there any bad pleasures? Can pleasure itself be bad, or only its source?
Qualitative hedonism, a form of ethical HEDONISM, says pleasures
differ in quality as well as quantity, and some are better than others.
How pleasure relates to happiness is also important for hedonism and
utilitarianism.

A particular set of problems concern pleasure and belief, and the
notion of being pleased that ... How is pleasure related to what one is
pleased at, by, etc., especially when the object is illusory? How are
the object and the cause of a pleasure related? And can pleasures

themselves ever be false, as against merely resting on false beliefs? Can one be mistaken about whether one is pleased, etc.? See also HAPPINESS, UTILITARIANISM.

J. Annas, 'Aristotle on pleasure and goodness', in A. O. Rorty (ed.), *Essays on Aristotle's Ethics*, California UP, 1980, particularly pp. 292–8. (Are pleasures commensurable? Are they subjective?)

Aristotle, *Nicomachean Ethics*, book 7, chapters 11–14, book 10, chapters 1–5. (Aristotle's two discussions of pleasure. The relations between them are disputed.)

J. Dybikowski, 'False pleasure and the Philebus', *Phronesis*, 1970. (False pleasure and Plato. Fairly difficult, with occasional Greek, but refers to other literature.)

R. B. Edwards, *Pleasure and Pain*, Cornell UP, 1979. (Defence of qualitative hedonism.)

J. C. B. Gosling, *Pleasure and Desire*, Oxford UP, 1969. (Discusses hedonism in light of modern treatments of pleasure.)

J. C. Hall, 'Quantity of pleasure', *Proceedings of the Aristotelian Society*, 1966–7. (Can pleasure be measured?)

D. A. Lloyd Thomas, 'Happiness', *Philosophical Quarterly*, 1968.

M. A. McCloskey, 'Pleasure', *Mind*, 1971. (Asymmetries between pleasure and pain.)

J. S. Mill, *Utilitarianism*, 1861, chapter 2. (Qualitative hedonism. See J. Plamenatz, *The English Utilitarians*, 1949, p. 137; this volume includes Mill.)

D. L. Perry, *The Concept of Pleasure*, Mouton, 1967. (General discussion of what pleasure is, and how it relates to neighbouring concepts and expressions.)

Plato, *Philebus*, particularly § 31–55. (Extended discussion, including on whether there are false pleasures.)

Plenitude (principle of). Principle that the universe, to be as perfect as possible, must be as full as possible: must contain the greatest possible diversity of kinds in the greatest possible profusion compatible with the laws of nature; cf. the idea that existence is a perfection (cf. ONTO-LOGICAL ARGUMENT). An alternative version is that nothing can remain a real but unactualized possibility throughout eternity.

Aristotle and Hobbes (see bibliography to MODALITIES).

J. Hintikka, *Time and Necessity*, Oxford UP, 1973, chapter 5. (Discusses principle in Aristotle, criticizing Lovejoy. Cf. review in *Journal of Hellenic Studies*, 1977, pp. 183–6. Cf. also under SUBSTANCE (bibliography), R. S. Woolhouse, p. 196 for brief discussion of some later views.)

A. O. Lovejoy, *The Great Chain of Being*, Harvard UP, 1936.

Plotinus. See NEOPLATONISTS.

Poisson's theorem. See NUMBERS (LAW OF LARGE).

Polar concepts. Concepts which allegedly only have application if their opposites have application, e.g. good and evil, if it is true that there could be nothing good in the universe unless there were something evil for it to contrast with, and vice versa.

> C. K. Grant, 'Polar concepts and metaphysical arguments', *Proceedings of the Aristotelian Society*, 1955–6. (Cf. also Heraclitus, fragments B23, 111 (in the standard Diels-Kranz numbering).)

Polish notation. Notation for propositional CALCULUS dispensing with special symbols. 'p', 'q', etc., stand for propositions. 'A' means 'or'. 'C' means 'materially IMPLIES'. 'E' means 'is materially equivalent to'. 'K' means 'and'. 'N' means 'not'. Constants precede the VARIABLES they govern. Punctuating is done entirely by ordering symbols (supplemented all too rarely by spacing). E.g. 'Apq' means 'p or q'; 'NApKqr' means 'neither p nor both q and r'. Convenient for typesetters but not for readers, beyond very short expressions.

Political philosophy. Political philosophy studies both substantive questions and concepts used in them, the former having returned to favour recently, as in ETHICS. The basic concern is with authority and sovereignty in groups of people not subject to further authority (sovereign states), and with associated organizational questions.

The notions of authority and obedience lead to two groups of questions. The first concerns the nature and purpose of the state, its ultimate justification or dispensability, and the relations between it and its citizens. Is the state a real entity with a life of its own? Is it founded on divine right, natural law, utility, or social contract – a contract whereby its citizens or their ancestors have somehow, perhaps by not emigrating, pledged themselves to behave in certain ways? Or might the contract be purely hypothetical (Rawls)? Does the state exist for its own sake? Or to promote the real or supposed interests of its citizens, or of some of them? Or to guarantee its citizens maximum freedom from mutual interference? Are there limits to the power it should have over its citizens, and can its citizens ever properly disobey, secede or engage in revolution?

The second group of questions, which is not independent of the first, concerns different types of constitution, and where sovereignty lies within them. Should only some citizens or inhabitants of the relevant area have the right to participate politically, and if so, which? By what methods may the sovereign body justifiably reach its decisions and, in particular, especially in modern times, what are the forms of direct and representative democracy, and how acceptable are they? How should the representatives be elected? How may a constitution be changed? What rights should belong to minorities and those excluded from participation? What are the basis and limits of property and privilege?

The two groups come together in questions about ideal states or utopias and ideals in general, like the various forms of liberty and equality, and the relations between them.

Further questions concern the use of force by the state and its citizens, internally and externally, the relations of sovereign states with each other, and transfers of sovereignty within and between sovereign states.

Political science studies actual past and present political institutions, and explains rather than justifies them. Political philosophy is often called political theory, especially when studied in departments of political science.

Aristotle, *Politics*. (Books 4–6 discuss different constitutions, books 7–8 ideal state, while book 2 criticizes Plato.)

S. I. Benn and R. S. Peters, *Social Principles and the Democratic State*, Allen and Unwin, 1959; American edn 1964, entitled *Principles of Political Thought*. (Full-scale general introduction.)

*R. Goodin and P. Pettit, *A Companion to Contemporary Political Philosophy*, Blackwell, 1993. (41 specially commissioned articles on whole range of contemporary issues.)

P. Laslett *et al.* (eds), *Philosophy, Politics and Society*, Blackwell, 5 vols, 1956, 1962, 1967, 1972, 1979. (Miscellaneous essays, reflecting development of subject since the war.)

R. Nozick, *Anarchy, State and Utopia*, Blackwell, 1974. (Argues for very slimmed-down version of state, based on just exchange of goods justly acquired. Influential on development of Thatcherism in UK. See also discussion in J. Wolff, *Robert Nozick: Property, Justice and the Minimal State*, Polity Press, 1991.)

Plato, *Crito* (obedience), *Republic* (ideal state), *Statesman* (or *Politicus*: different constitutions; cf. *Republic*, book 8), *Laws* (second-best state).

A. Quinton (ed.), *Political Philosophy*, Oxford UP, 1967. (Essays, with annotated bibliography.)

J. Rawls, *A Theory of Justice*, Oxford UP, 1972. (Influential version of contract theory.)

*J. Wolff, *An Introduction to Political Philosophy*, Oxford UP, 1996. (Good general introduction.)

Polyadic. See MONAD.

Polymorphous. Literally, having many forms. Concept introduced by Ryle and applied, in particular, to THINKING, though little referred to now. The general idea is that there is no particular action we must be engaged in to be thinking, and perhaps also that there is no overt action we could not engage in without thinking; but the detailed interpretation of polymorphousness is controversial.

D. L. Mouton, 'The concept of thinking', *Nous*, 1969. (Includes criticism of Ryle.)

J. O. Urmson, 'Polymorphous concepts', in O. P. Wood and G. Pitcher (eds), *Ryle*, Macmillan, 1970. (Cf. also ibid., pp. 77–8.)

Popper, Karl R. 1902–94. Austrian philosopher of science, and also political philosopher, born in Vienna. He was connected with the Vienna Circle (see POSITIVISM) in his youth but later migrated to New Zealand and then to England where he worked in London. He asserted that if a statement is to be scientific rather than metaphysical it must be falsifiable, but he did not, as the logical positivists did, dismiss metaphysical statements as meaningless. He then based his philosophy of science on the hypothetico-deductive method, claiming that enumerative INDUCTION is invalid, and indeed does not in fact occur, while verification and CONFIRMATION (as opposed to his own 'corroboration') are impossible. As his philosophy of science said we should aim to eliminate the false rather than establish the true, so, rather analogously, his political philosophy said we should aim to eliminate the bad rather than establish the good, and he opposed utopianism and any appeal to historical inevitability. *Logik der Forschung*, 1934–5, trans. with additions as *The Logic of Scientific Discovery*, 1959. *The Open Society and Its Enemies*, 1945. *The Poverty of Historicism*, 1957. *Conjectures and Refutations*, 1963. *Objective Knowledge*, 1972. See also BASIC STATEMENTS, CONCEPT, CONVENTIONALISM, EVIDENCE, FREEWILL, HISTORICISM, INSTRUMENTALISM, KUHN, PROBABILITY.

B. Magee, *Popper*, Fontana/Collins, 1973.

A. O'Hear, *Karl Popper*, Routledge, 1980.

310

Positivism. Doctrine associated with COMTE who adopted the term 'positive' to convey six features of things: being real, useful, certain, precise, organic, relative. He used it of his philosophy, which insisted on applying the scientific attitude not only to the sciences but also to human affairs. He saw the sciences as forming a natural sequence resting on mathematics and developing, both in order of logic and historically, through the physical and biological sciences to sociology (whose name he invented) and morals. Thought, he said, evolved from the theological attitude, explaining things by introducing gods, etc., through the metaphysical attitude involving a search for things-in-themselves and causes, to the scientific attitude stressing the observable. He emphasized synthesis, both of reason, feeling and action, which the two earlier attitudes had failed to balance, and of the various sciences, and even of the three attitudes, since the superseded ones still had their merits. This is why his list of features includes 'relative' and 'organic'. Positivism continued ever after to emphasize the unity of the sciences, and to confine science to the observable and manipulable. The evolutionary approach fitted well with nineteenth-century biological developments and with systems extending these to human affairs, like that of Herbert Spencer (1820–1903).

Comte, however, was more concerned to expound and apply scientific method than to examine it and ask what it presupposes. More critical, in the sense of stressing the limitations of what science can do, was MACH. For him, science aims at the most economical description of appearances, i.e. ultimately of our sense-experience, or sensations. Appearances are explained in the sense of being described in familiar terms, but no hidden entities or causes are postulated. Atoms, being unobservable, are treated as a mere *façon de parler* (cf. PHENOMENALISM). This goes beyond the earlier positivism by criticizing notions (e.g. those of physical object and atom) that seem proper to science itself, not merely to metaphysics. Mach's outlook, and the similar one of R. Avenarius (1843–96), are sometimes called empiriocriticism.

Logical positivism is primarily associated with the Vienna Circle of the 1920s, whose most famous members were M. Schlick, Carnap, O. Neurath and Waismann. Wittgenstein and Popper were on its fringes. C. Hempel and H. Reichenbach in Berlin, and later Ayer in England, were its allies. It also influenced philosophy in America, Holland and Scandinavia. Schlick preferred the name 'consistent empiricism', and 'logical empiricism' has a similar sense. The prefix 'logical' indicates partly that the topic for enquiry is meaning, partly that the doctrine is regarded as true as a matter of logic, and partly that logic is seen as the basic tool of philosophy. Under the influence of Mach, and also of Hume, the Circle concentrated on the general problem of MEANING, and developed the verification or verifiability principle. This said that something is meaningful if and only if it is either verifiable empirically, i.e. ultimately (not necessarily directly) by observation through the senses, or is a TAUTOLOGY of logic or mathematics, in which case it does not assert anything. The verification theory either identifies meaning with method of verification, or simply says that the verification principle is to be accepted.

Positivists have always tried to limit enquiry and belief to what can be firmly established. Following the empiricist tradition they have usually taken this to be primarily what we learn immediately from the senses. Metaphysics and theology they dismissed. Ethics and aesthetics they usually tried to assimilate as far as possible to sciences like psychology, later distinguishing different kinds of meaning (emotive, evaluative, prescriptive, etc.: see NATURALISM) to deal with what was left of them. But they found it difficult to deal with science, and most of everyday discourse (e.g. about material objects, other people, or the past), without letting metaphysics and other nonsense through. They sometimes required only verifiability in principle, not in practice. But then meaning can hardly be identified with the 'method' of verification, especially if in the end a statement is verifiable simply if we 'know what it would be like' for it to be true. And must verification be conclusive ('strong') or will mere provision of evidence ('weak' verification) suffice? Since few, if any, statements are conclusively verifiable, much energy was devoted to elaborating 'weak' forms of the principle and a theory of CONFIRMATION, especially by Ayer and Carnap.

'Verify' may mean either 'show to be true' or 'test for truth'. Carnap substituted 'test' for 'verify'. But Popper used the first sense, and argued that with universal affirmative statements like 'All swans are white', which he thought important for science, it is easier to falsify false ones than to verify true ones. He therefore emphasized falsifiability, not, however, as a criterion of meaningfulness but as demarcating scientific statements from metaphysical ones. He accepted both as meaningful.

Neurath and others thought that sentences could only properly be compared with sentences, not with the world. They therefore sympathized with the coherence theory of TRUTH. This sympathy was reinforced by the difficulty of showing general laws to be true.

Carnap emphasized the unity of science, and his physicalism claimed that all scientific statements could be translated into statements about physical objects, or space-time points (as against electrons, desires, social systems, etc.). He also insisted that meaningful statements must be verifiable publicly, not just by one person. 'Physicalism' is also used for the doctrine that all meaningful statements can be translated into the language of physics, and for the IDENTITY THEORY OF MIND; cf. MATERIALISM.

Among questions facing the verification principle is whether it is itself a tautology, empirical or meaningless. One answer treats it as a recommendation. Other problems concern necessary statements (see MODALITIES): if, as logical positivists think, they assert nothing, of what use are they?

Logical positivism itself has long been superseded (see PHILOSO-PHY AND ANALYSIS), but its spirit has to some extent been revived during the last third of the twentieth century in the form of antirealism (see REALISM).

Operationalism or operationism stems from P. Bridgman and treats concepts rather as one version of logical positivism treats statements: concepts must be defined in terms of the operations employed in applying them, e.g. length can be defined only in terms of techniques of measurement, so that length may be a different concept when applied to football pitches and stellar diameters (cf. PRAGMATISM).

Legal positivism names a complex variety of doctrines, only partly connected with positivism as above considered. The main connecting threads are emphasis on law as what is commanded or 'posited', and emphasis on law as it is (positive law) rather than as it should be (e.g. natural law). See also MEANING, REDUCTIONISM, CONFIRMATION, BASIC STATEMENTS, ANALYTIC.

*A. J. Ayer, *Language, Truth and Logic*, Gollancz, 1936, 2nd edn with important 'Introduction', 1946. (Classic statement in English of logical positivism.)

A. J. Ayer (ed.), *Logical Positivism*, Free Press, 1959. (General essays, including famous one by Hempel, and long bibliography.)

A. C. Benjamin, *Operationism*, Thomas, 1955. (General treatment.)

P. Bridgman, *The Logic of Modern Physics*, Macmillan, 1927. (Operationalism.)

R. Carnap, *The Unity of Science*, Kegan Paul, Trench, Trubner, 1932, trans. with Introduction by M. Black, 1934. (Classic statement of one form of physicalism.)

*A. Comte, *Introduction to Positive Philosophy*, Bobbs-Merrill, 1970, Hackett, 1988. (Translation of first two chapters of his *Cours de philosophie positive* of 1830, also translated with further selections from the *Cours* in *The Essential Comte*, Croom Helm/ Barnes and Noble, 1974.)

J. L. Evans, 'Meaning and verification', *Mind*, 1953. (Critical discussion of development and presuppositions of logical positivism, and different versions of verification principle.)

H. L. A. Hart, *The Concept of Law*, Oxford UP, 1961, particularly p. 253. (Legal positivism.)

C. Hempel, 'On the logical positivists' theory of truth', *Analysis*, vol. 2, 1935.

C. Hempel, 'A logical appraisal of operationism', *Scientific Monthly*, 1954, reprinted in his *Aspects of Scientific Explanation*, Free Press, 1965. (Sympathetic discussion. Popper (below), p. 440, briefly criticizes operationalism. Cf. also C. Taylor, *The Explanation of Behaviour*, RKP, 1964, chapter 4, and for some further references D. H. Mellor, *The Matter of Chance*, Cambridge UP, 1971, p. 76.)

D. Hume, *Enquiry concerning Human Understanding*, 1748. (Last paragraph is famous forerunner of verification principle.)

*L. Kolakowski, *Positivist Philosophy*, Penguin, 1966, trans. 1968. (Elementary introduction, mainly on earlier forms and related outlooks.)

*E. Mach, *Popular Scientific Lectures*, Open Court, 1898, chapter 9: 'The economic nature of physical inquiry'. (Popular exposition.)

D. Makinson, 'Nidditch's definition of verifiability', *Mind*, 1965. (Difficulties in formulating verifiability principle. Moderately technical. Nidditch himself, in *Mind*, 1961, is revising Ayer's formulation.)

K. R. Popper, *The Logic of Scientific Discovery*, Hutchinson, 1959 (German original, 1934). (Standard statement of Popper's falsificationist position.)

H. Putnam, 'Pragmatism', *Proceedings of the Aristotelian Society*, supplementary vol., 1995. (Assesses favourably a pragmatist version of verification.)

M. Schlick, 'Meaning and verification', *Philosophical Review*, 1936, reprinted in H. Feigl and W. Sellars (eds), *Readings in Philosophical Analysis*, Appleton-Century-Crofts, 1949. (Exposition and applications of verification theory, equating meaning with method of verification.)

Possibilism. See ACTUALISM.

Possible. See MODALITIES.

Possible worlds. A device going back to Leibniz but brought to prominence recently, especially by D. K. Lewis, for analysing necessity and possibility and related notions (see MODALITIES). Each of the infinitely many logically possible states of affairs is regarded as a 'world'. A proposition can then be called logically necessary if it is true in all possible worlds, and logically possible if it is true in at least one. Counterfactuals can be analysed in terms of possible worlds (see

CONDITIONALS), and so can propositions themselves: a proposition can be defined as a set of possible worlds, namely the set of those worlds in which it is true; see SENTENCE.

One problem arising concerns the status of possible worlds. Are they merely abstract possibilities, or have they some sort of reality of their own? The latter view is modal realism, and is represented in an extreme form (sometimes called concrete as opposed to abstract modal realism) by Lewis, for whom possible worlds are as real as the actual world (and are actual for themselves, though not for us), but they are spatiotemporally disconnected from the actual world and from each other, so that even in principle we cannot travel from one to another. (Sometimes 'modal realism' is confined to Lewis's view.) See also ACTUALISM.

But if possibilities have a reality of their own like this, how is it that we can come to know of them? And how can they concern or be about the things in our world? This latter problem is that of transworld identity. This is most acute for Lewis's version, and he has suggested that everything in the actual world has a counterpart in every possible world in which (speaking intuitively) 'it' exists at all. Counterpart theory then deals with the relations between these counterparts in the relevant different worlds.

A further problem concerns the use of possible worlds in analysing counterfactuals: this involves judgements of comparative similarity between them, so how are these to be made?

D. K. Lewis, *On the Plurality of Worlds*, Blackwell, 1986. (Develops his version of modal realism.)

M. J. Loux (ed.), *The Possible and the Actual*, Oxford UP, 1979. (Essays, mainly reprinted, on possible worlds and transworld identity.)

A. McMichael, 'A problem for actualism about possible worlds', *Philosophical Review*, 1983. (Includes expositions and discussions of various views about possible worlds.)

G. H. R. Parkinson, 'Philosophy of logic', in N. Jolley (ed.), *The Cambridge Companion to Leibniz*, Cambridge UP, 1995 (See pp. 212–16 for brief discussion of Leibniz on possible worlds: for more extended discussion, see B. Mates, *The Philosophy of Leibniz*, Oxford UP, 1986, chapter iv.)

A. Plantinga, *The Nature of Necessity*, Clarendon, 1974. (See chapter 5 for possible worlds.)

R. C. Stalnaker, 'Propositions', in A. F. MacKay and D. D. Merrill (eds), *Issues in the Philosophy of Language*, Yale UP, 1976, followed by critical 'Comments' by L. Powers, and developed in Stalnaker's *Inquiry*, MIT Press, 1984. (Propositions as sets of possible worlds. See also Stalnaker's

'Possible worlds', *Nous*, 1976, reprinted in Loux, and (with editorial introduction) in T. Honderich and M. F. Burnyeat (eds), *Philosophy As It Is*, Penguin, 1979, for his view of possible worlds themselves.)

Post hoc. 'After this'. Used of an explanation given after the event, with hindsight. The phrase *'post hoc ergo propter hoc'* (after this, therefore because of this) is used of a form of fallacious reasoning which claims that because one event happened after another, it must have been caused by that event; whereas, in fact, there might be no causal connection between the two events. 'After I received the lucky charm, I won the lottery'.

Potentiality. See ACTUALITY AND POTENTIALITY.

Pour soi. See BAD FAITH.

Practical ethics. See APPLIED ETHICS.

Pragmatics. See SEMANTICS.

Pragmatism. Originally developed as a theory of meaning by Peirce who was concerned with the meaning of concepts affecting the intellect, especially scientific concepts, rather than those confined to the senses (like red) or emotions. He thought the meaning of such concepts, and of statements in which they appeared, was exhausted by the effects they could have on our experience and actions. When the name became widely used for various related theories he used pragmaticism for his own particular version. This theory can be thought of as a looser form of operationalism (see POSITIVISM), and Peirce expressed an affinity for positivism.

Pragmatism is also often thought of as a theory of truth. Peirce made truth 'the opinion which is fated to be ultimately agreed to by all who investigate'. He seems to mean that truth is what would be believed if investigation continued indefinitely, whether or not it does continue; it is the limit where belief is finally stabilized. This side of pragmatism was developed by W. James, who differed from Peirce by including, and emphasizing, the effect of concepts on our senses and emotions. Truth, for James, is agreement with reality, but this means that it is what works or satisfies us, in the sense that it is whatever we ultimately find believable or consistent. But he allowed that our emotions might well, and properly, influence what we do ultimately so find.

Other philosophers who have been labelled pragmatists include DEWEY, F. C. S. Schiller (1864–1937), C. I. Lewis (1883–1964) and F. P. RAMSEY (1903–30). 'Pragmatism' is also sometimes used as a general label for views like CONVENTIONALISM and INSTRU-MENTALISM, though these (especially instrumentalism) perhaps replace truth, at least in certain contexts, rather than define it. See also SUPERASSERTABLE.

B. Aune, *Rationalism, Empiricism, and Pragmatism*, Random House, 1970. (Chapters 4 and 5 discuss modern versions of pragmatism. Cf. also D. H. Mellor (ed.), *Prospects for Pragmatism*, Cambridge UP, 1980, essays written in honour of F. P. Ramsey.)

A. J. Ayer, *The Origins of Pragmatism*, Macmillan, 1968. (Treats Peirce and James.)

J. Buchier (ed.), *The Philosophy of Peirce*, RKP, 1940. (Selections from Peirce. See especially chapters 2, 3 and 17, and for the quotation p. 38.)

W. B. Gallie, *Peirce and Pragmatism*, Penguin, 1952.

W. James, *Pragmatism*, 1907.

W. James, *The Meaning of Truth*, 1909. (Selected essays, issued to clarify Pragmatism.)

H. Putnam, 'Pragmatism', *Proceedings of the Aristotelian Society*, supplementary vol., 1995. (Assesses favourably a pragmatist version of verificationism.)

A. Rorty (ed.), *Pragmatic Philosophy*, 1966. (Anthology.)

Predicate. What is said of (predicated of) a SUBJECT. In 'Grass is green' 'grass' is the subject and 'is green' is the predicate. (But in traditional formal logic, and loosely elsewhere, the predicate would be 'green', not 'is green'.) A subject/predicate sentence is a sentence in which something is predicated of a subject as in 'Grass is green', as against, for example, conditional or existential sentences such as 'There are lions in Africa'. There is in certain contexts, notably in discussions of whether existence is a predicate, a certain ambiguity between whether a predicate is linguistic (a set of words) or non-linguistic (what the words in some sense stand for, or a property). Also 'logical predicate' has sometimes been used for what would be the grammatical predicate of a sentence when it is expressed in its proper logical form (cf. theory of DESCRIPTIONS). See also MONAD for some kinds of predicate, and for M-predicate and P-predicate see PERSON.

Predicative. See ATTRIBUTIVE.

Prediction paradox. Some boys are told they will be examined next week, but will not know on which day until it arrives. It cannot be Saturday, or they would know on Friday night. But if Friday is the last possible day, it cannot be Friday either, or they would know on Thursday night. By repeating the argument the other days too are eliminated. Apparently, therefore, the examination cannot occur, under the conditions stated. Many other examples are used.

M. Clark, *Paradoxes from A–Z*, London: Routledge, 2002.

D. J. O'Connor, 'Pragmatic paradoxes', *Mind*, 1948, followed by discussions (over many years) in subsequent issues of Mind.

W. V. O. Quine, *Ways of Paradox and other Essays*, Harvard UP, 1966, chapter 2. (Claims paradox is unreal.)

R. M. Sainsbury, *Paradoxes*, Cambridge UP, 1988. (See pp. 94–106 (pp. 91–103 in second edition, 1995) for elementary introduction.)

Preference. In UTILITARIANISM the assumption is made that we make choices between actions based on our preferences relating to the outcomes of the possible actions, in terms of the happiness, or pleasure, or benefit, or welfare, or utility of the outcome. But we may make choices based on our values or ideals, which surely cannot be seen as merely 'preferences'? Preference Logic studies the structures of preferences.

D. Parfit, *Reasons and Persons*, Oxford UP, 1984 (particularly Part 1, and Part 2, Chapter 8, section 60, 'Desires that depend on value judgments or ideals').

G. H. von Wright, *The Logic of Preference*, Edinburgh UP, 1963 (together with S. Halldén, *On the Logic of Better*, Lund: Library of Theoria, 1957, the pioneering works on Preference Logic).

Prescriptivism. See NATURALISM.

Presupposition. See IMPLICATION.

Price, Richard. 1723–91. Welsh philosopher and economist, born in Glamorgan, who worked as a clergyman in London. He supported the American and French revolutions. He was a leading representative of the 'intuitionist' school of moral philosophy, which opposed the 'MORAL SENSE' theory of HUTCHESON and others. He insisted that our knowledge of right and wrong was derived from reason, and that right and wrong themselves were 'real characters of actions', not 'only qualities of our minds'. *A Review of the Principle Questions in Morals*, 1758.

Primitive. In philosophy, 'basic', 'undefined', 'taken for granted'.

Principle. See LAWS.

Priority. Various different types of priority should be distinguished. If an event A (for example, the ringing of a bell in Manchester) is chronologically, or temporally prior to another, B, (workers in a factory in Birmingham going home) then it simply occurs before B. But if A is causally related to B, (where A is now the ringing of a bell in the Birmingham factory) it may be said to be explanatorily prior to B (the workers in that factory going home). If the concept of B cannot be understood with already having understood the concept of A, A is said to be logically, or conceptually, prior to B. Thus, what it is to be a sister cannot be understood without understanding what it is to have the same parents; parenthood might thus be said to be logically prior to sisterhood. Metaphysical priority is sometimes assimilated to logical priority, and sometimes to ontological priority. A is said to be ontologically prior to B if A in no way depends on B for its existence, but B does depend on A for its existence, or, to put it another way, A is ontologically prior to B if A's existence is a necessary condition of B's existence, but not vice versa. Epistemological priority depends upon the order in which we come to know things.

Prisoner's dilemma. Two prisoners are told that if both confess both will be gaoled for two years; if neither confesses both will be gaoled for one year; if one alone confesses he will be freed and the other gaoled for three years. What will rational prisoners do? Many variants are possible, but in general a prisoner's dilemma situation exists when it is better for each if each does A than if each does B, but better for each if he does B than if he does A. An example of the dilemma is disarmament negotiations, and it is important in general for game theory (see DECISION THEORY) and ethics. See also NEWCOMB'S PARADOX.

D. P. Gauthier, 'Morality and advantage', *Philosophical Review*, 1967, reprinted in J. Raz (ed.), *Practical Reasoning*, Oxford UP, 1978. (Uses dilemma to explore relations between these notions. Cf. also his (more technical) 'Reason and maximization', *Canadian Journal of Philosophy*, 1975.)

D. Parfit, 'Prudence, morality, and the prisoner's dilemma'. *Proceedings of the British Academy*, 1979, published separately, 1981. (Discusses some ramifications of dilemma. Cf. also his *Reasons and Persons*, Clarendon, 1984.)

*R. M. Sainsbury, *Paradoxes*, Cambridge UP, 1988. (See pp. 64–70 (pp. 66–72 in 2nd edn, 1995) for elementary introduction.)

Private language. Anyone can invent a private Esperanto for their diary, but can languages, or parts of languages, be private in a more radical sense? In particular, can a language contain elements which it is logically impossible for anyone but its speaker to learn or understand, e.g. can a language contain words which have meaning by standing for objects only accessible to the speaker? The importance of the question is that sensations, pains, etc., have been thought to be such objects, so that words which had meaning by standing for them would be private in the relevant sense. Three questions therefore are whether such a private language is possible, and, if not, how words like 'pain' do have meaning, and in what sense, if any, pains are private.

Wittgenstein seems to have argued that to use a language is to do something one may do correctly or incorrectly. One must therefore be able to check, at least in principle, that one is doing it correctly. But with a private language no such checking would be possible. It is disputed whether this argument is sound, and also whether the alternative account that Wittgenstein himself gave of how words like 'pain' have meaning commits him to some form of behaviourism. The issue is important in connection with various kinds of scepticism. See also ACCESS.

M. Budd, *Wittgenstein's Philosophy of Psychology*, Routledge 1989. (See particularly chapter 3.)

J. V. Canfield (ed.), *The Philosophy of Wittgenstein*, vol 9. *The Private Language Argument*, Garland. (Large collection of articles.)

*J. W. Cook, 'Human beings', in Winch, P. (ed.), *Studies in the Philosophy of Wittgenstein*, RKP, 1969.

O. R. Jones (ed.), *The Private Language Argument*, Macmillan, 1971. (Includes much of the important literature.)

A. Kenny, *Wittgenstein*, Penguin, 1973. (Chapter 10.)

S. Kripke, *Wittgenstein on Rules and Private Language: An Elementary Exposition*, Blackwell, 1982. (One famous though controversial interpretation of Wittgenstein.)

J. T. Saunders and D. F. Henze, *The Private-Language Problem*, Random House, 1967. (Presents opposing attitudes in dialogue form, finally offering solution.)

Privation. See NEGATION.

Probability. Probability theory or the calculus of chances or probabilities is the mathematical theory underlying probability arguments and most (though not all) theories of induction with a mathematical basis. (See CONFIRMATION, where the relation between confirmation and probability is also discussed.) This calculus contains elementary rules governing results to be expected from tossing dice or drawing marbles from a bag. It also covers BAYES'S THEOREM, and topics like the law of large numbers (see NUMBERS (LAW OF LARGE)). Results within this theory are purely mathematical, and are not predictions about what actual dice, etc. will do. Use of the theory simply draws out the logical implications of assumptions already made.

Various theories have been offered about the nature of probability. The classical theory defines an event's probability as the proportion of alternatives, among all those possible in a given situation, that include the event in question. There are 36 possible results of tossing two dice, of which 11 include at least one six, so the probability of getting at least one six in a throw of two dice is 11/36. But the alternatives must be equiprobable (equally probable) – or equispecific, if 'equiprobable' seems question-begging in an analysis of 'probable'. This is hard to ensure. Attempts to ensure it have often used the principle of INDIFFERENCE. Other difficulties concern the probability of theories, such as Darwinism, and cases where the alternatives are not obviously finite and definite in number, e.g. the probability that all swans including future ones are white; since we can breed swans the number of future swans could depend on our very probability calculations. BERTRAND'S BOX PARADOX becomes relevant here. Kneale's 'range' theory attempts to answer some of these difficulties. Range is used elsewhere too. For Carnap a proposition's range is the set of state-descriptions compatible with it (see CONFIRMATION).

The frequency theory defines probability in terms of the ratio of times something happens to times it might happen. If the proportion of smokers who die of cancer remains steady at 10 per cent then the probability of smokers dying of cancer is 10 per cent. Since most of the classes we are concerned with are open classes, the probability is defined as the limit, in the mathematical sense, to which the frequency tends in the long run. We often talk of the probability of single events, e.g. that Smith will die of cancer, and it is disputed how, if at all, the frequency theory can account for this. Also the notion of a limiting frequency raises a problem because in an infinite or open-ended series, such as tosses of a coin, any limiting frequency is compatible with any result in a finite run. If a penny falls heads a million times running the limiting frequency of heads could still be a half if it fell tails the next million, or indeed if it merely behaved normally the next million times. Therefore in applying the theory we seem to have to say things like 'Probably the limiting frequency is this' or 'Probably present trends of cancer among smokers will continue', where 'probably' is unexplained.

The propensity theory, substituted by Popper for the frequency theory, defines probability as a propensity of objects themselves, e.g. of a die to show a six. Popper claims propensities are no more 'mysterious' than gravitational fields, but one can still ask just what propensities are and how wide an area the theory covers. The word 'chance' can also be used for 'propensity', and for objective probability when this is distinguished from subjective degrees of belief (see below).

The logical relation theory makes probability a logical relation between evidence and a conclusion, rather like entailment (see IMPLICATION) only weaker (cf. CONFIRMATION). Probability is therefore always relative to evidence. Apart from the difficulty of finding such a relation, one defect of this theory as an analysis of 'probably' is that if we know a true proposition, p, which entails another, q, we can 'detach' q, i.e. assert it on its own, but if p only makes q probable, we can at best say 'Probably q', which leaves 'probably' unanalysed – and even that we cannot say if we know there is another true proposition which makes q improbable.

The subjectivist theory analyses probability in terms of degrees of belief. A crude version would simply identify the statement that something is probable with the statement that the speaker is more inclined to believe it than to disbelieve it. Degrees of belief may be measured in terms of the bets the believer would be willing to place, and more refined versions of the theory say one is only entitled to use 'probably' if one's bets are 'coherent', in the sense that one does not bet on contradictory propositions in such a way that one is bound to lose whatever happens, which can be expressed by saying that one does not let oneself have a 'Dutch book' made against one. This, however, still bases probability on the attitudes of the believer. Because 'coherence' is required, subjectivism is sometimes described as the view that probability is the degree of the rational person's belief. However, when this means that calling something probable is saying that it is rational to believe it, it is not subjectivist, since it no longer analyses probability in terms of beliefs actually held. It then has no special name.

Another version of the subjectivist theory is the speech act theory. To call something probable is not to describe one's belief but to express it. To say war is probable is to say, but only tentatively, that war will occur. Like other SPEECH ACT analyses (e.g. of 'good', 'true') this faces the objection at least prime facie (cf. GOOD), that it ignores cases like 'If war were probable we would emigrate', where it is not being even tentatively asserted that war will occur. It has never in fact been popular, and perhaps applies better to sentences like 'It may happen' than to 'It is probable that it will happen', or even 'It will probably happen'.

Between them these theories try to account for the ideas that probability is objective and not of our choosing, and yet is somehow relative to our knowledge, since things in the world are either so or not so, and not probably so (though quantum physics may provide an exception to this). Problems also arise over when to say something was probable, especially if eventually it never happened.

Many recent writers think that there is more than one kind of probability. They often distinguish between probability as a logical relation, where probability statements are true or false as a matter of logic (Carnap's probability$_1$), and probability as relative frequency, where probability statements are empirical statistical statements which form the material for the mathematical calculus of chances (Carnap's probability$_2$). Some, like the frequency theorist Reichenbach, hold the identity conception of probability, saying that these two kinds are really one. Surely, however, one should distinguish at least three kinds of statement: empirical statistical statements, like 'The probability of an Englishman being a Catholic is 10 per cent', where this just means that 10 per cent are so; purely mathematical statements, like 'The probability of a double six with two throws of a true die is 1/36', where this makes no prediction about any actual dice; and 'ordinary' probability statements, like 'The probability of Smith being a Catholic is high'; 'Smith is probably a Catholic'; 'The probability of a six with this die is low'; 'This die will probably not show six'; 'The probability of rain tomorrow is high'; 'The probability of Darwinism being true is high'. These 'ordinary' statements may of course themselves be of various kinds, and may rest on statistical or mathematical statements.

Probabilities are called absolute, a priori or prior if they are considered as relative either to nothing or to the general background of knowledge rather than to some real or assumed set of evidence statements; otherwise they are relative or conditional. When a certain probability is assumed, e.g. the probability of an a which is b being c, the probability of an *a* which is *c* being *b* is called the inverse probability (cf. BAYES'S THEOREM). This notion raises no problems itself, but has been put to controversial uses, as a result of which LIKELIHOOD has been introduced.

Probabilism is the view that scientists can and should seek to attach probabilities to their hypotheses, i.e. to confirm them. Popper's opposing view that this is impossible and that the scientist should seek the most improbable, i.e. the most easily falsifiable (though not yet falsified), hypothesis is sometimes called improbabilism. See also BAYES'S THEOREM, CONFIRMATION.

A. J. Ayer, *The Concept of a Person*, Macmillan, 1963. *Miscellaneous Essays*. (Chapter 7 discusses logical relation theory, and single events. Criticized by C. G. Hempel, *Aspects of Scientific Explanation*, Free Press, 1965, pp. 65–6).

R. Carnap, 'The two concepts of probability', *Philosophy and Phenomenological Research*, 1945, reprinted in H. Feigl and W. Sellars (eds), *Readings in Philosophical Analysis*, Appleton-Century-Crofts, 1949, and in H. Feigl and M. Brodbeck (eds) *Readings in the Philosophy of Science*, Appleton-Century-Crofts, 1953. (Cf. also his book *Logical Foundations of Probability*, 1950, and, for another version, J. O. Urmson, 'Two of the senses of "probable"', *Analysis*, vol. 8, 1947, reprinted in M. Macdonald (ed.), *Philosophy and Analysis*, Blackwell, 1954.)

B. de Finetti, 'Foresight: Its logical laws, its subjective sources', translated from 1937 French original in H. E. Kyburg and H. E. Smokier (eds), *Studies in Subjective Probability*, Wiley, 1964. (De Finetti is main representative of subjectivist theory.)

I. Hacking, *The Emergence of Probability*, Oxford UP, 1975. (Historical.)

J. M. Keynes, *A Treatise on Probability*, Macmillan, 1921. (Chapter 1 defends logical relation theory. See also chapter 4 for principle of indifference.)

*H. E. Kyburg, *Probability and Inductive Logic*, Macmillan, 1970. (Part I gives basis of calculus of chances and discusses various theories of probability. Includes exercises and bibliographies. Other elementary accounts of the calculus of chances include B. Mates, *Elementary Logic*, 2nd edn, Oxford UP, 1972, chapter 2, §5, H. C. Levinson, *The Science of Chance: From Probability to Statistics*, Faber and Faber, 1952, I. Copi, *Introduction to Logic*, Macmillan, 6th edn, 1982, chapter 14, R. Fogelin, *Understanding Arguments*, Harcourt, Brace, Jovanovich, 1978, 4th, revised, edn (with W. Sinnott-Armstrong), 1991, chapter 10.)

*R. von Mises, *Probability, Statistics and Truth*, William Hodge, 1939, revised (Allen and Unwin/Macmillan), 1957 (German original, 1928).

(Non-technical account of one version of frequency theory (first chapter), followed by discussion and applications.)

K. R. Popper, 'The propensity interpretation of probability', *British Journal for Philosophy of Science*, 1959. (Propensity theory. Cf. D. H. Mellor, *The Matter of Chance*, Cambridge UP, 1971, chapter 4, and A. O'Hear's review of Popper in *Mind*, 1985, pp. 463–9.)

H. Reichenbach, *Experience and Prediction*, Chicago UP, 1938, (§ 33 advocates identity conception, and discusses single events.)

R. Swinburne, *An introduction to Confirmation Theory*, Methuen, 1973. (First two chapters discuss kinds of probability.)

Problematic. See MODALITIES.

Process philosophy. An approach traceable back as far as Heraclitus (fifth century BC) whereby the basic reality is process rather than static substance.

D. Browning (ed.), *Philosophers of Process*, Random House, 1965. (Selections, with introductions, from nineteenth and twentieth century writers.)

Proof theory. See METAMATHEMATICS, LOGIC.

Proper. It is convenient to allow a whole to count as one of its parts, a class as one of its subclasses, etc. 'Proper' is used to exclude these special cases, e.g. a proper part is a part smaller than the whole, as a proper fraction is a fraction less than one.

Property. (i) Any characteristic. (ii) A characteristic relevant for the indiscernibility of identicals (see LEIBNIZ'S LAW). Tully is the same as Cicero, but 'Tully is hereby named by a five-letter name' is true, while 'Cicero is hereby named by a five-letter name' is false. So being hereby named by a five-letter name is not a single property in this sense. It may, however, be doubted whether it is a characteristic at all, when the 'hereby' is unspecified (in which case we need not posit characteristics not subject to Leibniz's law). (iii) A positive, as against negative, characteristic, e.g. being red, but not being not red (which is too indefinite in its application: does it apply to abstract things?). (iv) A non-relational characteristic, e.g. being red, but not being a brother. (v) The Aristotelian and medieval proprium: a characteristic following from, and unique to, the essence of a species, but not part of its definition. Able to laugh is a proprium of a human being, if only humans can have it but human being is not defined as a laughing animal. Other senses exist.

S. Shoemaker, *Identity, Cause, and Mind*, Cambridge UP, 1984, chapter 10. (Discusses sense near to (iv).)

Property dualism. See DOUBLE ASPECT THEORY.

Propositional acts, attitudes, verbs. See SENTENCES, CONTENT (on attitudes).

Propositions. See SENTENCES.

Proprium. See PROPERTY.

Protocol statements. See BASIC STATEMENTS.

Psycholinguistics. General term for the study of language from the point of view of psychology, though applied particularly to the movement which since the 1950s has involved intense study of generative grammar (roughly, what mental processes underlie the generating of sentences in natural languages, taking account of both syntax and semantics (see SEMIOTIC)).

*J. Caron, *An Introduction to Psycholinguistics* (trans. T. Pownall), Harvester Wheatsheaf and Toronto UP, 1992 (French original, 1989).
*D. D. Steinberg, *An Introduction to Psycholinguistics*, Longman, 1993. (Partly philosophical, including exposition and discussion of Chomsky, and partly empirical study of language-learning.)

Psychologism. See NATURALISM. In general terms psychologism is the appeal to psychological arguments to solve philosophical problems. Sometimes this is made through confusion and sometimes explicitly. Something may depend on whether the appeal to psychology is intended to answer or simply to replace a philosophical problem; was Hume a psychologizer in his treatments of causation and the external world? Psychologism has often, and especially in the first half of the twentieth century, been regarded as a mistake. For instance, Frege attacked the view that the concept of number, which mathematics is concerned with, can be analysed in terms of the mental processes by which we arrive at arithmetical judgements. Recently, however, as explained under NATURALISM, this attitude to psychologism has been modified.

'Psychologism' and also 'mentalism', can alternatively refer to the view, as against eliminative MATERIALISM and certain kinds of BEHAVIOURISM, that there are inner mental states.

Popper sometimes uses 'psychologism' for the view that 'Social laws must ultimately be reducible to psychological laws'.

N. Block, 'Psychologism and behaviourism', *Philosophical Review*, 1981. (Second sense of 'psychologism', defined as 'the doctrine that whether behaviour is intelligent depends on the internal information processing that produces it', p. 5.)

G. Frege, *The Foundations of Arithmetic* (trans. J. L. Austin from German original of 1884), Blackwell, 1950. (Often referred to by the German title *Grundlagen*. See pp. 33–9 for attack on psychologism about numbers.)

K. R. Popper, *The Open Society and its Enemies*, RKP, 1945, vol. 2, chapter 14. (See p. 90 for quotation. Elsewhere, Popper uses 'psychologism' more in the first sense above.)

Psychology (philosophical). See MIND.

Psychophysical parallelism. Doctrine, associated in one form with LEIBNIZ, that mental events and physical (in particular, bodily) events form separate chains, with causal relations holding or not holding within each chain, but not between the chains. The apparent connections between the chains can be attributed to God. Is it a mere coincidence that when a pin is stuck in my toe, I feel a pain? No, says Leibniz, because God has ordained a pre-established harmony between the two events. See also MALEBRANCH and OCCASIONALISM.

Putnam, Hilary. 1926–. Born in Chicago, he has worked mainly at Harvard. Like KRIPKE, he came to philosophy from mathematics; their causal theories of MEANING have much in common, with Putnam concentrating mainly on 'natural kind terms' (such as 'lemon' or 'water'). This has led him to an EXTERNALIST view of thinking and similar notions, with his slogan that '"meanings" just ain't in the head!', and to a realist approach to the philosophy of science. More recently he has widened his philosophical sympathies, adopting a still rigorous but less science-based approach, and he has become critical of so-called analytic philosophy and of the way it is tending. His publications include *Mind, Language and Reality*, 1975; *Mathematics, Matter and Method*, 1975; *Realism and Reason*, 1983; *Meaning and the Moral Sciences*, 1978; *Reason, Truth and History*, 1981 (chapter one of this is the locus classicus for the 'brain in a vat' image); *The Many Faces of Realism*, 1987; *Representation and Reality*, 1988; *Realism with a Human Face*, 1990; *Renewing Philosophy*, 1992; *Words and Life*, 1994.

M. de Gaynesford, *Hilary Putnam*, Acumen, 2006.

Psychosemantics. Term associated especially with Fodor for the study of meaning from the point of view of what is going on in the mind when we use language meaningfully or have propositional attitudes (believing, desiring, etc., which have a meaningful content). See also LANGUAGE OF THOUGHT.

> J. A. Fodor, *Psychosemantics: The Problem of Meaning in the Philosophy of Mind*, MIT Press, 1987, partly revised in his *The Elm and the Expert: Mentalese and its Semantics*, MIT Press, 1994. (Cf. his *A Theory of Content and Other Essays*, MIT Press, 1990 (mainly reprints), and also, B. Loewer and G. Rey (eds), *Meaning in Mind: Fodor and his Critics*, Blackwell, 1991, for critical discussions of his position, with replies by him and bibliography of works by and about him.)

Pythagoras. Late sixth century BC. Born in Samos, he migrated to south Italy and founded Pythagorean 'brotherhood' whose doctrines, even centuries later, were often attributed to him. Traditionally he was the first to see the connection between musical harmonies and ratios of string lengths, and he and his followers developed arithmetic and geometry (including 'Pythagoras' theorem'), and in various ways tried to explain reality itself in terms of numbers. They may have originated the ideas (though without providing compelling evidence) that the earth is spherical and not the centre of the universe. They also developed religious ideas about the soul and reincarnation, together with rules for a 'way of life'. Both their mathematical and their religious ideas are said to have influenced Plato. Recently, however, much scepticism has been expressed about their alleged mathematical and scientific contributions. See also METAPHYSICS, NIETZSCHE.

> W. Burkert, trans. E. L. Minar Jr., *Lore and Science in Ancient Pythogoreanism*, Harvard UP, 1972. (A monumental work of scholarship, debunking many of the myths about Pythagoras and his followers.)
> M. F. Burnyeat, 'Other lives', *London Review of Books*, 22 February 2007. (A useful discussion of recent Pythagorean scholarship).
> J. A. Philip, *Pythagoras and Early Pythagoreanism*, Toronto UP, 1966. (Balanced discussion taking account of scholarship later than Schrodinger.)
> E. Schrodinger, *Nature and the Greeks*, Cambridge UP, 1954. (Contains sympathetic appreciation by famous modern physicist, though predating recent scholarship.)

Q

Qua. 'As', or 'in the capacity of'.

Qualia. Singular: 'quale'. A quale, such as red, is a quality considered as it appears to consciousness rather than as science might define it. Qualia are like SENSE DATA, but universal, not particular. Etymologically 'quale' is to 'quality' as 'quantum' is to 'quantity'. Two associated problems concern 'absent qualia' (more accurately, the absence of qualia: might someone have no experiences at all but live like a human while really being a ZOMBIE?), and 'transposed qualia' (or 'the INVERTED SPECTRUM': whenever we both see something we both call red, might you be having an experience I would call green if I had it?). Accounting for these possibilities raises problems, especially for FUNCTIONALISM (see Shoemaker reference in bibliography there). Occasionally 'quale' is used for something like 'TROPE'.

J. Bennett, 'Substance, reality, and primary qualities', *American Philosophical Quarterly*, 1965, reprinted in C. B. Martin and D. M. Armstrong (eds), *Locke and Berkeley*, Macmillan, 1968, and in Bennett's *Locke, Berkeley, Hume: Central Themes*, Clarendon, 1971.

E. Conee, 'The possibility of absent qualia', *Philosophical Review*, 1985. (Could there be ZOMBIES?)

H. P. Grice (see bibliography for SENSES).

R. Kirk, *Raw Feeling*, Clarendon, 1994. (Includes extended treatment of transposed qualia problem, and claims there is no unbridgeable explanatory gap between qualia and brain states. Cf. A. Clark, *Sensory Qualities*, Clarendon, 1993, claiming that we can 'explain qualitative facts in terms that do not presuppose other qualitative facts' (p. vii).)

J. Levine, 'Materialism and qualia: The explanatory gap', *Pacific Philosophical Quarterly*, 64.4, 1983. (Claims that there is an unsolved epistemological problem in explaining why certain qualia are associated with certain neural states.)

T. Nagel, 'What is it like to be a bat?', *The Philosophical Review*, 1974, and reprinted many times.

S. Shoemaker, 'Qualia and consciousness', *Mind*, 1991. (Qualia are indispensable.)

M. Tye, 'Visual qualia and visual content', in T. Crane (ed.), *The Contents of Experience*, Cambridge UP, 1992. (Claims there are no visual qualia.)

Qualities (primary and secondary). A distinction as old as the Greeks, but first elaborated by Locke, between qualities like shape or velocity, which seem to belong to things independently of observers (primary), and those like colour or taste, which seem to depend on the existence of observers (secondary); the terms 'primary' and 'secondary' stem from the seventeenth century chemist R. Boyle. The distinction proves hard to elaborate in detail though is widely agreed to exist in some form. For tertiary qualities see SUPERVENIENCE.

J. Bennett (see bibliography to QUALIA).

J. Locke, *An Essay concerning Human Understanding*, 1690, book 2, chapter 8.

C. McGinn, *The Subjective View*, Oxford UP, 1983. (Compares secondary qualities with indexicals (see TOKEN-RELEXIVES).)

A. D. Smith, 'Of primary and secondary qualities', *Philosophical Review*, 1990. (General historical survey, defending secondary qualities but claiming 'primary quality' should be either dropped or kept for whatever qualities are fundamental for current science.)

M. D. Wilson, 'History of philosophy and philosophy today; and the case of sensible qualities', *Philosophical Review*, 1992. (See particularly pp. 209–33 for assessment of recent interpretations of Locke and others on primary and secondary qualities, and pp. 234–43 for effects on that topic of recent scientific and philosophical developments.)

Quality-word. See METAPHYSICS.

Quantification. Literally, specification as to quantity. Two kinds of proposition are very important for formal logic, those saying something about everything, or everything of a given kind, and those saying something about at least one thing, or at least one thing of a given kind. So there are two main quantifiers. (In what follows, x is an individual VARIABLE.) The universal quantifier 'binding' (see VARIABLE) x is read 'For all (any, every) x', and is symbolized '(x)'

or '$(\forall x)$', sometimes (Πx)'. The particular (or existential) quantifier is read 'For some (i.e. at least one) x' or 'There exists at least one x such that', and is symbolized '$(\exists x)$', sometimes '(Σx)'. (Except with '(x)' the brackets are sometimes dropped.) Thus, using 'Rx' for 'x is red', typical sentences might be '$(x)\ (Rx)$' meaning 'For all x, x is red', i.e. 'Everything is red', and '$(\exists x)\ (Rx)$' meaning 'For some x, x is red', i.e. 'There is at least one red thing'. The x in the first bracket in each case may or may not be counted as part of the quantifier. The bracket immediately following a quantifier ('(Rx)' in the above examples) defines its scope, i.e. how much of the ensuing discourse it governs, or how much of what follows is being said of the variable in it. (Precise conventions about brackets, etc. again vary.) Either of these quantifiers can be defined in terms of the other plus negation.

Other quantifiers exist, such as 'For most x', 'For exactly one x' (the singular quantifier), 'For exactly $2x$,' etc. These can be symbolized by subscripts: '$(\exists_2 x)$' would mean 'For exactly two x'.

The values of a VARIABLE bound by a quantifier are quantified over. In the above examples objects in general are quantified over, but sometimes the range of objects quantified over (the universe of discourse) is limited: see MANY-SORTED LOGIC. When predicates are quantified over, f or F usually replaces x; '$(\exists f)$' means 'There is at least one f such that'.

Quantification is objectual (or referential) if it is taken to imply the existence, as 'real objects', of the values of the variable (cf. the views of Quine). Otherwise it is substitutional. Consider 'John is tall.' Can we infer '$(\exists f)$ (John is f)'? To those who interpret quantification substitutionally this is harmless, and merely says that for some replacement for f, the sentence 'John is f' is true. But those who interpret it objectually may reject the inference because it seems to imply a realist view of universals like tallness, which they reject on other grounds.

J. A. Faris, *Quantification Theory*, RKP 1964. (Semi-elementary. See also any modern introduction to logic, e.g. I. Copi, *Introduction to Logic*, Macmillan 6th edn, 1982.)

R. B. Marcus, 'Interpreting quantification', *Inquiry*, 1962. (Objectual and substitutional quantification. See also W. V. O. Quine, *Philosophy of Logic*, Prentice-Hall, 1970, pp. 91–4, and for his views on logic and metaphysics, his 'On what there is' (see bibliography to BEING).)

Quantifier shift fallacy. The fallacy of arguing from 'Every nice girl loves a sailor' to 'Some (one) sailor is loved by every nice girl', i.e. of confusing 'For all x there is a y such that ... ' with 'There is a y such that for all *x* ... ' (see QUANTIFICATION). The latter implies, but is not implied by, the former.

Quantifier words. A group of words including 'all', 'any', 'each', 'every', 'some', 'no' and 'a', all concerned in various ways with the notion of quantity (cf. QUANTIFICATION).

Traditional formal logic dealt mainly with four kinds of proposition, universal affirmative (called A propositions: 'All cats are black'), universal negative (E propositions: 'No cats are black'), particular affirmative (I propositions: 'Some cats are black') and particular negative (O propositions: 'Some cats are not black'). These were pictured as the corners of the square of opposition, whose sides and diagonals represented logical relations between the propositions (provided all four had the same subject and the same predicate, 'cats' and 'black' in the above examples). Singular propositions ('This cat (or Tiddles) is black') were traditionally treated as universal, though complications arise. The affirmative/negative distinction is called one of quality, the universal/particular distinction one of quantity (cf. QUANTIFICATION).

Both in the square of opposition and in the SYLLOGISM it was assumed that 'All cats are black' entails (see IMPLICATION) 'Some cats are black'. 'Some' can mean 'Some and perhaps all' on the inclusive interpretation, or 'Some but not all' on the exclusive interpretation. Nearly all logicians have found the inclusive interpretation more convenient because it is simpler. It is also assumed that 'some' means 'at least one', i.e. 'Some cats are black' is still true if only one is. In 'Some tea is undrinkable' it means 'not none'. In the nineteenth century, however, a problem arose, known as that of existential import, about which, if any, of the above four propositions entail that there exist any cats (or any black things, though this was less emphasized). It appeared that no otherwise acceptable answer could preserve intact the square of opposition and the traditional list of valid syllogisms, though for purposes of formal logic it was, and still is, found convenient to interpret 'All cats are black' as existentially negative, i.e. as saying that nothing is a cat and not black. This is true if there are no cats, and so does not imply that there are any. But 'Some cats are black' was interpreted as existentially affirmative, i.e. as saying that there exists at least one thing which is both a cat and black. Clearly 'All cats are black' no longer then entails 'Some cats are black'.

To call 'All unicorns are black' true simply because there are no unicorns seems odd. One solution (Strawson) is to say that 'All unicorns are black' does not entail, but does presuppose, that there are unicorns (for this and related distinctions see IMPLICATION). If there are none it will then fail to be true, but in a way that need not upset the square of opposition (since it will not be false either, and the square only applies to what is true or false).

However, let us compare the following sentences: 'All coins in my pocket are silver.' 'All (of) the coins ... ' 'Some coins ... ' 'Some of the coins ... ' 'No coins ... ' 'None of the coins ... ' The cases containing 'the' imply (i.e. entail or presuppose) that coins exist in my pocket. ('The' may be implicit, as in 'All John's children', i.e. 'All the children of John'.) But these cases say nothing about coins that might be, but are not, in my pocket. The other cases, however, are rather ambiguous. 'All coins ... ' is perhaps most naturally taken to mean 'Were you to find any coins in my pocket (which you might or might not) they would be silver (I throw coppers away on principle)'. (Cf. LAWS for some issues relevant here.) 'Some coins ... ' could either mean 'Some of the ... ' or could be used in the same way as in the 'foxes' example below, according as 'some' is stressed or not. But 'some' does not mean 'some of the' in 'There are some unicorns' or 'Some water is needed' – nor in 'Some foxes entered my garden last night', where it is what is said about them that implies their existence; contrast: 'Some foxes would be useful to clear this field of rabbits.'

All this raises the question of whether some or all of the quantifier words, in at least some of their uses, form part of referring expressions. Does 'No cats are black' refer to all cats and say of them that they are not black? Does 'Some cats are black' refer to all cats and say that they are not all not black, or does it perhaps refer only to those that are black? All these views have difficulties, and some writers say quantifier words never have a referring role (cf. DISTRIBUTION, REFERRING).

It seems that one role of 'any' is to make clear that what is being said is more like a law than a factual statement, 'Any body unacted on by forces moves in a straight line' carries less suggestion that there are such bodies than 'All bodies ... ' 'Any', however, can imply existence when combined with 'the', as in 'Any of the ones in that box would have done', and has ambiguities of its own: Compare 'Is any (at least one) member ready to vote?' and 'Is any (old) member entitled to vote?' Only the latter can be answered with 'Yes, any member'.

Another main role of 'any' is to emphasize randomness or choice: 'Any you choose, no matter which.' This may explain why 'any' is allied to 'some' as well as to 'all', for choice may be relevant in either case. But it only partly explains the substitution of 'any' for 'some' in many negative, interrogative and conditional contexts: 'Have you any matches (I don't mind which, or of what kind)?' 'If I had any matches', 'I haven't any matches (no matter what kind you choose)', 'I have some matches (but I have no choice about which, or what kind they are)' – but why 'I want some matches' and not (by itself) 'I want any matches'? ('I want any matches' (stressed) means 'I want as many as you've got, no matter what they're like'.) The negation, etc., may be only implicit: 'It was too smooth to have any effect', 'I was ashamed to take any' (but: 'glad to take some'), 'The question whether (condition that) there is any'.

'Any' tends, more than 'all', to focus attention on the individuals rather than the mass. Suppose we know that nearly all swans are white but a few are black. Then 'All swans are probably white', on its most natural interpretation, will be false, while 'Any swan (you choose) will probably be white' may be true. Note too that, though 'Any swan is white' implies 'All swans are white', 'Any of the candidates may win' does not imply 'All of the candidates may win; but 'any of the swans is white (choose which you like)' does imply they all are.

'Each', too, emphasizes that the things in question are taken one by one, or distributively, while 'all' can be interpreted distributively ('All the soldiers were conscripts') or collectively ('I doubt if all the soldiers could defeat that enemy (much less each of them)'). 'They each gave a pound and presented him with a clock' is normally elliptical. The role of 'any', as against 'each', in selecting is seen by comparing 'I will take any of you on' with 'I will take each of you on'.

'Every' (from 'ever each', and apparently peculiar to English) is like 'each' in many respects. They both imply existence, and do not, like 'any', cover hypothetical cases. But whereas 'each' emphasizes taking the items separately, 'every' sometimes does not, but rather resembles 'all'. 'I told everybody to come', but not 'I told each person to come', is true if I told a crowd in which everybody was present. Similarly 'I will take every one of you on', like 'I will take all of you on', is ambiguous about whether I mean together or separately.

'A' is rather like 'any', though it only goes with the singular, and only with words that can be in the plural. Like 'any', though with these limitations, it can approximate to 'all' ('A whale breathes air') or to 'some' ('A man met me'). When approximating to 'all' it often signifies typicality rather than universality ('A cat usually likes fish'; in 'Any cat usually likes fish' the 'usually' limits the number of occasions, not the number of cats (unless there are commas round 'usually'), while in the former case it may limit either). 'A' also may or may not imply existence. 'I am looking for a dog' may or may not mean I have a definite dog in mind.

Other quantifier words include 'many', 'most', 'few', 'a few', 'several', 'one' (and numbers generally), and even 'the' in some uses ('The whale is a mammal'). 'The' perhaps gets its generalizing use from referring to species ('The species whale is a species of mammal'). Finally, this entry, after its first four paragraphs, illustrates an approach to philosophical questions typical of the movement known as linguistic PHILOSOPHY.

T. Czezowski, 'On certain peculiarities of singular propositions', *Mind*, 1955. (The place of singular propositions in traditional logic. Cf. J. L. Mackie, '"This" as a singular quantifier', *Mind*, 1958, L. Gumanski, 'Singular propositions and "this" as a quantifier', *Mind*, 1960.)

P. T. Geach, *Reference and Generality*, Cornell UP, 1962. (Contains discussions of quantifier words in connections with reference, and also with conjunction and disjunction, and with scope. Draws on medieval discussions.)

*J. N. Keynes, *Formal Logic*, 1884, 4th (revised) edn, 1906. (Standard account of traditional formal logic.)

E. S. Klima, 'Negation in English' in J. A. Fodor and I J. Katz (eds), *The Structure of Language*, Prentice-Hall, 1964. (Elaborate and technical, but see p. 294 for 'too' and p. 314 for 'ashamed' and 'glad'.)

W. V. O. Quine, *Word and Object*, Wiley, 1960, § 29. (Quantifier words and scope.)

P. F. Strawson, *Introduction to Logical Theory*, Methuen, 1952. (Chapter 6 discusses existential import.)

*Z. Vendler, 'Each and every, any and all', *Mind*, 1962. (Cf. also his article 'Any and all' in P. Edwards (ed.), *The Encyclopedia of Philosophy*, Crowell, Collier and Macmillan, Free Press, 1967, where he connects the topic with the philosophy of science.)

Quiddity. The essence of an object, from Latin 'quidditas' – 'whatness'. Used by SCHOLASTIC philosophers.

Quine, Willard V. O. 1908–2000. American mathematical logician, born in Akron, Ohio, and worked in Cambridge, Massachusetts. He has elaborated a system of logic, following RUSSELL, where singular terms can be eliminated, and has cast doubt upon the ANALYTIC/synthetic distinction and similar distinctions, and on the extent to which determinate TRANSLATION is possible between, or even within, languages. He denies the possibility of a formalized INTENSIONAL logic. His slogan 'To be is to be the value of a variable' offers a criterion for distinguishing between realists and nominalists (cf. BEING, METAPHYSICS). *Methods of Logic*, 1950 (part 4 eliminates singular terms). *From a Logical Point of View*, 1953 (contains 'On what there is', 1948 (the slogan), 'Two dogmas of empiricism', 1951 (analytic/synthetic), and articles relevant to meaning and intensional logic). *Word and Object*, 1960. *Ontological Relativity and other Essays*, 1969. *Philosophy of Logic*, 1970. *The Roots of Reference*, 1973. See also AMBIGUITY (bibliography), CONDITIONALS, INSCRIPTION (bibliography), INTUITIONISM (bibliography), LEIBNIZ'S LAW, MEANING, MODALITIES, QUANTIFICATION, QUANTIFIER (bibliography), REFERRING (bibliography), SATISFY (bibliography), SENTENCES, TOKEN-REFLEXIVES.

R

Radical interpretation and translation. See TRANSLATION.

Ramsey, Frank. 1903–30. British mathematician, philosopher, logician and economist, who died young, having made significant contributions in each of those disciplines. At the age of 19, translated WITTGENSTEIN's *Tractatus Logico-Philosophicus*, and when that work was submitted for the degree of PhD at Cambridge in 1929, Ramsey was Wittgenstein's supervisor. In philosophy, Ramsey made important contributions to epistemology, theories of TRUTH, formal logic, metaphysics, philosophy of science, semantics, and to probability and decision theory. See also BELIEF, DEFLATIONISM, PRAGMATISM, RAMSEY SENTENCE.

D. H. Mellor (ed.), *Prospects for Pragmatism: Essays in Memory of F. P. Ramsey*, Cambridge UP, 1980.

F. P. Ramsey, D. H. Mellor (ed.), *Philosophical Papers*, Cambridge UP, 1990. (Contains all of Ramsey's writings on philosophy and the foundations of mathematics.)

Ramsey sentence. A device for showing what a theory is committed to. Suppose we take all the sentences in a scientific theory that use a particular term ('electron' say), and then replace that term by a variable, x. Then, instead of a series of sentences ascribing properties to electrons, we can say that there is some thing, x, which has those properties. This Ramsey sentence avoids the implication that we already know what an electron is.

D. K. Lewis, 'How to define theoretical terms', *Journal of Philosophy*, 1970 (using ideas from F. P. Ramsey's 'Theories', reprinted in D. H. Mellor (ed.), *Philosophical Papers*, Cambridge UP, 1990.

Range. See PROBABILITY, VARIABLE.

Rationalism. Any view appealing to reason as a source of knowledge or justification. Reason can be contrasted with revelation, in religion, or with emotion and feeling as in ethics, but in philosophy it is usually contrasted with the senses (including introspection, but not intuitions). 'Rationalist' is to 'A PRIORI' somewhat as 'EMPIRI-CIST' is to 'empirical', though the empiricist is more likely to apply his view to all knowledge. Rationalism is an outlook which somehow emphasizes the a priori and also the INNATE. 'Rationalist' has a variety of interpretations corresponding to those of 'empiricist'. A philosopher can be both rationalist and empiricist, in different though important respects (e.g. Kant); but such philosophers are often thought to be best classified as neither.

'Continental rationalists' is a traditional label for Descartes, Spinoza and Leibniz, with various lesser figures of that period who are regarded as sharing their general outlook.

*J. Cottingham, *The Rationalists*, Oxford UP, 1988.

D. W. Hamlyn, *The Theory of Knowledge*, Macmillan, 1970. (Chapter 2 briefly discusses basis of rationalism as it appears in Descartes, Leibniz and Bradley (and then discusses empiricism).)

W. von Leyden, *Seventeenth-Century Metaphysics*, Duckworth, 1968. (Chapter 3 has general introduction to rationalism and empiricism.)

A. O. Lovejoy, *The Great Chain of Being*, Harvard UP, 1936; Harper and Row, 1960. (Chapter 5 brings out some features and conflicts of some developed rationalist philosophies (Leibniz and Spinoza). See also A PRIORI, EMPIRICIST.)

*J. Lyons, *Chomsky*, Fontana, 1970, expanded, 1977. (Elementary introduction to influential thinker who has revived some rationalist ideas in the sphere of language-learning.)

G. Ryle (see bibliography to EPISTEMOLOGY (second Ryle item)).

Rationality. Aristotle famously claimed that humans are rational animals, and it has often been claimed that this is what distinguishes human beings from other animals. What, then, is it to be rational? Is it to have reasons for one's actions? Is it to evaluate evidence according to rules? We must distinguish behaviour which is merely rule governed from behaviour which is rule guided. See REASON for more on this. There is also the question of how we judge whether another culture's practices are rational or not. Are standards of rationality culturally relative?

J. F. Bennett, *Rationality: An Essay towards an Analysis*, Routledge, 1965. (A short and very clear exposition of what rational behaviour is.)

D. Davidson, *Truth and Interpretation*, Oxford UP, 1984. (On the impossibility of incommensurable cultures.)

M. Hollis and S. Lukes, *Rationality and Relativism*, MIT Press, 1982. (Good collection of papers.)

Rawls, John. 1921–2002. American philosopher who worked mainly at Harvard. Rawls most influential work, *A Theory of Justice*, 1971, (revised edition 1999) argues for 'justice as fairness'. The main principles are the liberty principle, which, as for MILL, involves the greatest possible liberty for each citizen compatible with a like liberty for all others; fair equality of opportunity for all; and the idea that any inequalities maximally benefit the least advantaged. Rawls argues for these principles by appealing to a hypothetical social contract between all citizens known as the ORIGINAL POSITION: what principles would people choose for ordering society if they were ignorant of what their own position in that society was to be, if they had to choose from behind a 'veil of ignorance? See JUSTICE, POLITICAL PHILOSOPHY.

S. Freeman, *Rawls*, Routledge, 2007. (Good introduction to *Theory of Justice* and other works.)

Realism. Like 'real', 'realism' gets its senses largely from what it is contrasted with. Any view can be called realist which emphasizes the existence, reality or role, of some kind of thing or object (e.g. material objects, propositions, UNIVERSALS), in contrast to a view which dispenses with the things in question in favour of words (nominalism), ideas (idealism, conceptualism), or LOGICAL CONSTRUCTIONS (phenomenalism). Cf. PERCEPTION, IDENTITY, DEFINITION. For naive realism see PERCEPTION.

A question much debated recently is whether it makes sense to talk of truths that are real but can never be verified, and so are inaccessible to our knowledge. Realists, of the relevant kind, see no objection to this, and so allow that the meanings of individual sentences can be given simply in terms of TRUTH CONDITIONS (see MEANING). Antirealists refuse to accept unverifiable sentences, asking how we could acquire an understanding of them, or manifest it by asserting them on suitable occasions. They therefore insist on replacing truth conditions by assertibility conditions. Antirealism differs from traditional verificationism (see POSITIVISM) in not insisting on sense experience as the only means by which verification or assertibility can be achieved; it is not committed to saying, with the logical positivists, that a priori statements don't really say anything. Dummett in particular emphasizes the greater role allowed to inference in anti-realism, and follows Quine in blurring the ANALYTIC/synthetic distinction.

Putnam distinguishes internal from external or metaphysical realism. The latter is ordinary realism and postulates, in any relevant sphere, a fact of the matter independent of all theories; the former is weaker and only allows such postulations within a given theory.

'Irrealism' is sometimes used for the view that, 'of a given region of discourse ... no real properties answer to the central predicates'.

Moral realism is the theory that there are objective facts determining what counts as morally right or wrong, good or bad, and that these are facts which are quite independent of whatever beliefs we might hold about them, and about which we can be mistaken. Moral antirealism denies that there are such facts.

In aesthetics realism emphasizes the nature of things as they are in themselves, not as we see them. A realist art-form aims to portray things as they are, not as mediated by some attitude, etc. of the artist; cf. NATURALISM.

For modal realism see POSSIBLE WORLDS.

P. A. Boghossian, 'The status of content', *Philosophical Review*, 1990. (Irrealism, which he argues against. For quotation see p. 157.)

D. Davidson (see para. beginning with him in bibliography to MEANING for the realism/antirealism debate. Cf. also M. A. F. Dummett, *Truth and Other Enigmas*, 1978, particularly its Preface, and M. Platts (ed.), *Reference, Truth and Reality*, 1980, particularly item by C. McGinn. For Dummett on antirealism and logical positivism see G. Evans and J. McDowell (eds), *Truth and Meaning*, 1976, p. 111. The intelligibility of realism is defended against Dummett by A. H. Goldman, 'Fanciful arguments for realism', *Mind*, 1984).

Midwest Studies in Philosophy, vol. 12, 1988. (Single-topic journal issue entitled *Realism and Anti-Realism*. Also covers that topic in ethics.)

H. Putnam, *Reason, Truth and History*, Cambridge UP, 1981, chapter 3. (Internal and external realism. See also his *Meaning and the Moral Sciences*, Routledge, 1978, part 4.)

C. Wright, *Realism, Meaning and Truth*, 2nd edn, Blackwell, 1993. (Chapters 9 and 10 discuss antirealism and verificationism, favouring them in limited area.)

Reason. A general faculty, common to all or nearly all humans and sometimes regarded, either seriously or by poetic licence, as a sort of impersonal external power ('the dictates (truths) of reason'). This faculty has seemed to be of two sorts, a faculty of intuition by which one 'sees' truths or abstract things ('essences' or universals, etc.), and a faculty of reasoning, i.e. passing from premises to a conclusion (discursive reason). The verb 'reason' is confined to this latter sense, which is now anyway the commonest for the noun too, though the two senses are related (to pass from premises to conclusion is to intuit a connection between them).

Kant contrasts reason, which is concerned with mediate INFERENCES, and understanding and power of judgement, which are concerned with acquiring concepts and passing judgements, respectively.

Practical reason has been distinguished from theoretical or speculative reason since Aristotle, and raises problems: Is reason in the practical sphere 'the slave of the passions' (Hume), i.e. is it limited to showing us means to ends which the passions dictate?

How far can reason be distinguished from feeling, emotion, etc.? (This problem parallels that of relating theoretical reason to the senses: cf. PERCEPTION.) Can reason mediate between morals and self-interest ('A sacrifice beyond all reason')? Also how many kinds of reasoning are there apart from deductive reasoning? (Cf. LOGIC.)

A second group of uses of 'reason' allows the plural and involves expressions like 'a (the, his) reason'. A reason may be a cause as in 'the reason for the explosion', or a factor in an explanation as in 'the reason why there are infinitely many prime numbers', and again problems arise over the practical sphere: how are reasons for believing related to reasons for acting? Only the former are evidence, but Smith's honesty may be a reason for believing him, and also for rewarding him.

Can the reason why someone acts be a cause of his acting? This depends on whether actions can be caused but it is a further question whether his reason can be the cause. 'The' reason might be something he is unconscious of, which 'his' reason cannot be (cf. FREEWILL).

'He has a reason to act' may mean that acting would promote some purpose he has, or some interest he has, or some purpose he should morally have. An interest is perhaps a purpose he would or should rationally have if he knew certain facts. One can have a reason, even consciously, and act as it prescribes, without acting from it. Also the reason why Smith acted, whether or not it coincides with his reason, need not be a reason for acting, not even a poor reason. See also INCONTINENCE.

Aristotle, *De Anima* (*On the Soul*), (III, 4–8 (theoretical reason), III, 910; *Nicomachean Ethics*, VII, 1–10; *De Motu* (*Movement of Animals*), 701a, 7–25 (all these treat practical reason). (Classic though difficult discussions.)

J. Bennett, *Rationality*, Routledge, 1964. (Clear short discussion of what distinguishes rational animals from others.)

H. I. Brown, *Rationality*, Routledge, 1988. (Criticizes view that rationality consists in evaluating evidence by rules. Also criticizes FOUNDATIONALISM and social relativism.)

R. Edgley, *Reason in Theory and Practice*, Hutchinson, 1969. (Defends practical reason, discussing its relations with theoretical.)

D. Gauthier, 'Reason and maximization,' *Canadian Journal of Philosophy*, 1975. (How is maximizing utility related to rationality?)

D. Hume, *A Treatise of Human Nature*, 1739–40, book 2, part 3, § 3. (Reason as slave of passions; see p. 415 of edition by L. A. Selby-Bigge (Clarendon, 1888), and see also the indexes of this and Selby-Bigge's edition of Hume's *Enquiries* (Clarendon, 2nd edn, 1902) under 'reason' and 'reasoning' for Hume's general treatment of reason both theoretical and practical.)

I. Kant, *Critique of Pure Reason*, 1781, 2nd edn 1787. (See 'reason', 'understanding', 'judgment' in index to N. Kemp Smith's translation, 1929.)

J. Kemp, *Reason, Action and Morality*, RKP, 1964. (The place of reason in morals and conduct. Includes historical material.)

J. Raz (ed.), *Practical Reasoning*, Oxford UP, 1978. (Readings.)

Recursive. Said of a procedure which can be applied to a starting point to get a certain result, and then re-applied to that result to get a further result, and so on. Adding one is a recursive procedure for generating the natural numbers from zero. Recursion theory is a branch of mathematical logic studying FUNCTIONS definable by such procedures.

A set is recursively enumerable if there is a procedure for generating its members (not necessarily in any given order). If both a set and its complement (i.e. the set containing just those items in the relevant domain that are not members of the original set) are recursively enumerable then the set itself is called recursive. In that case there is a DECISION PROCEDURE for whether candidates for membership are or are not members: since there is a process for generating both members and non-members, we wait to see in which list the candidate item appears. With a merely recursively enumerable procedure we can prove that something is a member, if it is, but cannot prove it is not a member, if it is not. The predicate calculus, for instance (i.e. the set of its theorems), is recursively enumerable but not recursive. See also DEFINITION, INDUCTION.

Reductio ad absurdum. A method of argument, used in both mathematics and philosophy, which rejects a claim that, taken as a premise in a valid argument, leads to an absurd or self-contradictory conclusion.

Reduction. See PERCEPTION, PHENOMENOLOGY.

Reductionism. Also called reductivism. Tendency to reduce certain notions, whether everyday ones, like physical object, or theoretical ones in science, like electron, to allegedly simpler or more basic notions, or more empirically accessible ones, e.g. one might claim to dispense with the word 'electron' and talk only of vapour trails in cloud chambers. To reduce a theory or a science to another is to show that the latter can in principle yield all the results of the former, e.g. that everything psychology tells us we could in principle learn from physiology. Reductionism is a feature especially of PHENOMEN-ALISTS, and other empiricists, and of POSITIVISTS in philosophy of science. See also PHILOSOPHY.

But reduction can also, and in recent discussions usually must, be distinguished from elimination. 'Water is H_2O' reduces water to H_2O but does not say there is no water, while 'Demons are (really) viruses' does say that there are no demons. In reduction we get a straight definition of water, whereas demons are not, or not straightforwardly, defined in terms of viruses. Rather the phenomena once attributed to demons are now thought to be caused by viruses. Similarly MATERIAL-ISM may take a reductive or an eliminative attitude to mental phenomena. A third outlook, however, appeals to SUPERVENIENCE.

To sum up, we might reduce (say) A to B by saying that A is real, but what it is is B – there is only one thing there, which is both A and B, B having explanatory priority; or we might eliminate A, so that there is only B; or we might say that A is real and distinct from B, but supervenes on it.

PARFIT has advanced a form of psychological reductionism about persons: what matters is not personal identity, but psychological connectedness and continuity, and these features of individuals can be determined without any reference to persons.

Naturalist theories in ethics, claiming that ethical facts are simply facts about the world, can be referred to as reductive theories. See NATURALISM.

D. Charles and K. Lennon (eds), *Reduction, Explanation, and Realism*, Oxford UP, 1993. (Specially commissioned essays. See its 'Introduction' for relations between reduction, elimination and supervenience.)

P. Foot, *Virtues and Vices*, Oxford UP, 1978. (Defence of ethical naturalism.)

T. Horgan, 'From supervenience to superdupervenience', *Mind*, 1993. (See particularly p. 575 for reductive and eliminative materialism, and the possibility of a third kind, with many references.)

D. Parfit, *Reasons and Persons*, Oxford UP, 1984. (For psychological reductionism.)

Reduction sentences. A technical device introduced by Carnap, to avoid a difficulty that arises over definitions like '"is soluble" means "dissolves if immersed"'. With 'if' interpreted in terms of material IMPLICATION, as is usual in logic, this definition would make anything soluble that was never actually immersed. The general idea is to avoid giving a definition, but to give instead conditions under which something is soluble, and conditions under which it is not, which do not imply that everything which is never immersed is soluble.

R. Carnap, 'Testability and meaning', *Philosophy of Science*, 1936 and 1937, § 8.

Reference. See REFERRING, MEANING.

Referent. See REFERRING.

Referring. There is a group of terms, including 'refer', 'denote', 'name', 'designate', 'stand for', 'mention', 'be about', 'talk about', 'say of', 'apply to', 'be true of', which somehow seem to connect language with objects in the widest sense. Some of these terms are used varyingly, and sometimes interchangeably, but all have peculiarities.

Referring is done primarily by people. Words and sentences refer only in so far as people use them to do so, and therefore often differently on different occasions. (Cf. MEANING for referring and denoting, and for sense and reference. A sentence can 'refer' in this derivative way, by containing a term that refers, without having a 'reference' in the technical sense, i.e. without referring as a whole and in its own right.)

When does referring occur? 'Smith is tall' is true of many people. But if I say the words 'Smith is tall' I normally refer only to some Smith I have in mind. The context shows which. Suppose, however, I intend to refer to Smith, and in fact say things true only of him, but mistakenly use the name 'Jones'. Have I referred to Smith? If my audience realize the mistake, perhaps I have, although I referred to him as 'Jones'. But suppose they are deceived? Certainly I have not mentioned Smith, whereas I perhaps have mentioned one of the

Joneses, at any rate if there is exactly one reasonably relevant in the context. (Mentioning something involves at least using some name or description which actually applies to it – or would apply to it if it existed; see 'Alaska' example below.) A further case is when I deliberately use 'Jones' because I know (or believe) my audience wrongly thinks of Smith as 'Jones'. In general must I, to refer, secure uptake? These and other problems occur also when I use not names but descriptions, or words like 'someone' (cf. also QUANTIFIER WORDS).

So much for subject expressions, but do we refer in using predicates, and in identity statements? Suppose I say, perhaps mistakenly, 'That is my doctor': have I referred to, and have I mentioned, my doctor? Again we can mention and refer to universals ('Tallness is becoming commoner') but do I mention or refer to tallness in saying 'Smith is tall'. Confusions in this area may contribute to referential theories of MEANING. That we can refer to tallness, and that 'tall' as a predicate has some relation to tallness, may suggest that 'tall' always refers to tallness and has meaning by doing so. An ambiguity of 'stand for' may also cause confusion here: '"Tall" stands for tallness' may mean '"Tall" refers to tallness', or '"Tall" is the term to use when applying the concept tallness'. Other questions bearing on referential theories of meaning are how we can understand propositions which involve reference to objects we are not acquainted with, and whether we must be in some way causally related to things if we are to refer to them, i.e. whether we should accept a causal theory of reference (see also MEANING).

Many of these problems recur with about. 'Talk about' resembles 'refer to'. Talking about something may seem to involve more than 'merely referring to' it, but perhaps one can refer to something without talking about it only if one is interrupted in mid-sentence, etc. Of course talking about something here may amount simply to asking questions, etc., about it. 'Be about' applies mainly to statements, problems, etc., rather than people, and has a more technical air. It is not obvious where to draw the line between what a statement is and is not about, and there is a danger of any statement being about everything (Goodman).

So far we have distinguished referring from related notions, and have considered the effects of things like the role of the speaker's intentions and mistakes, and of the speaker's and hearer's beliefs. A special group of problems concern referring and existence. How can we refer to or talk about what does not exist, be it fictional (Pickwick), future (one's own death), a LOGICAL CONSTRUCTION (the average person), or simply a muddle (the round square)? Do such things have some sort of BEING SO (Meinong), or do we not 'really' refer to them (Russell. Cf. theory of DESCRIPTIONS)? Or is referring not, or not always, a relation (which requires real terms to relate)? Is the use of the 'objects' mentioned in the first sentence of this entry simply a linguistic device? Perhaps 'The king of Alaska is tall' mentions that non-existent king, but does this simply mean that a certain phrase is used – a phrase suitable for mentioning a real king if there were one?

The 'king of Alaska' example introduces a further group of problems: how far are notions like referring essential to language? Does the fact that the phrase is suitable for mentioning a real king if there were one mean that 'mentioning the king of Alaska' is a phrase we can only understand because we understand phrases like 'mentioning the Queen of England', where this is one? Are non-designative names possible only because we have designative names? We have asked whether it is only because their objects are sometimes real objects that referring, etc., are possible. One can ask whether at least some of these objects must be particulars and not UNIVERSALS. But one can further ask whether referring, etc., could be dispensed with, either in a language spoken by people who already knew a language containing them, or (more radically) in a people's first language. Could other devices in language, like predicating, be understood without these notions? Quine claims that we can eliminate singular terms in favour of found VARIABLES; but could we understand the role of these without first understanding that of singular terms? Could there be a language with quite different devices altogether?

A referent is what is referred to. A reference class (probability theory) is the population serving as a basis for statistical statements. In '10 per cent of Englishmen are Catholics' Englishmen form the reference class; in 'The probability of a double six is 1/36' the reference class may be throws of a die, or of a double die, according to context. For divided reference see MEANING.

K. Donnellan, 'Reference and definite descriptions', *Philosophical Review*, 1966. (Often reprinted. Influential distinction between attributive and referential ways of interpreting definite DESCRIPTIONS.)

G. Evans, *The Varieties of Reference*, 1982. (Thorough but difficult.)

P. T. Geach, *Reference and Generality*, Cornell UP, 1962. (Referring and allied notions, including discussion of QUANTIFIER WORDS. See particularly 'denoting' in index. Cf. also his *Mental Acts*, 1957.)

N. Goodman, 'About', *Mind*, 1961. (Mainly rather technical, but § 2 is good introduction to paradox concerning 'about'. Cf. also D. Holdcroft, 'A principle about "about"', *Mind*, 1968, M. Hodges, 'On "being about"', *Mind*, 1971, which both concern 'about' and existence. See Holdcroft, pp. 515–17 for whether sentences have references.)

L. Linsky, *Referring*, RKP, 1967. (Discusses referring in connection with existing and describing. More historical than Meiland, discussing Meinong, Frege, Russell, Strawson.)

G. McCulloch, *The Game of the Name: Introducing Logic, Language, and Mind*, Clarendon, 1989. (Introduction to many aspects of contemporary philosophy based on the topic of proper names. Presupposes elementary logic and some general appreciation at undergraduate level of aims of analytical philosophy. Each chapter has annotated bibliography.)

J. W. Meiland, *Talking about Particulars*, RKP, 1970. (General discussion of nature of referring.)

W. V. O. Quine, *Methods of Logic*, RKP, 1952. (Part 4 tries, following Russell, to eliminate singular terms, i.e. to eliminate referring except by bound variables (see QUANTIFICATION).)

R. M. Sainsbury, *Reference without Referents*, Oxford UP, 2005. (Defends its existence. Presupposes some knowledge of issues.)

P. F. Strawson, *Individuals*, Methuen, 1959. (Part 2 distinguishes referring and predicating. Stresses role of particulars and discusses eliminability of referring. Fairly difficult. Cf. I. Hacking, 'A language without particulars', *Mind*, 1968, claiming that a certain Amerindian language is such a language.)

Reflective equilibrium. The goal of a process of reconciling our native intuitions in a given area with a set of principles which we take to govern that area. The intuitions and the principles are balanced against each other, with the result that discordant intuitions are exposed as such and discounted, while the principles are adjusted and sophisticated to take account of and systematize as many of the intuitions as possible. In particular, moral and political philosophy, scientific reasoning, and questions about personal identity have provided fields for this process. See ETHICAL INTUITIONISM.

S. Darwall, A. Gibbard and P. Railton, 'Toward *fin de siècle* ethics: Some trends', *Philosophical Review*, 1992. (See pp. 168–74 for some relevant discussion.)

N. Goodman, *Fact, Fiction and Forecast*, Athlone Press and MIT Press, 1954; revised in later edns (see chapter 3, and section 2).

B. Hooker, *Ideal Code, Real World*, Oxford UP, 2003. (Defence of using reflective equilibrium as a test for the ideal moral code.)

J. Rawls, *A Theory of Justice*, Oxford UP, 1972. (See its index.)

H. Sidgwick, *The Methods of Ethics*, Macmillan 1874 (7th edn and final version, 1907). (Balances utilitarianism and other systems against the moral intuitions of common sense.)

Reflexive. A relation is reflexive if a term which has it at all must have it to itself (as old as). It is irreflexive or aliorelative if a term cannot have it to itself (older than), and non-reflexive if it may or may not have it to itself (fond of).

Refute. Successfully show to be false. But it is not necessary for hearer to be convinced. Not synonymous with 'deny', 'reject' or 'rebut'.

A. Flew, *An Introduction to Western Philosophy*, Thames and Hudson, 1971, revised edn, 1989, pp. 21–3.

Reid, Thomas. 1710–96. Born at Strachan, he worked mainly in Aberdeen and Glasgow. He is generally known as the founder of the 'Scottish school of common sense', which reacted against the sceptical conclusions of the 'British EMPIRICISTS'. Reid, like KANT, was particularly influenced by HUME (whom some scholars think he misinterpreted.) Being unable to accept Hume's sceptical conclusions, he attacked the basis from which Hume began, and substituted one based on our common-sense assumptions. *Essays on the Intellectual Powers of Man*, 1785 (epistemology). *Essays on the Active Powers of Man*, 1788 (psychology and ethics).

Relations (external and internal). A relation is internal to the things it relates (its terms) when they would not be the things they are unless related by it. Otherwise it is external. 'Orange is between red and yellow' expresses an internal relation, presumably, because these colours would not be what they are unless related in this way. Alternatively, a relation is internal if without it its terms would not have the qualities they have. If crimson is a dark colour and pink is a light colour, being darker than pink is internal to crimson, for if crimson were not darker than pink it would not be a dark colour. In a looser sense whether a relation is internal may depend on how its terms are described. Being married is internal to a husband, described as such, but not, presumably, to Smith. For the husband would not be a husband unless married, but Smith could be Smith whether married or not. Some philosophers, notably Bradley, held the doctrine of internal relations, that all relations are internal in one or both of the stricter senses. Bradley added that ultimately relations are unreal.

F. H. Bradley, *Appearance and Reality*, 2nd edn, 1897, Appendix B. (Cf. also chapter 3.)

G. E. Moore, *Philosophical Studies*, Kegan Paul, Trench, Trubner, 1922, chapter 9. (Criticizes doctrine).

Relativism. Any doctrine could be called relativism which holds that something exists, or has certain properties or features, or is true or in some sense obtains, not simply but only in relation to something else. Some form of relativism seems plausible for statements like 'Strawberries are nice' (for whose palate?); 'The angles of a triangle sum to two right angles' (in Euclidean or non-Euclidean geometry?); 'I am at rest' (relative to my car? the earth? the sun?). In practice two forms of relativism have been popular: cognitive and moral.

Cognitive relativism, so called as applying to knowledge claims in general rather than simply to claims about value, etc., can take the extreme form that all beliefs are true. If no proposition can be both true and false, then when A believes what B disbelieves we can call their disagreement merely apparent and say they are really thinking of different propositions; if A says 'X is red' and B says 'X is not red' they must really be saying (e.g. 'X looks red to me'). This could be avoided by saying they are talking of the same proposition, but each saying that it is true to him, not simply true; 'true' is replaced by 'true for'. This second doctrine can be called subjective relativism, and Plato attributes it to Protagoras (second half of fifth century BC).

Cognitive relativism is more plausible when applied not to individuals but to societies, cultures, or 'conceptual schemes' (cultural relativism). Individuals can then hold false beliefs if they misapply their own principles, as a Euclidean geometer could wrongly think the angles of a triangle sum to three right angles. Cultural relativism can also apply to principles of reasoning as well as to propositions believed, but a standard objection to all these relativisms is that the claim that relativism is true, or the argument by which it is supported, is itself surely put forward as being absolutely true or valid; do not the very notions of asserting and arguing involve those of absolute truth and absolute validity? Is not to assert something, or put forward an argument, to present it as being absolutely true or valid?

Could one then limit relativism to certain spheres? It has seemed especially plausible in science, partly because scientific theories seem to become accepted without their predecessors being straightforwardly refuted, and partly because it is claimed that different scientific systems are simply incommensurable (Kuhn) and scientific terms are THEORY-LADEN: 'mass' and 'time' mean something different for

Einstein from what they meant for Newton, so that Einstein couldn't show Newton was wrong in what he said. Relativism is encouraged by the holistic approach of Quine and others, where we can call any statement true or false if we make enough adjustments elsewhere in our theory (we can insist that the sun goes round the earth by making enough adjustments to our dynamics, etc.) But the related doctrine of the indeterminacy of TRANSLATION is different from incommensurability, and they may even be inconsistent (Hacking). Relativism may also seem inevitable if we cannot avoid taking for granted some background of theory or set of concepts (conceptual scheme) or PARADIGM; we cannot criticize everything at once. (But see Davidson on conceptual schemes.) But if we adopt relativism in science, will not the same reasons make us adopt it elsewhere, with the problems discussed above? Can we stop halfway?

Moral relativism, encouraged in both ancient and modern times by anthropological reports of cultural diversity, applies relativism to statements of value or duty, etc. As cognitive relativism may replace 'true' by 'true for', so moral relativism may replace 'right' by 'right for', saying, e.g. that cannibalism is right for certain primitives but wrong for Europeans. But relativism here must be distinguished from saying that cannibalism is thought by Europeans to be (absolutely) wrong, and from saying that cannibalism is (absolutely) wrong for Europeans but right for some other group, as someone might say it is right for the starving, or that smacking children is right for parents but wrong for teachers. Obviously one's role or circumstances can affect what it is right for one to do, and some doctrines are only improperly called relativism. Also one who thinks all moral judgements are relative to societies, etc., must not conclude it is (absolutely) right to live and let live (see Williams). We must distinguish saying something is (absolutely) right for those in certain circumstances and saying that 'right' has no meaning and must be replaced by a different term, 'right for' or 'right by such-and-such standards'; a relativist might say nothing can be right except by reference to some standard, and standards can only be judged by reference to other standards. How does 'right' compare with 'true' here? Another question is whether the relativist means that any act can only be judged by the standards of the agent or his society, or that any appraisal can be judged only by the standards of the appraiser or his society (Lyons). This may affect (e.g.) our assessment of one society's appraisal of another society. Suppose A approves and B disapproves of C's abortion: on the former view only that appraisal will be correct which accords with the norms of C's society; on the latter view both appraisals can be correct if they accord with the norms of A's and B's societies, respectively.

Relativism is not the same as SUBJECTIVISM, in any sphere. Some relativism may be subjectivist, but a relativist need not say that what seem to be assertions of the relevant kind are really disguised commands or expressions of attitude, etc., nor that they are really about the speaker's or someone else's beliefs or attitudes.

See also PERSPECTIVISM.

D. Davidson, *Inquiries into Truth and Interpretation*, Clarendon Press, 1984. (Contains his famous 1974 attack on relativism, 'On the very idea of a conceptual scheme' and other relevant articles.)

M. Giaquinto, 'Science and ideology', *Proceedings of the Aristotelian Society*, 1983–4. (How they differ and why science is better.)

M. Krausz and J. W. Meiland (eds), *Relativism: Cognitive and Moral*, Notre Dame UP, 1982. M. Hollis and S. Lukes (eds), *Rationality and Relativism*, Blackwell, 1982. (Two sets of readings, both with introduction and bibliography. First includes Davidson, Williams and Lyons: second includes Hacking.)

T. S. Kuhn and H. Putnam (see bibliography to SCIENCE).

Plato, *Theaetetus*, § 152–86. (Discussion of Protagoras. Cf. also Plato's dialogue, *Protagoras*.)

W. V. O. Quine, 'Two dogmas of empiricism' in his *From a Logical Point of View*, Harper and Row, 1953. (Classic source for his holistic approach.)

G. Sher, 'Moral relativism defended?', *Mind*, 1980 (Criticizes views of G. Harman in Krausz and Meiland (above).).

F. E. Snare, 'The diversity of morals', *Mind*, 1980. (Defends version of moral relativism.)

Relevance logic. See IMPLICATION.

Reliabilism. See EPISTEMOLOGY.

Religion (philosophy of). The study of general philosophical problems about religion and God. Particular religious doctrines belong rather to revealed or dogmatic theology or to comparative religion, though their logical, metaphysical, etc. implications belong to philosophy of religion.

An initial question is, what counts as a religion? Must there be one or more gods involved? What counts as a god, and in particular as the God of monotheism?

Natural theology is a part of philosophy of religion. Without using revelation it examines the existence, nature, properties and abilities of

God, and His relations to the world. Are there limits to His power? Can He perform logical impossibilities, or set Himself problems that He cannot solve (paradox of omnipotence)? Can He be omniscient compatibly with human, or indeed His own, freewill (paradoxes of omniscience)? Can He be both omnipotent and benevolent, the world being as it is (problem of evil)? Concerning His nature one can ask whether He exists necessarily, how His essence relates to His existence, and whether He has His predicates in the ordinary sense or analogically. An important question is whether God exists in time. If so, must He not in some way develop? And how does His existence fit in with relativity theory? If He is timeless, in what sense can He be a person or can He act? And can His omniscience include knowledge of facts involving temporal TOKEN-REFLEXIVES (see Sorabji)?

Arguments for God's existence include the ONTOLOGICAL ARGUMENT, the COSMOLOGICAL ARGUMENT, the argument from DESIGN and the argument from religious experience. The last has it that there is a special religious experience which guarantees or lets us infer the existence of God as its object.

On God and the world one can ask: Did He create the world, and if so, in what sense? Does He determine laws of nature, or of logic, or of morality? Does He intervene in the world with miracles, and what counts as a miracle?

Religious questions have been affected by the recent dominance of logic and semantics. How do religious words and discourse have meaning? Are religious statements to be interpreted literally or in some other way (the modern version of the medieval problem about analogical predication; see above)?

The field of religious experience suggests questions about mysticism, awe, the numinous and also faith: what is faith, how is it related to rational evidence and superstition, and can it be justified? Can there be a duty to believe? Religions promising immortality engender questions shared with philosophy of MIND. Problems peculiar to Christianity arise over concepts like the Trinity, the Incarnation, transubstantiation, salvation, grace and prayer, and their bearings on substance, causality, freewill again, and responsibility.

B. Davies, *Philosophy of Religion: A Guide and Anthology*, Oxford UP, 2000.

P. Helm (ed.), *Divine Commands and Morality*, Oxford UP, 1981.

*J. Hick, *Philosophy of Religion*, Prentice-Hall, 1963. (General introduction.)

A. Kenny, *The Five Ways*, RKP, 1969. (Aquinas' proofs for God's existence.)

R. Le Poidevin, *Arguing for Atheism*, Routledge, 1996. (Clear, introductory work that aims at provoking discussion.)

J. L. Mackie, 'Evil and omnipotence', *Mind*, 1955. (Problem of evil and paradox of omnipotence. Cf. discussions in succeeding volumes, and in Schlesinger (below). See also Mackie's *The Miracle of Theism*, Clarendon, 1982, discussing this and other arguments about God's existence.)

M. Martin, *Atheism: A Philosophical Justification*, Temple UP, 1989, and 1992. (Is what the title says.)

C. Meister and P. Copan (eds), *Routledge Companion to Philosophy of Religion*, Routledge, 2007. (Huge volume with a very wide range of topics and eminent contributors.)

*B. Mitchell (ed.), *The Philosophy of Religion*, Oxford UP, 1971. (Introductory anthology.)

A. O'Hear, *Experience, Explanation and Faith*, RKP, 1984. (Discusses arguments about God's existence falling in these areas.)

M. Palmer, *The question of God*, Routledge, 2001.

A. Plantinga, *Warranted Christian Belief*, Oxford UP, 2000. (Christian belief as warranted, rather than justified: follows his earlier books on the idea of 'warrant'.)

G. Schlesinger, *Religion and Scientific Method*, Reidel, 1977. (Offers new solution to problem of evil and claims that theism can be scientifically confirmed.)

R. K. Sorabji, *Time, Creation, and the Continuum*, Duckworth, 1983. (See chapter 16 on timelessness and omniscience, based on discussion of ancient writings.)

R. Swinburne, *Is there a God?* Oxford UP, 1997. (Swinburne has published many books, arguing that Christian faith is both rational and coherent. This is the most introductory.)

C. Taliaferro, *Contemporary Philosophy of Religion*, Blackwell, 1998.

Remembering. See MEMORY.

Resemblance. See UNIVERSALS.

Representation. Used in a variety of philosophical contexts. Political representation is a feature of modern democracies. In what way can a person or a party represent others? In aesthetics there is the question of what it is for a work of art to represent its subject: how can pencil marks on paper represent a face, for example? In cognitive science mental representations are taken to be mental objects with semantic properties – see INTENSIONALITY.

N. Goodman, *Languages of Art*, Hackett, 1976. (Discusses notion of representation in general, as well as in pictorial art.)

Resultance. See SUPERVENIENCE.

Results. See CAUSATION.

Richard's paradox. One of what are sometimes called the semantic PARADOXES (cf. RUSSELL'S PARADOX, TYPES). Take all decimal numbers between 0 and 1 specifiable in finitely many words. Each will have infinitely many digits. Those which apparently terminate are followed by endless 0's. Arrange these numbers in some order in a table, so that each number occupies a row and its digits appear in successive columns. Take the number formed by the diagonal of the table, starting from the top left. For any n, the n-th digit of this diagonal number will be the n-th digit of the n-th row in the table. Replace each digit in this diagonal number by its successor. (Assume the successor of 9 is 0.) The resulting number cannot appear in the table, yet is specifiable in finitely many words (we have just specified it).

This diagonal procedure was originally used by CANTOR to prove that there must be more decimal numbers than can be put in a table as above, even though such a table has infinitely many rows. Since the infinite number of decimals thus exceeds the infinite number of rows in such a table, in the sense that these numbers cannot be paired off with each other, there must be more than one 'transfinite' (i.e. infinite) number. This last result is not affected by solutions to Richard's paradox, which only concerns numbers specifiable in finitely many words.

M. Clark, *Paradoxes from A–Z*, London: Routledge, 2002.
E. Teensma, *The Paradoxes*, Van Gorcum, 1969, pp. 32–4.

Rorty, Richard. 1931–2007. American thinker, with wide-ranging interests in philosophy, literature and the humanities. He was trained in, but came to reject, analytic philosophy, moving instead towards a more pragmatist view. Influenced by the later thought of Wittgenstein he held that language and thought do not represent or mirror reality: they are ways of coping. He became interested in the continental tradition in philosophy, and argued that analytic and continental philosophy were not opposed, but essentially complemented each other. *Philosophy and the Mirror of Nature*, 1971. *Contingency, Irony, and Solidarity*, 1989. *Objectivity, Relativism and Truth: Philosophical Papers I*, 1991.

R. Brandom, *Rorty and his Critics*, Blackwell, 2000. (Responses to Rorty from leading philosophers including Habermas, Davidson, Putnam, Dennett, McDowell, Bernard Williams.)

Rousseau, Jean-Jacques. 1712–78. Political philosopher and philosopher of education, he was born in Geneva and lived largely in France, often under patronage (including that of HUME in England). He emphasized the corrupting effects of society on people in their natural condition. He thought that society must be considered to be founded on a social contract between people, and he elaborated a notion of the 'general will', which would be represented in the decisions made in a properly ordered society. The sovereign's decisions were legitimate only when they represented this general will, not (as with HOBBES) whenever the sovereign had effective power. He also set forth principles of education in line with his other views. *Discourse on the Arts and Sciences*, 1750. *Discourse on the Origin and Basis of Inequality Among Men*, 1755. *The Social Contract*, 1762. *Emile*, 1762 (on education).

Russell, Bertrand A. W. 1872–1970. Born at Ravenscroft, Gloucester, he worked mainly in England (especially Cambridge), sometimes in America. His early fame rested on two main contributions to logic, the theory of DESCRIPTIONS and the theory of TYPES. He taught Wittgenstein at Cambridge before the First World War. His later work concentrated mainly on EPISTEMOLOGY, metaphysics and philosophy of mind, where he based himself mainly on the empiricist tradition of HUME, MILL, etc., though he was notorious for changing his views. He also stressed the importance to philosophy of modern scientific developments. A prolific writer, Russell was also famous for his great political and social commitment. He wrote extensively on moral and political matters, but did not regard these writings as part of his philosophical work. Won the Nobel Prize for Literature in 1950. *The Principles of Mathematics*, 1903, revised, 1937. 'On denoting', *Mind*, 1905 (theory of descriptions). *Principia Mathematica*, 1910–13 (with WHITEHEAD. Theory of types). *Our Knowledge of the External World*, 1914. 'The philosophy of logical atomism', *Monist*, 1918. *The Analysis of Mind*, 1921. *An Inquiry into Meaning and Truth*, 1940.

See also BROAD, CALCULUS, CATEGORIES, CAUSATION, CLASS, FREGE, IMPLICATION, INDUCTION, INTENSIONALITY AND INTENTIONALITY, LANGUAGE (PHILOSOPHY OF), LOGICAL ATOMISM, LOGICAL CONSTRUCTIONS, MATHEMATICS (bibliography), MEANING, MONISM, PARADIGM CASE, PARADOX, PHENOMENALISM, PHILOSOPHY, QUINE, REFERRING, RUSSELL'S PARADOX, SENSE DATA, SENTENCES, STRAWSON, SUFFICIENT REASON, TOKEN-REFLEXIVES, TRUTH, UNIVERSALS, VARIABLE.

Russell's paradox. Most classes are not members of themselves (the class of cats is not a cat), but some classes are members of themselves (the class of classes is a class). Is the class of all classes that are not members of themselves a member of itself? If yes, no. If no, yes. This is the most famous of the logical PARADOXES. Russell invented his theory of TYPES in order to answer it.

M. Clark, *Paradoxes from A–Z*, London: Routledge, 2002.

R. M. Sainsbury, *Paradoxes*, Cambridge UP, 1988, revised, 1995. (Chapter 5 gives brief introduction.)

Ryle, Gilbert. 1900–76. British philosopher born at Brighton and working in Oxford, who was one of the early protagonists of 'linguistic PHILOSOPHY'. His main work was in philosophy of MIND and in philosophical LOGIC. He was particularly famous for criticizing the 'ghost in the machine' view of mind and body, which he attributed primarily to DESCARTES, and he analysed various mental concepts in terms of dispositions to behave in certain ways. In his youth he felt some affinity for PHENOMENOLOGY. *The Concept of Mind*, 1949. *Dilemmas*, 1954. See also CATEGORIES, CONDITIONALS (bibliography), DIALECTIC (bibliography), EPISTEMOLOGY, FEELING, FREEWILL (bibliography), HETEROLOGICAL, INFERENCE, LIAR, MATHEMATICS, NEGATION, POLYMORPHOUS, RATIONALISM, SCEPTICISM, SEEING, SENSATION, SENTENCES, THINKING, TOPIC-NEUTRAL.

S

Salva veritate. 'Preserving the truth'. See INTENSIONALITY.

Santayana, George. 1863–1952. Born in Madrid, he worked at Harvard and then in Europe, dying at Rome. An apparently paradoxical figure, a Catholic agnostic who attacked broad-churchmanship and religious and political liberalism, an aesthetically minded Platonist who called himself a materialist, a rejector of modern ideas of inevitable progress who admired the pragmatist William James, he accepted our impulses for what they were but treated reason as a further impulse, a neutral integrator of the rest. He believed in essences, but not as a superior realm. The ordinary world exists, and we must start from ordinary beliefs, and not seek the illusory foundations sought in vain by the sceptic. How far his philosophy changed in his later works is controversial. *The Sense of Beauty*, 1896. *The Life of Reason* (five volumes), 1905–6. *Winds of Doctrine*, 1913 (criticisms). *Scepticism and Animal Faith*, 1923. *Realms of Being* (four volumes, on Essence, Matter, Truth, Spirit), 1927–40, in single volume with new introduction, 1942. *Dominations and Powers*, 1951 (social philosophy).

Sartre, Jean-Paul. 1905–80. Born in Paris, he worked mostly in France, with some study in Germany. Famous both as a writer of novels and plays and as a philosopher, he represented one form of EXISTENTIALISM, though his later work tended towards Marxism. He was the most explicitly atheistic of existentialists, and took an active part in politics. *Sketch for a Theory of the Emotions*, 1939. *Being and Nothingness*, 1943. *Existentialism is a Humanism*, 1946 (popular, but often regarded as not representing his main thought). *Critique of Dialectical Reason*, 1960 (Marxist in tendency). See also BAD FAITH, MARCEL, MERLEAU-PONTY.

Satisfice. As an optimizing policy gets, or aims to get, the best results possible so a satisficing policy gets, or aims to get, results sufficient but not necessarily the best possible. The notion derives from the economist H. A. Simon (1916–2001).

> M. Slote and P. Pettit, 'Satisficing consequentialism', *Proceedings of the Aristotelian Society*, supplementary vol., 1984. (Some philosophical implications. Cf. also M. Slote, *Common Sense Morality and Consequentialism*, RKP, 1985, chapter 3.)

Satisfy. A notion introduced by Tarski to help construct his semantic definition of TRUTH for formalized languages. Consider a sentential FUNCTION 'x loves y' and suppose that John loves Mary. Then 'x loves y' is satisfied by any ordered sequence of objects whose first two terms are John and Mary taken in that order. In general, suppose a certain sentential function contains n different free VARIABLES (some of which may be repeated: 'x loves x' has only one). Then take any sequence of objects and assign its first n terms, taken in order, to the n variables, respectively, also taken in some order (usually alphabetical). Then the sequence satisfies the function if the first n terms of the sequence are related as the resulting sentence says they are. To ensure the sequence is long enough, it is convenient to take only infinite sequences and ignore all superfluous terms, i.e. all after the first n. A sentence, or closed sentential function, contains no free variables, so that all the terms in all sequences are superfluous. 'John loves Mary', therefore is (vacuously) satisfied by all sequences if he does, and by none if he doesn't. Tarski therefore defines truth by calling a sentence true if all sequences satisfy it and false if none do. The limitation to formalized languages has to do with problems like the LIAR PARADOX.

> W. V. O. Quine, *Philosophy of Logic*, Prentice-Hall, 1970, particularly chapter 3. (Priority of satisfaction over truth.)
> A. Tarski, 'The semantic conception of truth and the foundations of semantics', *Philosophy and Phenomenological Research*, 1944, reprinted in H. Feigl and W. Sellars (eds), *Readings in Philosophical Analysis*, Appleton-Century-Crofts, 1949. (See also the account by M. Black, 'The semantic definition of truth', *Analysis*, 1948, reprinted in M. MacDonald (ed.), *Philosophy and Analysis*, Blackwell, 1954.)

Saturated. See CONCEPT.

Scepticism. Any view involving doubt about whether something exists, or about whether we can know something, or about whether we are justified in arguing in certain ways. Throughout the ages many philosophers have held that unless we know some things for certain we cannot know anything at all, or even legitimately think anything probable (cf. FOUNDATIONALISM). Many of them, especially the Greek sceptics and Descartes, have therefore sought a sure mark or 'criterion' of when a proposition is true.

One can doubt whether knowledge can be had in certain spheres, or whether it can be had by certain methods. An extreme rationalist like Plato, sometimes, may doubt if we can ever get knowledge through the senses. An extreme empiricist like Hume may doubt if we can ever get it through reason, or through any reasoning except deductive (Hume again; see INDUCTION). Particular arguments may attack the reliability of particular kinds of alleged knowledge, e.g. memory, precognition, intuition.

The sceptic may doubt whether we can know something, or even have any reason to believe it (cf. agnostics). Less often he may deny that certain things exist, or that they could exist, even though he must then claim to know negative propositions (dogmatic scepticism; cf. atheists). He may deny or doubt the existence of God, of objects when not experienced (Berkeley), of any objects at all beyond our experiences themselves, i.e. beyond our SENSATIONS or SENSE DATA (Hume; cf. PERCEPTION), and that subjects like ethics contain any truths to be known (logical POSITIVISTS; cf. NATURALISM). Sceptics have asked how we could know of the past (Russell asked how we know we did not spring into existence, complete with 'memories', five minutes ago), or of minds other than our own. Descartes even tried, unsuccessfully, to doubt his own existence. Milder forms of scepticism allow that we can know something but only by certain methods: perhaps we can know that ordinary objects, or others' feelings, exist, but only by inference, not by direct observation.

The views that nothing exists outside one's own mind, or that nothing such can be known to exist, are called solipsism (literally, 'only-oneself-ism'). A weaker version of solipsism concerns merely the existence of other minds (one form of the other minds problem, though this problem also concerns what we can know, and how, about other minds, e.g. what others are thinking and feeling).

One particular question that the sceptic asks is how I can know that I am not now dreaming.

Methodological scepticism is the adoption of sceptical views not to defend them but as a starting point, departures from which are to be

justified. Thus Descartes' method of doubt involves doubting everything until something necessarily indubitable is found, on which
knowledge can be built. See also METHODOLOGICAL SOLIPSISM.

Radical forms of scepticism have often been unpopular on the
grounds that they cannot coherently be stated without presupposing
their own falsity (cf. TRANSCENDENTAL ARGUMENTS). See also
PRIVATE LANGUAGE ARGUMENT, ACCESS, INCORRIGIBLE,
PERCEPTION, SEXTUS EMPIRICUS.

J. L. Austin (see bibliography to SENSE DATA).

J. Bogen and M. Beckner, 'An empirical refutation of Cartesian scepticism',
Mind, 1979. (Attacks Descartes' argument from dreaming. For an earlier
and different attack see M. Macdonald, 'Sleeping and waking', Mind,
1953.)

M. F. Burnyeat (ed.), The Skeptical Tradition, California UP, 1983. (Historical
essays, half on ancient scepticism and half on modern reactions.)

A. P. Griffiths, 'Justifying moral principles', Proceedings of the Aristotelian
Society, 1957–8. (Tries to rescue morals from the sceptic.)

D. Hume, Treatise, 1739, and Enquiry concerning Human Understanding,
1748. (Nearest among great philosophers to scepticism.)

A. A. Long, Hellenistic Philosophy, Duckworth, 1974. (Includes treatment of
Greek sceptics.)

G. E. Moore, Philosophical Papers, Allen and Unwin/Macmillan, 1959. (Several
items attack scepticism.)

H. Putnam, 'Brains in a vat', chapter 1 of his Reason, Truth and History,
Cambridge UP, 1981. (How far can scepticism be coherently stated?)

G. Ryle, Dilemmas, Cambridge, UP, 1954, chapter 7. (Scepticism and
perception.)

B. Stroud, The Significance of Philosophical Scepticism, Clarendon, 1984.
(Sympathetic treatment of scepticism, emphasizing need to ask how the
problem arose and what the significance of philosophical scepticism is.)

P. Unger, Ignorance: A Case for Scepticism, Clarendon, 1975. (Defends
scepticism because of high standards required for knowledge.)

M. Williams (ed.), Scepticism, Dartmouth Publishing Company, 1993. (Reprinted
essays on issues connected with scepticism and the external world.)

M. D. Wilson, 'Skepticism without indubitability', Journal of Philosophy,
1984. (Significance of seventeenth-century scepticism. This and the adjacent
article by Stroud are summarized by R. J. Fogelin in the same issue, p. 552.)

J. Wisdom, J. L. Austin and A. J. Ayer, 'Other minds', Proceedings of the
Aristotelian Society, supplementary vol., 1946. Wisdom reprinted in his
Other Minds, Blackwell, 1952, and Austin in A. Flew (ed.), Logic and
Language, 2nd series, Blackwell, 1966.

Scholastic philosophy. So called from the 'schools' (i.e. universities) in which it flourished. The predominant form of European philosophy in the Middle Ages, reconciling Aristotelianism with Christian theology. Prominent scholastic philosophers included Abelard, Albert the Great, AQUINAS, OCKHAM and SCOTUS.

Schopenhauer, Arthur. 1788–1860. Born in Danzig and educated partly in France and England, he worked mostly in Germany. He admired KANT, but, like KIERKEGAARD, reacted against the prevalent philosophy of HEGEL. He saw his chief contribution to philosophy as the identification of the Kantian thing-in-itself with the will, and emphasized the role of will in the world, both animate and inanimate. His treatment of unconscious willing partly anticipated Freud. He combined this with an ethic of pessimistic resignation strongly influenced by Indian thought. *The Fourfold Root of the Principle of Sufficient Reason*, 1813, revised, 1847. *The World as Will and Idea* (or *Representation*), 1819. *Parerga und Paralipomena*, 1851 (miscellaneous essays).

C. Janaway, *Schopenhauer*, Oxford UP, 1994.
B. Magee, *The Philosophy of Schopenhauer*, Clarendon, 1983.

Science (philosophy of). The study of science in the broadest sense, its nature, aims, methods, tools, parts, range and relation to other subjects.

The study of how science works is normally taken as a fair guide to how it should. This study is often called methodology, a term which can also be relative, e.g. methodology of history. Literally 'methodology' means 'study of method'; a method is not itself a methodology. Inductive logic, or the logic of induction, is normally limited to the study of INDUCTION as a mode of reasoning. Whether strictly there is any inductive reasoning is a question philosophy of science shares with philosophy of logic. But philosophy of science itself studies the process, taken as a whole, whereby we start from premises about the world and reach, by rational means, conclusions about the world which cannot be reached from those premises by deduction alone. Everyday thinking also uses such a process, but science is more systematic and method-conscious, and so more often studied.

The 'mathematical' sciences, especially physics, need special mathematical techniques, but scientific argument in general is often taken to presuppose a mathematical apparatus for applying the notions of PROBABILITY and CONFIRMATION, both of which themselves raise many problems. The calculus of chances (see PROBABILITY), which underlies probability, is often, but not always, taken as the basis for scientific procedure.

When studying the nature of scientific reasoning we naturally ask how it can be justified, and what are its purposes. In what circumstances can a scientific statement properly be accepted? In particular what role does simplicity play, and when is one hypothesis simpler than another? Apart from prediction and control the main purpose of science is perhaps EXPLANATION, and an important part of philosophy of science concerns what this is and how it is achieved.

LAWS of nature, CAUSATION and scientific necessity (see MODALITIES) are important concepts here: what are they, and are they real or should they somehow be explained away or reduced to other notions?

The difficulties about acceptability, and about what laws of nature are, lead to questions about the nature of scientific systems. Are they perhaps abstract systems which we fit to the world as we might choose between alternative geometries (see SPACE)? Just as there are problems about a system as a whole, so there are about the terms in it. What sort of meaning and definition can they have? (Cf. POSITIVISM for operationalism.) Should so-called theoretical entities such as electrons, which cannot be directly observed, be postulated as really existing things, or should they be treated as LOGICAL CONSTRUCTIONS? These problems about the terms and structures of scientific hypotheses lead one to ask about the properties a good hypothesis should have, and about the respective roles of observation and experiment, and the nature and types of measurement (see MAGNITUDES).

Moreover, how does science develop? Is it through the orderly replacement of hypotheses found to be false by better ones, or in some other way? Does it progressively approach an absolute truth? And how far does science extend? Do geology, astronomy, psychology, sociology, even history, have equal claims with physics, chemistry and biology to be called sciences (cf. SOCIAL PHILOSOPHY, philosophy of HISTORY), and can they be reduced to a common basis, as physicalism (in one of the senses of that term: see POSITIVISM) asserts?

L. W. Beck (see bibliography to LOGICAL CONSTRUCTIONS).

R. Boyd, P. Gasper and J. D. Trout (eds), *The Philosophy of Science*, MIT Press, 1991. (41 collected essays, divided into sections with introduction to each.)

L. J. Cohen, *The Implications of Induction*, Methuen, 1970. (Develops alternative to calculus of chances as basis of confirmation.)

M. Giaquinto, 'Science and ideology', *Proceedings of the Aristotelian Society*, 1983–4. (Defends rationality of science against various irrationalist approaches without making this a mere matter of definition.)

*D. A. Gillies, *Philosophy of Science in the Twentieth Century: Four Central Themes*, Blackwell, 1993. (The themes are inductivism, conventionalism, observation, demarcation (of science as such).)

*I. Hacking (ed.), *Scientific Revolutions*, Oxford UP, 1981. (Essays stemming from the work of Kuhn.)

I. Hacking, *Representing and Intervening: Introductory Topics in the Philosophy of Natural Science*, Cambridge UP, 1983. (Discusses scientific objectivity ('representing') and experimental method ('intervening').)

T. S. Kuhn, *The Structure of Scientific Revolutions*, Chicago UP, 1962, 2nd edn with postscript, 1970. (One, controversial, view of how science develops. For criticism see I. Lakatos and A. Musgrave (eds), *Criticism and the Growth of Knowledge*, Cambridge UP, 1970, and Hacking (ed.) (above). See also P. Horwich (ed.), *World Changes: Thomas Kuhn and the Nature of Science*, MIT Press, 1993. (Conference papers reflecting Kuhn's influence and with 'Afterwords' by him.).)

P. Lipton, *Inference to the Best Explanation*, Routledge, 1993.

Midwest Studies in Philosophy, vol. 19, 1993. (Issue devoted to philosophy of science.)

S. Psillos and M. Curd (eds), *The Routledge Companion to Philosophy of Science*, Routledge, 2008. (Large collection of over 50 articles by distinguished contributors.)

H. Putnam, 'What is "realism"', *Proceedings of the Aristotelian Society*, 1975–6. (Science and truth. Explained in his *Meaning and the Moral Sciences*, RKP, 1978.)

Scientism. A general term, usually pejorative, emphasizing the value or self-sufficiency of science in a certain area, e.g. the view that philosophical problems require none but scientific techniques for answering them.

T. Sorell, *Scientism*, Routledge, 1991. (Treats the subject both inside and outside philosophy.)

Scope. See QUANTIFICATION.

Scotus, John Duns. c. 1266–1308. Born probably at Duns near Anglo-Scottish border. Scottish theologian and philosopher who probably worked in Cambridge, Oxford and Paris. His interests were in the same general area as those of AQUINAS, though somewhat less closely tied to ARISTOTLE. He held distinctive views on such questions as the nature of being, of matter, of relations, of transcendentals (see BEING), and on how individual members of a species are distinguished (where he introduces his notion of haecceitas ('thisness'); see HAEC-CEITY). He also introduced a fresh proof for God's existence. Among his authentic works are the *Opus Oxoniense* (a commentary on the *Sentences* of Peter Lombard), *Quaestiones Quodlibetales* (miscellaneous questions), *De Primo Principio*, and commentaries on Aristotle's metaphysics and logic. His philosophy, with that of his followers, is called Scotism. Not to be confused with John Scotus Erigena (ninth century), who was an Irish theologian and philosopher whose *De Divisione Naturae* shows NEOPLATONIC influence, and develops (following earlier Greek thinking) an idea similar to that of the analogical predication discussed by later thinkers.

See also OCKHAM.

A. B. Wolter (ed. and trans.), *John Duns Scotus: A Treatise on God as First Principle*, Franciscan Herald Press, 1961. (Has Latin text and English tradition.)

A. B. Wolter (ed. and trans.), *Duns Scotus: Philosophical Writings: A Selection*, Nelson, 1962, Hackett, 1987. (Has Latin text and English translation. Bobbs-Merrill published the English without the Latin in 1964.)

Searle, John. 1932–. American philosopher of language and mind. Was a Rhodes Scholar at Oxford as an undergraduate and graduate student, and has spent most of his career at the University of California, Berkeley. He developed AUSTIN's theory of illocutionary acts in *Speech Acts: An Essay in the Philosophy of Language*, 1969, and then further, in *Intentionality: An Essay in the Philosophy of Mind*, 1983. His CHINESE ROOM ARGUMENT against a strong Artificial Intelligence thesis has been influential. He has written on consciousness in *The Rediscovery of the Mind*, 1983, and in *Minds, Brains and Science*, 1984. *The Construction of Social Reality*, 1995. *Rationality in Action*, 2001.

See INTENSIONALITY AND INTENTIONALITY, SPEECH ACTS.

E. Lepore and R. Van Gulick (eds), *John Searle and his Critics*, Blackwell, 1991.

Seeing. Cf. PERCEPTION throughout. In general, seeing is having sight. We normally use eyes, but sight cannot be defined as perception through eyes if we allow that we might see with artificial eyes, or none. Would someone without eyes count as seeing if that person consistently knew the colours of surrounding objects? An interesting problem here concerns blindsight, where certain brain-damaged people can accurately report certain features of their environment apparently only accessible to sight but disclaim having any visual experiences. This leads on to the question of whether seeing something involves noticing and identifying it. Seeing as is important here. We can switch from seeing a certain ambiguous drawing as a picture of a duck to seeing it as a picture of a rabbit. Does this involve a change in belief, or in judgement, or what? How are seeing X, seeing X as Y (which may or may not be the same as X), judging X to be Y, and taking X to be Y, related together? The role of judgement or inference arises in other cases too. Our retinal image is two-dimensional. Must we therefore use inference in seeing the world as three-dimensional? We judge that a pillar-box looking grey in sodium light is red. But when the sun looks larger at sunset than at noon, though we know that even the visual image it subtends is not, is any judgement involved? And is there any non-epistemic seeing, i.e. seeing that does not involve belief in any way?

The things we see include objects, shadows, flashes, properties like 'the blue of her dress', relations, events, states of affairs, facts. Does this variety throw any light on whether seeing is a unitary notion, and if it is, what the conditions are for its occurrence? We may see literally or metaphorically ('the point of the joke', 'that his wits were failing'), and these can be hard to distinguish, when our evidence is largely visual.

Normally what we see must exist, though we see pink rats and 'see in the mind's eye' (see below). It is disputed whether we see whole objects in the same sense in which we see the parts of their surfaces in our line of vision.

Sometimes 'see' means 'catch sight of' or 'come to see', and so means something momentary ('suddenly he saw it'). But, as 'come to see' suggests, in another sense we can go on seeing something. This raises the question of how far 'see' is a 'success' or 'achievement' word, i.e. a word which does not, or not simply, refer to an activity, like 'run', but refers to a success or achievement, like 'win'.

Is visualizing a sort of inner seeing? If so, what is seen? Does it involve seeing or having mental images, and how, if so, are these related to what is visualized (which may be real or imaginary)?

Seeing differs from some of the other SENSES in certain ways. Colours seem to be 'in' objects in a way sounds or smells are not. Is the feel of velvet in the velvet? We 'catch sight of', or 'like the look of', something, but 'sights' and 'looks' are not things we see, in the way sounds are things we hear. How analogous is seeing the colour of something to hearing the sound of it? (Cf. SENSATION.)

Many of the questions about seeing might be summed up by asking how far seeing is a kind of experience and how far it is a source of knowledge.

T. Clarke, 'Seeing surfaces and physical objects', in M. Black (ed.), *Philosophy in America*, Allen and Unwin, 1965.

F. Dretske, *Seeing and Knowing*, RKP, 1969. (Relations between them. On seeing and believing see also M. Alcock and H. Jackson, 'Seeing and acquiring belief', *Mind*, 1979, D. Close, 'What is non-epistemic seeing?', *Mind*, 1976, 'More on non-epistemic seeing', *Mind*, 1980, J. Heil, 'Seeing is believing', *American Philosophical Quarterly*, 1982.)

C. L. Hardin, *Color for Philosophers*, Hackett, 1988. (Emphasizes the relevant scientific facts, along with philosophical discussion. Cf. also E. Thompson, *Colour Vision: A Study in Cognitive Science and the Philosophy of Perception*, Routledge, 1995, claiming to analyse colours as relations between persons and objects, avoiding extremes of objectivism and subjectivism.)

D. Lewis, 'Veridical hallucination and prosthetic vision', in J. Dancy (ed.), *Perceptual Knowledge*, Oxford UP, 1988.

E. J. Lowe, 'Experience and its objects', and M. G. F. Martin, 'Sight and touch', both in T. Crane (ed.), *The Contents of Experience*, Cambridge UP, 1992.

J. M. Shorter, 'Imagination', *Mind*, 1952, reprinted in O. P. Wood and G. Pitcher (eds), *Ryle*, Macmillan, 1970. (Seeing and visualizing, and the relation between imagination and mental images.)

M. Tye, *The Imagery Debate*, MIT Press, 1992. (Contains material relevant to both seeing and imagining. See particularly chapter 7 on visual qualia.)

G. N. A. Vesey, 'Seeing and seeing as', *Proceedings of the Aristotelian Society*, 1955–6, reprinted in R. J. Swartz (ed.), *Perceiving, Sensing, and Knowing*, Doubleday, 1965.

L. Wittgenstein, *Philosophical Investigations*, Blackwell, 1953, II, xi, pp. 193–214. ('Duck/rabbit', etc. Cf. review by P. F. Strawson in *Mind*, 1954, pp. 95–7, reprinted in G. Pitcher (ed.), *Wittgenstein*, Macmillan, 1966, pp. 59–61.)

Self-deception. See BAD FAITH.

Self-regarding. Attributed to desires or actions if aimed at affecting oneself. If aimed at affecting others, these are other-regarding. Self-regarding aims need not be selfish (e.g. improving one's own moral character is not), nor need other-regarding aims be altruistic (e.g. sadism is not). Actions may also be divided, irrespective of their aims, into self-affecting (affecting only the agent) and other-affecting

(affecting others too); both individual actions and types of action may be so divided.

C. D. Broad, 'Egoism as a theory of human motives', *Hibbert Journal*, vol. 48, 1949–50, reprinted in his *Ethics and the History of Philosophy*, 1952, and in D. Cheney (ed.) *Broad's Critical Essays in Moral Philosophy*, 1971; cf. also chapter 12 in this last.

J. S. Mill, *On Liberty*, 1859. (Advocates self-affecting/other-affecting distinction as basis for state interference with individual, but calls it self-regarding/not self-regarding.)

Semantic ascent. See FORMAL MODE.

Semantics. The general study of MEANING. Semantics is a species of the more general study of semiotics, the theory of signs, other species of which are syntactics and pragmatics. In each case philosophers study the notions in general and from an abstract point of view, while linguists study their application to particular languages and adopt an empirical approach to the more general questions, as in the case of semantics. Syntax or syntactics studies signs independently of their interpretation. In philosophy, it studies some of the properties of logical systems (see AXIOM). In linguistics, it studies the formal aspects of natural languages (e.g. why it is that 'the woman runs' is a well-formed string of words while 'the runs woman' is not). (This usage is rather different from that where syntax, as the study of sentences, contrasts with grammar, as the study of individual words.) Pragmatics studies signs in relation to what we do with them, given that they have the meaning they have (cf. pragmatic IMPLI-CATION). Semantics studies signs in relation to what, or how, they signify. It also studies meaning itself in so far as this depends on what we do with the signs (e.g. SPEECH ACT theories of meaning); here it fuses with semantics. (In this entry SIGN is used in its wide sense.)

N. Chomsky, *Aspects of the Theory of Syntax*, MIT Press, 1965. (Important source for his ideas at that time.)

T. Crane, 'The language of thought: No syntax without semantics', *Mind and Language*, 1990. (Claims that if there is a LANGUAGE OF THOUGHT it must have semantics as well as syntax, so that there cannot be a 'syntactical theory of the mind'.)

J. D. Fodor, *Semantics: Theories of Meaning in Generative Grammar*, Harvard UP, 1979.

H. P. Grice, *Studies in the Way of Words*, Harvard UP, 1989. (Collected essays on semantics and pragmatics by important contributor, especially to pragmatics.)

*R. K. Larson and G. M. A. Segal, *Knowledge of Meaning: Introduction to Semantic Theory*, MIT Press, 1995. (General introduction.)

C. W. Morris, *Signs, Languages and Behaviour*, Prentice-Hall, 1946, chapters 8 § 1. (Source of the distinctions.)

W. V. O. Quine, *Elementary Logic*, Ginn and Co., 1941. (One of many text books introducing basic ideas of formal logic.)

Semiotic. See SEMANTICS.

Sensa. See SENSE DATA.

Sensation. Either a kind of experience or a faculty, the latter including, in philosophy, the faculty of having 'pure experiences' (see PERCEPTION). Usually SENSE DATUM means an alleged object of experience distinct from the experiencing, while 'sensation' means the experience itself, but it is controversial how far there is a clear-cut distinction here. We hear sounds, but 'have' auditory sensations. Is this because sounds can exist independently of being heard? When we 'have' or 'feel' a sensation, 'sensation' is perhaps an 'internal accusative', like 'blow' in 'strike a blow'; whatever the case with sense data, sensations must presumably be had by some subjects. All this raises the question of what sensations are. Are they objects of some sort? Or properties of the subject which has them? Must the subject be conscious of them, or could (say) a pain exist without being present to consciousness, e.g. because the subject was distracted? Is pain representation of damage to the body?

Also are sensations located? Is a pain in the leg really in the leg even a 'phantom' pain felt when the leg has been amputated? And how do we know the location of a sensation, if it has one? Experiences seem to be called sensations primarily when either they have no external correlate, or they are of something rather general or obscure. Hearing a ringing in the ears is an auditory sensation. 'Seeing stars' and being dazzled, and perhaps being hallucinated, having after-images, and seeing a pure blue sky, are visual sensations, but we seldom talk of visual sensations of colour; cf. SEEING on the nature of colour. 'Sensation of' usually means 'consisting of' as in 'sensation of pain, giddiness, nausea', but it can mean 'apparently, or as if, caused by' as in 'sensation of hardness, falling', 'sensation of warmth' may be of the 'consisting of' kind as in fever or of the 'caused by' kind as when extending a hand to fire. 'Sensation' can apparently refer to a kind of experience like 'the sensation of falling' or to something datable such as 'the sensation I had just now', but phrases like 'I keep feeling that sensation' suggest that the 'datable' cases should really be analysed as 'kind' cases where 'had' means 'had an instance of'. This affects the question of whether several people can have the same sensation. (For a related important problem concerning sensations see PRIVATE LANGUAGE.)

Most sensations seem to be bodily, but some, like the sensation of being followed, are hard to classify. See also PERCEPTION, FEELINGS, SEEING.

D. W. Hamlyn, *The Theory of Knowledge*, Macmillan, 1970. (Chapter 6 has general discussion of sensation, sense data and perception.)

F. Jackson, 'The existence of mental objects,' in J. Dancy (ed.), *Perceptual Knowledge*, Oxford UP, 1988. (Defends it.)

C. Peacocke, *Sense and Content*, Oxford UP, 1993, chapter 1.

G. Ryle, 'Sensations,' in H. D. Lewis (ed.), *Contemporary British Philosophy*, 3rd series, 1956, reprinted in R. J. Swartz (ed.), *Perceiving, Sensing, and Knowing*, Doubleday, 1965. (One view of ambiguity of 'sensation' and role of sensations.)

*P. Smith and O. R. Jones, *The Philosophy of Mind: An Introduction*, Cambridge UP, 1986. (Chapters 14 and 15 defend functionalist account of pain.)

G. N. A. Vesey, 'Berkeley and sensations of heat', *Philosophical Review*, 1960. (Why we can call both objects and sensations hot.)

Sensationalism. Also called sensationism. A form of EMPIRICISM whereby all our knowledge rests ultimately on SENSATIONS or on SENSE DATA, which initially are given to us free from any element of interpretation or judgement.

P. Alexander, *Sensationalism and Scientific Explanation*, RKP, 1963.

Sense. See MEANING, REFERRING.

Sense data. Generally, entities which exist only when, and because, they are sensed. Many philosophers throughout history have thought that perception shares with memory, imagination, dreams, hallucinations, etc., a basis in 'pure experience' that is free from interpretation and error. This was usually treated as a special and infallible direct or immediate awareness, recently often called sensing, of things variously described as impressions, ideas, perceptions or sensations until Moore and Russell popularized the term 'sense data' (plural of 'sense datum', literally 'given to sense'). Sensa, plural of 'sensum', is also used (but see Price, p. 19). Usually it is held that sense data have all the properties they appear to have, and no others, and can only be sensed by one subject. Colour patches, sounds, smells, tastes, feelings of hardness or heat are typical examples. After-images, dream images, mental images, pains, kinaesthetic sensations, feelings of nausea, etc., are sometimes included, sometimes not.

In practice, however, it is hard to pick out and describe sense data, and to base our knowledge of physical objects on them (cf. PERCEPTION), and so conceptions of them vary. Often for sense data, as for Berkeley's ideas, to exist is to be sensed or perceived. But sometimes they are said to be public, and parts either of objects or of the surfaces of objects (Moore attacked Berkeley's 'To be is to be perceived'). They may then lack some properties they seem to have, or have others as well, discoverable on further inspection. Or they may be intrinsically vague in some respects. When one catches a quick glimpse of a speckled hen, does one's sense datum have a definite number of speckles? Those who try to connect sense data with physical objects sometimes suppose there could be merely possible sense data (sensibilia, plural of 'sensibile'), and that objects, even when not being perceived, consist of these. It is also hard to individuate sense data, i.e. say where one ends and the next begins, and hard to say if they can change. And are they substances, qualities, events, or what?

The act/object view of sensing so far discussed, where sensing is an act directed upon sense data as objects, is sometimes replaced by the allegedly less objectionable adverbial view, where 'I am sensing a red sense datum' is replaced by 'I am sensing redly'. Another view is that talk of sense data is a mere linguistic convenience, providing a noun for talking about appearances, so that on seeing a red dress in sodium light one says 'I sense a grey sense datum' instead of 'I seem to see something grey'. Recently sense data, after being unpopular for some time, have undergone a certain rehabilitation.

See also SENSATION, PHENOMENALISM, QUALIA.

J. L. Austin, *Sense and Sensibilia*, Oxford UP, 1962. (Attacks sense datum theory held by A. J. Ayer in his *Foundations of Empirical Knowledge*, Macmillan, 1940, who replies in 'Has Austin refuted the sense-datum theory?', *Synthèse*, 1967, reprinted in Ayer's *Metaphysics and Common Sense*, Macmillan, 1969, and (with discussions) in K. T. Fann (ed.), *Symposium on J. L. Austin*, 1969.)

A. J. Ayer, *The Central Questions of Philosophy*, Weidenfeld and Nicolson, 1973. (See pp. 70–2 for some terminological points.)

J. F. Bennett, *Locke, Berkeley, Hume: Central Themes*, Oxford UP, 1971. (II, 5, pp 31–35 'How not to reify sense-data'.)

T. Crane (ed.), *The Contents of Experience*, Cambridge UP, 1992. (Contains partial rehabilitation of sense data. See pp. 2–5 of its Introduction, and E. J. Lowe's paper 'Experience and its objects', pp. 86–7.)

R. Hall, 'The term "sense-datum"', *Mind*, 1964. (Origin of the term.)

R. J. Hirst, *Problems of Perception*, Allen and Unwin/Humanities Press, 1959. (First four chapters criticize arguments for sense data.)

G. E. Moore, 'The refutation of idealism', *Mind*, 1903. (Attacks Berkeley's 'To be is to be perceived'. For his own view of sense data cf. his 'A defence of common sense', in J. H. Muirhead (ed.), *Contemporary British Philosophy*, 2nd series, Allen and Unwin, 1925, reprinted in Moore's *Philosophical Papers*, Allen and Unwin, 1959, and discussed by Bouwsma in Warnock (below).)

*H. H. Price, *Perception*, Methuen, 1932, 1950, Greenwood Press, 1981. (Chapter 1 introduces and defends sense data, which form basis for rest of book.)

*B. Russell, *The Problems of Philosophy*, Home University Library, 1912.

T. L. S. Sprigge, *Facts, Words and Beliefs*, RKP, 1970, chapter 1. (Defends sense data. Cf. also F. Jackson, *Perception*, Cambridge UP, 1977, H. Robinson, *Perception*, Routledge, 1994. Jackson is criticized by C. L. Hardin, *Color for Philosophers*, Hackett, 1988, pp. 96–112.)

R. J. Swartz (ed.), *Perceiving, Sensing and Knowing*, Doubleday, 1965. (Part 2 contains relevant articles, including G. A. Paul, 'Is there a problem about sense data?', *Proceedings of the Aristotelian Society*, supplementary vol., 1936 (defending linguistic view), and Quinton (below).)

G. J. Warnock (ed.), *Philosophy of Perception*, Oxford UP, 1967. (Various relevant articles. See particularly those by O. K. Bouwsma, R. J. Hirst, R. Wollheim, A. M. Quinton.)

Senses. Normally the faculties of sight, hearing, touch, taste, smell. Occasionally the sense organs are called 'senses'. The kinaesthetic sense, sense of muscular movement, can be included, though not normally the sense of balance, nor the MORAL SENSE, nor things like a sense of rhythm, beauty, responsibility, etc.

Should the senses be distinguished and defined in terms of their objects, or of their organs, or of how they operate? How far do they parallel each other? E.g. do we hear and smell objects as directly as we apparently see them? How can they apparently trespass on each other's territory? How can ice which feels cold, look cold? (Cf. SEEING.)

Because of problems like 'trespassing', various philosophers since Aristotle have distinguished the senses' special or proper objects (or special or proper sensibles; but for 'sensibilia' see SENSE DATA) from others. Various views of these proper objects are possible. They may be (i) those primarily accessible only to one sense, such as tastes, sounds, etc.; or (ii) those a sense cannot be mistaken about; or (iii) those a sense must perceive if it perceives anything (perhaps we cannot see without seeing shapes, though shapes can also be felt); or (iv) those a sense perceives directly, without interpretation or inference. (i) is the commonest view. Those objects accessible to more than one sense, as shape is accessible to sight and touch, are then called common sensibles. Aristotle postulated a common sense (*sensus communis*) for them to be the proper objects of. The nature and roles of this 'common sense', which has no connection with shrewdness, etc., are disputed. It seems to have been a sort of unifying general sense which acted through all the sense organs. See QUALIA.

T. Crane (ed.), *The Contents of Experience*, Cambridge UP, 1992. (See particularly an article in it by M. G. F. Martin, 'Sight and touch'.)

H. P. Grice, 'Some remarks about the senses' in R. J. Butler (ed.), *Analytical Philosophy, First Series*, Oxford UP, 1962. (Intuitive distinctions between the various senses support the existence of qualia.)

D. W. Hamlyn, *Sensation and Perception*, RKP, 1961. (Proper objects, etc. See index under 'sense-objects'.)

B. J. O'Shaughnessy, 'The sense of touch', *Australasian Journal of Philosophy*, 1989. (Argues for primacy of touch among the senses.)

R. Sorabji, 'Aristotle on demarcating the five senses', *Philosophical Review*, 1971.

Sensibilia. See SENSE DATA.

Sensing. See SENSE DATA.

Sentences, propositions, statements. A sentence is a set of one or more words in a natural or artificial language, provided the set is constructed according to the grammatical rules and can be used by itself for asserting, asking, commanding, etc., so far as its structure goes, though it need not be meaningful: 'Saturday is in bed' is a sentence. Sentences may be individuated syntactically (so that 'I saw wood' is one sentence with two meanings, that I cut or sighted it) or semantically (so that 'I saw wood' becomes two sentences). One sentence, as syntactically defined, may play different roles: 'The company will parade at noon' may be a prediction or an order. In artificial languages of the kind used in formal logic, sentences (including open ones: see below) are often called well-formed formulae (see AXIOM), and the grammatical rules are called formation or syntactical rules. Such languages are normally designed to exclude as ungrammatical the meaningless, and also the paradoxical (e.g. 'This sentence is false': cf. LIAR PARADOX). An open sentence is a sentential FUNCTION. An eternal sentence (Quine) is one without tenses and other TOKEN-REFLEXIVES, and having its verbs in the 'timeless present' ('Chaucer comes before Shakespeare'), so that if anyone using it on a certain occasion speaks truly, anyone else using it on any other occasion will also speak truly. (Contrast 'The weather is hot', which may be true today and false tomorrow.) Philosophers have in fact been mainly concerned with indicative or declarative sentences, i.e. those fitted for making assertions.

In natural languages, sentences have usually been defined and distinguished in ways allowing them to suffer from various kinds of ambiguity and meaninglessness. Propositions have therefore been introduced. They have provided something common to sentences, in the same or different languages, which mean the same ('I am hot' and 'J'ai chaud'), or to utterances which do not mean the same, but say the same thing ('I am hot' said by me and 'You are hot' said to me by you), or to an assertion and the corresponding question or command, etc. ('The door is shut'/'Is the door shut?'/'Shut the door!') In this last use propositions resemble PHRASTICS, but are expressed in the indicative, and so, unlike phrastics, can represent what is assertable but unasserted ('Snow is white' can be asserted, but is unasserted in 'If snow is white ... '). Whether propositions can similarly represent unasked questions, uncommanded commands, etc., is another question. Propositions have also served as what can be true or false, and what logical relations like entailment relate. Finally they have served as what is believed, wished, judged, etc. (Believing and wishing, etc., are propositional attitudes. Things like judging, which occur at a definite time, are propositional acts. All these verbs are propositional verbs.)

A big difficulty with propositions is how they are to be individuated, i.e. when do we have one and when another? This difficulty can be avoided, or at least mitigated, if we take a proposition to be a sentence in one of its meanings, assuming it is clear when a sentence has one meaning and when another. This is how propositions were usually treated before the problems they were later supposed to solve became urgent. It makes them less useful for explaining things like translation and wordless thoughts where either more than one sentence, or no sentence, seems to be involved. Another difficulty concerns how many roles propositions can play at once. To take the above examples, can they provide both something common for 'I am hot' and 'J'ai chaud', and something common for 'I am hot' and 'You are hot', when the latter is said to me by you?

Various views have been held about the nature of propositions. Ayer has treated them as LOGICAL CONSTRUCTIONS out of synonymous sentences. For Russell, at one time, the constituents of a proposition were the actual objects it was about, which anyone believing the proposition must be acquainted with; propositions apparently about nonexistent things, or things the believer could not be acquainted with, were really about something else (e.g. sense data or universals). Frege introduced his notion of 'sense' to account for how propositions mentioning the same object twice could be informative (see MEANING), and held that the constituents of a proposition (or thought – 'Gedanke' as he called it) were the senses of the terms in it. More recently too propositions have been often regarded as structured entities whose constituents are either the objects and properties they are about or modes of presentation of these. Sometimes propositions are called coarse-grained if they are interpreted in a *de re* or transparent way (see MODALITIES, INTENSIONALITY), so that if terms in them are replaced by other terms referring to or describing the same things, or true of the same things, we still have the same proposition. If they are interpreted in a *de dicto* or opaque way, so that such substitutions cannot be made without getting a different proposition, they are fine-grained. Propositions are also sometimes equated with sets of POSSIBLE WORLDS, namely those in which they are true, so that those propositions which are true in exactly the same possible worlds are the same proposition, and so too are propositions which entail (see IMPLICATION) one another.

Propositions are standardly represented by 'that'-clauses ('That all cats are black'), and are often treated as the CONTENT of propositional attitudes (see BELIEF). But 'that'-clauses themselves raise problems about their interpretation (Davidson).

Some of these difficulties have led to the introduction of statements either instead of or in addition to propositions. Statements which are usually thought to be what is true or false, are either datable statings which are fairly easy to individuate ('His statement was made before lunch'), or they are the content of such statings, or what is stated ('That statement has been often made'). The flavour of the 'datable statings' view shows itself in the feeling that something assertable but unasserted (cf. 'Snow is white' above) is better called a proposition than a statement, and in the fact that statements, rather than propositions, are contrasted with questions, commands, etc. One way of accepting both statements and propositions is to treat statements as what is common to 'I am hot' and 'You are hot', said of the same person, and propositions as what is common to 'I am hot' and 'J'ai chaud', or 'I am hot' said by different people (Lemmon).

Individual uses of 'proposition' and 'statement' are legion (for a further use of 'statement' see Ayer), but it is largely in connection with natural languages that they need to be distinguished from each other and from 'sentence'. This is because of TOKEN-REFLEXIVES, whereby a sentence may not only be ambiguous, but may be true or false, or neither, according to who utters it when. Therefore the distinctions are not needed in formal systems (see AXIOM), nor in discussing ordinary language so far as we can assimilate this to formal systems by translation, or ignore the differences. For many purposes the three terms, and especially 'proposition' and 'statement', are used interchangeably (as often in this dictionary).

Singular statements or propositions predicate something of a single subject as in 'Socrates is wise', 'Socrates is not wiser than Plato', and are contrasted with general ones, which may be universal: 'All cats are black' ('All John's cats … ' is universal for most but not all purposes), or particular: 'Some cats are black', 'There exist black cats' (cf. QUANTIFIER WORDS). A multiply general statement contains each of the two main quantifiers (see QUANTIFICATION) or their defined equivalents ('Every person has some faults'). 'General' is sometimes used for 'universal'. For atomic and molecular see LOGICAL ATOMISM. See also JUDGEMENT, FACTS, SPEECH ACTS.

A. J. Ayer, *Language, Truth and Logic*, Gollancz, 1936. (See index to 1946 edition.)

R. Carnap, *Introduction to Semantics*, Harvard UP, 1942, § 37. (Ambiguity in 'proposition'.)

A. Church, 'On Carnap's analysis of statements of assertion and belief', *Analysis*, vol. 10, 1950, reprinted with Carnap's reply, 'On belief sentences', in M. Macdonald (ed.), *Philosophy and Analysis*, Blackwell, 1954. (Pro substantial propositions.) D. Davidson, 'On saying that', *Synthèse*, vol. 19, 1968–9, reprinted in D. Davidson and J. Hintikka (eds), *Words and Objections*, Reidel, 1969 (with Quine's comment at pp. 333–5), and in Davidson's *Inquiries into Truth and Interpretation*, Clarendon, 1984.

G. Frege, 'The thought: a logical inquiry', *Mind*, 1956 (German original, 1918–19), reprinted in Salmon and Soames.

P. Horwich, *Truth*, Blackwell, 1990. (See pp. 94–6 for brief exposition of Frege and Russell on propositions, in context of treating them as the CONTENT of BELIEF, to which the believer is related.)

E. J. Lemmon, 'Sentences, statements and propositions', in B. A. O. Williams and A. Montefiore (eds), *British Analytical Philosophy*, RKP, 1966. (Criticized by R. T. Garner, 'Lemmon on sentences, statements and propositions', *Analysis*, vol. 30, 1970.)

R. B. Marcus, 'Rationality and believing the impossible', *Journal of Philosophy*, 1983. (Includes discussions, with references, of various views of propositions.)

G. E. Moore, *Some Main Problems of Philosophy*, Allen and Unwin, 1953, Collier Books, 1962, written much earlier. (Contains important discussions of propositions. See pp. 262–6 for a difficulty over false propositions.)

W. V. O. Quine, *Word and Object*, Wiley, 1960. (See p. 35–6 for accounts of occasion and standing sentences.)

B. Russell, *Logic and Knowledge*, Allen and Unwin, 1956. ('The philosophy of logical atomism' and 'On propositions' in this volume discuss propositions, the latter giving his later view. See pp. 222–4 for difficulty over false propositions.)

G. Ryle, 'Are there propositions?', *Proceedings of the Aristotelian Society*, 1929–30. (Pros and cons of substantial propositions.)

N. Salmon and S. Soames (eds), *Propositions and Attitudes*, Oxford UP, 1988. (Important collection with accessible introduction.)

R. C. Stalnaker (see bibliography to POSSIBLE WORLDS).

A. Stroll, 'Statements' in A. Stroll (ed.), *Epistemology*, Harper and Row, 1967.

Serial relation. Relation which is CONNECTED, TRANSITIVE and asymmetric (see SYMMETRIC), thus uniting a series. 'Less than' is a serial relation which unites the natural numbers into a single series.

Set. See CLASS.

Set theory. See CALCULUS.

Sextus Empiricus. Wrote c.200 AD in unknown location. Generally considered the main representative of ancient SCEPTICISM, of an agnostic rather than dogmatic kind (i.e. he rejected the view that knowledge was demonstrably impossible, and insisted on keeping an open mind on this as on other questions). He was influenced by the earlier sceptic Pyrrho of Elis (wrote c.300 BC) and used logical modes of argument ('tropes') deriving from Aenesidemus of Knossos (1st century BC). He is also a major source for our knowledge of STOIC logic (which he opposed). His main works are *Outlines of Pyrrhonism* and *Against the Learned* (with variously titled subdivisions).

Shaftesbury, Third Earl of. 1671–1713. Also called Anthony Ashley Cooper, he was born in London, lived mostly in England, and died at Naples. His early education was entrusted to LOCKE. He was an early representative of the MORAL SENSE school, believing in a 'natural sense of right and wrong'. He emphasized the existence of altruistic sentiments, and gave a utilitarian basis for morality, which could be reinforced by religion but was not dependent upon it. *An Inquiry concerning Virtue or Merit*, 1699. *Characteristics of Men, Manners, Opinions, Times*, 1711 (collected treatises, including the *Inquiry*). See also HUTCHESON.

Sidgwick, Henry. 1838–1900. Born in Yorkshire, he worked in Cambridge, and is best known as a leading UTILITARIAN. He claimed that a kind of HEDONISTIC utilitarianism underlies common sense morality. He also wrote on economics, the nature of philosophy, and the philosophy of Kant, and was interested in psychical research (cf. BROAD, H. H. PRICE). *The Methods of Ethics*, 1874 (7th edition and final version, 1907). *The Principles of Political Economy*, 1883. *The Elements of Politics*, 1891. See also INTUITION.

Sign and symbol. Some distinguish these, saying that signs operate through a natural or causal connection as in 'Clouds are a sign of rain', while symbols are conventional as in 'A broken line is a symbol for a footpath'. The convention need not be explicit. Symbols may be chosen, or arise, because of their causal associations: a scarifying bang may be used as a danger-warning. Symbols relying on resemblance are sometimes called icons. But 'sign' is often used in a wide sense to include symbols.

H. H. Price, *Thinking and Experience*, Hutchinson, 1953, particularly chapter 6.

Singer, Peter. 1946–. Australian moral philosopher, educated at the Universities of Melbourne and Oxford. Spent much of his career at the University of Melbourne, but since 1999 has been at Princeton. Singer applies utilitarian principles to the field of applied ethics, for example, to the issues of our treatment of animals, of world poverty, of abortion, euthanasia and infanticide. 'Famine, affluence, and

morality', *Philosophy and Public Affairs*, 1972. *Animal Liberation*, 1975. *Practical Ethics*, 1979. *Rethinking Life and Death: The Collapse of Our Traditional Ethics*, 1994. *Unsanctifying Human Life: Essays on Ethics*, 2001. *One World: The Ethics of Globalization*, 2002. *The Life You Can Save: Acting Now to End World Poverty*, 2009.
See PRACTICAL ETHICS.

Sinn. See MEANING.

Slingshot. See FREGE ARGUMENT.

Slippery slope. A form of argument in which a position is criticized because it is alleged that accepting it would make it more likely (or even inevitable) that a more extreme view would be adopted. This may, indeed, sometimes be the case, and the argument good, for example, where some clear principle has been breached, for example, that torture is never justified. But the argument can be misused where there is, in fact, no such likelihood or inevitability. Similar to saying that accepting the initial position is just 'the thin end of the wedge'.

Smith, Adam. 1723–90. Moral philosopher and economist, who was born at Kirkcaldy and worked mainly in Scotland, including Glasgow University. Though primarily known for his economic theory based on an individualistic system of free enterprise, he also developed a system of moral philosophy in his first book. This system was primarily founded on that sympathy which, he said, we feel for the motives of moral agents and for the gratitude or resentment of those affected by the actions of such agents. He also criticized the 'moral sense' theory of his teacher HUTCHESON. There is some dispute about how far a single view of human nature underlies Smith's two main books. *The Theory of Moral Sentiments*, 1759. *An Inquiry into the Nature and Causes of the Wealth of Nations*, 1776.

J. R. Weinstein, *On Adam Smith*, Wadsworth, 2000. (Introductory.)

Social contract. See POLITICAL PHILOSOPHY.

Social philosophy. The study of philosophical problems arising from economics, anthropology, sociology and social psychology. It borders on philosophy of mind since it studies concepts involved in action like motive, intention, freewill, responsibility. However, it emphasizes the agent's role as a member of a group, and the group as itself an agent. Hence it considers ethical problems like that of collective responsibility, and metaphysical and methodological problems concerning the nature of groups and features of their behaviour. How far can group behaviour be caused or predicted, or described in terms of general laws? How far can it be reduced to the play of economic forces, and what kinds of EXPLANATION can be given of it? How does a social scientist form the concepts he uses? What counts as a society or social behaviour, and how are these related to individuals and individual behaviour? How far can one be objective in collecting and assessing evidence in the social sciences, and in general how far can or should these sciences resemble the natural sciences?

The 'rational man' is often used as a model in economics. This leads to problems about his behaviour, especially in competitive situations (game theory, DECISION THEORY). The notions of preference and voting behaviour can be studied by means of logical systems which formalize these notions. Such systems show how various electoral procedures work and study problems like the VOTING PARADOX and variants of it.

Social philosophy shares with ethics and political philosophy problems about things like the rights of a group acting in self-defence against members or outsiders, what constitutes the interests of a group as such, how these interests relate to members' and outsiders' interests, how it is legitimate to achieve them, and how decisions are to be taken.

The methodological, as against ethical, political and psychological, parts of the subject are often called the philosophy of the social sciences. See also HISTORY.

M. Brodbeck (ed.), *Readings in the Philosophy of the Social Sciences*, Macmillan and Collier-Macmillan, 1968.

J. Feinberg, *Social Philosophy*, Prentice-Hall, 1973. (Mainly on freedom, rights, justice.)

D.-H. Ruben, *The Metaphysics of the Social World*, RKP, 1985. (Criticizes versions of individualism in social philosophy.)

R. S. Rudner, *Philosophy of Social Science*, Prentice-Hall, 1966. (Emphasizes classificatory questions, objectivity, functionalism.)

A. Ryan, *The Philosophy of the Social Sciences*, Macmillan, 1970. (Emphasizes connections with general methodology.)

B. Turner (ed.), *The New Blackwell Companion to Social Theory*, Blackwell, 2008. (Collection of articles: see Part 1, Section 3, 'Philosophy of the Social Sciences.)

Socrates. c. 469–399 BC. Mentor of PLATO and of several so-called 'Socratic schools' (Megarians, Cynics, Cyrenaics). Probably scarcely left Athens except on military service. Executed for 'corrupting the youth and introducing strange gods'. He apparently wrote nothing, and is known to us mainly through Plato and Xenophon (and a caricature in Aristophanes' contemporary comedy, *The Clouds*). ARISTOTLE, who never met him, regards him as mainly interested in ethics, but as laying the basis for Plato's theory of 'Forms'. See DIALECTIC, INCONTINENCE, SOPHISTS.

H. H. Benson (ed.), *Essays on the Philosophy of Socrates*, Oxford UP, 1992. (Collection of recent essays, with excellent bibliographies.)

T. C. Brickhouse and N. D. Smith, *Plato's Socrates*, Oxford UP, 1995 and *The Philosophy of Socrates*, Westview, 2000. (Clear introductions.)

W. Prior (ed.), *Socrates: Critical Assessments*, Routledge, 1996 (4-volume collection of the best work on Socrates since the 1940s.)

C. C. W. Taylor, *Socrates: A Very Short Introduction*, Oxford UP, 2000. (What it says.)

G. Vlastos, *Socrates: Ironist and Moral Philosopher*, Cornell UP, 1991, and *Socratic Studies*, Cambridge UP, 1994. (Seminal books by the most influential writer on Greek philosophy.)

Socratic paradox. See INCONTINENCE.

Solipsism. See SCEPTICISM.

Sophists. A movement of itinerant professional lecturers on many topics, including philosophical ones, who flourished in Greece, mainly in the last half of the fifth century BC. They differed widely in outlook, though many shared a tendency to scepticism. They emphasized the study of human affairs rather than natural science or abstract metaphysics, and they were responsible for many initiatives in ethics and political philosophy, and also philosophy of language, philosophy of mind and epistemology. They were accused, especially by PLATO, of logic-chopping and subversiveness, but also of pandering to popular tastes. Leading sophists, all active in this period, include Protagoras of Abdera, Gorgias of Leontini, Prodicus of Ceos, Hippias of Elis, Antiphon of Athens. After the fifth century the movement continued but declined in quality.

J. De Romilly, *The Great Sophists of Periclean Athens*, Clarendon, 1992, French original, 1988. (Balanced discussion from point of view of history of ideas rather than philosophy and emphasizing both destructive and reconstructive sides of sophists.)

W. K. C. Guthrie, *A History of Greek Philosophy*, Cambridge UP, Vol. 3, 1969. (Covers Sophists and Socrates in two sections, which are also published separately.)

G. B. Kerferd, *The Sophistic Movement*, Cambridge UP, 1981.

Sorites. See HEAP.

Sortal. A UNIVERSAL which provides a principle for distinguishing, counting and reidentifying particulars (see UNIVERSALS), i.e. for saying of what sort they are. If a sortal applies to an object at any time, then it applies to that object throughout its existence. Cat is a sortal. Thing, red thing, snow, are not sortals (but patch of snow perhaps is: Strawson, p. 202). Cf. COUNT NOUN.

P. F. Strawson, *Individuals*, Methuen, 1959. (See 'universals' in index. Cf. also M. Dummett, *Frege: Philosophy of Language*, Duckworth, 1973, p. 76. For potentially wider usage cf. J. Locke, *An Essay concerning Human Understanding*, 1690, 3.3.15. See also N. Griffin, *Relative Identity*, Oxford UP, 1977, chapter 3.)

Sosein. See BEING.

Sound. See VALID.

Space and time. Some problems concern space or time individually, while others concern both. These latter have become more prominent recently.

How are space and matter related? Parmenides (see ELEATECS) thought that to say empty space exists would be to say that what is not exists. Aristotle and Descartes too, among others, rejected it. Modern physics blurs the issue by allowing matter and energy to be intertransformed in certain circumstances, and emphasizing fields of force. General relativity theory treats gravity as a property of space rather than of matter, and quantum mechanics complicates the distinction between space and matter.

Until about two centuries ago Euclidean geometry was thought to be unique, and so the geometry of space. It relied on the axiom of parallels, that through a given point not on a given straight line exactly one straight line could be drawn parallel to the given one. But then it was realized that not only was this independent of the other axioms, but consistent systems could be developed if it were replaced by an axiom saying either that more than one such line, or that none, could be drawn. These replacements yield geometries often called hyperbolic or Lobachevskian (N. I. Lobachevsky, 1793–1856) and elliptic or Riemannian (G. E B. Riemann, 1826–66), respectively. In these systems space is regarded as curved, negatively in Lobachevskian and positively in Riemannian geometry, because it has in three dimensions properties analogous to those of the surfaces of a saddle-back and sphere, respectively, in two dimensions. It now becomes an open question of what kind of geometry applies to real space, and geometries can be developed for imaginary spaces, which need not be limited to three dimensions. Real space evidently has three, but is this logically necessary (cf. MODALITIES, ANALYTIC)? And what makes a dimension specifically spatial as against merely a parameter or independent variable for some measuring system? Spaces studied by mathematics are metrical if they allow of measurement and topological if they do not. Some transformations of spatial things affect shape and size, and so disturb measurements, but leave relations of betweenness undisturbed: if b was between a and c before the transformation, it remains so afterwards. Topology studies these transformations. The topological transformations of a rubber ball, for example, are those possible with stretching and squeezing but without tearing.

Logical space is a term used by Wittgenstein in his difficult discussion of logical possibility. A place in logical space is given by the sense of an atomic sentence (see LOGICAL ATOMISM), which then describes that place. A rough example: the question whether my cat is black constitutes a place in logical space. When I say that it is black, I describe that place as being of a certain sort. The logical relations between propositions and between the terms in them can then be treated as having some analogy with spatial relations. Later this 'mapping' of relations between concepts was often called logical geography. This use of 'space' is metaphorical but it suggests the question what makes the analogy an apt one (cf. the above question about dimensions).

The notion of empty space suggests that of time without change. This, however, has been more generally rejected (but see Shoemaker), presumably because there seems to be no analogue here of the effects of perspective. Would the progressive fading of memory serve as an analogue? But this is unreliable and seems to depend in fact, though not in principle, on changes.

Time, more than space, seemed not to be real or measurable because most, if not all of it so far as it consists of periods rather than moments, seems not to exist at any given moment, and what fails to exist now has seemed less real than what merely fails to exist here. Augustine, following Aristotle and Sextus Empiricus (in what is sometimes known as his 'whittling argument'), argued that since there is no indivisible unit of time, and the present is at the meeting point of past and future, so there is no present time. If past times no longer exist, future times have yet to exist, and the present time does not exist, then time does not exist.

Another famous attack on the reality of time was made by McTaggart, who distinguished two series of temporal positions. The A series contains notions like past, present, future, which apply to different events at different times. The B series contains notions like earlier than, simultaneous with, after, which permanently link whatever events they do link. He then argues that the B series by itself, without the A series, cannot account for change, and so for time, while the A series involves either a contradiction or a vicious regress. Some try to make the B series basic by defining 'present' as 'simultaneous with this utterance' (cf. discussion by Broad in Smart, pp. 334–8).

It is hard to describe the 'passing of time', for whether time itself flows or we move in time, how fast do these things happen? They seem to need second-order time to occur in (Dunne), but this makes doubtful sense, and only leads to a regress. A further problem arises over our consciousness of change, if we can only experience the present and this is strictly momentary (cf. Augustine's problem about measuring time when only one instant of it is there to measure). To deal with this, the specious present was used by various psychologists who claimed empirical evidence for it, and philosophers. 'Specious' suggests it only appeared to be present. It was usually claimed that the specious present was some short period ending at the present and forming the object of an act of awareness occurring at the present instant. The awareness itself was momentary, but it was awareness of a period of time. The stream of experience was then founded, in complex and controversial ways, on such acts. It has been argued, however, that the whole idea of analysing experience into successive units is mistaken; perhaps the momentary present is only a myth. There still remains the general question of how we acquire our ideas of time and space – e.g. are memory and perception involved? Bergson distinguishes time as viewed by science, which is 'spatialized' into a series of moments, like cinema frames albeit mathematically dense, from 'duration' as experienced by consciousness, which cannot be so split up.

Time, unlike space, has only one dimension (but see MacBeath), and an apparently irreversible direction. This topic is controversial, but on one view this irreversibility is connected with the second law of thermodynamics, which says that entropy, or lack of organization, tends towards a maximum in isolated systems. For time to be reversed would thus be for this law to be broken. This law can be analysed as an effect of the statistical probabilities governing matter in motion: of all the possible configurations of a set of particles that can follow after a given state the vast majority correspond to a higher degree of disorder than exists in that state. Therefore it seems that the irreversibility of time is guaranteed by, and is simply a reflection of, a mathematical law of probability. But a difficulty arises because this law is symmetrical with respect to time: the above statement of it will hold equally if we replace 'follow after' by 'precede'. Another view analyses the direction of time in terms of that of causation.

Einstein's special theory of relativity treats space and time together as space–time. The main point of this is that in certain cases whether one event precedes another depends on the observer's motion relative to the two events, and motion involves both space and time.

A different and historically earlier, though not completely separate, issue is whether space and time are absolute or relational ('relative' is also used, but often kept for the Einstein view). Are space and time independent of the objects in them, as the absolute view says, or are they merely sets of relations between objects, so that it does not make sense to talk of absolute directions or absolute motion? The questions mentioned above about empty space, and time without change, are relevant again here. The question about motion has largely centred round rotation and centrifugal force, i.e. the relations between force and acceleration.

Also, are space and time parallel, in the sense that all, or nearly all, that can be said of the one can be said of the other, e.g. can a thing move around in time as it can in space? This raises questions about the relations between objects and events.

A question that has had some discussion recently is whether space and time are necessarily unique. Could there be a set of objects spatially and temporally related to each other but not to us? (For a different use of the same idea cf. D. K. Lewis's treatment of POSSIBLE WORLDS.) And could there be duplicate universes in space or time? If we went off in a rocket, travelling in what by all available tests was a straight line, and eventually reached what appeared to be a second earth, could we decide whether it really was another one or whether we had somehow come back to this earth? Similarly, could there be a 'mirror universe', i.e. could the universe contain a point or axis of symmetry (cf. INCONGRUENT)? The 'duplicate universe' question was asked earlier about time than about space (cf. METAPHYSICS for the doctrine of eternal recurrence, and in general cf. LEIBNIZ'S LAW). Finally could time be closed or circular? And could it have a beginning or an end?

On the infinite divisibility of space and time see ZENO'S PARADOXES.

H. G. Alexander (ed.), *The Leibniz–Clarke Correspondence*, Manchester UP, 1956. (Clarke defended Newton's absolute view in a series of letters to Leibniz, who defended the relational view. Alexander's introduction discusses later writers too.)

Aristotle, *Physics*, iv. (Place, void and time.)

H. L. Bergson, *Time and Free Will*, Allen and Unwin, 1910 (French original, 1889), chapter 2. (Duration. His later works ascribe it to the world itself as well as to consciousness.)

B. Dainton, *Time and Space*, Acumen, 2001. (Clear and comprehensive introduction.)

J. W. Dunne, *An Experiment with Time*, 1927, 3rd (revised) edn, Faber, 1934, revised edn, Macmillan, 1981.

R. Flood and M. Lockwood (eds), *The Nature of Time*, Blackwell, 1986. (Series of lectures, taking account of modern physics.)

Paul Horwich, *Asymmetries in Time*, MIT Press, 1987. (Offers a unified treatment of various areas where asymmetries of time arise.)

*R. Le Poidevin and M. MacBeath (eds), *The Philosophy of Time*, Oxford UP, 1993. (Mainly reprinted essays, including McTaggart, Quinton and Shoemaker. Has annotated bibliography.)

M. MacBeath, 'Time's square' in Le Poidevin and MacBeath. (Could time have more than one dimension?)

D. H. Mellor, *Real Time*, Cambridge UP, 1981. (Defends McTaggart's attack on A series, and rejects tensed facts, but keeps B series.) *Real Time II*, Routledge, 1998.

*W. Newton Smith, *The Structure of Time*, RKP, 1980. (General introduction.)

G. Plumer, 'The myth of the specious present', *Mind*, 1985. (Discussion, with references. Cf. also R. M. Gale, 'Has the present any duration?', *Nous*, 1971.)

A. Quinton, 'Spaces and times', *Philosophy*, 1962, reprinted in Le Poidevin and MacBeath. (Are space and time unique? Cf. also K. Ward, 'The unity of space and time', M. Hollis, 'Box and Cox', *Philosophy*, 1967.)

C. Ray, *Time, Space and Philosophy*, Routledge, 1991. (Introduction to various problems arising from modern science.)

H. Reichenbach, *The Philosophy of Space and Time*, Dover, 1958, and *The Direction of Time*, University of California Press, 1991.

E. Reif, *Statistical Physics*, McGraw Hill, 1965 (vol. 5 of Berkeley Physics course), chapter 1. (Elementary account of the view that irreversibility of time is related to statistical physics.)

W. C. Salmon, *Space, Time and Motion: A Philosophical Introduction*, Minnesota UP, 2nd edn, 1980. (Moderately elementary introduction to issues from modern physics.)

L. Sklar, *Space, Time and Spacetime*, California UP, 1974. (Extended introduction to effects of modern science on philosophy of space and time. Requires some fairly elementary mathematics.)

J. C. C. Smart (ed.), *Problems of Space and Time*, Macmillan, 1964, R. Gale (ed.), *The Philosophy of Time*, Macmillan, 1968. (These two volumes contain, with some overlap, many relevant discussions, with editorial introductions. Several of the authors mentioned above are included, including McTaggart in Gale.)

R. K. Sorabji, *Matter, Space, and Motion*, Duckworth, 1988, chapter 10. (Could time be circular?)

R. Swinburne (ed.), *Space, Time and Causality*, Reidel, 1983. (Discussions, often technical, of absolute versus relative, time and causation, quantum mechanics, the Einstein–Podolski–Rosen paradox.)

R. Taylor, 'Spatial and temporal analogies and the concept of identity', *Journal of Philosophy*, 1955, reprinted in Smart. (Defends parallelism of space and time. Cf. also J. M. Shorter, 'Space and time', *Mind*, 1981. On objects and events see F. I. Dretske, 'Can events move?', *Mind*, 1967, A. Quinton, 'Objects and events', *Mind*, 1979, P. M. S. Hacker, 'Events and objects in space and time', *Mind*, 1982.)

P. Turetzky, *Time*, Routledge, 1998. (History of philosophy of time.)

B. Van Fraassen, *An Introduction to the Philosophy of Space and Time*, Random House, 1970

L. Wittgenstein, *Tractatus*, 1921, trans. D. F. Pears and B. F. McGuinness, RKP, 1961. (Logical space. Very difficult.)

Specious present. See SPACE.

Speech acts. When we speak there are many things we may be doing. We are normally saying something meaningful. We may be stating, ordering, promising, etc. And we may hope to achieve certain ends such as frightening someone. The systematic study of what we do in or by speaking dates mainly from J. L. AUSTIN, who distinguished three main levels of what he called 'speech acts': locutionary acts, or locutions, are acts of uttering meaningful sentence; illocutionary acts, or illocutions, are what we do in saying things, e.g. stating, promising; perlocutionary acts, or perlocutions, are what we do by saying things, e.g. persuading, frightening. (The words 'in' and 'by' are only rough guides: Austin, chapter 10.) Austin thinks illocutions rely on conventions and can usually be made explicit with 'hereby': 'I hereby warn (order) you … ' Perlocutions depend on natural or causal processes. etc.', we cannot say, 'I hereby persuade you.'

These distinctions grew out of the breakdown, or apparent breakdown, of an earlier distinction between constatives, or utterances which state something, and so can be true or false, and performatives, or utterances which do something other than stating. To say 'I promise' is to promise, not to say that one is promising.

The related notions of performatives and illocutions have been used to try and explain the meaning of certain terms like GOOD, TRUE, PROBABLE, by reference to the 'force' of utterances containing them, i.e. what these utterances normally achieve (cf. NATURALISM). To explain a term's meaning in this way is to offer a speech act analysis of its meaning.

Of Austin's three main terms 'illocution' is the most important, but whether meaning can ever be explained in terms of illocutionary force is disputed. Whether illocutionary force is something distinct from meaning, and whether there are locutions, as distinct from illocutions, have also been disputed. Other problems concern how successful a speech act must be to count as a speech act, and what the speaker must intend. Must the hearer hear and understand the speaker? Must the speaker intend the hearer to believe or understand something, and if so, what (cf. REFERRING)? The use of 'act' in this way has been objected to as a term of art which here rests on confusion (Cerf, § iv, in Fann).

J. L. Austin, *How to Do Things with Words*, Oxford UP, 1962.

K. T. Fann (ed.), *Symposium on J. L. Austin*, 1969, part 4. (Six relevant discussions.)

H. Fingarette, 'Performatives', *American Philosophical Quarterly*, 1967, J. D. B. Walker, 'Statements and performatives', *American Philosophical Quarterly*, 1969. (Both these defend Austin's earlier constative/performative distinction.)

J. R. Searle (see bibliography to GOOD. Cf. also his 'Austin on locutionary and illocutionary acts', *Philosophical Review*, 1968, criticizing notion of locution.)

J. R. Searle (ed.), *The Philosophy of Language*, Oxford UP, 1971. (First four items are relevant).

Spinoza, Baruch (Benedict). 1632–77. Jewish philosopher who was born and lived in Holland, working as a lens-grinder. He is usually counted among the Continental RATIONALISTS, and his main work is his *Ethics*. In this he sets out to give a systematic exposition of philosophy in general on the model of Euclid, culminating in ethics. The result concerns metaphysics at least as much, and shows much Cartesian influence, though he replaces DESCARTES' body/mind dualism by a monism in which there is but a single SUBSTANCE, known as 'God or nature'. He was also a rigid determinist. *Tractatus Theologico-Politicus*, 1670. *Ethics*, 1677. *Treatise on the Improvement of the Understanding*, 1677. See also DOUBLE ASPECT, IDENTITY THEORY.

E. M. Curley (ed. and trans.), *The Collected Works of Spinoza*, vol. 1, Princeton UP, 1985. (Includes *Ethics*, etc. For political work see R. H. M. Elwes (ed. and trans.), *The Chief Works of Benedict de Spinoza*, vol. 1, Dover, 1951, vol. 1.)

J. F. Bennett, *A Study of Spinoza's Ethics*, Hackett, 1984.

J. F. Bennett, *Learning from Six Philosophers: Descartes, Spinoza, Leibniz, Locke, Berkeley, Hume*, Oxford UP, 2001.

Square of opposition. See QUANTIFIER WORDS.

Stadium. See ZENO'S PARADOXES.

Stand for. See REFERRING.

State-description. See CONFIRMATION.

Statements. See SENTENCES.

Stochastic. Concerning or involving conjecture or randomness. A stochastic process is one in which the outcome is unpredictable, or is not determined, even though some outcomes may be more probable than others. This may be because not all the causes of the outcome are known. Predicting the weather and predicting human behaviour are examples of stochastic processes. See INDUCTION and PROBABILITY.

Stoics. Movement founded by Zeno of Citium (c.336–c.264 BC; different from Zeno the ELEATIC), and named from the porch ('stoa') in Athens where he taught. Stoics treated knowledge under three heads: logic, physics, ethics. They developed propositional LOGIC and the theory of IMPLICATION, and tried to discover a sure mark ('CRITERION') of truth. They developed a thoroughgoing materialism, treating matter as a continuum (as opposed to Epicurean atomism), but added a rather nonmaterial flavour with their pantheism and notions such as the 'tension' ('tonos') that matter was subject to. In ethics (to which the later Stoics largely confined themselves) they held determinist views and advocated acceptance of fate, based on self-sufficiency and a realization that 'virtue' was the only ultimate value. Leading Stoics include also Chrysippus (c.280–c.206 BC), Posidonius (c.135–c.51 BC), Seneca (c.4 BC–AD 65), Epictetus (c.AD50–c.138), Marcus Aurelius (AD121–80). Cicero (106–43 BC), though not a Stoic himself, is an important source for their views.

See also CATEGORIES, DIALECTIC, EPICUREANS, IDEA, METAPHYSICS, NIETZSCHE, PHILOSOPHY, SEXTUS.

A. A. Long, *Hellenistic Philosophy*, Duckworth, 1974.

A. A. Long and D. N. Sedley, *The Hellenistic Philosophers*, Cambridge UP, 1987. (Vol. 1 contains translated texts and vol. 2 Greek and Latin texts with commentary.)

Strawson, Peter F. 1919–2006. British philosopher born in London and worked in Oxford, who was a leading member of the later phase of 'linguistic philosophy'. He both earned the strictures of RUSSELL for his attention to 'ordinary language' in criticizing Russell's theory of DESCRIPTIONS, and cautiously led linguistic philosophy back to METAPHYSICS along lines laid down by KANT. He also made notable contributions to the theory of truth and to the mind/body problem (cf. MIND, NO-OWNERSHIP, PERSON). 'On referring', *Mind*, 1950 (criticizes Russell). *Individuals*, 1959 (return to metaphysics). *The Bounds of Sense*, 1966 (commentary on Kant). *Subject and Predicate in Logic and Grammar*, 1974. *Skepticism and Naturalism: Some Varieties*, 1985. *Analysis and Metaphysics: An Introduction to Philosophy*, 1992. *Entity and Identity*, 1997. See also CATEGORIES, CONDITIONALS, CONJUNCTION, FACTS, FEATURE-PLACING, FORM, IMPLICATION, INDIVIDUALS, LANGUAGE (PHILOSOPHY OF), LEIBNIZ'S LAW, LOGIC, QUANTIFIER, REFERRING, SEEING, SORTAL.

Structure (deep and surface). The surface structures of a phrase or sentence, studied by surface grammar, are its grammatical analysis or analyses as it stands. Its deep structures, studied by depth grammar, are the abstract structures underlying given interpretations of it and determining them, e.g. 'Pretty little girls' camp' has two surface structures (according to whether 'pretty' is adjective or adverb (cf.

'fairly')) but five possible deep structures: it has five interpretations, two with 'pretty' as adverb and three with it as adjective (see AMBIGUITY). See also GRAMMARS.

N. Chomsky, *Cartesian Linguistics: A Chapter in the History of Rationalist Thought*, Harper and Row, 1966, pp. 31 ff. (See n. 80 for deep structure and logical FORM. Later, however, he revised his views in *Reflections on Language*, Fontana, 1976, pp. 81–4, where he abandons the term 'deep structure', as unduly conflating syntactic and semantic considerations; cf. also pp. 93–105, on logical form, and his later *Knowledge of Language: Its Nature, Origins and Use*, Praeger, 1986.)

G. Harman (ed.), *On Noam Chomsky: Critical Essays*, Doubleday Anchor, 1974. (For logical form, etc., see index under 'Logical analysis', and also J. D. Atlas, 'On presupposing', *Mind*, 1978 (criticizing equation of logical form with deep structure).)

L. Wittgenstein, *Philosophical Investigations*, Blackwell, 1953, § 664.

Structure-description. See CONFIRMATION.

Sub-contraries. See CONTRADICTION.

Subject. The subject of experience, the one who has the experience, is to be distinguished from the object of experience, what the experience is of, or about. See OBJECT. In a grammatical context, subject and PREDICATE are distinguished.

Subjectivism. View or views which claim that what appear to be objective truths or rules in certain spheres, notably ethics, are really disguised commands or expressions of attitude, etc., e.g. 'Lying is wrong' would be regarded not as stating an objective fact, but as really being the command 'Never lie!', or an expression of the speaker's hostility to lying, like 'Lying! Grr!' (cf. NATURALISM). An alternative version of subjectivism says that the utterances in question do express objective truths, but only about human minds, wishes, beliefs, experiences, etc., whether these be of the speaker or of people in general. 'Lying is wrong' would then mean 'I, or perhaps people generally, disapprove of lying'. Berkeley's IDEALISM is called 'subjective' because it holds that physical objects are really ideas in the mind, even though the mind in question may be that of God.

Objectivist views, by contrast, claim of certain things that they exist independently of the mind, or that there are, in the relevant sphere, truths independent of human wishes and beliefs, or that there are similarly independent ways of establishing certain truths or answering certain questions (e.g. on how to act, or how to argue rationally). See also INTERSUBJECTIVE, RELATIVISM, PROBABILITY, COGNITIVISM.

F. Jackson, G. Oppy and M. Smith, 'Minimalism and truth aptness' *Mind*, 1994. (Claims that one cannot defend the status of various ethical and other utterances as true or false by watering down the notion of truth.)

Subjunctive conditional. See CONDITIONALS and POSSIBLE WORLDS.

Sublime. In aesthetics, the quality of overwhelming size or greatness, particularly in nature, inspiring awe, wonder or respect. The concept originates with Longinus (1st century AD) who uses it to describe lofty or elevated language: then in the eighteenth century it was used by the Earl of SHAFTESBURY of nature, and Joseph Addison of the Alps, which 'fill the mind with an agreeable horror'. Edmund Burke contrasted the sublime with the beautiful in our experience of both art and nature and connects it to a sense of terror. Kant restricts the sublime to nature.

E. Burke, *A Philosophical Enquiry into the Origin of our Ideas of the Sublime and the Beautiful*, 1757, Blackwell, 1987.

I. Kant, *Observations on the Feeling of the Beautiful and Sublime*, 1764, University of California Press, 1960.

S. H. Monk, *The Sublime*, Michigan UP, 1960.

T. Weiskel, *The Romantic Sublime*, Johns Hopkins UP, 1976.

Subsist. See BEING.

Substance. Parmenides (cf. ELEATICS) gave an apparent logical demonstration that reality must be one. He seems to have thought that anything real must exist at all times and in all places, and there were many attempts in the next century or so to distinguish between the real, which obeyed one or both of these demands, and the merely apparent or derivative. In the atomism of the late fifth century BC, as in the EPICUREAN system which derived from it, the atoms of which things were made were real, while their shifting colours and temperatures were merely attributed to them by us. Against this background, the notion of substance as one of the CATEGORIES is first explicitly discussed by Aristotle. 'Substance' is the traditional

translation, followed here, for the Greek ousia. Some scholars, however, think 'substance' a bad translation, partly because of its later
treatment by Locke (see below). They prefer terms like 'being' or
'entity' or 'essence'.

Aristotle seems to use 'substance' in two main senses (though some
see instead two kinds of substance here). In the first sense a substance
is a particular concrete object, like Socrates or this horse, while in the
second sense it is the FORM or essence which makes a substance in
the first sense the thing it is. Socrates is what he is because the flesh of
which he is made has taken on the form of human and not, say, that
of horse. In his *Categories*, Aristotle uses primary substance for the
former sense of 'substance' and secondary substance for the latter
sense (or rather for something approximating to that). Socrates is a
primary substance and man is a secondary substance. There is, however, a problem about this second sense of 'substance', where a
substance is a form, for it is not clear how forms are related to
UNIVERSALS. Aristotle denies, in his *Metaphysics*, that anything
universal can be a substance. The modern sense of 'substance' as
'stuff' (water, iron, etc.), though uncommon in philosophy, seems to
be an amalgam of these two senses.

There is, however, a third possible sense of 'substance', which
Aristotle mentions but dismisses, namely matter, or what remains
when one removes the form or properties of something. For Locke, as
traditionally interpreted, the substance of something is the substrate
which remains when we remove all its properties, a rather mysterious
'something ... we know not what' which underlies the 'accidents' or
properties of things. We can only know something by describing it, i.
e. giving its properties, which is impossible if it itself has none. But
this interpretation of Locke has been challenged, and anyway substances (plural) for him were the things themselves, including their
properties.

Descartes defined substances as what can exist without depending
on anything else, except God, who alone can create or destroy them
and who Himself is the only substance in the strictest sense. For
Descartes therefore, as for Parmenides, substance was permanent, so
that the material world formed but a single substance, since only it,
not things in it, was permanent (once God had created it). Properties,
or attributes and modes, as they were called, depended for their existence on the substances in which they inhere. A substance therefore is
a substrate for properties, but for Descartes it is not something isolated somehow from all its properties and so unknowable. Modes are,
roughly, ways in which an attribute can be possessed, rather like the

DETERMINATE of a determinable. Leibniz, who thought of substances as living things, connected substance with the notions of actuality and activity. These thinkers disputed about the number and kinds of substances, the main classification being into material and spiritual substances, though Spinoza claimed that there could be only one substance, generally known as 'God or nature'.

This notion of a substance as what exists in its own right or independently raises certain difficulties. Firstly, what things are distinguishable and definite enough to count? Cloud? Rainbows? Shadows? Secondly, what sort of independence is in question? Is a hand a substance although it must be a hand of someone? Is a father a substance when described as 'father', or only when described as 'person', since a father must be the father of children? In other words, do fathers as such form one kind of substance as people or horses do? Or is the independence not logical, as here, but of some other kind – perhaps metaphysical, as Descartes thought in calling God the only substance in the full sense, other things being only derivatively so because they owe their existence to God? In what sense is substance prior, since one can no more have a substance without attributes than attributes without a substance? How indeed is substance related to attribute? Is a substance a mere bundle of attributes? If so, what binds the bundle together? Or does a substance underlie all its attributes, which leads back to the unsatisfactory view of an unknowable substrate? If substrate are what attributes apply to, what can be said about attributes of attributes? Surely we can say of an attribute, as well as of a substance, that it is desirable, or rare, or say that scarlet is brighter than crimson.

These considerations suggest a further ambiguity in the term 'substance'. Is there perhaps an absolute or metaphysical sense where the contents of the world are divided into substances and other things (attributes, relations, etc.), and a relative or logical sense where whatever we are talking about is the substance and what we say about it are the attributes (cf. CATEGORIES)? Some philosophers have rejected the metaphysical sense and supposed that substance is at bottom a linguistic notion (cf. METAPHYSICS. This is one form of nominalism). But if we accept the metaphysical notion of substance, should we count among substances any abstract things like UNIVERSALS or propositions (see SENTENCES)?

See also PROCESS PHILOSOPHY.

Aristotle, *Categories*, (trans. with commentary by J. L. Ackrill in Clarendon Aristotle series, 1963, translation but not commentary reprinted in J. Barnes (ed.), *Oxford Translation of Aristotle*, 2nd edn, Princeton UP, 1984), particularly chapter 5 but cf. chapter 7, *Metaphysics*, books 7 (or Z), 8 (or H), 12 (or Λ).

M. Ayers, 'Substance: Prolegomena to a realist theory of identity', *Journal of Philosophy*, 1991. (Defends a notion of substance based on six criteria.)

Descartes, *Principles of Philosophy*, part I, § 51–3, 56. Cf. also § 5 of appendix to *Replies to Objections*, II. (For substance as permanent see J. Bennett, *Kant's Dialectic*, Cambridge UP, 1974, §§ 19–21.)

W. C. Kneale, 'The notion of a substance', *Proceedings of the Aristotelian Society*, 1939–40. (General historical discussion, followed by tentative defence of substance.)

J. Locke, *Essay*, book 2, chapter 23. (For challenge see M. R. Ayers, *Locke*, Routledge, 1991, vol. 2, part 1, and also J. Bennett, 'Substance, reality, and primary qualities', *American Philosophical Quarterly*, 1965, reprinted in C. B. Martin and D. M. Armstrong (eds), *Locke and Berkeley*, Macmillan, n.d.)

D. M. MacKinnon, 'Aristotle's conception of substance', in R. Bambrough (ed.), *New Essays on Plato and Aristotle*, RKP, 1965.

G. Martin, *Leibniz: Logic and Metaphysics*, Manchester UP, 1960, trans. 1964, § 28. (Leibniz on substance.)

A. Quinton, *The Nature of Things*, RKP, 1973. (Extended modern treatment of four relevant problems.)

R. D. Sykes, 'Form in Aristotle: Universal or particular?', *Philosophy*, 1975. (Can serve as elementary introduction to these topics in Aristotle.)

D. Wiggins, *Sameness and Substance*, Blackwell, 1980. (Fairly difficult modern treatment of substance.)

R. S. Woolhouse, *Descartes, Spinoza, Leibniz: The Concept of Substance in Seventeenth-Century Metaphysics*, Routledge, 1993.

Substrate. See SUBSTANCE.

Sufficient conditions. See NECESSARY AND SUFFICIENT CONDITIONS.

Sufficient reason (principle of). Principle that nothing can be so without a reason, causal or otherwise, why it is so. Nothing occurs by 'blind chance', and, in particular, two apparent alternatives such as our universe and a 'mirror universe' like ours but with right and left interchanged, are not really alternatives unless there is enough difference between them for God to have had a reason to create one rather than the other. The principle is associated mainly with Leibniz, for whom it forms one of the two main principles of reasoning, and governs 'truths of fact'. His other principle is the principle of

CONTRADICTION, which governs 'truths of reason'. A third principle, the principle of the best, or of perfection, explains why one rather than another possibility is actualized by saying that the actual world is the best of all possible worlds. The principle, however, has far older roots. Democritus (fifth century BC), for instance, is said to have made his atoms come in all possible shapes because it would be arbitrary for them to come in some and not others, and in the Middle Ages Buridan's ass (though not to be found in the works of Jean Buridan (c.1295–1356)) starved to death because equally placed between two exactly similar and equally attractive bales of hay between which it could not choose.

G. W. Leibniz, *Monadology*, 1714, particularly § 32–6, 53–4. (Leibniz's 5th paper to S. Clarke, 1716, § 21 (in H, G. Alexander (ed.), *The Leibniz–Clarke Correspondence*, Manchester UP, 1956) derives identity of indiscernibles (see LEIBNIZ'S LAW) from sufficient reason principle.)

N. Rescher, *The Philosophy of Leibniz*, Prentice-Hall, 1967, chapter 2. (Schematizes relations between the three principles.)

B. Russell, *A Critical Exposition of the Philosophy of Leibniz*, 1900, § 14–45. (Claims Leibniz only partly distinguishes sufficient reason and perfection principles. Cf. G. H. R. Parkinson, *Logic and Reality in Leibniz Metaphysics*, Clarendon, 1965, pp. 105–6.)

Simplicius, *Commentary on Aristotle's Physics*, transl. J.O. Urmson, with notes by P. Lautner, Cornell UP, 1997, 28. 25–6. (Democritus on shapes of atoms.)

Summum bonum. See GOOD.

Superassertable. Term introduced by C. Wright for use in the REALIST/antirealist debate. A proposition is superassertable if not only is there a warrant for asserting it available on investigation but any further investigation, no matter how long continued, would still warrant its assertion. Superassertability thus provides a step beyond mere warranted assertibility towards the realists' truth that can transcend all verification. It is akin to Peirce's idea of truth as what will ultimately be agreed on, especially if 'will' is read as 'would be', but does not presuppose that we know what an ultimate ideal state of knowledge would be like. (See also PRAGMATISM.)

C. Wright, *Truth and Objectivity*, Harvard UP, 1992 (particularly pp. 47–8). (See also review by J. Edwards in *Mind*, 1994, particularly pp. 62–3.)

Supererogation. Doing more than duty requires, 'going the extra mile'.

J. O. Urmson, 'Saints and heroes', in A. I. Melden (ed.), *Essays in Moral Philosophy*, University of Washington Press, 1958.

Superman. See ÜBERMENSCH.

Supervaluation. A device offered for solving the HEAP paradox. This paradox involves a conditional premise of the form: 'If n grains form a heap so do n-1 grains.' The supervaluational account claims to reject this premise by insisting, first, that the predicate 'is a heap' always can be arbitrarily sharpened in indefinitely many ways. One way would say that 100 or more grains form a heap while 99 or less do not; another would say that 99 or more do while 98 or less do not; and so on. The account then treats the conditional premise as true (absolutely), if, but only if, it is true for all such sharpenings of the predicate.

But now suppose we have, say, 100 grains before us. We cannot say 'If 100 grains form a heap, so do 99', since there will be a sharpening of 'is a heap' where this will not hold, namely just that sharpening which says that 100 grains or more form a heap while 99 or less do not. The same argument applies of course to whatever number of grains we have before us. We can therefore block the paradox without having to decide on any particular sharpening for 'is a heap', though at the cost of not allowing it to remain as an ultimately vague predicate, and indeed of not allowing any ultimately vague predicates (Sainsbury offers 'is an adult' as a predicate that may be importantly vague in certain social contexts).

R. M. Sainsbury, *Paradoxes*, Cambridge UP, revised edn, 1995, pp. 33–9 (revised from 1st edn, 1988, pp. 31–40).

Supervenience. Supervenient characteristics or properties, etc. (in older literature often called consequential characteristics; occasionally tertiary qualities) are characteristics which in a certain way come along ('-vene') on top of a situation of or in addition to ('super-') certain other characteristics without needing to be logically entailed by them (see IMPLICATION). One or two examples may illustrate some of the complexities that arise. Take right and red. Two otherwise exactly similar actions done in exactly similar circumstances by exactly similar people (or the same person perhaps) cannot differ by one being right and the other wrong; their rightness or wrongness cannot be the only feature that distinguishes them. Two objects exactly similar in all their physical and chemical properties cannot in fact differ just by one being red and the other not red. Right and red are therefore candidates for being supervenient properties, though there are differences between them: it seems to make sense to suppose that two otherwise indistinguishable objects should be one red and the other not, even if only by magic, while this does not make sense in the case of right. We can always ask of an action 'What's right about it?', while we can't ask of an object 'What's red about it?' (where we are not referring to parts or features, etc.). This suggests that supervenience comes in degrees, and weak and strong versions of it have been suggested (along with other distinctions: see Horgan section 5). Yet even with rightness, those properties of the action on which the rightness supervenes (called subvenient) do not logically entail that it is right. Different people may hold different views on its rightness (as even more obviously they may on something's beauty or niceness, to take two further candidates for being supervenient properties), but what is necessary is that they must, if they are to be intelligible, make the same judgements about each of the things being compared.

If something's having a certain property at a certain time counts as an EVENT, then the event of its having a certain supervenient property will itself supervene on the event(s) of its having the relevant subvenient property or properties. On other views of events, however, such as Davidson's (see below), there will only be one event here.

As the above examples show, supervenience can be used to classify secondary QUALIA and various value terms. Supervenience can also be used to relate certain properties to what constitutes them: being water or having water's properties may be said to supervene on being H_2O, if being water is regarded as a different property from being H_2O; but see also REDUCTIONISM.

A particularly important role has been played by supervenience during the last third of the twentieth century in philosophy of mind, to explain how psychological properties (having toothache, believing that it's raining, envying one's boss, etc.) are related to properties of the body, especially of the brain. A pioneer in this has been Davidson, whose anomalous MONISM says that any individual mental event is identical with some physical event, but that the mental properties involved will not be identical with, but will supervene on, the physical properties involved. The point is that two creatures in exactly the same mental state could be in different physical states. However, the distinction between narrow and broad CONTENT raises a difficulty here and has led to a distinction whereby supervenience is global or local according as it applies only to a whole context or world, or to individual items in that world; cf. INTERNALISM AND EXTERNALISM.

Supervenience then is not the same as identity. Whether mental properties can supervene on physical properties without psychology (as the science of mental properties) being reducible to the relevant physical sciences is disputed (see Horgan, especially p. 575.) A further distinction has been made between supervenience, where two things cannot differ merely in a supervenient property, and resultance, where one property results from or is somehow grounded in others (e.g. by Dancy, who thinks resultance more important and also discusses the relations between supervenience and universability.)

On some non-COGNITIVIST ethical views, what supervenes on certain ordinary properties is a commitment to certain reactions, e.g. that when confronted with two similar actions one of which one has blamed one must also blame the other (or else point to some relevant difference between them). When this is not so, but what supervenes is a genuinely objective property or fact, the supervenience can be called ontological (Horgan, p. 563), Horgan goes on to insist that if supervenience is to support a materialist view of the mind (in the way outlined above), it must be ontological and its being so in that relevant area must admit of explanation (in which case it can be dubbed superdupervenience: p. 566 and section 8; cf. Dancy's emphasis on resultance).

S. Blackburn, 'Supervenience revisited', in I. Hacking (ed.), *Exercises in Analysis*, Cambridge UP, 1985, reprinted in Blackburn's *Essays in Quasi-Realism*, Oxford UP, 1993. (Discusses significance of a strong and a weak sense of supervenience in connection with his rejection of moral realism's claim that there are objective moral truths independent of any of our attitudes. Fairly difficult.)

J. Dancy, 'On moral properties', *Mind*, 1981. (Distinguishes supervenience from resultance and universability, concentrating on ethics.)

D. Davidson, *Essays on Actions and Events*, Clarendon, 1980. (Reprinted essays which include his main contributions to philosophy of mind. Cf. particularly essays 11 and 13. Some of the essays are criticized, with Davidson's replies, in B. Vermazen and M. B. Hintikka (eds), *Essays on Davidson: Actions and Events*, Clarendon, 1985.)

J. Griffin, 'Values: Reduction, supervenience and explanation by ascent', in D. Charles and K. Lennon (eds), *Reduction, Explanation and Realism*, Clarendon, 1992. (Doubts the supervenience of values: what exactly supervenes on what?)

*R. M. Hare, 'Supervenience', *Proceedings of the Aristotelian Society*, supplementary vol., 1984. (General discussion of it and its applications by a leading representative of its non-ontological use in ethics. Cf. brief discussions in *Mind* by A. J. Dale (1985) and H. Spector (1987).)

*T. Horgan, 'From supervenience to superdupervenience: Meeting the demands of the material world', *Mind*, 1993. (Full discussion, tracing the notion's historical development from 'emergentist' scientific views, and discussing various types and applications of it, and prospects for its usefulness. Includes extensive bibliography. (*Applies to first 16 pp., after which it gets more technical, discussing applications and complications.)

J. Kim, *Supervenience and Mind: Selected Philosophical Essays*, Cambridge UP, 1993. (Essays on supervenience and its applications in philosophy of mind. On weak, strong and global supervenience see particularly chapter 5, chapter 9, section 3. For another definition of weak supervenience, see J. Haugeland, 'Weak supervenience', *American Philosophy Quarterly*, 1982, especially p. 97.)

*G. E. Moore, *Principia Ethica*, Cambridge UP, 1903. (Classic pioneering attempt to apply ontological supervenience, though not so called, in analysing good.)

Southern Journal of Philosophy, supplement to vol. 22, 1984. (Symposium papers on supervenience, with comments.)

Ü. D. Yalçin and E. E. Savellos (eds), *Supervenience: New Essays*, Cambridge UP, 1995. (Discussions covering types of supervenience, their relations to each other, to reduction, and to ontological priority, whether supervenient properties can have causal powers, and whether any explanation can be given of how a supervenient property relates to its subvenient properties.)

Support. See CONFIRMATION.

Supremum bonum. See GOOD.

Sustain. See CONDITIONALS.

Syllogism. A valid or invalid argument in which a conclusion connecting two terms is deduced from two premises connecting those terms to a third term, called the middle term. The subject of the conclusion is called the minor term, and is connected to the middle term in the minor premise. The predicate of the conclusion, the major term, is connected to the middle term in the major premise, conventionally written first. Only four types of proposition are allowed (see QUANTIFIER WORDS). In 'All men are mortal; all Greeks are men; so all Greeks are mortal', men is the middle term, Greeks the minor term and mortal the major term.

The middle term may be either subject or predicate in each premise, giving accordingly four different figures of syllogism (Aristotle, who first formalized the syllogism, only recognized three as distinct). Since the three propositions in a syllogism can each be of four kinds, each figure will contain $4^3 = 64$ kinds of syllogism, called moods, giving 256 moods for the four figures together.

Only a few moods are valid (the number can be predicted mathematically, given certain assumptions; cf. also DISTRIBUTION). If some of these are assumed to be valid the rest can be derived from them, or reduced to them, in an AXIOM SYSTEM. The gist of the assumed moods, especially the only valid mood with universal affirmative conclusion, exemplified above, can then be given by the syllogistic principle. The traditional 'dictum de omni et nullo' ('the maxim of all and none') is one form of this principle; taking two first-figure moods as basic it says that whatever applies to all, or none, of a given class applies to all, or none, respectively, of a given sub-class of it. In the above example, mortal applies to all men and so to all Greeks.

All the above syllogisms are categorical. 'All' is closely related to the material IMPLICATION sense of 'if'. 'All cats are black' is similar in meaning to 'If anything is a cat, it is black'. Hypothetical syllogisms have at least one premise in this hypothetical form (but see Keynes).

Modal syllogisms contain, in at least one premise, or in the conclusion, at least one modal term (see MODALITIES), e.g. 'Necessarily all cats are black'.

Three main criticisms have been made of the syllogism: that as an argument it begs the question because the conclusion is already contained in the premises (cf. INFERENCE); that it is unclear whether the four allowed kinds of proposition entail the existence of things of the kinds they mention (the problem of existential import: does 'All unicorns are black' entail that there are unicorns? (cf. QUANTIFIER WORDS)); that it is very limited in scope, and in particular ignores the logic of relations by using 'be' as its only verb (cf. LOGIC).

Aristotle's practical syllogism is a subject of dispute. It is like an ordinary syllogism but has for conclusion an action, or perhaps an utterance closely related to one, such as a resolve: 'All sweet things are good to eat; this is sweet; therefore let me eat it.' Cf. practical REASON, INCONTINENCE, IMPERATIVE.

J. N. Keynes, Formal Logic, 1884, 4th (revised) edn 1906. (Full treatment from traditional viewpoint.)

J. Lukasiewicz, *Aristotle's Syllogistic*, Clarendon, 1951, enlarged 1957. (Treats Aristotle historically and from viewpoint of modern logic. 2nd edn 1957 includes modal syllogisms.)

J. S. Mill, *A System of Logic*, Longmans, Green, 1843, book 2, chapter 3. (Famous attack on syllogism's usefulness.)

M. Nussbaum, *Aristotle's De Motu*, Princeton UP, 1978. (See Essay iv for classic discussion of practical syllogism.)

L. E. Rose, 'Aristotle's syllogistic and the fourth figure', *Mind*, 1965.

G. H. von Wright, *Explanation and Understanding*, RKP, 1971. (Practical syllogism. See its index under 'practical inference'.)

Symbol. See SIGN.

Symmetric. A relation holding from *a* to *b* is symmetric if it must hold from *b* to *a* (sibling of). It is asymmetric if it cannot (parent of), and non-symmetric if it may or may not (brother of). 'Non-symmetric' occasionally includes 'asymmetric'. It is anti-symmetric if its holding from *a* to *b* and from *b* to *a* implies that *a* and *b* are the same object. 'Not greater' than among numbers is anti-symmetric, but 'not older than among people' is not, but only non-symmetric: different people can have the same age, but different numbers cannot have the same size, so if *a* is not greater than *b* nor *b* than *a*, then *a* and *b* are the same number. Sometimes 'weak anti-symmetric' is used for this, with 'anti-symmetric' replacing 'asymmetric'.

Symptom. See CRITERION.

Synechism. Any view emphasizing continuity as against discontinuity or atomism. In particular, a term associated with Peirce.

J. A. Passmore, *A Hundred Years of Philosophy*, Duckworth, 1957, 2nd edn, 1966. (See pp. 104–5 (pp. 103–4 in Penguin edn, 1968).)

Synonymy. See MEANING.

Syntax, syntactics. See SEMANTICS.

Synthetic. See ANALYTIC.

T

Tacit and implicit knowledge. Two terms associated especially, though not exclusively, with two very different philosophers, M. Polanyi (1891–1976) and M. Dummett. The terms are often used interchangeably, though Polanyi uses 'tacit'.

Polanyi starts from such facts as that we can recognize faces without knowing how we do so, and can be specially trained to respond to certain perceived stimuli without knowing just what we are responding to. He claims that we transfer our attention from e.g. the specific features of a face to the face as a whole (we attend from the former to the latter, as he puts it), and thereby have tacit knowledge of the former. The idea is then developed to cover the foreshadowing by which a scientist sees first a problem and then a possible solution to it in his data. What matters is not that the tacit knowledge be unconscious but that it be what we attend from.

For Dummett implicit knowledge is that knowledge which speakers must have of a language. The knowledge is the propositions which constitute a theory of meaning for the language (roughly, what the individual words mean and how they combine to form sentences), but such knowledge obviously is not explicit in most speakers, and it would be circular to demand that they can formulate it in the language. Such knowledge, however, does not, for Dummett, consist in some inner psychological state which can causally explain our ability to use the language. Rather it is manifested simply in the speaking itself, and to give the content of what is known is simply to give a detailed account of the language itself. For Chomsky, on the other hand, who also uses the notion, it does consist in an inner psychological state.

Tacit knowledge has also been important recently in connection with both descriptionalist accounts of mental IMAGERY and psychological accounts of mental competences.

M. Davies, 'Tacit knowledge and subdoxastic states', in A. George (ed.), *Reflections on Chomsky*, Blackwell, 1989. (See particularly section one for the relation between these terms, and also on Chomsky's views. Davies develops his views in his *Tacit Knowledge*, Blackwell, 1996.)

M. Dummett, 'What is a theory of meaning? (II)', in G. Evans and J. McDowell (eds), *Truth and Meaning*, Oxford UP, 1976. (See particularly pp. 70–2, and cf. also B. Smith, 'Understanding language', *Proceedings of the Aristotelian Society*, 1992, particularly section v. Later, however, Dummett rejected this notion; see the Preface to his *The Seas of Language*, Clarendon, 1993, especially pp. x–xii.)

J. Fodor, 'The appeal to tacit knowledge in psychological explanations', *Journal of Philosophy*, 1968, reprinted in his *Representations*, Harvester Press, 1981. (Defends an 'intellectualist' or rule-following account of mental competences in terms of tacit knowledge.)

M. Polanyi, *The Tacit Dimension*, Doubleday, 1966, particularly chapter 1.

Z. Pylyshyn, 'The imagery debate: Analog media versus tacit knowledge', in N. Block (ed.), *Imagery*, MIT Press, 1981.

Tarski, Alfred. 1901–83. Mathematician and logician, born in Warsaw where he worked until 1939, and after that at Berkeley, California. His work relevant to philosophy was mainly in his formalization of semantics. This led to his 'semantic theory' of TRUTH, whose formulation was importantly affected by the LIAR paradox. He also contributed to the formal treatment of logical and mathematical MODELS. 'Der Wahrheitsbegriff in den formalisierten Sprachen', *Studia Philosophica*, 1935 (translated from Polish book of 1933). 'The semantic conception of truth and the foundations of semantics', *Journal of Philosophy and Phenomenological Research*, 1944 (shorter version of above). *Logic, Semantics, Metamathematics*, 1956 (collected logical papers from 1923 to 1938 in translation, including 'Wahrheitsbegriff'). *Introduction to Logic and to the Methodology of the Deductive Sciences*, 1941 (translated and revised from Polish original of 1936).

Tautology. Literally; saying the same thing. Loosely, any ANALYTIC truth. More strictly, and usually, either any logical truth, i.e. any statement true in virtue of its form (see ANALYTIC), or a truth-functional logical truth, such as 'Snow is white or snow is not white'. (Not 'Everything is white or not white', which is logically true, but is not such that its truth can be inferred from the truth or falsity of its parts for it has no relevant parts.) The sense of mere repetition, whereby 'I took his life and killed him' becomes a tautology, does not occur in philosophy.

Teleological. Having to do with design or purpose. See also ETHICS, EXPLANATION, and for teleological argument, DESIGN.

Temporal parts. See GENIDENTITY.

Term. Sometimes a word or phrase ('Always define your terms'), and sometimes objects or things, such as the terms of a relation. (If John loves Joan the relation loving has the people John and Joan as its terms.)

Tertiary qualities. See SUPERVENIENCE.

Tertium non datur. See EXCLUDED MIDDLE.

Testimony. As well as our own sense perception, memory and reasoning, another source of knowledge – indeed a very common one – is from what other people tell us. Some try to justify the testimony of others as knowledge only when it can be reduced to the individual's own sense perception, memory and reasoning, and thus regard it as only a second-order source of knowledge.

> C. A. J. Coady, *Testimony: A Philosophical Study*, Oxford UP, 1992. (Defends a non-reductionist account.)

Theodicy. The justification of God's ways and especially the reconciliation of divine providence with the existence of evil and sin, the so-called 'problem of evil'.

> J. L. Mackie, 'Evil and omnipotence', *Mind*, 1955. (Anthologized many times, for example, in W. L. Rowe, *God and the Problem of Evil*, Blackwell, 2001, which also contains 'The free will defense', Plantinga's response to Mackie, which is also in A. Plantinga, *Nature and Necessity*, Clarendon, 1971.)
> M. Tooley, 'The Problem of Evil', *The Stanford Encyclopedia of Philosophy* (Winter 2008 Edition), Edward N. Zalta (ed.). Available at: http://plato.stanford.edu/archives/win2008/entries/evil/ (accessed 1 March 2009).

Theorem. See AXIOM.

Theory. See LAWS.

Theory-laden. Applied to a term if its use can only be understood in terms of some theory. 'He has an anal-retentive personality', for example, only makes sense against a background of Freudianism. It is sometimes claimed that many more terms are theory-laden or theory-loaded than appear so at first sight.

N. R. Hanson, *Patterns of Discovery*, Cambridge UP, 1958. (See index.)

Thick and thin concepts. Terms used especially in recent ethics. Thick concepts are those which seem to combine a purely descriptive element with an element of evaluation or prescription, such as 'cowardly', 'heroic', 'treacherous', 'loyal', 'brutal', 'lewd', while thin terms embody only an evaluative or prescriptive element, such as 'good' 'evil', 'ought', 'right'. It seems hard for someone who does not accept the relevant values or prescriptions to decide whether to call attributions of the thick concepts true or false. However, the correct analysis of the thick concepts is disputed.

A related contrast is that between concepts of causation according to whether they do or do not go beyond mere regular sequence, and concepts of meaning according to whether they do or do not go beyond mere truth conditions. 'Robust', and 'modest' (sometimes 'minimalist') are widely used to make this sort of contrast in various fields.

A. Gibbard and S. Blackburn, 'Morality and thick concepts', *Proceedings of the Aristotelian Society*, supplementary vol., 1992.

B. A. O. Williams, *Ethics and the Limits of Philosophy*, Fontana, 1985 (particularly pp. 129–30 with context).

Thing-in-itself. See NOUMENON.

Thing-word. See METAPHYSICS.

Thinking. In the seventeenth century 'thinking' was often used to cover mental phenomena in general, including feeling, with the result that Descartes and others could distinguish between substances according to whether they had extension or thinking as their defining attributes (giving material objects and minds, respectively). This usage is no longer current.

Thinking can take many forms: at least those of believing, imagining, pondering, calculating, deliberating, ruminating, assuming, evaluating; it can be something occurring at a given time or a state we can be in; and it can concern theoretical or practical matters (cf. practical REASON). Whether or not all these cases are equally central

(Urmson; see Sibley ref. below), it seems hopeless to try to isolate any one activity as that of thinking. Moreover, it may be thought that thinking is never manifested except in other activities that could occur without it. Kicking a football involves thinking, but the same leg-movements could result from a reflex. Here one can in various degrees be 'thinking what one is doing', but the thinking is not, or need not be, a separate activity. For these reasons thinking has sometimes been called POLYMORPHOUS. This in turn suggests an 'adverbial' view of thinking, whereby there is no activity, or even set of activities, to be called thinking, but activities in general can be carried out thoughtfully or thoughtlessly, intelligently or unintelligently, etc. However, this will hardly cover all cases. One cannot calculate thoughtlessly, except in the sense of 'He thoughtlessly went on calculating while the kettle boiled dry'. This example shows that intelligence or thoughtfulness, like care, deliberation, etc., can be manifested in the fact that something is done, as well as in the manner in which it is done. But it also shows that calculating, even if done hastily or carelessly, essentially involves thinking, while being an activity in its own right (not a mere synonym of 'thinking').

Such activities, and especially silent thought, and occasions when thoughts dawn on one or flash across the mind, have at various times occupied much attention. A recently popular theory is that we have here simply physical events in the brain seen from a certain point of view (IDENTITY THEORY OF MIND). More longstanding are disputes about the role of mental images, language and behaviour. Behaviour, if it involves overt movements, seems irrelevant in many of the cases we are considering. Hypothetical behaviour might seem to be involved, in the sense that the thinker would behave in certain ways if certain things happened, e.g. would give certain answers if asked certain questions. But this does not explain what does happen at the definite time when the thought occurs. Language seems involved, in that anything properly called a thought must presumably be expressible in language. But we often have the thought before finding words to express it. It may be true, however, that thoughts involving abstract things can only occur to a being possessing a language which could express them. Mental images here need not be full-blooded pictures, but may be confused patches of colour, or sounds, or incipient sensations of moving the vocal chords, or anything that might be called material for experience. It seems hard to conceive of thought occurring without any such elements at all. But it seems equally hard to see what relevance such imagery has if it does occur, since it seems that one could have any amount of such imagery without having the relevant thought. If the topic of 'Unageless thought' has been less discussed recently this seems to be rather through despair at finding an answer than for any other reason.

All this suggests two further questions. First, how is thinking related to time? A train of thought takes time, and can be interrupted and left incomplete, but can any of this happen in the case of a single thought that flashes on one? In expressing a thought one may, for example, first say the subject and then the predicate, but does one think them in this or any order? How, in fact, is the structure of a thought, if it has one, related to that of a sentence expressing it? We must distinguish here a thought as a datable occurrence from a thought as the context common to many such occurrences. But how are they related? Have they a common structure? The second question is how far thoughts, in either sense, can be described. Thoughts as contents can be true, valid, fallacious, misleading, sombre, illuminating, commonplace, though some of these terms will only apply to them relative to a context. Thoughts as occurrences can be dated and put into words, but descriptions of them seem either to borrow from descriptions of the content, or to be peripheral and not reaching the heart of the thought itself. Descriptions like 'hasty', 'sudden', 'unexpected' seem to presuppose other descriptions, which yet are not forthcoming.

The question of the structure of a thought raises the question of how thinking a whole thought or proposition is related to thinking of an object, e.g. something which the thought was about. In particular, which is prior? Does one think thoughts by, for example, thinking of objects and attributes and somehow putting them together, as by thinking of the cat and of black, and putting them together to get the thought that the cat is black? Or is thinking of an object something that can only be abstracted from a whole thought, so that one can only think of an object by thinking something about it?

Another important question about thinking concerns the things we think about. If I think about Caesar, does this constitute a relation between me and him? But perhaps Caesar never existed, so that I could not have been related to him; does my thinking still remain what it was? This raises the question of internalist and externalist analyses (see INTERNALISM AND EXTERNALISM) of mental states, and issues about the nature of their CONTENT. Also, what happens if I think something false of Caesar, e.g. that he had a beard when in fact he did not? This, with the fact that Caesar no longer exists to be thought of, may suggest that I must use a representative of him to do my thinking with, e.g. a mental image, which can exist now, and be bearded. But even if such an image were always present on these occasions, how would the image itself be related to Caesar? What would make it an image of him? For it is Caesar, not the image, that we are supposed to be thinking about, and we must surely know what we are thinking about (it seems), which would be difficult if there were just the image. This whole question remains wide open. With the idea that thought requires a representative cf. the representative theory PERCEPTION. For further questions about thinking and the objects it has cf. INTENSIONALITY AND INTENTION-ALITY (see the 'Cicero' example there), and MODALITIES on the *de re/de dicto* distinction.

A further question we can ask is what it is that thinks? Must a thought belong to a continuing thinker? When Descartes said 'I think, therefore I am', what sort of an 'I' did he prove the existence of? Could we say with G. C. Lichtenberg (1742–99) 'It is thinking', as we say 'it is raining'? And how are Smith's thoughts related to Smith? Are they properties of him? Do they help to constitute him? Must a thinker indeed be human at all? Could machines or computers think, and if not, what condition is it that they fail to satisfy? How far can mental processes be modelled artificially?

See also JUDGEMENT, REFERRING.

R. M. Chisholm, 'Sentences about believing', *Proceedings of the Aristotelian Society*, 1955–6. (Discusses cases like the 'Cicero' example in INTENSIONALITY.)

*T. Crane, *The Mechanical Mind: A Philosophical Introduction to Minds, Machines and Representation*, Penguin, 1995. (Elementary introduction, including such questions as whether computers can think.)

M. de Gaynesford, 'How wrong can one be?', *Proceedings of the Aristotelian Society*, 1996. (Must we know what we are thinking about? See first footnote for many references.)

P. T. Geach, *Mental Acts*, RKP, 1971. (Exploration of the analogy between thinking and speaking. Cf. also his *God and the Soul*, RKP, 1969, chapter 3.)

W. J. Ginnane, 'Thoughts', *Mind*, 1960. (Clear exposition of the problem of analysing sudden thoughts. For defence of imageless thought see also G. Humphrey, *Thinking: An Introduction to Its Experimental Psychology*, Methuen, 1951, Wiley 1963, pp. 122–31, 225–30.)

G. C. Lichtenberg, *Aphorisms*, trans. R. J. Hollingdale, Penguin, 1990, new edn 2002.

D. L. Mouton, 'Thinking and time', *Mind*, 1969. (Refers to Ginnane and Geach.)

G. Myro, 'Thinking', in H. Robinson (ed.), *Objections to Physicalism*, Clarendon, 1993. (Lecture given about 1980 on nature of thinking and our knowledge of it.)

H. H. Price, *Thinking and Experience*, Hutchinson, 1953. (General study.)

A. N. Prior, *Objects of Thought*, Oxford UP, 1971. (Part I discusses the direct objects ('accusatives'), if any, of thinking (propositions, etc.) and requires a fair knowledge of logic. Part II uses less logic (but with some POLISH NOTATION) to discuss examples like the Caesar one above.)

J. Ross, 'Immaterial aspects of thought', *Journal of Philosophy*, 1992. (Claims thinking cannot be identical with any physical process or any function of one.)

F. N. Sibley 'Ryle and thinking', in O. P. Wood and G. Pitcher (eds), *Ryle*, Macmillan, 1970. (Thinking and the many uses of 'think'. Cf. J. O. Urmson, 'Polymorphous concepts', in same volume, and also A. R. White, *The Philosophy of Mind*, Random House, 1967, chapter 4.)

*P. Smith and O. R. Jones, *The Philosophy of Mind: An Introduction*, Cambridge UP, 1986. (Chapter 16 gives elementary introduction.)

T. L. S. Sprigge, *Facts, Words and Beliefs*, RKP, 1970. (Complex and sophisticated attempt to analyse thinking in terms of images.)

A. Woodfield (ed.), *Thought and Object: Essays on Intentionality*, Clarendon, 1982. (Essays on the nature, types, structure and roles of the contents of thoughts. D. C. Dennett's 'Beyond belief' is reprinted with afterthoughts in his *The Intentional Stance*, MIT Press, 1987; see particularly pp. 54ff. (pp. 168 ff in reprint) for difficulties in *de re/de dicto* distinction.)

Third man argument. Argument named by Aristotle but deriving from Plato, who offered it as a criticism of his own theory of Forms (see IDEA, UNIVERSALS). The term 'man' can apparently be applied to both Socrates and the Form Man, so we need a third 'man' to explain what these have in common. The term 'man' will then apply to this third entity, and so we shall need a fourth, and so on. The theory of Forms therefore seems to lead on to an infinite regress. The detailed interpretation of the argument is highly controversial (Plato himself uses the example, 'large', which may or may not be significantly different), but the argument can be widened to cover the relations between universals and particulars in general.

D. M. Armstrong, *Universals: An Opinionated Introduction*, Westview Press, 1989, pp. 53–7. (Widens the argument, without explicitly naming it.)

C. C. Meinwald, 'Goodbye to the third man', in R. Kraut (ed.), *The Cambridge Companion to Plato*, Cambridge UP, 1992. (Offers a solution to the argument, integrating it with general development of Plato's thought, drawing on her *Plato's Parmenides*, Oxford UP, 1991. See n. 13 for references to literature generated by Vlastos.)

J. A. Passmore, *Philosophical Reasoning*, Duckworth, 1961, chapter 2. (Treats the argument from modern point of view, though again without explicitly naming it.)

Plato, *Parmenides* 131e–3a. (For commentary see e.g. R. G. Allen, *Plato's Parmenides*, Minnesota UP and Blackwell, 1983.)

G. Vlastos, 'The third man argument in the *Parmenides*', *Philosophical Review*, 1954, variously reprinted. (Classic discussion which has generated immense literature.)

Thought experiment. A form of reasoning that asks 'What if ... ?'. Philosophers imagine different hypothetical situations to test their ideas, concepts, theories, moral rules. For example, suppose some thinking beings had no senses other than that of hearing, would they have the concept of space? See CHINESE ROOM ARGUMENT for another example.

R. A. Sorenson, *Thought Experiments*, Oxford UP, 1992. (Lots of examples.)

P. F. Strawson, *Individuals*, Methuen, 1959, Routledge, 1990. (Part I, Section 2 for the hearing and space example.)

Time. See SPACE.

Time-slice. See GENIDENTITY.

Token. See UNIVERSALS, TOKEN-REFLEXIVES.

Token-reflexives. When a sentence contains phrases like 'here', 'now', 'this', 'I', 'last year, 'in January', or tenses of verbs, we cannot fully know what was said by someone uttering the sentence, unless we know something about that particular utterance like its date, place, utterer, etc. Particular utterances of a word or sentence are called tokens (see UNIVERSALS), and so these phrases, which as it were point back to the token sentences in which they appear, are called token-reflexives. Alternative names for them include demonstratives, egocentric particulars (Russell), indicator terms, indexicals (but Putnam calls words for natural kinds, like 'water' indexical, as sharing certain features with ordinary indexicals).

An important issue, which affects what propositions (see SEN-TENCES) are, and what sort of things can be true or false, is whether token-reflexives can be eliminated, i.e. whether sentences containing them can be translated into what Quine calls eternal SENTENCES.

J. N. Findlay, 'An examination of tenses', in H. D. Lewis (ed.), *Contemporary British Philosophy*, III, Allen and Unwin, 1956. (Difficulties in eliminating tenses.)

C. McGinn, *The Subjective View*, Oxford UP, 1983. (Compares indexicals with secondary QUALITIES.)

J. Perry 'The problem of the essential indexical', *Nous*, 1979, reprinted in N. Salmon and S. Soames (eds), *Propositions and Attitudes*, Oxford UP 1988. (Difficulties raised by the fact that some beliefs seem to involve indexicals or token-reflexives essentially.)

H. Putnam, 'Meaning and reference', *Journal of Philosophy*, 1973, particularly pp. 709–11.

W. V. O. Quine, *Word and Object*, Wiley, 1960. (Largely follows Russell. See index under 'indicator word'. See § 36 for tenses, and p. 107n. for terminology.)

B. Russell, *An Inquiry into Meaning and Truth*, Allen and Unwin, 1940, (Chapter 7 claims that 'egocentric particulars' can be eliminated. R. M. Gale (ed.), *The Philosophy of Time*, Macmillan, 1968, pp. 296–8, distinguishes token-reflexives as linguistic entities from egocentric particulars as private entities.)

C. Sayward, 'Propositions and eternal sentences', *Mind*, 1968. (Token-reflexives in general cannot be eliminated.)

P. Yourgran (ed.), *Demonstratives*, Oxford UP, 1990. (Reprinted essays on various relevant topics. See particularly items by Perry and Evans.)

Topic-neutral. Expressions, such as the logical constants (e.g. 'and', 'or', 'not') which contribute to the structure of a language rather than to the content of what it is being used to express, so that they are neutral as between different subject matters. Sometimes they may merely be neutral regarding the subject matter under discussion: 'I am thinking now', for example, says that something is happening, but says nothing about the process, and is therefore topic-neutral in the philosophy of mind. Identifying such expressions raises problems. When understood in the first way they might be called the subject matter of logic. The notion was introduced by Ryle, and used by, e.g. Smart in defending his version of the identity theory of mind. See also FORM, RAMSEY SENTENCE.

G. Ryle, *Dilemmas*, Cambridge UP, 1954, chapter 8. (See p. 116 for his own definition.)

J. J. C. Smart, 'Sensations and brain processes', *Philosophical Review*, 1959, reprinted in V. C. Chappell (ed.), *The Philosophy of Mind*, Prentice-Hall, 1962, C. V. Borst (ed.), *The Mind/Brain Identity Theory*, Macmillan, 1970. (See reply to objection 3. Borst reprint has footnote referring to criticisms and Smart's reply.)

Topological. See SPACE.

Total evidence requirement. See CONFIRMATION.

Tracking. See NOZICK.

Transcendental arguments. Primarily, an argument which shows of some proposition not that it is true but that it must be assumed to be true if some sphere of thought or discourse, especially an indispensable sphere, is to be possible. An early example is Aristotle's argument that the law of contradiction cannot be proved, since any proof involves it, but that it must be assumed by anyone who asserts anything at all, and therefore by anyone asserting that the law is false. Kant thought such arguments could also justify non-formal conditions of objective thought (his CATEGORIES). The law of contradiction is a formal condition: see FORM.

Since Kant, transcendental arguments have been popular as a weapon against various kinds of sceptic. The sceptic, it is claimed, cannot state his position without assuming what he is claiming to be sceptical of. His position is therefore parasitic on that of his opponent.

However, there is much dispute about exactly how transcendental arguments work, how they are to be distinguished from other kinds of argument, how many kinds of them there are, and what sort of things they can be used to establish. They may concern not only whether propositions are true, but whether terms are meaningful; whether concepts have application or usefulness; whether arguments are valid; and whether things of a certain kind exist though we cannot construct instances of those kinds.

Transcendental arguments are perhaps a strengthened form of PARADIGM CASE ARGUMENTS. A transcendental argument for something like the legitimacy of INDUCTION would say that a whole sphere of our thought or language presupposes its legitimacy, whether or not we have even heard of induction. A paradigm case argument for it points simply to the fact that we regard some arguments as legitimate inductive ones.

Aristotle, *Metaphysics*, book 4 (or Γ), chapter 4.

P. Bieri, R.-P. Horstmann and L. Krüger (eds), *Transcendental Arguments and Science: Essays in Epistemology*, Reidel, 1979. (Essays, with comments, on nature of transcendental arguments, and their bearing on how far science could attain to absolute truth.)

A. P. Griffiths and J. J. MacIntosh, 'Transcendental arguments', *Proceedings of the Aristotelian Society*, supplementary vol., 1969. (Griffiths defends them with examples. MacIntosh is critical.)

R. Rorty, 'Verificationism and transcendental arguments', *Nous*, 1971. (Moderate defence, but stressing limitations, M. S. Gram, 'Transcendental arguments', ibid., is relevant but difficult.)

Transcendentals. See BEING.

Transformation rules. See AXIOM.

Transitive. A relation holding from *a* to *b* and from *b* to *c* is transitive if it must hold from *a* to *c*, whatever *a*, *b* and *c* may be ('ancestor of'). It is intransitive if it cannot ('father of'), and non-transitive if it may or may not ('fond of'). 'Non-transitive' occasionally includes 'intransitive'. (The qualification 'whatever *a*, *b* and *c* may be' is needed to exclude certain rogue cases like 'results in less than ten when added to', which looks transitive if *a*, *b* and *c* are, respectively, 2, 3 and 4, but is not if they are, respectively, 6, 2 and 7.)

Translation (indeterminacy of). Quine claims that assured translation between any two languages, or even within one language, is impossible in principle. There are certain exceptions, namely certain occasion sentences, which are covered by stimulus synonymy, and also truth-functional TAUTOLOGIES (but on these see Roth under Quine ref.). To translate, in general, we must construct analytical hypotheses, which say that an element in one language is equivalent to, or analysable in terms of, an element in the other. But Quine thinks it is impossible in principle to justify choosing one such hypothesis against another, and our choice may affect the truth of the sentence being translated. Quine claims that this raises fatal difficulties for determinate notions of meaning, synonymy and translation.

Translation of this kind is called radical translation. A related, though different, notion is radical interpretation, which the truth-conditions theory of MEANING must use in constructing a theory of what a speaker's words and sentences mean on the basis of the contexts in which they are uttered. Such interpretation uses the principles of CHARITY or humanity. It differs from Quine's radical translation because it does not envisage different speakers having incommensurable conceptual schemes (see RELATIVISM), but rather may sometimes make one choose between attributing false beliefs to speakers and taking them to mean something different from what they seem to mean.

D. Davidson, 'Radical interpretation', *Dialectica*, 1973, reprinted in his *Inquiries into Truth and Interpretation*, Clarendon, 1984.

H. J. Glock, *Quine and Davidson on Language, Thought and Reality*, Cambridge UP, 2003. (Clear exposition and discussion. See Sections 6 and 7.)

R. Kirk, 'Translation and indeterminacy' and 'Quine's indeterminacy thesis', *Mind*, 1969. (Critical. Answered by A. Hyslop, 'Kirk on Quine on bilingualism' and P. Harris, 'Translation into Martian', *Mind*, 1972.)

A. C. Lambert and P. D. Shaw, 'Quine on meaning and translation', *Mind*, 1971. (Critical.)

W. V. O. Quine, *Word and Object*, Wiley, 1960, chapter 2. (See pp. 35–6 for occasion sentences, and pp. 32–3, 46 for stimulus synonymy. Cf. discussion in D. Davidson and J. Hintikka (eds), *Words and Objections*, Reidel, 1969, and also P. A. Roth, 'Theories of nature and the nature of theories', *Mind*, 1980.)

Transparent. See INTENSIONALITY AND INTENTIONALITY.

Transposition. See CONTRAPOSITION.

Tripartite analysis of knowledge. The traditional, classical, analysis of knowledge, with its origins in Plato (who gives it and rejects it in the *Theaetetus*). A person, X, is said to know a proposition, p, if, and only if, (1) p is true; (2) X believes that p; and (3) X is justified in believing that p. Sometimes referred to as the JTB, or Justified True Belief, analysis of knowledge. GETTIER produced counter-examples to this analysis: see bibliography. See EPISTEMOLOGY.

Plato, *Theaetetus*, 201c–201d.

Trope. Property or relation considered as it appears in a single instance, so that it is a particular (see UNIVERSALS). The being brown of this table, which it shares with no other object, would be a trope. If Tom, John and Bill are brothers, the being a brother of Bill that Tom possesses would be a trope, as would that possessed by John, and also the being brothers possessed by the three of them. The name 'trope' has recently become established; other names have included 'individual accidents', 'abstract particulars', 'unit-properties', 'property-instances', and others. The notion goes back to Aristotle, but whether there really are such things, and if so, whether they are additional to or replace universals, are disputed questions.

In Greek philosophy 'trope' (which literally means 'way', 'method' or 'mode') refers especially to the ten modes of argument attributed to Aenesidemus, writing probably in the first century BC.

Aristotle, *Categories*, chapter 2.

D. M. Armstrong, *Universals: An Opinionated Introduction*, Westview Press, 1989. (Includes extended discussion of various trope theories.)

J. Bennett, *Events and Their Names*, Oxford UP, 1988. (Chapter 6 analyses events as tropes. See also p. 15 n. 7 for references to further discussions.)

K. Campbell, *Abstract Particulars*, Blackwell, 1990. (Makes tropes the basic building-blocks of a metaphysical system.)

A. A. Long and D. N. Sedley (eds), *The Hellenistic Philosophers*, vol. 1. Cambridge UP, 1987. (See its index of philosophers for Aenesidemus and his modes (as they are called there).)

P. A. Simons, 'Particulars in particular clothing: Three trope theories of substance', *Philosophy and Phenomenological Research*, 1994. (Defends a 'nuclear' view of tropes, combining 'bundle' and 'substratum' views.)

Tropic. See PHRASTIC.

Truth and falsity. Truth is something we all approve of, and aim, or should aim, to achieve. But just what is it? What we say may be criticized in many ways, only one of which is for failing to state the truth (see below). But failure to do that seems somehow to be the most basic kind of failure. What then is it that we want to achieve? Is truth a relation between what we say and the subject matter we say it about? Or between different things we do or could say? Or is to call something true simply a way of repeating it? Or perhaps of expressing a certain kind of approval of it or willingness to endorse it? Or is something true if, in a certain sense, it works or produces satisfaction? Various theories exist corresponding to such views.

The correspondence theory is perhaps the commonest theory of truth, partly because 'correspondence' can be interpreted strictly or loosely. In its strictest form, primarily associated with Moore and Russell, this theory involves a relation between two things, that which is true (a proposition, belief, judgement, etc.) and that which makes it true (a fact, or perhaps a state of affairs or event). The fact has a structure which the proposition, etc., copies or pictures. But finding pairs of things which correspond in this way is difficult, especially since the sort of structure that a proposition might have, involving the relations between things like nouns and verbs, or subjects and predicates, seems entirely different from any features of the outer world. Subjects and predicates are different (linguistic) things in a way that objects and properties are not; and how would one distinguish the correlates of 'Snow is white' and 'For snow to be white'? Similar difficulties confront correspondence, or picture, theories of how sentences or propositions have MEANING. Also if all we know is propositions, and propositions picture the world, how can we compare the propositions with the world itself to see if they picture it accurately? (Cf. PERCEPTION on the difficulty of knowing about an external world if we must begin from 'pure experience'.)

There is a less strict form of the theory, which no longer requires that each part of the proposition should correspond to a part of reality. On this view, something is true if it can be correlated with a fact and false if not, or if its negation can be correlated with a fact. A still looser form calls something true if it simply 'says things as they are'. This leads naturally to F. P. Ramsey's redundancy (also occasionally called no truth) theory, whereby to call something true is simply to repeat what it says. On this view, truth is not a property of anything, but the use of 'true' provides a shorthand way of referring to things said. A development of this is Strawson's performative (occasionally, ditto) theory, which is a SPEECH ACT theory. Here when we call something 'true' we perform an act of agreeing to, repeating, or conceding it – we say 'ditto' to it. These theories, which are often called deflationary, have been criticized as unable to cover all senses of 'true', and loose correspondence theories have been returned to and defended by Austin and, in a modified form, Hamlyn. Recently deflationism has been revived by Horwich's minimal theory.

A recent variant of the correspondence theory is Tarski's semantic theory. This is primarily designed for, though not confined to, artificial languages, whose elements or 'words' may be infinitely many but are of definite kinds and have definite roles. Sentences in a given language, L, are called 'true-in-L' (not to be confused with 'L-true', Carnap's symbol for 'logically true': see ANALYTIC, VALID) when their elements are so combined as to state what is the case, e.g. 'Snow is white' is true in English if and only if snow is white. This avoids treating propositions and facts as entities, and is easy to develop in a rigorous and formal way. But there are limits to how far it can be applied without great complication, even to formal languages, for reasons connected with the LIAR PARADOX and Gödel's THEOREMS.

The correspondence theory suits philosophers who make a sharp distinction between knower and known. Those who refuse to do this, notably IDEALISTS, often favour the coherence theory. The basic idea of this is that something is true if it coheres or is logically consistent with a wider system than any of its rivals cohere with. This theory presupposes that CONSISTENCY can be defined independently of truth, and also that one of the various possible consistent systems of propositions is wider than any of the others. Idealists who hold this theory, however, say that strictly only the system taken as a whole is true. Single propositions in it give only partial approximations to the truth. Can we really understand 'Caesar crossed the Rubicon', it might be asked, and so be in a position to call it true, until we appreciate all its causes and consequences, even to the end of time? The theory is therefore sometimes called a degrees of truth theory. Another reason for thinking truth has degrees is that we cannot know whether something belongs to the widest coherent system, if there is one, without examining every proposition, so in practice we must be satisfied with something less. (See also below.) Moreover, in advanced sciences like cosmology it is often difficult to decide between different but consistent ways of describing the universe. All the known celestial movements can be explained on a geocentric theory, if it is sufficiently complex. The coherence theory can be supplemented by devices like adopting the simplest out of several competing hypotheses. It is then attractive in those regions of science where immediate verification is impossible. Perhaps partly for this reason it was favoured by some positivists (Neurath, Hempel). Cf. also CONVENTIONALISM, INSTRUMENTALISM, POSITIVISM.

This sort of consideration also lies behind the pragmatic theory, for which see PRAGMATISM.

What sort of things can be true? Is 'true' properly or primarily applied to mental acts and states such as acts of utterance, judgements, beliefs, or to linguistic things, such as indicative sentences, or to certain abstract things such as propositions (see SENTENCES)? 'Statement' can be a convenient non-committal word. How we answer this will affect what we say about how truth is related to time and tense: can something, like the sentence 'I am hot', become true?

Is everything which is of the right kind to be true or false actually true or false, as one form of the law of EXCLUDED MIDDLE asserts? Is 'My wife is asleep', said by a bachelor, false (Russell) or neither true nor false (Strawson)? Strawson's view claims that there are 'truth-value gaps', i.e. an absence of TRUTH-VALUES where one might expect them. Some have said certain statements about the future are neither true nor false, since the future is not yet determined. Cf. FREEWILL (for logical determinism).

Compare also cases in fiction and mythology, like 'Unicorns are vegetarian', where the legends give no evidence. There are other things which seem to be of the right kind to be true or false but are sometimes thought to be neither, or to be not really of that kind. Examples include value statements, laws of nature and counterfactual CONDITIONALS. It seems, then, that some things fail to be true or false because they are not of the right kind, while others may be not false but wrong for some other reason ('My wife is asleep', said by a bachelor). Metaphors and comparisons, etc., raise again the question of degrees of truth, e.g. should exaggerations be described as nearly true, or fairly true, or containing some truth? The HEAP paradox has also been thought to call for degrees of truth.

Special problems arise in certain cases. What is it for a logical or mathematical statement to be true? How is 'true' related to 'provable'? (Cf. GÖDEL'S THEOREMS, mathematical INTUITIONISM.)

A distinction is often drawn, though also often ignored, between the meaning of 'true' and the CRITERIA of truth. It is sometimes unclear to which of these a given theory is intended to apply.

Another use of 'true' and 'false' is that whereby predicates can be true or false of subjects. Linguistic PHILOSOPHERS sometimes ask what significance there is in such facts as that artificial teeth, but not artificial silk, are called false, while no teeth are true. See also SATISFY, TRUTH-VALUE, FACTS, VALID, LIAR PARADOX, philosophy of MATHEMATICS.

*M. Black, 'The semantic definition of truth', *Analysis*, vol. 8, 1948, reprinted in M. Macdonald (ed.), *Philosophy and Analysis*, Blackwell, 1954. (On Tarski. Easier than Tarski though it presupposes elementary knowledge of logic.)

D. Davidson, 'The structure and content of truth', *Journal of Philosophy*, 1990. (Discusses Tarskian truth, and rejects both deflationist and correspondence theories, and also antirealist theories (such as the coherence theory and pragmatism), changing some of his earlier views, and finally proposing a further theory of his own.)

D. W. Hamlyn, 'The correspondence theory of truth', *Philosophical Quarterly*, 1962. (Fairly difficult defence of loose correspondence theory.)

P. Horwich, *Truth*, Blackwell, 1990. (States a deflationary theory, calling it 'minimal', though distinguishing it from redundancy theory at pp. 39–41; then defends it against thirty-nine objections.)

H. Joachim, *The Nature of Truth*, 1905. (Coherence.)

W. Künne, *Conceptions of Truth*, Clarendon, 2003. (Comprehensive survey of theories, together with his own 'modest account' of truth.)

D. H. Mellor, *Real Time*, Cambridge UP, 1981, 2nd edn, *Real Time II*, Routledge, 1998. (See chapter 2 on relations between truth and time: is truth timeless in all cases?)

G. E. Moore, *Some Main Problems of Philosophy*, Allen and Unwin, 1953, Collier Books, 1962, written much earlier.

G. Pitcher (ed.), *Truth*, Prentice-Hall, 1964. (Contains papers by J. L. Austin, P. F. Strawson, G. J. Warnock, M. Dummett, with excerpt from F. P. Ramsey, *On Dummett* cf. bibliography to TRUTH-VALUE.)

*B. Russell, *The Problems of Philosophy*, Home University Library, 1912, chapter 12. (Cf. also Russell in bibliography to LOGICAL ATOMISM.)

R. M. Sainsbury, 'Degrees of belief and degrees of truth', *Philosophical Papers*, 1986. (Defends degrees of truth in connection with heap paradox.)

S. Soames, 'What is a theory of truth?', *Journal of Philosophy*, 1984. (See particularly p. 411 for brief statement of three things a theory of truth has tried to do.)

P. F. Strawson, *Logico-Linguistic Papers*, Methuen, 1971. (Includes several relevant items. For truth-value gaps see chapters 1, 4.)

A. Tarski, 'The semantic conception of truth', *Philosophy and Phenomenological Research*, 1944, reprinted in H. Feigl and M. Sellars (eds), *Readings in Philosophical Analysis*, Appleton-Century-Crofts, 1949.

Truth conditions. Conditions for a given sentence, proposition, etc., to be true; e.g. when p and q represent propositions which we assume must be true or false, the truth conditions of 'Not (p without q)' are that p and q be both true, or both false, or p be false and q true. To call something 'one of the truth conditions' of something else is ambiguous. It may mean that the first thing is adequate by itself to guarantee the truth of the second, but other things would be so too. (In the above example three such alternative truth conditions are given.) Or it may mean that the first thing is one of a set of things which are adequate for this if taken together (e.g. the truth of p is one of the truth conditions for 'p and q').

Truth conditions have also been used to give the meaning of terms like 'now' by those who think there is no property of presentness.

See also MEANING.

D. H. Mellor, *Real Time*, Cambridge UP, 1981, 2nd edn, *Real Time II*, Routledge, 1998. (See particularly pp. 74–8 for meaning of 'now', etc.)

Truth function. A truth function of a given proposition, or set of them, is a proposition whose TRUTH VALUE can be inferred given theirs, e.g. 'p or f' (but not 'p because f') is a truth function of p and f. The truth function of a complex expression, consisting of a number of linked propositions ('John will only come to the party if Bill is not invited and the weather is good'), can be determined by means of a TRUTH TABLE.

Truth table. One among the decision procedures (see DECIDABLE) for the propositional CALCULUS. The TRUTH-VALUE, normally true or false, of a complex expression in the propositional calculus depends on the truth-values assigned to the VARIABLES in it. A truth table is a systematic expression of all possible combinations of such assignments for the expression in question. Each combination occupies a row in the table, with the resulting truth-value for the whole expression placed, for example, at one end of the row. These truth-values for the whole expression form a column, from which various properties of the expression can be read off, e.g. the expression is logically true if this column contains no truth-value but true.

The following example of a truth table for 'Not (p and not q)' (where p and q represent propositions, and '1' means 'true' and '0' means 'false') is written out at unnecessary length to show how it is constructed. Various alternative presentations are possible. In the present case each row should be read from left to right, and the final column shows that the whole expression is false when p is true and q is false, and true in all other eases.

p	q	not q	p and not q	not (p and not q)
1	1	0	0	1
1	0	1	1	0
0	1	0	0	1
0	0	1	0	1

Truth-value. True and false are known as the two main truth-values. For a two-valued logic they, are in practice the only truth-values, though theoretically any two could be chosen. Three-valued and in general many-valued logics use three or more values accordingly, adding to true and false or replacing them. When they add to them, as in the first example below, or as degrees of truth do, they reject bivalence (see EXCLUDED MIDDLE). Examples are true/false/

indeterminate, known to be true/known to be false/unknown, necessarily true/necessarily false/contingent; certainly true/99 per cent probable/ ... /certainly false (this last group, like that of degrees of truth, could contain infinitely many values). Sometimes a set of truth-values falls into two groups with important logical properties analogous to those of true and false, respectively. Those analogous to true are then called designated values, and those analogous to false are called undesignated values.

> M. Dummett, 'Truth', *Proceedings of the Aristotelian Society*, 1958–9, reprinted in G. Pitcher (ed.), *Truth*, Prentice-Hall, 1964, in P. F. Strawson (ed.), *Philosophical Logic*, Oxford UP, 1967, and in Dummett's *Truth and Other Enigmas*, Duckworth, 1978. (Includes explanation of designated and undesignated values).

Truth-value gaps. See TRUTH AND FALSITY.

T-sentence. See MEANING.

Turing, Alan. 1912–54. British mathematician, logician and computer pioneer. Before the Second World War, he wrote several influential papers on the mathematical theory of computing, and developed the idea of a TURING MACHINE. During the War, he worked at the top secret British code breaking centre at Bletchley Park, where he helped to design an electro-mechanical machine, the bombe, to break the German codes. After the War he worked on developing the first real computer at the University of Manchester. He presciently foresaw the future of computers and devised the TURING TEST of when we might say of a machine that it thinks. He committed suicide in 1954, after having hormone injections following his conviction in 1952 for homosexuality (then illegal).

> A. Hodges, *Alan Turing: The Enigma of Intelligence*, Burnett, 1983. (A sympathetic and admirably clear exposition of his life and work.)
>
> P. Millican and A. Clark (eds), *The Legacy of Alan Turing, Volume 1: Machines and Thought*, and *The Legacy of Alan Turing, Volume 2: Connectionism, Concepts and Folk Psychology*, Oxford UP, 1997.

Turing machine. A device due to TURING for solving any problem which can be solved by computation. An indefinitely long tape extends through a point on the machine which reads symbols on it, normally in the form of noughts and ones, or some equivalent (e.g.

negative and positive charge). The machine can carry out just four operations: move the tape one step to the left; move the tape one step to the right; replace a nought on the tape with a one; replace a one with a nought. It also can be in any of a finite number of possible states, each containing instructions (varying from state to state) for carrying out the operations in the light of what it reads on the tape, and for passing from one state to another. The problem to be solved, together with any relevant data, is then coded on to the tape (the rest of the tape being filled with noughts) and fed into the machine. Different machines will have different repertoires (i.e. sets of possible states), according to the problem to be solved, but there can also be a universal Turing machine which can be programmed to take on the repertoires of any given machine and so to replace it. However, since the tape must be indefinitely long, and both the number of possible states and the sequence of operations needed indefinitely large (though finite), a Turing machine must be thought of as an idealized blueprint rather than a practicable construction. The idea is important because it makes precise what a computable function is. Any function (in the mathematical sense) that can be effectively computed by a computer at all can be computed by a Turing machine. This lets us distinguish the sort of problems that can, and the sort that cannot, be in principle solved by a computer.

T. Crane, *The Mechanical Mind: A Philosophical Introduction to Minds, Machines and Mental Representation*, Penguin, 1995, chapter 3. (Elementary introduction).

R. Penrose, *The Emperor's New Mind*, Oxford UP, 1989, chapter 2, particularly pp. 46–56, 67–75.

Turing test. Test devised by TURING for helping us to answer, or rather to provide a more precise substitute for, the question 'Can machines think?' The test takes the form of an imitation game. A human and a machine, both hidden behind a screen, confront an interlocutor who asks them a series of questions to find out which is which. The machine is programmed to deceive the interlocutor for as long as possible by imitating the sort of responses a human would give (its answers need not be true), while the human tries to help the interlocutor. If the machine succeeds over some pre-assigned period, it wins the imitation game and passes the Turing test. Turing thought, overoptimistically, that machines capable of a modest success rate (30 per cent) would be a practical possibility by the end of the twentieth century.

N. Block, 'The computer model of the mind', in D. Osherson and B. E. Smith (eds), *An Invitation to Cognitive Science*, vol. III, MIT Press, 1990, particularly pp. 248–53.

R. Epstein, G. Roberts and G. Beber (eds), *Parsing the Turing Test: Philosophical and Methodological Issues in the Quest for the Thinking*, Springer-Verlag, 2008. (30 articles, by, among others, Searle, Chomsky, Churchland, surveying and discussing 55 years of the Turing Test.)

A. M. Turing, 'Computing machinery and intelligence', *Mind*, 1950, reprinted in A. R. Anderson (ed.), *Minds and Machines*, Prentice-Hall, 1964, along with various articles discussing the significance of Turing's article, and in numerous other places.

Types (theory of). Towards the end of the nineteenth century interest revived in the logical PARADOXES, from which the semantic ones were not yet distinguished. To cope with RUSSELL'S PARADOX and others, Russell enunciated the vicious circle principle: 'If, provided a certain collection had a total, it would have members only definable in terms of that total, then the said collection has no total', i.e. we cannot talk of the totality of its members. Classes form such a collection, for him. There are, he said, first-type, or first-level, classes whose members are ordinary objects, second-type classes whose members are first-type classes, and so on. The class of cats and the class of dogs are animal classes. They are first-type classes themselves, and are members of the second-type class of animal classes. There is a class of all classes of a given type which will itself be one type higher, but no class of all classes (see also CATEGORIES). Ordinary objects are of type zero. The hierarchy of types also applies to properties: A property of properties of objects belongs to the second type. Black is a property of some cats. It has the property of applying to some cats. Applying to some cats is therefore a second-type property of the first-type property black.

In 'Napoleon had all the properties of a great general', having all the properties of a great general is a property of Napoleon, and so is of the first type. But it refers to properties, so is said to be of the second order. It attributes to Napoleon only the relevant first-order properties (on this theory). The addition of the hierarchy of orders to that of types gives us the ramified as against simple theory of types. (But words like 'second-order' are normally used more loosely.) Propositions too are distinguished into orders. A proposition referring to no other propositions is of the first order. One referring to propositions of the first order (e.g. 'Some first-order propositions are false') is of the second order, and so on. The ramified theory was used to solve the semantic PARADOXES, e.g. the LIAR.

Since the ramified theory invalidates certain mathematical procedures, Russell introduced the controversial axiom of reducibility, saying that any higher-order property or proposition could be replaced by some first-order one.

Classes, etc., defined in ways violating the vicious circle principle are said to have impredicative definitions (for an example see Carnap, p. 37–8).

One disadvantage of the theory is that many words, e.g. 'class', 'proposition', 'true', become systematically, or 'typically', AMBIGUOUS, with different senses for each type or order.

R. Carnap, 'The logicist foundations of mathematics' in P. Benacerraf and H. Putnam (eds), *Philosophy of Mathematics*, Blackwell, 1964, pp. 31–41. (Elementary but illuminating.)

I. M. Copi, *The Theory of Logical Types*, RKP, 1971. (Fuller treatment.)

A. Whitehead and B. Russell, *Principia Mathematica*, Cambridge UP, vol. 1, 1910. (See Introduction, chapter 2, § 1, for vicious circle principle, repeated (though not there so called) in Russell's *Logic and Knowledge*, Allen and Unwin, 1956, p. 63.)

Type/token. See UNIVERSALS.

U

Übermensch. In NIETZSCHE, the 'one who transcends humanity' (literally) or 'new man' (sometimes misleadingly translated as 'super-man') of the future, who willingly overcomes or goes beyond humanity's existing constraints, such as traditional morality.

Uncertainty principle. See CAUSATION.

Unexpected examination paradox. See PREDICTION.

Universalizability. An important part of morality seems to lie in the idea that what is right for one person must be right for anyone else in the same position. This can be expressed by saying that a moral judgement must be universalizable. Kant made such a claim in one of his formulations of the categorical IMPERATIVE: 'Act only on that maxim which you can at the same time will to become a universal law'. If I say that you ought not to lie, I commit myself to saying that anyone else in your position ought not to lie. Similarly, if I call someone's action a good deed I must allow that anyone else who did the same thing in the same circumstances did a good deed.

Universalizability is not the same as generality. 'Everyone ought to give 1 per cent of his income to blind cripples over sixty' is very specific but quite universal. It refers to all who have an income and all blind cripples over sixty since all such cripples are put on a level. In spite of this, 'generalize' is sometimes used for 'universalize', as by Singer.

Judgements may be universal in a stricter or a looser sense. The looser kind may mention individual people, places, etc. Thus 'Everyone should fight for his country' is universal in the stricter sense, since no particular country is mentioned. On the other hand, 'Everyone should fight for England', 'Every Englishman should fight for

England,' 'Every Englishman should be kind to animals', are all universal only in the looser sense.

Those who make universalizability important for ethics may hold either of two views. The first view uses universalizability to distinguish the MORAL from the non-moral. Someone's principle is a moral principle, on this view, if he is willing to universalize it. In this way universalizability helps to define morality, providing either a necessary condition for it (Hare) or a sufficient condition, or both (see NECESSARY AND SUFFICIENT CONDITIONS). The second view (Kant, Singer) tries to distinguish the moral from the immoral, by saying that what makes a principle moral is basically that it is universalizable, in the sense that there is no inconsistency in supposing everyone to act on it. 'Inconsistency' here may mean the kind of inconsistency involved in frustrating one's own ends (it is inconsistent to commit oneself to accepting that all promises should be broken, if they would then no longer be regarded as promises, so that one's purpose in making them would be frustrated, whatever that purpose might be). Or it may mean simply the frustration of something which is, or should be, a general end of human action, e.g. maximizing happiness.

There are difficulties in the notion of universalizing. What counts as universalizing a judgement? Suppose that whatever applies to me must apply to everyone like me: how like me must they be? Can I not describe my case in such a way that no one is like me? Remembering that very specific judgements can still be universalized, I might say: 'Although people in general ought not to lie, I myself may lie, because I will allow that anyone may lie if he is just six feet tall, has a scar on his left knee, etc., etc.', listing so many of my characteristics that no one else has them all. Also, do desires, etc., count as relevant characteristics? If so, I might say: 'You ought to help the poor, and so ought anyone like you, but I need not because I am not like you. I do not desire to help them, as you do.'

One way of expressing the need for universalizability is by saying that whatever is a reason for one person to act must be a reason for anyone else in the same position to act in the same way. This may give a necessary condition for morality, but it is not peculiar to morality, since it is a mere principle of logical consistency. If danger to health is a reason for Smith not to smoke, it is presumably a reason for everyone like him not to smoke – though again it may be hard to describe how 'like' him they must be.

It has been disputed how many kinds of universalizability there are. Universalizability in the sense of mere logical consistency is, as we

have just seen, too wide to define morality completely. Universalizability in the sense of impartiality (in particular, not favouring
oneself) seems to be a principle which marks the moral from the
immoral, rather than the moral from the non-moral. But this principle
too, as we have seen, is not easy to formulate. How far universalizability is relevant to morality, therefore, whether as helping to define
it or as contributing to its content, is unclear. (Another notion
important here is that of SUPERVENIENCE.)

For moral particularism see ETHICS.

J. Dancy, 'On moral properties', *Mind*, 1981. (Universalizability and allied
notions.)

A. Gewirth, 'Categorial consistency in ethics', *Philosophical Quarterly*, 1967.
(Discusses how far universalizability can he used for moral attack on
racialism. Criticized by N. Fotion, 'Gewirth and categorial consistency',
Philosophical Quarterly, 1968.)

R. M. Hare, *The Language of Morals*, Oxford UP, 1952, *Freedom and
Reason*, Clarendon, 1963. (Claims universalizability gives necessary
condition (not sufficient, but important), for defining morality.)

*W. D. Hudson, *Modern Moral Philosophy*, Macmillan, 1970. (General
introduction, including discussions of universalizability in connection
with Hare.)

I. Kant, *The Moral Law: Kant's Groundwork of the Metaphysic of Morals*,
H. J. Paton (trans.), Hutchinson, 1948. (For Kant's formulations of the
Categorical Imperative. Probably best translation of Kant's *Grundlegung*,
1785, earliest and most famous major attempt to base morality on
universalizability. Difficult.)

D. Locke, 'The trivializability of universalizability', *Philosophical Review*,
1968. (Distinguishes several senses of 'universalizability', and claims that
most of them are of little importance to ethics.)

D. H. Monro, 'Impartiality and consistency', *Philosophy* 1961 (cf. his
Empiricism in Ethics, Cambridge UP, 1967, chapter 16.) (Distinguishes
these. Criticized by S. B. Thomas, 'The status of the generalization
principle', *American Philosophical Quarterly*, 1968.)

M. G. Singer, *Generalization in Ethics*, Eyre and Spottiswoode, 1963.
(Elaborate modern development of Kant's view, claiming that generalization (i.e. universalization) is 'the fundamental principle of
morality' (Preface). Studies in detail the implications of the question.
'What would happen if everyone did that?' Shorter version in his
'Moral rules and principles', in A. I. Melden (ed.), *Essays in Moral Philosophy*, Washington UP, 1958, stressing difference between rules and
principles.)

Universals and particulars. Objects around us share features with other objects. It is in the nature of most such features that they can characterize indefinitely many objects. Because of this the features are called universals and the main problem is to describe their status. Exceptions, such as 'being the tallest of men', can be included for convenience. The objects are called their instances. The problem is often called, especially in Greek philosophy, the one-many or one-over-many problem. Traditionally three kinds of answer have been given: realism, conceptualism and nominalism. Realism in this sense is primarily associated with Plato, who treated universals as objects (cf. FORM, IDEA), separate from their instances, and faced great difficulties over what they were like and how they related to these instances. Plato's Forms, in so far as they are treated rather as particulars (see below), are often said not to be universals, though doing duty for them. Platonism is nowadays any view which treats things like universals, propositions, numbers, etc., as independent objects. Frege is a noted modern Platonist. Another form of realism, often attributed to Aristotle though the interpretation of Aristotle is very controversial, denies that universals are objects or separate from their instances, but nevertheless makes them real things which somehow exist just by being instantiated. It is unclear how this view treats things like unicornhood. The labels *universalia ante rem* or *res*: universals prior to the object(s), and *universalia in re* or *rebus*: universals in the object(s), are often applied to Plato's and Aristotle's views respectively. *Universalia post rem* or *res*: universals, after, or derivative from, the object(s), normally applies to nominalism, though it could apply to conceptualism. The term 'substantial universals' is applied, like 'realism', primarily to Plato's view, though sometimes also to Aristotle's. It could, but usually does not, denote universals corresponding to substances, e.g. tablehood, as against qualitative universals like hardness. Realists often limit universals to only some general features.

For conceptualism, universals are thoughts or ideas in and constructed by the mind. This view, summarily rejected by Plato, is largely associated with the British EMPIRICISTS. It may explain human thinking and the MEANING of many words, but it can no longer explain why the world itself is as it is (which Plato claimed his Forms explained). The view thus avoids Plato's dilemma that the universal is either outside its instances and so irrelevant to them, or inside them and so split up. But what sort of thing is this thought or idea? Does it involve images, and if so, of what sort? Can the same idea be shared by different people, which splits the universal up again, or have they similar but distinct ideas, which leads to the difficulty associated with PRIVATE LANGUAGES? Some writers include conceptualism under nominalism, e.g. Armstrong, who talks of 'conceptual nominalism'.

For nominalism, represented especially by Ockham in the middle ages and so by many recent writers, there are only general words like 'dog', and no universals in the sense of entities like doghood. Cf. MEANING, and also below on 'types' and 'tokens'. (For N. Goodman nominalism means recognizing only INDIVIDUALS (second sense), which for him may be abstract but cannot include classes.)

There are two ways of defining a class of objects. One can define it extensionally or in extension, by listing its members, or one can define it as containing all those things which have a certain property or set of properties (called defining it intensionally or in intension; see INTENSIONALITY). The former way makes it impossible for a class, once it is defined, to acquire new members, and is of little use. The latter way leaves open how many members, if any, a class has; the class of dogs contains whatever things have the properties necessary for being a dog. Nominalism now faces a difficulty, for if there are no universals, i.e. no properties, what determines whether something belongs to the class of dogs or not? This is another version of Plato's demand for Forms to account for the world's being as it is. The main nominalist answer to this difficulty uses the notion of resemblance. An object is a dog if it resembles some given dog which is chosen as a standard or paradigm. Two disputed objections to this are that resemblance itself seems to be an indispensable universal, and that resemblance involves partial identity, for to resemble something is to have something, though not necessarily everything, in common with it; the common feature is then presumably a universal.

A variant on the use of resemblance is Wittgenstein's notion of family resemblance, whereby there need be nothing common to all the members of a class, nor need any member be taken as the paradigm, but the members form 'a complicated network of similarities overlapping and criss-crossing' like the fibres that make up a thread. An example Wittgenstein takes is that of a game: have all games got something in common? A somewhat related notion is that of clusters (Gasking).

Particulars, which are not always the same as INDIVIDUALS, cannot be instantiated, and cannot appear as a whole at separated places simultaneously though their parts may be spatially separate. A particular can perhaps appear as a whole at different moments of time (though see GENIDENTITY), but these must normally be linked into a stream – though an intermittent sound may constitute one and the same particular, and see Burke. A particular's parts may be constantly changing, as with a flame, and it need not be 'solid' (shadows, rainbows, clouds, can all be particulars, and perhaps the sky). It must, however, be identifiable and distinguishable from other particulars, so clouds, etc., are not always particulars. Particulars can be abstract, provided the conditions about space and time are preserved (e.g. an action or event, like the Renaissance. Rarely non-spatiotemporal things like numbers are included.) Bare particulars are particulars considered as independent of all their properties. It is therefore hard to identify or refer to them.

Particulars are like SUBSTANCES in the first Aristotelian sense of that term though the emphasis is on being unique in space and time rather than, as with Aristotle on existing in their own right as the bearers of attributes and subjects of change. Therefore, shadows and actions are more easily called particulars than substances, while Platonist universals are more naturally called substances than particulars, especially since particulars cannot be instantiated.

As an adjective 'particular' has its everyday sense, and also that given under SENTENCE.

We have seen that universals are sometimes treated rather as particulars. Idealism's concrete universal is also a kind of particular. It is a system of instances, treated as a developing individual, e.g. man in 'Man has evolved slowly'. Bradley treats ordinary particulars as concrete universals, since they are developing individuals, though really the universe is the sole individual. He uses 'particular' in a more restricted sense than the present entry.

Universals, like particulars, are of many kinds. Some universals (relations) can only be instantiated in ordered pairs or triplets, etc., of objects. Others, like 'round square', cannot be instantiated at all, even in thought. Some can be instantiated together with their opposites: an object can be both beautiful and ugly, in different respects; or the object may instantiate the universal only if described in a certain way: something may be large if described as a mouse, but not if described as an animal (see ATTRIBUTIVE); and the instances may themselves be universals, for a universal may have universals as its instance: red may have the property of being beautiful. Moreover, stuffs, like water, are not particulars but presumably instantiate universals (though wateriness rather characterizes other things resembling water). Logically, then, it is the notion of an instance that is correlative to that of a universal, though instances are no doubt usually particulars.

A distinction closely related to that between universals and parti-culars, and revealing some of the complications in this field, is that between types and tokens, introduced by Peirce. The word 'in' appears twice in the present sentence, yet it is only one word. Peirce would call these two appearances in any one copy of the present book, two tokens of a single type. A word as found in the dictionary is therefore a type with indefinitely many tokens (written, spoken, etc.). Only types can be derived from Latin. Only tokens can be ille-gible. A token may be ambiguous, and then so must its type. A type may be polysyllabic, and then so must all its tokens. The distinction is significant for nominalists, for when they say there are only words and no universals, do they mean types or tokens? Also, the distinction is not sufficient by itself, for the words in a speech cannot be types, for types are not limited to a single speech, nor yet tokens, since the speech, and therefore the same words, can be recorded many times (Cohen). It is disputed how closely this distinction resembles that between universals and particulars. 'Word' as a universal has instan-ces (several hundred on this page); as a type it has tokens (each of just four letters). Also to what spheres, apart from words, is it relevant? Is the Union Jack, or the lion in 'The lion is carnivorous', a type or a universal or what? Is the lion a concrete universal? Spheres where the distinction has been used include aesthetics, in the analysis of works of art, and in the IDENTITY THEORY OF MIND. See also REALISM, CONCEPT, IDEA, SENTENCES, TROPE, THIRD MAN ARGUMENT.

R. I. Aaron, *The Theory of Universals*, Clarendon, 1952, revised 1967. (Universals as 'natural recurrences' and 'principles of grouping'. Some history.)

E. B. Allaire, 'Bare particulars', *Philosophical Studies*, 1963, reprinted with discussion in Loux (below).

Aristotle, *Metaphysics*, book 7 (or Z), chapters 13–16, *Posterior Analy-tics*, book 2, chapter 19. (Cf. also Aristotle references under SUBSTANCE.)

D. M. Armstrong, *Universals and Scientific Realism*, vol. 1: *Nominalism and Realism*, vol. 2: *A Theory of Universals*, Cambridge UP, 1978. (Important modern work. See also his *Universals: An Opinionated Introduction*, Westview Press, 1989, which is shorter than his earlier work but contains important revisions.)

F. H. Bradley, *The Principles of Logic*. 1993, book 1, chapter 2, § 4, chapter 6, § 30–6. (Concrete universals. Cf. R. M. Eaton, *General Logic*, Scribner's Sons 1931, pp. 269–72.)

M. B. Burke, 'Cohabitation, stuff and intermittent existence', *Mind*, 1980. (Material objects can exist intermittently.)

W. Charlton, *Aesthetics*, Hutchinson, 1970, pp. 27–9. (Types and universals. Relevance to aesthetics. Cf. also R. A. Dipert, 'Types and tokens: A reply to Sharpe', *Mind*, 1980; Sharpe replies in *Mind*, 1982.)

L. J. Cohen, *The Diversity of Meaning*, Methuen, 1962, pp. 4–5. (Brief discussion of types and tokens.)

D. Gasking, 'Clusters', *Australasian Journal of Philosophy*, 1960.

N. Goodman, 'A world of individuals', in I. M. Bochenski *et al.*, *The Problem of Universals*, 1956, reprinted in P. Benacerraf and H. Putnam (eds), *Philosophy of Mathematics*, Blackwell, 1964 (cf. also ibid., pp. 21–3), and in C. Landesman (ed.), *The Problem of Universals*, Basic Books, 1971. (Goodman's nominalism.)

D. K. Lewis, 'New work for a theory of universals', *Australasian Journal of Philosophy*, 1983. (Discuss Armstrong's earlier work, claiming universals are indeed needed, but for reasons different from Armstrong's. Difficult.)

M. Loux, *Metaphysics: A Contemporary Introduction*, Routledge, 1998. (Good introduction.)

M. J. Loux (ed.), *Universals and Particulars*, Anchor Books, 1970. (Selected readings.)

A. Oliver, 'The metaphysics of properties', *Mind*, 1996. (Extended survey article, with references, on recent views on the nature and role of properties, concentrating especially on Armstrong's treatment of properties as immanent universals.)

Plato, *Phaedo, Republic*, § 596, *Parmenides*, particularly down to § 135c. (These are among the important passages. The *Parmenides* includes what seems to be strong self-criticism, including the 'third man argument'.)

H. H. Price, *Thinking and Experience*, Hutchinson, 1953, chapter 1, reprinted in Landesman (above). (Moderate defence of resemblance theory, reconciling it with *'universalia in rebus'* theory.)

W. V. O. Quine, 'On what there is' (see bibliography to BEING). (Offers a criterion for deciding whether there are universals or not.)

A. B. Schoedinger (ed.) *The Problem of Universals*, Humanities Press, 1992. (General anthology.)

M. A. Simon, 'When is a resemblance a family resemblance?', *Mind*, 1969. (Critical discussion of family resemblance view.)

*H. Staniland, *Universals*, Doubleday Anchor, 1972. (Elementary introduction, if inevitably a bit dated.)

L. Wittgenstein, *Philosophical Investigations*, Blackwell, 1953, §§ 65–77. (Family resemblance view.)

Universe of discourse. See QUANTIFICATION.

Utilitarianism. Moral theories about what we ought to do are commonly, if not uncontroversially, divided into deontological and teleological ones (see ETHICS). The main, though not the only, teleological (or CONSEQUENTIALIST) theory is utilitarianism, which in its most general form is to the effect that we always ought to do what will produce the greatest good. But 'utilitarianism' is sometimes restricted to hedonistic utilitarianism, which holds that the good is pleasure, or perhaps happiness. Early utilitarians seldom distinguished these. Ideal utilitarianism, notably represented by Moore, allows other things to be good, or even to be the main goods (for Moore personal relations and aesthetic experiences). Most early utilitarians were hedonistic, though contemporary ones are harder to classify, and often appeal to preference or satisfaction of desire rather than to pleasure. Utilitarianism has never held, as its name may suggest, that one should pursue only the useful and not the good in itself, nor that one should pursue only 'low-grade' pleasures; when Bentham said that if the pleasure is equal pushpin is as good as poetry, one should not ignore the 'if'-clause.

Though the idea of utilitarianism goes back to the Greeks, its most famous exponents have been Bentham and J. S. Mill, Bentham's greatest happiness principle says that one should pursue 'the greatest good, or greatest happiness, of the greatest number'. The formula is imprecise, because if we try to spread happiness to many people we may produce less happiness overall than if we confine it to fewer people. Faced with this difficulty, utilitarians have usually said that one should aim for the greatest happiness overall, however distributed. It is therefore often objected that they cannot account for our intuitions about justice. It is also doubted whether they can account for our normal views on promise-keeping, truth-telling, etc. Also utilitarianism faces difficulties in connection with such things as the double-effect doctrine (see ETHICS) or the distinction between (e.g.) killing and letting die.

Utilitarianism may be attacked in a weak or a strong way. The weak way grants that we always ought to aim for the greatest happiness, but says we have other duties too, e.g. to distribute it in certain ways. The strong attack says that some of our duties not only go beyond utilitarianism, but are inconsistent with it, because they involve producing less happiness than other courses of action would produce.

Recently utilitarians have split into two camps. Act utilitarians (also called extreme or direct utilitarians; notably J. J. C. Smart) say that on each occasion we should do whatever act will produce the greatest good. Rule utilitarians (also called restricted or indirect utilitarians) say that we should obey those rules which would produce the greatest happiness if generally followed. These are other versions of rule utilitarianism. Suppose I ignore a red traffic light and, by some fluke, thereby prevent an accident which would otherwise have occurred. Then, whatever my motive, on act utilitarianism I did right, but on rule utilitarianism I did wrong, assuming that general obedience to the traffic laws produces better results than general disobedience to them.

Motive utilitarianism is the view that 'one pattern of motivation is morally better than another to the extent that the former has more utility than the latter' (Adams).

One difficulty for utilitarianism is how we can ever know what we ought to do. Not only can we never know the total consequences of any act, but much may depend on what others do, and they in turn must take account of what we may do (cf. DECISION THEORY, FREEWILL (on self-prediction)). Rule utilitarianism is partly intended to overcome this difficulty, but has difficulties of its own.

The question whether we should aim at what we think best or at what is really best raises a difficulty shared by other theories.

An interesting recent question concerns population policy. Normally utilitarians have concerned themselves with problems about creating goods and distributing them among a given population, but further questions obviously arise when we can decide how large that population shall be, and which of various alternative populations shall exist. Negative utilitarianism says we should aim only to remove evil, not to produce good. Ordinary utilitarianism says we should both remove evil and produce good, aiming at the greatest overall balance of good.

See also HEDONISM, PLEASURE, SIDGWICK, UNIVERSALIZABILITY, and bibliography for CONSEQUENTIALISM.

H. B. Acton and J. W. N. Watkins, 'Negative utilitarianism', *Proceedings of the Aristotelian Society*, supplementary vol., 1963.

R. M. Adams, 'Motive utilitarianism', *Journal of Philosophy*, 1976, reprinted P. Pettit (ed.), *Consequentialism*, Dartmouth Publishing Co., 1993. (For quotation see p. 470 (p. 74 in reprint).)

J. Annas, 'Aristotle on pleasure and goodness', in A. O. Rorty (ed.), *Essays on Aristotle's Ethics*, California UP, 1980. (Uses Aristotle as basis for attacking some of the fundamental assumptions of utilitarianism. Cf. also in same volume J. McDowell, 'The role of *end* in Aristotle's ethics', and the two articles by D. Wiggins, particularly pp. 258–61; all quite difficult and Wiggins uses some technicalities.)

G. E. M. Anscombe, 'Modern moral philosophy', *Philosophy*, 1958, reprinted in C. Wallace and A. D. M. Walker (eds), *The Definition of Morality*, Methuen, 1970, with additional bibliography, and in W. D. Hudson (ed.), *The Is/Ought Question*, Macmillan, 1969. (Criticizes utilitarianism.)

R. B. Brandt, *A Theory of the Good and the Right*, Clarendon, 1979. (Revised edition, Prometheus 1998, with foreword by Singer.) (Influential defence of utilitarianism.)

B. Hooker, *Ideal Code, Real World*, Oxford UP, 2003. (Detailed and sophisticated defence of rule consequentialism.)

D. Lyons, *Forms and Limits of Utilitarianism*, Oxford UP, 1965. (Discusses relations between versions of act and rule utilitarianism. Discussed by B. A. Brody, 'The equivalence of act and rule utilitarianism', *Philosophical Studies*, 1967.)

*J. S. Mill, *Utilitarianism*, 1861. (Classic and provocative defence.)

G. E. Moore, *Principia Ethica*, Oxford UP, 1903. (Ideal utilitarianism.)

I. Narveson, 'Utilitarianism and new generations', *Mind*, 1967. (Population control. Discussed by T. L. S. Sprigge, 'Professor Narveson's utilitarianism', *Inquiry*, 1968 (§2), and H. Vetter, 'Utilitarianism and new generations', *Mind*, 1971.)

D. Parfit, *Reasons and Persons*, Oxford UP, 1984. (Part I discusses consequentialism in general. Part 4 discusses questions about population policy.)

A. Sen and B. A. O. Williams (eds), *Utilitarianism and Beyond*, Cambridge UP, 1982. (Mainly specially written essays, covering philosophy and economics.)

H. Sidgwick, *Methods of Ethics*, 1874 (7th edition and final version, 1907), facsimile reprint, Hackett, 1981. (Classic, highly detailed, treatment of different ethical theories, and defence of utilitarianism.)

J. J. C. Smart, 'Extreme and restricted utilitarianism', in P. Foot (ed.), *Theories of Ethics*, Oxford UP, 1967. (Act utilitarianism. See also J. Rawls, 'Two concepts of rules', ibid.)

*J. C. C. Smart and B. A. O. Williams, *Utilitarianism For and Against*, Cambridge UP, 1973. (Debate with annotated bibliography).

V

Vacuous. In logic certain statements, notably universal statements (see SENTENCES), and CONDITIONALS, are often interpreted more widely than in ordinary thought. 'All unicorns are black' means 'There are no non-black unicorns', and so is true if there are no unicorns. 'If p then q', where p and q are propositions, means 'Not (p without q)', and so is true if p is false. Statements true simply because their subject terms are empty or (in the case of conditionals) their antecedents false, or for certain other 'irrelevant' reasons, are called vacuously true. Their contradictions can be called vacuously false. A term occurs vacuously in a statement if the truth or falsity of the statement remains unaffected when the term is replaced by any other term meaningfully admissible in that context. 'Red' for instance occurs vacuously in 'This table is either red or not red'. Normally (though not always: see Quine) a term not occurring vacuously occurs essentially.

W. V. O. Quine, 'Truth by convention', in H. Feigl and W. Sellars (eds), *Readings in Philosophical Analysis*, Appleton-Century Crofts, 1949. (Vacuous occurrence.)

Vagueness. To be distinguished from AMBIGUITY and OPEN TEXTURE.

Problems about vagueness arise especially from the HEAP (or sorites) paradox, and mainly concern how far it affects TRUTH and the law of EXCLUDED MIDDLE, and whether it is an objective feature of the world, or simply a feature, perhaps unavoidable, of our language, or is an illusion depending on our ignorance.

G. Evans, 'Can there be vague objects?', *Analysis*, 1978. (One-page article raising problem for view that there can. NB: The symbol '∇' means 'it is vague whether' and 'Δ' means 'it is definite whether'. Cf. also (difficult) discussion by S. A. Rasmussen in *Mind*, 1986.)

T. Parsons and P. Woodruff, 'Worldly indeterminacy of identity', *Proceedings of the Aristotelian Society*, 1995. (Vagueness is an objective feature of the world. Cf. also M. Tye, 'Vague objects', *Mind*, 1990.)

T. Williams, *Vagueness*, Routledge, 1994. (General treatment, including historical material and defending the view that vagueness depends on our ignorance. See also bibliography to HEAP.)

Valid. An inference or an argument is valid if its conclusion follows deductively from its premises. The premises may be false, but if they are true the conclusion must be true. An inference is invalid if it is not valid. It is contravalid if an inference from the same premises to the opposite conclusion would be valid. Sometimes, however, a valid argument is simply defined as one where it is logically impossible for all the premises to be true and the conclusion false. This raises the same 'paradoxes' as strict IMPLICATION. With inductive, etc., inferences, 'valid' may be used as above, in which case they are all invalid, but it may mean simply 'meeting the standards proper to them'. A formula (propositional FUNCTION, open SENTENCE) is valid if it is true for every value of its VARIABLES. Otherwise it is invalid. It is contravalid if it is false for every value. Logically true propositions, i.e. propositions instantiating valid propositional functions, are sometimes called valid, and logically false ones contravalid. Sound, applied to an inference, means either 'valid, and having all its premises true' or just 'valid'. An interpretation of an AXIOM SYSTEM is sound if, under it, all the axioms and theorems are truths. Alternatively, it is sound if whatever is derivable in it from certain premises really follows from those premises. A proof system of any kind can similarly be called sound. Soundness is similar to but not identical with CONSISTENCY.

A. Church, *Introduction to Mathematical Logic*, vol. 1, Princeton UP, 1956, p. 55. (Soundness.)

B. Mates, *Elementary Logic*, Oxford UP, 1965. (See index. Soundness and consistency.)

Value. See VARIABLE.

Variable. Symbol used to stand indefinitely for any one of a set of things or notions. It ranges over the members of the set. The members are its values and the set is its range. Individual variables, propositional variables, etc., range, respectively, over INDIVIDUALS, propositions, etc. Syntactical variables range over syntactical (i.e. logical) OPERA-TORS. A symbol assumed to stand for one thing alone throughout a given context is a constant. The thing in question may be unspecified. But with logical constants it is specified. The logical constants are terms like 'and', 'or', 'not', 'implies'. They are a subclass of logical operators (which go beyond them by including things like quantifiers (see QUANTIFICATION)). In school algebra, x, y, etc., are numerical variables, ranging over numbers; a, b, etc., are numerical constants; and '+', '×' etc., correspond to logical constants.

A variable is bound or, occasionally, apparent, if it occurs within the scope of a quantifier containing the same variable (see QUANTI-FICATION); a bound variable is rather like a pronoun. Otherwise it is free or, occasionally, real; though the variable within the quantifier itself is sometimes called bound, sometimes neither. In (x) (Fxy), the second x is bound while the y is free: the first x can be called bound or neither. In mathematics, a 'real variable' is one ranging over 'real', as against imaginary or complex, numbers.

For intervening variables see LOGICAL CONSTRUCTIONS.

A hidden variable is something unobserved but postulated to explain, by its variations, variations in observed phenomena that we cannot otherwise account for.

I. Copi, *Introduction to Logic*, 6th edn, Macmillan, 1982. (Elementary intro-duction, See its index under 'variable'. For fuller treatment see, with its index, his *Symbolic Logic*, 5th edn, Macmillan, 1979 (treatment differs somewhat in different editions).)

Veil of ignorance. See ORIGINAL POSITION.

Veil of perception. Bennett's name for a doctrine, or perhaps just assumption, which he attributes to Locke in particular. This is that we are in effect separated by a veil from the world outside our minds, so that we can only perceive things outside us by having IDEAS which copy and resemble those things.

J. Bennett, 'Substance, reality and primary qualities', in C. B. Martin and D. M. Armstrong (eds), *Locke and Berkeley*, Macmillan, 1968, and in Bennett's *Locke, Berkeley and Hume: Central Themes*, Clarendon, 1971.

Verification. See POSITIVISM.

Vicious circle principle. See TYPES (THEORY OF).

Vico, Giambattista. 1668–1744. Born in Naples, he worked mainly there. His main work lay in speculative philosophy of HISTORY, where he elaborated a theory of how civilizations independently undergo a certain kind of development, which occurs under divine providence. He influenced CROCE among others. *The New Science*, 1725 (revised in later editions).

Vienna circle. See POSITIVISM.

Vindication. See INDUCTION.

Virtue. In Greek ethics, virtue (*arete*) was a dominant concept. Socrates and the Sophists were much concerned with its nature and value, and how it might be acquired. Plato devoted several early dialogues to individual virtues. For Aristotle, the human good was to live in accordance with virtue, or with the highest if there was more than one. For the Stoics, virtue was the only unconditional good. Christianity substituted a duty to obey the will of God, and in more modern times, ethical outlooks have largely divided into the deontological, making duty the primary concept, and teleological, emphasizing the pursuit of certain ends; see ETHICS.

Recently, however, there has been a revival of interest in virtue as a basis for ethics, under the name 'virtue ethics'. The prescribed aim is to promote the virtues in oneself and others, and the emphasis is on what sort of a person one is. Virtues may or may not be MORAL, and what makes them so when they are is disputed. Are courage, tenacity, prudence, moral virtues? Are laziness, carelessness, stubbornness, moral vices? And what of intellectual virtues like wisdom, intelligence, quick-wittedness? For Aristotle, the main intellectual virtues, at least, ranked higher than the moral ones. Further questions concern whether the nature or value of virtues depends on physical or social conditions (would meekness be a virtue in a caveman?), and how far virtue ethics can cater for all our moral intuitions.

Virtue epistemology has been a recent application of virtue ethics to the attempt to resolve disputes between different accounts of truth and justification, such as FOUNDATIONALISM and coherentism, by focussing on the intellectual virtues of the individual, such as honesty, inquisitiveness and creativity.

Aristotle, *Nicomachean Ethics*.

*R. Crisp and M. Slote (eds), Virtue Ethics, Oxford UP, 1997, and R. Crisp (ed.), *How Should One Live? Essays on the Virtues*, Oxford UP, 1998. (Two useful collections of articles.)

J. Greco, 'Virtue Epistemology', *The Stanford Encyclopedia of Philosophy* (Fall 2008 Edition), Edward N. Zalta (ed.). Available at: http://plato. stanford.edu/archives/fall2008/entries/epistemology-virtue/ (accessed 1 March 2009).

*R. Hursthouse, 'Virtue Ethics', *The Stanford Encyclopedia of Philosophy* (Fall 2008 Edition), Edward N. Zalta (ed.). Available at: http://plato. stanford.edu/archives/fall2008/entries/ethics-virtue/ (accessed 1 March 2009). (Excellent introduction and summary.)

*R. Hursthouse, *On Virtue Ethics*, Oxford UP, 1999. (Clear exposition and defence of virtue ethics.)

A. Macintyre, *After Virtue*, Duckworth, 1981. (Historical discussion of how Greek ethics was superseded by more modern attempts to justify morality, themselves superseded by Nietzsche's emphasis on the will and by recent developments from that, as a result we are so far removed from Greek ethics as only to half understand it.)

O. O'Neill, *Duty and Virtue*, Dartmouth Publishing co., 1993.

*G. Pence, 'Virtue theory', in P. Singer (ed.), *A Companion to Ethics*, Blackwell, 1991. (Brief introduction, with short but useful bibliography.); 'Recent work on virtues', *American Philosophical Quarterly*, 1984. (Critical survey of various recent books and articles. NB Asterisk only refers to first of Pence's publications.)

M. Slote, *From Morality to Virtue*, Oxford UP, 1992. (See also summary, discussions, and Slote's reply, in *Philosophy and Phenomenological Research*, 1994.)

E. Sosa, 'For the love of truth?', in *Virtue Epistemology: Essays on Epistemic Virtue and Responsibility*, A. Fairweather and L. Zagzebski (eds), Oxford UP, 2001. (Contains many other contributions to virtue epistemology, as also does L. Zagzebski and Michael DePaul (eds), *Intellectual Virtue: Perspectives from Ethics and Epistemology*, Clarendon, 2003.)

L. Zagzebski, *Virtues of the Mind: An Inquiry into the Nature of Virtue and the Ethical Foundations of Knowledge*, Cambridge UP, 1996. (Virtue epistemology.)

Voting paradox. Let three issues A, B, C, be voted on by three voters whose respective orders of preference are ABC, BCA, CAB. If the first vote is on two issues, and the second vote on the winner and the third issue, the third issue will always win, so that the winner will depend on the order in which the issues are voted on. This example also shows that majority preference is not TRANSITIVE, even when that of each individual is; for a majority prefers A to B, and a majority prefers B to C, but also a majority prefers C to A. This second feature shows that an electorate can be irrational in a way that none of its members need be. It is sometimes called Arrow's paradox because he used it to prove his 'impossibility theorem', that four plausibly desirable conditions cannot be satisfied together by any voting system.

Another paradox sometimes called the voting paradox, or paradox of democracy, asks how we can consistently hold, when outvoted, both that our favoured policy ought to be enacted and that the policy favoured by the majority ought to be enacted.

K. J. Arrow, 'Values and collective decision-making', in P. Laslett *et al* (eds), *Philosophy, Politics and Society*, 3rd series, Blackwell, 1967, § iv.

M. Clark, *Paradoxes from A–Z*, Routledge, 2002.

R. Wollheim, 'A paradox in the theory of democracy', in P. Laslett *et al.* (eds), *Philosophy, Politics and Society*, 2nd series, Blackwell, 1962.

W

Warrant. Roughly, a belief is warranted if it is justified. But some (e.g. Plantinga) have drawn a distinction between warrant and justification. See also EPISTEMOLOGY.

> A. Plantinga, *Warranted Christian Belief*, Oxford UP, 2000. (Christian belief as warranted, rather than justified: follows his earlier books on the idea of 'warrant', e.g. *Warrant: The Current Debate*, Oxford, 1993.)

Waismann, Friedrich. 1896–1959. Austrian logical positivist who was born in Vienna and migrated to Oxford. He was originally a member of the Vienna Circle, but in Oxford he became a leader of 'linguistic philosophy', emphasizing the fuzziness in various respects of ordinary language. In particular, he criticized the sharpness of the ANALYTIC/synthetic distinction, and introduced the notion of OPEN TEXTURE. He also argued for CONVENTIONALISM in mathematics. Collections of his lectures and articles were published posthumously. *The Principles of Linguistic Philosophy*, 1965. *How I see Philosophy*, 1968 (articles, including six-part article on 'Analytic', originally published in *Analysis*, 1949–53). See also LOGIC.

Weakness of will. See INCONTINENCE.

Well-formed formula. See AXIOM.

Weyl's paradox. See HETEROLOGICAL.

WFF. See AXIOM.

Whewell, William. 1794–1866. Born in Lancaster, he worked in Cambridge, where he became Master of Trinity College. He taught minerology and moral philosophy, but is mainly known for his work in philosophy of science, where he developed the hypothetico-deductive method (see INDUCTION), while accepting also certain fundamental principles which were innate but became self-evident only after reflection. He was opposed by J. S. MILL. In ethics he developed a system based rights, themselves based on human nature. *History of the Inductive Sciences, from the Earliest to the Present Time,* 1837. *Philosophy of the Inductive Sciences, Founded upon Their History,* 1840, expanded in 3rd edition into three parts: *History of Scientific Ideas,* 1858, *Novum Organon Renovatum,* 1858. *On the Philosophy of Discovery,* 1860. *Elements of Morality, Including Polity,* 1845.

Whitehead, Alfred N. 1861–1947. Born in Thanet, he worked mainly in Cambridge, London and Harvard. His early work was in mathematics and logic, in which he taught, and then collaborated with, RUSSELL. Later he turned more to METAPHYSICS, and developed a philosophy based on processes and events rather than on material objects. His work was influenced by developments in physics then current, and was also relevant to philosophy of science on topics such as laws of nature. *Principia Mathematica,* 1910–13 (with Russell, Whitehead concentrating mainly on the mathematical parts, Russell on the philosophical). *Science and the Modern World,* 1925. *Process and Reality,* 1929 (often regarded as his main philosophical book, but difficult). *Adventures of Ideas,* 1933.

Williams, Bernard. 1929–2003. British philosopher who worked in Oxford, Cambridge, London and at Berkeley. He had a wide range of interests, both within philosophy and generally. He sat on Royal Commissions on gambling, drug abuse and private schools, and chaired one on obscenity and film censorship. He believed philosophy should not be studied in isolation from history, general culture and human psychology. His own work drew strongly on Greek philosophy, and he made important contributions to personal identity and, specially, to moral philosophy. He was critical of utilitarianism and all consequentialist theories, and also of Kantian moral philosophy. He introduced the term MORAL LUCK, and wrote on virtue ethics and truth. *Morality: An Introduction to Ethics,* 1972. *Problems of the Self,* 1973. *Utilitarianism: For and Against,* (with J. J. C. Smart), 1973. *Descartes: The Project of Pure Enquiry,* 1978. *Moral Luck,* 1981. *Ethics and the Limits of Philosophy,* 1985. *Shame and Necessity,* 1993. *Truth and Truthfulness: An Essay in Genealogy,* 2002.

Winch, Peter. 1926–97. British philosopher, who worked in Swansea, London and the University of Illinois, Urbana-Champaign. His best known work is *The Idea of a Social Science*, 1958, which was influenced by Collingwood, whose *The Idea of History* was an important model, and, especially, Wittgenstein, whose ideas Winch applied to ethics and religion as well as to the study of the social sciences.

Wittgenstein, Ludwig, J. J. 1889–1951. Austrian philosopher, born in Vienna, who taught in Cambridge. Both his main works (the first two mentioned below) were leading contributions to philosophical movements, the first to LOGICAL ATOMISM and the second (influential through oral dissemination before publication) to linguistic PHILO-SOPHY. All his works but the first were published posthumously. In the first he tried to preserve an extensionalist logic (see INTEN-SIONALITY AND INTENTIONALITY), which led him to trace the limits of what could be stated explicitly and what could only be shown. The second revolves around his rejection of the view that there can be words which have meaning by standing for inner experiences private to the experiencer; this led him to think that philosophical puzzlement in general grew out of misunderstandings of how language works. *Tractatus Logico-Philosophicus*, 1921, trans 1922 and (better) 1961. *Philosophical Investigations*, 1953. *Remarks on the Foundations of Mathematics*, 1967, *On Certainty*, 1969. *Remarks on the Philosophy of Psychology* (2 vols) 1980. See also CRITERION, EPISTEMOLOGY, FINITISM, LANGUAGE GAME, MEANING, POSITIVISM, PRIVATE LANGUAGE, SEEING, SPACE, STRUCTURE, UNIVERSALS.

There is a huge literature on Wittgenstein. Among the best recent introductions to his philosophy are A. C. Grayling, *Wittgenstein: A Very Short Introduction*, Oxford UP, 2001, and R. Monk and S. Critchley, *How to Read Wittgenstein*, Norton, 2005.

Z

Zeno of Citium. See STOICS.

Zeno's paradoxes. The surviving paradoxes of Zeno of Elea (see ELEATICS) fall mainly into two groups, concerning plurality and motion, though these groups are related. Their interpretation and significance is to some extent controversial.

The idea behind the former group seems to be as follows: to have no size is to be nothing, while to have size is to be divisible (whether in reality or only in principle is left unclear). But the parts resulting from division must themselves either lack size, and so be nothing, or have size, and so be further divisible. Therefore we must end with nothing or with infinitely many parts. If these infinitely many parts lack size they cannot contribute to the whole, which will itself lack size; but if they have size, however small, the whole they form will be infinitely large.

The paradoxes of motion seem intended to argue that space and time can be neither atomic (made of indivisible points and moments) nor continuous. The Moving Rows paradox seems to argue that if both space and time are atomic there is a maximum velocity, namely one point per moment – but anything moving at this velocity relative to one object can always be shown to be moving faster relative to some other object, so there is no maximum velocity. The argument can be made to cover the cases where only one of space and time is atomic. Aristotle, however, who is our source for this paradox, treats it as simply confusing relative and absolute motion. The above version, whether or not historically accurate, is stronger than Aristotle's. There are other versions.

The Achilles and the Tortoise paradox argues that if space and time are both continuous, then if Achilles allows the tortoise a start in a race he can never overtake it. He takes at least some time to reach the tortoise's start, during which the tortoise moves at least some distance. While Achilles covers this distance the tortoise moves some more. While Achilles covers this 'more' the tortoise moves again. Clearly the argument can be repeated indefinitely: even though the successive stages get shorter and are covered over more quickly, at the end of any given stage Achilles is still behind the tortoise. How can he reach the end of an endless series of stages? The Dichotomy is a variant of the Achilles, saying that one can never cover a distance, because one must first cover the first half, then the third quarter, and so on, constantly bisecting the remaining distance. In a more general form the paradox claims that if two objects are separated by a certain distance at a certain time they can never be separated by a different distance at any other time. The name Stadium is ambiguous, sometimes meaning the Dichotomy, sometimes the Moving Rows.

The Flying Arrow argues that, since at any moment an arrow occupies a definite position, and since between two moments there is nothing but other moments the arrow can only be in positions and never move from one to another.

The Grain of Millet, on a different topic, argues that a single grain in falling makes no sound, but a thousand grains make a sound, so a thousand nothings become something, which is absurd, cf. HEAP.

Modern discussions centre on the Achilles, of which many variants have been developed. Its full solution is still disputed.

M. Clark, *Paradoxes from A–Z*, Routledge, 2002.

R. M. Sainsbury, *Paradoxes*, Cambridge UP, 1988 (revised, 1995), chapter 1.

W. C. Salmon (ed.), *Zeno's Paradoxes*, Bobbs-Merrill, 1970. (Modern discussions, with extensive bibliography. On the Moving Rows cf. also J. Immerwahr, 'An interpretation of Zeno's stadium paradox', *Phronesis*, 1978.)

Zero sum game. Concept used in game theory and DECISION THEORY. A zero sum game (or situation in general) is one in which the total gains of all the participants equals the total losses of all the participants. For any situation in the game, if someone gains, another, or others, lose the same amount. Situations in which everyone gains, or suffers, are non-zero sum: for example, giving something I want to get rid of to someone who wants it is a non-zero sum, or win-win situation.

Zombie. As used by philosophers, creature looking and behaving exactly like a human but having no conscious experiences. See also QUALIA.

Guide to Philosophy Online

All websites mentioned in this section were last accessed on 7 March 2009.

Introduction

The internet is constantly changing and evolving. It is likely that some sites mentioned here will no longer exist by the time you try them: others will certainly have started. Not only do sites appear and disappear: the content of those sites that remain can change, and sometimes drastically so. What was, at one time, a good site might later become worthless. For this reason, some websites archive their entries, so that, even if the site is changed at a later date, the site as it was when you accessed it is available online permanently. For example, the *Stanford Encyclopedia of Philosophy*, see below, does this.

When using the internet, it is always important to use your discretion and judgement: not everything you read on the internet is true or reliable (nor, of course, is everything you read in a book). The first place many will turn to is Wikipedia, but caution should be exercised. Wikipedia is an amazing resource which has great advantages combined with many drawbacks, both the advantages and the drawbacks arising from the way in which entries can be posted and changed. It has entries for a vast number of different philosophers and topics in philosophy. These vary in quality. Many are very good, but sometimes, inevitably in an enterprise as large and open as this, there are errors or distortions.

Finding articles in journals online

If you are searching for an article which has appeared in an academic journal, you may very well find it online through JSTOR. JSTOR is an online archive of scholarly journals, covering many disciplines, and including most of the major English language philosophy journals. It is possible to access JSTOR in a variety of ways. Most University libraries provide access, as do many public libraries (whether or not you are a member of that library). You can find out more information about JSTOR by asking at your library, or by going to http://www.jstor.org/.

Citing an online source

If you use online material in preparing an essay or an article, you should cite your sources just as you would have done for a printed source. The normal method of citing an on-line source is to give the URL and the date accessed, as follows: N. Bostrom, 'anthropic-principle.com', www. anthropic-principle.com/ (accessed 6 March 2009). Note that all web sites in this Guide were accessed on 7 March 2009: to save repetition, this is not noted for each one.

All the sites listed below are free, and do not require registration.

General philosophy sites

Two excellent online philosophy encyclopedias, with original articles by specialist philosophers, chosen and refereed by distinguished editorial boards and peer reviewers, updated when appropriate, and with good bibliographies are the *Stanford Encyclopedia of Philosophy*, http://plato. stanford.edu/, and *The Internet Encyclopedia of Philosophy*, www.iep. utm.edu/.

Episteme, www.epistemelinks.com/, is a large and very useful resource which includes over 20,000 links to philosophy resources online, with many additional features. The links are categorized by philosopher, by topic and by time period. From this site you can also search many other sites, including the *Stanford* and *Internet Encyclopaedias*, as well as specially chosen entries in other places such as Wikipedia and Encarta. *Episteme* casts its net very wide, so the links vary in quality. For a more focussed search, which cuts out many irrelevant links from other search sites, *Noesis*, http://noesis.evansville.edu/, is very useful. It searches for Philosophy sites, books, texts and reviews in a way that minimizes the chances of including irrelevant or poor quality links.

Two outstanding general philosophical sites maintained by individual philosophers are Peter King's *Philosophy Around the Web*, http://users. ox.ac.uk/~worc0337/phil_index.html, and Garth Kemerling's *Philosophy Pages*, www.philosophypages.com/. King's site is a treasure trove, and, among many other features, provides usefully annotated links to sites arranged by topic and by philosopher. Kemerling includes *A Dictionary of Philosophical Terms and Names* at www.philosophypages.com/dy/index.htm. The site contains excellent short summaries of the life and works of great philosophers.

David Chalmers and David Bourget have just (January 2009) launched http://philpapers.org/, a comprehensive directory of over 200,000 online philosophy articles and books by academic philosophers, which promises to be a very valuable new resource. For Chalmers' explanation of its aims, see http://fragments.consc.net/djc/2009/01/philp.html. Chalmers, one of the leading philosophers of mind, and Bourget have also compiled a very good set of categorized links to over 2,500 papers on consciousness at http://consc.net/online.html.

Complete texts of classic works by Bacon, Hobbes, Descartes, Spinoza, Locke, Berkeley, Hume, Kant, Leibniz and many other philosophers can be found at Carl Mickelsen's website, www.class.uidaho.edu/mickelsen/readings.htm. The University of Adelaide's site, http://etext.library.adelaide.edu.au/, also contains many classic philosophical texts.

Classic texts in philosophy can provide many problems for the contemporary reader. Language can provide a problem, of course, but even for those texts originally written in English, the style and vocabulary may prove difficult for the modern reader. The philosopher Jonathan Bennett has provided a remarkable service to philosophy by providing translations of very many of the works of British philosophers of the early modern era (such as – but not only – Bacon, Hobbes, Locke, Berkeley and Hume) into modern English, and making these translations available free of charge online. The site also includes new translations of philosophers who wrote in languages other than English, including Descartes, Spinoza, Leibniz and Kant. Bennett's website is www.earlymoderntexts.com/index.html. For his justification of his project, see his 'On translating Locke, Berkeley and Hume into English', *Teaching Philosophy* 17 (1994, pp. 261–69), available at www.earlymoderntexts.com/jfb/translating.html. Bennett continues to add works to the site, and all the texts are fully searchable.

David Edmonds and Nigel Warburton at *Philosophy Bites*, www.philosophybites.com/, have nearly 100 podcast interviews with contemporary philosophers, and a good set of links as well. See http://nigelwarburton.typepad.com/philosophy_bites/past_programmes.html for the complete list of interviews.

Specific philosophers

Here are some recommended web sites for individual philosophers, usually with links to other sites for the same philosopher. See *Episteme*

Links, Garth Kemerling's *Philosophy Pages* and the *Stanford* and *Internet Encyclopedias* (see above for details of these sites) for further coverage of these and other philosophers.

Anscombe. www.unav.es/filosofia/jmtorralba/anscombe_bibliography.htm. Useful bibliography.

Augustine. http://ccat.sas.upenn.edu/jod/augustine.html.

Avicenna. www.muslimphilosophy.com/sina/. Comprehensive set of links to both Arabic and English sites.

Bentham. www.ucl.ac.uk/Bentham-Project/index.htm.

Berkeley. www.georgeberkeley.org.uk/links.htm. Large collection of links.

Broad. www.ditext.com/broad/cdbroad.html. Useful introduction and bibliography.

Derrida. http://hydra.humanities.uci.edu/derrida/. Useful bibliography and other links.

Descartes. www.philosophypages.com/ph/desc.htm. Good introduction and suggestions for further reading.

Dewey. http://dewey.pragmatism.org/.

Frege. www.ocf.berkeley.edu/~brianwc/frege/. Comprehensive set of links.

Gödel. www.sm.luth.se/~torkel/eget/godel.html. Corrects some misconceptions.

Hegel. www.hegel.net/en/e0.htm. Lively site, answers FAQ about Hegel. www.hegel.org/links.html. Large set of links.

Heidegger. www.webcom.com/~paf/ereignis.html. Lots of links to sources in English and more.

Hume. www.davidhume.org/. Good introductory material, and links and bibliography.

Husserl. www.husserlpage.com/. Comprehensive coverage.

William James. www.des.emory.edu/mfp/james.html. Comprehensive coverage.

Kant. http://comp.uark.edu/~rlee/semiau96/kantlink.html. Guide to electronic Kant texts, and to much secondary literature.

Kierkegaard. http://sorenkierkegaard.org/comment.htm. Texts, summaries, commentaries and comprehensive bibliographies for all of his works.

Leibniz http://mally.stanford.edu/leibniz.html. Brief summary of publications, life and further reading (but no links).

Levinas. http://home.pacbell.net/atterton/levinas/index.htm. Extensive bibliography.

Locke. www.philosophypages.com/ph/lock.htm. Brief introduction to his work with suggestions for further reading.

Merleau-Ponty. www.mythosandlogos.com/MerleauPonty.html. Brief introduction to his thought and good set of links.

Mill. www.cpm.ll.ehime-u.ac.jp/AkamacHomePage/Akamac_E-text_Links/Mill.html. Links to texts and other web pages.

Nietzsche. www.philosophypages.com/ph/niet.htm. Brief introduction to his work with suggestions for further reading.

Peirce. www.peirce.org/. Biography, hypertexts and other links.

Quine. www.wvquine.org/. Comprehensive resource, created and maintained by his son.

Ramsey. www.fil.lu.se/sahlin/ramsey/. Introduction to his thought, some links.

Russell. www.mcmaster.ca/russdocs/russell.htm. Searchable site concerned with Russell's considerable output of writings, and books about Russell. You can listen to his voice.

Santayana. www.iupui.edu/~santedit/. Details of his works, and useful links.

Sartre. www.geocities.com/sartresite/. Biography, quotations, influences, links and summaries of his philosophy.

Sidgwick. www.utilitarian.net/sidgwick/. Links to his works and writings about him.

Singer. www.utilitarian.net/singer/. Comprehensive list of and links to writings by and about Singer.

Spinoza. http://frank.mtsu.edu/~rbombard/RB/spinoza.new.html. Links to texts, other sites and background material.

Turing. www.turing.org.uk/. Fascinating site about Turing's life and work maintained by Andrew Hodges, author of the excellent biography. www. alanturing.net/. Archive of the history of computing, with facsimiles of documents by Turing and others in AI, and articles about him and AI.

Wittgenstein. www.philosophypages.com/ph/witt.htm. Short introduction to his work, with suggestions for further reading. www.wittgen-cam.ac.uk/cgi-bin/ forms/home.cgi. The Cambridge Wittgenstein Archive pages: some interesting material about his life.